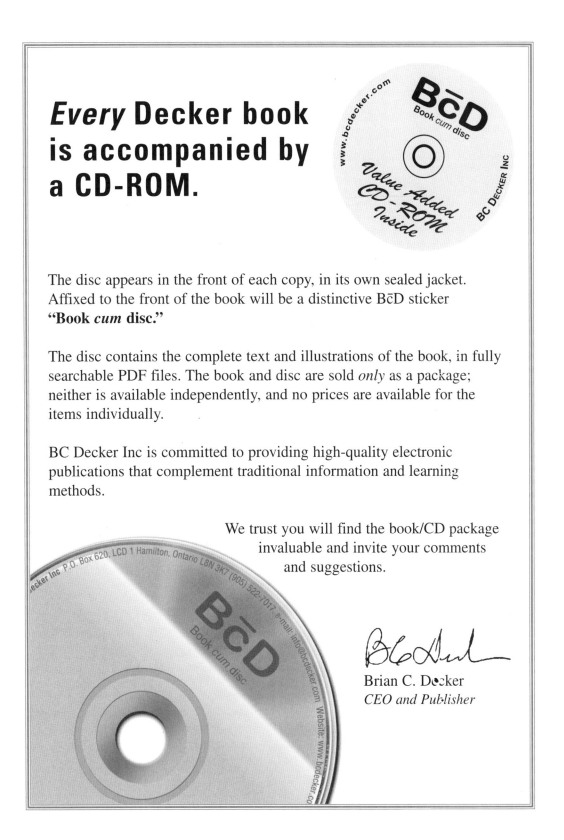

American Cancer Society

Atlas of Clinical Oncology

Published

Blumgart, Fong, Jarnagin	*Hepatobiliary Cancer (2001)*
Cameron	*Pancreatic Cancer (2001)*
Carroll, Grossfeld	*Prostate Cancer (2002)*
Char	*Tumors of the Eye and Ocular Adnexa (2001)*
Clark, Duh, Jahan, Perrier	*Endocrine Tumors (2003)*
Droller	*Urothelial Tumors (2003)*
Eifel, Levenback	*Cancer of the Female Lower Genital Tract (2001)*
Fuller, Seiden, Young	*Uterine and Endometrial Cancer (2003)*
Ginsberg	*Lung Cancer (2002)*
Grossbard	*Malignant Lymphomas (2002)*
Ozols	*Ovarian Cancer (2003)*
Pollock	*Soft Tissue Sarcomas (2002)*
Posner, Vokes, Weichselbaum	*Cancer of the Upper Gastrointestinal Tract (2002)*
Prados	*Brain Cancer (2002)*
Raghavan	*Germ Cell Tumors (2003)*
Shah	*Cancer of the Head and Neck (2001)*
Silverman	*Oral Cancer 5th Edition (2003)*
Wiernik	*Adult Leukemias (2001)*
Willett	*Cancer of Lower Gastrointestinal Tract (2001)*
Winchester, Winchester	*Breast Cancer (2000)*

Forthcoming

Richie, Steele	*Kidney Tumors (2004)*
Volberding	*Viral and Immunological Malignancies (2004)*
Yasko	*Bone Tumors (2004)*

American Cancer Society

Atlas of

Clinical Oncology

Editors

GLENN D. STEELE JR, MD
Geisinger Health System

THEODORE L. PHILLIPS, MD
University of California

BRUCE A. CHABNER, MD
Harvard Medical School

Managing Editor

TED S. GANSLER, MD, MBA
Director of Health Content, American Cancer Society

American Cancer Society
Atlas of
Clinical Oncology

Germ Cell Tumors

Derek Raghavan, MD, PhD

Professor of Medicine and Urology
Chief, Division of Oncology
University of Southern California
Norris Comprehensive Cancer Center
Los Angeles, California

2003
BC Decker Inc
Hamilton • London

BC Decker Inc
P.O. Box 620, LCD 1
Hamilton, Ontario L8N 3K7
Tel: 905-522-7017; 1-800-568-7281
Fax: 905-522-7839; 1-888-311-4987
E-mail: info@bcdecker.com
www.bcdecker.com

ISBN 1–55009–082–8
Printed in Spain

Sales and Distribution

United States
BC Decker Inc
P.O. Box 785
Lewiston, NY 14092-0785
Tel: 905-522-7017; 800-568-7281
Fax: 905-522-7839; 888-311-4987
E-mail: info@bcdecker.com
www.bcdecker.com

Canada
BC Decker Inc
20 Hughson Street South
P.O. Box 620, LCD 1
Hamilton, Ontario L8N 3K7
Tel: 905-522-7017; 800-568-7281
Fax: 905-522-7839; 888-311-4987
E-mail: info@bcdecker.com
www.bcdecker.com

Foreign Rights
John Scott & Company
International Publishers' Agency
P.O. Box 878
Kimberton, PA 19442
Tel: 610-827-1640
Fax: 610-827-1671
E-mail: jsco@voicenet.com

Argentina
CLM (Cuspide Libros Medicos)
Av. Córdoba 2067 – (1120)
Buenos Aires, Argentina
Tel: (5411) 4961-0042/(5411) 4964-0848
Fax: (5411) 4963-7988
E-mail: clm@cuspide.com

Japan
Igaku-Shoin Ltd.
Foreign Publications Department
3-24-17 Hongo
Bunkyo-ku, Tokyo, Japan 113-8719
Tel: 3 3817 5680
Fax: 3 3815 6776
E-mail: fd@igaku-shoin.co.jp

U.K., Europe, Scandinavia,
Middle East
Elsevier Science
Customer Service Department
Foots Cray High Street
Sidcup, Kent
DA14 5HP, UK
Tel: 44 (0) 208 308 5760
Fax: 44 (0) 181 308 5702
E-mail: cservice@harcourt.com

Singapore, Malaysia, Thailand,
Philippines, Indonesia, Vietnam,
Pacific Rim, Korea
Elsevier Science Asia
583 Orchard Road
#09/01, Forum
Singapore 238884
Tel: 65-737-3593
Fax: 65-753-2145

Australia, New Zealand
Elsevier Science Australia
Customer Service Department
STM Division
Locked Bag 16
St. Peters, New South Wales, 2044
Australia
Tel: 61 02 9517-8999
Fax: 61 02 9517-2249
E-mail: stmp@harcourt.com.au
Web site: www.harcourt.com.au

Mexico and Central America
ETM SA de CV
Calle de Tula 59
Colonia Condesa
06140 Mexico DF, Mexico
Tel: 52-5-5553-6657
Fax: 52-5-5211-8468
E-mail: editoresdetextosmex@prodigy.net.mx

Brazil
Tecmedd
Av. Maurílio Biagi, 2850
City Ribeirão Preto – SP – CEP: 14021-000
Tel: 0800 992236
Fax: (16) 3993-9000
E-mail: tecmedd@tecmedd.com.br

Dedication

This volume honors the following dedicated clinicians and researchers who taught me about the biology and treatment of germ cell tumors: A. Munro Neville, MD, PhD; Sir Michael Peckham, MD; Eadie Heyderman, MD; Ann Barrett, MD; Timothy McElwain, MD (deceased); B. J. Kennedy, MD; Elwin E. Fraley, MD; and Paul Lange, MD. It also reflects my continuing affection and respect for my patients, who have battled this disease and who have helped to overcome it for future generations.

Derek Raghavan, MD, PhD
Los Angeles, January 2003

Foreword

This first edition of *Germ Cell Tumors,* containing state-of-the-art information about testicular cancer, is really a book about the lives of patients. As you may know, I was one of those patients and am a survivor of advanced testicular cancer. This textbook discusses many elements of the cancer experience that have challenged me both physically and psychologically, from my diagnoses through to my recovery and even now.

What I appreciate most about this book is that it discusses not only technical advances but the totality of testicular cancer care, including early detection, initial therapy decisions, improved surgery, disease follow-up, salvage therapy, resources for patients, and psychological stress. Many physicians overlook these last two areas, failing to provide insight and assistance to their patients and their patients' families. Psychological and social issues can last longer than the physical side effects of treatment and can continue to affect patients well after their disease has been treated. The host of issues introduced to a person's life once he or she is diagnosed with cancer and the experience of living through and beyond a cancer diagnosis is termed survivorship. It is to the individuals and families experiencing cancer survivorship that the Lance Armstrong Foundation, which I have been privileged to establish, has been dedicated. I should also mention that Dr. Derek Raghavan, the editor of this book, has served the Foundation since his appointment as an initial member of the Scientific Advisory Committee.

Although I am not a cancer expert, it is clear to me that the technical chapters outline all of the advances that have occurred in the treatment of testicular cancer and that it is hoped will occur in the treatment of other cancers that are not now commonly considered "curable." This book describes the history of chemotherapy, from a time when a cure for advanced disease was unheard of to the present, when every patient, even those with disease as threatening as mine, has an opportunity to be cured. Even those who are not successfully treated the first time still have a second chance at a successful recovery. Had I developed my cancer prior to the availability of platinum and other drugs, I would not have had the opportunity to have a family, to continue my cycling career, and to win a few bike races.

I am very grateful for the care that I received and for the medical advances that give hope to testicular cancer patients. I have accepted the challenge of "the obligation of the cured"—issued to me by my physician, Dr. Craig Nichols—to give back and to provide hope and an example to others currently living with cancer. This book describes how the science of testicular cancer has given me and other patients the opportunity to embrace that responsibility.

Lance Armstrong
October 2002

Contents

Preface

The management of testicular cancer has become one of the modern paradigms of successful cancer care. In less than 50 years, some of the modern legends of the world of genitourinary cancer research and treatment have created an environment in which young men with metastatic germ cell tumors can expect a cure rate of 80 to 90%, which has replaced a previous cancer-related mortality rate of similar magnitude.

In a series of logical intellectual steps supported by carefully constructed preclinical and clinical studies, physicians have acquired a much clearer understanding of the molecular biology of germ cell neoplasia, with identified stem cell origins, a classic marker chromosome, characteristic gene abnormalities, and biochemical markers of tumor presence and progression. The typing of germ cell tumors by conventional light microscopy has become more sophisticated, augmented by the techniques of electron microscopy, immunohistochemistry, and fluorescent in situ hybridization. Invasive imaging and staging techniques have been supplanted by computed tomography, magnetic resonance imaging, and positron emission tomography, and germ cell tumors have been one of the "stalking horses" for the development of each of these modalities. The indications and templates for surgery and radiotherapy have been refined and refocused. The early days of cytotoxic chemotherapy, initially ineffective and then replaced by active but toxic regimens, have given way to an era of curative strategies with dramatically reduced toxicity. Patients with good-risk characteristics have been identified who can be cured by orchiectomy alone, with follow-up provided by well-structured surveillance protocols. Against this background of success, current investigations have been more heavily focused on the long-term consequences of curative treatment.

Today, the presenting patient can expect an excellent prognosis and highly refined information regarding diagnosis, treatment, and prognosis. Improved understanding of the demographic, epidemiologic, and social issues pertaining to germ cell tumors has allowed the development of a vastly superior system of patient management and support, culminating in the broad availability of easily accessed resources for the lay population and clinicians alike.

This volume of the American Cancer Society Atlas of Clinical Oncology, focusing on advances in the diagnosis and management of germ cell tumors in males, is a celebration of these many advances and has been written by many of the contributors to the current state of the art. (Germ cell tumors in females are reviewed in a companion volume on cancers of the ovary.) It covers all of the topics listed above, describing the progress to date and identifying the remaining issues that require resolution. Added to this scientific and clinical review is a series of detailed discussions on psychosocial issues, patient support, and the management of the occasional problem cases that do not result in cure. In a series of thoughtfully conceived essays with extensive illustration, the contributors to this volume have chronicled the interplay between laboratory and clinical science, which has culminated in a success story of which all who work in the field of cancer care can be proud.

Derek Raghavan, MD, PhD
Los Angeles, California

Contributors

TOMASZ M. BEER, MD
Department of Medicine
Oregon Health and Science University
Portland, Oregon
Salvage Chemotherapy and New Drugs

RICHARD BIHRLE, MD
Department of Urology
Indiana University
Indianapolis, Indiana
Surgery of the Retroperitoneum

MICHAEL J. BOYER, MBBS, PhD, FRACP
Department of Medicine
University of Sydney
Sydney, Australia
Acute Toxicity of Chemotherapy

THOMAS C. CHEN, MD
Department of Neurosurgery
University of Southern California
Central Nervous System Metastases

TIMOTHY J. CHRISTMAS, MD, FRCS
Academic Urology Unit
The Royal Marsden Hospital
London, United Kingdom
Presentation of Germ Cell Tumors

GARY J. R. COOK, MSc, MD, FRCP, FRCR
Department of Radioisotope Physics
University of London
London, United Kingdom
Radiologic Investigation

VICTORIA CORTESSIS, PhD
Department of Preventative Medicine
Keck School of Medicine
University of Southern California
Los Angeles, California
*Epidemiologic Insights into the Occurrence
   and Causes of Testicular Cancer*

IVAN DAMJANOV, MD, PhD
Department of Pathology
University of Kansas School of Medicine
Kansas City, Kansas
Pathology

SIAMAK DANESHMAND, MD
Department of Urology
Keck School of Medicine
University of Southern California
Los Angeles, California
*Surgery for Testicular Cancer: Radical
   Orchiectomy*

GEDSKE DAUGAARD, MD
Department of Oncology
Rigshospitalet
Copenhagen, Denmark
*Active Surveillance for Stage I
   Nonseminomatous Germ Cell Tumors*

JOHN P. DONOHUE, MD
Department of Urology
Indiana University
Indianapolis, Indiana
Surgery of the Retroperitoneum

RICHARD S. FOSTER, MD
Department of Urology
Indiana University
Indianapolis, Indiana
Surgery of the Retroperitoneum

MARY K. GOSPODAROWICZ, MD, FRCPC, FRCR
(Hon)
Department of Radiation Oncology
University of Toronto
Toronto, Ontario
*Approach to the Management of Stage I
Seminoma*

ELLEN R. GRITZ, PhD
Department of Behavioral Science
MD Anderson Cancer Center
University of Texas
Houston, Texas
*Psychosocial Outcomes after Testicular
Cancer Treatment*

OMID HAMID, MD
Department of Medicine
University of Southern California
Los Angeles, California
Central Nervous System Metastases

PATRICIA HARRISON, MD
Department of Anesthesiology and Pain
Management
Kaiser Permanente Hospital
Los Angeles, California
Pain Management Techniques

LISA G. HORVATH, MBBS, FRACP
Department of Medical Oncology
Sydney Cancer Centre
Sydney, Australia
Acute Toxicity of Chemotherapy

ALAN HORWICH, PhD, FRCR, FRCP
Department of Radiotherapy
Institute of Cancer Research
London, United Kingdom
*Presentation of Germ Cell Tumors and
Chemotherapy for Metastatic Seminoma*

ROBERT P. HUBEN, MD
Department of Urologic Oncology
Roswell Park Cancer Institute
Buffalo, New York
Surgical Anatomy

JANET E. S. HUSBAND, OBE, FMedSci, FRCP, FRCR
Department of Diagnostic Radiology
Institute of Cancer Research
University of London
London, United Kingdom
Radiologic Investigation

JANE M. INGHAM, MB, BS, FRACP
Departments of Medicine and Oncology
Georgetown University
Washington, DC
*End-of-Life Considerations for Patients
with Germ Cell Tumors*

AVRUM I. JACOBSON, MD
Department of Urology
University of Washington
Seattle, Washington
*Tumor Markers in Germ Cell Tumors of
the Testis*

A. ROBERT KAGAN, MD
Department of Radiation Oncology
Kaiser Permanente Hospital
Los Angeles, California
Irradiation for Seminoma

PHILIP KANTOFF, MD
Division of Solid Tumor Oncology
Dana-Farber Cancer Institute
Harvard University Medical School
Boston, Massachusetts
Management of Extragonadal Germ Cell Tumors

DOW-MU KOH, MRCP, FRCR
Department of Clinical Magnetic Resonance
Institute of Cancer Research
London, United Kingdom
Radiologic Investigation

ARZU KOVANLIKAYA, MD
Department of Radiology
University of Southern California
Los Angeles, California
Pediatric Germ Cell Tumors

PAUL H. LANGE, MD, FACS
Department of Urology
University of Washington
Seattle, Washington
*Tumor Markers in Germ Cell Tumors
    of the Testis*

STACEY B. LEIBOWITZ, MD
Department of Medical Oncology
Dana-Farber Cancer Institute
Harvard University Medical School
Boston, Massachusetts
Management of Extragonadal Germ Cell Tumors

MARCIO H. MALOGOLOWKIN, MD
Department of Pediatrics
Keck School of Medicine
University of Southern California
Los Angeles, California
Pediatric Germ Cell Tumors

KIM MARGOLIN, MD
Department of Medical Oncology
City of Hope National Medical Center
Duarte, California
*High-Dose Chemotherapy and Stem Cell
    Support in the Treatment of Poor-Risk
    Germ Cell Cancer*

HECTOR L. MONFORTE, MD
Department of Pathology
University of Southern California
Los Angeles, California
Pediatric Germ Cell Tumors

A. MUNRO NEVILLE, MD, PhD, FRCPATH
Ludwig Institute for Cancer Research
London, United Kingdom
Biology of Germ Cell Tumors

EDWARD S. NEWLANDS, MD, PhD, FRCP
Department of Medical Oncology
Imperial College School of Medicine
London, United Kingdom
*Management of Nonseminomatous Testicular
    Cancer*
*Chemotherapy for Poor-Risk Patients:
    Standard-Dose Therapy*

CRAIG R. NICHOLS, MD
Department of Medicine
Oregon Health and Sciences University
Portland, Oregon
*Prognostic Factors in Disseminated Germ Cell
    Tumors*

IRENE PANAGIOTOU, MD
Department of Medicine
Oregon Health and Sciences University
Portland, Oregon
Salvage Chemotherapy and New Drugs

GIORGIO PIZZOCARO, MD
Department of Surgery
National Cancer Institute
Milan, Italy
Surgery of Metastic Disease after Chemotherapy

DAVID I. QUINN, MBBS, PhD, FRACP
Department of Medical Oncology
University of Southern California
Los Angeles, California
Central Nervous System Metastases

DEREK RAGHAVAN, MD, PhD
Division of Oncology
USC Norris Comprehensive Cancer Center
Los Angeles, California
Biology of Germ Cell Tumors and *Late Toxicity
    of Chemotherapy*

MIKAEL RØRTH, MD
Department of Oncology
Rigshospitalet
Copenhagen, Denmark
*Active Surveillance for Stage I Nonseminomatous
    Germ Cell Tumors*

RAMESH A. SHIVDASANI, MD, PhD
Department of Medicine
Dana-Farber Cancer Institute
Harvard Medical School
Boston, Massachusetts
Management of Extragonadal Germ Cell Tumors

STUART E. SIEGEL, MD
Department of Pediatrics
Keck School of Medicine
University of Southern California
Los Angeles, California
Pediatric Germ Cell Tumors

ERIC A. SINGER, MA
School of Medicine
Georgetown University
Washington, DC
*End-of-Life Considerations for Patients
    with Germ Cell Tumors*

EILA C. SKINNER, MD
Department of Urology
Keck School of Medicine
University of Southern California
Los Angeles, California
*Surgery for Testicular Cancer: Radical
    Orchiectomy*

OSCAR E. STREETER JR, MD
Department of Radiation Oncology
Keck School of Medicine
Unversity of Southern California
Los Angeles, California
Central Nervous System Metastases

CHRISTOPHER SWEENEY, MBBS
Department of Medicine
Indiana University
Indianapolis, Indiana
Late Toxicity of Chemotherapy

GUY C. TONER, MD, FRACP
Peter MacCallum Cancer Centre
University of Melbourne
Melbourne, Australia
*Management of Nonseminomatous Germ Cell
    Tumors: Chemotherapy for Patients with a
    Good Prognosis*

DAMON J. VIDRINE, DrPH
Department of Behavioral Science
MD Anderson Cancer Center
University of Texas
Houston, Texas
*Psychosocial Outcomes after Testicular Cancer
    Treatment*

PADRAIG R. WARDE, MB, MRCPI, FRCPC
Department of Radiation Oncology
University of Toronto
Toronto, Ontario
Approach to the Management of Stage I Seminoma

STEVEN N. WOLFF, MD
Lance Armstrong Foundation
Austin, Texas
Resources for the Patient with Testicular Cancer

Biology of Germ Cell Tumors

DEREK RAGHAVAN, MD, PhD
A. MUNRO NEVILLE, MD, PhD, FRCPath

Germ cell tumors, which constitute one of the most fascinating groups of malignancies, represent a curious interface between cancer and differentiation. Their embryologic complexity and structural diversity have made these tumors the focus of intense clinicopathologic and molecular scrutiny.[1] Just a quarter of a century ago, metastatic testicular cancer caused death in the vast majority of patients. With the evolution of effective chemotherapy and the development of a more rational approach to surgery, as well as an improved understanding of the clinical biology of the disease, this pattern has changed to one in which more than 80% of patients with advanced disease should expect to be cured. Nevertheless, one of the most curious aspects of this disease is that despite the success in achieving cure, clinicians and scientists do not really understand the basis of these results at a biologic level, and the basis of the delicate balance between differentiation and dedifferentiation remains something of an enigma. The information that is available on some of the key factors that regulate oncogenesis and ontogenesis is reviewed in this chapter.

CLASSIFICATION AND FUNCTIONAL PATHOLOGY

The two major variants of germ cell tumors are seminomas and nonseminomatous germ cell tumors (NSGCTs). As discussed in Chapter 4, these tumors, while histogenetically related, have distinct morphologic features. The most common variant of germ cell malignancy is the classic seminoma (see Chapter 4, Figure 4–2), which is characterized by large, round, or polyhedral cells, arranged with a uniform morphology; large centrally located spherical hyperchromatic nuclei with irregular outlines; and one or more basophilic nucleoli and intense histochemical staining for alkaline phosphatase. Thus, this cell type closely resembles the normal or primordial germ cell, and this has led to the concept that the primordial germ cell gives rise to seminoma. Seminoma is characterized by occurrence in patients of a somewhat older age and by an exquisite responsiveness to radiotherapy and chemotherapy. A well-characterized variant is anaplastic seminoma, which is less differentiated and to which a worse prognosis has been attributed in some series (see below and Chapters 18 and 19).

Spermatocytic seminoma, which was traditionally viewed as a variant of classic seminoma, actually has a distinct lineage and histogenesis. Spermatocytic seminoma is also clinically distinct as it tends to present in elderly men, is usually associated with radiologic evidence of intratumoral calcification, and is rarely associated with metastasis.

NSGCTs, or malignant teratomas, include embryonal carcinoma, choriocarcinoma, and teratoma (mature and immature) (see Chapter 4, Figures 4–3, 4–5, and 4–6). Teratomas are characterized by somatic differentiation and may include elements of glandular tissue, hair, and cartilage, as well as components of extraembryonic differentiation (as in yolk sac tumor and choriocarcinoma). Embryonal carcinomas and teratomas are reminiscent of embryologic structures and have a spectrum of histologic patterns, ranging from those that resemble aspects of the developing fetus to one of completely disorganized sheets of anaplastic cells.

Some of the different components of these tumors elaborate a series of tumor markers (see Chapter 7).

A variant of embryonal carcinoma, the yolk sac tumor (or endodermal sinus tumor), produces α-fetoprotein (AFP). Human chorionic gonadotropin (hCG) and placental alkaline phosphatase are classically produced by elements with placental or trophoblastic differentiation, including choriocarcinoma and syncytiotrophoblastic giant cells.

The demonstration of AFP production by a solid neoplasm that morphologically resembles seminoma but that is functionally and ultrastructurally distinct (Figures 1–1 and 1–2) has added some credence to the theory that seminoma and NSGCT have a common origin.[2,3] Other marker proteins (including lactic acid dehydrogenase, alkaline phosphatase, and carcinoembryonic antigen) and genes are expressed by both seminoma and nonseminoma[4] (see Chapter 7) although fibronectin appears to be more limited to nonseminomas.[5] By contrast, it appears

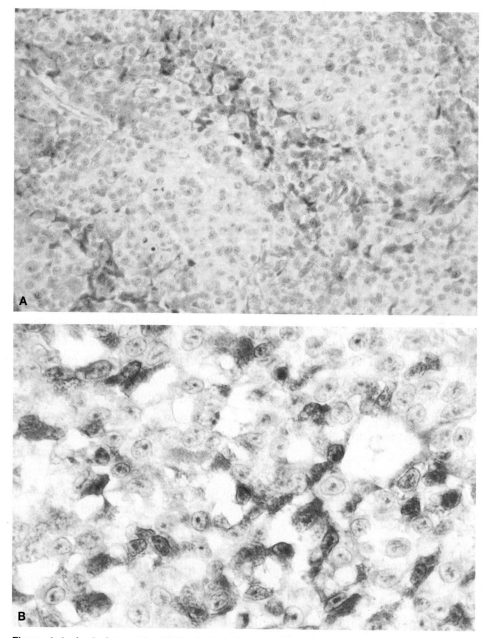

Figure 1–1. An "α-fetoprotein (AFP)–producing" seminoma xenograft. *A,* Low-power micrograph. Note classic architecture, with intermingled production of AFP. *B,* High-power micrograph. Note cytoplasmic staining of AFP. (Photographs courtesy of Dr. Eadie Heyderman, Dr. Derek Raghavan, and Prof. A. M. Neville.)

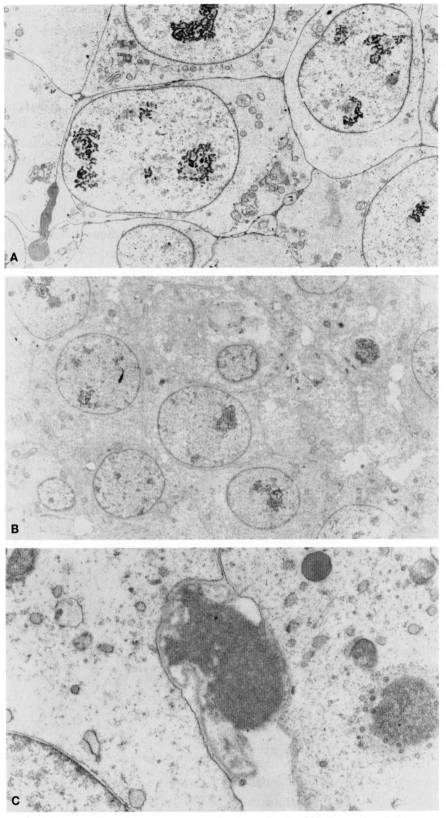

Figure 1–2. An "α-fetoprotein (AFP)-producing" seminoma xenograft. *A,* Electron micrograph of classic seminoma (for purposes of comparison). *B,* Electron micrograph of an "AFP-producing" seminoma xenograft. Note the similarity of architecture. *C,* Electron micrograph of electron-dense extracellular material from the xenograft shown in B. (Electron micrographs courtesy of Dr. Paul Monaghan, Dr. Derek Raghavan, and Prof. A. M. Neville.)

that *MAGE-A4*, a member of a family of genes that encode for tumor antigens that can be recognized by tumor-specific cytolytic T lymphocytes derived from patients with malignant disease, is found in classic seminoma but not in anaplastic seminoma or NSGCT.[6] It should be recalled that one of the features of classic seminoma is a lymphocytic infiltration, which theoretically could explain this phenomenon. Similarly, *c-kit* expression is found predominantly in seminoma rather than in NSGCT,[7] as discussed below.

Thus, by morphologic and functional criteria, it appears most likely that the majority of testicular cancers, including the variants of seminoma and the NSGCTs, share a common origin from primordial germ cells, via the intermediary step of atypical germ cells or carcinoma in situ (CIS). The mechanism of this transition has been the subject of considerable preclinical and clinical investigation, as outlined below.

HISTOGENESIS

Gonadal Germ Cell Tumors

There is now a consensus that seminomas and teratomas (or NSGCTs) arise from germ cells, based on their morphologic, histochemical, functional, and ultrastructural features. However, the precise stage of development of the germinal tissue that gives rise to germ cell tumors remains uncertain. Electron microscopy shows that seminomas are composed of a broad spectrum of cells with features of spermatocytes, spermatogonia, and undifferentiated cells, and it has thus been proposed that seminoma is a tumor of seminiferous epithelium, arising from stem cells that are committed to spermatocytic differentiation.[8]

In opposition to the generally accepted concept of a germ cell origin of classic seminoma, Masson ascribed the features of the precursors of spermatozoa to spermatocytic seminoma and suggested that this variant was derived directly from these cells.[9] Today, the consensus is that classic seminoma is derived from primordial germ cells and that the origin of spermatocytic seminoma is different (but as yet undefined). It is likely that spermatocytic seminoma also originates from the germ cell but perhaps at a different stage of embryologic development.

The histogenesis of malignant teratomas has been a more controversial subject although it is now agreed that these varied tumors also arise from germ cells (Figure 1–3); this has led to their designation as NSGCTs. Their unusual histologic appearance, with a range of tissues of varied differentiation and with the presence of elements of up to three germinal layers, initially led to many different theories of histogenesis. For example, in 1926, Budde[10] suggested that the formation of teratomas was the result of a malfunction of the primary embryonic organizers, with cells being released from normal developmental control at the primitive stalk stage. It was also suggested that teratomas represented suppressed twins or were caused by dysfunction of the cellular organizers during embryogenesis. Willis[11] showed that teratomas lack somatic distribution of tissues and that there is no organization in relation to the spinal column, thus discounting these theories, but he did believe that blastomeres, displaced in early embryonic development and having escaped the influence of cellular organizers, give rise to teratomas. However, for many years, the British school of pathologists viewed seminomas and teratomas as having distinct histogenetic origins.[12]

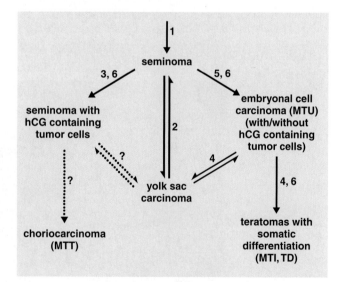

Figure 1–3. Schema of histogenesis of germ cell tumors. Note interrelationships between pathways of development of seminoma and nonseminomatous germ cell tumor (NSGCT). *1,* Origin of seminoma from an atypical germ cell. *2,* Overlap of seminoma and solid variant of yolk sac carcinoma (morphologic?/functional?). *3,* Concurrent evolution of seminoma plus STGC. *4,* Developmental linkages (potentially reversible) between variants of NSGCT. *5,* Atypical germ cell giving rise directly to NSGCT. *6,* Potential for seminoma to be the originator of all tumor types, as intermediary after rise of atypical germ cells. (Reproduced with permission from Raghavan D, Neville AM.[1])

Askanazy, in 1907, was the first to propose that totipotential undifferentiated cells could undergo a metamorphosis to produce teratomas.[13] Several clinicopathologic studies in the following half century supported this fundamental concept,[1,14–16] as did a series of preclinical studies (see below). In particular, support for the germ cell origin of testicular cancer has been provided by the demonstration of a preinvasive intratubular carcinoma in situ, or "atypical germ cell."[17,18] These atypical cells, which differ from normal germ cells in their increased size, irregular chromatin patterns, increased deoxyribonucleic acid (DNA) content, and mitotic index,[19] have been found in infertile males,[19,20] in the contralateral testes of patients with germ cell tumors,[21] in cryptorchid and ectopic testicles,[22] and in "normal" tissue adjacent to germ cell tumors.[23]

Friedman believed that the germinoma (seminoma) was the precursor of undifferentiated malignant teratoma (embryonal carcinoma), which, in turn, gave rise to malignant teratomas with varying degrees of somatic differentiation and to tumors with extraembryonic differentiation.[24] The frequent coexistence of elements of seminoma and NSGCT within extragonadal germ cell tumors is often interpreted as support for commonality of origin, but Dixon and Moore[14] noted the absence of transition stages in these sites and suggested that this favored parallel origins for the two elements. However, transitional morphologic patterns were subsequently identified; for example, Friedman and Pearlman described the "seminoma with trophocarcinoma," a classic seminoma with widely dispersed small foci of embryonal carcinoma, which manifested radioresistance and had an intermediate prognosis between those of seminoma and embryonal carcinoma.[25] This seems to reflect a phenomenon similar to that found in studies (that my colleagues and I conducted) of a solid variant of yolk sac tumor with AFP production that morphologically resembles classic seminoma, as noted above.[2]

Similarly, the place of anaplastic seminoma in the histogenetic scheme of testicular cancer is not clear. This pattern is less differentiated than classic seminoma, but there is considerable controversy as to whether it actually has a different natural history, therapeutic responsiveness, and prognosis[26–29] (see also Chapters 18 and 19). Given the variability of criteria used to define this entity, it is likely that anaplastic seminoma actually represents a series of different tumors, from classic seminoma with reduced differentiation through the spectrum to embryonal carcinoma. This entity further supports the germ cell theory of the origin of these tumors.

Ultimately, it appears that the primordial germ cell gives rise to an atypical germ cell (or carcinoma in situ) that is associated with most types of testicular tumors. Primordial germ cells are first seen in the gastrula,[30] and they subsequently migrate to the genital ridges via the endoderm (Figure 1–4). In humans, they develop within the gonad early in the first trimester, giving rise to spermatogonia during the second and third trimesters. The spermatogonia then undergo a series of mitoses that produce type A, intermediate, and type B spermatogonial cells. The type B cells go on to form primary spermatocytes after further replication and meiosis and eventually produce four haploid cells that form spermatids and spermatozoa. Many of these cells die, and the process of apoptosis is prominently identified, both in the mouse and in humans. The factors that control evolution to malignancy or, alternatively, that lead to apoptosis and limitation of the process of germ cell division have not yet been defined. Several genes have been identified as being involved somehow in

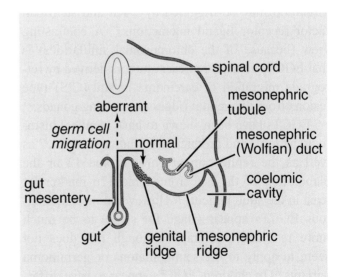

Figure 1–4. The migration of germ cells from the endoderm to sites of genital ridges and the aberrant pathway of migration that leads to the development of extragonadal germ cell tumors. (Reproduced with permission from Raghavan D, Neville AM.[1])

this process, including aberrations of chromosome 12, mutations of *c-kit*, and (possibly) expression of the D2 cyclins (see below).

Extragonadal Germ Cell Tumors

Although extragonadal germ cell tumors (EGCTs) are histologically identical to germ cell tumors derived from primary gonadal sites, their biology is substantially different, for reasons that are not clear. Initially, it was suggested that EGCTs arise from a local dislocation of tissues during embryogenesis, with neoplasia developing in primitive rests of totipotential cells left during the blastular or morular phase.[31] Analogous to the theory of the origins of testicular germ cell tumors, this theory was subsequently discounted and replaced by a theory of germinal origin.[24] The basic concept of the evolution of EGCTs is that they are derived from germ cells with an aberrant path of migration from the yolk sac to the genital ridges (see Figure 1–4). During the first trimester of pregnancy, germ cells normally migrate from the yolk to the genital ridges, leading ultimately to the formation of the gonads.

In the instance of EGCTs, it is postulated that these cells have an aberrant path of migration in the midline,[32] as a consequence of which they lodge in the pineal gland, mediastinum, retroperitoneum, or sacrococcygeum.[33] It has been proposed that this migration may be triggered by c-Kit and stem cell factor receptor–ligand interactions.[34] A contrasting view (because of the chromosomal similarities) is that EGCTs actually represent tumors derived by retrograde migration of carcinoma in situ (CIS)–type lesions from the genital ridges or evolving gonads.[35]

EGCTs have been shown to have identical histologic patterns and production of tumor markers,[33] as well as the replication of chromosome 12 or the elaboration of the isochromosome 12p marker (at least in the adult patient).[36] However, nonseminomatous EGCTs appear (stage for stage) to be much more resistant to therapy although this does not seem to apply to the seminomatous or germinoma variants.[33] In children, EGCTs appear to have different genetic characteristics, with alterations of chromosomes 1 and 6 and usually an absence of changes of chromosome 12p.[37] It may well be that infantile and adult EGCTs develop from germ cells at different stages of their development.

Schneider and colleagues examined germ cell tumors (GCTs) of gonadal and extragonadal origin to assess whether loss of imprinting reflects origin from different stages of germ cell development.[38] They studied DNA methylation of CpG dinucleotides as this represents the most significant biochemical marker of imprinting and allows the identification of maternal and paternal alleles. These workers hypothesized that primordial germ cells erase their inherited imprint and establish a new gender-specific imprinting pattern. If GCTs preserve the original imprinting status of their cell of origin, it would be reasonable to assume that GCTs arising from primordial germ cells before entry into the gonadal ridges and GCTs arising from premeiotic germ cells show erased imprinting; by contrast, if GCTs arise from primordial germ cells that have already entered meiosis (in the genital ridges), they should display a gender-specific gametic imprinting pattern.[38] These studies showed that (1) both gonadal and extragonadal GCTs share a common cell of origin, the primordial germ cell, that has already erased its imprinting; (2) the pattern of erasure is different between adult and infant patients; and (3) ovarian and extragonadal teratomas may arise from germ cells that are more advanced in their development.

MODELS OF GERM CELL DIFFERENTIATION: ONTOGENESIS AND ONCOGENESIS

Murine Germ Cell Evolution

Murine spermatogenesis potentially offers a model of cellular regulation in germ cell neoplasia. During mouse embryogenesis, primordial germ cells migrate from the yolk sac through the hindgut and dorsal mesentery to the genital ridges, where they are seen by the eleventh day of gestation. During migration, they undergo mitosis, and their number increases from around 100 to about 25,000.[39] While incomplete, some data are available regarding molecular factors regulating this process. It appears that *BMP4* is required for the generation of primordial germ cells[40] and that *OCT4* may be required in the establishment of their multipotentiality.[41]

The level of mitotic activity decreases after arrival at the genital ridges, and differentiation of the gonad begins. Subsequently, spermatogonia proliferate, and some undergo meiosis, producing haploid spermatids. These give rise to spermatozoa. Several different types of spermatogonia have been identified although the regulation of their proliferation and differentiation has not been clearly defined. In this context, it should also be noted that there are important differences between the development of germ cells in the female and in the male. Female germ cells proliferate by mitosis and enter meiosis in the embryo, arresting in prophase of the first meiosis and remaining dormant until puberty. At that time, the first meiotic division is completed, but growth is again arrested at the second metaphase, until fertilization.[42] However, in males, the germ cells undergo a few mitotic divisions in the embryo and then remain dormant until puberty, when the spermatogonial stem cells divide by mitosis and then commence meiosis, culminating in the formation of haploid spermatids.

In the mouse, the presence of two mutant alleles initially identified as causing coat color mutations, at either the dominant-white spotting (W) locus (producing the c-Kit receptor) or the Steel (*Sl*) locus (which controls the stem cell factor or c-Kit ligand), can cause sterility, marrow hypoplasia, depletion of mast cells, and reduction of melanocytes.[43] As noted elsewhere in this chapter, c-Kit is a member of the type III receptor tyrosine kinase family; interaction of the c-Kit receptor with the Steel factor leads to activation of tyrosine kinase and phosphorylation of the receptor, which allows binding to sulfhydryl moieties.[44] The mutation in the dominant-white spotting (W) locus leads to a defect in precursor cells that leads to the depletion of differentiated germ cells whereas the mutation of the *Steel* gene causes a defect in the tissue microenvironment, perhaps through a defect in the *MGF* gene, which encodes a growth factor similar to epidermal growth factor (EGF).[45] Mutation of the *Sl* gene also leads to depletion of germ cells. Sertoli's cells produce stem cell factor in the testis whereas c-Kit is expressed on several evolving stages of spermatogonia (but not on the undifferentiated type A spermatogonia).[46] This process can be studied by a technique in which donor mouse germ cells are injected into seminiferous tubules; when spermatogenesis results, the recipient mouse transmits the donor haplotype to the offspring.[43] Such studies have confirmed the expression of c-Kit in evolving stages of spermatogenesis (with the exception of undifferentiated type A spermatogonia) and suggest that stem cell factor may be a prerequisite for the maintenance of c-Kit–positive differentiated germ cells.[43] Orr-Urtreger and colleagues showed that c-Kit is expressed in primordial germ cells before and after migration into the genital ridges during embryogenesis.[47] The model developed by Ohta and colleagues also suggests that the undifferentiated type A spermatogonia in *Sl*-mutant testes may be the putative stem cells that can proliferate and differentiate.[43] Potten and Loeffler[48] proposed that these stem cells occupy a special environmental site, or niche, generated by adjacent cells, which facilitates self-renewal, and it appears that this niche may reside physically in the surrounds of the basement membrane of the testis. It may be no accident that atypical germ cells (carcinoma in situ) are characterized by a migration away from the basement membrane.

However, the process is complex, especially in a context in which the series of observations from Stevens and colleagues suggests that it is unlikely that simple inactivation of the *MGF/c-kit* pathway leads to increased susceptibility to germ cell tumors per se.[54] It has been suggested that an additional relevant gene may reside in the region of the *Sl* deletions. This region of murine chromosome 10 is homologous to the critical 12q22 chromosomal locus in humans.

Also of interest, the interactions between the spermatogonial precursors and the Sertoli's cells are very similar to the interactions between the hematopoietic stem cells and the surrounding stroma.[43] Hematopoiesis may be mediated by the interaction of c-Kit with a transmembrane 4 superfamily protein complex and integrin family proteins.[49] Steel factor is a potent co-stimulating cytokine that participates in growth stimulation of the hematopoietic progenitors. The similarity of these interactions between stem cells and the microenvironment may explain the occasional overlap of leukemia and germ cell malignancy in the same patient.

Another set of potential regulators of mammalian spermatogenesis are the A-type cyclins.[50] Cyclins and cyclin-dependent kinases (CDKs) have important roles in DNA synthesis and cell division, functioning variously at G_1–S and mitosis.[51] There are two vertebrate cyclin genes, *cyclin A1* and *cyclin A2*, which have different patterns of expression; *cyclin A1* functions in germline and early embryonic cells, and *cyclin A2* functions in somatic cells.[52,53] Immunohistochemical studies have identified *cyclin A1* only in male germ cells prior to or during the first meiotic division but not associated with the second division. *Cyclin A2* ribonucleic acid (RNA) has been identified in murine testicular germ cells, including spermatogonia and preleptotene spermatocytes (which are destined for meiosis) and in both ovarian germline and somatic cells.[50] Cyclin A1 binds both cyclin-dependent kinases 1 (CDK1) and 2 (CDK2), but cyclin A2 binds only CDK2.[50] Although it should not be forgotten that the mere identification of messenger RNA (mRNA) does not necessarily have functional implications, these data suggest different functions for cyclin A1 and cyclin A2 in the initiation of meiosis for germ cells and in the regulation of germ cell evolution. The marked differences in cyclin A1 and A2 expression during spermatogenesis may thus provide a model for the exploration of the regulation of the different types of germ cell tumors (Figure 1–5).

Teratomas in the 129 Strain Mouse

The 129/Sv inbred strain mouse model is characterized by a susceptibility to spontaneous germ cell tumors, with an incidence of up to about 10% in mice that are 3 to 4 weeks old. This model, developed by Leroy Stevens, was initially used to characterize the biology of teratomas and embryonic stem cells.[54,55] Analogous to human NSGCTs, 129 strain murine teratomas are composed of disorganized aggregations of malignant cells arranged in sheets, rosettes, and organoid formations although the pattern varies with the age of the mice.[55] For example, in fetal and neonatal mice, the tumors are composed predominantly of undifferentiated sheets of embryonal carcinoma whereas adult mice have tumors composed predominantly of differentiated tissues.

Kleinsmith and Pierce cloned these cells and demonstrated their multipotentiality by showing variable differentiation after their injection into different somatic sites.[15] Pierce and colleagues initially demonstrated in this system the presence of embryoid bodies (aggregates of embryonal carcinoma surrounded by mesenchymal and endodermal cells) that resembled mouse embryos.[56] These aggregates, when transplanted subcutaneously, gave rise to teratomas and teratocarcinomas, also supporting the potential reversibility of the malignant process in this model. Mintz and Illmensee provided added evidence regarding the potential reversibility of malignancy by producing phenotypically normal but genetically mosaic mice by injection of 129 strain teratocarcinoma cells into murine blastocysts.[57]

Stevens[55] demonstrated a time dependence of the ability to form GCTs by grafting genital ridges into ectopic sites, leading to the concept that the maximal time of tumorigenesis in this system is around the twelfth day of gestation. In addition, Stevens demonstrated the importance of mutation of the *Steel* (*Sl*) gene in this system: mice that are homozygous for mutation of this gene lack primordial germ cells and consequently fail to develop these murine teratomas. Sexual differentiation is also critical, as germ cell tumors arise in males in this model, perhaps because of the differences in the evolution of normal germ cells (see above) or perhaps because of hormonal factors. Also of relevance, primordial germ cells are still undergoing mitosis at the eleventh and twelfth days of gestation, but this decreases substantially after that. This time of maximum mitotic activity parallels the time at which GCTs arise maximally. Of relevance, the 129/Sv Ter strain, in which there is a very high incidence of GCTs, has an abnormally prolonged period of mitotic activity.[58]

Several genes and resulting proteins with involvement in tumorigenesis in other systems (such as tumor necrosis factor, transforming growth factor-β, and basic fibroblast growth factor) are involved in germ cell proliferation and are candidates for being involved in the genesis of murine GCTs (see also below). Of particular interest, mutant genes that appear to be involved with susceptibility to murine GCTs include *Ter*, *Steel*, and *TCGT1*, and specific involvements have been mapped to chromosomes 13 and 19.[58–60] The *Ter* mutation increases the risk of 129 strain mice developing GCTs, with more than 90% of *Ter/Ter* male mice being affected. *Ter/Ter* mutant mice also show a deficiency of primordial germ cells, but they also continue to exhibit prolonged mitosis, which suggests that normal Ter protein may modulate mitotic arrest.

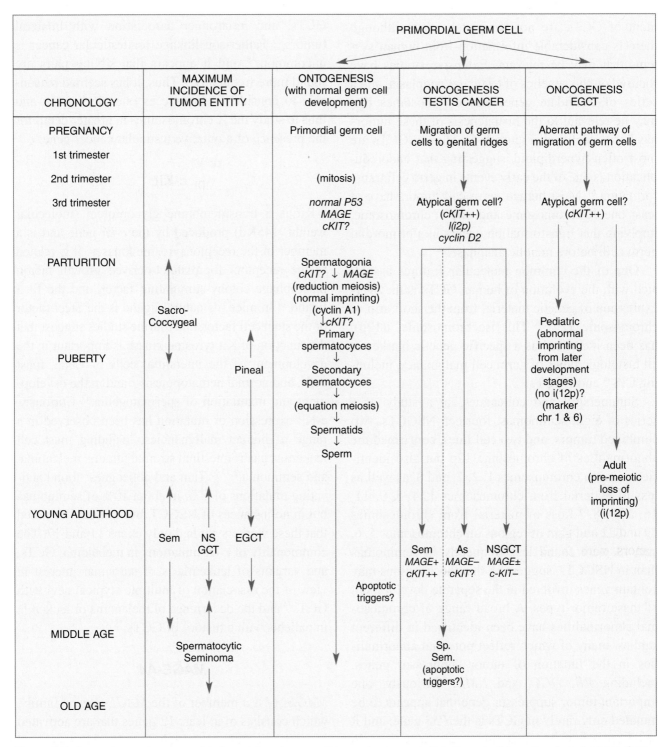

Figure 1–5. Spermatogenesis as a model of regulation of germ cell tumor development. Note the potential overlap of mechanisms. Sem = seminoma; NSGCT = nonseminoma germ cell tumor; EGCT = extragonadal germ cell tumor; AS = anaplastic seminoma; Sp.Sem = spermatocytic seminoma.

MOLECULAR CORRELATES OF GERM CELL TUMOR DEVELOPMENT AND FUNCTION IN HUMANS

The steps between the process of normal sperm formation and the aberrations that lead to the development of GCTs are not completely clear although there is considerable information from human systems that may be relevant. Extensive studies have focused on the genetics of testicular neoplasia, and a series of candidate genes and chromosomes that may be relevant to the histogenesis of these tumors has been identified (Figure 1–5). Human GCTs are most often hyperdiploid, suggesting that endoreduplication is one of the early events in germ cell transformation.[61] Most human germ cell tumors have at least one X chromosome and one Y chromosome, implying that transformation occurs in a primordial germ cell, before meiotic anaphase.[62]

One of the common molecular features associated with the evolution of human GCTs is the overexpression of genetic material from the short arm of chromosome 12.[62,63] This isochromosome, i(12p), has been identified as a specific genetic marker in all histologic types of germ cell malignancy, including CIS[64] and EGCTs.[36]

Summersgill and colleagues, in a study of a series of eight seminomas, fourteen NSGCTs, two combined tumors, and two cell lines, confirmed the abnormalities of chromosome 12p but also identified gains in chromosomes 1, 2, 7, and 8, as well as loss of material from chromosomes 1, 4, 5, 9, 11, 16, and 18.[65] Loss of material from chromosomes 19 and 22 and gain of regions on chromosomes 5, 6, and 13 were found less frequently in seminomas than in NSGCTs, suggesting that these regions may contain genes involved in the separate development of these tumor types. A broad range of chromosomal abnormalities have been identified in different studies, many of which reflect potential abnormalities in the function of tumor suppressor genes, including *RB*, *DCC*, and *NME*. Curiously, one important tumor suppressor gene that appears to be mutated only rarely in GCTs is the *P53* gene, and it has been suggested that this may partly explain these tumors' exquisite sensitivity to radiation therapy and chemotherapy.[66]

Another potential susceptibility gene for testicular GCTs has been localized to the Xq27 chromosome. Rapley and colleagues studied 134 families with two or more cases of testicular cancer and found an association between this chromosomal region and testicular maldescent, an association with testicular GCTs, and a stronger association with bilateral tumors.[67] Father-son linkage for testicular cancer is uncommon,[68] and it appears that sibling pairs are found more frequently.[69] Thus, it has seemed reasonable to consider X linkage as one mechanism and thus to study the X chromosomes in greater detail for the presence of a putative testicular cancer gene.

c-Kit

c-Kit is a transmembrane glycoprotein (molecular weight, 145Kd) produced by the *c-kit* gene and is a member of the receptor tyrosine kinases. It is related to the receptors for platelet-derived growth factor, macrophage colony-stimulating factor, and the flt 3 ligand.[70] In mice, its natural ligand is the Steel factor or the stem cell factor, and murine studies suggest that the function of Kit tyrosine kinase is important in the development of the interstitial cells of Cajal, mast cells, and normal hematopoiesis[71] and in the development and maturation of spermatogonia.[43] Curiously, c-Kit expression or mutation has been observed in a range of human malignancies, including mast cell leukemia, gastrointestinal stromal tumors, melanoma, and seminoma.[7,72,73] Tian and colleagues[7] found activating mutations of *c-kit* in about 10% of seminomas but in no instances of NSGCT, but it should be noted that these workers studied only exons 11 and 17. The commonality of *c-kit* mutations in melanoma, GCTs, and variants of leukemia is of particular interest in view of the association of multiple atypical nevi with GCTs[74] and the occurrence of melanoma or leukemia in patients with a history of GCTs.[75]

MAGE-A4

MAGE-A4 is a member of the *MAGE-A* gene family, which consists of at least 12 genes that are activated in various tumors, including melanoma and GCTs.[6,76–79] These genes encode for tumor antigens that can be recognized by tumor-specific cytolytic T lymphocytes, and they appear to have a role in clinical immunity in some tumors. Takahashi and colleagues demonstrated the expression of MAGE proteins in human spermatogonia and (to a lesser extent) in human primary spermatocytes.[80] Aubry and colleagues[6] confirmed these results and also showed that Sertoli's cells and spermatids did not express MAGE-A4 immunohistochemically. These workers showed an absence of MAGE-A4 reactivity in embryonic and fetal gonads at up to 15 weeks of gestation, weak positive staining at 17 weeks, and strong staining by 28 weeks. These data suggest that the second meiotic division may interfere with the expression of this gene.

In an extensive study, Aubry and colleagues[6] reported expression of *MAGE-A4* in 12 of 12 classic seminomas, 0 of 5 anaplastic seminomas, 0 of 10 NSGCTs, in the seminomatous regions of two mixed tumors (seminoma/NSGCT), and in 0 of 2 Leydig cell tumors and 0 of 1 Sertoli cell tumor. Of particular interest, they also showed expression of this gene in some elements of CIS associated with seminoma and NSGCT, but with considerable heterogeneity of expression in different regions of the testis. Others have shown greater heterogeneity of expression in seminoma.[77–79] Hara and colleagues, using a polymerase chain reaction technique, reported the expression of MAGE-A4 in NSGCTs[78] although this observation could reflect contamination by nonmalignant germline elements within the tumor-bearing testis. Nevertheless, Aubry and colleagues hypothesized that MAGE-A4 is expressed in premeiotic germ cells and GCTs that express classic germ cell lineage but not in tumors with embryonic, extraembryonic, or somatic differentiation, perhaps yielding important information about the differential lineage of seminoma and NSGCT.[6] However, at the time of reporting, it was too early to assess whether MAGE-A4 had any functional role in the progression from the primordial germ cell to the malignant state.

Cyclin D2

The D-type cyclins (D1, D2, and D3) are important regulators of cell cycle function, particularly the G_1 phase. In a series of experiments in knockout mice, Sicinski and colleagues showed that cyclin D2 defi-

ciency leads to sterility because of the failure of ovarian granulosa cells to proliferate normally in response to follicle-stimulating hormone (FSH).[81] Males deficient in the D cyclins have testicular hypoplasia. Sicinski and colleagues showed that GCT cell lines often express high levels of cyclin D2 mRNA but very little or no cyclin D1 and D3 and that an increased copy number of the cyclin D2 gene is often present in these cell lines.[81] Extra copies of the chromosomal region 12p13, which contains the *cyclin D2* gene, are very common in testicular GCTs and presumably are provided by i(12p). These data suggest that the expression of a cyclin that is essential for the development of a specific tissue is particularly susceptible to being subverted during oncogenesis in the same tissue.[81]

CLINICAL EPIDEMIOLOGY AND ETIOLOGY: IMPLICATIONS FOR HISTOGENESIS

The epidemiology of GCTs is reviewed in detail in Chapter 2. To some extent, what is known about the clinical epidemiology of these tumors is revealing of their histogenesis. One of the more dramatic aspects of the epidemiology of this disease is the clear evidence of increasing incidence during the past century, with a rise from around 2 to 3 new cases per 100,000 males per year to the current level of 6 to 8 new cases per 100,000 males per year in some populations. There is a definite racial predominance, with a white-to-black ratio of up to 40:1.[82] The highest incidences are found in Scandinavia and New Zealand, but the basis of this is unknown. The most common traditional etiologic association is the linkage between cryptorchidism and the genesis of testicular cancer. As noted previously, an unexpectedly frequent association is the concurrence of atypical cutaneous nevi and germ cell malignancies, which appears to be more common than the linkage of testicular maldescent and GCTs.[74] While a potential mechanism via altered signaling of *c-kit* offers an attractive explanation, no finite data have been reported on this issue. A possible model of relevance may again be provided by the 129 strain mouse, bearing the lethal yellow allele of the agouti locus (A^y) in this instance. This variant shows a *reduced* incidence of GCTs but an increased frequency of other solid tumors.[55] Of particular interest is the observation that the agouti gene product may inhibit function of melanocortin receptors,[83] which may provide a mechanism linking the biology of GCTs and that of pigmented skin tumors.

Most of the etiologic and epidemiologic associations appear to point to an origin in atypical germ cells. The association of testicular maldescent and the formation of testicular tumors has been known for more than 200 years,[84,85] and atypical germ cells have been identified in cryptorchid testicles.[22] Similarly, testicular cancer is found more commonly in patients with testicular dysgenesis, infertility, and Kleinfelter's syndrome (with expression of an XXY chromosome). Additional epidemiologic associations include reduced body muscle mass and a lower prevalence of male pattern baldness, which may imply lower circulating testosterone levels, as either a cause or an effect of testicular cancer.[86] Although testicular trauma and mumps orchitis have largely been discounted as antecedents of GCTs,[87,88] earlier studies suggested that both could have mechanisms of oncogenesis predicated on testicular atrophy and the consequent evolution of atypical germ cells. Similar mechanisms have been considered to be involved in studies that have suggested that the ingestion of estrogens during the first trimester of pregnancy may be associated with an increased risk of testicular cancer in the offspring.[89] It thus appears that subjects with reproductive disorders associated with a relative deficiency of androgen function are at increased risk of testicular cancer. As increases in the length of a trinucleotide repeat cytidine, adenine, guanine (CAG) in the androgen receptor gene may lead to reduced transactivation of this gene, King and colleagues[90] assessed a series of 11 testicular cancer cell lines for expanded (CAG)n tracts in DNA and identified this phenomenon in five lines. In addition, they found expanded CAG repeats in 1 of 11 sporadic testicular tumors. However, when comparing the expression of this repeat in patients with testicular cancer and in control subjects, Rajpert-De Meyts and colleagues did not reveal any significant differences in prevalence of CAG repeats in the androgen receptor genes between the two populations.[91] Further studies are needed to clarify this important issue.

As an extension of this concept of genetic transmission, family clustering has occasionally been reported, with a possible increased incidence in father-son and sibling pairs.[68,92,93] In theory, this phenomenon could reflect a heritable pattern of CAG repeats with associated alterations in the function of the androgen receptor gene within sequential generations of affected families. This could also explain the racial differences in the incidence of testicular cancer. My colleagues and I postulated the potential for genetic anticipation in germ cell malignancy about 20 years ago, based on a limited database of father-son pairs.[68] Recently, Han and Peschel[94] have updated the literature, identifying 52 father-son pairs with testicular germ cell tumors, and have suggested that genetic anticipation does, in fact, occur in this disease. They have dealt with the issue of case ascertainment bias to some extent, noting that fathers have tended to present later and with less aggressive disease than have their offspring. In this study, earlier presentation and the presence of NSGCT (rather than seminoma) were identified as parameters of genetic anticipation and increased aggression. However, it should be noted that seminoma per se is not necessarily a less aggressive tumor than NSGCT and that the improved results of therapy reflect greater responsiveness to radiation therapy and, perhaps, to chemotherapy. In addition, this study did not take into consideration the potential impact of the development of effective chemotherapy for advanced disease; in the past 20 years, the potential for patients with more aggressive disease to survive and to produce children has changed dramatically. In addition, hormonal factors may confound the process, as discussed below. Thus, the real situation in regard to the impact of genetic anticipation in germ cell malignancy remains unresolved.

As noted above, several parameters of testicular dysfunction and infertility are associated with the development of GCTs. The prevalence of high circulating levels of FSH may explain some of the populations that have an increased incidence of GCTs, with one of the putative mechanisms being altered expression or function of the cyclin D proteins. Of relevance, one study found that male dizygotic twins are three times more likely to develop testicular GCTs than are male monozygotic twins although it should be noted that zygosity was determined by questionnaire in this study.[95] A potential explanation of this finding may be the association of FSH hypersecretion in the mothers of dizygotic twins, a marked similarity between the geographic distribution in the occurrence of dizygotic twinning and testicular cancer, the apparent linkage of high levels of cyclin D2 and FSH, and the association between Down syndrome, FSH hypersecretion, and testicular cancer.[96] This leads to the hypothesis that chronic FSH hypersecretion may be causative of testicular cancer.[96] This may also be a mechanism for the familial aggregation of GCTs as noted above, analogous to the putative familial hormone patterns that lead to the familial aggregation of male pattern baldness (it should not be forgotten that in patients with testicular cancer, baldness is in fact less common).

It should also be noted that a direct hormonal association of testicular dysfunction, hormonal levels, and testicular cancer is not the only putative mechanism. For example, many of the epidemiologic observations in testicular cancer patients could be explained on the basis of a transmitted carcinogen. For example, Schwartz has hypothesized that ochratoxin A, a mycotoxin found as a contaminant of various foods, may cause testicular cancer.[97] Ochratoxin A is a known genotoxic carcinogen and has been shown in animal experiments to cause adducts in testicular DNA. Thus, this is another potential mechanism for familial aggregation, given the tendency for clustering of familial dietary patterns. This association has not been proved for GCTs in human studies, but it is a reminder that much current epidemiologic information is circumstantial and that the exact origins and histogenetic mechanisms in the formation of GCTs remain unclear.

SUMMARY

Germ cell tumors remain a biologic enigma. Despite improved knowledge of mechanisms for cure, the fundamental understanding of their biology remains incomplete. Extensive data derived from the murine teratoma model provide an intriguing window into teratoma biology although there is controversy regarding the usefulness of this information in the context of human disease. Several social, epidemiologic, and molecular factors that appear to regulate the growth and development of normal and malignant human germ cells have been identified. However, the specific linkages remain to be both biologically and clinically elucidated. It is clear that these tumors are associated with germ cell origins, predominantly young populations, cryptorchidism, infertility, a range of abnormal hormonal factors, multiple atypical nevi, and abnormalities of genetic expression. Whether there is a unifying hypothesis that explains these curiosities remains to be determined.

REFERENCES

1. Raghavan D, Neville AM. The biology of testicular tumours. In: Innes-Williams D, Chisholm G, editors. Scientific foundations of urology. 2nd ed. London: William Heinemann Medical Books; 1982. p. 785–96.
2. Raghavan D, Sullivan AL, Peckham M, Neville AM. Elevated serum alphafetoprotein and seminoma: clinical evidence for a histologic continuum? Cancer 1982;50:982–9.
3. Monaghan P, Raghavan D, Neville AM. Ultrastructural studies of xenografted human germ cell tumors. Cancer 1982;49:683–97.
4. Raghavan D, Lange PH. Endocrine aspects of genitourinary neoplasia. In: Shearman RP, editor. Clinical reproductive endocrinology. London: Longmans; 1985. p. 727–52.
5. Ruoslahti E, Jalanko H, Comings D, et al. Fibronectin from human germ cell tumors resembles amniotic fluid fibronectin. Int J Cancer 1981;27:763–7.
6. Aubry F, Satie AP, Rioux-Leclercq N, et al. MAGE-A4, a germ cell specific marker, is expressed differentially in testicular tumors. Cancer 2001;92:2778–85.
7. Tian Q, Frierson HF Jr, Krystal GW, Moskaluk CA. Activating c-kit gene mutations in human germ cell tumors. Am J Pathol 1999;154:1643–7.
8. Pierce GB Jr. Ultrastructure of human testicular tumors. Cancer 1966;19:1963–83.
9. Masson P. Etude sur le seminome. Rev Can Biol 1946;5:361–87.
10. Budde M. Origin of fetal inclusions, complicated dermoids and teratomas and their interrelations. Monatsschr F Geburtsch U Gynak 1926;74:276–83.
11. Willis RA. The borderland of embryology and pathology. 2nd ed. London: Butterworth; 1962.
12. Pugh RCB. Combined tumours. In: Pugh RCB. Pathology of the testis. Oxford and London: Blackwell Scientific Publications; 1976. p. 139–59.
13. Askanazy M. Die Teratome nach ihrem Bau, ihrem Verlauf, ihrer Genese und in Vergleich zum experimentellen Teratoid. Verh Dtsch Ges Path 1907;11:39–82.
14. Dixon FJ, Moore RA. Testicular tumors: a clinicopathological study. Cancer 1953;6:427–54.
15. Kleinsmith LJ, Pierce GB. Multipotentiality of single embryonal carcinoma cells. Cancer Res 1964;24:1544–52.
16. Teilum G. Special tumours of ovary and testis. Copenhagen: Munksgaard; 1971.

17. Bunge RG, Bradbury JT. An early human seminoma. JAMA 1965;193:960–2.
18. Skakkebaek NE. Possible carcinoma-in-situ of the testis. Lancet 1972;ii:516–7.
19. Skakkebaek NE. Carcinoma-in-situ of the testis: frequency and relationship to invasive germ cell tumours in infertile men. Histopathology 1978;2:157–70.
20. Nuesch-Bachman IH, Hedinger C. Atypische Spermatogonien als Prakanzerose. Schweiz Med Wochenschr 1977; 107:795–801.
21. Berthelsen JG, Skakkebaek NE, Morgensen P, Sorensen BL. Incidence of carcinoma in situ of germ cells in contralateral testis of men with testicular tumours. BMJ 1979; 2:363–4.
22. Waxman M. Malignant germ cell tumor in situ in a cryptorchid testis. Cancer 1976;38:1452–6.
23. Skakkebaek NE. Atypical germ cells in the adjacent "normal" tissue of testicular tumours. Acta Pathol Microbiol Scand 1975;83:127–30.
24. Friedman NB. The comparative morphogenesis of extragenital and gonadal teratoid tumors. Cancer 1951;4:265–76.
25. Friedman M, Pearlman AW. Seminoma with trophocarcinoma: a clinical variant of seminoma. Cancer 1970;26:46–64.
26. Maier JG, Sulak MH. Radiation therapy in malignant testis tumors. Cancer 1973;32:1212–6.
27. Johnson DE, Gomez JJ, Ayala A. Anaplastic seminoma. J Urol 1975;114:80–2.
28. Kademian M, Bosch A, Caldwell WL, Jaeschke W. Anaplastic seminoma. Cancer 1977;40:3082–6.
29. Percarpio B, Clements JC, McLeod DG, et al. Anaplastic seminoma: an analysis of 77 patients. Cancer 1979;43: 2510–3.
30. Skakkebaek NE, Rajpert-de Meyts E, Jorgensen N, et al. Germ cell cancer and disorders of spermatogenesis: an environmental connection? Acta Pathol Microbiol Immunol Scand 1998;106:3–12.
31. Schlumberger HG. Teratoma of the anterior mediastinum in the group of military age. Arch Pathol 1946;41:398–444.
32. Witschi E. Migration of the germ cells of human embryos from the yolk sac to the primitive gonadal folds. Contr Embryol Carnegie Inst 1948;32:67–80.
33. Boyer MJ, Raghavan D. Extragonadal germ cell tumors. In: Peckham MJ, Pinedo H, Veronesi U, editors. Oxford textbook of oncology. Oxford: Oxford University Press; 1995. p. 2169–89.
34. Wylie C. Germ cells. Cell 1999;96:165–74.
35. Chaganti RS, Houldsworth J. The cytogenetic theory of the pathogenesis of adult male germ cell tumors. Acta Pathol Microbiol Immunol Scand 1998;106:80–4.
36. Chaganti RS, Rodriguez E, Mathew S. Origin of adult male mediastinal germ-cell tumours. Lancet 1994;343:1130–2.
37. Perlman EJ, Cushing B, Hawkins E, Griffin CA. Cytogenetic analysis of childhood endodermal sinus tumors: a Pediatric Oncology Group study. Pediatr Pathol 1994;14:695–708.
38. Schneider DT, Schuster AE, Fritsch MK, et al. Multipoint imprinting analysis indicates a common precursor cell for gonadal and nongonadal pediatric germ cell tumors. Cancer Res 2001;61:7268–76.
39. Tam PP, Snow MH. Proliferation and migration of primordial germ cells during compensatory growth in mouse embryos. J Embryol Exp Morphol 1981;64:133–45.
40. Lawson KA, Dunn NR, Roelen BA, et al. BMP4 is required for the generation of primordial germ cells in the mouse embryo. Genes Dev 1999;13:424–36.
41. Nichols J, Zevnik B, Anastassiadis K, et al. Formation of pluripotent stem cells in the mammalian embryo depends on the POU transcription factor Oct4. Cell 1998;95:379–91.
42. Peters H. The development of the mouse ovary from birth to maturity. Acta Endocrinol 1969;62:98–116.
43. Ohta H, Yomogida K, Dohmae K, Nishimune Y. Regulation of proliferation and differentiation in spermatogonial stem cells: the role of c-kit and its ligand SCF. Development 2000;127:2125–31.
44. Rottapel R, Reedijk M, Williams DE, et al. The steel/W transduction pathway: kit autophosphorylation and its association with a unique subset of cytoplasmic signaling proteins is induced by the steel factor. Mol Cell Biol 1991;11:3043–51.
45. Zsebo KM, Williams DA, Geissler EN, et al. Stem cell factor is encoded at the Sl locus of the mouse and is the ligand for the c-kit tyrosine kinase receptor. Cell 1990;63:213–24.
46. Motro B, van der Kooy D, Rossant J, et al. Contiguous patterns of c-kit and steel expression: analysis of mutations at the W and Sl loci. Development 1991;113:1207–21.
47. Orr-Urtreger A, Avivi A, Zimmer Y, et al. Developmental expression of c-kit, a proto-oncogene encoded by the W locus. Development 1990;109:911–23.
48. Potten CS, Loeffler M. Stem cells: attributes, k cycles, spirals, pitfalls and uncertainties. Lessons for and from the crypt. Development 1990;110:1001–20.
49. Anzai N, Lee Y, Youn B-S, et al. c-kit associated with the transmembrane 4 superfamily proteins constitutes a functionally distinct subunit in human hematopoietic progenitors. Blood 2002;99:4413–21.
50. Ravnik SE, Wolgemuth DJ. Regulation of meiosis during mammalian spermatogenesis: the A-type cyclins and their associated cyclin-dependent kinases are differentially expressed in the germ-cell lineage. Dev Biol 1999;207:408–18.
51. Pines J. Cyclin and cyclin-dependent kinases: take your partners. Trends Biochem Sci 1993;18:195–7.
52. Howe JA, Howell M, Hunt T, Newport JW. Identification of a developmental timer regulating the stability of embryonic cyclin A and a new somatic A-type cyclin at gastrulation. Genes Dev 1995;9:1164–75.
53. Sweeney CS, Murphy M, Kubelka M, et al. A distinct cyclin A gene is expressed in germ cells and during early embryogenesis in the mouse. Development 1996;122:53–64.
54. Stevens LC, Hummel KP. A description of spontaneous congenital testicular teratomas in strain 129 mice. J Natl Cancer Inst 1957;27:719–47.
55. Stevens LC. The biology of teratomas. Adv Morphog 1967; 6:1–31.
56. Pierce GB, Dixon FJ, Verney EL. Teratocarcinogenic and tissue forming potentialities of the cell types comprising neoplastic embryoid bodies. Lab Invest 1960;9:583–90.
57. Mintz B, Illmensee K. Normal genetically mosaic mice produced from malignant teratocarcinoma cells. Proc Natl Acad Sci U S A 1975;72:3585–9.
58. Noguchi T, Noguchi M. A recessive mutation TER causing germ cell deficiency and a high incidence of congenital testicular teratomas in 129/Sv-ter mice. J Natl Cancer Inst 1985;75:385–91.

59. Matin A, Collin GB, Asada Y, et al. Susceptibility to testicular germ-cell tumours in a 129 MOLF – Chr 19 chromosome substitution strain. Nat Genet 1999;23:237–40.

60. Muller AJ, Teresky AK, Levine AJ. A male germ cell tumor-susceptibility-determining locus, PGCT1, identified on murine chromosome 13. Proc Natl Acad Sci U S A 2000; 97:8421–6.

61. de Jong B, Oosterhuis JW, Castedo SM, et al. Pathogenesis of adult testicular germ cell tumors: a cytogenetic model. Cancer Genet Cytogenet 1990;48:143–67.

62. Chaganti RSK, Rodriguez E, Bosl GJ. Cytogenetics of male germ-cell tumors. Urol Clin North Am 1993;20:55–66.

63. Atkin NB, Baker MC. i(12p): specific chromosomal marker in seminoma and malignant teratoma of the testis? Cancer Genet Cytogenet 1983;10:199–204.

64. Rodriguez E, Mathew S, Reuter V, et al. Cytogenetic analysis of 124 prospectively ascertained male germ cell tumors. Cancer Res 1992;52:2285–91.

65. Summersgill B, Goker H, Weber-Hall S, et al. Molecular cytogenetic analysis of adult testicular germ cell tumours and identification of regions of consensus copy number change. Br J Cancer 1998;77:305–13.

66. Kersemaekers A-MF, Mayer F, Molier M, et al. Role of P53 and MDM2 in treatment response of human germ cell tumors. J Clin Oncol 2002;20:1551–61.

67. Rapley EA, Crockford GP, Teare D, et al. Localization to Xq27 of a susceptibility gene for testicular germ-cell tumours. Nat Genet 2000;24:197–200.

68. Raghavan D, Jelihovsky T, Fox RM. Father-son testicular malignancy: does genetic anticipation occur? Cancer 1980;45:1005–9.

69. Forman D, Oliver RT, Brett AR, et al. Familial testicular cancer: a report of the UK family register, estimation of risk and HLA class 1 sib-pair analysis. Br J Cancer 1992;65:255–62.

70. Rousset D, Agnres F, Lachaume P, et al. Molecular evolution of the genes encoding receptor tyrosine kinase with immunoglobulinlike domains. J Mol Evol 1995;41:421–9.

71. Fleischman RA. From white spots to stems cells: the role of the kit receptor in mammalian development. Trends Genet 1993;9:285–90.

72. Bokemeyer C, Kuczyk MA, Dunn T. Expression of stem-cell factor and its receptor c-kit proto-oncogene in germ cell tumours. J Pathol 1996;122:301–6.

73. Hirota S, Isozaki K, Moriyama Y, et al. Gain-of-function mutations of c-kit in human gastrointestinal stromal tumors. Science 1998;279:577–80.

74. Raghavan D, Zalcberg J, Grygiel JJ, et al. Multiple atypical nevi: a cutaneous marker of germ cell tumors. J Clin Oncol 1994;12:2284–7.

75. Travis LB, Curtis RE, Storm H, et al. Risk of second malignant neoplasms among long-term survivors of testicular cancer. J Natl Cancer Inst 1997;89:1429–39.

76. Van der Bruggen P, Traversari C, Chomez P, et al. A gene encoding an antigen recognized by cytolytic T lymphocytes on a human melanoma. Science 1991;254:1643–7.

77. Cheville JC, Roche PC. MAGE-1 and MAGE-3 tumor rejection antigens in human germ cell tumors. Mod Pathol 1999;12:974–8.

78. Hara I, Hara S, Miyake H, et al. Expression of MAGE genes in testicular germ cell tumors. Urology 1999;53:843–7.

79. Jungbluth AA, Busam KJ, Kolb D, et al. Expression of MAGE-antigen in normal tissues and cancer. Int J Cancer 2000;85:460–5.

80. Takahashi K, Shichijo S, Noguchi M, et al. Identification of MAGE-1 and MAGE-4 proteins in spermatogonia and primary spermatocytes of testis. Cancer Res 1995;55: 3478–82.

81. Sicinski P, Donaher JL, Geng Y, et al. Cyclin D2 is an FSH-responsive gene involved in gonadal cell proliferation and oncogenesis. Nature 1996;384:470–4.

82. Daniels JL, Stutzman RE, McLeod DG. A comparison of testicular tumors in black and white patients. J Urol 1981;125:341–2.

83. Dinulescu DM, Cone RD. Agouti and agouti-related protein: analogies and contrasts. J Biol Chem 2000;63:175–85.

84. Pott P. The chirurgical works of Percivall Pott. London: Lowndes, Johnson, Robinson, Cadell, Evans, Fox, Vew and Hayes; 1779.

85. Gilbert JB, Hamilton JB. Studies in malignant testis tumors; incidence and nature of tumors in ectopic testes. Surg Gynecol Obstet 1940;71:731–43.

86. Petridou E, Roukas KI, Dessypris N, et al. Baldness and other correlates of sex hormones in relation to testicular cancer. Int J Cancer 1997;71:982–5.

87. Field TE. The role of trauma in the aetiology of testicular neoplasms. J R Army Med Corps 1963;109:1.

88. Henderson BE, Benton BDA, Waver PT, et al. Stilbestrol and uro-genital tract cancer in adolescents and young adults. N Engl J Med 1979;288:354.

89. Cosgrove MD, Benton B, Henderson BE. Male genitourinary abnormalities and maternal diethylstilbestrol. J Urol 1977;117:220–2.

90. King BL, Peng HO, Goss P, et al. Repeat expansion detection analysis of (CAG)n tracts in tumor cell lines, testicular tumors, and testicular cancer families. Cancer Res 1997;57:209–14.

91. Rajpert-De Meyts E, Leffers H, Daugaard G, et al. Analysis of the polymorphic CAG repeat length in the androgen receptor gene in patients with testicular germ cell cancer. Int J Cancer 2002;102:201–4.

92. Gordon-Taylor G, Wyndham NR. On malignant tumours of the testicle. Br J Surg 1947;35:6–7.

93. Salm R, Adlington SR. Seminoma in identical twins. Br Med J 1962;2:964.

94. Han S, Peschel RE. Father-son testicular tumors: evidence for genetic anticipation? Case report and review of the literature. Cancer 2000;88:2319–25.

95. Swerdlow AJ, De Stavola BL, Swanwick MA, Maconochie NEW. Risks of breast and testicular cancers in young adult twins in England and Wales: evidence on prenatal and genetic aetiology. Lancet 1997;350:1723–8.

96. Lambalk CB, Boomsma DI. Genetic risk factors in tumours of the testis: lessons from twin studies. Twin Res 1998;1:154–5.

97. Schwartz GG. Hypothesis: does ochratoxin A cause testicular cancer? Cancer Causes Control 2002;13:91–100.

Epidemiologic Insights into the Occurrence and Causes of Testicular Cancer

VICTORIA CORTESSIS, PhD

Epidemiologic research has described the population distribution of testicular cancer and has suggested pathophysiologic mechanisms that are being investigated. Descriptive studies show that testicular cancer is becoming more common and that it occurs primarily in young men. This unusual age distribution accounts for much of the impact of disease and suggests some etiologic hypotheses. Analytic research has provided etiologic insights suggesting that testicular germ cell carcinoma has both environmental and genetic origins.

PATTERNS OF OCCURRENCE

Time Trends

The lifetime risk of testicular cancer is less than 1%. Unlike the more common cancers, testicular cancer primarily affects young men (Figures 2–1 and 2–2). Among men between the ages of 20 and 35 years, testicular cancer was the most common cancer until it was surpassed by Kaposi's sarcoma, a cancer related to acquired immunodeficiency syndrome (AIDS). The occurrence of testicular cancer has been increasing for decades,[1–14] and where accurate incidence data have been collected, the rates have been found to have increased by a factor of three or four in the last 50 years. Incidence rates in the United States nearly doubled from 1973 to 1999, as shown by data collected by nine registries of the Sur-

veillance, Epidemiology, and End Results (SEER) program (Figure 2–3). Because the increases have been so rapid and substantial, they are attributed to increasingly prevalent environmental exposures although the specific agents remain elusive.

Studies that distinguish between period and cohort effects[3,9,10,12,15–18] have found that year of birth is a more important determinant of risk than year of diagnosis. These birth-cohort effects suggest that important exposures occur early in life, perhaps in utero.

SEER data show steadier rates in the 1990s among white males in the United States and even suggest a decline in the late 1990s among men aged 20 to 24 years.[19] It is tempting to interpret this report as a hint that the epidemic may be abating, but past instances of stabilized rates proved to be only perturbations in the general upward trend. Rates have traditionally been more stable at the extremes of age, that is, among boys and among men over 60 years of age. One study found that the incidence of testicular cancer in boys (up to 4 years of age) and very young men (15 to 19 years of age) did not increase in Denmark, Norway, and Sweden during the period of 1960 to 1985.[18] However, the authors noted that age-specific incidence continued to rise in all other age groups throughout this period, and they concluded that these younger cases may differ etiologically from the others. An additional set of analyses[9,15,16] showed stabilization of risk in several cohorts born around the time of the Second World War. However, this lull was not sustained, and risk to successive cohorts climbed thereafter.

In recent decades, remarkable advances in treatment have led to dramatically improved survival of testicular cancer patients in the industrialized world. In the United States, the improvement has been greatest among white persons, and survival is associated with socioeconomic status in many areas.[3,14,20,21] However, it is now evident that survivors are at an elevated risk of several undesirable sequelae, including infertility,[22,23] sexual dysfunction,[24] other types of cancer,[25,26] and second occurrences of testicular cancer.[26-35] (See also Chapters 27 and 28.)

Geographic and Racial/Ethnic Distribution

There is significant variation in the geographic and racial/ethnic distribution of testicular cancer. In the United States, incidence is highest among non-Hispanic white persons (Figure 2–1). Worldwide, rates are relatively high in the United Kingdom and in northern Europe.[36] There are, however, noteworthy differences even among these predominantly white groups. For example, the highest age-adjusted rates have for some time been observed in Denmark (11.1 per 100,000 in 1995) whereas in nearby Finland, rates

are substantially lower (2.8 per 100,000 in 1995).[36] Traditionally, rates have been far lower in Africa and Asia and among those of African and Asian descent in the United States. Schottenfeld and Warshauer concluded that underreporting does not appear to explain the lower rates in Africa, as elevated rates of other cancers were concomitantly observed.[1]

In humans, the vast majority of testicular tumors arise in germ cells. In Los Angeles County, rates of germ cell carcinoma for the period of 1972 to 1999 were highest among the non-Hispanic white population, followed by the Hispanic population and then several groups of Asian ancestry; rates were lowest among African Americans (Figure 2–4). These patterns were similar for subgroups of tumors defined by histologic type (nonseminoma, mixed germ cell tumor, and seminoma).

Age Distribution

Testicular germ cell tumors have a distinctive pattern of age at onset, with a small spike in the first few years of life and with a second broad peak beginning just after puberty. This characteristic shape of the age-incidence curve is observed for all racial and ethnic groups (as shown by the "total"

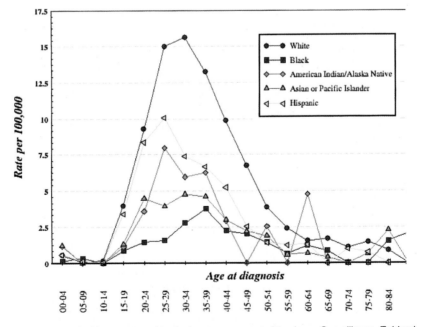

Figure 2–1. Incidence rates of testicular cancer reported to eleven Surveillance, Epidemiology, and End Results (SEER) registries, 1995 to 1999, for five racial/ethnic groups (group-specific spikes at 54, 64, and 84 years interpreted as statistical variation in small populations).

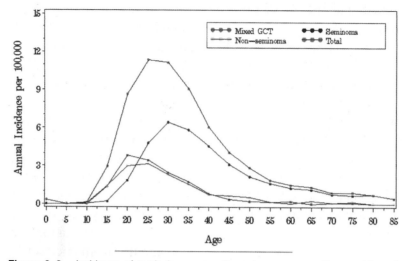

Figure 2–2. Incidence of testicular germ cell carcinoma among the non-Hispanic white population in Los Angeles County, 1972 to 1999, showing age distribution of all tumors and of three categories of histologic types. (GCT = germ cell tumor.)

curve in Figure 2–4) and could be seen in past decades even as age-specific rates were rising.

There are some measurable differences in the age distribution of histologic subtypes. Germ cell tumors of early childhood are limited to nonseminoma (predominantly yolk sac tumors). Nonseminoma and mixed germ cell tumors are more common among adolescents and the youngest adults whereas seminoma predominates among men who are in their early twenties and older (see Figure 2–2). The age-incidence pattern for all germ cell tumors (total curve in Figure 2–2) results from the age-dependent distributions of these histologic subgroups.

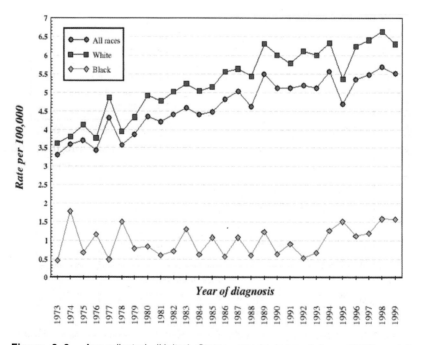

Figure 2–3. Age-adjusted (United States standard population, 2000) racial group–specific incidence rates of testicular cancer reported to nine Surveillance, Epidemiology, and End Results (SEER) registries, 1973 to 1999.

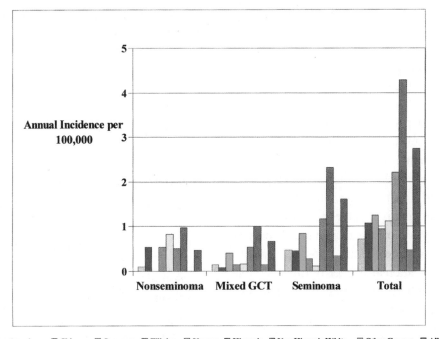

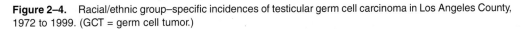

Figure 2–4. Racial/ethnic group–specific incidences of testicular germ cell carcinoma in Los Angeles County, 1972 to 1999. (GCT = germ cell tumor.)

Several etiologic models have been proposed to account for the unusual age distribution of testicular germ cell tumors, which shows a preponderance of occurrence in early adulthood.

In 1983, Henderson and colleagues[37] proposed a biologic model with two critical periods. The initial event occurs in utero if elevated levels of free estrogen (and perhaps other steroids) are present when testicular germ cells begin to differentiate. This event is postulated to alter germ cells permanently, and they then remain dormant throughout childhood. The second critical period is puberty, when the altered germ cells are stimulated to multiply by rising levels of hormones, presumably gonadotropins. At the time it was proposed, this model could account for all germ cell tumors except the small fraction occurring during early childhood, prior to the events of puberty. It is now apparent, however, that even this early group accords with the model because more recent research[38,39] has demonstrated that male infants experience a transient elevation in both testosterone and gonadotropins, with levels approaching those of puberty. However, this model does not account for the lower incidence of testicular cancer that is observed in later decades of life.

Paradoxically, this is a time when age-related biologic processes are presumed to enhance carcinogenic processes, leading to the dramatic rise in the incidence of most adult tumors.

In 1999, Aalen and Tretli[40] described a mathematical model that addresses both the lower incidence of testicular cancer seen in later decades of life and the increasing temporal trends. Underlying their model is the idea that a subgroup of men is susceptible to testicular cancer and that the susceptibility results from a combination of genetic and environmental factors during fetal life. It is presumed that susceptible individuals develop testicular cancer after the hormonal processes of puberty begin. By fitting their model to testicular cancer incidence data collected in Norway from 1953 through 1993, they estimated the proportion of susceptible men among cohorts born between 1885 and 1975. They inferred that (1) a very small proportion of men in each cohort were born with susceptibility to either seminoma or nonseminoma (0.6% and 0.5%, respectively, for the most recent cohort) and that (2) the proportion of susceptible men increased in successive birth cohorts, rising by a factor of 10 during the 90-year period. The dramatic increase in the proportion of susceptible individuals explains the temporal trend in population rates, which would rise as birth cohorts with successively higher proportions of susceptible individuals completed puberty.

The two models taken together offer an explanation of why testicular cancer occurs primarily in young men. The model of Henderson and colleagues explains that incidence rises early in adulthood because the onset of disease follows puberty. The results of Aalen and Tretli explain why age-specific incidence rates fall again in later decades.[40] They found that the proportion of susceptible individuals in any birth cohort is extremely small. Most susceptible individuals develop testicular cancer during the first few decades after puberty, resulting in a relatively high incidence in early adulthood. By the time a birth cohort reaches older ages, however, very few susceptible individuals remain disease free, so rates fall.

In 1995, Buetow[41] reviewed components of an unrelated hypothesis suggesting that the age distribution of testicular cancer results from a viral etiology. This explanation has its roots in an earlier observation that testicular cancer shares epidemiologic features with Hodgkin's disease, for which a similar mechanism had been suggested. According to this model, infection at an early age has low pathogenicity and imparts immunity but delayed infection results in neoplasm.

Impressions from Descriptive Data

The patterns of occurrence described above were observed in data collected and compiled by cancer registries. The long histories of some registries and the high quality of the incidence and demographic data that have been collected allow one to confidently conclude that (1) testicular cancer is primarily a disease of young men and has different geographic and racial/ethnic distributions; (2) its incidence increased dramatically during the twentieth century, at least partly due to birth cohort effects; and (3) its mortality has decreased more recently in industrialized countries. The first two sets of observations provide some hints about the etiology of testicular cancer. However, to find specific causes and develop preventive measures, analytic studies that measure causal factors at the individual level are needed. The

analytic studies described in the next section have identified a series of conditions that seem to occur more frequently among individuals with testicular cancer. These conditions include the major known risk factor, cryptorchidism. Family history of testicular cancer is the only other well-established risk factor (although analytic studies have begun to explore the possible etiologic role of additional factors).

UROGENITAL CONDITIONS ASSOCIATED WITH TESTICULAR CANCER

Cryptorchidism

Cryptorchidism is a common congenital disorder in which one or both testicles fail to descend into the scrotum before birth. Over half of the boys who are born with cryptorchidism experience spontaneous testicular descent during the first year of life. A history of persistent cryptorchidism, in which spontaneous descent does not occur, is the major established risk factor for testicular cancer. Epidemiologic studies consistently find associations between a personal history of cryptorchidism and risk of testicular cancer, and reported estimates of relative risk range from 2.5 to 18.[1,5,11,42–60] Some studies found cryptorchidism to be more strongly associated with seminoma than with other histologic types.

The specific mechanisms whereby a history of cryptorchidism predisposes an individual to testicular cancer are not known although two general scenarios have been postulated. The "abdominal-location hypothesis" asserts that pathogenic effects of the suprascrotal position are responsible for malignant transformation of germ cells. Often taken as support for this hypothesis is the observation that among men with a history of cryptorchidism, the risk of testicular cancer is lower for those who were treated for cryptorchidism at an early age. However, an alternate explanation is that groups treated at earlier ages include higher proportions of boys who would have otherwise experienced spontaneous testicular descent—and who are presumably at lower risk for testicular cancer.

A second set of observations interpreted as supporting this hypothesis comes from surgical models of cryptorchidism in rodents. In these experiments, histologic and molecular changes were observed in testes that were presumed to be normal until they were surgically retained or elevated into the abdomen. Changes included an increased apoptosis of primary spermatocytes[61] and spermatids[62]; a significant and permanent decrease in testosterone levels; and the induction of messenger ribonucleic acids (mRNAs) encoding transforming growth factor (TGF)-β_2, TGF-β_3, tumor necrosis factor (TNF)-α receptor, Fas,[62] and an ovarian-specific transcript of the luteinizing hormone (LH) receptor.[63] While it is clear that prolonged periods in a suprascrotal position can induce numerous changes, mechanistic studies are needed to determine which changes (if any) contribute to the malignant potential of rodent or human testes.

The alternative "common-cause hypothesis" suggests that one or more factors cause both testicular cancer and cryptorchidism. Several sets of findings are consistent with this possibility. First, among men with a history of unilateral cryptorchidism, elevated rates of neoplasm occur even in contralateral normally descended testicles.[5,46,51,53] Second, several specific factors have been implicated in the etiologies of both conditions. These include low birth weight and several indicators of in utero exposure to high levels of free estrogen.[46,64–66] Finally, a few observations suggest that while a prolonged suprascrotal position may induce a variety of germ cell changes, very early germ cell changes in undescended testes of cryptorchid boys do not necessarily result from the suprascrotal position. For example, in a series of boys with cryptorchidism who were under a year old, germ cell hypoplasia was found in the suprascrotal testes of boys who were without a symptomatic inguinal hernia but not in the suprascrotal testes of those who had this accompanying condition.[67] The authors of the study suggest that the latter group may be interpreted as being made up of boys with normal testes in whom the descent of the testes was inhibited mechanically by the hernia.

It would be instructive to compare temporal trends in the incidence of testicular cancer with temporal trends in the prevalence of cryptorchidism. Unfortunately, the occurrence of cryptorchidism is not well documented. Data from birth defect registries are inadequate, for two reasons. First, some registries classify cryptorchidism as a minor malformation and record it only when it occurs in conjunction with an additional major malformation. Second, the frequent occurrence of spontaneous testicular descent complicates the determination of persistently undescended testes. As a result, limited inferences about the occurrence of cryptorchidism are usually based on follow-up studies of boys born with cryptorchidism in selected hospitals. One study of this type suggests that 3 to 4% of boys born in the United States have undescended testicles and that about two-thirds of these boys experience spontaneous descent in infancy, leaving about 1% with persistent cryptorchidism at 1 year of age.[68] More comprehensive data from the United Kingdom show that more than 1% of males have persistent cryptorchidism and that the condition has become more common since 1960. Some part of the increased prevalence may be attributable to the increased survival of premature infants. However, in two large studies, the elevated prevalence of persistent cryptorchidism among boys who were born prematurely appeared to be attributable to low birth weight rather than to early gestational age when these variables were adjusted for each other.[65,69] Two recently published extensive reviews of occurrence data suggest that where reliable data have been collected over time, cryptorchidism has become more prevalent in recent decades.[70,71] Of relevance to the etiology of testicular cancer is the recent report that the prevalence of cryptorchidism in Denmark is about twice that in Finland.[72]*

Hypospadias

Hypospadias is a congenital condition in which the urethral opening is abnormally located. Several epidemiologic studies report an association between history of hypospadias and the occurrence of testicular cancer.[11] Registry data for

---

*Editor's note: In a case-control study in Australia, cryptorchidism occurred statistically significantly more often in patients with germ cell tumors (GCT) than in healthy males without cancer, but it was also noted that the occurrence of multiple atypical cutaneous nevi was a more frequent association, an observation that was confirmed in the Netherlands (see Chapter 1).

hypospadias are not reliable, largely because variation in the severity of this condition leads to inconsistent reporting of cases. Limited data suggest that hypospadias has become more common in parts of Europe and the United States in recent decades and that prevalence varies geographically.[70,71] Hypospadias and cryptorchidism occur together more often than would be expected by chance[66] and so may share etiologic features.

Other Congenital Conditions

Results of studies of inguinal hernia and testicular cancer have been inconsistent although the weight of the evidence suggests an association.[11,51,59,73]

There are numerous reports of testicular cancer in individuals with testicular atrophy, various forms of gonadal dysgenesis, and conditions such as renal abnormalities that are often undiagnosed. Although these reports are intriguing because of the postulated fetal origins of testicular cancer, systematic studies of associations between testicular cancer and the conditions mentioned above are not available.

Poor Semen Quality and Subfertility

Testicular cancer is associated with poor semen quality and may be associated with infertility and reduced fertility. Studies of spermatogenesis in men with testicular cancer prior to orchiectomy were reviewed by Petersen and colleagues,[74] who concluded that the majority of patients with testicular germ cell carcinoma have very poor semen quality. Two case-control studies found significant associations with infertility[50,59]; two others did not.[20,75] A single case-control study found nearly twice the risk of testicular cancer among men with low relative fertility, a measure based on the number of children each man fathered. However, it is not clear that any of these conditions existed before the onset of subclinical disease. Significantly impaired testicular function is observed even in men with carcinoma in situ, the presumptive precursor to germ cell carcinoma.[76] Therefore, one cannot rule out the possibility that the observed associations between these reproductive variables and testicular cancer result from the effects of undetected neoplasia.

Explanations for the Occurrence of Testicular Cancer with Other Urogential Conditions

Two related hypotheses that address associations between testicular cancer and the conditions discussed above have recently been proposed.

The "endocrine disruptor" hypothesis suggests that some chemicals in the environment disrupt endocrine function, resulting in numerous adverse effects that may include testicular cancer, cryptorchidism, hypospadias, and poor semen quality.[77] Compounds postulated to have this property are termed endocrine disruptors, and developing organisms are thought to be particularly susceptible to their effects.

Boisen and colleagues[78] suggest that male genital abnormalities—testicular cancer, reduced semen quality, and subfertility—are elements of a common entity they term the testicular dysgenesis syndrome, which results from a disruption of embryonal programming and gonadal development during fetal life. They suggest that the prevalence of this syndrome is rising and that the increases are causally linked to endocrine disrupters that are affecting genetically susceptible individuals.

While these hypotheses are unproven, they provide intriguing explanations for numerous observed patterns and also provide a theoretical framework that may be useful in future etiologic and mechanistic studies of testicular cancer.

ETIOLOGY

The dramatically increased occurrence of testicular cancer in this century suggests that environmental causes have become more prevalent, and observed cohort effects suggest that some factors act early in life. Patterns of familial occurrence suggest that inherited genetic factors also predispose to testicular cancer. Accordingly, etiologic studies have addressed environmental, perinatal, and genetic factors.

Perinatal Factors

A series of epidemiologic studies found the risk of testicular cancer to be associated with a history of in utero exposure to exogenous steroid hormones.[1,43,79]

An individual can be exposed in utero if his mother takes oral contraceptives during an unrecognized pregnancy. In years past, estrogens and (sometimes) progestins were administered as a test for pregnancy and were included in preparations prescribed as "supplements" or were taken in an attempt to avert abortion during a recognized pregnancy. In a cohort of men known to have been exposed in utero to the estrogen analogue diethylstilbestrol (DES), testicular cancer occurred at two to three times the expected frequency (although this excess was not statistically significant).[80] Case-control studies addressing the role of DES had additional limitations but reported essentially consistent findings.[1,43,47,79]

Associations with factors that are indicators of high levels of free estrogen early in a woman's pregnancy have also been reported. For example, risk is elevated among men who were firstborn children,[73,81] and free estradiol is higher in a woman's first pregnancy than in her second.[82,83] Risk is elevated among men whose mothers had high body weight,[79] and heavy women are presumed to produce more estradiol by aromatization of testosterone in adipose tissue. Risk is also elevated among sons of women who experienced excessive nausea and vomiting during pregnancy,[43,84] and elevated free estradiol is found in women with severe hyperemesis during pregnancy.

Several epidemiologic studies have found low birth weight to be associated with the occurrence of testicular cancer,[20,85] cryptorchidism,[65,69] and hypospadias.[66,86]

These observed associations of perinatal factors with the later occurrence of testicular cancer are consistent with the model proposed by Henderson and colleagues[37] and underscore the etiologic importance of events in early life. However, epidemiologic studies can rarely establish the timing and dose of harmful hormone exposures, so the mechanistic inferences that can be drawn from these results are limited. However, experiments in which estradiol was administered to pregnant mice during carefully timed intervals not only demonstrated that in utero exposure can cause cryptorchidism but also identified a period of susceptibility in this species. Exposure on the thirteenth day of pregnancy (embryonic day 13 [E13], when sexual differentiation is beginning) causes cryptorchidism in immature male mouse pups,[87] and in utero exposure

was associated with increased frequency of testicular teratoma in one study.[88]

Exposures of Adolescence and Early Adulthood

A number of studies have explored the effects of hormones whose levels rise in puberty. In some of the studies, levels of testosterone, LH, and follicle-stimulating hormone (FSH) were measured. In others, factors that can be interpreted as proxies for androgens and gonadotropins were measured instead. In a study conducted among men with diagnosed unilateral testicular cancer, investigators examined the contralateral testicle for the presence of carcinoma in situ (CIS). Men with both testicular cancer and CIS at the time of diagnosis tended to have lower levels of testosterone and higher levels of both LH and FSH[76] than men with only testicular cancer. However, the implications of this result are not clear. One possibility is that this hormone profile confers greater susceptibility to disease, indicated by carcinogenic processes that are under way in both testicles of men with CIS. Alternatively, this hormone profile may result from disease processes that are occurring in both testicles of men with CIS. To distinguish causes from effects of disease, proxy measures of hormone levels that can be recalled from the past are of value.

Possible associations with androgen levels have been explored, using proxies. Two presumed proxies for testosterone levels are a history of severe acne during puberty and male pattern baldness as both are associated with somewhat higher testosterone levels. A history of both conditions may be less frequent among men who develop testicular cancer.[84] In addition, testicular germ cell tumors and CIS are observed in patients who are in a low-androgen state.[89] While animal experiments show that androgen is required for testicular descent,[90] a limited number of epidemiologic studies suggest that a high proportion of boys with cryptorchidism have normal androgen action and response.[91,92] Some cases of hypospadias have been attributed to defects of androgen action or response, but this mechanism appears to account for only a small proportion of nonsyndromic cases.[93,94]

Possible effects of FSH levels have also been addressed, using proxy measures. Dizygous twinning may be a proxy for elevated FSH levels. Dizygous twinning is known to be associated with elevated maternal FSH levels[95,96] and is a familial trait.[97,98] Risk of testicular cancer is reportedly elevated among dizygous twins.[99–101] One explanation for the association is that these twins inherit from their mothers a tendency to have elevated FSH levels, which promotes testicular carcinogenesis after puberty. (An alternate explanation is that estrogen levels are especially high during pregnancies that produce twins.) Further suggestion of an effect of FSH comes from case reports in which testicular cancer was diagnosed in men following gonadotropin treatment[102] and from the observation that patients with Kallmann's syndrome (who have insufficient gonadotropin secretion) do not develop testicular cancer, in spite of frequent cryptorchidism.[89]

Although indirect, these observations are consistent with patterns of lower testosterone and high gonadotropin levels in individuals who develop testicular cancer. Rajpert-De Meyts and Skakkebaek[89] provided an elegant discussion of possible mechanisms whereby sex hormones may mediate germ cell carcinogenesis. The possibility that elevated gonadotropins may be a risk factor accords well with the effects of puberty that were hypothesized by Henderson and colleagues[37] and suggests that FSH-responsive genes may play a role in those phases of testicular carcinogenesis that occur in adulthood.

Additional and nonhormonal exposures occurring in adulthood have also been implicated in testicular cancer etiology. Numerous small studies have investigated infectious agents, but most of these studies were conducted with relatively small samples and are inconclusive. An adequately sized retrospective study that is under way at the time of this publication will explore both hormonal and viral causes of testicular cancer. This study uses the US Department of Defense serum depository, which includes samples collected before the onset of testicular cancer and which may prove to be an exceptional resource for resolving these hypotheses.

A claim offered in support of a viral etiology is the increased occurrence of testicular cancer among men infected with human immunodeficiency virus (HIV), who are clearly at an elevated risk for cancers that involve viral infections, namely, Kaposi's sarcoma (which has been linked to human herpesvirus 8) and non-Hodgkin's lymphoma (which is linked to Epstein-Barr virus). However, the suggestion that men infected with HIV are at an elevated risk for testicular cancer is based on a small number of cases occurring in men with AIDS, among whom a doubling of the expected occurrence was seen only for seminoma.[103] Even if occurrence is elevated, a relative risk of 2 suggests quite a different dynamic than do the reported AIDS-associated relative risks of 300 for Kaposi's sarcoma and < 100 for non-Hodgkin's lymphoma.

A single report indicates that antibodies to the endogenous retrovirus K10 can be detected in 50 to 60% of patients with testicular cancer and that titers resolve with treatment.[104] Although further work is needed to learn whether expression of K10 is part of the pathophysiologic process and whether antibodies can be used to monitor disease processes, this report is intriguing because of the novelty of the agent.

Studies exploring the number of sexual partners and related variables have not shown a pattern of association with a measured or presumptive history of sexually transmitted disease.

Etiologies that involve elevated scrotal temperature and testicular trauma have been postulated. Although both associations seem plausible, it is hard to imagine how either of these factors could be measured retrospectively without introducing recall bias. Exercise and regular participation in specific sports activities have been suggested as proxies for both scrotal temperature and testicular trauma. However, a recent review of the eight epidemiologic studies of the effect of physical activity on the risk of testicular cancer indicated that there is currently insufficient evidence from which to draw any conclusions.[105]

A series of studies of occupation and investigations of testicular cancer clusters, recently reviewed by McGlynn,[106] has not pointed to specific occupational hazards. However, numerous reports indicate that testicular cancer has for some time tended to occur disproportionately among men of high socioeconomic status and among sons of women of high socioeconomic status.[1,85] These associations are not understood but are observed consistently enough to warrant further investigation.

Genetic Factors

Specific genes that confer an elevated risk of testicular cancer have not yet been found. However, numerous studies strongly suggest that inherited genetic predisposition plays an important role. A positive family history of germ cell carcinoma is invariably found to be a risk factor, and estimates of relative risk are large, ranging from 3 to over 12 for first-degree relatives.[26,107–116] These estimates of familial relative risk are greater than for most other cancers[117] and indicate that inherited genetic factors almost surely play an important role. Although family members tend to share environmental exposures, statistical arguments show that familial relative risks of this magnitude are unlikely to arise from shared environment alone.[118,119] Studies that distinguish between types of first-degree relatives reported higher relative risks for brothers than for fathers or sons.

A single genetic segregation analysis of testicular cancer[120] supported a major gene model over models that incorporate a polygenic effect only. This result suggests the existence of one or more major susceptibility genes, defined as individual genes responsible for a substantial variation in risk.

Studies of genetic linkage are conducted in families to identify chromosomal regions that contain major susceptibility genes. In linkage studies that have been completed to date, the International Testicular Cancer Linkage Consortium has identified (1) four autosomal regions with preliminary suggestions of genetic linkage[121,122] and (2) a region on chromosome Xq27 with significant evidence of linkage among families in which one member has a history of bilateral testicular cancer.[123] These studies are currently being extended to additional families, whose participation may clarify linkage relationships in the autosomal regions and identify a susceptibility locus on Xq27.

A small number of candidate gene studies that have been completed to date have not suggested particularly promising susceptibility loci.[108,124,125] However, the finding of genetic linkage to chromosome Xq27 and elsewhere in the genome will help investigators focus future association studies on positional candidate genes that have a greater prior probability of involvement in testicular cancer.

Candidate genes for cryptorchidism were recently suggested by the observation of bilateral undescended testes in mice with targeted disruption in each of six genes. The products of these genes are (1) Leydig insulin-like hormone (Insl3), a presumed signaling molecule that is expressed in a sex-specific pattern[126]; (2) a novel G protein–coupled receptor (now called G protein–coupled receptor affecting testis descent [Great]) with an expression pattern in embryonic gonads and gubernacula[127]; (3) three abdominally expressed Hox proteins[128–130]; and (4) a regulatory molecule with a basic helix-loop-helix DNA-binding motif.[131] Overbeek and colleagues postulated that Great is the Insl3 receptor.[127] Nef and colleagues suggest that Insl3 mediates estrogen-induced cryptorchidism, based on their finding that in utero administration of estradiol-17β or DES at E13 both causes cryptorchidism and specifically down-regulates Insl3 expression in embryonic Leydig's cells.[87] Epidemiologic studies examining human homologues of these genes are very preliminary and have not yet found a pattern of involvement in human cryptorchidism.

Cytogenetic analyses have identified numerous karyotypic abnormalities in germ cell tumors. The most consistent finding is an isochromosome, i(12p), on the short arm of chromosome 12 that is described in over 80% of published germ cell tumor karyotypes. It is now recognized that virtually all germ cell tumors have an increased 12p copy number, present as either one or more copies of i(12p), tandem duplications, or elements transposed to other regions of the genome.[132] Because increased 12p copy number is observed even in the presumptive precursor lesion (carcinoma in situ), it may be one of the earliest somatic gene changes in the genesis of testicular germ cell tumors.[133]

A series of candidate genes on 12p are actively being investigated. Based on a review of functional analyses, Chaganti and Houldsworth[133] recently suggested that *CCND2* is a 12p gene whose deregulated expression leads to germ cell transformation. This gene encodes cyclin D2, a protein that (with its catalytic partners CDK4 and CDK6) controls the G_1–S cell cycle checkpoint by phosphorylating the retinoblastoma protein (pRB). Cyclin D2 shows suggestive patterns of expression in established germ cell tumor cell lines, germ cell tumors, and CIS. It is plausible that overexpression of *CCND2* could mediate critical events in puberty because cyclin D2 protein appears to be required for the maturation of FSH-responsive gonadal cells during sexual maturation.

Although the significance of cytogenetic changes seen in germ cell carcinoma is not yet understood, more recent studies, employing molecular genetic techniques, have begun to describe corresponding patterns in gene expression[134] and to identify additional promising candidate genes.[135,136]

SUMMARY

Testicular germ cell carcinoma is a disease of young men. Although treatment has improved dramatically in recent decades, some groups of men have not benefited fully from these advances, and survivors remain at risk for numerous subsequent problems. The incidence of testicular cancer has been rising steadily for decades. This temporal trend is attributed to changing patterns of exposure to risk factors, but specific environmental agents responsible for the increasing rates have not been identified. The two established risk factors are cryptorchidism and family history of testicular cancer. A distinctive age distribution and reported birth cohort effects suggest that critical events that contribute to the pathophysiology of testicular cancer may occur early in life and again at about the time of puberty. Both environmental and genetic factors are believed to be important. Genetic effects seem to operate both by inherited predisposition and by acquired chromosomal changes leading to deregulated gene expression. Although chromosomal regions have been implicated in both processes, the responsible genes and their mechanisms of action have not been identified. Taken together, these observations suggest several causal hypotheses that are being explored by using proxy measures of past exposures and by newer techniques of genetics and molecular biology.

REFERENCES

1. Schottenfeld D, Warshauer ME, Sherlock S. The epidemiology of testicular cancer in young adults. Am J Epidemiol 1980;112(2):232–46.
2. Boyle P, Kaye SB, Robertson AG. Changes in testicular cancer in Scotland. Eur J Cancer Clin Oncol 1987;23(6):827–30.
3. Osterlind A. Diverging trends in incidence and mortality of testicular cancer in Denmark, 1943-1982. Br J Cancer 1986;53(4):501–5.
4. Brown LM, Pottern LM, Hoover RN. Testicular cancer in young men: the search for causes of the epidemic increase in the United States. J Epidemiol Community Health 1987;41(4):349–54.
5. Stone JM, Cruickshank DG, Sandeman TF, Matthews JP. Trebling of the incidence of testicular cancer in Victoria, Australia (1950-1985). Cancer 1991;68(1):211–9.
6. Adami HO, Bergstrom R, Sparen P, Baron J. Increasing cancer risk in younger birth cohorts in Sweden. Lancet 1993;341:773–777.
7. Adami HO, Bergstrom R, Mohner M, et al. Testicular cancer in nine northern European countries. Int J Cancer 1994; 59(1):33–8.
8. Gilliland FD, Key CR. Male genital cancers. Cancer 1995; 75(1 Suppl):295–315.
9. Wanderas EH, Tretli S, Fossa SD. Trends in incidence of testicular cancer in Norway 1955-1992. Eur J Cancer 1995; 31A(12):2044–8.
10. Ekbom A, Akre O. Increasing incidence of testicular cancer–birth cohort effects. APMIS 1998;106(1):225–9; discussion 229–31.
11. Prener A, Engholm G, Jensen OM. Genital anomalies and risk for testicular cancer in Danish men. Epidemiology 1996;7(1):14–9.
12. Liu S, Semenciw R, Waters C. Clues to the aetiological heterogeneity of testicular seminomas and non-seminomas: time trends and age-period-cohort effects. Int J Epidemiol 2000;29:826–31.
13. Moller H. Trends in incidence of testicular cancer and prostate cancer in Denmark. Hum Reprod 2001;16(5):1007–11.
14. Power DA, Brown RS, Brock CS, et al. Trends in testicular carcinoma in England and Wales, 1971-99. BJU Int 2001; 87(4):361–5.
15. Zheng T, Holford TR, Ma JZ, et al. Continuing increase in incidence of germ-cell testis cancer in young adults: experience from Connecticut, USA, 1935-1992. Int J Cancer 1996;65(6):723–9.
16. Bergstrom R, Adami HO, Mohner M, et al. Increase in testicular cancer incidence in six European countries: a birth cohort phenomenon. J Natl Cancer Inst 1996;88(11):727–33.
17. Liu S, Wen SW, Mao Y, et al. Birth cohort effects underlying the increasing testicular cancer incidence in Canada. Can J Public Health 1999;90(3):176–80.
18. Moller H, Jorgensen N, Forman D. Trends in incidence of testicular cancer in boys and adolescent men. Int J Cancer 1995;61(6):761–4.
19. Pharris-Ciurej ND, Cook LS, Weiss NS. Incidence of testicular cancer in the United States: has the epidemic begun to abate? Am J Epidemiol 1999;150(1):45–6.
20. Brown LM, Pottern LM, Hoover RN, et al. Testicular cancer in the United States: trends in incidence and mortality. Int J Epidemiol 1986;15(2):164–70.
21. Schottenfeld D. Testicular cancer. In: Schottenfeld D, Fraumeni JF, editors. Cancer epidemiology and prevention. New York: Oxford University Press; 1996. p. 1207–18.
22. Pont J, Albrecht W. Fertility after chemotherapy for testicular germ cell cancer. Fertil Steril 1997;68(1):1–5.

23. Jacobsen R, Bostofte E, Engholm G, et al. Fertility and off-spring sex ratio of men who develop testicular cancer: a record linkage study. Hum Reprod 2000;15(9):1958–61.

24. Jonker-Pool G, van Basten JP, Hoekstra HJ, et al. Sexual functioning after treatment for testicular cancer: comparison of treatment modalities. Cancer 1997;80(3):454–64.

25. Klein FA, Melamed MR, Whitmore WF Jr. Intratubular malignant germ cells (carcinoma in situ) accompanying invasive testicular germ cell tumors. J Urol 1985;133(3):413–5.

26. Dong C, Lonnstedt I, Hemminki K. Familial testicular cancer and second primary cancers in testicular cancer patients by histological type. Eur J Cancer 2001;37(15):1878–85.

27. Dieckmann KP, Boeckmann W, Brosig W, et al. Bilateral testicular germ cell tumors. Report of nine cases and review of the literature. Cancer 1986;57(6):1254–8.

28. Scheiber K, Ackermann D, Studer UE. Bilateral testicular germ cell tumors: a report of 20 cases. J Urol 1987;138(1):73–6.

29. Thompson J, Williams, CJ, Whitehouse JM, Mead GM. Bilateral testicular germ cell tumors: an increasing incidence and prevention by chemotherapy. Br J Urol 1988;62:374–6.

30. Hellbardt A, Mirimanoff RO, Obradovic M, et al. The risk of second cancer (SC) in patients treated for testicular seminoma. Int J Radiat Oncol 1990;18:1327–31.

31. Patel SR, Richardson RL, Kvols L. Synchronous and metachronous bilateral testicular tumors. Mayo Clinic experience. Cancer 1990;65(1):1–4.

32. Osterlind A, Berthelsen JG, Ablidgaard N, et al. Risk of bilateral testicular germ cell cancer in Denmark: 1960-1984. J Natl Cancer Inst 1991;83(19):1391–5.

33. Colls BM, Harvey VJ, Skelton L, et al. Bilateral germ cell testicular tumors in New Zealand: experience in Auckland and Christchurch 1978–1994. J Clin Oncol 1996;14(7):2061–5.

34. Wanderas EH, Grotmol T, Fossa SD, Tretli S. Maternal health and pre- and perinatal characteristics in the etiology of testicular cancer: a prospective population- and register-based study on Norwegian males born between 1967 and 1995. Cancer Causes Control 1998;9(5):475–86.

35. Tekin A, Aygun YC, Aki FT, Ozen H. Bilateral germ cell cancer of the testis: a report of 11 patients with a long-term follow-up. BJU Int 2000;85(7):864–8.

36. Bray F, Sankila R, Ferlay J, et al. Estimates of cancer incidence and mortality in Europe in 1995. Eur J Cancer 2002;38(1):99–166.

37. Henderson BE, Ross RK, Pike MC, Depue RH, et al. Epidemiology of testis cancer. In: Skinner DG, editor. Urological cancer. New York: Grune and Stratton;1983. p. 237–50.

38. Forest M. Pituitary gonadotropin and sex steroid secretion during the first two years of life. In: Grumbach MM, Sizonenko PC, Aubert ML, editors. Control of the onset of puberty II. Lippincott, Williams & Wilkins; 1990. p. 451–770.

39. Mann DR, Fraser HM. The neonatal period: a critical interval in male primate development. J Endocrinol 1996;149(2):191–7.

40. Aalen OO, Tretli S. Analyzing incidence of testis cancer by means of a frailty model. Cancer Causes Control 1999;10(4):285–92.

41. Buetow SA. Epidemiology of testicular cancer. Epidemiol Rev 1995;17(2):433–49.

42. Morrison AS. Cryptorchidism, hernia, and cancer of the testis. J Natl Cancer Inst 1976;56(4):731–3.

43. Henderson BE, Benton B, Jing J, et al. Risk factors for cancer of the testis in young men. Int J Cancer 1979;23(5):598–602.

44. Gallagher RP, Huchcroft S, Phillips N, et al. Physical activity, medical history, and risk of testicular cancer (Alberta and British Columbia, Canada). Cancer Causes Control 1995;6(5):398–406.

45. Pottern LM, Hoover RN, Brown LM. Prenatal and perinatal risk factors for testicular cancer. Cancer Res 1986;46(9):4812–6.

46. Depue RH, Pike MC, Henderson BE. Cryptorchidism and testicular cancer. J Natl Cancer Inst 1986;77(3):830–3.

47. Moss AR, Osmond D, Bacchetti P, et al. Hormonal risk factors in testicular cancer. A case-control study. Am J Epidemiol 1986;124(1):39–52.

48. Giwercman A, Berthelsen JG, Muller J, et al. Screening for carcinoma-in-situ of the testis. Int J Androl 1987;10(1):173–80.

49. Strader CH, Weiss NS, Daling JR, et al. Cryptorchism, orchiopexy, and the risk of testicular cancer. Am J Epidemiol 1988;127(5):1013–8.

50. Haughey BP, Graham S, Brasure J, et al. The epidemiology of testicular cancer in upstate New York. Am J Epidemiol 1989;130(1):25–36.

51. Pinczowski D, McLaughlin JK, Lackgren G, et al. Occurrence of testicular cancer in patients operated on for cryptorchidism and inguinal hernia. J Urol 1991;146(5):1291–4.

52. Forman D, Pike MC, Davey G, et al. Aetiology of testicular cancer: association with congenital abnormalities, age at puberty, infertility and exercise. BMJ 1994;303:1393–9.

53. Swerdlow AJ, Higgins CD, Pike MC. Risk of testicular cancer in cohort of boys with cryptorchidism. BMJ 1997;314(7093):1507.

54. Moller H, Skakkebaek NE. Testicular cancer and cryptorchidism in relation to prenatal factors: case-control studies in Denmark. Cancer Causes Control 1997;8(6):904–12.

55. Coupland CA, Chilvers CE, Davey G, et al. Risk factors for testicular germ cell tumours by histological tumour type. United Kingdom Testicular Cancer Study Group. Br J Cancer 1999;80(11):1859–63.

56. Weir HK, Marrett LD, Kreiger N, et al. Pre-natal and perinatal exposures and risk of testicular germ-cell cancer. Int J Cancer 2000;87(3):438–43.

57. Stang A, Ahren W, Bromen K, et al. Undescended testis and the risk of testicular cancer: importance of source and classification of exposure information. Int J Epidemiol 2001;30(5):1050–6.

58. Benson RC Jr, Beard CM, Kelalis PP, Kurland LT. Malignant potential of the cryptorchid testis. Mayo Clin Proc 1991;66(4):372–8.

59. Aetiology of testicular cancer: association with congenital abnormalities, age at puberty, infertility, and exercise. United Kingdom Testicular Cancer Study Group. BMJ 1994;308(6941):1393–9.

60. Moller H, Prener A, Skakkebaek NE. Testicular cancer, cryptorchidism, inguinal hernia, testicular atrophy, and genital malformations: case-control studies in Denmark. Cancer Causes Control 1996;7(2):264–74.

61. Shikone T, Billig H, Hsueh AJ. Experimentally induced cryp-

torchidism increases apoptosis in rat testis. Biol Reprod 1994;51(5):865–72.

62. Ohta Y, Nishikawa A, Fukazawa Y, et al. Apoptosis in adult mouse testis induced by experimental cryptorchidism. Acta Anat 1996;157(3):195–204.

63. Iizuka A, Park MK, Mori T. Effects of unilateral cryptorchidism on the expression of gonadotropin receptor mRNA. Biochem Biophys Res Commun 1996;221(2):290–4.

64. Swerdlow AJ, Wood KH, Smith PG. A case-control study of the aetiology of cryptorchidism. J Epidemiol Community Health 1983;37(3):238–44.

65. Jones ME, Swerdlow AJ, Griffith M, Goldacre MJ. Prenatal risk factors for cryptorchidism: a record linkage study. Paediatr Perinat Epidemiol 1998;12:383–96.

66. Weidner IS, Moller H, Jensen TK, Skakkebaek NE. Risk factors for cryptorchidism and hypospadias. J Urol 1999; 161(5):1606–9.

67. Cortes D, Thorup JM, Beck BL. Quantitative histology of germ cells in the undescended testes of human fetuses, neonates and infants. J Urol 1995;154(3):1188–92.

68. Berkowitz GS, Lapinski RH, Dolgin SE, et al. Prevalence and natural history of cryptorchidism. Pediatrics 1993;92(1):44–9.

69. Hjertkvist M, Damber JE, Bergh A. Cryptorchidism: a registry based study in Sweden on some factors of possible aetiological importance. J Epidemiol Community Health 1989;43(4):324–9.

70. Paulozzi LJ. International trends in rates of hypospadias and cryptorchidism. Environ Health Perspect 1999;107(4):297–302.

71. Toppari J, Kaleva M, Virtanen HE. Trends in the incidence of cryptorchidism and hypospadias, and methodological limitations of registry-based data. APMIS 2001;109 (103 Suppl):S37–42.

72. Kavela MM, Haavisto A-M, Schmidt IM, et al. Higher incidence of cryptorichidism in Denmark than in Finland. In Proceedings of the International Congress of Endocrinology; 2000; Sydney, Australia.

73. Swerdlow AJ, Huttly SR, Smith PG. Testicular cancer and antecedent diseases. Br J Cancer 1987;55(1):97–103.

74. Petersen PM, Skakkebaek NE, Giwercman A. Gonadal function in men with testicular cancer: biological and clinical aspects. APMIS 1998;106(1):24–34; discussion 34–6.

75. Swerdlow AJ, Huttly SR, Smith PG. Testis cancer: post-natal hormonal factors, sexual behaviour and fertility. Int J Cancer 1989;43(4):549–53.

76. Petersen PM, Giwercman A, Hansen SW, et al. Impaired testicular function in patients with carcinoma-in-situ of the testis. J Clin Oncol 1999;17(1):173–9.

77. Barlow S, Kavlock RJ, Moore JA, et al. Teratology Society Public Affairs Committee position paper: developmental toxicity of endocrine disruptors to humans. Teratology 1999;60(6):365–75.

78. Boisen KA, Main KM, Rajpert-De Meyts E, Skakkebaek NE. Are male reproductive disorders a common entity? The testicular dysgenesis syndrome. Ann N Y Acad Sci 2001;948:90–9.

79. Depue RH, Pike MC, Henderson BE. Estrogen exposure during gestation and risk of testicular cancer. J Natl Cancer Inst 1983;71(6):1151–5.

80. Strohsnitter WC, Noller KL, Hoover RN, et al. Cancer risk in men exposed in utero to diethylstilbestrol. J Natl Cancer Inst 2001;93(7):545–51.

81. Prener A, Hsieh CC, Engholm G, et al. Birth order and risk of testicular cancer. Cancer Causes Control 1992;3(3):265–72.

82. Bernstein L, Pike MC, Depue RH, et al. Maternal hormone levels in early gestation of cryptorchid males: a case-control study. Br J Cancer 1988;58(3):379–81.

83. Bernstein L, Depue RH, Ross RK, et al. Higher maternal levels of free estradiol in first compared to second pregnancy: early gestational differences. J Natl Cancer Inst 1986;76(6):1035–9.

84. Petridou E, Roukas KI, Dessypris N, et al. Baldness and other correlates of sex hormones in relation to testicular cancer. Int J Cancer 1997;71(6):982–5.

85. Akre O, Ekbom A, Hsieh CC, et al. Testicular nonseminoma and seminoma in relation to perinatal characteristics. J Natl Cancer Inst 1996;88(13):883–9.

86. Fredell L, et al. Hypospadias is related to birth weight in discordant monozygotic twins. J Urol 1998;160(6 Pt 1):2197–9.

87. Nef S, Shipman T, Parada LF. A molecular basis for estrogen-induced cryptorchidism. Dev Biol 2000;224(2):354–61.

88. Walker AH, Bernstein L, Warren DW, et al. The effect of in utero ethinyl oestradiol exposure on the risk of cryptorchid testis and testicular teratoma in mice. Br J Cancer 1990;62(4):599–602.

89. Rajpert-De Meyts E, Skakkebaek NE. The possible role of sex hormones in the development of testicular cancer. Eur Urol 1993;23(1):54–9; discussion 60–1.

90. Emmen JM, McLuskey A, Adham IM, et al. Hormonal control of gubernaculum development during testis descent: gubernaculum outgrowth in vitro requires both insulin-like factor and androgen. Endocrinology 2000;141(12):4720–7.

91. Brown TR, Berkovitz GD, Gearhart JP. Androgen receptors in boys with isolated bilateral cryptorchidism. Am J Dis Child 1988;142(9):933–6.

92. Lim HN, Nixon RM, Chen H, et al. Evidence that longer androgen receptor polyglutamine repeats are a causal factor for genital abnormalities. J Clin Endocrinol Metab 2001;6(7):3207–10.

93. Sutherland RW, Wiener JS, Hicks JP, et al. Androgen receptor gene mutations are rarely associated with isolated penile hypospadias. J Urol 1996;156(2 Pt 2):828–31.

94. Aaronson IA, Cakmak MA, Murat A, Key LL. Defects of the testosterone biosynthetic pathway in boys with hypospadias. J Urol 1997;157(5):1884–8.

95. Martin NG, Robertson DM, Chenevix-Trench G, et al. Elevation of follicular phase inhibin and luteinizing hormone levels in mothers of dizygotic twins suggests nonovarian control of human multiple ovulation. Fertil Steril 1991;56(3):469–74.

96. Lambalk CB, De Koning CH, Braat DD. The endocrinology of dizygotic twinning in the human. Mol Cell Endocrinol 1998;145(1-2):97–102.

97. Parisi P, Gatti M, Prinzi G, Caperna G. Familial incidence of twinning. Nature 1983;304(5927):626–8.

98. Lichtenstein P, Olausson PO, Kallen AJ. Twin births to mothers who are twins: a registry based study. BMJ 1996; 312(7035):879–81.

99. Braun MM, Ahlbom A, Floderus B, et al. Effect of twinship on incidence of cancer of the testis, breast, and other sites (Sweden). Cancer Causes Control 1995;6(6):519–24.

100. Swerdlow AJ, De Stavola BL, Swanwick MA, Maconochie NE. Risks of breast and testicular cancers in young adult twins in England and Wales: evidence on prenatal and genetic aetiology. Lancet 1997;350(9093):1723–8.

101. Lambalk CB, Boomsma DI. Twinning, cancer, and genetics [letter]. Lancet 1998;351(9106):909–10.

102. Neoptolemos JP, Locke TJ, Fossard DP. Testicular tumour associated with hormonal treatment for oligospermia. Lancet 1981;2(8249):754.

103. Goedert JJ, Cote TR, Virgo P, et al. Spectrum of AIDS-associated malignant disorders. Lancet 1998;351(9119):1833–9.

104. Goedert JJ, Sauter ME, Jacobson LP, et al. High prevalence of antibodies against HERV-K10 in patients with testicular cancer but not with AIDS. Cancer Epidemiol Biomarkers Prev 1999;8(4 Pt 1):293–6.

105. Friedenreich CM. Physical activity and cancer prevention: from observational to intervention research. Cancer Epidemiol Biomarkers Prev 2001;10(4):287–301.

106. McGlynn KA. Environmental and host factors in testicular germ cell tumors. Cancer Invest 2001;19(8):842–53.

107. Tollerud DJ, Blattner WA, Fraser MC, et al. Familial testicular cancer and urogenital developmental anomalies. Cancer 1985;55(8):1849–54.

108. Forman D, Oliver RT, Brett AR, et al. Familial testicular cancer: a report of the UK family register, estimation of risk and an HLA class 1 sib-pair analysis. Br J Cancer 1992;65(2):255–62.

109. Westergaard T, Olsen JH, Frisch M, et al. Cancer risk in fathers and brothers of testicular cancer patients in Denmark. A population-based study. Int J Cancer 1996;66(5):627–31.

110. Heimdal K, Olsson H, Tretli S, et al. Risk of cancer in relatives of testicular cancer patients. Br J Cancer 1996;73(7):970–3.

111. Dieckmann KP, Pichlmeier U. The prevalence of familial testicular cancer: an analysis of two patient populations and a review of the literature. Cancer 1997;80(10):1954–60.

112. Hemminki K, Vaittinen P, Kyyronen P. Age-specific familial risks in common cancers of the offspring. Int J Cancer 1998;78(2):172–5.

113. Hemminki K, Vaittinen P. Familial cancers in a nationwide family cancer database: age distribution and prevalence. Eur J Cancer 1999;35(7):1109–17.

114. Sonneveld DJ, Lonnstedt I, Hemminki K. Familial testicular cancer in a single-centre population. Eur J Cancer 1999;35(9):1368–73.

115. Dong C, Hemminki K. Modification of cancer risks in offspring by sibling and parental cancers from 2,112,616 nuclear families. Int J Cancer 2001;92(1):144–50.

116. Spermon JR, Witjes JA, Nap M, Kiemeney LA. Cancer incidence in relatives of patients with testicular cancer in the eastern part of The Netherlands. Urology 2001;57(4):747–52.

117. Easton D, Peto J. The contribution of inherited predisposition to cancer incidence. Cancer Surv 1990;9(3):395–416.

118. Khoury MJ, Beaty TH, Liang KY. Can familial aggregation of disease be explained by familial aggregation of environmental risk factors? Am J Epidemiol 1988;127(3):674–83.

119. Aalen OO. Modelling the influence of risk factors on familial aggregation of disease. Biometrics 1991;47(3):933–45.

120. Heimdal K, Olsson H, Tretli S, et al. A segregation analysis of testicular cancer based on Norwegian and Swedish families. Br J Cancer 1997;75(7):1084–7.

121. Leahy MG, Tonks S, Moses JH, et al. Candidate regions for a testicular cancer susceptibility gene. Hum Mol Genet 1995;4(9):1551–5.

122. Candidate regions for testicular cancer susceptibility genes. The International Testicular Cancer Linkage Consortium. APMIS 1998;106(1):64–70; discussion 71–2.

123. Rapley EA, Crockford GP, Teare D, et al. Localization to Xq27 of a susceptibility gene for testicular germ-cell tumours. Nat Genet 2000;24(2):197–200.

124. Heimdal K, Anderson TI, Skrede M, et al. Association studies of estrogen receptor polymorphisms in a Norwegian testicular cancer population. Cancer Epidemiol Biomarkers Prev 1995;4(2):123–6.

125. Harries LW. Identification of genetic polymorphisms at the glutathione S-transferase Pi locus and association with susceptibility to bladder, testicular and prostate cancer. Carcinogenesis 1997;18(4):641–4.

126. Nef S, Parada LF. Cryptorchidism in mice mutant for Insl3. Nat Genet 1999;22(3):295–9.

127. Overbeek PA, Gorlov IP, Sutherland RW, et al. A transgenic insertion causing cryptorchidism in mice. Genesis 2001;30:26–35.

128. Rijli F, Matyas R, Pelligrini M, et al. Cryptorchidism and homeotic transformations of spinal nerves and vertebrae in Hoxa-10 mutant mice. Proc Natl Acad Sci U S A 1995;92(18):8185–9.

129. Satokata I, Benson G, Maas R. Sexually dimorphic sterility phenotypes in Hoxa10-deficient mice. Nature 1995;374(6521):460–3.

130. Hsieh-Li HM, Witte DP, Weinstein M, et al. Hoxa 11 structure, extensive antisense transcription, and function in male and female fertility. Development 1995;121(5):1373–85.

131. Good DJ, Porter FD, Mahon KA, et al. Hypogonadism and obesity in mice with a targeted deletion of the Nhlh2 gene. Nat Genet 1997;15(4):397–401.

132. Chaganti RS, Rodriguez E, Bosl GJ. Cytogenetics of male germ-cell tumors. Urol Clin North Am 1993;20(1):55–66.

133. Chaganti RS, Houldsworth J. Genetics and biology of adult human male germ cell tumors. Cancer Res 2000;60(6):1475–82.

134. Kraggerud SM, Skotheim RI, Szymanska J, et al. Genome profiles of familial/bilateral and sporadic testicular germ cell tumors. Genes Chromosomes Cancer 2002;34(2):168–74.

135. Zafarana G, Gillis AJ, van Gurp RJ, et al. Coamplification of DAD-R, SOX5, and EKI1 in human testicular seminomas, with specific overexpression of DAD-R, correlates with reduced levels of apoptosis and earlier clinical manifestation. Cancer Res 2002;62(6):1822–31.

136. Qiao D, Zeeman AM, Deng W, et al. Molecular characterization of hiwi, a human member of the piwi gene family whose overexpression is correlated to seminomas. Oncogene 2002;21(25):3988–99.

Surgical Anatomy

ROBERT P. HUBEN, MD

The two surgical procedures that are performed routinely in the treatment of germ cell malignancies are radical orchiectomy and retroperitoneal lymph node dissection. Both procedures require a thorough knowledge of the anatomic areas involved, which include the testis itself, the scrotum, the inguinal canal, and the retroperitoneum. In addition, it is important to understand the development and descent of the testis in order to understand the nature of the vascular and lymphatic supply of the testis as the early spread of testicular cancer is via lymphatic pathways. For this reason, the embryologic development and migration of the testis will also be reviewed.

TESTES

Embryology

The gonads are induced to develop by the primordial germ cells that migrate from the yolk sac via the dorsal mesentery to populate the mesenchyme of the posterior body wall in the fifth week.[1] The primordial germ cells induce cells in the mesonephros and adjacent coelomic epithelium, at about the tenth thoracic level, to grow and form a pair of gonadal or genital ridges medial to the developing mesonephros (Figure 3–1, *A*). During the sixth week, the primitive sex cords develop, with both cortical and medullary regions, and a new pair of ducts (the paramesonephric or müllerian ducts) begin to form just lateral to the mesonephric or wolffian ducts. The indifferent phase of gonadal development ends at 6 weeks. The subsequent phases of sexual development are controlled by sex chromosome genes, hormones, and other factors, most of which are encoded on the autosomes.[1] Cells in the medullary region of the primitive sex cords differentiate into Sertoli's

cells while the cells of the cortical sex cords regress (Figure 3–2, *A*). During the seventh week, the Sertoli's cells organize to form the testis cords, which become canalized at puberty and differentiate into the seminiferous tubules. The testis cords distal to the seminiferous tubules also canalize at puberty and differentiate into a series of thin-walled ducts called the rete testis (see Figure 3–2, *B*). The rete testis connects with five to twelve residual mesonephric tubes to form the spermatic ducts while the remaining portion of the mesonephric duct forms the vas deferens (see Figure 3–2, *B*). During the seventh week, the testis starts to become round, and degenerating cortical sex cords become separated from the coelomic epithelium by a layer of connective tissue called the tunica albuginea.[1]

Antimüllerian hormone (AMH) secreted by the pre-Sertoli cells controls several steps in male genital development.[1] AMH causes the paramesonephric ducts to regress rapidly between the eighth and tenth weeks. A paramesonephric duct remnant persists as a small cap of tissue at the cephalad junction of the testis and epididymis and is called the appendix testis or hydatid of Morgagni.[2] Another müllerian duct remnant forms the prostatic utricle within the prostatic urethra.

In the ninth or tenth week, Leydig's cells differentiate from mesenchymal cells within the genital ridges.[1] Testosterone produced by the Leydig's cells stimulates the mesonephric ducts to transform into the spermatic ducts called the vasa deferentia. The most cephalad end of each mesonephric duct regresses, and the appendix epididymis persists as a remnant. The portion of vas deferens adjacent to the testis becomes the epididymis. During the ninth week, five to twelve mesonephric ducts in the area

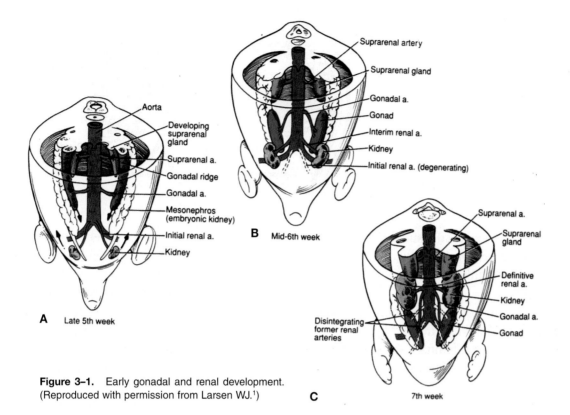

Figure 3–1. Early gonadal and renal development. (Reproduced with permission from Larsen WJ.[1])

of the epididymis make contact with the rete testis. These tubules do not fuse with the rete testis until the third month, after which they are called the efferent ductules. At the same time, the mesonephric tubules at the lower pole of the testis degenerate while a small remnant persists as the paradidymis (see Figure 3–2, *B*).[1]

The testis is initially located at the tenth thoracic level, and it descends into the scrotum between birth and the second week of life. The descent of the testis depends on a ligamentous cord, the gubernaculum, which forms within a longitudinal fold on either side of the vertebral column.[1] The superior end of this cord attaches to the testis, and the inferior end attaches to the fascia between the developing external and internal oblique muscles. A slight evagination of the peritoneum, the processus vaginalis, develops at the same time near the inferior base of the gubernaculum. The inguinal canal is formed when the processus vaginalis grows inferiorly, pushing out an evagination of the various layers of the abdominal wall.

The inguinal canal conveys the testis to the developing scrotum and forms the sheath of the spermatic cord.[1] The processus vaginalis begins to elongate candally during the eighth week, bringing the bulb of the gubernaculum with it. Three layers of the developing abdominal wall are encountered by the elongating processus. The first layer is the fascia transversalis, which becomes the internal spermatic fascia of the spermatic cord (Figure 3–3). The next layer is the internal oblique muscle, which becomes the cremasteric fascia of the spermatic cord. Lastly, the external oblique muscle is encountered; it becomes the external spermatic fascia. The superior rim of the canal, the site of eversion of the fascia transversalis, is called the deep ring of the inguinal canal. (Figure 3–4).[3] The lower and more medial rim of the canal, the site of eversion of the external oblique muscle, is called the superficial ring of the inguinal canal (see Figure 3–4).

The testis descends to the level of the deep inguinal ring by the third month, and descent is completed in the seventh to ninth months due to further shortening of the gubernaculum.[4] Movement of the testis through the inguinal canal is also promoted by increasing abdominal pressure due to growth of the abdominal viscera. The testis has completely entered the scrotal sac by the ninth month, and the gubernaculum becomes a small band connecting the inferior pole of the testis to the floor of the scrotum.

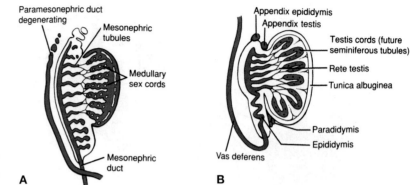

Figure 3–2. Development of the testis, (*A*) at 7 weeks, (*B*) at birth. (Adapted, with permission, from Larsen WJ.[1])

Given the complexity of normal testicular descent, it is understandable that cryptorchidism, or failure of such descent to occur fully, is a common developmental abnormality.

The superior portion of the processus vaginalis usually becomes obliterated within the first year of birth, leaving only a distal remnant sac. This remnant, the tunica vaginalis, lies anterior to the testis and normally does not contain fluid.

Failure of the processus vaginalis to obliterate may lead to an open communication between the abdominal cavity and the scrotal sac. A communicating hydrocele may result. Additionally, loops of bowel may herniate through a patent processus vaginalis, leading to the development of an indirect inguinal hernia.[2]

Anatomy

Each testis measures about $5.0 \times 3.0 \times 2.5$ cm and is covered by a fibrous constricting covering, the tunica albuginea.[5] The tunica albuginea sends numerous fibrous septa into the interior of the gland, dividing it into small testicular lobules (Figure 3–5).

Each testis contains about 300 lobules, each of which contains 1 to 4 seminiferous tubules.[5] The seminiferous tubules connect to 15 to 20 straight tubules (tubuli recti), which coalesce in the posterior mediastinum of the testis to form the rete testis. From the rete, 15 to 20 efferent ductules penetrate the tunica albuginea to open into the head of the epididymis, which is attached to the upper pole of the testis. The pathologic staging of tumors within the testis is shown in Table 3–1.[6]

Blood supply to the testis is from the testicular artery, both of which arises from the aorta below the renal arteries. Each courses anteriorly to the psoas muscle and through the deep inguinal ring to enter the spermatic cord. Veins emerging from the testis form the dense pampiniform plexus, which merges to form the testicular vein. The right testicular vein drains into the inferior vena cava while the left testicular vein drains into the left renal vein.

The lymphatic vessels of the testis have both superficial and deep components.[2] The superficial set arises from the surface of the tunica vaginalis while the deep set arises from the epididymis and body of the testis. Both sets form several large trunks that ascend within the spermatic cord to accompany the testicular vessels through the inguinal canal. These lymphatics terminate in the lumbar or para-aortic nodes below the renal vessels.

Innervation of the testis is from sympathetic nerves from the aortic and renal plexuses.[5] Parasympathetic nerves from the prostatic plexus supply the vas deferens and the epididymis.

Afferent fibers travel to the spinal cord via the

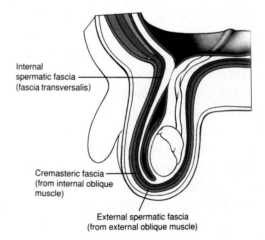

Figure 3–3. Development of the spermatic fascia. (Reproduced with permission from Larsen WJ.[1])

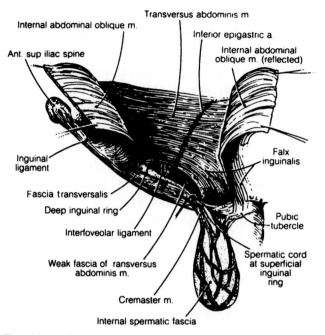

Figure 3–4. The inguinal canal. (Reproduced with permission from Woodburne RT, Burkel WE.[3])

sympathetic pathways, parallel to the testicular vessels. These fibers pass through the aorticorenal plexus, then through the lesser and least splanchnic nerves to spinal segments T10 to T12[5]; they also pass, via lumbar splanchnic nerves, to spinal segments L1 to L2. Testicular pain is referred to the middle and lower abdominal wall.[5]

INGUINAL CANAL

The nerves of the abdominal wall muscles are the seventh through eleventh intercostal nerves and the sub-

costal, iliohypogastric, and ilioinguinal nerves.[3] The iliohypogastric nerve penetrates the internal abdominal oblique muscle several centimeters medial to the anterior superior iliac spine and continues medially below the external abdominal oblique muscle. After giving off a lateral cutaneous branch, the iliohypogastric nerve terminates with an anterior cutaneous branch, which penetrates the external oblique muscle several centimeters above the superficial inguinal ring. The ilioinguinal nerve penetrates the internal oblique muscle near the deep inguinal ring and runs medially through the inguinal canal. The nerve becomes superficial at the superficial inguinal ring and supplies the upper and medial portions of the thigh. An anterior scrotal branch supplies the skin of the root of the penis and the anterior scrotum.[3]

The components and boundaries of the inguinal canal are shown in Figure 3–4. The inguinal ligament forms the floor of the canal while the lacunar ligament forms the medial floor. The external oblique aponeurosis is superficial to the entire canal. The fascia transversalis forms a layer posterior to the entire length of the canal. The internal oblique muscle arises from the inguinal ligament in front of the deep ring and inserts behind and medial to the superficial ring (see Figure 3–4); thus, it forms a part of the anterior wall of the canal laterally, a part of the posterior wall medially, and a "roof" for the canal centrally.[3]

The elements of the spermatic cord pass through the inguinal canal. These include the ductus deferens, the deferential artery and vein, the testicular artery, the pampiniform plexus of veins, the lym-

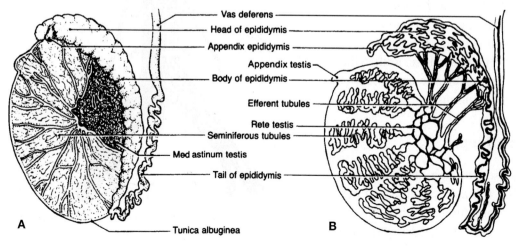

Figure 3–5. Anatomy of the testis. *A,* Parasagittal view. *B,* Duct system. (Reproduced with permission from April EW.[5])

Table 3–1. PATHOLOGIC STAGING OF TUMORS WITHIN THE TESTIS	
Stage	Description
pTis	Intratubular germ cell neoplasia (carcinoma in situ).
pT$_1$	Tumor limited to testis and epididymis, without vascular/lymphatic invasion. Tumor may invade into tunica albuginea but not the tunica vaginalis.
pT$_2$	Tumor limited to testis and epididymis with vascular/lymphatic invasion, or tumor extending through the tunica albuginea with involvement of the tunica vaginalis.
pT$_3$	Tumor invades spermatic cord, with or without vascular/lymphatic invasion.
pT$_4$	Tumor invades the scrotum, with or without vascular/lymphatic invasion.

Adapted from American Joint Committee on Cancer.[6]

phatics, and the autonomic nerves of the testis.

The ilioinguinal nerve and the genital branch of the genitofemoral nerve also pass through the canal. The latter is sensory to the anterior skin of the scrotum and motor to the cremaster muscle.[5] The cremasteric artery arises from the inferior epigastric artery, which lies behind the canal; it penetrates the posterior wall of the inguinal canal and emerges with the spermatic cord at the superficial inguinal ring.[3] The elements of the spermatic cord are covered all the way through the canal by the internal spermatic fascia. Additional covering comes from the cremaster muscle and fascia in the middle of the canal. These coverings are joined by the external spermatic fascia as they emerge through the superficial inguinal ring.[1]

THE RETROPERITONEUM

The distribution of metastases from each testis to the retroperitoneal lymph nodes has been described definitively.[7] The technique of retroperitoneal lymph node dissection is the topic of a subsequent chapter (see Chapter 10) and will not be addressed here. Rather, the major blood vessels and the autonomic nerve supply of the retroperitoneum will be discussed.

Blood Supply

The abdominal aorta passes through the diaphragm at the level of the twelfth thoracic vertebra and lies in front of the anterior longitudinal ligament that covers the lumbar vertebrae.[4] It divides into two

common iliac arteries at the fourth lumbar vertebra. The branches of the abdominal aorta may be divided into paired arteries to the body wall, arteries to paired viscera, and unpaired midline branches to the digestive tract (Figure 3–6).[4]

The body wall branches are segmental arteries in series with the posterior intercostal branches of the thoracic aorta.[4] The inferior phrenic arteries supply the diaphragm and may send a branch to the adrenal gland. There are four pairs of lumbar arteries, which arise from the posterior abdominal aorta at the bodies of the four upper lumbar vertebrae. They pass laterally and posteriorly against the bodies of the vertebrae, posterior to the sympathetic trunk and posterior to the inferior vena cava on the right side as well.[4] The anterior branches of the lumbar arteries are small and barely extend beyond the lateral border of the musculus quadratus lumborum. Each artery also has a large posterior branch that accompanies the dorsal ramus of the corresponding spinal nerve and divides into spinal and muscular branches. The spinal branch passes through the intervertebral foramen and supplies the

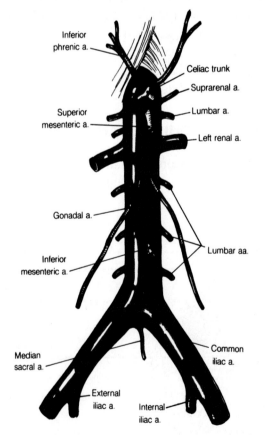

Figure 3–6.   Branches of the abdominal aorta. (Reproduced with permission from Hall-Craggs EC.[4])

spinal cord, the meninges, and the vertebrae.[2] The large muscular branches supply the muscles of the back and the overlying skin and subcutaneous tissues. Because of extensive collateral circulation in the younger age group of men undergoing retroperitoneal lymph node dissection, sacrifice of the lumbar arteries has not been associated with adverse neurologic sequelae to the spinal cord itself.

Branches of the abdominal aorta to paired viscera are the middle adrenal (suprarenal) arteries, the renal arteries, and the gonadal arteries to the testes. The suprarenal arteries supply the adrenal glands directly from the aorta.[1] The renal arteries arise just below the level of the superior mesenteric artery. The right artery passes behind the inferior vena cava and right renal vein to the kidney. The shorter left renal artery passes posterior to the left renal vein. Small inferior adrenal branches are given off by both arteries.

Figure 3–1 illustrated the embryologic development of the lateral branches of the abdominal aorta. Lateral sprouts vascularize the adrenal glands, the testes, and the kidneys. At about the sixth week, the gonads begin to descend while the kidneys ascend. The gonadal artery lengthens as the testis descends, but the ascending kidney is vascularized by a series of new and more-cephalad sprouts from the aorta (see Figure 3–1). This complex process largely explains why variations in the number and location of renal arteries and veins are so common. This variability in renal vasculature often presents one of the most challenging aspects of retroperitoneal lymph node dissection.

The unpaired branches of the abdominal aorta to the digestive tract are the celiac trunk, the superior mesenteric artery, and the inferior mesenteric artery. It is the superior mesenteric artery that limits the upward extent of retroperitoneal lymph node dissection. This artery supplies the whole length of the small intestine as well as the ascending and transverse colon.[2] Injury to this vessel is catastrophic. The inferior mesenteric artery supplies the descending and sigmoid flexure of the colon and most of the rectum.[2]

There is extensive collateral circulation in these areas of the bowel, so the inferior mesenteric artery may be sacrificed in more extensive dissections, without adverse consequences.

The inferior vena cava is formed to the right of and behind the bifurcation of the aorta, by the junction of the two common iliac veins. The tributaries of the inferior vena cava do not correspond to those of the aorta in several respects.[4] There are no veins from the digestive tract since these drain into the hepatic portal system. Only the right gonadal vein drains directly into the inferior vena cava; the left gonadal vein drains into the left renal vein. Lastly, the short hepatic veins drain directly into the inferior vena cava posterior to the liver.

Autonomic Innervation of the Retroperitoneum and Pelvic Viscera

Sympathetic innervation to the pelvic viscera arises from spinal segments T12 to L2 (Figure 3–7).[4] White rami communicantes carry the preganglionic sympathetic motor neurons from the lowest thoracic and upper lumbar spinal nerves to the sympathetic chain of paravertebral ganglia.[4] Some of the neurons

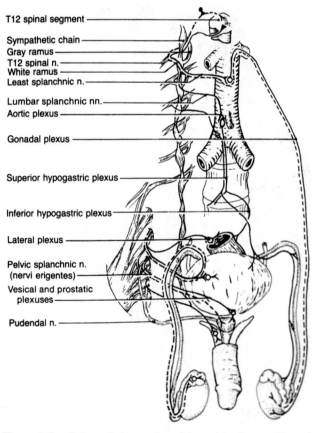

T12 spinal segment
Sympathetic chain
Gray ramus
T12 spinal n.
White ramus
Least splanchnic n.
Lumbar splanchnic nn.
Aortic plexus
Gonadal plexus
Superior hypogastric plexus
Inferior hypogastric plexus
Lateral plexus
Pelvic splanchnic n. (nervi erigentes)
Vesical and prostatic plexuses
Pudendal n.

Figure 3–7. Autonomic innervation of the pelvic viscera. Visceral afferent fibers are shown as dashed lines. (Reproduced with permission from April EW.[5])

may synapse within the paravertebral ganglia before leaving via the lumbar splanchic nerves to join the aortic plexus. The superior hypogastric plexus is the continuation of the aortic plexus; injury to this plexus results in retrograde ejaculation.

The superior hypogastric plexus consists of a broad flattened band of intercommunicating nerve bundles that descend over the bifurcation of the aorta.[3] The relationship of the plexus to the aorta and vena cava is shown in Figure 3–8.[8] Opposite the first sacral segment, the plexus divides into left and right hypogastric nerves. There are few (if any) parasympathetic neurons in the superior hypogastric plexus. The hypogastric nerves (also called the inferior hypogastric plexuses) run along the anterior surface of the sacrum to provide sympathetic innervation to the pelvic plexus on the walls of the rectum.

Parasympathetic innervation to the pelvic viscera arises from spinal segments S2 to S4.[4] The pelvic splanchnic nerves represent the sacral portion of the craniosacral (parasympathetic) portion of the autonomic nervous system.[4]

These preganglionic nerves supply the parasympathetic innervation of all the pelvic and perineal viscera and the abdominal viscera supplied by the inferior mesenteric artery.[3] The pelvic splanchnic nerves arise from the ventral rami of the second, third, and fourth sacral nerves as they emerge from the pelvic sacral foramina. The third sacral nerve usually provides the largest contribution; three to ten strands of nerves pass forward and become incorporated into the inferior hypogastric plexus.[3] The fibers synapse in the ganglia of the inferior hypogastric plexus and ganglia in the muscular walls of the pelvic viscera.[4]

SUMMARY

The embryology and surgical anatomy of the testis are important features that govern the natural history and pattern of spread of testicular cancer and also define the surgical approaches required for curative treatment of this disease. Knowledge of these aspects of the pathobiology of testicular cancer is critical to avoiding unnecessary surgical complications and to limiting the morbidity of the requisite surgical procedures. The application of these important principles is reviewed in Chapter 9 (in the discussion of the principles of orchiectomy) and in Chapter 10 (in the discussion of retroperitoneal lymph node dissection).

REFERENCES

1. Larsen WJ. Human embryology. 2nd ed. Philadelphia: Churchill Livingstone; 1997.
2. Gray H, Clemente CD, editors. Gray's anatomy of the human body. 30th ed. New York: Lea & Febiger; 1984.
3. Woodburne RT, Burkel WE. Essentials of human anatomy. 9th ed. New York: Oxford University Press; 1994.
4. Hall-Craggs EC. Anatomy as a basis for clinical medicine. 3rd ed. Baltimore (MD): Williams & Wilkins; 1995.
5. April EW. Anatomy. 2nd ed. (NY) John Wiley & Sons; 1990.
6. Greene FL, Balch CM, Page DL, et al, editors. American Joint Committee on Cancer (AJCC) Cancer staging manual 6th ed. New York: Springer-Verlag 2002. p. 317–22.
7. Donohue JP, Zachary JM, Maynard BR. Distribution of nodal metastases in nonseminomatous testis cancer. J Urol 1982;128:315–20.
8. Foster RS, Donohue JP. Retroperitoneal lymph node dissection. In: Vogelzang, Shipley WU, Scardino PT, et al, editors. Comprehensive textbook of genitourinary oncology. 2nd ed. Philadelphia: Lippincott Williams & Wilkins; 2000. p. 955–67.

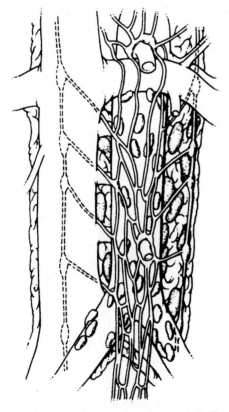

Figure 3–8. Anatomy of retroperitoneal sympathetic fibers. (Reproduced with permission from Foster RS, Donohue JP.[8]

4

Pathology

IVAN DAMJANOV, MD, PhD

Germ cell tumors (GCTs), as their name implies, originate from germ cells. Such tumors can arise from gonads, as well as in extragonadal sites. Extragonadal GCTs are most often located in the midline and are typically found in the retroperitoneum, sacrococcygeal region, anterior mediastinum, or intracranial areas (usually in the pituitary region). Less commonly, GCTs are found in other regions, such as the neck, extremities, or internal organs (Table 4–1).

Germ cell tumors of the gonads have essentially the same microscopic features as those found in other locations. With some notable exceptions, all of these tumors can be classified according to the same principles, suggesting that all of them share the same biology and are most likely derived from germ cells in an identical manner. Unfortunately, despite considerable progress, our understanding of the basic aspects of the pathogenesis of GCT remains incomplete, and the crucial events leading to tumor formation remain obscure. This chapter will briefly reviews the current views of the histogenesis of GCTs in general, including the experimental data supporting various theories of carcinogenesis. The pathology of the most common forms of germ cell neoplasia in humans is then reviewed.

HISTOGENESIS

Even though it is almost intuitively self-evident that GCTs originate from germ cells, this point of view was ardently disputed for many years. In this respect, it is quite instructive to read the 1911 paper of James Ewing, the leading American pathologist of the day. He reviewed the theories of germ cell neoplasia of the testis that were considered at that time and noted that essentially all cells of the testis had been deemed by some authorities as potential progenitors of testicular GCTs.[1] For more than 100 years, teratomas, the most intriguing of all germ cell neoplasms, were considered by some pathologists to be derived from germ cells whereas others considered them to be derived from misplaced embryonic cells.[2] Finally, even when the gonadal GCT became histogenetically linked to the germ cells residing in the gonads, controversy remained about the exact provenance of GCT in extragonadal sites. Finally, even though most GCTs seem to arise from germ cells, there is no doubt that some of the congenital sacrococcygeal teratomas represent parasitic incompletely separated fetal twins and are not true neoplasms but a form of a fetus in fetu.[3]

Carcinoma in Situ of the Testis

The earliest forms of testicular GCT have been identified (by Skakkebaek)[4] inside the seminiferous tubules of infertile men. Subsequent studies by Skakkebaek and his associates in Denmark, followed by observations in other laboratories in the United States and Europe, proved beyond any reasonable doubt that the atypical germ cells in the seminiferous tubules represent the precursors of

Table 4–1. ANATOMIC LOCATIONS OF GERM CELL TUMORS		
Common	Less Common	Uncommon
Testis	Sacrococcygeal region	Neck region
Ovary	Retroperitoneal region	Intracranial compartments
	Mediastinum	Internal organs

invasive GCTs.[5] This preinvasive form of neoplasia, named carcinoma in situ (CIS) by Skakkebaek, became known also as testicular intratubular germ cell neoplasia (ITGCN), a term that has received greatest acceptance in North America.[6]

ITGCN occurs in the testis many years before the GCT becomes clinically evident. Such isolated lesions are usually discovered in specimens of biopsies performed for the elucidation of infertility or in surgically resected testes removed for some other reason. If the preinvasive neoplasia is left untreated, the neoplastic cells will give rise to invasive GCT over a variable period of time. The invasive neoplasms originating from CIS are mostly of two kinds, seminomas or nonseminomatous germ cell tumors (NSGCTs). CIS can be found adjacent to almost all invasive testicular GCTs of the adult testis, except in testes harboring spermatocytic seminomas. Spermatocytic seminomas seem to arise through a different mechanism than do classic seminomas and NSGCTs, and they differ from these other two forms of GCT in that they are not preceded by or associated with CIS.[7] Most testicular yolk sac tumors of infancy and prepubertal teratomas also do not originate from CIS, and the invasive tumors are not associated with intratubular neoplasia in the adjacent testis.[8]

Intratubular CIS can be easily recognized in histologic sections (Figure 4–1). The neoplastic cells are typically found in seminiferous tubules that have thickened basement membranes and are devoid of spermatogenesis. The neoplastic germ cells have large centrally located nuclei surrounded by clear glycogen-rich cytoplasm. The nuclei of CIS are larger than those of normal spermatogonia and contain distinct nucleoli. In contrast to normal spermatogonia, which are diploid, CIS cells are often aneuploid, usually in the hypertriploid or hypotetraploid range.[9]

Intratubular malignant germ cells express placental-like alkaline phosphatase (PLAP), which is closely related to the germ cell–specific alkaline phosphatatase (GCAP) found in fetal and early postnatal germ cells.[10] Commercial antibodies to PLAP do not distinguish this isoenzyme from the GCAP; accordingly, such antibodies can be used in the daily practice of pathology for proving the presence of CIS in seminiferous tubules by immunohistochemical means.

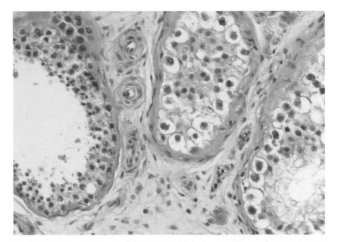

Figure 4–1. Testicular carcinoma in situ (intratubular germ cell neoplasia). The tubules containing the atypical neoplastic cells have thickened basement membranes (hematoxylin and eosin; ×180 original magnification).

Intratubular malignant germ cells express several other genes and their protein products, which can be used as immunohistochemical markers of germ cell neoplasia. Among others, CIS expresses CD117 (also known as *c-kit* proto-oncogene protein), which is also found in fetal and infantile gonocytes.[5,11] During normal development of the testis, *c-kit* gene is involved in the migration of germ cells and their early differentiation. This gene is not expressed in the adult testis. Persistence or aberrant expression of *c-kit* gene in CIS may be a sign of abnormal persistence of the unstable fetal phenotype in germ cell or a lack of the adult type of differentiation, which may render such cells more susceptible to malignant transformation. It remains to be determined whether c-Kit product contributes to the development of invasive GCT.

The products of other genes found to be expressed in CIS are the apoptosis-inducing proteins, such as Fas-L,[12] and the evolutionarily highly conserved protein VASA.[13] CIS cells also express CD30 (a transmembrane glycoprotein belonging to the tumor necrosis factor receptor/nerve growth factor superfamily) and *P53* (a well-known tumor suppressor gene located on chromosome 17p13.1). Overexpression of cyclin D2 has been detected in CIS.[14] At the present time, there is not enough evidence to indicate that any of these genes or their products play a crucial role in testicular carcinogenesis.[15] It is also not known how these endogenous factors interact with exogenous, hormonal, and environmental factors that are suspected to promote the development of testicular tumors.[16]

Ovarian Germ Cell Tumor Precursors

In contrast to the well-characterized precursor lesions in the testis, ovarian precursors of GCTs have not been identified in humans. Nevertheless, there is considerable support for the so-called parthenogenetic theory, which implies that most (if not all) ovarian teratomas and other GCTs arise from parthenogenetically activated oocytes.

The theory linking ovarian teratomas to parthenogenesis is best supported by the experimental data on LT mice, an inbred strain of mice showing a genetic predisposition for the parthenogenetic activation of intraovarian oocytes and the formation of ovarian teratomas.[17] Approximately 50% of LT mice develop ovarian teratomas by puberty. A genetic locus designated Ots1 (ovarian teratoma susceptibility) on chromosome 6 of these mice was identified as the single locus responsible for the formation of teratomas in this mouse strain in a semidominant manner.[18] No equivalent human genes have been identified. Nevertheless, parthenogenetic activation of ovarian germ cells remains the most likely explanation for the occurrence of most ovarian teratomas, even though no parthenogenesis has been recorded in humans. Supporting this theory are observations of parthenogenetically activated oocytes during in vitro fertilization procedures. The experimental data on embryonic stem cells from parthenogenetically activated oocytes of nonhuman primates[19] represent yet another indirect argument supporting the theory on the parthenogenetic origin of ovarian GCT.

Chromosomal studies performed on human ovarian GCTs indicate that such tumors could originate from premeioitic, meiotic, or postmeiotic oocytes.[20] Although abnormal oocytes are easily identified as the precursors of teratomas in the ovaries of LT mice, abnormal oocytes have not been identified in human ovaries. The significance of so-called dysgenetic or polyovular primordial follicles, frequently found in the ovaries of neonates and infants and occasionally seen in ovaries harboring GCTs, remains enigmatic.[21]

Origin of Extragonadal Germ Cell Tumors

Most extragonadal GCTs are located in the midline. This fact has been used to argue that such tumors originate from primordial germ cells misplaced on their route from the yolk sac to the final destination in the gonads; stray germ cells can be found in fetuses of experimental animals, but it is not clear whether such an event takes place during human fetal development.

Some extragonadal GCTs, especially those diagnosed in utero or in early postnatal life, represent parasitic conjoined twins.[3] Teratomas of this kind are most often located in the sacrococcygeal region but can be found in many other locations, including the intrascrotal space, internal abdominal or thoracic sites, and the cranium.

The theory advocating that many GCTs arise from displaced developmentally pluripotent embryonic cells has been supported by experimental data obtained by transplanting early mouse embryos to extrauterine sites.[22,23] Teratomas and teratocarcinoma derived from such ectopically transplanted mouse embryos resemble human germ cells. The stem cells of these tumors are also called embryonal carcinoma cells, in analogy to the stem cells of human NSGCTs. The study of these cells has contributed to the understanding of the differentiation of malignant stem cells and the formation of various somatic and extraembryonic tissues in human GCTs.[24]

HISTOPATHOLOGY OF TESTICULAR GERM CELL TUMORS

Testicular GCTs account for less than 1% of all internal organ malignancies in adult males.[25] Nevertheless, these tumors are important because they typically affect young adult males and men in their most productive years. Furthermore, testicular GCTs are readily curable if diagnosed on time and treated appropriately.

GCTs account for more than 90% of all testicular tumors. These tumors have many features in common. Thus, they have a peak incidence in the 25- to 40-year age group. All GCTs of adult testes, with the exception of spermatocytic seminoma, originate from intratubular CIS. All testicular tumors tend to metastasize first to the periaortic lymph nodes but can disseminate later hematogenously to other major organs as well. Currently, over 90% of all testicular GCTs are curable by modern therapeutic approaches.[26]

For clinical purposes, adult testicular GCTs should be separated from the testicular tumors of infancy and childhood. In the adult testes, two types of GCT predominate: seminomas, which account for 40% of all GCTs, and NSGCTs, which account for 35%. If one adds to them the third entity—NSGCT combined with seminoma (accounting for about 15% of all GCTs)—it becomes evident that seminomas and NSGCTs form the vast majority of all tumors of the adult testis. Spermatocytic seminomas, pure yolk sac tumors, pure choriocarcinomas, and teratomas of postpubertal or adult testes are rare. The same holds true for sex cord tumors such as Sertoli cell tumors and Leydig cell tumors. Most of the testicular tumors of infancy and childhood are classified as yolk sac tumors and teratomas.

Seminoma

Seminoma is the most common GCT of the testis.[6] This tumor is composed of a single cell type. The neoplastic cells resemble spermatogonia and have vesicular nuclei and well-developed cytoplasm filled with glycogen. The cells are arranged into nests surrounded by fibrous septa infiltrated with lymphocytes (Figure 4–2).Tumor cells may grow in the form of cords, solid sheets, or distinct nodules or may present in a tubular, reticular, cystic, or cribriform pattern.[6] Tumors invade or replace the adjacent testicular tissue, but occasionally the cells grow between the seminiferous tubules. Intratubular spread is found in one-third of all tumors. Invasion of the rete testis, often in a pagetoid manner, is seen in 40% of cases and may be accompanied by intratubular extension into the epididymis. Most seminomas show brisk mitotic activity, but there is no evidence that counting mitoses has any prognostic significance.[6]

Immunohistochemistry is useful in distinguishing seminomas from embryonal carcinoma. Typi-

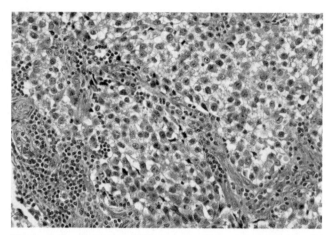

Figure 4–2. Seminoma. The tumor cells are arranged in solid nests surrounded by lymphocyte-rich fibrous septa (hematoxylin and eosin; ×160 original magnification).

cally, most seminomas express PLAP and do not stain with antibodies to keratin (AE1/AE3) whereas embryonal carcinoma cells are PLAP negative and keratin positive.[6,14] Furthermore, most seminomas express CD117 and do not express CD30 whereas most embryonal carcinomas are CD117 negative and CD30 positive.[27]

Human chorionic gonadotropin–positive multinucleated syncytiotrophoblastic cells are present in appoximately 25% of all seminomas.[6] Cytogenetic studies show a marker chromosome, i(12p), in the majority of cases.

Nonseminomatous Germ Cell Tumors

NSGCTs comprise a group of neoplasms that may present in the following several histologic forms: (1) pure embryonal carcinoma; (2) mixed germ cell tumors (also known as teratocarcinomas), composed of embryonal carcinoma, somatic tissues, and extraembryonic tissues equivalent to yolk sac carcinoma and choriocarcinoma; (3) pure yolk sac tumor; (4) pure choriocarcinoma; (5) NSGCT combined with seminoma; and (6) teratoma of postpubertal testes.

Embryonal Carcinoma

The term "embryonal carcinoma" is used for a cell type as well as for a subtype of NSGCT. Embryonal carcinoma (EC) cells are undifferentiated malignant cells resembling the developmentally pluripotential and uncommitted cells from early stages of embryogenesis. Embryonal carcinoma cells that have lost their capacity to differentiate form monomorphic tumors composed of single cell type. Such pure embryonal carcinomas, account for 2 to 3% of all GCTs. Developmentally pluripotent EC cells form the stem cells of mixed GCTs (teratocarcinomas), which account for 30 to 35% of all testicular GCTs. In British classification systems, teratocarcinoma is also known as malignant teratoma [immature].

EC cells are usually polygonal, columnar, or cuboidal and have indistinct borders, contributing to the crowding of nuclei in histologic sections. Because the cytoplasm is scant, the nuclei appear as overlapping one another. These tumor cells may be arranged into solid sheets or into papillary, gland-like, or tubular structures (Figure 4–3). The mitotic rate is high, and the tumor cells often undergo apoptosis. Broad areas of necrosis, intratubular invasion, vascular invasion, and distant metastases (found in 60% of cases) are common.

Immunohistochemically, ECs are positive for keratin, CD30, and (quite often) PLAP. They are negative for CD117 and epithelial membrane antigen (EMA).[6,27] Cytogenetic study will usually reveal an isochromosome, i(12p). Syncytiotrophoblastic cells positive for chorionic gonadotropin are commonly found adjacent to EC cells, but the finding of such cells is still compatible with the diagnosis of EC.

Mixed Germ Cell Tumor (Teratocarcinoma)

Mixed GCTs are NSGCTs that are composed of (1) malignant stem cells equivalent to EC, (2) a teratomatous portion composed of somatic tissues, and (3) extraembryonic tissues such as choriocarcinoma and yolk sac carcinoma. Apparently, these EC cells have retained their capacity to differentiate, like their equivalent embryonic cells in the pre-implantation embryos. EC differentiating into somatic tissues such as neural tissue, cartilage, bone, and glands gives rise to the teratomatous part of such tumors. EC cells differentiating into extraembryonic tissues form the parts of the tumor composed of yolk sac and choriocarcinoma components.

For clinical purposes, there are no significant differences between EC cells that form monomorphous

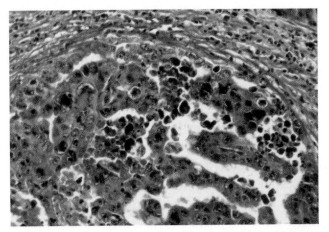

Figure 4–3. Embryonal carcinoma. Tumor cells form solid sheets and papillary structures (hematoxylin and eosin; ×180 original magnification).

tumors and those that have retained their capacity to differentiate into other tissues. The EC cells that are developmentally "nullipotent" are cytologically indistinguishable from those found in mixed GCTs considered to be pluripotent. The only significant difference is that mixed GCTs containing yolk sac carcinoma elements usually secrete α-fetoprotein (AFP), and those containing trophoblastic elements secrete human chorionic gonadotropin (hCG) into the blood. On the other hand, patients harboring pure EC may be serologically negative for AFP and hCG.

Yolk Sac Tumor

The cells that form the yolk sac tumor (also known as endodermal sinus tumor or "Teilum tumor") resemble the cells found in the extraembryonic structures corresponding to visceral embryonic endoderm of the peri-implantation–stage germinal disc, extraembryonic yolk sac, allantois, and related extraembryonic mesenchyme (magma reticulare). Yolk sac components are typically found in about 65% of all mixed GCTs,[6] but they may exceptionally be the only element of adult NSGCTs.[28,29] Pure yolk sac tumor is the most common testicular tumor of infancy and early childhood.[6] Infantile yolk sac tumors appear to be biologically distinct from yolk sac tumors of adults[29,30] and should not be included among the NSGCTs.

Yolk sac tumor components of NSGCTs in adults have the same histologic features as the pure infantile yolk sac tumors. Ulbright and colleagues[6] list 11 different patterns: (1) a reticular pattern, composed of a network of interlacing elongated cells, microcystic clear spaces, and vacuolated cells resembling fat cells; (2) a macrocystic pattern, in which larger empty spaces are lined by flattened cells; (3) an endodermal sinus pattern, in which cuboidal or columnar cells are attached to vascular papillary cores (often described as "festooned") or line tissue spaces in a labyrinthine pattern (resembling the endodermal sinus of the murine placenta) and/or form glomeruloid bodies (Schiller-Duval bodies); (4) a papillary pattern resembling mesothelioma or other micropapillary tumors; (5) a solid pattern composed of solid sheets of epithelial cells; (6) a glandular/alveolar pattern, in which cuboidal or columnar cells form structures resembling intestinal or endometrioid glands or line acinar and cystic spaces; (7) a polyvesicular vitelline pattern composed of cuboidal or flat epithelium-lined cysts surrounded by generally loose mesenchyme; (8) a myxomatous pattern composed of spindle-shaped or stellate cells lying in a loose myxomatous stroma containing prominent thin-walled blood vessels; (9) a sarcomatoid pattern composed of anaplastic spindle cells; (10) a hepatoid pattern resembling fetal liver; and (11) a parietal yolk sac pattern, in which the extracellular basement membrane material predominates. The reticular pattern is most commonly seen, followed by the solid and endodermal sinus patterns (Figure 4–4).

Immunohistochemically, most yolk sac tumors stain with antibodies to AFP. Epithelial cells are positive for keratins. Staining for CD34 is often positive, allowing one to distinguish yolk sac tumors from seminomas and EC, which are negative. Staining for PLAP may give positive or negative results and is of limited value. EMA is typically negative and is helpful in distinguishing yolk sac tumors from adenocarcinomas. Other immunohistochemical stains are of lesser diagnostic value.

Choriocarcinoma

Choriocarcinomas are composed of cells resembling syncytiotrophoblastic and cytotrophoblastic cells that line the chorionic villi. Pure testicular chorio-

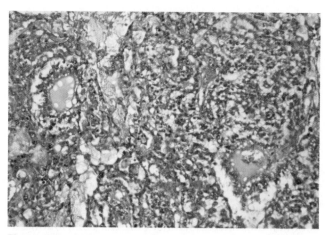

Figure 4–4. Yolk sac tumor. The tumor consists of inter-anastomosing strands. Focally, the tumor cells form glomeruloid structures (Schiller-Duval bodies) (hematoxylin and eosin; ×120 original magnification).

carcinomas are extremely rare, accounting for 0.3% of all testicular tumors.[6] Focal choriocarcinoma cells can be found in 8% of all NSGCTs.[30]

Choriocarcinoma cells tend to destroy tissue and invade blood vessels, causing necrosis and hemorrhage. Such foci typically contain (1) mononuclear cytotrophoblastic cells with clear cytoplasm and (2) multinucleated syncytiotrophoblastic cells (Figure 4–5).

Combined Seminoma and NSGCT

The combined seminoma and NSGCT is included under the heading of mixed GCTs in some texts[6]

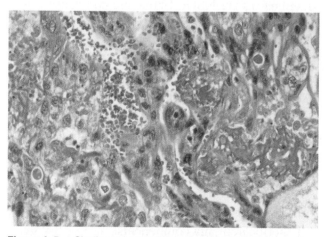

Figure 4–5. Choriocarcinoma. The tumor consists of mononuclear cytotrophoblastic and multinucleated syncytiotrophoblastic cells (hematoxylin and eosin; ×180 original magnification).

whereas other texts place them in a separate category.[31] Such combined tumors provide an interesting insight into the histogenesis of GCTs, indicating that some NSGCTs arise from preexisting seminomas.[32] However, another published interpretation is that seminoma and NSGCT both arise from a common precursor germ cell (see Chapter 1).

Combined tumors account for 15% of testicular GCTs. Most often these tumors consist of seminoma admixed with embryonal carcinoma cells. However, seminoma may be admixed with other NSGCT components, such as teratoma, yolk sac, and choriocarcinoma, which may be present in varying proportions. For practical purposes, these combined tumors are treated as NSGCTs. By convention, pure seminomas containing syncytiotrophoblastic cells are not included in this category.

Teratoma of Postpubertal Testis

Teratomas of the postpubertal testis, also known as mature teratomas, are composed of somatic tissues. In contrast to mixed NSGCTs (teratocarcinomas), these teratomas do not contain EC cells.

Even though these tumors do not contain EC cells, they occasionally produce metastases that may be composed of somatic tissues (mature metastasizing teratoma) or that consist of EC cells.[6,33] It seems that most of these metastases are derived from small foci of EC that have not been recognized in the primary testicular tumor. These teratomas are thus best considered fully differentiated forms of mixed NSGCTs (teratocarcinoma) in which almost all EC cells have differentiated into somatic tissue. Since one cannot be entirely sure that a large tumor does not contain EC cells in a part that was not examined histologically, or that some EC cells have already metastasized before the tumor was resected, all teratomas of postpubertal testes should be considered as being potentially malignant.

In the seminiferous tubules adjacent to these teratomas, there are atypical germ cells corresponding to CIS or ITGCN. Such intratubular neoplastic cells are not found in the seminiferous tubules adjacent to testicular teratomas of infancy or in the testes adjacent to dermoid cysts of postpubertal testes.[34] These findings indicate that the teratomas of adult testes are histogenetically more akin to NSGCTs and seminomas than to teratomas of prepubertal testes and dermoid cysts, which are benign tumors that are unrelated to intratubular malignant germ cells.

Spermatocytic Seminoma

Spermatocytic seminoma is a tumor composed of cells that show signs of spermatogenic differentiation. This tumor accounts for 2% of all testicular GCTs. In contrast to other GCTs, it has a peak incidence in the sixth decade.[35] Most tumors are benign, but some may undergo secondary malignant transformation and give rise to sarcoma.

The tumors are composed of polymorphous neoplastic cells arranged into solid sheets interrupted by broad acellular fibrous strands. Three cell types can be recognized: small cells with round nuclei superficially resembling lymphocytes, intermediate cells with large vesicular nuclei and well-developed eosinophilic or basophilic cytoplasm, and large cells with loosely structured chromatin resembling spireme chromatin in primary spermatocytes in meiotic prophase.[6] Intratubular CIS is not present in adjacent seminiferous tubules, suggesting that the histogenesis of these tumors is different from that of seminomas and NSGCTs. In contrast to classic seminomas that are associated with EC and other NSGCT elements in 15% of cases, spermatocytic seminomas never progress into other NSGCTs.

Testicular Tumors of Infancy and Childhood

Most testicular tumors of infancy and childhood are classified as yolk sac tumors or teratomas.[36–38] Histologically, these tumors have the same features as the equivalent tumors in adult testes. In contrast to seminomas, NSGCTs, and teratomas of postpubertal or adult testes, prepubertal testicular tumors usually are not associated with atypical germ cells in the adjacent seminiferous tubules. These findings suggest that the histogenesis of prepubertal GCTs is different from that of postpubertal tumors.

Teratomas arising in prepubertal testes are invariably benign. Yolk sac tumors removed in the early stages of development have an excellent prognosis, but even tumors that have metastasized are curable with proper treatment.[39] In the series analyzed by Grady and colleagues,[39] which contained 212 prepubertal yolk sac tumors, 33 tumors had metastasized. The metastases were into the abdominal lymph nodes in 9 cases, were hematogenous in 13 cases, and were combined lymphogenous and hematogenous in 6 cases. The pattern of metastasis of prepubertal yolk sac tumors differs thus from the usual route of spread of postpubertal GCTs.

OVARIAN GERM CELL TUMORS

Ovarian GCTs account for approximately 25 to 30% of all ovarian tumors. The classification of the World Health Organization recognizes several entities that roughly correspond to testicular GCTs (Table 4–2).

Most ovarian GCTs are classified as benign teratomas (dermoid cysts), which account for 95% of all ovarian GCTs.[21] Most patients are younger than 30 years of age. In the first two decades, ovarian GCTs account for 60% of all ovarian tumors, one-third of which are malignant.[40,41]

Dysgerminoma

Dysgerminoma is the ovarian equivalent of testicular seminoma. It accounts for 1% of all ovarian GCTs and for close to 50% of all ovarian malignant GCTs. Most of the tumors occur in the second and third decade of life and are rarely found in persons under the age of 10 years or over the age of 50 years. In 15% of cases, the tumors are bilateral.[21]

Microscopically, the tumor is composed of uniform, round, or polygonal cells with vesicular nuclei

Table 4–2. CLASSIFICATION OF OVARIAN GERM CELL TUMORS*
Dysgerminoma
Yolk sac tumor
Embryonal carcinoma
Polyembryoma
Choriocarcinoma
Teratoma
Immature
Mature
Monodermal
Mixed tumor

*World Health Organization classification.

and clear cytoplasm. As in testicular seminomas, these cells are arranged into nests, sheets, or cords enclosed by fibrous septa containing lymphocytes. The septa may contain plasma cells, macrophages, and giant cells, arranged into granulomas in some cases. Scattered multinucleated syncytiotrophoblastic cells that stain with antibodies to hCG are found in 3% of tumors.[21,40] In approximately 15% of tumors initially thought to represent dysgerminomas, additional examination may reveal components of other GCTs, such as EC or yolk sac tumor; accordingly, such tumors are classified as mixed GCTs.[21]

Immunohistochemically, dysgerminoma cells react positively with antibodies to PLAP and inhibin/activin but are usually unreactive with antibodies to keratins, EMA, and AFP.[21,42]

Yolk Sac Tumor

Yolk sac tumors are rare malignant tumors, accounting for approximately 0.5% of all ovarian GCTs and 20% of all malignant ovarian GCTs.[21,40,41] Most tumors are diagnosed in the immediate postpubertal period, the mean age of patients at diagnosis being 16 to 19 years.[41] These tumors are almost invariably unilateral and large (> 15 cm in diameter) and have a ruptured surface in 30% of cases.[21] The patient's blood typically contains AFP in high concentration.

Microscopically, yolk sac tumors of the ovary have the same features as testicular yolk sac tumors. Round hyaline globules are often evident in the extracellular spaces. AFP can be demonstrated in tumor cells. In about 15% of cases, the tumors contain elements of other GCTs, most often squamous epithelium from dermoid cysts.[41]

Embryonal Carcinoma and Mixed Germ Cell Tumors

Ovarian ECs are equivalent to testicular ECs. Like the testicular tumors, ovarian ECs are composed exclusively of EC cells. Such tumors are extremely rare, and most tumors show some form of differentiation of EC cells into teratoma, yolk sac tumor, or choriocarcinoma. Such tumors are then classified as mixed GCTs, and the pathologist is expected to list the various components identified microscopically.

ECs and mixed GCTs are very rare. They typically occur in young girls and women in the age group of 4 to 28 years (median, 12 years).[41] Microscopically, ovarian EC cells are identical to testicular EC cells. Mixed GCTs contain hCG-positive syncytiotrophoblastic cells, AFP-positive yolk sac tumor cells, and various somatic tissues of teratoma.

Polyembryoma

Polyembryomas are extremely rare malignant tumors composed of EC cells arranged into bodies that resemble early embryos. In addition to these embryoid bodies, these tumors usually contain other mixed germ cell elements. The recent review by Jondle and colleagues[43] shows that fewer than 15 polyembryomas have been reported in the last 60 years since the first case was described by Peyron.

Choriocarcinoma

Choriocarcinomas are tumors showing trophoblastic differentiation. Pure nongestational choriocarcinomas of the ovary are extremely rare but highly malignant.[40,41] Microscopically, the tumors are composed of mononuclear cytotrophoblastic and multinucleated syncytiotrophoblastic cells. Tumors are typically unilateral, but the contralateral ovary may contain teratomas.[44]

Teratoma

Teratomas are tumors that are composed of somatic tissues arranged in a haphazard manner. Three forms of teratoma are recognized: (1) immature teratoma, (2) mature teratoma, and (3) monodermal teratoma. Teratomas account for 98% of all ovarian GCTs, and most of these (95%) are classified as mature teratomas.[21] Teratomas are tumors of young women, most of whom are diagnosed before 30 years of age.

Immature Teratomas

Immature teratomas make up 3% of all ovarian teratomas. Typically, they present as solid ovarian tumors in girls and young women under the age of 20 years. In addition to mature somatic tissues, these tumors invariably contain embryonic neuroectodermal structures (Figure 4–6) and/or glial tissue resembling brain tumors such as astrocytoma, glioblastoma multiforme, or ependymoma. Squamous epithelium of the dermoid cyst is found in about 20% of tumors.

Immature teratomas can be graded histologically by quantifying the amount of immature neural tissue in the tumor. Using this approach, these tumors can be classified as low grade or high grade.[21] Low-grade tumors contain less than one low-magnification microscopic field in any one microscopic slide. High-grade tumors contain immature neuroepithelial tissue exceeding one lower-power microscopic field per slide. Extraovarian spread typically takes place in the form of peritoneal implantation of glial tissue. Other embryonic malignancies, such as rhabdomyosarcoma,[45] may arise occasionally from immature teratomas.

Mature Teratomas

Mature teratomas are cystic in 80% of cases (Figure 4–7) and solid in the remaining 20% of cases. Mature solid teratomas occur in younger women and must be distinguished from immature teratomas, with which they share many features. Cystic teratomas represent the most common ovarian GCT. These teratomas can be diagnosed during a woman's entire reproductive life and even after menopause.

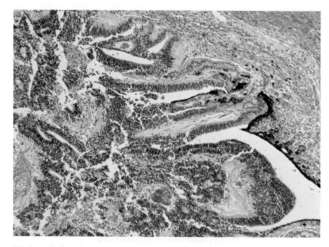

Figure 4–6. Immature teratoma of the ovary. The small blue cells correspond to immature neural precursor cells forming tube-like structures and protrusions (hematoxylin and eosin; ×130 original magnification).

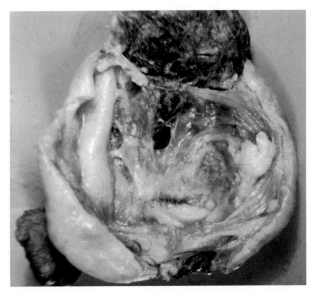

Figure 4–7. Benign cystic teratoma. The open cyst is lined by skinlike squamous epithelium focally covered with hair. There is also a tooth protruding into the lumen of the cyst.

Most teratomas involve only one ovary, but bilaterality is found in about 15% of cases. Histologically, the solid teratomas are composed of various mature somatic tissues derived from all three embryonic germ layers. Glial and neural tissue may be prominent, but in contrast to immature teratomas, there are no embryonic neuroectodermal structures. Cystic teratomas are predominantly composed of skin and skin appendages, including hair and sebaceous glands. Teeth, neural tissue, retinal epithelium, many mesenchymal tissues (such as cartilage, bone, fat tissue, and muscles), and endodermal derivatives (such as bronchial and intestinal components) may be found. Thyroid tissue is the most common endocrine tissue found. Occasionally, teratomas may be associated with benign tumors such as Brenner tumor.[46]

Mature teratomas are benign tumors. In some cases, however, these tumors may undergo malignant transformation and give rise to carcinomas and sarcomas. The most common malignant tumors originating in cystic teratomas are squamous cell carcinomas.[21] Melanomas and sarcomas also may arise from these tumors.[21,47]

Monodermal Teratomas

Monodermal teratomas are composed almost exclusively of a single tissue and include entities such as struma ovarii, carcinoid tumors, and the neuroectodermal tumors, including ependymoma, neuroblastoma, medulloblastoma, and glioblastoma multiforme.[40,41]

Struma ovarii, composed of thyroid tissue, represents the most common monodermal teratoma (Figure 4–8). These tumors are usually solid but may be cystic, and they are often confused with other ovarian tumors.[48] Tumors may be composed of typical thyroid tissue or may resemble thyroid only superficially (see Figure 4–8). Occasionally, struma may recur many years after the removal of the original tumor, even though the tumor appeared histologically benign. Peritoneal implants (strumosis peritonei) are a rare complication.

SACROCOCCYGEAL TERATOMAS

Sacrococcygeal teratomas (see also Chapter 22 by Malogolowkin and colleagues) are the most common congenital tumors, occurring in 1 of 40,000 neonates.[49] These tumors occur four times more often in females than in males. The tumors show an age-dependent malignancy that increases with the age of the patients. Thus, 7% of tumors diagnosed at birth, 37% of tumors diagnosed by the age of 1 year, and 50% of tumors diagnosed at the age of 2 years are malignant.[50]

Congenital tumors present as masses protruding from the rump of the neonate (Figure 4–9). These tumors are classified into four groups according to the presacral and/or abdominal extension of neo-

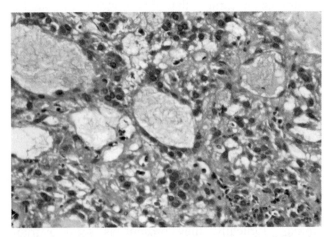

Figure 4–8. Struma ovarii. The tumor consists of cells forming solid areas and only focally lining colloid-filled acini (hematoxylin and eosin; ×180 original magnification).

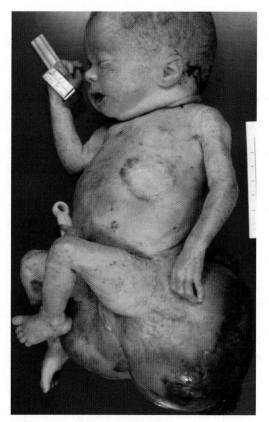

Figure 4–9. Sacrococcygeal teratoma in a neonate who died shortly after birth. A large tumor mass protrudes from the infant's rump.

plastic masses.[49] Type I tumors have only a minimal presacral component; type II tumors are predominantly external but have a definitive intra-abdominal component; type III tumors are mostly in the abdomen, with a very small external component; and type IV tumors are entirely intra-abdominal and presacral, and there is no external tumor.

Overall, benign tumors predominate.[51] Approximately 65% are classified as mature solid teratomas, 25% as immature teratomas, and 10% as malignant mixed GCTs. The latter tumors contain EC and yolk sac tumor components. Tumors treated in specialized surgical centers have an excellent prognosis.[52]

GERM CELL TUMORS OF OTHER LOCATIONS

Mediastinal Germ Cell Tumors

Mediastinal GCTs (see also Chapter 21) typically occur in the anterior part of the mediastinum and account for appoximately 15% of all tumors and cysts at this site.[53–57] The tumors are typically connected to the thymus, and it is assumed that they originate from displaced germ cells retained in that location. In the neonatal period, mediastinal teratomas are often intrapericardial or intracardiac.[51]

Mediastinal GCTs predominantly affect young males, and the mean age at diagnosis is about 28 years.[57] For no obvious reasons, patients with Klinefelter's syndrome are at a higher risk of developing mediastinal GCTs than are other males. In infants and prepubertal children, males and females are affected at the same rate.

Overall, benign tumors predominate. Approximately 45% of tumors are classified as benign cystic or solid teratomas, 20% are classified as seminomas, and 25% are classified as mixed GCTs. The remaining 10% are histologically classified as pure ECs, yolk sac tumors, or choriocarcinomas. Teratomas are not associated with chromosomal abnormalities in tumor cells, but the NSGCT cells show always some chromosomal disturbances.[58]

Approximately 2% of patients who have mediastinal NSGCTs (especially those that contain yolk sac tumor elements) develop hematologic malignancies, such as acute leukemia and myelodysplastic and myeloproliferative disorders.[59] The hematopoietic malignant cells contain the GCT chromosomal marker i(12)p, indicating that they are derived from the mediastinal GCTs. In analogy with normal hematopoietic stem cells that originate in the fetal yolk sac, it is assumed that the neoplastic hematopoietic cells originate in the yolk sac components of the mediastinal NSGCT. Treatment of seminomas is associated with good results in 88% of cases whereas the NSGCTs respond in only 49% of cases.[60] Patients with mediastinal NSGCTs are at an increased risk for developing metachronous testicular tumors.[61]

Retroperitoneal Germ Cell Tumors

Tumors originating in the space delineated by the posterior sheath of the peritoneum and the posterior abdominal wall, extending from the diaphragm to the upper rim of the pelvis, are classified as retroperitoneal. Retroperitoneal GCTs account for approximately 1 to 2% of all GCTs. Approximately

70% of tumors are found in children under the age of 10 years, and one-half of these are diagnosed in children under the age of 1 year.[50] Childhood tumors are mostly benign. Retroperitoneal GCTs in adult males are mostly malignant.[62]

The nature of primary malignant retroperitoneal GCTs in adult males is a matter of controversy. A significant number of patients diagnosed with retroperitoneal GCTs are subsequently found to have testicular GCTs, suggesting that many (if not all) retroperitoneal tumors are metastases from a primary testicular neoplasm.[61,62] Histopathologic examination of testes of patients diagnosed with retroperitoneal GCTs will almost invariably disclose some abnormalities, such as hyalinization of seminiferous tubules, extensive fibrosis, or calcification, suggesting that the presumptive testicular primary GCTs might have involuted following the metastasis of tumor cells to retroperitoneal space, where a new tumor is formed. Some retroperitoneal tumors develop many years after orchiectomy for a testicular tumor, further giving credence to the belief that most retroperitoneal GCTs are actually metastases.[63]

Intracranial Germ Cell Tumors

GCTs account for 0.3% of all intracranial tumors (see Chapter 21). More than 90% of tumors are found in children and in adolescents younger than 20 years.[64] Two-thirds of tumors are found in the second decade. In children, GCTs make up 3% of all intracranial tumors. Intracranial GCTs have their highest incidence in East Asia, accounting for up to 15% of childhood neoplasms in Japan and Taiwan.[65] In Western countries, the tumors are 2.5 times more common in males than in females, but in Japan, the male-to-female ratio is 9:1.[66]

Most intracranial tumors are located in the pineal region, followed by the suprasellar compartment.[64] Most tumors are classified as germinomas, accounting for 60% of all intracranial GCTs.[65,66] These tumors correspond histologically to testicular seminomas, and they are highly radiosensitive. About 10% of intracranial GCTs are benign teratomas. Mixed GCTs, pure ECs, pure yolk sac carcinomas, and choriocarcinomas are equally represented, accounting for the remaining 30% of GCTs.

Intracranial GCTs have the same morphology and share many (if not most) of the molecular biologic features of testicular and ovarian GCTs.[67]

Germ Cell Tumors in Unusual Locations

GCTs have been described in essentially all major anatomic regions and internal organs.[50] Many of these pharyngeal, orbital, and gastric teratomas are found in children, but some have been encountered in adults as well. From the point of view of pathology, these tumors resemble those found in the gonads.

SUMMARY

Germ cell tumors are characterized by similar histologic appearances, whether they arise at gonadal or extragonadal sites, and they may display a broad range of somatic and germinal differentiation. Important advances in histologic assessment have been augmented by immunohistochemical and molecular analysis, leading to a histologic classification that reflects the biology of the disease.

REFERENCES

1. Ewing J. Teratoma testis and its derivatives. Surg Gynecol Obstet 1911;12:230–61.
2. Damjanov I, Solter D. Experimental teratoma. Curr Top Pathol 1974;59:69–130.
3. Spencer R. Parasitic conjoined twins: external, internal (fetus in fetu and teratomas), and detached (acardiacs). Clin Anat 2001;14:428–44.
4. Skakkebaek NE. Possible carcinoma-in-situ of the testis. Lancet 1972;ii:516–7.
5. Rørth M, Rajpert-De Meyts E, Andersson L, et al. Carcinoma in situ in the testis. Scand J Urol Nephrol 2000;34 Suppl 205:166–86.
6. Ulbright TM, Amin MB, Young RH. Tumors of the testis, adnexa, spermatic cord, and scrotum. Atlas of tumor pathology. Third series, fascicle 25. Washington (DC): Armed Forces Institute of Pathology; 1999.
7. Stoop H, Van Gurp, De Krijger R, et al. Reactivity of germ cell maturation stage-specific markers in spermatocytic seminoma: diagnostic and etiological implications. Lab Invest 2001;81:919–28.
8. Manivel JC, Simonton S, Wold LE, Dehner LP. Absence of intratubular germ cell neoplasia in testicular yolk sac tumors in children. A histochemical and immunohistochemical study. Arch Pathol Lab Med 1988;112:641–5.
9. Oosterhuis JW, Castedo SMMJ, De Jong B, et al. Ploidy of primary germ cell tumors of the testis: pathogenetic and clinical relevance. Lab Invest 1989;60:14–20.

10. Roelofs H, Manes T, Millan JL, et al. Heterogeneity in alkaline phsophatase isoenzyme expression in human testicular germ cell tumors. An enzyme-immunohistochemical and molecular analysis. J Pathol 1999;189:236–44.

11. Horie K, Fujita J, Takakura H, et al. The expression of c-kit protein in human adult and fetal tissues. Human Reprod 1993;8:1955–62.

12. Kersemaekers A-MF, van Weeren PC, Ooosterhuis JW, Looijenga LHJ. Involvement of the Fas/FasL pathway in the pathogenesis of germ cell tumours of the adult testis. J Pathol 2002;196:423–9.

13. Zeeman A-M, Stoop H, Boter M, et al. VASA is a specific marker for both normal and malignant human germ cells. Lab Invest 2002;82:159–66.

14. Houldsworth J, Reuter V, Bosl GJ, et al. Aberrant expression of cyclin D2 is an early event in human male germ cell tumorigenesis. Cell Growth Differ 1997;8:293–9.

15. Looijenga LHJ, Oosterhuis JW. Pathogenesis of testicular germ cell tumors. Rev Reprod 1999;4:90–100.

16. McGlynn KA. Environmental and host factors in testicular germ cell tumors. Cancer Invest 2001;19:842–53.

17. Stevens LC, Varnum D. The development of teratomas from parthenogenetically activated ovarian eggs. Dev Biol 1974;37:369–80.

18. Lee GH, Bugni JM, Obata M, et al. Genetic dissection of susceptibility to murine ovarian teratomas that originate from parthenogenetic oocytes. Cancer Res 1997;57:590–3.

19. Cibelli JB, Grants KA, Chapman KB, et al. Parthenogenetic stem cells in nonhuman primates. Science 2002;295:819.

20. Dahl N, Gustavson KH, Rune C, et al. Benign ovarian teratomas. An analysis of their cellular origin. Cancer Genet Cytogenet 1990;46:115–23.

21. Russell P, Robboy SJ, Anderson MC. Ovary: germ cell tumors. In: Robboy SJ, Anderson MC, Russell P, editors. Pathology of the female reproductive tract. London: Churchill Livingstone; 2002. p. 641–90.

22. Stevens LC. The development of transplantable teratocarcinomas from intratesticular grafts of pre- and post-implantation mouse embryos. Dev Biol 1970;21:364–81.

23. Solter D, Skreb N, Damjanov I. Extrauterine growth of mouse egg-cylinders results in malignant teratoma. Nature 1970;227:503–4.

24. Pierce GB Jr, Abell MR. Embryonal carcinoma of the testis. Pathol Annu 1970;5:27–60.

25. Jemal A, Thomas A, Murray T, Thun M. Cancer statistics, 2002. CA Cancer J Clin 2002;52:23–47.

26. Krege S, Souchon R, Schmoll HJ, et al. Interdisciplinary consensus on diagnosis and treatment of testicular germ cell tumors: results of an update conference on evidence-based medicine (EBM). Eur Urol 2001;40:372–91.

27. Leroy X, Augusto D, Leteurte E, Gosselin B. CD30 and CD117 (c-kit) used in combination are useful for distinguishing embryonal carcinoma from seminoma. J Histochem Cytochem 2002;50:283–5.

28. Medica M, Germinale F, Giglio F, et al. Adult pure yolk sac tumor. Urol Int 2001;67:94–6.

29. Foster RS, Hermans B, Bihrler R, Donohue JP. Clinical stage I pure yolk sac tumor of the testis in adults has different clinical behavior than juvenile yolk sac tumor. J Urol 2000;164:1943–4.

30. Jacobsen GK, Barlebo H, Olsen J, et al. Testicular germ cell tumors in Denmark 1976-1980. Pathology of 1058 consecutive cases. Acta Radiol Oncol 1984;23:239–47.

31. Damjanov I. Male reproductive system. In: Damjanov I, Linder J, editors. Anderson's Pathology. 10th ed. St. Louis (MO): Mosby; 1996. p. 2166–230.

32. Srigley JR, Mackay B, Toth P, Ayala A. The ultrastructure and histogenesis of male germ cell neoplasia with emphasis on seminoma with early carcinomatous features. Ultrastruct Pathol 1988;12:67–86.

33. Simmonds PD, Lee AH, Theaker JM, et al. Primary pure teratomas of the testis. J Urol 1996;155:939–42.

34. Ulbright TM, Srigley JR. Dermoid cyst of the testis: a study of five postpubertal cases, including a pilomatrixoma-like variant, with evidence supporting its separate classifiction from mature testicular teratoma. Am J Surg Pathol 2001;25:788–93.

35. Eble J. Spermatocytic seminoma. Hum Pathol 1994;25:1035–42.

36. Kay R. Prepubertal testicular tumor registry. J Urol 1993;150:671–4.

37. Gobel U, Calaminus G, Engert J, et al. Teratomas of infancy and childhood. Med Pediatr Oncol 1998;31:8–15.

38. Gobel U, Schneider DT, Calaminus G, et al. Germ-cell tumor in childhood and adolescence. GPII and MAKEI and the MAHO group. Ann Oncol 2002;11:263–71.

39. Grady RW, Ross JH, Kay R. Patterns of metastatic spread in prepubertal yolk sac tumor of testis. J Urol 1995;153:1259–61.

40. Scully RE, Young RH, Clement PB. Tumors of the ovary, maldeveloped gonads, fallopian tube, and broad ligament. Atlas of tumor pathology. Third series, fascicle 23. Washington (DC): Armed Forces Institute of Pathology; 1996.

41. Clement PB, Young RH. Atlas of gynecologic surgical pathology. Philadelphia (PA): W. B. Saunders; 2000.

42. Cabellis J, Cataldi P, Reis FM, et al. Gonadal malignant germ cell tumor express immunoreactive inhibin/activin subunits. Eur J Endocrinol 2001;145:779–84.

43. Jondle DM, Shahin MS, Sorosky J, Benda JA. Ovarian mixed germ cell tumor with predominance of polyembryoma: a case report with literature review. Int J Gynecol Pathol 2001;21:78–81.

44. Goswami D, Sharma K, Zutchi V, et al. Nongestational pure choriocarcinoma with contralateral teratoma. Gynecol Oncol 2001;80:262–6.

45. Yanai H, Matsuura H, Kawasaki M, et al. Immature teratomas of the ovary with a minor rhabdomyosarcomatous component and fatal rhabdomyosarcomatous metastases: the first case in a child. Int J Gynecol Pathol 2001;21:82–5.

46. Burg J, Kommoss F, Bittinger F, et al. Mature cystic teratoma of the ovary with struma and benign Brenner tumor: a case report with immunohistochemical characterization. Int J Gynecol Pathol 2002;21:74–7.

47. Kruger S, Schmidt H, Kupker W, et al. Fibrosarcoma associated with benign cystic teratoma of the ovary. Gynecol Oncol 2002;84:150–4.

48. Szyfelbein WM, Young RH, Scully RE. Struma ovarii stimulating ovarian tumors of other types: a report of 30 cases. Am J Surg Pathol 1995;19:21–9.

49. Schropp KP, Lobe TE, Rao B, et al. Sacrococcygeal ter-

atomas:the experience of four decades. J Pediatr Surg 1992;27:1075–9.

50. Damjanov I, Knowles BB, Solter D. The human teratomas: experimental and clinical biology. Clifton (NJ): Humana Press; 1983.

51. Isaacs H Jr. Tumors of the newborn and infant. St. Louis (MO): Mosby-Year Book; 1991.

52. De Backer A, Erpicum P, Phillipe P, et al. Sacrococcygeal teratomas: results of retrospective multicentric study in Belgium and Luxembourg. Eur J Pediatr Surg 2001;11:182–5.

53. Moran CA, Suster S. Primary germ cell tumors of the mediastinum. I. Analysis of 322 cases with special emphasis on teratomatous lesions and new proposal for histopathologic classification and clinical staging. Cancer 1997;80:681–90.

54. Moran CA, Suster S, Przygodzki RM, Koss MN. Primary germ cell tumors of the medistinum. II. Mediastinal seminomas: a clinicopathologic and immunohistochemical study of 120 cases. Cancer 1997;80:691–8.

55. Moran CA, Suster S, Koss MN. Primary germ cell tumors of the mediastinum. III. Primary yolk sac tumor, embryonal carcinoma, and combined non-teratomatous germ cell tumors: a clinicopathological and immunohitochemical study of 64 cases. Cancer 1997;80:699–707.

56. Moran C. Germ cell tumors of the mediastinum. Pathol Res Pract 1999;195:583–7.

57. Weidner N. Germ-cell tumors of the mediastinum. Semin Diagn Pathol 1999;16:42–50.

58. Schneider DT, Schuster AE, Fritsch MK, et al. Genetic analysis of mediastinal nonseminomatous germ cell tumors in children and adolescents. Genes Chromosomes Cancer 2002;34:115–25.

59. Hartmann JT, Nichols CR, Droz JP, et al. Hematologic disorders associated with primary mediastinal nonseminomatous germ cell tumors. J Natl Cancer Inst 2000;92:54–61.

60. Bokemeyer C, Nichols CR, Droz JP, et al. Extragonadal germ cell tumors of the mediastinum and retroperitoneum: results from an international analysis. J Clin Oncol 2002; 20:1864–73.

61. Hartmann JT, Fossa SD, Nichols CR, et al. Incidence of metachronous testicular cancer in patients with extragonadal germ cell tumors. J Natl Cancer Inst 2001;21:1733–8.

62. Scholz M, Zehender M, Thalmann GN, et al. Extragonadal retroperitoneal germ cell tumor: evidence of origin in the testis. Ann Oncol 2002;13:121–4.

63. Lehman J, Ritz M, Nurnberg N, et al. Retroperitoneal mature teratoma 15 years after initial treatment of testicular mixed germ cell tumor. Eur Urol 2000;38:644–8.

64. Rosenblum MK, Matsutani M, Van Meir EG. CNS germ cell tumours. In: Kleihues P, Cavanee WK, editors. Pathology and genetics of tumours of the nervous system. Lyon, France: International Agency for Research on Cancer; 2000. p. 208–14.

65. Nomura K. Epidemiology of germ cell tumors in Asia of pineal region tumor. J Neurooncol 2001;54:211–7.

66. Hirato J, Nakazato Y. Pathology of pineal region tumors. J Neurooncol 2001;54:239–49.

5

Presentation of Germ Cell Tumors

TIMOTHY J. CHRISTMAS, MD, FRCS
ALAN HORWICH, PhD, FRCR, FRCP

In the male, the classic presenting symptom of a germ cell tumor (GCT) is a painless hard swelling within the body of the testis in a young man. In the United States, the lifetime risk for developing a testicular tumor is about 1 in 300, and the incidence has been increasing.[1]

The swelling within the testis may be noticed by the patient or his sexual partner. The presence of testicular atrophy, which is a predisposing factor for GCT, may make the swelling more readily apparent. Atrophy of the testis can occur as a result of cryptorchidism (especially when it has not been corrected until late childhood), infection (particularly mumps orchitis), or torsion or local trauma. Some men with testicular tumors and atrophic testes may present to an infertility clinic and be diagnosed on examination in that setting.[2]

The age pattern of testicular cancer is unusual. The incidence of germ cell tumors rises sharply from late teens to a peak just under 30 years of age for nonseminoma and between 30 and 35 years of age for seminoma. There is a fall in the incidence of germ cell tumors at older ages, and they are distinctly uncommon in those aged over 65 years. Spermatocytic seminoma occurs typically in older men, but the most common testicular tumor in the older age group is lymphoma.

CRYPTORCHIDISM

The incidence of cryptorchidism is 3.4% in neonates weighing > 2.5 kg and is 0.8% in the adult population.[3] A history of testicular maldescent increases the risk approximately fivefold, and abdominal testes are 35 to 48 times more likely to undergo malignant change than a normal testis; approximately 10% of testicular tumors develop within testes with a history of cryptorchidism.[4,5] Delayed recognition of a cryptorchid testis can increase the risk of malignancy. In the developed world, the great majority of cryptorchid testes are diagnosed in childhood and are corrected by orchiopexy. A previously cryptorchid testis needs close follow-up later in life, and this can be done by palpation if the testis has been successfully transferred to the scrotum. However, in some cases, the diagnosis is delayed or the testis cannot be surgically translocated to the scrotum, and these patients require close follow-up. Testes within the superficial inguinal pouch can still be palpated but may also require imaging with ultrasonography or magnetic resonance imaging (MRI)

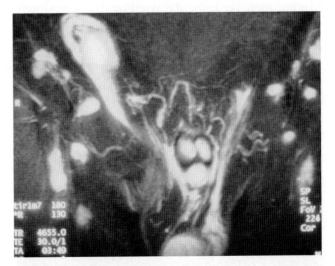

Figure 5–1. Magnetic resonance imaging scan of a cryptorchid right testis within the superficial inguinal pouch in a 35-year-old man. The left testis lies in the scrotum.

to ensure that malignant change has not occurred. When cryptorchid testes remain intra-abdominal, they may present late after undergoing malignant change, with lower abdominal or back pain and a palpable mass (Figure 5–2). These tumors can grow to a massive size (Figure 5–3) and can metastasize (Figure 5–4).[6] Local invasion of adjacent pelvic structures may occur, leading to presentation with unexpected symptoms such as hematuria.[7]

CARCINOMA IN SITU

There is a recognized preinvasive condition of the testes called carcinoma in situ. At present, however, this condition must be diagnosed by testicular biopsy, a procedure that does not lend itself to screening. Carcinoma in situ is found in less than 1% of subfertile men, about 5% of patients with corrected testicular maldescent, and in the contralateral testes of about 5% of men who have had an orchiectomy for a germ cell tumor. If the contralateral testis is atrophic, the risk of its containing carcinoma in situ is as high as 20 to 25%. An observational study has determined that the conversion of carcinoma in situ to invasive testicular cancer appears to occur at a rate of about 50% within 5 years. Although the condition is diagnosed definitively by biopsy, suspicion is increased by the ultrasonographic finding of macrocalcification.

DIAGNOSIS

In some men, the testicular swelling develops slowly while the rate of growth may be very rapid in others.

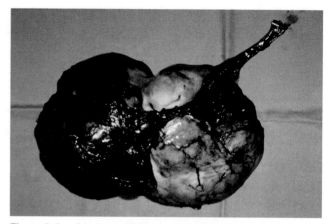

Figure 5–3. A large undifferentiated malignant teratoma that developed within an abdominal testis in a 19-year-old man.

A dull ache may be present within the testis or the scrotum in up to 30% of cases; in 10% of cases, acute pain may be the presenting symptom. In up to 30% of cases, there is an apparent history of scrotal injury. When scrotal pain is present or when there is a history of injury, the diagnosis may be less obvious, and other diagnoses should be considered, such as torsion of the testis or epididymo-orchitis. The differential diagnosis for testicular tumors is shown in Table 5–1. In young men who develop a rapidly growing hydrocele, there should be a high index of suspicion for the presence of an underlying testicular tumor (Figure 5–5). When clinical examination and tumor marker assays fail to provide a definitive diagnosis, then further confirmatory investigations such as scrotal ultrasonography (Figures 5–6 and 5–7),[8] computed tomography (CT) (Figure 5–8), or MRI are indicated.

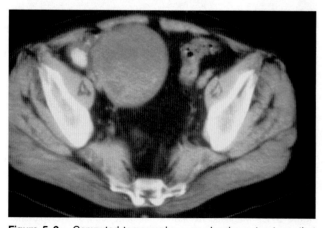

Figure 5–2. Computed tomography scan showing a teratoma that has developed within a cryptorchid testis on the right side of the pelvis.

Figure 5–4. Teratoma within an abdominal testis, with para-aortic lymph node metastases attached.

Table 5–1. DIFFERENTIAL DIAGNOSIS FOR TESTICULAR TUMORS

Epididymo-orchitis
Torsion of the testis
Hydrocele
Epididymal cyst
Hematoma
Inguinoscrotal hernia
Varicocele
Tuberculosis of the testis
Gumma of the testis

Delay in Diagnosis

Since both intensity of treatment and prognosis relate to the extent of disease at presentation, it is important that testicular diagnosis is not delayed. In the past, lack of physician awareness, compounded by ignorance of the disease in the young male population, led to substantial intervals between first symptoms and the start of treatment. For example, in patients presenting in the early 1980s, the average delay was just under 3 months, and there is evidence that those who suffered delays of more than 100 days presented with a more advanced pattern of disease.[9] There is also evidence for an impact on prognosis. A multi-institution study of chemotherapy results conducted by the Medical Research Council in the United Kingdom showed that the 3-year survival rate for men with a history of less than 3 months was 81%, compared with 61% in those with a history of more than 3 months ($p = .02$).

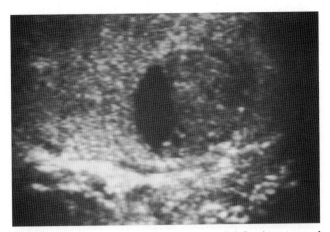

Figure 5–6. Scrotal sonogram showing a well-defined teratoma of the testis.

Presentation with Systemic Symptoms

In a few cases, GCT of the testis can present with systemic symptoms secondary to endocrine effects of the primary tumor itself. Gynecomastia (Figure 5–9) is a presenting feature in up to 5% of men with testicular tumors, due to an imbalance resulting from a relative deficiency of androgenic suppression and the predominance of estrogenic stimulation of the growth of breast tissue. This can be mediated by an increase in gonadotropin level, particularly that of human chorionic gonadotropin (hCG), and an increase in estradiol levels. Another factor is the low level of androgens produced by some men with testicular atrophy, particularly those with a history of bilateral cryptorchidism. Interstitial cell testicular tumors such as Leydig cell and Sertoli cell tumors can manufacture hormones and raise estradiol levels, leading to gynecomastia.

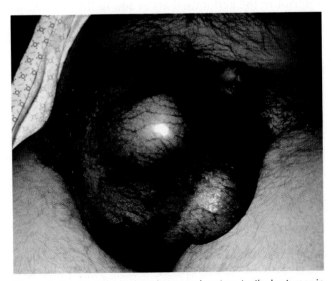

Figure 5–5. Massive hydrocele secondary to a testicular tumor in a 30-year-old man.

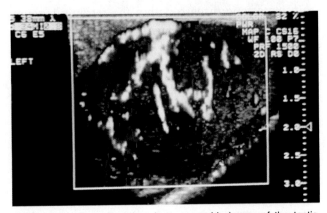

Figure 5–7. Color Doppler ultrasonographic image of the testis, showing enhanced blood supply to a testicular teratoma.

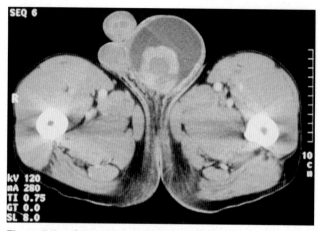

Figure 5–8. Computed tomography scan showing a large hydrocele secondary to an impalpable seminoma.

Presentation with Symptoms from Metastases

In 10% or more of cases, the presentation of testicular GCT is a result of symptoms derived from metastatic disease. In some cases, this is due to the presence of a small primary tumor but massive fast-growing metastases. The most common first site for the development of metastatic disease is within retroperitoneal lymph nodes. The sentinel nodes from right-sided tumors are in the aortocaval area; those from left-sided tumors are in the para- and preaortic areas, most frequently on the ipsilateral side. Nodal enlargement may cause local symptoms such as backache and loin pain, which may be more extreme when there is obstruction of the ureter, leading to hydronephrosis (Figure 5–10) or invasion of the psoas muscle and/or the spine (Figures 5–11 and 5–12).* Compression of nerve roots can lead to leg weakness and muscle wasting. Nodal enlargement from metastatic disease within the retroperitoneum can also cause compression of the inferior vena cava (Figure 5–13), which in turn promotes the development of deep venous thrombosis within the iliac veins and, hence, swelling of the lower limbs. Compression or invasion of the third part of the duodenum by lymph node metastases is a fortunately rare

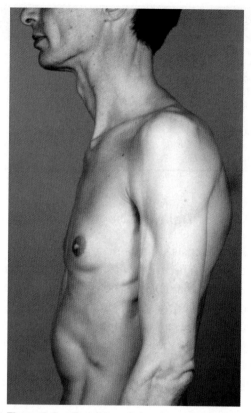

Figure 5–9. Gynecomastia in a man with a testicular tumor.

complication that is more likely with right-sided testicular tumors and that presents with either bowel obstruction or gastrointestinal bleeding. Ejaculation and antegrade seminal emission in the male are dependent on the sympathetic nervous system and, in particular, the postganglionic nerve fibers that lie anterior to the abdominal aorta and in the aortocaval groove. Patients with testicular GCT have presented

---

*Editor's note: Occasionally, ipsilateral flank pain will be caused by a large primary tumor, with dragging on the spermatic cord without evidence of lymph node metastases; thus, flank pain may not always denote metastatic disease.

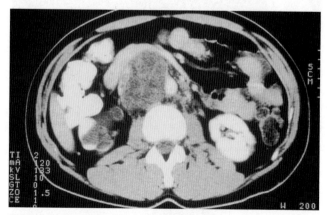

Figure 5–10. Computed tomography scan showing aortocaval lymph node metastases that have compressed the ureter, leading to hydronephrosis and atrophy of the right kidney.

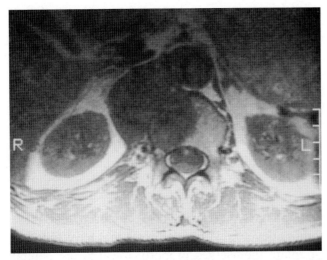

Figure 5–11. Right retroperitoneal nodal metastases invading the L1 vertebra and psoas muscle, with imminent spinal cord compression.

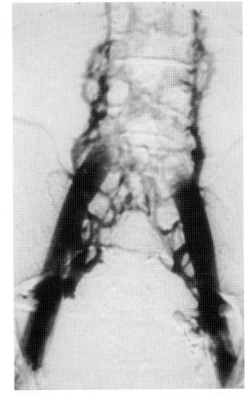

Figure 5–13. Venacavogram showing complete occlusion of the inferior vena cava by nodal metastases. The blood is finding alternative routes along collateral vessels.

with loss of ejaculation and anorgasmia, owing to compression of these nerves (Figure 5–14).

Previous inguinal surgery can disturb the usual pattern of nodal spread, with initial metastasis in inguinal or pelvic nodes. Pulmonary metastases can advance rapidly in young men with GCT, and the initial presentation may be as an acute shortness of breath, hemoptysis, or even pulmonary embolus after direct invasion of the right atrium. In these circumstances, the chest radiograph made at presentation may be dramatic (Figure 5–15). These patients are in urgent need of chemotherapy since the majority of them can survive if treated with modern regimens.

Presentation of metastatic testicular GCT within the head and neck is less common but can take two

forms. Lymph node metastases within the neck are most often found in the supraclavicular fossa. It is important to scrutinize the testes and to check the tumor markers (α-fetoprotein [AFP] and hCG) in all young men who present with nodal masses in the neck. Fine-needle aspiration is often unhelpful, and nodal excision biopsy should be avoided until a tes-

Figure 5–12. Intraoperative picture after excision of nodal mass shown in Figure 5–11. The L1 vertebra has been replaced by a metal cage and bone grafts.

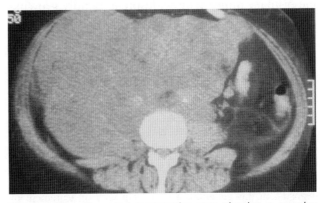

Figure 5–14. Computed tomography scan showing a massive retroperitoneal nodal mass from testicular teratoma that initially presented with loss of ejaculation secondary to sympathetic nerve fiber compression.

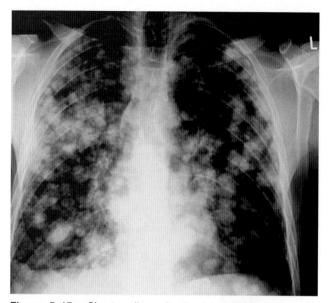

Figure 5–15. Chest radiograph showing multiple pulmonary metastases from a testicular germ cell tumor in a patient who initially presented with shortness of breath.

ticular primary tumor has been excluded. The second form of presentation is with brain metastasis (Figure 5–16), which causes headaches, visual disturbance, drowsiness, or epileptic seizures. As with those who present with metastases in the neck, all young men presenting with a solid brain lesion that might be a metastasis should be investigated for a possible primary testicular tumor.*

Rapid referral and diagnosis are particularly important in cases involving a subset of germ cell tumors that proliferate most rapidly. Typically, these tumors contain choriocarcinomatous elements. The presentation of this subtype of germ cell tumor is a syndrome often associated with a small or impalpable primary tumor with widespread rapidly growing metastases affecting retroperitoneal nodes, the lung fields bilaterally, and often the liver and the central nervous system. The serum concentration of hCG is usually > 100,000 U/L. The rapid growth of numer-

*Editor's note: Occasionally choriocarcinoma presents with carcinomatous infiltration of the meninges without solid deposits; this will be found in a patient with headache and/or central neurologic syndromes without evidence of cortical deposits. In this situation, a spinal tap with measurement of cerebrospinal fluid (CSF) tumor markers may reveal the diagnosis, particularly when the blood hCG to cerebrospinal fluid hCG ratio is less than 30 to 40:1.

ous lung metastases can lead to respiratory failure within days; therefore, this presentation represents an indication for emergency chemotherapy.[10]

EXTRAGONADAL GERM CELL TUMORS

After the testis, the next most common site for primary GCTs in males is the retroperitoneum, the anterior mediastinum, the pineal gland region, and the pre-sacrococcygeal area. There are several theories to explain the derivation of these tumors (see also Chapter 1). Some have proposed that these tumors develop within cell rests that have failed to orientate themselves properly towards the genital ridge in the embryo. In males, retroperitoneal GCTs may actually represent metastases from a testicular primary that has regressed. Mediastinal GCTs are rare, and nonseminomas are more common than seminomas. Individuals with these tumors present with shortness of breath, cough, and local discomfort and appear to have a worse prognosis than those with germ cell tumors arising at other sites.[11]

Primary retroperitoneal GCTs present as an abdominal mass or an obstruction of the renal or gastrointestinal tract. In practice, it can be difficult to distinguish retroperitoneal primary GCTs from occult primaries causing abdominal metastasis although the latter may have associated carcinoma in situ. A testicular ultrasound examination should be

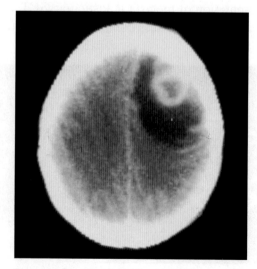

Figure 5–16. Computed tomography scan of the head, showing a left frontal lobe metastasis from a testicular germ cell tumor.

part of the assessment. The prognosis is similar to that of an equivalent testicular primary.[12]

A recent retrospective review of an international series of 635 patients with extragonadal GCTs of the mediastinum and retroperitoneum[13] included 341 patients with primary mediastinal GCTs and 283 patients with retroperitoneal GCTs. Fifty-one of the mediastinal tumors were seminomas, of which 13 had cervical lymph node metastases but only 3 had extranodal disease. In contrast, mediastinal primary tumors metastasized commonly to lungs, abdominal lymph nodes, liver, bone, and the central nervous system and were frequently associated with high serum concentrations of either AFP or hCG. Similarly, only 51 of the 283 patients with GCTs in the retroperitoneum had seminomas. The majority of these were good-prognosis presentations. Retroperitoneal nonseminomas metastasized widely to lung, liver, and cervical nodes. The survival rate of patients presenting with seminomatous extragonadal GCTs was equivalent to that of those with testicular primaries, with a reported 88% 5-year survival rate and no difference between mediastinal and retroperitoneal presentations. For patients with nonseminomas, the 5-year survival rate was 49%, compared to 63% for those with retroperitoneal nonseminomas. There is an association between primary mediastinal nonseminomas and hematologic malignancies. Such malignancies occurred in 17 of the 290 patients with mediastinal nonseminoma and occurred within 5 years of the GCT.[14] The most common disorders were acute megakaryoblastic leukemia (number [n] = 5) and myelodysplasia (n = 5). Analysis of leukemic blasts for the GCT marker chromosome i(12p) revealed its presence in 5 (38% of the hematologic malignancies analyzed).

Primary intracranial GCTs occur in the pineal and suprasellar regions[15] (see also Chapter 28). They represent approximately 1% of all primary intracranial cancers, and may be slightly more common in Japan and Taiwan. These tumors also may be either seminomas or nonseminomas. The presentation of pineal tumors is usually with headache, nausea and vomiting, and evidence of raised intracranial pressure. There may be signs of Parinaud's syndrome (paralysis of conjugate upward gaze). The usual early symptoms of suprasellar tumors are those of visual disturbances, and there may be polyuria, polydipsia, lethargy, somnolence, and evidence of hypopituitarism and loss of visual field. These tumors may metastasize to the meninges and also may metastasize systemically.

REFERENCES

1. Ries LAG, Eisner MP, Kosary CL, et al. SEER cancer statistics review, 1973–1999, National Cancer Institute. Bethesda, MD. http://seer.cancer.gov/csr/1973_1999/, 2002 (accessed Dec 02, 2002).
2. Moller H, Skakkebaek N. Risk of testicular cancer in subfertile men: case-control study. BMJ 1999;318:559–62.
3. Levitt SB, Kogan SG, Engel RM, et al. The impalpable testis: a rational approach to management. J Urol 1978;120:515–20.
4. Strader CH, Weiss NS, Daling JR, et al. Cryptorchism, orchiopexy, and the risk of testicular cancer. Am J Epidemiol 1988;127:1013–8
5. Leissner J, Filipas D, Wolf HK, Fisch M. The undescended testis: considerations and impact on fertility. Br J Urol 1999;83:885–92.
6. Kulkarni JN, Desai SM, Phadke GK, Tongaonkar HB. Improved management of abdominal undescended testicular tumours with bulky confluent retro-peritoneal nodal metastases. J Urol 1996;156:1341–4.
7. Walker R, Rogers H, Christmas TJ. Seminoma in an undescended testis presenting with frank haematuria. Br J Urol 1997;79:290–1.
8. Fuse H, Shimazaki J, Katayama T. Ultrasonography of testicular tumors. Eur Urol 1990;17:273–5.
9. Chilvers CE, Saunders M, Bliss JM, et al. Influence of delay in diagnosis on prognosis in testicular teratoma. Br J Cancer 1989;59:126–8.
10. Andreyev HJN, Dearnaley DP, Horwich A. Testicular nonseminoma with high serum human chorionic gonadotrophin: The trophoblastic teratoma syndrome. Diagn Oncol 1993;3:67–71.
11. Childs WJ, Goldstraw P, Nicholls JE, et al. Primary malignant mediastinal germ cell tumours: improved prognosis with platinum-based chemotherapy and surgery. Br J Cancer 1993;67:1098–101.
12. McAleer JJA, Nicholls J, Horwich A. Does extragonadal presentation impart a worse prognosis to abdominal germ-cell tumors? Eur J Cancer 1992;28:825–8.
13. Bokemeyer C, Nichols CR, Droz JP, et al. Extragonadal germ cell tumors of the mediastinum and retroperitoneum; results from an international analysis. J Clin Oncol; 2002; 7:1864–73.
14. Bokemeyer C, Kollmannsberge C, Harstrick A, et al. Treatment of patients with cisplatin-refractory testicular germ-cell cancer. German Testicular Cancer Study Group (GTCSG). Int J Cancer 2000;83:848–51.
15. Jennings MT, Gelman R, Hochberg F. Intracranial germ cell tumours; natural history and pathogenesis. J Neurosurg 1985;63:155–67.

6

Radiologic Investigation

JANET E. S. HUSBAND, OBE, FMedSci, FRCP, FRCR
DOW-MU KOH, MRCP, FRCR
GARY J. R. COOK, MSc, MD, FRCP, FRCR

OVERVIEW

Oncologic imaging is a rapidly evolving subspecialty of general diagnostic radiology, its birth and continued growth being a much needed response to the importance of imaging in the management of patients with cancer. The radiologist undertaking examinations in patients with testicular tumors should have a special interest in oncology, should have a detailed knowledge of the patterns of spread of testicular tumors and the characteristic appearances of metastatic disease at different sites, and should be familiar with the many diagnostic pitfalls that may make the difference between treating a patient unnecessarily or missing early curable disease. Equally important, the effective use of all imaging relies on meticulous imaging techniques and protocols.

Although imaging techniques have been developed and refined over recent years, computed tomography (CT), first used for staging testicular tumors in the late 1970s, remains the standard method of investigation and follow-up. The major advantage of CT is that it is ideally suited to the examination of the most common sites of tumor spread, that is, the lymph nodes and lungs. Following orchiectomy, CT is performed for staging to identify the presence and extent of metastatic disease and also to provide an overall estimate of tumor burden. During follow-up, CT remains the imaging method of choice.

Magnetic resonance imaging (MRI) has advanced enormously during recent years and has many applications in body imaging. However, in the management of testicular tumors, MRI is mainly used for certain specific indications or as a problem-solving exercise. For example, MRI is the technique of choice in the staging investigation of patients who are at high risk of developing brain metastases. MRI is also useful with patients who are undergoing resection of retroperitoneal masses when there is concern regarding the presence or extent of inferior vena caval involvement. As a problem-solving technique, MRI can be helpful in characterizing focal liver lesions, in detecting suspected bone involvement, and in elucidating the cause of unusual neurologic features.[1] The results on an MRI of the testis can distinguish seminomas from nonseminomatous germ cell tumors (NSGCTs) preoperatively.[2] It may also be used to distinguish solid primary testicular tumors from cysts but is less frequently used than ultrasonography.[3]

Ultrasonography is useful in ascertaining the nature of a testicular swelling (Figure 6–1, A) and is particularly helpful with patients who present with metastatic disease when an occult primary tumor of the testis is suspected and for examining the contralateral testis in patients with an obvious primary tumor (in order to identify bilateral synchronous tumors).[4,5] Although large retroperitoneal nodal masses may be visualized on ultrasonography (see Figure 6–1, B), the technique is not used to detect lymph node disease or for staging the extent of tumor spread because it is generally unreliable for detecting small-volume deepseated lesions. (Lymph nodes are more clearly delineated by CT, as shown in Figure 6–1, C.)

Plain-film chest radiography can show metastases ≥ 1 cm in diameter and, in addition to CT, have always played an important role in the staging and routine follow-up of patients with testicular tumors. Recently, however, the routine use of both chest radiography and chest CT in the follow-up of patients with NSGCTs has been questioned.[6,7] White and colleagues[6] suggest that in low-risk pure seminoma (normal abdominal CT and marker negative), follow-up chest CT can be avoided safely and chest radiography alone is required.

An exciting new development is the introduction of positron emission tomography (PET). While this technique is still at an early stage of clinical evaluation in regard to testicular tumors, several studies have already demonstrated that PET may provide useful additional information for staging and that the technique may be an important prognostic indicator. Early reports suggest that PET may have a useful role in assessing treatment response and in determining residual tumor viability.

Most testicular cancers demonstrate avid uptake of 18-fluoro-2-deoxyglucose (FDG), except for mature teratomas, in which metabolic activity is relatively low. As uptake of this radiopharmaceutical is high in metastatic testicular tumor tissue compared to background tissues, PET is a sensitive technique for demonstrating metastatic disease. The inclusion of PET in the management of patients with testicular cancer can alter management in up to 57% of cases.[8,9]

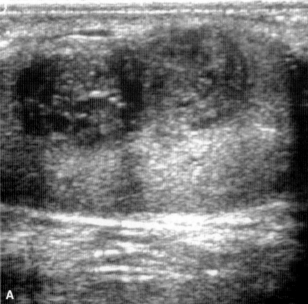

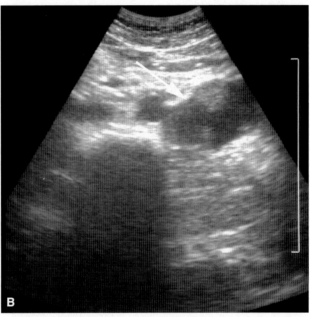

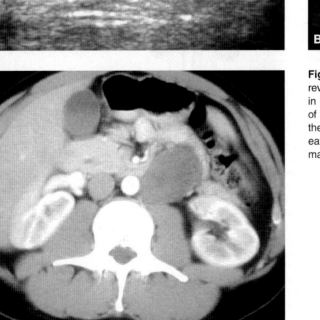

Figure 6–1. Mixed germ cell testicular tumor. *A,* Ultrasonography revealed a 3.5 cm mass of mixed echogenicity within the left testis, in keeping with a germ cell tumor. *B,* Ultrasonographic examination of the abdomen demonstrated a hypoechoic nodal mass (*arrow*) in the left para-aortic region. *C,* The nodal disease was better delineated by computed tomography, as a low-density left para-aortic mass just below the level of the left renal vein.

PATTERNS OF TUMOR SPREAD

The presence of lymphatic or vascular invasion documented on histologic examination is an important prognostic indicator of primary testicular tumors because these are the pathways of metastatic spread.

Lymphatic invasion leads to tumor spread along four to eight efferent lymphatic channels that accompany the spermatic cord. These channels pass through the internal inguinal ring, where they join together to form major lymphatic channels accompanying the testicular vessels. These major vessels cross the ureter at the pelvic brim and then fan out into several branches to enter the retroperitoneal lymph nodes (Figure 6–2).

Right-sided testicular tumors spread to the right paracaval and retrocaval nodes as well as to the precaval nodes and interaorticocaval lymph nodes (Figure 6–3, A).

Left-sided tumors also spread to lymph nodes around the great vessels. Those nodes that are first involved are usually the lymph nodes in the left para-aortic region below the left renal vein (see Figure 6–3, B). In general, lymph nodes involved in right-sided tumors tend to be lower in the retroperitoneum than those involved in left-sided tumors. This simply reflects the anatomic arrangement of normal retroperitoneal lymph node chains. Crossover of lymph node involvement will occa-

sionally be seen, but this is relatively uncommon (see Figure 6–3, C).

Further spread of disease extends above the renal vessels in the retroperitoneal and retrocrural spaces. Lymphatic spread may also extend to nodes lateral to the paracaval and para-aortic groups; these nodes are are sometimes referred to as "echelon nodes." The so-called echelon node on the right was first described by the anatomist Rouvière, in his elegant description of anatomic dissection.[10] An echelon node on the left has also been described. With the knowledge derived from CT, it is now clear that these echelon nodes lie on the anterior surface of the iliopsoas and, although an unusual site of disease, may be a first site of relapse (Figure 6–4).[11]

The pattern of tumor spread in testicular tumors is characteristic and is usually contiguous below the diaphragm; thus, the consistency with which right-sided tumors spread to the right-sided retroperitoneal nodes and left-sided tumors spread to left-sided nodes is extremely high.[12] If a single node that is deemed to be enlarged is demonstrated on the contralateral side to the primary tumor, then histologic verification of metastatic disease is recommended prior to therapy. However, direct spread of tumor from one side to the other, via communicating lymphatics, is common particularly if several nodes are involved or if there is a large coalescent nodal

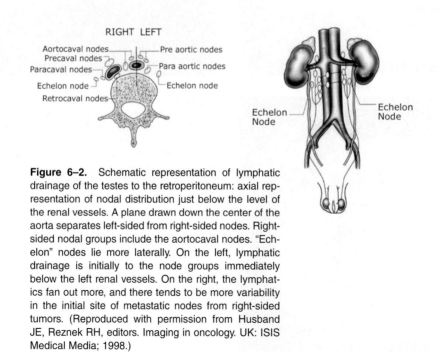

Figure 6–2. Schematic representation of lymphatic drainage of the testes to the retroperitoneum: axial representation of nodal distribution just below the level of the renal vessels. A plane drawn down the center of the aorta separates left-sided from right-sided nodes. Right-sided nodal groups include the aortocaval nodes. "Echelon" nodes lie more laterally. On the left, lymphatic drainage is initially to the node groups immediately below the left renal vessels. On the right, the lymphatics fan out more, and there tends to be more variability in the initial site of metastatic nodes from right-sided tumors. (Reproduced with permission from Husband JE, Reznek RH, editors. Imaging in oncology. UK: ISIS Medical Media; 1998.)

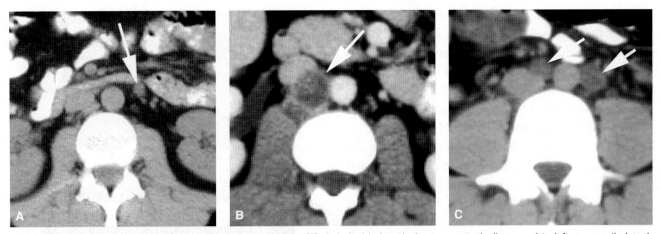

Figure 6–3. Retroperitoneal nodal disease demonstrated on CT. *A,* Left-sided testicular tumors typically spread to left para-aortic lymph nodes just below the level of the left renal vein (*arrow*). *B,* Right-sided tumors usually spread to the retrocaval (*arrow*), paracaval, precaval, or aortocaval lymph nodes. *C,* The presence of crossover lymphatic trunks can result in dissemination of disease from a right-sided testicular tumor to nodes on the left. Note the enlarged right-sided aortocaval and left-sided para-aortic nodes (*arrow*).

mass.[12] Crossover occurs more commonly from right to left than from left to right. This may be due to the fact that lymph nodes on the right are situated lower in the retroperitoneum and that lymphatic flow is generally in a cranial direction (see Figure 6–3, *C*).

Pelvic nodal disease is uncommon but may occur in certain specific situations. In patients with large retroperitoneal masses, retrograde flow of tumor cells through the lymphatics may result in nodal disease. Cryptorchidism and previous scrotal surgery are also risk factors for nodal disease in the pelvis (Figure 6–5).[13]

Mediastinal nodal disease usually occurs by direct contiguous spread of tumor via the thoracic duct into the posterior mediastinum through the diaphragmatic hiatus in seminoma (Figure 6–6), but with an NSGCT, tumor spread is more random.[14] Not infrequently, however, nodal disease is seen in the anterior mediastinum, aortopulmonary window, or hilar regions, without any evidence of posterior mediastinal or subcarinal involvement. This is more commonly seen in cases of NSGCT than in cases of seminoma. Tumor spread of disease to the supraclavicular fossae and to lymph nodes in the neck is also more common in cases of NSGCT. Pleural masses and effusions are well-recognized features of seminoma[15] and are usually accompanied by other manifestations of metastatic spread.

Vascular invasion of the primary tumor results in hematogenous spread predominantly to the lungs.

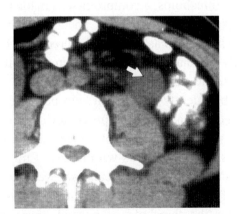

Figure 6–4. An "echelon" node on CT. In this man with relapsed seminoma, there was an enlarged echelon node (*arrow*) lying anterior to the left psoas muscle. (Reproduced with permission from Husband JE, Reznek RH, editors. Imaging in oncology. UK: ISIS Medical Media; 1998.)

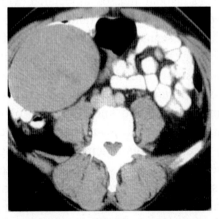

Figure 6–5. Pelvic disease. This 47-year-old man with a history of right orchiectomy for undescended testes developed a large seminomatous mass within the right pelvis. The mass appears to be of near uniform density on this computed tomography (CT) scan.

Hematogenous spread is more common in cases of NSGCT than in cases of seminoma. It should also be remembered that nodal masses may contribute to hematogenous spread as tumor cells may also invade the blood vessels that supply lymph node deposits. This is more likely to occur in large nodal masses that have spread beyond the lymph node capsule.

Other sites of bloodborne metastases include the brain, the liver, and bone. Metastases in unusual sites may be identified in patients with both seminomas and NSGCTs. Unusual sites of disease are most commonly seen in relapsed patients who have undergone previous treatment for metastatic disease. It is therefore important that the radiologist be aware of the patient's previous history and current clinical symptoms. Unusual sites include the kidneys, adrenal glands, muscles, spleen, prostate, pericardium, pleura, and peritoneum (Figure 6–7).[16]

STAGING

Lymph Node Metastases

Lymph node metastases in patients with testicular tumors vary in size, from nodal masses that are < 2 cm in diameter to huge retroperitoneal masses. The character of nodal masses is related to histology; on CT, seminoma nodal deposits are usually of soft-tissue density whereas NSGCTs are often heterogeneous since they contain areas of necrosis and cystic degeneration (see Figures 6–1, C, and 6–6). Homogeneous low-density "cystic" lesions may be a feature of NSGCTs. Nodal masses associated with seminoma and nonseminomatous tumor may also calcify.

Staging CT scans are reviewed to identify nodal disease, lung metastases, and (in patients with advanced disease) bloodborne metastases in other sites. It is important that the radiologist interpreting the examination should know the side of the primary tumor in order to give appropriate weight to any equivocal findings. Edema and scarring in the groin are usually obvious on CT. The detection of nodal disease relies on size criteria, and over the last two decades there has been much discussion regarding the appropriate threshold for the upper limit of normal for retroperitoneal nodes. There is now, however, a general consensus that nodes > 8 mm in

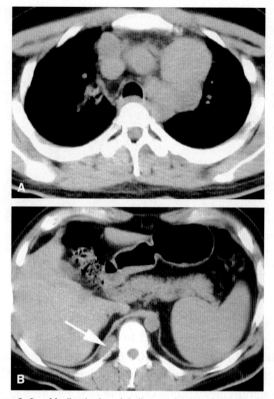

Figure 6–6. Mediastinal nodal disease in a patient with disseminated testicular seminoma. *A,* There was bulky anterior mediastinal lymphadenopathy, which appeared of homogeneous soft-tissue density on computed tomography (CT) scan. *B,* There was contiguous spread of disease from the abdomen, with an enlarged right retrocrural node (*arrow*) measuring more than 6 mm.

short-axis diameter in the upper retroperitoneum should be considered enlarged whereas a 10 mm short-axis diameter is generally regarded as the upper limit of normal in the lower retroperitoneum. Nevertheless, it should be recognized that by defining such thresholds, a compromise is made between higher sensitivity and lower specificity and vice versa. This issue has been considered in two histologically correlated studies.[17,18] Lien and colleagues reviewed the abdominal CT scans of 90 patients who subsequently underwent retroperitoneal lymphadenectomy as a staging procedure. In this study, which included all patients with abnormal CT scans, as well as patients with nodes of up to 2 cm in diameter, lymph node metastases were identified in 38 of the 90 patients. Applying various upper limits for the threshold of normal, these authors demonstrated the variation in sensitivities and specificities that result from the chosen criteria. Thus, if the upper limit of normal were taken as 15

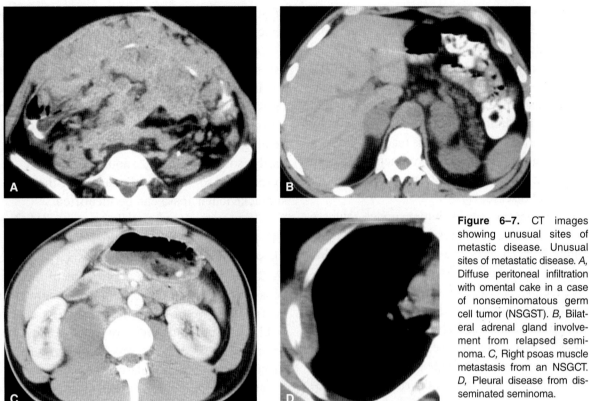

Figure 6–7. CT images showing unusual sites of metastic disease. Unusual sites of metastatic disease. *A,* Diffuse peritoneal infiltration with omental cake in a case of nonseminomatous germ cell tumor (NSGST). *B,* Bilateral adrenal gland involvement from relapsed seminoma. *C,* Right psoas muscle metastasis from an NSGCT. *D,* Pleural disease from disseminated seminoma.

mm in diameter, the sensitivity would be only 37% but the specificity would be 98% whereas an upper limit of 10 mm would provide a sensitivity of 47% and a lower specificity of 87%. Other investigators have shown similar results.[18,19] The adoption of a threshold of 10 or 15 mm accepts false-negative rates of between 30 and 45%. Hilton and colleagues[20] have shown that if an even lower threshold of 4 mm is used, the false-negative rate may be reduced from 63% (with a 10 mm threshold) to 7%. They concluded that nodes > 4 mm in diameter (especially those located anterior to the midline of the aorta) should be regarded as suspicious.

Although different institutions adopt different thresholds of the upper limit of normal, the most important factor is to be consistent within a managed group of patients. At the Royal Marsden Hospital, a lymph node that is > 10 mm in diameter (maximum short-axis diameter [MSAD]) is regarded as definitely enlarged whereas a node that is between 8 and 10 mm in MSAD is considered to be only suspicious. The subsequent decision pathway for such a patient then depends upon other clinical factors. For example, if the patient is at high risk, with histologic evi-

dence of vascular and lymphatic invasion, then chemotherapy will be given routinely and subsequent follow-up will give a good indication as to whether the suspicious node was involved or not, depending upon its behavior on follow-up. However, in patients who are at low risk, further procedures (such as fine-needle aspiration) may be performed.

It is important to recognize that enlarged nodes may be due to benign hyperplasia and inflammatory reaction as well as to metastatic disease. Therefore, a single enlarged node without other clinical evidence of metastatic spread should be viewed cautiously before a definitive diagnosis is made. All the limitations of CT outlined above are well established and are unlikely to be overcome even in this new era of multichannel CT.

Lymph node masses may be discretely enlarged with well-defined contours, and several enlarged nodes may be found in a cluster around the great vessels. In patients with advanced disease, tumor breaks through the lymph node capsule into the adjacent tissues, and many nodes may then coalesce (Figure 6–8). Because of the retroperitoneal pathway of metastatic spread, nodal masses are frequently closely related or involve adjacent vessels. Thus, the inferior vena cava is frequently displaced either posteriorly or anteriorly by an enlarging mass, and the renal veins may be compressed and attenuated. MRI is superior to CT in demonstrating the vascular anatomy, on account of its multiplanar capability and high-contrast resolution (Figure 6–9). Tumor may invade the inferior vena cava; this is readily shown on contrast-enhanced CT or MRI. Hydronephrosis is an important and common complication of advanced retroperitoneal disease.

In the retrocrural space, lymph nodes that are > 6 mm in diameter are presumed to be enlarged (see Figure 6–6, B). It is rare to see retrocrural disease without evidence of disease in the retroperitoneum caudally. As in other sites, retrocrural nodal disease may be either of soft-tissue density or cystic.

At the time of staging, pelvic CT should be performed to exclude nodal disease, but pelvic CT is not recommended in follow-up if the staging scan is normal and the patient has none of the risk factors associated with pelvic relapse.[21] Pelvic CT should be performed down to the level of the pubic symphysis.

In patients who relapse following previous courses of chemotherapy, or in patients who have undergone radical lymphadenectomy, lymph node involvement may be seen at unusual sites. It is important to carefully assess the peritoneum and mesenteric regions[22]

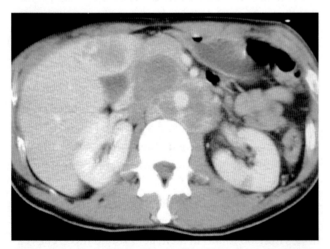

Figure 6–8. Coalescent nodal disease. Computed tomographic imaging in a man with disseminated nonseminomatous germ cell tumor showed a coalescent nodal mass surrounding the abdominal aorta. The mass was displacing the inferior vena cava to the right, with a widening of the aortocaval distance. There was also a low-attenuation metastasis in the left lobe of the liver. A small incidental cyst was noted within the left kidney.

of such patients to look for psoas nodes[18] and to review the pelvis (Figure 6–10).

Lymph node involvement within the mediastinum is readily detected by using contrast-enhanced CT. The characteristics of nodal metastases in the mediastinum are similar to those in the retroperitoneum and may be of soft-tissue density or heterogeneous masses that are partly cystic and partly solid. Scanning should commence in the lower neck so that nodal masses in the neck and supraclavicular fossa can be identified.

There are many pitfalls in the diagnosis of retroperitoneal and mediastinal lymphadenopathy. These include vascular anomalies such as a retro- or circum-aortic renal vein, duplication of the inferior vena cava, left ascending lumbar communicating veins, and a left-sided inferior vena cava (Figure 6–11).[23,24] Such anomalies are usually easily seen on contrast-enhanced CT scans but occasionally can cause confusion, particularly if an intravenous contrast medium has not been used. It is important to note these anomalies in all patients at the time of staging as such information is important for planning therapy, whether it be surgery or radiotherapy. Other errors relate to the misinterpretation of normal structures (such as small-bowel loops or diaphragmatic crura) and to the misinterpretation of postsurgical changes after staging lymphadenectomy (Figure 6–12).[25]

All of these patterns of disease are shown well on CT, and generally there is no need to undertake other investigations such as MRI or ultrasonography at the time of staging. However, if MRI is being performed to assess the liver or another questionable site of spread, then retroperitoneal nodal metastases can be identified by using MRI in a manner similar to that of CT. On MRI, enlarged lymph nodes have a relatively low signal intensity on T1-weighted sequences, intermediate to high signal intensity on T2-weighted sequences, and a high signal intensity on inversion recovery sequences (eg, short-tau inversion recovery [STIR]).

PET is not undertaken as a routine staging investigation in patients with testicular tumors. However, emerging evidence suggests that PET using FDG may identify disease not detected on staging CT. Early reports suggest that PET shows advantages with respect to sensitivity compared to CT but that specificity is similar.[26,27]

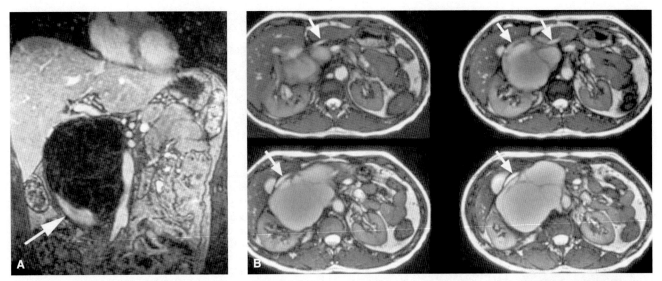

Figure 6–9. Displacement of the inferior vena cava by nodal disease as shown by magnetic resonance imaging (MRI) in a patient with a testicular nonseminomatous germ cell tumor. Coronal fast imaging with steady procession (FISP) (*A*) and axial T2-weighted images (*B*) showed a large multiloculated cystic mass within the right peritoneum, displacing the inferior vena cava (*arrows*) anteriorly and laterally. The distortion of the vascular anatomy within the retroperitoneum was best appreciated with multiplanar MRI.

Lung Metastases

Chest CT is generally regarded as an essential staging investigation for all germ cell tumors. It is the most sensitive imaging technique for detecting pulmonary nodules, and metastases down to the size of 3 to 4 mm can be diagnosed. However, the appearance of benign nodules is identical to that of small metastases, and in countries where there is a high incidence of granulomatous disease (such as the United States), false-positive results may be a problem.[28] If one or more suspicious lesions are detected,

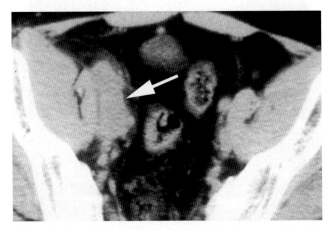

Figure 6–10. Pelvic nodal relapse. Computed tomography in this man with relapsed seminoma after successful treatment of retroperitoneal nodal disease showed enlarged nodes along the right external iliac vessels (*arrow*).

then rescanning after an interval to observe growth is required if there are no other clinical or imaging features to indicate stage IV disease.

Lung metastases in patients with NSGCTs are more common than in patients with seminoma. CT can detect lung metastases down to the size of 3 to 4 mm, and there is substantial evidence to show that CT is more sensitive than chest radiography in the detection of metastatic disease in these patients.[6,29] However, the use of chest radiography for cases of both seminoma and NSGCT continues and has been the subject of considerable debate. Some authors advocate the use of chest radiography alone in the staging of seminoma and in NSGCT patients with normal abdominal CT scans[28,30] whereas others continue to use CT for staging all patients.

In NSGCT patients, pulmonary metastases usually appear as well-defined spherical lesions (Figure 6–13) that vary in size from tiny nodules less than a centimeter in diameter to large lobulated masses, indistinguishable from many other types of pulmonary metastases. In patients with seminoma, lung metastases tend to be large and grow more slowly than those in patients with NSGCTs. Pleural tumors may be identified on a CT more readily than by chest radiography and are seen as a discrete mass or as a plaquelike sheet of tissue within the pleural space (see Figure 6–7, *D*).[15] Pleural effusions are

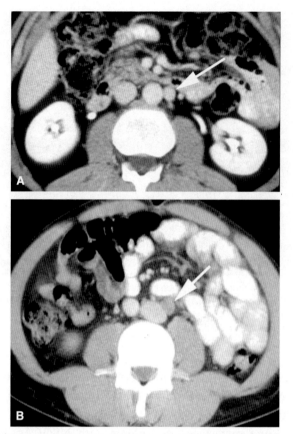

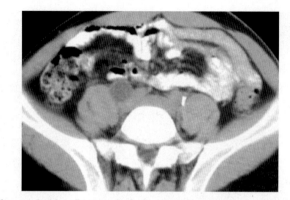

Figure 6–12. Postsurgical change. This patient underwent retroperitoneal nodal dissection following chemotherapy for stage II nonseminomatous germ cell tumor. Early postsurgical computed tomography showed a 2 cm well-defined cystic lesion within the right retroperitoneum (*arrow*), in keeping with a lymphocele. Note the surgical clip adjacent to the left psoas muscle.

Figure 6–11. Vascular anomalies. *A,* A duplicated inferior vena cava (*arrow*) may be mistaken for a left para-aortic node by computed tomography if imaging is performed without intravenous contrast enhancement. *B,* In this example of a patient with a left-sided inferior vena cava, a low-density lymph node was seen adjacent to the cava (*arrow*). Vascular anomalies should be brought to the attention of the urologic surgeon, particularly if surgery is contemplated.

embryonal carcinoma elements, or with vascular invasion and lymphatic invasion) may harbor occult brain metastases. Such metastases are usually hemorrhagic and therefore have characteristic appearances on both MRI and CT.[31] They have very high

common in patients with intrathoracic metastases but may not necessarily be malignant.

Other Sites of Metastasis

The liver is an unusual site of metastasis but is a more common site in NSGCT cases than in seminoma cases. In patients with NSGCTs, metastases can be mistaken for simple cysts because these metastases may be low-density (cystic) lesions (see Figure 6–13). If doubt exists regarding the presence or character of a lesion, then ultrasonography or MRI may provide useful additional information. Ultrasonography is also useful for guiding biopsies of focal lesions in the liver that are suspected of representing metastases.

Although MRI is the preferred technique for investigating brain metastases, CT is an excellent alternative. Patients who are at high risk (with

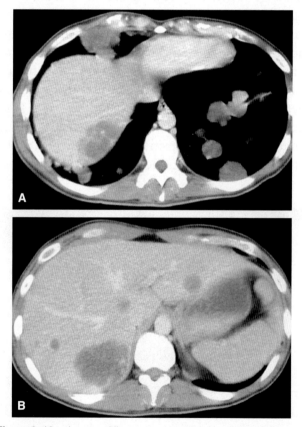

Figure 6–13. Lung and liver metastases in a 45-year-old man with nonseminomatous germ cell tumor. *A,* Computed tomography (CT) demonstrated multiple rounded metastases within the lung bases. *B,* CT also showed several low-density metastases within the liver.

signal intensity on T1-weighted unenhanced MRI (Figure 6–14) and frequently have a low-signal-intensity peripheral rim representing hemosiderin and other degradation products from the hemorrhage. On unenhanced CT, these metastases have a very high density due to hemorrhage. On contrast-enhanced imaging with CT and MRI, these metastases enhance, and, similarly to other brain metastases, the lesions are usually surrounded by edema on both unenhanced and enhanced CT and MRI.

Metastases to bone are relatively rare and are usually suspected on the basis of clinical features. Radionuclide bone scanning, plain-film radiography, CT, and MRI all have a place in diagnosis and will demonstrate the characteristic features of bone metastases. There are no imaging findings that distinguish testicular tumor bone metastases from other primary sites of disease. Bone deposits are usually destructive lesions, and CT or MRI may show an associated soft-tissue mass.

Although rare at the time of staging, metastases may develop in any site, and scans should be carefully scrutinized to cover all areas. It is also important to recognize incidental disease that may mimic metastases, such as an incidental renal carcinoma or

a nonfunctioning adrenal tumor.[32]

MONITORING TUMOR RESPONSE

While surgery and platinum-based chemotherapy remain the mainstay of treatment, efforts are now focused on refining chemotherapy regimens in order to limit unnecessary treatment and reduce toxicity without compromising the chance of cure. CT remains the workhorse for monitoring chemotherapeutic response and for follow-up of all patients with testicular tumors. Radiotherapy still has a role in the management of testicular tumors (particularly seminomas), and CT provides not only a method of assessing response to radiotherapy but also information for radiotherapy planning. The introduction of PET using FDG (FDG-PET) has been met with much excitement because this new functional imaging technique may prove to be particularly valuable in the assessment of disease response. All of these diagnostic and therapeutic advances open the way to a more tailored approach to patient management in which imaging will play an increasingly critical role.

The objective of CT during and following chemotherapy is to document response to therapy at all known sites of disease, to measure changes in tumor size where appropriate, and to delineate the presence and extent of residual masses (Figures 6–15 and 6–16). In patients who have NSGCTs and disease confined to the retroperitoneal nodes and who are treated with chemotherapy, the size of the residual mass is a key factor in determining the need for surgical intervention. In general, masses that are > 1 cm in diameter are resected because there is a risk of subsequent relapse. However, where residual masses are < 1 cm in diameter, evidence indicates that the vast majority of such lesions represent necrosis and fibrosis.[33,34] In a recent series reported by Steyerberg and colleagues,[35] the size of the mass before treatment did not appear to be related to post-treatment histology. However, the percentage regression of the mass during treatment does appear to be an important indicator of residual activity. Steyerberg and colleagues found that the combination of radiologic parameters (size of residual mass and tumor regression) and clinical parameters (histology of primary tumor, serum markers) provided the best prediction of residual-tumor status. In a study

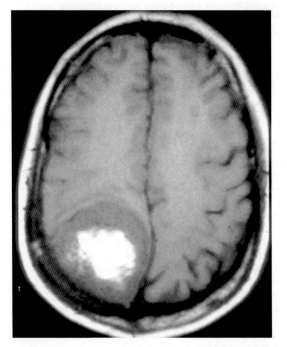

Figure 6–14. Hemorrhagic brain metastasis. Unenhanced axial T1-weighted magnetic resonance imaging through the brain revealed a high-signal lesion surrounded by a rim of relatively low-signal edema within the right parietal lobe, typical of a hemorrhagic metastasis.

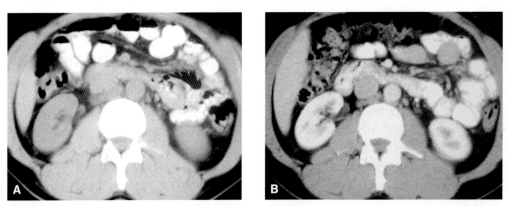

Figure 6–15. Partial response to treatment in a man with stage II seminoma of the right testis. *A,* Pretreatment computed tomography (CT) showed a 40 mm × 8 mm retrocaval node. *B,* After chemotherapy, repeat CT showed regression of the node, measuring 25 mm × 4 mm.

of 40 patients with NSGCTs, Dexeus and colleagues [36] found that those with initial masses that were < 2 cm in diameter had a low frequency of residual masses (14%), compared with much higher frequencies of 59% for masses of 2 to 5 cm and 75% for masses that were > 5 cm. Another approach is to undertake a limited scan of the site of nodal enlargement after 21 days of chemotherapy, in an attempt to predict good responders who may require less chemotherapy. [37]

In patients with NSGCTs, "cystic" change may be seen by CT during therapy (Figure 6–17), and although less frequently observed now than in the early days of CT, enlargement of such masses may also be seen in follow-up. [38] There is also evidence to suggest that tumor density as measured by CT is related to persistent active malignancy. [38] A simple low-density "cystic" lesion after therapy is likely to represent mature differentiated teratoma. [38,39] On CT, residual masses in the retroperitoneum vary from large cystic/solid lesions to poorly defined soft-tissue

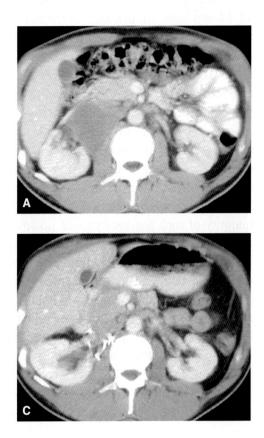

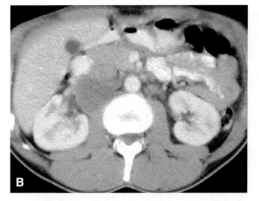

Figure 6–16. Monitoring of tumor response in a 37-year-old man with nonseminomatous germ cell tumor of the right testis. *A,* Staging computed tomography (CT) showed a large low-density paracaval nodal mass. *B,* Following radiotherapy and chemotherapy, CT demonstrated a partial response, but there was a 3 cm residual mass. *C,* The residual mass was removed at surgery. On the postsurgical CT scan, surgical clips are visible in the right retroperitoneum, but there was no evidence of residual or recurrent disease.

residuas closely related to the major vessels. Management is complex in many patients who have undergone multiple relapses and even previous excisions of residual disease, and the role of the radiologist in defining the precise extent of disease and its relationship to the great vessels becomes extremely important. In many cases, the retroperitoneal structures are blurred, bowel is tethered to the retroperitoneum, and surgical clips degrade the image.[40] Seminomatous residual masses in patients are usually free of active cancer, contain only fibrosis and necrosis, and may show calcifications on CT (Figure 6–18). Therefore, excision of these masses is not undertaken routinely.

Pulmonary metastases usually respond to treatment in the same manner as the patient's retroperitoneal disease. Reduction in size is frequently followed by complete regression in small metastases. However, scars at the site of previous metastases may be observed during follow-up, and in NSGCT cases, metastases may cavitate, leaving air-containing spaces surrounded by a thin rim of surrounding soft tissue (Figure 6–19).[41]

Bearing in mind that patients with testicular tumors have a high chance of cure and are usually young at the time of diagnosis, it is important to consider ways of reducing the radiation dose associated with CT. Thus, the timing of CT in relation to treatment and the extent of scanning to be performed needs to be considered carefully. Clearly, scanning before and after therapy is required, but it may be possible to limit the exposure by only scanning those areas which were involved at presentation rather than routinely scanning the whole thorax, abdomen, and pelvis.

FDG-PET may demonstrate changes in tumor function before changes in tumor size have occurred, and the technique may also have an important place in assessing posttreatment tumor viability, thereby reducing the need for surgery after chemotherapy.[42] Due to the complementary functional information available with PET, positive and negative predictive values in excess of 90% have been reported in the evaluation of residual masses.[8,42] However, it is generally not possible to differentiate posttreatment necrosis and scarring from mature teratoma unless a more complex kinetic

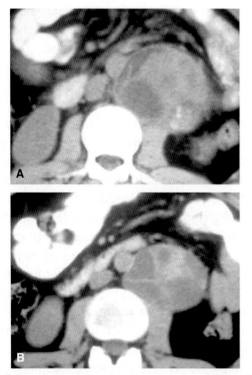

Figure 6–17. Cystic change in nonseminomatous germ cell tumor (NSGCT) following treatment in a 40-year-old man with NSGCT. *A,* Pretreatment computed tomography showed a left para-aortic nodal mass of mixed density. *B,* After chemoradiotherapy, there was a reduction in the size of the lesion. In addition, a greater degree of cystic change within the mass was observed.

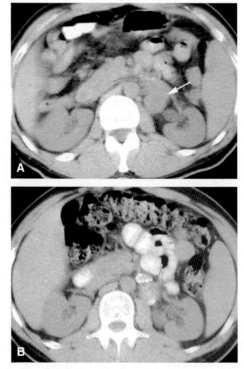

Figure 6–18. Calcified residual mass in a 35-year-old man with seminoma of the left testis. *A,* Unenhanced pretreatment computed tomography (CT) demonstrated left para-aortic lymph nodes (*arrow*). *B,* Following successful treatment, repeat unenhanced CT showed calcifications within the nodes. The appearance of these remained stable on subsequent imaging.

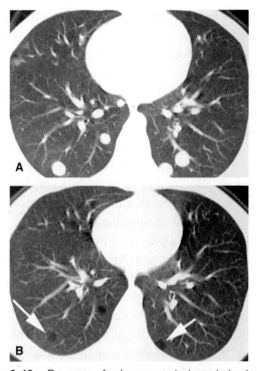

Figure 6–19. Response of pulmonary metastases to treatment in a 45-year-old man with nonseminomatous germ cell tumor. *A,* Staging computed tomography revealed multiple lung metastases measuring 1 to 2 cm. *B,* Following successful chemotherapy, there was complete resolution of the metastases, with small air-containing spaces remaining in the positions of previous disease (*arrows*).

analysis of FDG uptake is made.[43] Such analysis is probably not practical in a routine clinical setting. For greatest accuracy, it is recommended that FDG-PET be performed at least 2 weeks following the completion of therapy.[44] Early reports have suggested that FDG-PET is better at predicting treatment response to high-dose chemotherapy after two or three cycles than are radiologic or serum tumor marker monitoring.[45]

SURVEILLANCE

Surveillance for patients with stage I NSGCTs is now routine practice at many centers, and CT plays a critical role in this policy.[46,47] The number of CT studies undertaken during a 5-year surveillance schedule and the timing of such CT studies vary from center to center, but in general, CT is performed every three to six months for the first 2 or 3 years. Further follow-up with CT is carried out either annually or only if there is a rise in serum markers or there is other evidence that suggests relapse. Chest radiography is omitted from the surveillance program at many centers now because there is good evidence that results from x-ray films do not contribute to management decisions, provided CT is being carried out on a regular basis.[48]

Although CT for staging should include the chest, abdomen, and pelvis, follow-up scanning for patients on surveillance should not include pelvic CT unless there are special risk factors, such as bulky retroperitoneal adenopathy (> 2 cm in short axis), prior history of scrotal surgery, and invasion of tunica vaginalis by a tumor.[49] PET is likely to have an important role in assessing patients on surveillance as small nodal deposits or other subtle or equivocal findings on follow-up may be assessed with PET, and a definitive diagnosis of relapse can be made more quickly than by simply waiting for a further follow-up CT study. Rising markers may be observed without demonstrable CT findings, and in this group of patients, it is likely that PET will be a valuable adjunct. In this scenario, PET is very specific, having a positive predictive value in excess of 90% but a negative predictive value of only 50% (Figure 6–20).[8] This reflects the fact that even functional imaging techniques cannot detect microscopic volumes of disease. Nevertheless, PET remains more sensitive than anatomic techniques and is frequently the first modality to identify the site of previously marker-positive occult disease.[8]

IMAGING TREATED DISEASE

Even in patients with advanced disease at diagnosis, excellent response to treatment can be achieved today. As a result, imaging is now frequently performed in patients who have undergone multiple courses of chemotherapy and multiple relapses. In such patients, the imaging findings are more complex and difficult to interpret than at the time of staging. For example, such patients also frequently have undergone previous surgery; scarring in the lungs or in other tissues adds to the difficulties of identifying relapse. Furthermore, previous treatment with radiotherapy may not only cause radiation fibrosis in the treated tissue volume but may also influence the site of subsequent relapse. For example, in patients with stage I seminoma who have undergone radiotherapy to the para-aortic nodes (without pelvic node irradiation), the pelvis is a common site of relapse and therefore a group who should receive surveillance pelvic CT scans.[50]

Complications of chemotherapy, such as lung infection or bleomycin lung damage, may render the interpretation of follow-up CT scans extremely difficult, and the radiologist must be aware of all previous sites of disease and the patient's current clinical status before attempting to interpret the examination. Similarly, rebound thymic hyperplasia (Figure 6–21), an unusual complication of chemotherapy, may be misinterpreted as relapse. However, although the thymus is enlarged, its normal shape is maintained, and careful evaluation of the CT study should usually permit the distinction of these two entities.[51,52]

FDG-PET is also expected to play a central role in elucidating problems in previously treated patients, problems not only in the chest and abdomen but also in the more unusual sites of tumor relapse.

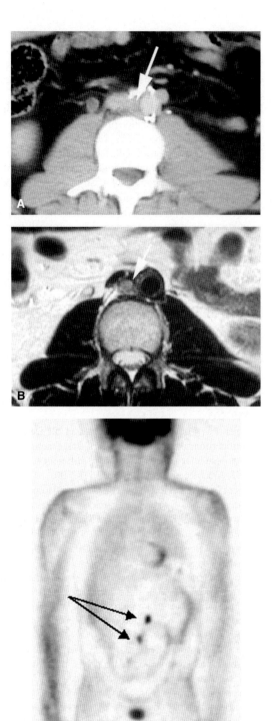

Figure 6–20. Follow-up imaging. This 37-year-old man had a history of nonseminomatous germ cell tumor and nodal relapse in the retroperitoneum, treated with chemoradiotherapy and surgical dissection. A rising level of serum beta–human chorionic gonadotropin was detected during follow-up. *A,* Computed tomography (CT) showed some residual soft tissue in the aortocaval space (*arrow*), just above the aortic bifurcation. *B,* The residual tissue was better visualized by T2-weighted magnetic resonance imaging, owing to the superior contrast resolution (*arrow*). *C,* Positron emission tomography using 18-fluoro-2-deoxyglucose revealed two areas of increased metabolic activity within the retroperitoneum (*arrows*). The inferior focus corresponded to the area of CT abnormality.

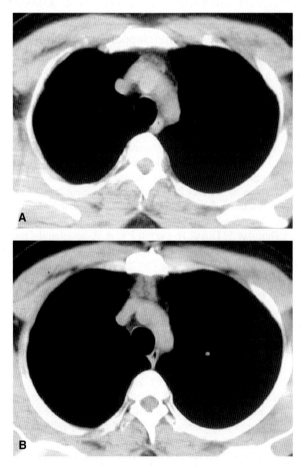

Figure 6–21. Rebound thymic hyperplasia. This 22-year-old man with testicular seminoma was treated with chemotherapy. *A,* computed tomography (CT) of the thorax prior to treatment showed involuting thymic tissue within the prevascular space. *B,* Three months after the completion of chemotherapy, CT revealed diffuse enlargement of the thymus. Note the normal configuration of the gland.

CONCLUSION

Over the last decade, major advances in the treatment of testicular tumors have led to improved cure rates and prolonged survival. This, together with major advances in imaging, has led to a greater understanding of how imaging should be used appropriately at staging and during follow-up. Questions regarding the risks associated with radiation therapy are being addressed as long-term follow-up reveals an increased risk of second primary cancers. The newer imaging techniques of both MRI and FDG-PET are likely to have an increasing role in the future. Currently, MRI cannot be used to image the lungs in the routine clinical setting, but the technique could replace CT for staging nodal disease. It is possible, therefore, that abdominal MRI could be used for follow-up in low-risk patients for whom chest CT is considered unnecessary. The important role of FDG-PET in the management of testicular tumors is rapidly becoming apparent, and confirmation of initial exciting results is awaited with optimism and enthusiasm.

REFERENCES

1. Arnold PM, Morgan CJ, Morantz RA, et al. Metastatic testicular cancer presenting as spinal cord compression: report of two cases. Surg Neurol 2000;54:27–33.
2. Johnson JO, Mattrey RF, Phillipson J. Differentiation of seminomatous from nonseminomatous testicular tumors with MR imaging. AJR Am J Roentgenol 1990;154:539–43.
3. Thurnher S, Hricak H, Carroll PR, et al. Imaging the testis: comparison between MR imaging and US. Radiology 1988;167:631–6.
4. Grantham JG, Charboneau JW, James EM, et al. Testicular neoplasms: 29 tumors studied by high-resolution US. Radiology 1985;157:775–80.
5. Senay BA, Stein BS. Testicular neoplasm diagnosed by ultrasound. J Surg Oncol 1986;32:110–2.
6. White PM, Adamson DJ, Howard GC, et al. Imaging of the thorax in the management of germ cell testicular tumours. Clin Radiol 1999;54:207–11.
7. Harvey ML, Geldart TR, Duell R, et al. Routine computerised tomographic scans of the thorax in surveillance of stage I testicular non-seminomatous germ-cell cancer—a necessary risk? Ann Oncol 2002;13:237–42.
8. Hain SF, O'Doherty MJ, Timothy AR, et al. Fluorodeoxyglucose positron emission tomography in the evaluation of germ cell tumours at relapse. Br J Cancer 2000;83:863–9.
9. Gambhir SS, Czernin J, Schwimmer J, et al. A tabulated summary of the FDG PET literature. J Nucl Med 2001;42:1S–93S.
10. Rouviere H. Anatomy of the human lymphatic system . Ann Arbor: Edwards Brothers;1938.
11. Williams MP, Cook JV, Duchesne GM. Psoas nodes—an overlooked site of metastasis from testicular tumours. Clin Radiol 1989;40:607–9.
12. Dixon AK, Ellis M, Sikora K. Computed tomography of testicular tumours: distribution of abdominal lymphadenopathy. Clin Radiol 1986;37:519–23.
13. Mason MD, Featherstone T, Olliff J, et al. Inguinal and iliac lymph node involvement in germ cell tumours of the testis: implications for radiological investigation and for therapy. Clin Oncol (R Coll Radiol) 1991;3:147–50.
14. Wood A, Robson N, Tung K, et al. Patterns of supradiaphragmatic metastases in testicular germ cell tumours. Clin Radiol 1996;51:273–6.
15. Williams MP, Husband JE, Heron CW. Intrathoracic manifestations of metastatic testicular seminoma: a comparison of chest radiographic and CT findings. AJR Am J Roentgenol 1987;149:473–5.
16. Husband JE, Bellamy EA. Unusual thoracoabdominal sites of metastases in testicular tumors. AJR Am J Roentgenol 1985;145:1165–71.
17. Lien HH, Stenwig AE, Ous S, et al. Influence of different criteria for abnormal lymph node size on reliability of computed tomography in patients with non-seminomatous testicular tumor. Acta Radiol Diagn (Stockh) 1986;27:199–203.
18. Stomper PC, Fung CY, Socinski MA, et al. Detection of retroperitoneal metastases in early-stage nonseminomatous testicular cancer: analysis of different CT criteria. AJR Am J Roentgenol 1987;149:1187–90.
19. Forsberg L, Dale L, Hoiem L, et al. Computed tomography in early stages of testicular carcinoma. Size of normal retroperitoneal lymph nodes and lymph nodes in patients with metastases in stage II A. A SWENOTECA study: Swedish-Norwegian Testicular Cancer Project. Acta Radiol Diagn (Stockh) 1986;27:569–74.
20. Hilton S, Herr HW, Teitcher JB, et al. CT detection of retroperitoneal lymph node metastases in patients with clinical stage I testicular nonseminomatous germ cell cancer: assessment of size and distribution criteria. AJR Am J Roentgenol 1997;169:521–5.
21. White PM, Howard GC, Best JJ, et al. The role of computed tomographic examination of the pelvis in the management of testicular germ cell tumours. Clin Radiol 1997;52:124–9.
22. Barakos JA, Jeffrey RB Jr, McAninch JW, et al. Computerized tomography diagnosis of diffuse intraperitoneal metastases after retroperitoneal lymphadenectomy for testicular carcinoma. J Urol 1986;136:680–1.
23. Baumuller A, Billmann P. Retroperitoneal lymph node metastasis from testicular tumor hidden by vena cava transposition. Eur Urol 1985;11:206–8.
24. Moul JW, Maggio MI, Hardy MR, et al. Retroaortic left renal vein in testicular cancer patient: potential staging and treatment pitfall. J Urol 1992;147:454–6.
25. Cohen SI, Hochsztein P, Cambio J, et al. Duplicated inferior vena cava misinterpreted by computerized tomography as metastatic retroperitoneal testicular tumor. J Urol 1982;128:389–91.
26. Hain SF, O'Doherty MJ, Timothy AR, et al. Fluorodeoxyglu-

cose PET in the initial staging of germ cell tumours. Eur J Nucl Med 2000;27:590–4.

27. Cremerius U, Wildberger JE, Borchers H, et al. Does positron emission tomography using 18-fluoro-2-deoxyglucose improve clinical staging of testicular cancer? Results of a study in 50 patients. Urology 1999;54:900–4.

28. Moul JW. Proper staging techniques in testicular cancer patients. Tech Urol 1995;1:126–32.

29. Lien HH, Lindskold L, Fossa SD, et al. Computed tomography and conventional radiography in intrathoracic metastases from non-seminomatous testicular tumor. Acta Radiol 1988;29:547–9.

30. Fernandez EB, Colon E, McLeod DG, et al. Efficacy of radiographic chest imaging in patients with testicular cancer. Urology 1994;44:243–8; discussion 8–9.

31. Guest PJ, Guy R, Wilkins PR, et al. Haemorrhagic cerebral metastases from malignant testicular teratoma. Clin Radiol 1992;45:190–4.

32. Olliff JF, Eeles R, Williams MP. Mimics of metastases from testicular tumours. Clin Radiol 1990;41:395–9.

33. Hendry WF, A'Hern RP, Hetherington JW, et al. Para-aortic lymphadenectomy after chemotherapy for metastatic non-seminomatous germ cell tumours: prognostic value and therapeutic benefit. Br J Urol 1993;71:208–13.

34. Stomper PC, Jochelson MS, Garnick MB, et al. Residual abdominal masses after chemotherapy for nonseminomatous testicular cancer: correlation of CT and histology. AJR Am J Roentgenol 1985;145:743–6.

35. Steyerberg EW, Keizer HJ, Sleijfer DT, et al. Retroperitoneal metastases in testicular cancer: role of CT measurements of residual masses in decision making for resection after chemotherapy. Radiology 2000;215:437–44.

36. Dexeus FH, Shirkhoda A, Logothetis CJ, et al. Clinical and radiological correlation of retroperitoneal metastasis from nonseminomatous testicular cancer treated with chemotherapy. Eur J Cancer Clin Oncol 1989;25:35–43.

37. Tsetis D, Sharma A, Easty M, et al. Potential of limited day 21 post-chemotherapy CT scan in predicting need for post-chemotherapy surgery in nonseminomatous testicular germ cell cancer. Urol Int 1998;61:22–6.

38. Husband JE, Hawkes DJ, Peckham MJ. CT estimations of mean attenuation values and volume in testicular tumors: a comparison with surgical and histologic findings. Radiology 1982;144:553–8.

39. MacVicar D, Horwich A, Fisher C, et al. MRI of post chemotherapy residual masses in metastatic testicular teratoma. Clin Radiol 1992;46 Suppl:430.

40. von Krogh J, Lien HH, Ous S, et al. Alterations in the CT image following retroperitoneal lymphadenectomy in early stage non-seminomatous testicular tumor. Acta Radiol Diagn (Stockh) 1985;26:187–91.

41. Charig MJ, Williams MP. Pulmonary lacunae: sequelae of metastases following chemotherapy. Clin Radiol 1990;42: 93–6.

42. De Santis M, Bokemeyer C, Becherer A, et al. Predictive impact of 2-18fluoro-2-deoxy-D-glucose positron emission tomography for residual postchemotherapy masses in patients with bulky seminoma. J Clin Oncol 2001;19: 3740–4.

43. Sugawara Y, Zasadny KR, Grossman HB, et al. Germ cell tumor: differentiation of viable tumor, mature teratoma, and necrotic tissue with FDG PET and kinetic modeling. Radiology 1999;211:249–56.

44. Cremerius U, Effert PJ, Adam G, et al. FDG PET for detection and therapy control of metastatic germ cell tumor. J Nucl Med 1998;39:815–22.

45. Bokemeyer C, Kollmannsberger C, Oechsle K, et al. Early prediction of treatment response to high-dose salvage chemotherapy in patients with relapsed germ cell cancer using [(18)F]FDG PET. Br J Cancer 2002;86:506–11.

46. Francis R, Bower M, Brunstrom G, et al. Surveillance for stage I testicular germ cell tumours: results and cost benefit analysis of management options. Eur J Cancer 2000;36:1925–32.

47. Segal R, Lukka H, Klotz LH, et al. Surveillance programs for early stage non-seminomatous testicular cancer: a practice guideline. Can J Urol 2001;8:1184–92.

48. Gels ME, Hoekstra HJ, Sleijfer DT, et al. Detection of recurrence in patients with clinical stage I nonseminomatous testicular germ cell tumors and consequences for further follow-up: a single-center 10-year experience. J Clin Oncol 1995;13:1188–94.

49. Wright AR, White PM. Testicular cancer—who needs surveillance pelvic CT? Clin Radiol 1999;54:78.

50. Taylor MB, Carrington BM, Livsey JE, et al. The effect of radiotherapy treatment changes on sites of relapse in stage I testicular seminoma. Clin Radiol 2001;56:116–9.

51. Kissin CM, Husband JE, Nicholas D, et al. Benign thymic enlargement in adults after chemotherapy: CT demonstration. Radiology 1987;163:67–70.

52. Tait DM, Goldstraw P, Husband JE. Thymic rebound in an adult following chemotherapy for testicular cancer. Eur J Surg Oncol 1986;12:385–7.

7

Tumor Markers in Germ Cell Tumors of the Testis

AVRUM I. JACOBSON, MD
PAUL H. LANGE, MD, FACS

Tumor markers are biologic attributes of malignant cells, that help to distinguish those malignant cells from normal cells. These can be divided into three categories: (1) protein markers, (2) chromosomal markers, and (3) other molecular markers, including abnormal expression of oncogenes and tumor suppressor genes. Markers may be uniquely identified with certain neoplasms, or they may be normal constituents that, in the face of a tumor, are expressed in abnormal locations and/or quantities or display abnormal functions. They may be located intracellularly, on the cell surface, or they may be excreted, at times being detectable in bodily fluids such as urine or serum. In germ cell tumors (GCTs), serum protein markers such as α-fetoprotein (AFP), human chorionic gonadotropin (hCG), and lactate dehydrogenase (LDH) dominate and will therefore be the focus of this chapter.

GCTs were among the first tumors for which serum markers were applied. The first step was taken in 1930, when hCG was detected in the urine of men with choriocarcinoma.[1] Since that time, they have acquired increasing importance in the management of GCTs. In fact, today it is impossible to discuss almost any aspect of GCTs without a thorough understanding of the role of these serum markers. They provide critical information for diagnosis, prognosis, staging, monitoring response to therapy, and diagnosing recurrence; each of these functions will be addressed in this chapter.

SERUM MARKERS

α-Fetoprotein

The biochemistry and biology of AFP has been well described. AFP is a 70 kD single-chained glycoprotein that was first found in normal human fetal serum in 1954.[2] It is a dominant serum protein of the early embryo, accounting for almost one-third of total serum protein. Concentrations peak at 12 to 14 weeks of gestation and decline after week 16. Although detectable at birth, serum levels fall by 1 year of age to the minimal level (< 10 ng/dL) usually seen in adults. AFP belongs to a superfamily of proteins that includes albumin and vitamin D–binding protein and is produced in the yolk sac, liver, and intestines of the fetus (Figure 7–1). It functions as a carrier protein and has been shown to bind fatty acids, estrogen, thyroid hormone, and retinoic acid.

Although AFP functions as a tumor marker, it is important to recognize other potential sources of serum elevation. AFP was first shown to be elevated in hepatocellular carcinomas.[3] Other malignancies that have been associated with elevated AFP levels include pancreatic, gastric, and pulmonary malignancies.[4] However, elevated serum levels of AFP do not necessarily denote malignancy. Certain benign processes, including benign liver disease, pregnancy, ataxia telangiectasia, and tyrosinemia, have

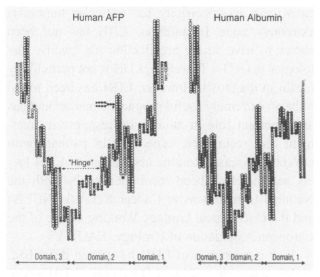

Figure 7–1. The structure of AFP is similar to that of Albumin. (Adapted from: Mizejewski GJ. AFP structure and function. Relevance to isoforms, epitopes, and conformational variants. Experimental Biology and Medicine 2001;226:377–408)

also been shown to be potential sources of elevated AFP.[4,5] However, in the clinical context of GCTs, these other disease sources for AFP almost never present a problem.

The detection of AFP in cases of GCTs was first demonstrated in 1974.[6] Cells of yolk sac origin are responsible for its production, implying reexpression of repressed genes or malignant transformation of a pluripotential cell. These elements are present in embryonal carcinoma, teratocarcinoma, and yolk sac tumors; they are, however, never present in pure seminoma or choriocarcinoma (Figure 7–2).[7] This has important ramifications, especially in cases of pure seminoma: even when these elements cannot be histologically demonstrated in such cases, they must be assumed to be present in the face of elevated AFP levels, and the tumor must be treated as a nonseminomatous GCT.[8]

Human Chorionic Gonadotropin

Human chorionic gonadotropin is a 38 kD hormone secreted by placental syncytiotrophoblasts, whose function is to maintain the corpus luteum. It consists of two subunits, an α subunit and a β subunit. The α subunit is closely related to the α subunit of anterior pituitary hormones such as

luteinizing hormone (LH), follicle-stimulating hormone (FSH), and thyroid-stimulating hormone (TSH). The β subunit is biologically active and structurally and antigenically distinct, allowing for the production of specific antibodies used in immunoassays.[9] However, at times, these antibodies may cross-react with the β subunit of LH, which is 70% homologous to that of hCG. In addition, hCG, at high levels, may clinically mimic these pituitary hormones. Hyperthyroidism has been reported,[10] and the 5% of GCT patients who develop gynecomastia are believed to do so secondary to a testosterone/estrogen imbalance caused by the effect of hCG on the Leydig's cells.

Tumors, in addition to producing intact hCG subunits, may produce so-called "nicked" free β subunits. These nicked molecules are biologically inactive, lack certain intra-amino acid bonds, and are therefore unstable and can be quickly degraded. The nicked isoforms and degradation products are not recognized by certain immunoassay antibodies and may be a source of false-negative study results or underestimation of the hCG level (Figure 7–3).[11]

Only minute amounts of hCG (< 5 IU/L) are detectable in healthy adults. Levels of hCG are elevated in pregnancy and in gestational disorders. As well, elevated serum concentrations have been reported in cases of hepatic, pancreatic, gastric, pulmonary, breast, renal, and bladder tumors and in cases of multiple myeloma.[4] However, concentrations > 10,000 IU/L are seen only in pregnancy and

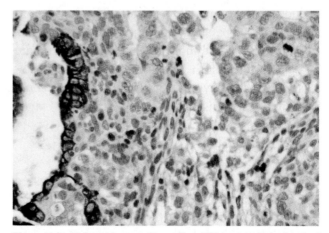

Figure 7–2. Yolk-sac tumor with positive AFP immunohistochemical staining. (Note Schiller-Duval body to the left of the image.)

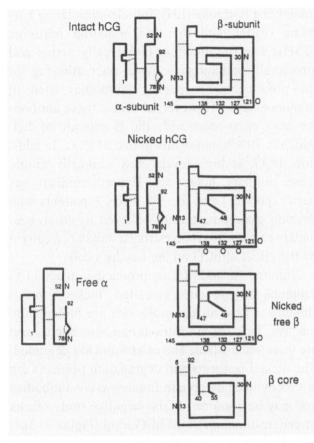

Figure 7–3. Structure of hCG and its breakdown products. (Adapted from Bower M, Rustin GJS. Serum tumor markers and their role in monitoring germ cell cancers of the testis. In: Comprehensive textbook of genitourinary oncology, ed 2. Philadelphia, Lippincott, Williams & Williams 1999: p. 927–8.)

eases, and its specificity for testicular tumors is extremely poor. In addition, LDH has not been shown to have strong predilection for specific histologies in GCTs. Therefore, LDH is not particularly useful in diagnosis. However, LDH has been found to be an extremely useful prognostic marker and has an important role in monitoring response to treatment and recurrence, especially in patients with advanced disease. Routine assessment of LDH levels has therefore been recommended by both the National Comprehensive Cancer Network (NCCN) and the Oncological Urology Working Group of the European Association of Urology (EAU).[14,15]

Five isoenzymes of LDH have been described; each is a tetramer of two LD subunits. LDH isoenzyme 1 (LDH-1) consists of four LD-β subunits. In testicular cancer, LDH-1 is the most commonly elevated isoenzyme[16] and has been shown to pre-

in patients with GCTs, gestational trophoblastic disease, and (rarely) trophoblastic differentiation of lung or gastric primaries.[12] Of patients with GCTs, 40 to 60% will have elevated hCG levels; this includes essentially all patients with choriocarcinoma, 80% of patients with embryonal carcinoma, and 10 to 25% of those with seminoma (Figure 7–4).[13] Elevated hCG levels imply syncytiotrophoblastic elements, even when these elements cannot be demonstrated histologically.

Lactate Dehydrogenase

LDH is a 134 kD cellular protein highly expressed in skeletal, cardiac, and smooth muscle as well as in liver, kidney, and brain. It functions in both aerobic and anaerobic metabolism, converting lactate to pyruvate in the former and pyruvate to lactate in the latter. LDH is elevated in a wide spectrum of dis-

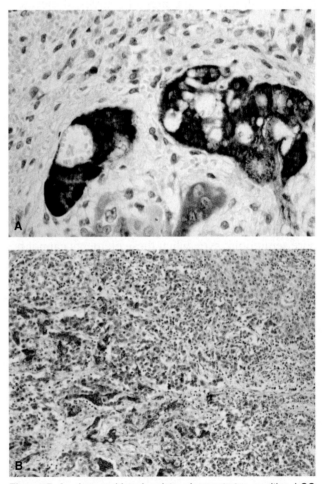

Figure 7–4. Immunohistochemistry demonstrates positive hCG staining of syncytiotrophoblastic elements in choriocarcinoma (*A*) and in seminoma (*B*).

dict response to therapy, relapse-free survival, and overall survival.[16–19]

Placental Alkaline Phosphatase

Placental alkaline phosphatase (PLAP) is the fetal isoenzyme of the ubiquitous adult alkaline phosphatase. It is normally expressed in utero and in children less than 1 year of age and functions as a protein phosphotyrosine phosphatase, catalyzing the abstraction of inorganic phosphate from phosphate esters. Although widely accepted as a reliable histologic marker for seminoma, its merit as a serum tumor marker is uncertain (Figure 7–5). In seminoma, serum PLAP levels are elevated in 50 to 72% of patients, with higher stages more frequently presenting with elevated levels.[20–22] In one multicenter prospective trial, the incidence of elevated PLAP in seminoma was greater than that of hCG or LDH (56% vs 35% and 34%, respectively). In addition, PLAP was found to have the highest sensitivity for detecting metastasis.[23] Specificity, however, is poor. Elevated levels can be seen in smokers and in persons with other malignancies, including, lung, ovary, breast, and gastrointestinal malignancies[24,25]; even in nonsmokers, the positive predictive value has been shown to be less than 50%.[25] Overall, PLAP has not proven to be a clinically beneficial serum marker for testicular neoplasms, and most centers have abandoned its routine use for that purpose.

Other Serum Markers

A variety of potential GCT serum markers have been explored. Of these, perhaps the best investigated is neuron-specific enolase (NSE). NSE is the neuroendocrine isoenzyme of the glycolytic enzyme enolase. In cases of carcinoid tumor, medullary thyroid carcinoma, neuroblastoma, and small cell carcinoma of the lung, NSE has been found to be a useful tumor marker. In GCTs, and especially seminoma, NSE has shown some promise. In one study, NSE was elevated in 6 of 21 patients with stage I seminoma and in 11 of 16 patients with metastatic disease; in all cases, levels fell with treatment, and no false positives were noted. In addition, marker positivity was noted in 10 patients in whom the more conventional markers were negative.[26]

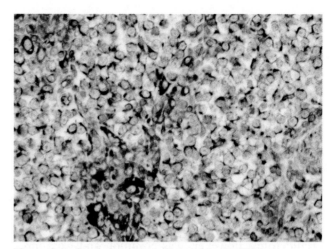

Figure 7–5. Seminoma with positive staining for PLAP.

However, in a larger study which investigated the use of NSE for 100 GCT patients, including 58 patients with seminoma, NSE was not found to be a valuable tumor marker. Less than 20% of patients were NSE positive, and both false-positive and false-negative values were identified.[27] In general, there is insufficient evidence to merit a role for NSE in the management of testicular GCTs, and even investigational interest appears to have waned.

Other potential serum markers that have been proposed include carcinoembryonic antigen (CEA), pregnancy-specific B1-glycoprotein (SP-1), and terato-related antigen (TRA)-1-60. At present, none have been proven to be clinically beneficial. CEA is a fetal gastrointestinal epithelial-membrane glycoprotein that is elevated in numerous malignant and benign conditions and is widely recognized as an important marker in gastrointestinal malignancies. Applying CEA measurement to GCTs, however, has been disappointing; levels are rarely elevated,[28,29] and even when they are elevated, there is no correlation with disease activity.[30,31] As a tumor marker for GCTs, SP-1 has also been disappointing. Although both seminomas and nonseminomatous germ cell tumors (NSGCTs) may at times secrete SP-1, marker positivity rates are significantly lower than for conventional markers. Also, elevated levels are seen in the same patients who have elevated hCG levels.[32–34] The addition of SP-1 to the arsenal of markers, therefore, provides no important additional information.

TRA-1-60 is the most recent addition to the GCT marker "scene." Characterized by Badcock and colleagues, TRA-1-60 is a keratan sulphate proteoglycan expressed on the surface of embryonal carcinoma progenitor cells.[35] Serum levels are elevated in approximately 80% of disseminated GCTs and fall significantly with chemotherapy. However, failure to return to normal levels was seen in 4 (17%) of 23 patients with NSGCT and in 3 (30%) of 10 patients with seminoma. These persistent elevated levels did not correlate with persistent disease. In stage I disease, 57% of patients with NSGCT and 13% of patients with SGCT presented with elevated serum TRA-1-60. Failure of levels to normalize after orchiectomy, however, was common and was unrelated to disease recurrence.[36] At present, TRA-1-60 cannot be recommended as a useful GCT marker.

CYTOGENETIC MARKERS

Some progress has been made in the search for genetic markers in GCTs. In 1983, Atkin and Baker located the first specific chromosomal abnormality associated with GCTs.[37] They noted duplication of the short arm of chromosome 12, designated i(12p), in four patients with testicular neoplasms. Larger series later confirmed extra copies of i(12p) in 83% of male GCTs; moreover, its presence was noted in all histologic types, including 89% of SGCTs and 81% of NSGCTs, and in all pathologic stages.[38] The occurrence of this cytogenic marker in other tumors is unusual, making it an ideal candidate for a useful histologic tumor marker.[13] Indeed, in one study, i(12p) was used to make the definitive diagnosis in 28% of patients with poorly differentiated carcinomas of unknown origin.[39] Also, there is some evidence that the presence of more than three copies of i(12p) predicts a poor response to chemotherapy.[40] On a more experimental front, a recent study by Summersgill and colleagues found a gain of i(12p) material in invasive tumors but not in testicular carcinoma in situ (CIS)[41]; this suggested a role in progression to invasion. Others, however, have found rare cases of CIS exhibiting i(12p); this has been interpreted as evidence of a key and early role for i(12p) in tumorigenesis.[42] One possible explanation for this defect is that its mechanism of action is exerted through the proto-oncogenes cyclin D and parathyroid hormone–like hormone (PTHLH), both of which are localized on 12p. These oncogenes, however, have yet to be shown to have a significant impact in GCTs. Obviously, the exact clinical value of i(12p) is still evolving.

Parenthetically, other chromosome alterations, involving loci on chromosomes 1 to 13, 17, 18, 22, and X, have been implicated in GCT pathogenesis and prognosis.[38–48] This important work, however, is still in its infancy, and detailed discussion of each of these loci is beyond the scope of this chapter.

ONCOGENES AND TUMOR SUPPRESSOR GENES

Like the study of cytogenetic markers, the study of molecular markers is in its infancy. At present, despite extensive study of numerous proto-oncogenes, few have been implicated in testicular germ cell tumorigenesis. Two potentially responsible genes are *hst*-1 and *c-kit*. The *hst*-1 gene is located on the long arm of chromosome 11 and encodes fibroblast growth factor. Expression has been shown in 63% of NSGCT tissue samples but in only 4% of seminomas. In contrast, *c-kit*, which encodes a tyrosine kinase growth factor receptor, is expressed predominantly in seminoma tissue (*c-kit* expressed in 80% seminoma vs 7% NSGCT).[49] The interaction of *c-kit* with its natural ligand, stem cell factor (SCF), has been implicated in enhanced tumor growth. It has been suggested that the binding of SCF to cells expressing *c-kit* increases cell survival, and alteration of SCF expression has been seen in GCTs.[50] This is of particular interest as the SCF gene is located at region 12q22, an area known to have loss of heterozygosity in over 40% of GCTs.[48]

The role of tumor suppressor genes in testicular cancer has not been widely studied and is a potential fertile area of future investigation. Despite the limited information available, the retinoblastoma gene (*RB*) and *p53* have shown potential as markers for GCTs. Strohmeyer and colleagues found decreased *RB* ribonucleic acid in all GCTs and found no RB protein product in seminomas, embryonal carcinomas, and choriocarcinomas. *RB* gene mutations, however, could not be identified, suggesting a missed subtle gene micromutation or a mechanism at the level of transcription.[51] Sequencing of the *p53* gene in GCTs rarely reveals mutations. In a recent review, in only

6.7% of 281 tumors sequenced was a mutation found.[52–54] Again, however, the gene product has been shown to be abnormal. Wild-type p53 protein product has a very short half-life and is almost undetectable by immunohistochemistry. Mutated p53 protein, in contrast, is more stable and is therefore detectable. The p53 product has been detected in 77% of GCTs, again suggesting a transcriptional or posttranscriptional mechanism.[54] *P53* has been shown to be involved in triggering apoptosis induced by DNA-damaging agents.[55] The data supporting the role of *p53* as a clinical chemosensitizing agent in metastatic GCT are conflicting. Baltaci and colleagues showed that *p53* levels were significantly related to complete response, partial response, and treatment failure. Kersemaekers and colleagues, however, failed to show a correlation between *p53* levels and treatment response.[56] Both studies, unfortunately, were limited by their small population: 24 and 35 patients, respectively. *P53* has also been investigated in clinical stage I disease. In 149 patients, *p53* levels did not appear to predict pathologic stage II disease.[57]

DIAGNOSIS

Although testicular cancer is the most common malignancy in men between the ages of 15 and 34 years, the incidence is still quite low, being estimated at 5 in 100,000 (National Cancer Institute's cancer results, 1995–1999). Screening with serum markers would not be practical, given the poor specificity of the existing markers, as false-positive values would far outnumber true positives for screening. Nonetheless, tumor markers retain an important role in diagnosis. Nowhere is this more evident than in extragonadal GCTs, which can often present as poorly differentiated cancer of unknown origin. In the setting where normal histologic criteria are absent, positive immunohistochemical staining for AFP or hCG (or even elevated serum levels) can confirm the diagnosis and allow appropriate therapy. Finally, i(12p), which is expressed in more than 80% of GCTs and is rarely expressed in other malignancies, may be an additional aid.

In testicular primaries, markers sometimes have an important diagnostic role as well. Patients with NSGCTs present with elevated AFP or hCG in 85%

of cases (AFP alone in 40% of cases, hCG alone in 50 to 60%).[58] Seminoma patients, on the other hand, never present with elevated AFP, but 10 to 25% present with detectable hCG, which implies syncytiotrophoblastic elements, even if not visible by routine microscopy. In the common presentation of a painless testicular mass, elevated markers are practically pathognomonic of GCT and can predict histology to a degree. AFP suggests the presence of embryonal or yolk sac elements, and hCG, especially at high levels, suggests elements of choriocarcinoma. Elevated AFP levels in the face of a histologic diagnosis of seminoma mean that NSGCT elements exist somewhere in the primary tumor and/or metastasis. In these cases, management should be conducted as though the diagnosis were NSGCT.

PROGNOSIS AND STAGING

For many years, it has been recognized that tumor markers correlate with underlying biologic aggressiveness, and indeed, all markers have been shown to be more commonly elevated in higher-stage disease. LDH, in particular, has been shown to be not only a reflection of tumor burden[59] but also an independent significant prognostic factor for growth rate and disease-specific survival.[60,61] Predicting how individual patients will respond to therapy is key, and as cure rates improve, the issue of reducing treatment toxicity in lower-risk patients becomes even more important. Many systems of risk stratification have been proposed, with varying success. However, because of the variability and lack of consensus, the International Germ Cell Cancer Collaborative Group (IGCCCG) was formed. This panel of leading experts from around the world studied 5,662 patients with metastatic testicular cancer, 5,202 with NSGCTs and 660 with SGCTs. Based on three factors—site of primary, level of marker elevation, and the presence of nonpulmonary visceral metastasis—patients were stratified into good-, intermediate-, or poor-risk groups (Table 7–1) (see also Chapter 8). In terms of patient numbers, marked elevation of markers was by far the most important reason for allocating patients into the different prognostic groups. Sixty percent of all patients were categorized as having a good prognosis, and 26% and 14% were respectively classed as intermediate- and poor-prognosis patients.

Table 7–1.   INTERNATIONAL GERM CELL CONSENSUS CLASSIFICATION PROGNOSIS CRITERIA FOR TESTICULAR CANCER

	Nonseminoma	Seminoma
Good Prognosis*†	Testicular/retroperitoneal primary and No nonpulmonary visceral metastasis and Good markers (all): AFP < 1,000 ng/mL, hCG < 5,000 IU/L (1,000 ng/mL), and LDH < 1.5 × upper limit of N	Any primary site and No nonpulmonary visceral metastasis and Normal AFP, any hCG, any LDH
Intermediate Prognosis‡§	Testicular/retroperitoneal primary and No nonpulmonary visceral metastasis and Intermediate markers (any 1): AFP > 1,000 ng/mL and < 10,000 ng/mL, or hCG > 5,000 IU/L and < 50,000 IU/L, or LDH > 1.5 × N and < 10 × N	Any primary site and Nonpulmonary visceral metastasis and Normal AFP, any hCG, any LDH
Poor Prognosis‖	Mediastinal primary or Pulmonary visceral metastases or Intermediate markers (any 1): AFP > 10,000 ng/mL, or hCG > 50,000 IU/L (10,000 ng/mL), or LDH > 10 × upper limit of N	—

AFP = a-fetoprotein; hCG = human chorionic gonadotropin; LDH = lactate dehydrogenase; N = normal; (Adapted from The International Germ Cell Collaborative Group.[62])
*For nonseminomas: 5-year progression-free survival (PFS), 89%; 5-year survival, 92%.
†For seminomas: 5-year PFS, 82%; 5-year survival, 86%.
‡For nonseminomas: 5-year PFS, 75%; 5-year survival, 80%.
§For seminomas: 5-year PFS, 67%; 5-year survival, 72%.
‖For nonseminomas; 5-year PFS, 41%; 5-year survival; 48%.

Interestingly, no patient with seminoma was classified as having a poor risk.[62]

The IGCCCG categories have been widely accepted and have been used to dictate treatment. They have even been incorporated into the tumor-node-metastasis (TNM) staging system by the American Joint Committee on Cancer (Table 7–2).[63] The serum tumor marker category, labeled S, is unique since no other malignancy incorporates markers into staging. While the standard three cycles of bleomycin, etoposide, and cisplatin (BEP) are recommended for good-prognosis patients with metastases, S2 and S3 patients should either receive at least an additional cycle or be placed on an aggressive clinical protocol.[14,15] Patients without evidence of metastatic disease and who have persistent marker elevation post orchiectomy are labeled stage IS and are discussed in the next section.

MONITORING

Response to Therapy

The ability to monitor response to therapy is among GCT markers' most important roles. In a disease in which rapid growth and progression to a worse prognostic group or even to incurability are potential threats, early indication of ineffectual treatment may allow a more aggressive therapy to be instituted in a more timely fashion. After complete surgical excision of all viable tumor, one would expect that each marker would decline according to its half-life ($t_{1/2}$), which is known to be 4.5 days for AFP, 16 to 24 hours for hCG, and 1 day for LDH. Chemotherapy, on the other hand, does not immediately eliminate all disease; therefore, the rate of decline is more complex. Although many criteria have been published, there is no consensus on which of these criteria should be used. Empirically, a 10-fold decrease in serum marker levels seen over a 3-week period has been consistent with a good disease response.[58] The group at Memorial Sloan-Kettering Cancer Center proposed that a satisfactory $t_{1/2}$ after chemotherapy was < 3 days for hCG and < 7 days for AFP. They found that patients with a satisfactory marker decrease as defined by this criterion had complete remission rates of 89%, compared to only 9% for patients with a slower regression.[64] Another strategy used the ratio between marker levels at the initiation of chemotherapy and levels on day 22 of the first cycle. A 200-fold

Table 7–2. AMERICAN JOINT COMMITTEE ON CANCER STAGING FOR TESTICULAR GERM CELL TUMORS		
	Stage	Criteria
Serum Tumor Markers	Sx	NA
	S0	Normal serum markers
	S1	LDH < 1.5 × upper limit of normal hCG < 5,000 (IU/L) AFP < 1,000 (ng/mL)
	S2	LDH 1.5–10 × upper limit of normal hCG = 5,000–50,000 (IU/L) AFP = 1,000–10,000 (ng/mL)
	S3	LDH > 10 × upper limit of normal HCG > 50,000 (IU/L) AFP > 10,000 (ng/mL)
TMN Staging	0	pTis, N0, M0, S0
	I	pT1–4, N0, M0, SX
	IA	pT1, N0, M0, S0
	IB	PT2–4, N0, M0, S0
	IS	Any T, N0, M0, S1–3
	II	Any T, N1–3, M0, SX
	IIA	Any T, N1, M0, S0–1
	IIB	Any T, N2, M0, S0–1
	IIC	Any T, N3, M0, S0–1
	III	Any T, any N, M1, SX
	IIIA	Any T, any N, M1a, S0–1
	IIIB	Any T, N1–3, M0, S2
	IIIB	Any T, any N, M1a, S2
	IIIC	Any T, N1–3, M0, S3
	IIIC	Any T, any N, M1a, S3
	IIIC	Any T, any N, M1b, any S

AFP = α-fetoprotein; hCG = human chorionic gonadotropin; LDH = lactate dehydrogenase; M = metastasis; N = regional node; NA = not available; T = primary tumor.

or greater decrease was associated with complete response in 91% of cases whereas patients with smaller decreases were shown to have an incomplete response to the treatment in 94% of cases.[65]

When calculating marker half-life after chemotherapy, one must remember that there is often a dramatic increase in serum marker levels at the start of chemotherapy, probably because of cell lysis from the chemotherapy. Consequently, calculation of half-life must begin at the apogee of serum marker levels after the induction of chemotherapy (Figure 7–6).[66]

What, then, should be done with a patient who has persistent marker elevation? With the rare exception, persistent markers imply persistent disease and warrant further therapy even in the absence of a localizable mass. The opposite, unfortunately, is not true; 20 to 30% of patients with stage I NSGCTs will relapse after orchiectomy despite normal markers, and 10 to 20% of patients undergoing postchemotherapy retroperitoneal lymph node dissection will be found

to have viable tumor despite negative markers (Figure 7–7).[4] Patients with elevated markers after orchiectomy and no metastasis seen on imaging are classified as stage IS. These patients are almost always found to have disseminated disease and are better treated with chemotherapy than with surgery.[67] Patients with positive markers after first-line chemotherapy should be treated with salvage chemotherapy[14,68] (as discussed in detail in Chapter 16). In the less common case, where markers rise more than 2 years after initial chemotherapy, the lesion(s) causing the marker elevation can usually be identified and possibly treated initially with cytoreductive surgery.[14]

Although the presence of persistent markers implies persistent tumor in the vast majority of cases, there are instances in which persistently elevated markers should be considered with caution. In particular, a hypergonadotropic hypogonadic state is not uncommon after chemotherapy.[69,70] The marked elevation of luteinizing hormone (LH) may be misinter-

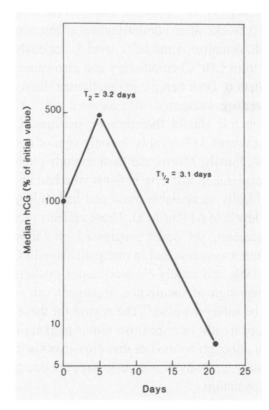

Figure 7–6. Mean slopes of the hCG values during induction chemotherapy in 37 patients with germ cell cancer. (Adapted from Vogelzang NJ, Lange PH, Goldman A, et al. Acute changes of alpha-fetoprotein and human chorionic gonadotropin during induction chemotherapy of germ cell tumors. Cancer Research 1982;42: 4855–61.)

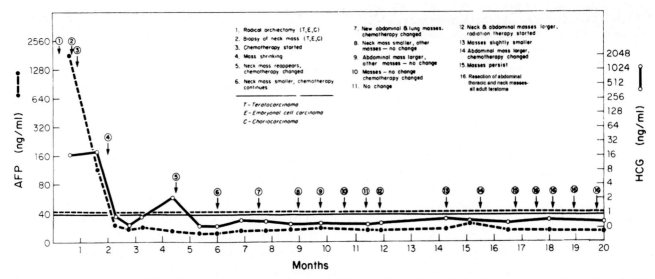

Figure 7–7. α-Fetoprotein (AFP) and human chorionic gonadotropin (hCG) levels in a patient with multiple recurrences. At the time of original publication, it was not known that recurrences could occur without elevated tumor markers.

preted as elevated hCG by insufficiently specific immunoassays. Today, most hCG assays have little cross-reactivity with LH, but in situations where cross-reactivity is suspected, hCG levels, assessed again 2 weeks after administration of testosterone, should normalize if the hCG level is seriously elevated from LH.[4] Chemotherapy can also cause liver dysfunction. Both benign and malignant diseases of the liver are associated with elevated AFP. A liver function test should therefore be performed in a patient whose AFP level is the only sign of residual disease. Finally, Morris and Bosl recently published their experience with five patients who had no radiographically identifiable mass and had mildly elevated levels of AFP or hCG. These patients received no treatment, yet never progressed on follow-up. The authors suggest that in rare patients with GCTs with stable and mildly elevated tumor markers and no other sign of recurrence, treatment can sometimes be safely avoided.[71] The reason for these low-level apparently false-positive tumor markers is not known although antibodies that cross-react with the secondary antibody in immunoassays are one possible explanation.

Recurrence

Serum tumor markers are absolutely critical in the proper follow-up of patients with testicular cancer. Rising serum tumor markers can herald recurrence long before a localizable mass can be identified, and early detection can significantly improve prognosis. AFP and hCG are the first indications of recurrence in 50% of patients and have a combined sensitivity of 86%; as well, specificity is near 100%, notwithstanding the rare exceptions mentioned above.[72] LDH is also of key value; although less specific, an elevated LDH level may be the only biochemical abnormality at the time of recurrence in 10% of NSGCT patients.[73] Indeed, GCT is one of the few cancers for which therapy (including chemotherapy) can be initiated, continued, or resumed on the basis of positive marker status without confirmation by biopsy when such confirmation would require significant surgical intervention.

Prior marker status should not change the approach to follow-up. Just as the histology of the initial tumor often differs from that of the recurrence, so too can marker statuses differ. Disease that is initially marker negative may recur with elevated serum marker levels, and disease that is initially marker positive may present without the expression of tumor markers or even with the expression of a different pattern of markers. Therefore, all protocols should recommend that AFP, hCG, and LDH levels in patients with GCTs should be monitored carefully regardless of histology or original marker status.[14,15] At our institution, the NCCN guidelines are followed (Tables 7–3 and 7–4). Only when a longer disease-

| Table 7–3. GUIDELINES FOR SURVEILLANCE OF NONSEMINOMATOUS GERM CELL TUMORS* | | |
Year	History/PE, Markers, CXR	Abdomino-pelvic CT
Stages IA and IB after Observation		
1	q 1–2 mo	q 3–4 mo
2	q 2 mo	q 3–4 mo
3	q 3 mo	q 4 mo
4	q 4 mo	q 6 mo
5	q 6 mo	q 12 mo
6	q 12 mo	q 12 mo
7	q 12 mo	q 12 mo
After Complete Response to Chemotherapy and/or RPLND		
1	q 1–2 mo	q 6 mo
2	q 2 mo	q 6 mo
3	q 3 mo	q 12 mo
4	q 4 mo	q 12 mo
5	q 6 mo	q 12 mo
6	q 12 mo	q 12 mo
7	q 12 mo	q 12 mo

CXR = chest radiography; CT = computed tomography; PE = physical examination; q = every; RPLND = retroperitoneal lymph node dissection.
*National Comprehensive Cancer Network guidelines.

| Table 7–4. GUIDELINES FOR SURVEILLANCE OF SEMINOMA GERM CELL TUMORS* | | |
Year	History/PE, Markers, Abdominopelvic CT	CXR
Stages IA, IB, and IS after Observation		
1	q 4 mo	q 8 mo
2	q 4 mo	q 8 mo
3	q 4 mo	q 8 mo
4	q 6 mo	q 12 mo
5	q 6 mo	q 12 mo
6	q 6 mo	q 12 mo
7	q 6 mo	q 12 mo
8	q 12 mo	q 24 mo
9	q 12 mo	q 24 mo
10	q 12 mo	q 24 mo
Stages IA, IB, and IS after XRT (25–30 Gy)		
1	q 3 mo	q 12 mo
2	q 4 mo	q 12 mo
3	q 6 mo	q 12 mo
4	q 6 mo	—
5	q 6 mo	—
6	q 12 mo	—
7	q 12 mo	—
8	q 12 mo	—
9	q 12 mo	—
10	q 12 mo	—
Stages IIA and IIB after XRT (35–40 Gy)		
1	q 2 mo	at 4th mo
2	q 3 mo	—
3	q 4 mo	—
4	q 6 Mo	—
5	q 12 mo	—
6	q 12 mo	—
7	q 12 mo	—
8	q 12 mo	—
9	q 12 mo	—
10	q 12 mo	—
Stages IIC and III after Chemo ± RPLND ± XRT		
1	q 2 mo	4 mo after surgery; otherwise, q 3 mo until stable
2	q 3 mo	—
3	q 4 mo	—
4	q 6 mo	—
5	q 12 mo	—
6	q 12 mo	—
7	q 12 mo	—
8	q 12 mo	—
9	q 12 mo	—
10	q 12 mo	—

Chemo = chemotherapy; CT = computed tomography; CXR = chest radiography; PE = physical examination; q = every; RPLND = retroperitoneal lymph node dissection; XRT = radiation therapy.
*National Comprehensive Cancer Network guidelines.

free interval is seen and recurrence becomes less likely can the frequency of serum marker determinations be reduced. In a recent study of 1,263 GCT patients, 79% of the patients whose disease recurred had the recurrence within 2 years. After 5 years, recurrence rates drop to approximately 1% per year, and recurrences are seen almost entirely in patients with nonseminomatous disease.[74]

CONCLUSION

In the past 50 years, the biology of tumor marker production has been studied extensively, and the concepts arising from these investigations are now incorporated routinely into clinical practice. The measurement of AFP, hCG, and LDH levels is critically important for optimal management, and serial assays of these proteins are routinely used for diagnosis, monitoring, and the attribution of prognosis. Of importance, it is now recognized that tumor marker production may be variable and that formerly "silent" tumors may relapse with the production of a new marker. Thus, routine clinical follow-up of treated patients requires regular assessment of circulating tumor marker levels for the duration of the period of surveillance.

REFERENCES

1. Zondek B. Versuch einer biologischen (hormonalen) Diagnostik beim mailgnen Hodentumor. Chirurg 1930;2:1072–80.

2. Bergstrand CG, Czar B. Demonstration of new protein from carcinoma of the colon. J Urol 1954;72:712.

3. Abelev GI, Perova SD, Kramkova NI, et al. Production of embryonal alpha I globulin by transplantable mouse hepatomas. Transplantation 1963;1:174.

4. Richie JP. Neoplasms of the testis. In: Walsh PC, Retik AB, Stamey TA, Vaughn ED, editors. Campbell's urology. 6th ed. Philadelphia: W.B. Saunders; 1992. p. 1222–63.

5. Bloomer JR, Waldmann TA, McIntire KR, et al. Serum alpha-fetoprotein levels in patients with non-neoplastic liver disease. Gastroen 1973;65:530.

6. Abelev GI. Alpha-fetoprotein as a marker of embryo-specific differentiations in normal and tumor tissues. Transplant Rev 1974;20:137–45.

7. Raghavan D, Sullivan AL, Peckham MJ, Neville AM. Elevated serum alphafetoprotein and seminoma: clinical evidence for a histologic continuum? Cancer 1982;50:982–9.

8. Lange PH, Nochomovich LE, Rosai J, et al. The role of alpha-fetoprotein and human chorionic gonadotrophin in patients with seminoma. J Urol 1991;124:472–8.

9. Vaitukaitis JL. Human chorionic gonadotropin: a hormone secreted for many reasons. N Engl J Med 1979;301:324.

10. Giralt SA, Dexeus F, Amato R, et al. Hyperthyroidism in men with germ cell tumors and high levels of beta human chorionic gonadotrophin. Cancer 1992;69:1286.

11. Kardana A, Cole LA. Polypeptide nicks cause erroneous results in assays of human chorionic gonadotrophin free beta subunits. Clin Chem 1992;38:26.

12. Bower M, Rustin GJS. Serum tumor markers and their role in monitoring germ cell cancers of the testis. In: Vogelzang NJ, Shipley WU, Scardino PT, et al, editors. Genitourinary oncology. 2nd ed. Philadelphia: Lippincott Williams and Wilkins; 1999. p. 927–38.

13. Klein EA. Tumor markers in testis cancer. Urol Clin North Am 1993;20:67–73.

14. National Comprehensive Cancer Network practice guidelines in oncology. Vol 1; Rockledge, PA. Testicular cancer 2003.

15. Laguna MP, Pizzocarro G, Klepp O, et al. EAU guidelines on testicular cancer. Eur Urol 2001;40:102–10.

16. von Eyben FE, Liu FJ, Amato RJ, Fritsche HA. Lactate dehydrogenase isoenzyme 1 is the most important LD isoenzyme in patients with testicular germ cell tumor. Acta Oncol 2000;39:509–17.

17. von Eyben FE, Blaabjerg O, Madsen EL, et al. Serum lactate dehydrogenase isoenzyme 1 and tumor volume are indications of response to treatment and predictors of prognosis in metastatic testicular germ cell tumors. Eur J Cancer 1992;238:410–5.

18. von Eyben FE, Madsen EL, Blaabjerg O, et al. Serum lactate dehydrogenase isoenzyme 1 and relapse in patients with nonseminomatous testicular germ cell tumors clinical stage 1. Acta Oncol 2001;40(4):536–40.

19. von Eyben FE, Blaabjerg O, Petersen PH, et al. Serum lactate dehydrogenase isoenzyme 1 and prediction of death in patients with metastatic testicular germ cell tumors. Clin Chem Lab Med 2001;39(1):38–44.

20. Albrecht W, Bonner E, Jeschke K, et al. PLAP as a marker for germ cell tumors. In: Jones NG, Appleyard I, Harnden P, Joffe JK, editors. Germ cell tumours IV. London: John Libbey & Co; 1998. p. 105–9.

21. Koshida K, Nishino A, Yamamoto H, et al. The role of alkaline phophatase isoenzymes as a tumor marker for testicular germ cell tumors. J Urol 1991;146:57.

22. Lange PH, Millan JL, Stigbrand T, et al. Placental alkaline phosphatase as a tumor marker for seminoma. Cancer Res 1982;42:3244.

23. Weissbach L, Bussar-Maatz R, Mann K. The value of tumor markers in testicular seminomas. Results of a prospective multicenter study. Eur Urol 1997;32(1):16–22.

24. Muensch HA, Maslow WC, Azama F, et al. Placental-like alkaline phosphatase. Re-evaluation of the tumor marker with exclusion of smokers. Cancer 1986;58:1689.

25. Nielsen OS, Muntro AJ, Duncan W, et al. Is placental alkaline phosphatase (PLAP) a useful marker for seminoma? Eur J Cancer 1990;26(10):1049–54.

26. Fossa SD, Klepp O, Paus E. Neuron-specific enolas—a serum marker in seminoma? Br J Cancer 1992;65(2):297–9.

27. Gross AJ, Dieckmann KP. Neuron-specific enolase: a serum marker in malignant germ-cell tumors? Eur Urol 1993;24(2):277–8.

28. Hitchins RN, Rustin GJ, Mitchell HD, et al. Carcinoembryonic antigen levels in germ cell tumours. Int J Biol Markers 1989;41(1):31–4.

29. Blacker C, Feinstein MC, Roger M, Scholler R. Evaluation of PS beta 1G and other markers in germ cell tumors of the testis. Andrologia 1981;13(5):458–67.

30. Talerman A, van der Pompe WB, Haije WG, Baggerman L. Alpha-fetoprotein and carcinoembryonic antigen in germ cell neoplasms. Br J Cancer 1977;35(3):288–91.

31. Suurmeijer AJ, Oosterhuis JW, Marrink J, et al. Non-seminomatous germ cell tumors of the testis. Analysis of CEA production in primary tumors and in retroperitoneal lymph node metastasis after PVB chemotherapy. Eur J Cancer Clin Oncol 1984;20(5):601–8.

32. Steffens J, Friedman W, Nagel R. Immunohistochemical and radioimmunological determination of beta-HCG and pregnancy-specific beta1-protein in seminomas. Urol Int 1985;40(2):72–5.

33. De Bruijn HW, Suurmeijer AJ, Sleijfer DT, et al. Evaluation of pregnancy-specific beta 1-glycoprotein with non-seminomatous testicular germ cell tumors. Eur J Cancer Clin Oncol 1982;18(10):911–6.

34. Suurmeijer AJ, De Bruijn HW, Oosterhuis JW, et al. Non-seminomatous germ cell tumors of the testis. Immunohistochemical localization and serum levels of human chorionic gonadotrophin (HCG) and pregnancy-specific beta-1 glycoprotein (SP-1); value of SP-1 as a tumor marker. Oncodev Biol Med 1982;3(5-6):409–22.

35. Badcock G, Pigott C, Goepel J, Andrews PW. The human embryonal carcinoma marker antigen TRA-1-60 is a sialylated keratan sulfate proteoglycan. Cancer Res 1999;59:4715–9.

36. Lajer H, Daugaard G, Andersson AM, Skakkebaek NE. Clinical use of serum TRA-1-60 as a tumor marker in patients with germ cell cancer. Int J Cancer 2002;100:244–6.

37. Atkin NB, Baker MC. Specific chromosomal marker in seminoma and malignant teratoma of the testis? Cancer Genet Cytogenet 1983;10:199–204.

38. Samaniego F, Rodriguez E, Houldsworth J, et al. Cytogenetic and molecular analysis of human male germ cell tumors:

chromosome 12 abnormalities and gene amplification. Genes Chromosomes Cancer 1990;1:289–92.

39. Motzer RJ, Rodriguez E, Reuter VR, et al. Molecular and cytogenetic studies in the diagnosis of patients with poorly differentiated carcinomas of unknown primary site. J Clin Oncol 1995;13:274.

40. Bosl GJ, Dimitrovsky E, Reuter VE, et al. Isochromosome of chromosome 12: a clinically useful marker for male germ cell tumors. J Natl Cancer Inst 1989;24:1874–8.

41. Summersgill BM, Jafer O, Wang R, et al. Definition of chromosomal aberrations in testicular germ cell tumor cell lines by 24-color karyotyping and complementary molecular cytogenetic analysis. Cancer Genet Cytogenet 2001; 128(2):120–9.

42. Vos A, Oosterhuis W, de Jong B, et al. Cytogenetics of carcinoma in situ of the testis. Cancer Genet Cytogenet 1990; 46:75–81.

43. Summersgill B, Osin P, Lu YJ, et al. Chromosomal imbalances associated with carcinoma in situ and associated testicular germ cell tumours of adolescents and adults. Br J Cancer 2001;82:213–20.

44. Skotheim RI, Monni O, Mousses S, et al. New insights into testicular germ cell tumorigenesis from gene expression profiling. Cancer Res 2002;62:2359–64.

45. Smith RC, Rukstalis DB. Frequent loss of heterozygosity at 11p loci in testicular cancer. J Urol 1995;153:1684.

46. Murtry VVVS, Chaganti RSK. Allelotyping of male germ cell tumors. Am J Hum Genet 1991;49:122.

47. Rodriguez E, Mathew S, Reuter V, et al. Cytogenetic analysis of 124 prospectively ascertained male germ cell tumors. Cancer Res 1992;52:2285.

48. Murtry VVVS, Houldsworth J, Baldwin S, et al. Allelic deletions in the long arm of chromosome 12 identify sites of candidate tumor suppressor genes in male germ cell tumors. Proc Natl Acad Sci U S A 1992;89:11106.

49. Stohmeyer T, Peter S, Hartmann M, et al. Expression of the hst-1 and c-kit protooncogenes in human germ cell tumors. Cancer Res 1991;51(7):1811–6.

50. Stohmeyer T, Reese D, Press M, et al. Expression of the c-kit proto-oncogene and its ligand stem cell factor (SCF) in normal and malignant human testicular tissue. J Urol 1995;153:511.

51. Stohmeyer T, Reissmann P, Cordon-Cardo C, et al. Correlation between retinoblastoma gene expression and differentiation in human testicular tumors. Proc Natl Acad Sci U S A 1991;88:6662.

52. Fleischhacker M, Stohmeyer T, Imai Y, et al. Mutations of the p53 gene are not detectable in human testicular tumors. J Urol 1994;152:1133.

53. Peng HQ, Hogg D, Malkin D, et al. Mutations of the p53 gene do not occur in testis cancer. Cancer Res 1993;53:3574.

54. Kersemaekers AF, Mayer F, Molier M, et al. Role of P53 and MDM2 in treatment response of human germ cell tumors. J Clin Oncol 2002;20(6):1551–61.

55. Chresta CM, Masters JRW, Hickman JA. Hypersensitivity of human testicular cell tumors to etoposide-induced apoptosis associated with functional p53 and high bax:bcl-2 ratio. Cancer Res 1996;56:1834–41.

56. Baltaci S, Orhan D, Turkolmez K, et al. P53, bcl-2, and bax immunoreactivity as predicators or response and outcome after chemotherapy for metastic germ cell testicular tumours. BJU Intl 2001;87(7):661–6.

57. Heidenreich A, Sesterhenn IA, Mostofi FK, et al. Prognostic risk factors that identify patients with clinical stage I non-seminomatous germ cell tumors at low risk and high risk for metastasis. Cancer 1998;83:1002–11.

58. Small EJ, Torti FM. Testes. In: Abeloff MD, Armitage JO, Lichter AS, Niederhuber JE, editors. Abeloff clinical oncology. 2nd ed. Philadelphia: Churchill Livingston Inc.; 2000. p. 1906–45.

59. Boyle LE, Samuels ML. Serum LDH activity and isoenzyme patterns in nonseminomatous germinal (NSG) testis tumors. Proc Am Soc Clin Oncol 1977;18:278.

60. Mencel PJ, Motzer RJ, Mazumdar M, et al. Advanced seminoma; treatment results, survival, and prognostic factor in 142 patients. J Clin Oncol 1994;12:120–6.

61. Stoter G, Bosl GJ, Droz JP, et al. Prognostic factors in metstatic germ cell tumors. Prog Clin Biol Res 1990;357:313–9.

62. The International Germ Cell Collaborative Group. International germ cell consensus classification: a prognostic factor-based staging system for metastatic germ cell cancers. J Clin Oncol 1997;15(2):594–603.

63. Green FL, Balch CM, Page DL, et al, editors. American Joint Committee on Cancer (AJCC) Cancer Staging manual. 6th ed. New York: Springer-Verlag; 2002. p. 77–87.

64. Toner GC, Geller NL, Tan C, et al. Serum tumor marker half-life during chemotherapy allows early prediction of complete response and survival in nonseminomatous germ cell tumors. Cancer Res 1990;50:5904–10.

65. Picozzi VJ Jr, Freiha F, Hannigan JF, Torti FM. Prognostic significance of a decline in serum human chorionic gonadotropin levels after initial chemotherapy for advanced germ-cell carcinoma. Ann Intern Med 1984;100:183.

66. Lange PH, Vogelzang NJ, Goldman A, et al. Marker half-life analysis as a prognostic tool in testicular cancer. J Urol 1982;128:70.

67. Davis BE, Herr HW, Fair WR, et al. The management of patients with nonseminomatous germ-cell tumors of the testis with serologic disease only after orchiectomy. J Urol 1994;152:111–4.

68. Loehrer PJ, Gonin R, Nichols CR, et al. Vinblastin plus ifosfamide plus cisplatin as initial salvage therapy in recurrent germ-cell tumors. J Clin Oncol 1998;16:2500–4.

69. Leitner SP, Bose GJ, Bajororjmas D. Gonadal dysfunction in patients treated for metastatic germ cell tumors. J Clin Oncol 1986;4:1580.

70. Drasga RE, Einhorn LH, Williams SD, et al. Fertility after chemotherapy for testicular cancer. J Clin Oncol 1983;1:179.

71. Morris MJ, Bosl GJ. Recognizing abnormal marker results that do not reflect disease in patients with germ cell tumors. J Urol 2000;163(3):796.

72. De Bruijn HWA, Sleijfer DTH, Koops HS, et al. Significance of human chorionic gonadotropin, alpha fetoprotein and pregnancy specific B1-glycoprotein in the detection of tumor relapse and partial remission in 126 patients with non-seminomatous testicular germ cell tumors. Cancer 1985;55:829–35.

73. Skinner DG, Scardino PT. Relevance of biochemical tumor markers and lymphadenectomy in management of non-seminomatous testis tumors: current perspective. J Urol 1980;123:378.

74. Shahidi M, Norman AR, Dearnaley DP, et al. Late recurrence in 1263 men with testicular germ cell tumors; multivariate analysis of risk factors and implications for management. Cancer 2002;95:520–30.

8

Prognostic Factors in Disseminated Germ Cell Tumors

CRAIG NICHOLS, MD

With more clinical experience in germ cell tumors, investigators have become increasingly able to identify patients with good risk features and who are suitable for therapies of diminished intensity, as well as less fortunate patients who present with poor-risk features and for whom more-intense and higher-risk approaches are warranted. As therapy for poor-risk disease evolves, treatment is becoming more complex and intense and is associated with increased short-term and long-term complications. Therefore, the imperative to properly identify a patient's risk category has taken on increased importance.

The history of prognostication in cases of disseminated germ cell tumors began with early attempts to correlate pathologic features and clinical presentation with outcome. From the mid-1970s to the mid-1980s, patients with disseminated disease were all treated similarly irrespective of predicted outcomes based on institutional data. By the mid-1980s, sufficient clinical experience had accrued to allow investigators to develop relatively reliable classification systems (such as the Indiana University system), to apply lesser therapies in those patients with a good or moderate expectation of cure, and to intensify therapy in those with a poor anticipated outcome.[1] This has been the goal of prognostic systems since then. Most recently, new clinical parameters, molecular and biologic determinants of outcome, dynamic prognostic modeling, large database research, and specific prognostic systems for specialized subsets have all been investigated.

PROGNOSTIC CLASSIFICATION

To develop a new prognostic model for disseminated disease, an international consortium recently collected clinical data on patients receiving platinum-based therapy for metastatic germ cell tumor (Table 8–1 and Figure 8–1 and 8–2).[2] Data on 5,202 patients with nonseminomatous germ cell tumor and 660 patients with seminoma were analyzed, and it was found that independent predictors of outcome by univariate analysis included mediastinal primary site; degree of α-fetoprotein (AFP), human chorionic gonadotropin (hCG), and lactate dehydrogenase (LDH) elevation; and the presence of nonpulmonary visceral metastasis. Using these factors, prognostic categories were derived. Good-risk nonseminomatous patients were those with a testicular or retroperitoneal primary, favorable markers, and no nonpulmonary visceral metastases (an anticipated progression-free survival rate of 90%). Poor-prognosis patients included those patients with mediastinal primary nonseminoma, patients with nonpulmonary visceral metastases, or those with an unfavorable elevation in tumor markers (an anticipated progression-free survival rate of 40%). An intermediate group had an anticipated progression-free survival rate of 75%. For seminoma, only groups of good and intermediate risk were identified, with these risk categories being differentiated by the absence or presence of nonpulmonary visceral metastases. This classification is now the stan-

Table 8–1. INTERNATIONAL GERM CELL TUMOR CONSENSUS CONFERENCE CLASSIFICATION		
	Nonseminoma	**Seminoma**

Good Prognosis	Testis/retroperitoneal primary and
	  No nonpulmonary visceral metastases and
	  Good markers: AFP < 1,000 ng/mL, hCG < 5,000 IU/L, and
	  LDH < 1.5 × upper limit of normal
		Any primary site and
		  No nonpulmonary visceral metastases and
		  Normal AFP, any hCG, any LDH

	56% of nonseminomas 5-yr PFS = 89% 5-yr survival = 92%	90% of seminomas 5-yr PFS = 82% 5-yr survival = 86%

Intermediate prognosis	Testis/retroperitoneal primary and
	  No nonpulmonary visceral metastases and
	  Intermediate markers: any of AFP ≥ 1,000
	  and ≤ 50,000 IU/L, or hCG ≥ 5,000
	  and ≤ 50,000 IU/L, or LDH ≥ 1.5 × N and ≤ 10 × N
		Any primary site and
		  Nonpulmonary visceral metastases and
		  Normal AFP, any hCG, any LDH

	28% of nonseminomas 5-yr PFS = 75% 5-yr survival = 80%	10% of seminomas 5= yr PFS = 67% 5-yr survival = 72%

Poor Prognosis	Mediastinal primary or
	  Nonpulmonary visceral metastases or
	  Poor markers: any of AFP > 10,000 ng/mL,
	  hCG > 50,000 IU/L (10,000 ng/mL), or
	  LDH > 10 × upper limit of normal
		No patients classified as poor prognosis

	16% of nonseminomas 5-yr PFS = 41% 5-yr survival = 48%	

AFP = α-fetoprotein; hCG = human chorionic gonadotropin; LDH = lactase dehydrogenase; N = normal; PFS = progression-free survival.

dard classification system for the comparison of results of clinical studies done at various institutions.

Two separate large studies partially validate the findings of the International Germ Cell Consensus Classification (IGCCC) group. Saxman and colleagues at Indiana University reviewed the long-term outcome of patients entering the minimal/moderate–risk disseminated disease study, comparing four cycles of bleomycin, etoposide, and cisplatin (BEP) to three cycles of BEP.[3] Patients were entered in this study on the basis of having a minimal or moderate extent of disease according to the Indiana University staging system, a system that includes only extent of disease, size of disease, and involvement of nonpulmonary visceral organs in the assignment of prognosis. The primary conclusion was that the results of four versus three cycles of therapy were equivalent in these good-prognosis patients. However, a subset of patients with an otherwise good prognosis by disease extent but who had hCG elevations of > 1,000 mIU/mL were found to have a particularly poor outcome with either three or four cycles of BEP. There were 5 disease-related deaths among the 14 patients with hCG levels > 1,000 mIU/mL, compared

to 2 disease-related deaths in the 104 patients with hCG levels < 1,000 mIU/mL ($p < .001$).

Bajorin and colleagues reviewed clinical data from 796 patients with disseminated germ cell tumors.[4] Independently significant factors for response included mediastinal primary tumors, metastases to nonpulmonary visceral metastases (liver, bone, brain), pretreatment elevations of LDH and hCG, and pure seminoma histology. As with the IGCCC system, good-, intermediate-, and poor-risk groups were identified, with complete response (CR) rates of 92%, 76%, and 39%, respectively. Only pure seminoma histology was associated with an increased percentage of CR; all of the other factors reduced the proportion of CRs.

TUMOR MARKER DECLINE AS A PROGNOSTIC FACTOR

Investigators at Memorial Sloan-Kettering Cancer Center (MSKCC) have emphasized the prognostic role of tumor marker decline following the first cycle of chemotherapy.[5] A prognostic model was performed at MSKCC. The half-life of the tumor marker was calculated between the first two values measured after day 7 from the start of chemotherapy. The cutoff values for the half-lives of hCG and AFP were 3 and 7 days, respectively.

This study included 189 patients with good-, intermediate-, and poor-risk disseminated germ cell tumors as determined by the IGCCC. Patients with a normal half-life clearance of AFP and hCG had a CR proportion of 92%, a 2-year event-free survival rate of 91%, and a 2-year overall survival rate of 95%, compared to the group with unsatisfactory marker decline, in whom the CR proportion was 62%, the 2-year event-free survival rate was 69%, and the 2-year overall survival rate was 72% ($p < .0001$). Marker decline remained a significant variable for all three end points when adjusted for risk ($p < .01$), with outcome differences being most pronounced in the poor-risk subset.

Fizazi and colleagues reviewed marker decline during the first 4 weeks of chemotherapy in the context of the IGCCC.[6] Data from 695 patients who had been treated from 1987 to 2000 were studied. Serum tumor markers were determined prior to chemotherapy and at the 19- to 28-day mark after the first cycle of treatment. Decline rates were calculated (using a logarithmic formula) and were expressed as a time to theoretical normalization. By the IGCCC, 388 patients (60%) were good-risk

patients, 120 (19%) were intermediate-risk patients, and 139 (21%) were poor-risk patients. The median follow-up was 39 months. The 5-year survival rate was 97%, 83%, and 64% for good-, intermediate-, and poor-risk patients, respectively. In this study, cutoff points for the theoretical time to normalization of 9 weeks for AFP and 6 weeks for hCG were applied. Among poor-risk patients, those with a favorable pattern of normalization (both markers' time to normalization being lower than cutoff values) had a significantly better overall survival rate than those with a prolonged normalization (81% vs 59%, $p = .02$). Similar results were seen with relapse-free survival rates (73% vs 46%). Tumor marker decline had no impact on the predicting of outcome in patients with good- or intermediate-risk metastatic germ cell tumor.

Further studies failed to confirm this observation, however.[7,8] Likewise, the Indiana University study by Zon and colleagues suggests that tumor decline is somewhat erratic in the subset of patients with very high elevations of hCG, making mathematical prediction hazardous.[9]

Difficulty in accepting tumor marker decline as a firm predictor of outcome is the retrospective nature of both the analysis and the patient selection bias. This question is being addressed prospectively in the US Intergroup trial of poor-risk disease being under-

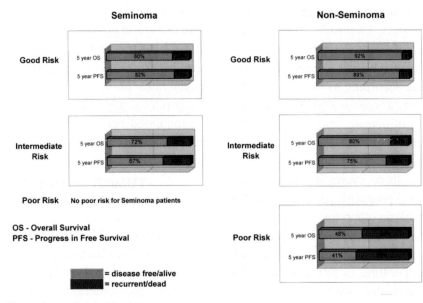

Figure 8–1.   Survival by risk category.

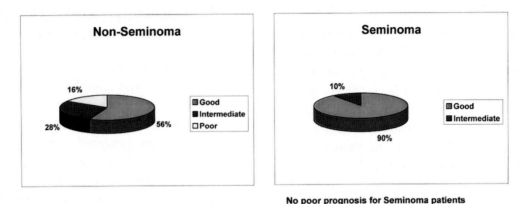

Figure 8–2. Distribution of risk groups.

taken at the time of this publication, in which frequent marker determination is required for all patients entering the trial.

BIOLOGIC PREDICTORS OF OUTCOME

The ability to assign risk on the basis of currently available clinical parameters has been maximized. One can argue as to which system is the most accurate, but most commonly employed systems can assign prognosis correctly for the vast majority of patients. The internationally defined prognostic system may assist in supplementing local prognostic schemes and allows for accurate comparison of results across studies. However, the next level of prognostication will likely come from the measurement of currently available (and some experimental) biologic predictors of outcome. None of these biologic parameters have been investigated thoroughly enough to be recommended for widespread use, but future prognostic systems will almost certainly incorporate one or more of the parameters.

Ploidy and proliferative index have been investigated as prognostic parameters for a variety of tumors, including germ cell tumors. Sledge and colleagues have analyzed ploidy and proliferative index as predictors of outcome in advanced disease, as defined by the Indiana University staging system.[10] In this study, ploidy was not predictive of survival, but proliferative index appeared to be a strong predictor of outcome. In the group of patients with proliferative indexes greater than the mean, survival was 37.7 ± 11.0 months, as compared with a mean survival of 85.6 ± 7.6 months for patients with

indexes less than the mean. In a multivariate analysis, proliferative index remained the most significant variable in the model ($p < .001$, compared with log [hCG] [$p = .016$], histology [$p = .045$], treatment employed [$p = $ not significant], or deoxyribonucleic acid index [$p = $ not significant]). Further attempts are being made to validate these preliminary findings in the recently completed Eastern Cooperative Oncology Group study of cisplatin and etoposide with either bleomycin or ifosfamide in the treatment of advanced germ cell tumors.

Other groups are using similar approaches to assess the impact of cytogenetic findings and oncogene expression on the determination of outcome. The discovery of a nonrandom chromosomal abnormality in the majority of germ cell tumors has renewed hope that a new understanding of the molecular mechanisms of this disease may be attainable in the near future, with an attendant benefit for therapy for patients with advanced disease. The identification of an isochromosome of the short arm of chromosome 12, i(12p), was initially reported by Atkin and Baker and is present in as many as 90% of germ cell tumor specimens.[11,12] Its identification in numerous tumor cell types, including seminoma, nonseminoma, and mature teratoma, as well as in both testicular and extragonadal primary lesions and even in carcinoma in situ of the testis, strongly suggests a role for this chromosomal event in the process of transformation.

Additionally, Bosl and colleagues have suggested that the number of copies of i(12p) present has prognostic importance.[13] In their analysis, 4 of 11 patients (36%) with a normal karyotype or with fewer than two additional copies of i(12p) had residual viable carcinoma after chemotherapy or failed induction therapy, as compared with 6 of 6 patients with more than three copies ($p = .035$). Importantly, three of these six patients had been categorized as good-risk patients by the Memorial Hospital prognostic model. Further confirmation of these observations in large clinical trials in patients with advanced disease will be required. However, this cytogenetic abnormality may ultimately prove to be an independent prognostic factor.

Investigators have begun to analyze host-related factors as predictors of outcome in cases of germ cell tumors. In no other malignancy is the identification of resistance to a single chemotherapeutic agent—cisplatin, in this case—so closely related to poor outcome. The ability to identify inherent (de novo) resistance to cisplatin at the time of diagnosis would allow (1) the identification of patients destined to fail standard treatment and (2) the early entry of such patients into clinical trials of novel therapeutic approaches. The analysis of potential mechanisms of cisplatin resistance can be broadly grouped into studies of platinum adduct formation, excision/repair capacity, and endogenous thiol content. Recently completed and ongoing investigations of the role of cisplatin resistance in predicting poor outcome offer some hope for the identification of such patients early in the course of treatment.[14,15] It is hoped that such studies will lead to a biologically based prognostic system or a hybrid classification with clinical and biologic parameters accurately explaining the diversity of response seen in patients with germ cell tumors.

Efforts to incorporate newer biologic markers into the field of prognostication are in development. Investigators at Indiana University have looked at deoxyribonucleic acid (DNA) repair enzyme expression and transcription of transcription regulators (Genesis) and at the presence of i(12p) in patients who experience late relapse.[16] Investigators at Memorial Sloan-Kettering Cancer Center have used multivariate cluster analysis to explore the role of p53, Ki67 expression, and apoptosis markers in predicting outcomes in patients with disseminated germ cell tumors.[17] A study of genetic analysis by microarray is also under way.

PROGNOSTICATION AFTER CHEMOTHERAPY

Much experience has been gained in predicting outcomes of patients who complete chemotherapy and in regard to adjunctive therapies following chemotherapy. In particular, post-chemotherapy surgical findings have been analyzed in efforts to identify those who are at high risk for additional events.

Foster and colleagues recently reported the role of retroperitoneal lymph node dissection (RPLND) in patients with persistently elevated markers after the completion of standard chemotherapy for disseminated disease. Of those patients with persistently elevated markers and residual radiographic abnormalities, all were able to undergo complete resection. Approximately one-third of the patients were disease free with either surgery alone or surgery plus post-surgery chemotherapy, with a minimum follow-up of 24 months.[18]

Patients who have an incomplete radiographic response to chemotherapy but a normalization of elevated serum biomarkers frequently undergo post-chemotherapy resection of residual disease. A number of attempts to characterize the nature of postchemotherapy radiographic abnormalities have been undertaken. The histologic characteristics of the primary, the percentage of radiographic response, and the IGCCC designation can provide rough guidelines as to the chances of finding residual cancer or teratoma, but the performance characteristics of these predictive parameters are insufficiently precise to be useful in the day-to-day management of patients. However, it is well known that histologic findings at postchemotherapy surgery are predictive of risk of relapse. Patients who undergo resection of large-volume teratoma have a significant chance (up to 30%) of developing recurrent teratoma and require additional surgery. Patients who have residual viable germ cell elements have up to a one-in-three chance of developing recurrent germ cell tumor. Therefore, the current recommendation at Indiana University is that additional chemotherapy (usually two additional cycles of EP) should be administered to those patients with residual germ cell cancer in the resected specimen after primary chemotherapy. The absolute contribution of additional chemotherapy in this setting is somewhat speculative, but this represents the standard of care at Indiana University.

New functional imaging modalities such as positron emission tomography (PET) have been investigated in attempts to characterize postchemotherapy residual masses. To date, PET has been insufficiently discriminatory, especially in being able to distinguish teratoma from residual cancer in order to guide decisions regarding surgery after chemotherapy.[19](See also Chapters 6 and 11.)

PREDICTIVE FACTORS IN SALVAGE THERAPY

Many of the same parameters that predict outcome for primary chemotherapy predict outcome for salvage therapy. In addition to primary site and serum marker elevation, various investigators have suggested prior best response, degree of cisplatin resistance, and the presence of brain metastases as important prognostic factors for salvage chemotherapy. Currently, many investigators divide patients into poor-risk patients with recurrent disease and good-risk patients with recurrent disease, the former group consisting of those patients with prior incomplete response to primary therapy, mediastinal primary nonseminoma, and high hCG levels. Investigators at Memorial Sloan-Kettering Cancer Center divide patients by these parameters to assign either treatment with experimental high-dose therapy or more conventional salvage treatment with cisplatin, ifosfamide, and paclitaxel and standard high-dose therapy.

SPECIAL SITUATIONS

Late Relapse

Patients with late recurrence of germ cell tumor have a unique biologic profile and behavior. The patients frequently have elevated AFP as the associated serum biomarker and frequently have characteristic histopathologic findings of yolk sac tumor. The malignant germ cell elements tend to be much more resistant to chemotherapy than are de novo germ cell tumors.

The prognosis for the small subset of patients who experience late recurrence of germ cell tumor (more than 2 years beyond initial treatment) is tied largely to the histologic composition of the late recurrent disease. For those with recurrent teratoma, the overall prognosis for aggressive resection undertaken by an experienced surgeon is good. Resection is likewise a primary consideration for those patients with recurrent germ cell elements or malignant non–germ cell elements.

Extragonadal Primaries

The behavior of extragonadal seminomas is identical to that of testicular primary seminomas of similar volume (see Chapter 21). Patients with extragonadal nonseminoma (especially those with mediastinal primary nonseminoma) have a significantly worse prognosis with both primary and salvage chemotherapy. The reasons for the poor prognosis in cases of mediastinal primary nonseminoma are not entirely clear but certainly are partly related to the associated biologic conditions (hematologic malignancies and non–germ cell elements) and the higher incidence of resistance to chemotherapy. Overall, only 40 to 50% of patients with mediastinal nonseminoma survive the illness; for those patients presenting with mediastinal primary disease and extramediastinal spread, the outcome is dismal. It is appropriate that all mediastinal nonseminoma primary patients be entered into trials designed for patients with a poor prognosis.

CONCLUSION

The ability to refine prognoses on the basis of clinical parameters has been largely maximized. With the possible exception of dynamic determination of marker decline, it is unlikely that readily available clinical data will contribute significantly to newer or better prognostic systems. The advent of molecular oncology and the ability to perform biologic assessments of these fascinating tumors open the door to investigations of markers of proliferation, apoptosis, and gene expression as newer, more precise, and more therapeutically relevant end points. The same large cooperative efforts that led to the IGCCC system with clinical parameters may be required to validate these unfolding biologic parameters.

REFERENCES

1. Einhorn LH. Testicular cancer as a model for a curable neoplasm: the Richard and Hinda Rosenthal Foundation Award Lecture. Cancer Res 1981;41:3275–80.

2. International Germ Cell Consensus Classification: a new prognostic factor-based staging system for metastatic germ cell cancers. J Clin Oncol 1997;15:594–603.

3. Saxman S, Finch D, Gonin R, et al. Long-term follow-up of a phase III study of three versus four cycles of bleomycin, etoposide, and cisplatin in favorable-prognosis germ-cell tumors: the Indiana University experience. J Clin Oncol 1998;16:702–6.

4. Bajorin D, Mazumdar M, Meyers M, et al. Metastatic germ cell tumors: modeling for response to chemotherapy. J Clin Oncol 1998;16:707–15.

5. Toner G, Geller N, Tan C, et al. Serum tumor marker half-life during chemotherapy allows early prediction of complete response and survival in nonseminomatous germ cell tumors. Cancer Res 1990;50:5904–10.

6. Fizazi K, Kramer A, Culine S, et al. The early decline of tumor markers predicts outcome in poor prognosis non-seminomatous germ-cell tumors (NSGCT): results of a multi-institutional study [abstract 739]. Proc Am Soc Clin Oncol 2002;21:185a.

7. Horwich A, Peckham M. Serum tumor marker regression rate following chemotherapy for malignant teratoma. Eur J Cancer Clin Oncol 1984;20:1463–70.

8. Lange P, Vogelzang N, Goldman A, et al. Marker half-life analysis as a prognostic tool in testicular cancer. J Urol 1982;128:708–11.

9. Zon R, Nichols C, Einhorn L. Management of strategies and outcomes of germ cell tumor patients with very high human chorionic gonadotropin levels. J Clin Oncol 1998; 16(4):1294–7.

10. Sledge G, Eble J, Roth B, et al. Relation of proliferative activity to survival in patients with advanced germ cell cancer. Cancer Res 1988;48:3864–8.

11. Atkin N, Baker M. Specific chromosome change, i(12p) in testicular tumors? Lancet 1982;ii:1349.

12. Atkin N, Baker M. i(12p): specific chromosomal marker in seminoma and malignant teratoma of the testis? Cancer Genet Cytogenet 1983;10:199–204.

13. Bosl G, Dmitrovsky E, Reuter V, et al. Isochromosome of chromosome 12: useful marker for male germ cell tumors. J Natl Cancer Inst 1989;81:1874–8.

14. Reed E, Ozols R, Tarone R, et al. Platinum-DNA adducts in leucocyte DNA correlate with disease response in ovarian cancer patients receiving platinum-based chemotherapy. Proc Natl Acad Sci U S A 1987;84:5024–8.

15. Reed E, Ozols R, Tarone R, et al. The measure of cisplatin-DNA adduct levels in testicular cancer patients. Carcinogenesis 1988;9:1909–11.

16. George D, Foster R, Hromas R, et al. Update on late relapse of germ cell tumors: a clinical and molecular analysis [abstract 689]. Proc Am Soc Clin Oncol 2001; 20:173a.

17. Mazumdar M, Bacik J, Dobrzynski D, et al. Cluster analysis of p53 and KI 67 expression, apoptosis, alphafetoprotein and human chorionic gonadotropin in nonseminomatous germ cell tumors (NSGCT) discovers a prognostic subgroup within embryonal carcinoma [abstract 710]. Proc Am Soc Clin Oncol 2001;20:178a.

18. Foster R, Bihrle R. Current status of retroperitoneal lymph node dissection for testicular cancer: when to operate. Cancer Contol 2002;9:277–83.

19. Stephens A, Gonin R, Hutchins G, et al. Positron emission tomography evaluation of residual radiographic abnormalities in postchemotherapy germ cell tumor patients. J Clin Oncol 1996;14:1637–41.

9

Surgery for Testicular Cancer: Radical Orchiectomy

SIAMAK DANESHMAND, MD

EILA C. SKINNER, MD

Testicular cancer remains the most curable solid tumor in men. Careful histologic diagnosis and prompt evaluation for metastatic disease are essential for the selection of appropriate treatment. The first surgical step in the management of testicular cancer is inguinal orchiectomy. In the past, before the advent of good techniques for testicular imaging, inguinal exploration with open biopsy of the testis was the primary method of making a definitive diagnosis of testicular cancer. Now, scrotal ultrasonography is nearly 100% accurate in identifying a tumor in the testis, and it is rarely necessary to perform a truly "exploratory" surgery.[1,2]

PRESENTATION OF TESTICULAR CANCER

The clinical presentation of testicular cancer is usually quite obvious. The typical patient is a man aged 17 to 45 years who notices a growing and relatively painless mass in the scrotum and seeks medical attention. However, as many as 10% of patients present with atypical complaints, such as sudden pain in the scrotum, a new-onset hydrocele, or recent trauma. Some patients are misdiagnosed as having epididymitis, causing an unnecessary delay in diagnosis. A high index of suspicion is required when evaluating any man in this age group with testicular complaints, and the possibility of testicular cancer must be in the differential diagnosis. Patients diagnosed with presumed epididymitis should be observed until the testicular examination result returns to normal, which might take several months. Any patient with nonspecific

orchialgia who is completely normal on examination should probably have at least one follow-up examination in 3 to 6 months to ensure that a small tumor was not missed. Because these cancers grow rapidly, there is little concern in regard to diagnosing subclinical tumors. Finally, a small percentage of patients present with symptoms of metastatic disease, such as a neck mass, back pain, hemoptysis, or gynecomastia. These patients may be unaware of the abnormality in the testis. Unless the physician considers testicular cancer in the differential diagnosis of these symptoms, the appropriate treatment may be unnecessarily delayed.

The widespread availability of high-quality scrotal ultrasonography with Doppler blood flow analysis has nearly eliminated much of the diagnostic difficulty for these patients. Today, patients who are misdiagnosed are mostly those for whom ultrasonography was not ordered. The caveat of the availability of ultrasonography, however, has been an increase in the finding of minor abnormalities such as microcalcifications, which has caused considerable anxiety and debate recently. A number of studies have shown that testicular microcalcifications are commonly found by modern ultrasonography, and their presence does not indicate an increased risk of subsequent testicular cancer.[3–5]

TIMING OF METASTATIC EVALUATION

Once the clinical diagnosis of testicular cancer has been made (based on examination and scrotal ultrasonography), the standard metastatic work-up can be completed, either before or after the orchiectomy. Tumor markers α-fetoprotein (AFP) and beta–human chorionic gonadotropin must be drawn prior to orchiectomy in order to establish the baseline value. Staging computed tomography (CT) of the abdomen and pelvis and chest radiography (or chest CT) are required for every patient. In most centers, it has been standard practice to perform the orchiectomy first and to delay the metastatic work-up until the tissue diagnosis has been obtained. This practice largely arose in the days when the clinical diagnosis was much less certain and CT was not readily available. There are two reasons to consider performing CT and marker evaluation prior to radical orchiectomy:

1. In the case of a patient with widespread symptomatic metastases and elevated serum AFP, the diagnosis of nonseminomatous germ cell tumor is certain. This patient might reasonably be treated initially with chemotherapy, delaying the orchiectomy until he has had a clinical response or until a subsequent planned retroperitoneal lymph node dissection is performed.
2. There is a small but significant risk of a retroperitoneal hemorrhage following an inguinal orchiectomy, and there are reported cases in which this hemorrhage was misdiagnosed as adenopathy and resulted in unnecessary chemotherapy.[6] This is certainly a rare situation but is one that can be avoided by performing CT prior to the orchiectomy.

For the vast majority of patients who present with a solid testicular mass, the timing of the CT scanning is not important. The interpretation of the scan is much more significant.

Percutaneous core or needle biopsy of the testis is not necessary and should be avoided in almost all cases. A possible exception is the young patient with an established diagnosis of leukemia who has suspected leukemic involvement of the testis. In any patient with a questionable mass in the testis, a safer approach includes an inguinal exploration and open biopsy.

BASIC SURGICAL APPROACH

The rationale for an inguinal orchiectomy in a patient with scrotal cancer is well established. This approach allows for high ligation of the spermatic cord, without any significant risk of scrotal contamination. A transscrotal approach would potentially place the inguinal lymph nodes at risk for metastases, which could have a significant impact on treatment. The surgery is well tolerated and is easily adjusted to deal with very large masses or scrotal skin involvement.

The surgery can be performed under general or regional anesthesia. The patient is placed supine, and the genitalia and lower abdomen are prepared. The surgeon must have direct access to the scrotum during the procedure. The incision is made transversely, beginning approximately 2 cm lateral to the pubic tubercle (Figure 9–1). The length of the incision depends on the size of the involved testis. In most cases, an incision of 3 to 5 cm in length is adequate. In a patient with a huge tumor, the incision can be curved down on the medial end to extend down onto the proximal scrotum (Figure 9–2). This will effectively open the incision to any size required to deliver the specimen.

After the subcutaneous tissues are divided, the external oblique fascia is opened between its longitudinal fibers, ending in the external ring (Figure 9–3). The fascia is lifted off the underlying spermatic cord structures. The ilioinguinal nerve is encountered, usually slightly lateral to the cord (Figure 9–4); it needs to be carefully mobilized and protected during the remainder of the dissection. At this point, the cord is mobilized within the inguinal canal, and a small plastic drain is passed around it for retraction. If there is uncertainty about the diagnosis, the cord can be temporarily clamped while the testis is deliv-

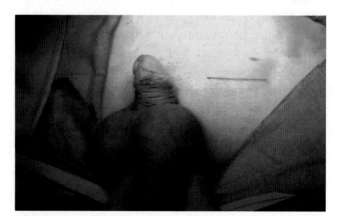

Figure 9–1.   Transverse incision for inguinal orchiectomy.

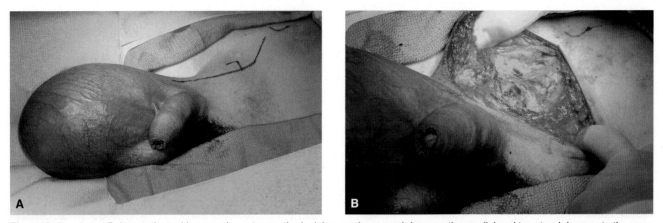

Figure 9–2. *A and B,* In a patient with a very large tumor, the incision can be curved down on the medial end to extend down onto the proximal scrotum.

ered. We do this by passing the plastic Penrose drain around the cord twice and securing it tightly with a clamp (Figure 9–5). This should provide venous and lymphatic control without affecting the arterial inflow. In most cases, however, when the diagnosis is certain, it is preferable to simply ligate and divide the cord completely prior to delivering the testis.

The cord must be mobilized to well inside the internal inguinal ring before it is ligated. This requires applying traction on the cord and sweeping off the surrounding soft tissues. The vas deferens can be separated from the cord and tied separately. The remaining cord structures are then clamped in one or two sections and tied with a double 2-0 silk suture ligature (Figure 9–6). Care must be taken to ensure complete hemostasis before the cord stump is allowed to retract into the ring. To ensure this, it is

wise to leave a long suture on the stump until just before wound closure. Finally, it is important that a large nonabsorbable suture be used on the stump so that the end can be easily identified from inside if the patient subsequently undergoes a retroperitoneal node dissection.

The testis is then delivered up into the inguinal incision from the scrotum. This requires blunt pressure from below and gentle traction on the distal cord (Figure 9–7, *A*). Once the testis is delivered, the gubernacular attachments to the inferior scrotum are divided (see Figure 9–7, *B*). Again, care must be taken to provide excellent hemostasis so that the patient does not develop a large postoperative scrotal hematoma.

If a diagnostic biopsy is planned, the wound should be carefully draped off, the tunica vaginalis

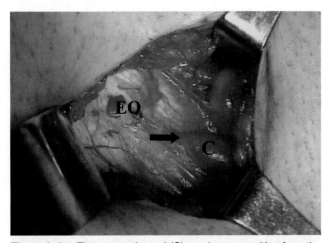

Figure 9–3. The spermatic cord (C) can be seen exiting from the superficial inguinal ring, formed by the edges of the external oblique aponeurosis (EO).

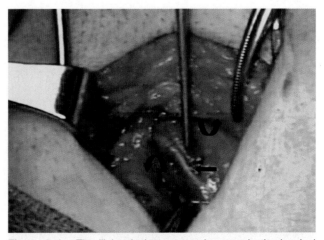

Figure 9–4. The ilioinguinal nerve can be seen in the inguinal canal (*straight arrow*) after the external oblique aponeurosis has been incised and reflected (*curved arrows*).

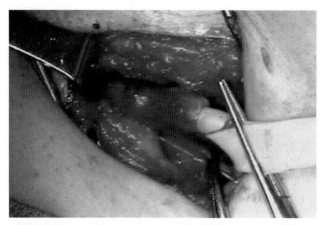

Figure 9–5. A Penrose drain is wrapped around the cord and secured tightly with a clamp to provide venous and lymphatic control.

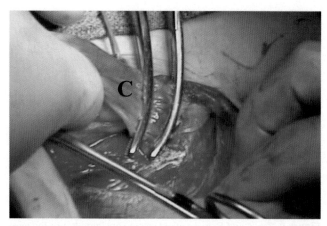

Figure 9–6. The spermatic cord (C) is clamped and then divided and doubly ligated with silk suture.

opened, and the testis examined. Biopsy is performed, and in the case of benign disease, the testis can be returned to the scrotum. We would generally perform a "bottleneck" procedure, everting and suturing the tunica vaginalis together behind the epididymis to avoid potential hydrocele formation in this situation. In most cases, the testis is simply removed, the scrotum is irrigated, and the wound is closed. A single figure-of-eight suture can be placed to obliterate the internal inguinal ring if it seems capacious, to avoid possible hernia. The external oblique fascia is closed with an absorbable suture, taking care to avoid injury to the ilioinguinal nerve. The subcutaneous tissues and skin are approximated in the usual way. This is an ideal situation for using tissue sealants rather than suture material for the skin (although the cost is still somewhat prohibitive).

Patients who have had prior scrotal surgery and who present with a testicular mass may have alterations in lymphatic drainage. Although these patients may have an increased risk of inguinal node metastasis, the initial approach should still be radical inguinal orchiectomy.[7]

A testicular prosthesis may be placed into the scrotum at the time of inguinal orchiectomy if the patient wishes. Such prostheses are available from a number of companies (now often called silicone carving blocks). They should be fixed to the lower dartos fascia with a single suture (to help keep them in a good position) and irrigated with antibiotic prior to closure.[8] The patient must be warned that sometimes these prostheses become encapsulated and very hard over time, which makes them aesthetically less natural in texture. Nevertheless, some patients clearly prefer to have a prosthesis placed if possible.

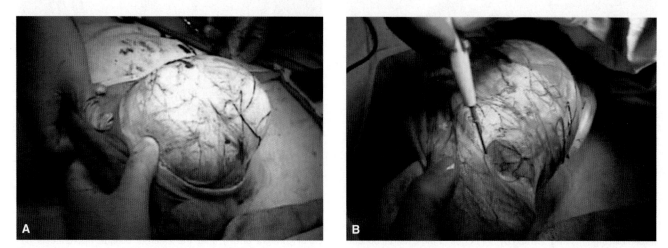

Figure 9–7. *A,* The mass is delivered into the inguinal incision from the scrotum. *B,* The gubernacular attachments are divided.

MANAGEMENT OF SCROTAL CONTAMINATION

The possibility of testicular cancer must be entertained before performing any scrotal surgery on a man between 17 and 45 years of age. However, diagnostic errors do occur. It was previously thought that scrotal surgery markedly increased the risk of local recurrence and inguinal node metastasis.[9] However, more recent evidence suggests that the local recurrence rate ranges from 0 to 6.4%.[10,11] A meta-analysis of 1,182 total cases, 206 with scrotal violation, showed that the risk of local recurrence increased from 0.4 to 2.9% but that it was a significant risk only when there was gross tumor spill.[12] The authors could not demonstrate a clear advantage of any adjuvant treatment regimen in this situation.

The management of scrotal violation requires several steps, as follows:

1. When the cancer is recognized, the surgeon should immediately drape off the testis (placement in a sterile glove is an easy way to do this) and ligate and divide the cord as high as possible in the scrotum, preferably at the external inguinal ring. A second inguinal incision is not required as the contamination has already occurred.

2. If the pathology and staging show stage I pure seminoma, the patient should receive prophylactic retroperitoneal radiation with an extended field to cover the hemiscrotum. This does increase the risk of azospermia, so such a patient may consider sperm banking prior to treatment.[13] Alternatively, a formal hemiscrotectomy can be performed.

3. If the pathology shows stage I nonseminoma, the previous scrotal scar should be widely excised at the time of retroperitoneal node dissection, along with the remaining spermatic cord. If a node dissection is not planned, this excision should be performed as a separate procedure. In the case of gross scrotal contamination, a formal hemiscrotectomy should be performed.

4. In advanced disease treated with systemic chemotherapy, no further treatment of the scrotum is necessary.

In all of these cases, the inguinal lymph nodes must be followed carefully by palpation at each visit to the clinic.

COMPLICATIONS

The procedure can usually be done on an outpatient basis, and there are few complications. As mentioned above, the most worrisome complication is a scrotal or retroperitoneal hematoma. This is completely avoidable with careful surgical technique. Wound infection, subcutaneous seroma, or long-term pain are very rare complications of this surgery.[14]

REFERENCES

1. Benson CB. The role of ultrasound in diagnosis and staging of testicular cancer. Semin Urol 1988;6:189–202.

2. Lenz S. Cancer of the testicle diagnosed by ultrasound and the ultrasonic appearance of the contralateral testicle. Scand J Urol Nephrol Suppl 1991;137:135–8.

3. Peterson AC, Bauman JM, Light DE, et al. The prevalence of testicular microlithiasis in an asymptomatic population of men 18 to 35 years old. J Urol 2001;166:2061–4.

4. Hobarth K, Susani M, Szabo N. Incidence of testicular microlithiasis. Urology 1992;40:464–7.

5. Kessaris DN, Mellinger BC. Incidence and implications of testicular microlithiasis detected by scrotal duplex sonography in a select group of infertile men. J Urol 1994;152:1560–1.

6. Bochner BH, Lerner SP, Kawachi M, et al. Postradical orchiectomy hemorrhage: should an alteration in staging strategy for testicular cancer be considered? Urology 1995;46:408–11.

7. Wheeler JS Jr, Babayan RK, Hong WK, Krane RJ. Inguinal node metastases from testicular tumors in patients with prior orchiopexy. J Urol 1983;129(6):1245–7.

8. Incrocci L, Bosch JL, Slob AK. Testicular prostheses: body image and sexual functioning. BJU Int 1999;84(9):1043–5.

9. Markland C, Kedia K, Fraley EE. Inadequate orchiectomy for patients with testicular tumors. JAMA 1973;224:1025–6.

10. Leibovitch I, Baniel J, Foster RS, Donohue JP. The clinical implications of procedural deviations during orchiectomy for nonseminomatous testis cancer. J Urol 1995;154(3):935–9.

11. Aki FT, Bilen CY, Tekin MI, Ozen H. Is scrotal violation per se a risk factor for local relapse and metastases in stage I nonseminomatous testicular cancer? Urology 2000;56(3):459–62.

12. Capelouto CC, Clark PE, Ransil BJ, Loughlin KR. A review of scrotal violation in testicular cancer: is adjuvant local therapy necessary? J Urol 1995;153(3 Pt 2):981–5.

13. Amelar RD, Dubin L, Hotchkiss RS. Restoration of fertility following unilateral orchiectomy and radiation therapy for testicular tumors. J Urol 1971;106:714–8.

14. Moul JW, Robertson JE, George SL, et al. Complications of therapy for testicular cancer. J Urol 1989;142(6):1491–6.

Surgery of the Retroperitoneum

RICHARD S. FOSTER, MD
RICHARD BIHRLE, MD
JOHN P. DONOHUE, MD

With the introduction of cisplatin-based chemotherapy in the 1970s, testicular cancer became one of the most chemosensitive tumors.

Over the years, medical oncologists have refined chemotherapeutic regimens in order to optimize efficacy and minimize toxicity. Currently, metastatic testicular cancer can be treated with chemotherapy in an outpatient setting, and the previously severe toxicities of nausea and vomiting are minimized with the use of modern antiemetics. Hence, over the last two decades, the efficacy of chemotherapy has been maintained and its toxicity has been minimized.

What is sometimes underappreciated in regard to therapy for testicular cancer is that not only is metastatic testicular cancer chemosensitive, it is also "surgery sensitive." The surgical removal of metastatic testicular cancer of the retroperitoneum, pelvis, lungs, mediastinum, or visceral organs is curative from 30 to 75% of the time, depending on the site of metastasis and the clinical situation. When one compares this ability to cure with surgical removal alone in cases of testicular cancer with the ability of surgical removal to cure in cases of other cancers (such as breast cancer, colon cancer, melanoma, etc), one can recognize that testicular cancer is unique from a surgical point of view. Furthermore, testicular cancer is amenable to surgical cure not only in patients at a low stage of disease but also in those patients who have completed chemotherapy or are resistant to chemotherapy. Even in the setting of chemorefractory disease localized to the retroperitoneum, cure at the 30 to 40% level is possible with surgical removal. Finally, even one of the most chemoresistant situa-

tions in testicular cancer, late relapse, is curable in as many as 40 to 50% of cases via surgical resection by expert hands (Figure 10–1). Therefore, testicular cancer is unique from a surgical point of view, and surgical therapy remains very important in the treatment of this disease.

As noted, the morbidity from the administration of systemic chemotherapy for testicular cancer has decreased over the last two decades; as the refinements in surgical technique occurred over the same time period, the morbidity from surgery has similarly decreased. In the 1970s and 1980s, the hospitalization period for patients undergoing retroperitoneal lymph node dissection (RPLND) for

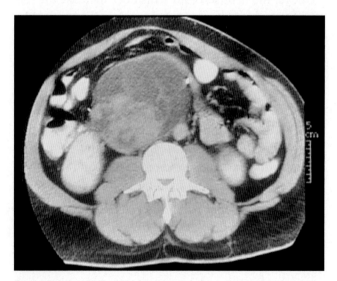

Figure 10–1. Computed tomography shows late relapse of testicular cancer is seen as a large precaval mass. Systemic chemotherapy is largely ineffective in treating this entity, and surgical resection remains the preferred therapy.

low-stage disease was 5 to 7 days; currently, it is 3 to 5 days. Currently, as nerve-sparing technique in conjunction with the complete removal of lymphatic tissue should be mandatory in cases of low-stage disease, loss of emission and ejaculation (such loss being due to the interruption of retroperitoneal sympathetic fibers) should not occur (Figure 10–2). Furthermore, in selected postchemotherapy patients who are candidates for RPLND, nerve sparing is also possible, and emission and ejaculation can be maintained at a level of 70 to 80%. Finally, the perioperative management of pain has improved with the introduction of the intrathecal administration of narcotics and local anesthetics and the routine use of patient-controlled analgesia at the bedside. Therefore, not only has the morbidity of chemotherapy diminished over the last two decades, the morbidity of surgery has decreased while the efficacy of surgical removal of metastatic testicular cancer has been maintained. As noted, this applies to both low-stage and high-stage (postchemotherapy) testicular cancer (see also Chapter 11).

SURGICAL ANATOMY

The lymphatic drainage of the testis is to the retroperitoneum. The region of lymphatics draining the testicles includes that area bordered by the crus of the diaphragm superiorly, the bifurcation of the iliac arteries inferiorly, and the ureters laterally. The lymphatic drainage of the testicles is usually very predictable, and metastatic disease reliably involves the area described above. However, exceptions do occur; when metastatic disease is found in the retroperitoneum of patients with low-stage disease, it is located in an aberrant drainage area approximately 5% of the time.

Formerly, RPLND for low-stage disease included a full bilateral template, which involved the removal of all lymphatic tissue from the crus of the diaphragm to the bifurcation to iliac arteries, from ureter to ureter. This procedure universally resulted in the loss of emission and ejaculation since no effort was made to preserve sympathetic fibers. Because the aorta and the vena cava are in the field of dissection, they must be adequately mobilized in order to completely remove lymphatic tissue that is posterior to these vessels. Therefore, in the course of RPLND, lumbar arteries and veins, which attach the great vessels to the posterior body wall, must be divided. Thus, in full bilateral RPLND, complete mobilization of the great vessels, the renal artery and vein, and the ureters is performed, followed by the removal of lymphatics from the posterior body wall (Figure 10–3). Donohue has called this concept of the mobilization of structures away from the lymphatic tissue and the subsequent removal of tissue from the posterior body wall the "subtraction" concept.

In the 1970s, surgical oncologists recognized that the lymphatic drainage of the testis was unique, depending on the side of the primary. For instance, a right-sided testicular primary drains predominantly to the interaortocaval, precaval, and right paracaval lymphatics whereas a left-sided primary drains primarily to the left para-aortic and preaortic lymphatic areas. Mapping studies performed by experienced surgeons have verified this unilateralness and pre-

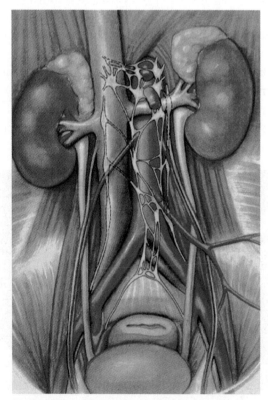

Figure 10–2. The anatomy of retroperitoneal sympathetic fibers in relationship to the great vessels is shown. Right- and left-sided efferent sympathetic fibers coalesce in the preaortic area at the bifurcation. With experience, these fibers can be identified prospectively prior to the removal of lymphatic tissue.

Figure 10–3. This completed full bilateral dissection illustrates the "subtraction" concept. The ureters, aorta, vena cava, and renal arteries are dissected away from lymphatic tissue. This is followed by removal of the lymphatic tissue from the posterior body wall. In this photograph, the aorta and vena cava are retracted laterally, and the anterior spinous ligament is seen posteriorly between these two great vessels. Division of lumbar arteries and veins is necessary to fully mobilize the aorta and the vena cava.

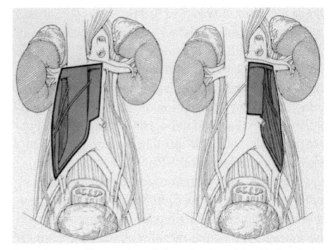

Figure 10–4. The template of dissection for a right-sided testicular primary is shown on the left. The template of dissection for a left-sided primary is shown on the right.

dictability of lymphatic drainage[1]; that is, the lymphatic drainage is unilateral and predictable if minimal to moderate metastatic disease is present in the retroperitoneum, but it becomes relatively unpredictable with higher volumes of metastatic tumor. Therefore, based on these mapping studies and a desire to preserve unilaterally the sympathetic fibers in order to preserve emission and ejaculation, so-called modified templates were introduced. These modified templates limited the scale of the dissection and preserved emission and ejaculation in 60 to 75% of patients,[2,3] thereby decreasing the morbidity of the procedure by decreasing the operative time and by limiting and decreasing the loss of emission and ejaculation (Figure 10–4).

The next step in the evolution of technique also related to anatomy. In the early 1980s, experienced surgeons who were involved in the care of patients with testicular cancer realized that the anatomy of sympathetic fibers in the retroperitoneum was not haphazard and unpredictable but was actually predictable within certain guidelines.[4,5] Surgeons began developing nerve-sparing techniques whereby the prospective dissection of sympathetic efferent fibers was carried out, followed by the mobilization of the great vessels, ureter, and renal vessels from the lymphatic tissue and the subsequent template removal of

lymphatics from the posterior body wall. Certain surgical maneuvers allow the prospective identification and dissection of these efferent sympathetic fibers to be done in a reliable and reproducible fashion. Learning these nerve-sparing techniques is not difficult; hence, these techniques have been widely applied in surgical therapy for low-stage testicular cancer (Figure 10–5).

The "subtraction" concept has thus been refined over the last two decades. Conceptually, RPLND for low-stage disease involves, as a first step, the prospective identification and dissection of efferent

Figure 10–5. A completed right modified nerve-sparing retroperitoneal lymph node dissection as viewed from the left side of the patient. The efferent sympathetic fibers are seen in vessel loops, and there is a retro-aortic left renal vein in this particular patient. The anterior spinous ligament is seen posteriorly after the completed resection of lymphatic tissue.

sympathetic fibers away from the lymphatic tissue. The second step is to mobilize the great vessels from the posterior body wall by dividing the lumbar arteries and/or veins, followed by the dissection of the ureter, the renal artery, and the renal veins from the lymphatic tissue. What then remains is to harvest the lymphatic packages from the posterior body wall since this is the only remaining attachment of the lymphatics after mobilization of the other structures. This concept and technique make RPLND a very reproducible and teachable procedure. It is not an ad hoc tour of the retroperitoneum, involving the removal of abnormal-appearing lymph nodes; rather, it is a systematic reproducible surgical procedure that is highly effective therapeutically.

SELECTION OF PATIENTS FOR PRIMARY RPLND

Primary RPLND is used in patients with nonseminoma who are at clinical stage I or who have a low- to moderate-volume clinical stage II tumor. At Indiana University, patients are staged with the determination of serum α-fetoprotein and beta–human chorionic gonadotropin (hCG) and with computed tomography (CT) of the retroperitoneum and chest. Some have disputed the use of chest CT for clinical stage I disease because of false-positive evaluations of CT scans of the chest.[6] Currently, at Indiana University, CT of the chest remains useful if the interpreter of the scans is experienced in the delineation of indicators of true positive metastatic disease. For instance, minimal abnormalities in the anterior mediastinum are very unlikely to be related to testicular cancer. Testicular cancer metastatic to the chest is usually pulmonary or posterior mediastinal in location. Knowledge of such factors is very useful in the interpretation of chest scans.*

Another important caveat is that a persistently elevated α-fetoprotein or hCG level in a patient who is otherwise at clinical stage I is a powerful indicator of occult systemic metastasis.[7,8] Such a patient is not a candidate for RPLND, and the appropriate treatment is systemic chemotherapy.

Approximately 30% of patients with clinical stage I nonseminoma will have occult metastatic disease, which is usually in the retroperitoneum. The rationale behind nerve-sparing RPLND in this population is that the surgical removal of metastatic disease is curative 50 to 75% of the time, depending on the amount of metastasis. Similarly, since nerve-sparing technique is used, the morbidity of the procedure does not include the loss of emission and ejaculation. The morbidity of the procedure is essentially that of a laparotomy and includes an approximate 1 to 2% chance of a small-bowel obstruction related to postoperative adhesions and an approximate 2 to 5% chance of developing an incisional hernia.[9] In patients with clinical stage II nonseminoma, the main advantage of primary RPLND is that it is therapeutic 50 to 70% of the time (depending upon the volume of metastasis) and that treatment with chemotherapy is thereby avoided. Nerve-sparing techniques can usually be used in clinical stage II patients, and there is therefore no postoperative loss of emission and ejaculation. Furthermore, there is a false-positive rate of 15 to 23% for clinical stage II disease. Primary RPLND will correctly determine whether or not there is metastatic disease; therefore, there is also a staging benefit for these clinical stage II patients.

Another advantage of primary RPLND for clinical stage I and II disease (in addition to its efficacy for germ cell cancerous elements) is that it is also the therapy of choice for teratoma in the retroperitoneum. Teratoma is not eradicated by chemotherapy, and it commonly exists in retroperitoneal nodes admixed with germ cell cancer. The probability of teratoma in the retroperitoneum increases with increasing volumes of tumor in the retroperitoneum and with the presence of teratoma in the orchiectomy specimen.[10] Some investigators use these criteria to predict the probability of retroperitoneal teratoma and thus to select patients with clinical stage I or II disease for RPLND.

---

*Editor's Note: In some centers, such as the University of Southern California, gallium scanning or positron emission tomography (PET) will occasionally be used as a tiebreaker when there is uncertainty regarding mediastinal involvement in a patient with an equivocal CT or magnetic resonance imaging (MRI) scan and negative tumor markers. A gallium or PET scan evaluated as abnormal may occasionally lead to the use of systemic chemotherapy but more often leads to a further biopsy procedure. Clearly, this is an issue of concern as false-positive evaluations may occur with gallium scanning or PET and further studies are urgently required.

SURGICAL TECHNIQUE

Right-Sided Testicular Primary

After administration of the anesthetic, the patient is placed in the supine position, and a Foley catheter is anchored. After preparing the abdomen, a midline incision is made, and a self-retaining Bookwalter retractor is used. The abdomen is routinely inspected and palpated, and if minimal or no metastatic disease is encountered, a right-sided template dissection is performed, with ipsilateral nerve sparing. If a higher volume of metastatic disease to the retroperitoneum is encountered, a full bilateral dissection is necessary since increasing amounts of retroperitoneal metastases are associated with a less predicable unilateral distribution.

If minimal or no retroperitoneal tumor is found, an incision is made in the posterior peritoneum, from the cecum along the root of the small bowel superiorly to the inferior mesenteric vein. For low-stage disease, it is not usually necessary to divide the inferior mesenteric vein. The root of the small bowel and the duodenum are reflected off of the retroperitoneum and held in place with a self-retaining retractor. The retroperitoneum is again inspected. The first step is to mobilize lymphatic tissue from the inferior aspect of the left renal vein as it crosses the aorta. The anterior aspect of the aorta is identified, and the "split" maneuver is performed at the twelve-o'clock position on the aorta from the crossing of the left renal vein to the origin of the inferior mesenteric artery (Figure 10–6). This split maneuver involves the division of lymphatic tissue at the twelve-o'clock position on the aorta and is the initial step in the vascular isolation of the aorta. The lymphatic tissue is then "rolled" medially into the interaortocaval area, and the surgeon inspects the aorta to determine if a lower-pole right renal artery is present. These lower-pole renal arteries usually pass anterior to the vena cava, and prospectively identifying these prior to the division of lymphatic tissue on the anterior aspect of the vena cava will avoid the inadvertent division of a lower-pole renal artery.

The next step is to perform the split of lymphatic tissue on the anterior aspect of the vena cava, from

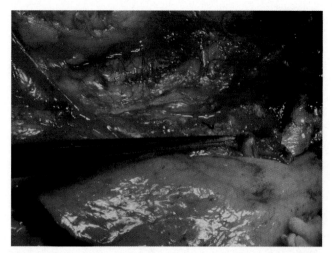

Figure 10–6. The initial steps of a right modified nerve-sparing retroperitoneal lymph node dissection as viewed from the patient's left side. Lymphatic tissue has been rolled from the left renal vein, and the beginning of the "split" maneuver at the anterior aspect of the aorta is seen. The surgical instruments are used to retract the lymphatic tissue medially and laterally after the initiation of the split maneuver.

origin of the left renal vein to the crossing of the right common iliac artery (Figure 10–7). The right gonadal vein is identified and is divided at its origin at the vena cava (Figure 10–8). It is dissected distally to the internal ring, at which point the vas deferens is seen coursing from the pelvis to the internal ring. The vas deferens is divided between ties, and the cord stump is mobilized from the internal ring. The right gonadal vein is thus harvested for pathology. The rationale for removing the right gonadal vein is

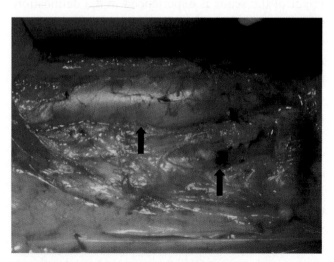

Figure 10–7. The completed initial steps of a right modified nerve-sparing retroperitoneal lymph node dissection as viewed from the patient's left side. The arrows depict the initial split of lymphatic tissue over the anterior aspect of the aorta and the vena cava.

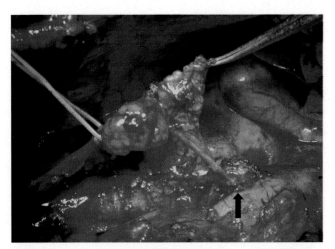

Figure 10–8. In this postchemotherapy dissection, metastatic teratoma along the right gonadal vein is seen. This illustrates the necessity of completely removing the right gonadal vein in a patient who presents with a right-sided testicular primary. The vessel loop and surgical instrument show the gonadal vein with the metastatic teratoma; the arrow indicates the entrance of the right gonadal vein into the vena cava. Although this is a postchemotherapy dissection, the principle of removing the right gonadal vein for a right-sided testicular primary holds for patients with low-stage disease.

that the lymphatics that drain the right testis pass to the retroperitoneum along the right gonadal vein.

Attention is then turned back to the vena cava. Lymphatic tissue is dissected medially and laterally off the vena cava, allowing the surgeon to identify the lumbar veins that attach the vena cava to the posterior body wall (Figure 10–9). These veins are dissected, ligated, and divided, which allows the surgeon to retract the vena cava anteriorly with vein retractors. At this point, the sympathetic chain is identified on the right side. The efferent sympathetic fibers passing from the sympathetic chain to the interaortocaval area and then into the pelvis are prospectively identified and dissected away from lymphatic tissue (Figure 10–10). After this dissection has been performed, attention is then turned back to the aorta. The remaining split of lymphatic tissue along the distal aorta and the right common iliac artery is now performed. Since the sympathetic fibers have previously been mobilized and placed in vessel loops, they are not injured during this distal aortic dissection. Lymphatic tissue is rolled off the aorta into the interaortocaval area, and the right-sided lumbar arteries are prospectively identified, dissected, and divided between ties. Superiorly, the renal artery is identified and is dissected away from lymphatic tissue as it

passes anterior to the crus of the diaphragm (Figure 10–11). Laterally, the right ureter is dissected away from lymphatic tissue, and hence, the "subtraction" of the aorta, the vena cava, the efferent sympathetic fibers, and the ureter has occurred. The surgeon then harvests the right paracaval and interaortocaval packages from the posterior body wall (Figure 10–12). Lumbar arteries and veins are controlled with clips or cautery as they enter the posterior body wall. Clips are used to secure lymphatics, especially at the diaphragmatic hiatus, in order to prevent lymphatic leaks from the cisterna chyli. The retroperitoneum is then closed, using a running absorbable suture. The midline incision is similarly closed, again using a running absorbable suture.

Left-Sided Testicular Primary

After the administration of the anesthetic, a Foley catheter is anchored and the abdomen is prepared. The midline incision is made, and a self-retaining Bookwalter retractor is used. Inspection of the abdomen and retroperitoneum is carried out; if a higher-volume retroperitoneal tumor is identified, a full bilateral dissection is performed, as in the case of right-sided disease. If minimal or no retroperitoneal tumor is identified, an incision is made in the posterior peritoneum lateral to the left colon. The left colon is then mobilized medially, exposing the

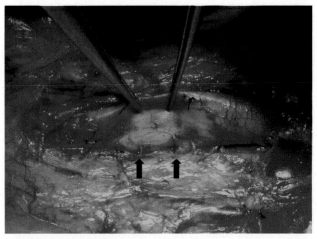

Figure 10–9. In this same dissection, as seen in Figure 10–8, this figure is the dissection from the patient's left side. The vena cava is being retracted anteriorly, and the arrows indicate lumbar veins that pass from the vena cava to the lumbar foramina in the posterior body wall. These lumbar veins must be dissected and divided to allow complete mobilization of the vena cava.

Figure 10–10. As viewed from the patient's left side, the vena cava is retracted anteriorly, thus exposing the right-sided sympathetic chain. Efferent sympathetic fibers are held in vessel loops, and the anterior spinous ligament is seen posteriorly at the completion of the lymphatic dissection.

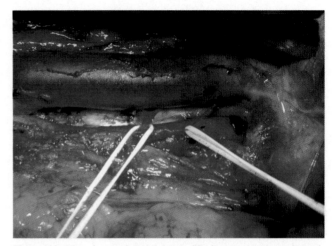

Figure 10–12. A completed right modified nerve-sparing retroperitoneal lymph node dissection as seen from the patient's left side. The lymphatic tissue has been completely removed, as indicated by the lack of lymphatic tissue in the right paracaval, precaval, and interaortocaval areas. The vessel loops hold efferent sympathetic fibers, and the anterior spinous ligament is seen posteriorly between the aorta and the vena cava.

left side of the retroperitoneum. The identification of the efferent sympathetic fibers on the left side is somewhat more difficult than on the right side. With experience, the efferent fibers can be identified as they pass anterior to the left common iliac artery and can be encircled with a vessel loop (Figure 10–13). They can then be dissected proximally and identified as they enter the left-sided sympathetic trunk. Alternatively, the efferent sympathetic fibers can be identified by dissecting on the psoas laterally and mobilizing the lymphatic tissue anteriorly until the

sympathetic chain is identified. The chain is fully exposed, which allows the identification of the efferent fibers. They are then dissected distally as they pass over the left common iliac artery. Since the anatomy of the efferent sympathetic fibers on the left side is more variable than that of those on the right side, it is very important to determine this neuroanatomy early in the procedure in order to avoid

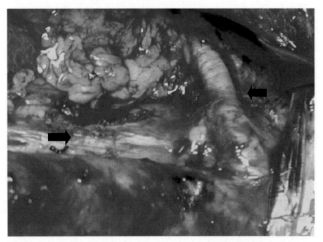

Figure 10–11. Also as viewed from the patient's left side, retractors hold the vena cava laterally and retract the origin of the left renal vein to the vena cava superiorly. The leftward-facing arrow indicates the right renal artery, which has been dissected from lymphatic tissue; the rightward-facing arrow indicates the insertion of the crus of the diaphragm to the posterior body wall at the anterior spinous ligament.

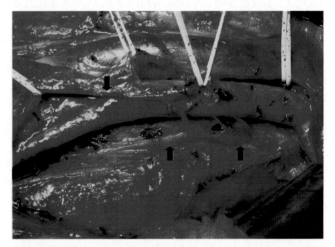

Figure 10–13. In this full bilateral dissection, the surgical anatomy of left-sided efferent sympathetic fibers is shown. The upward-pointing arrows show the left-sided sympathetic chain, and the downward-pointing arrow indicates the left-sided sympathetic efferent fibers as they pass anterior to the left common iliac artery. In this particular patient, right-sided sympathetic fibers were also preserved, and the confluence of right- and left-sided fibers is seen at the bifurcation of the aorta.

injury to the fibers. The preferred technique is to initially identify the fibers as they pass anterior to the left common iliac artery.

After the nerves have been identified, the lymphatic tissue overlying the left renal vein is divided and is rolled inferiorly. The origin of the left gonadal vein is identified and dissected (Figure 10–14). The left gonadal vein is divided from the left renal vein and dissected distally to the internal ring. At this point, the vas deferens is seen passing from the pelvis to the internal ring. The vas deferens is dissected and divided. The cord stump is mobilized from the internal ring, and this specimen, the left gonadal vein, is sent to pathology for permanent section (Figure 10–15).

The next step is to dissect the aorta. The anterior aspect of the aorta is identified as it passes posterior to the left renal vein. The lymphatic tissue on the aorta is split at the twelve-o'clock position, from the crossing of the left renal vein distally to the bifurcation of the left common iliac artery. Lymphatic tissue is dissected laterally away from the aortic wall into the left para-aortic area, with special care taken to identify lower-pole renal arteries to the left kidney (Figure 10–16). Since the sympathetic fibers have been previously identified and placed in vessel loops, injury to them is prevented. The left-sided lumbar arteries are then identified, dissected, and divided between ties (Figure 10–17). This allows the aorta to be retracted anteriorly and allows the sur-

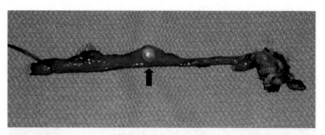

Figure 10–15. The resected left gonadal vein. On the right, the resected stump of the cord is seen; on the left, a silk tie has been placed to divide the left gonadal vein from its origin at the renal vein. The arrow illustrates metastatic tumor along the lymphatics of the left gonadal vein.

geon to perform a complete removal of lymphatic tissue. Next, the left ureter is dissected laterally from left periaortic lymphatic tissue. Finally, the left renal artery is sharply mobilized from lymphatic tissue to expose the crus of the diaphragm on the left (Figure 10–18). At this point, the "subtraction" technique has been performed, and the only remaining attachment of lymphatic tissue is to the posterior body wall. This lymphatic tissue is then harvested off the psoas muscle and anterior spinous ligament, with special care being taken to preserve the sympathetic chain and efferent fibers on the left side. The lumbar arteries and veins that typically enter the posterior

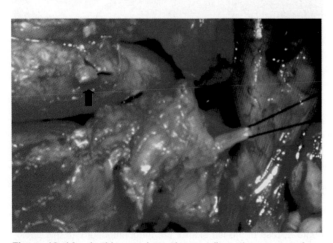

Figure 10–14. In this postchemotherapy dissection as seen from the patient's left side, the left gonadal vein is seen at its origin at the left renal vein. It has been encircled with a silk tie. The arrow indicates the divided inferior mesenteric artery as this was a full bilateral postchemotherapy dissection.

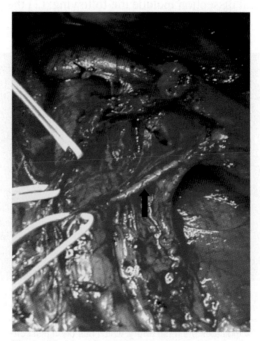

Figure 10–16. Viewed from the pelvis, a left lower-pole renal artery is indicated by the arrow. Vessel loops encircle sympathetic fibers in the initial stages of the dissection.

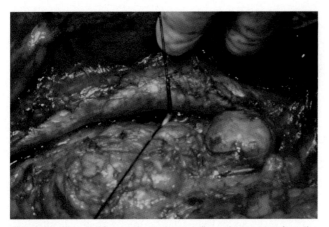

Figure 10–17. In this postchemotherapy dissection as seen from the patient's left side, one of the lumbar arteries on the left side has been dissected and ligated between silk ties. Metastatic tumor is seen on the right side, in the superior aspect of the left para-aortic zone.

body wall medial to the sympathetic chain are controlled with clips, ties, or cautery. The left colon is then placed back in anatomic position, and the abdomen is closed with a running absorbable suture.

Full Bilateral Dissection

If moderate-volume retroperitoneal tumor is identified at laparotomy, a full dissection is appropriate. The salient points regarding the technique of a full bilateral dissection include the following: (1) the pos-

terior peritoneal incision is from the cecum to the inferior mesenteric vein; (2) the inferior mesenteric vein is divided, which allows more complete mobilization of the left mesocolon from the retroperitoneum; and (3) the inferior mesenteric artery is also divided, which allows this complete mobilization of the left mesocolon to be performed (Figure 10–19). This enables the surgeon to have access to the entire retroperitoneum through a single approach. The mobilization of the renal arteries and renal veins is bilateral, and the division of lumbar arteries and veins is similarly bilateral. Nerve sparing may be performed unilaterally or bilaterally and is contingent upon findings at laparotomy (Figure 10–20). If an involved lymph node encompasses an efferent sympathetic fiber, the fiber is removed with the nodal package since the primary goal of the procedure is complete therapeutic removal of involved lymph nodes. Testicular cancer has the ability to implant if spilled intraperitoneally; therefore, the preservation of efferent sympathetic fibers is secondary to the complete and total removal of lymphatic tissue.

POSTOPERATIVE CONSIDERATIONS

Over the last two decades, there has been an evolution in the postoperative care of patients who

Figure 10–18. Anatomy of the left renal vein and left renal artery, as viewed from the patient's pelvis, looking superiorly. The leftward-facing arrow indicates the divided left gonadal vein. The upward-facing arrow indicates the renal artery, which has been dissected away from lymphatic tissue as it passes over the crus of the diaphragm. Inferiorly, the rightward-pointing arrow indicates the divided inferior mesenteric artery as this was a full bilateral dissection in a patient with residual tumor after chemotherapy.

Figure 10–19. When a full bilateral dissection is performed, the inferior mesenteric artery is usually divided in order to provide adequate access to the left side of the retroperitoneum. In this photograph, the arrow indicates the divided inferior mesenteric artery. The left mesocolon is held in the surgical instrument, showing how the mobilization of the left mesocolon exposes the left side of the retroperitoneum. In this patient, the right-sided nerves were preserved (they are held in the vessel loop).

Figure 10–20. A full bilateral retroperitoneal lymph node dissection, performed with bilateral nerve sparing. The "subtraction" concept is well illustrated. The ureters, the sympathetic fibers, the aorta, and the vena cava have all been mobilized from the posterior body wall, and all lymphatic tissue has been resected.

undergo primary RPLND. In the 1970s and early 1980s, nasogastric tubes were routinely used for 3 to 5 days, and hospitalization ranged from 5 to 7 days. Because it is now recognized that postoperative ileus is minimal, nasogastric tubes are not used after primary RPLND, and the patient is given clear liquids on postoperative day one. Techniques of pain control have similarly evolved, and the routine intrathecal administration of narcotics and anesthetics has improved the control of pain. Currently, the average hospitalization period for these patients is 3 to 4 days. The patient is not crossmatched for blood for these procedures because the early control of the great vessels minimizes the likelihood of blood loss. Return to full activity is possible in 3 to 6 weeks, depending on the age of the patient.

Formerly, patients who underwent primary RPLND and were found to be at pathologic stage II were frequently given two courses of postoperative adjuvant chemotherapy.[11,12] The rationale for this in the 1970s and 1980s was that the morbidity of two courses of chemotherapy was significantly less than the morbidity of four courses of chemotherapy, which would be recommended if the patient were observed postoperatively and disease subsequently recurred. Patients given two postoperative adjuvant chemotherapy courses avoided the morbidity of having four courses that is given for documented metastic disease. Hence, the morbidity of chemotherapy was minimized.

The argument for giving postoperative adjuvant chemotherapy to all pathologic stage II patients is not as defensible in current practice.[13] Since the standard of care for the treatment of metastatic tumor is three courses of bleomycin, etoposide, and cisplatin (BEP) and since antiemetics and growth factors have minimized the morbidity of administering three courses of chemotherapy, the argument for routinely administering postoperative adjuvant chemotherapy is not as strong. Many patients have chosen RPLND to avoid the potential side effects of chemotherapy, including that of diminished spermatogenesis in the contralateral testis. Therefore, it is the current recommendation at Indiana University that patients who are found to be at pathologic stage II at RPLND strongly consider postoperative observation alone. In the postoperative period, patients are presented the option of observation or two courses of adjuvant BEP. If observation is chosen and recurrence is found during follow-up, three courses of BEP are given. The only compelling argument for adjuvant chemotherapy is a suspected poor compliance with follow-up.

MODIFICATIONS OF TECHNIQUE FOR POSTCHEMOTHERAPY DISSECTION

The technique for RPLND for postchemotherapy tumor is an extension of the same techniques used for primary RPLND (see also Chapter 11). The "subtraction" concept holds in postchemotherapy disease, and the operation remains essentially a vascular procedure. The great vessels are mobilized from the tumor and posterior body wall by dividing lumbar arteries and veins. The ureters and renal vascular structures are similarly dissected away from the retroperitoneal lymphatics. After chemotherapy, residual tumor is frequently adherent to retroperitoneal structures such as the aorta and the vena cava. Hence, surgeons embarking upon postchemotherapy RPLND should have at their disposal a full array of vascular techniques and capabilities (Figure 10–21). It is interesting that the therapeutic capability of RPLND is retained in cases of disease after chemotherapy. The surgical removal of tumor after chemotherapy is curative in 30 to 80% of cases, depending on the clinical situation and the pathology of the resected tumor.

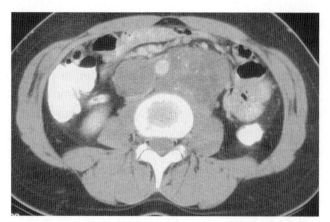

Figure 10–21.   Computed tomography scan illustrates the common circumstance of retroperitoneal postchemotherapy tumor existing adjacent to the aorta and the vena cava. In this patient, the vena cava is compressed posteriorly whereas the aorta is encircled with metastatic tumor. The degree of adherence of tumor to these structures is unpredictable, and surgeons performing these types of dissections should be fully versed in the techniques of vascular control and repair.

DISCUSSION

This chapter has discussed the rationale and technique for primary RPLND. It is well recognized that for patients with low-stage metastatic nonseminomatous testicular cancer, alternative treatments exist. Currently, patients at Indiana University who have clinical stage I nonseminoma are presented with options and may choose between surveillance or nerve-sparing RPLND. Fertility considerations and the avoidance of chemotherapy are the reasons most patients choose RPLND; the avoidance of any therapy, if appropriate, is usually the reason cited for choosing surveillance.

For patients with clinical stage II disease, the presence or absence of teratoma in the orchiectomy specimen and the volume of retroperitoneal tumor are decisive factors that may push a patient toward RPLND or primary chemotherapy. Patients with clinical stage II nonseminoma choose one of those two therapeutic options.

Factors that may cause the treating physician to recommend RPLND more strongly for a patient with clinical stage I disease include the presence of nongerm cell cancerous elements in the orchiectomy specimen, the lack of available health care facilities to perform the surveillance strategy, and a suspicion that the patient will not be compliant with follow-up on a surveillance strategy.

In conclusion, RPLND with nerve-sparing techniques remains a very valuable technique in the management of low-stage testicular cancer. Much as the morbidity of chemotherapy has decreased over the last two decades, so too has the morbidity of surgery decreased. Both surgery and chemotherapy remain very important in the treatment of metastatic testicular cancer.

REFERENCES

1. Donohue J, Zachary J, Maynard B. Distribution of nodal metastases in non-seminomatous testis cancer. J Urol 1982;128:315–20.
2. Richie JP. Modified retroperitoneal lymphadenectomy for patients with clinical stage I testicular cancer. Semin Urol 1988;6(3):216–22
3. Donohue JP, Thornhill JA, Foster RS. Retroperitoneal lymphadenectomy for clinical stage A testis cancer (1965 to 1989): modifications of technique and impact on ejaculation. J Urol 1993;149:237–43.
4. Jewett M, Kong Y, Goldberg J, et al. Retroperitoneal lymphadenectomy for testis tumor with nerve-sparing for ejaculation. J Urol 1988;139:1220–4.
5. Donohue JP, Foster RS, Rowland RG, et al. Nerve-sparing retroperitoneal lymphadenectomy with preservation of ejaculation. J Urol 1990;144:287–91.
6. See WA, Woxie L. Chest staging in testis cancer patients: image modality selection based upon risk assessment as determined by abdominal CT scan results. J Urol 1993;150:874.
7. Saxman SB, Nichols CR, Foster RS, et al. The management of patients with clinical stage I non-seminomatous testicular tumors and persistently elevated serologic markers. J Urol 1996;155:587–9.
8. Davis BE, Herr HW, Fai WR, et al. The management of patients with non-seminomatous germ cell tumor of the testis with serologic disease only after orchiectomy. J Urol 1994;152:111–3.
9. Baniel J, Foster RS, Rowland RG, et al. Complications of primary retroperitoneal lymph node dissection. J Urol 1994;152:424–7.
10. Foster RS, Baniel J, Leibovitch I, et al. Teratoma in the orchiectomy specimen and volume of metastasis are predictors of retroperitoneal teratoma in low stage non-seminomatous testis cancer. J Urol 1996;155:1943.
11. Williams SD, Stalein DM, Einhorn LH, et al. Immediate adjuvant chemotherapy versus observation with treatment at relapse in pathological stage II testicular cancer. N Engl J Med 1987;317:1433–8.
12. Behnia M, Foster R, Einhorn LH, et al. Adjuvant belomycin, etoposide and cisplatin in pathological stage II non-seminomatous testicular cancer: the Indiana University experience. Eur J Cancer 2000;36:472–5.
13. Rabbani F, Sheinfeld J, Farivar-Mohseni H, et al. Low-volume nodal metastases detected at retroperitoneal lymphadenectomy for testicular cancer: pattern and prognostic factors for relapse. J Clin Oncol 2001;12:2020–5.

11

Surgery of Metastatic Disease after Chemotherapy

GIORGIO PIZZOCARO, MD

GENERAL CONSIDERATIONS

The treatment of metastatic nonseminomatous germ cell tumors (NSGCTs) of the testis has become standardized during 25 years of experience with cisplatin-based chemotherapy. As outlined in Chapter 13, three or four courses of bleomycin, etoposide, and cisplatin (BEP) are given respectively to good-risk or to intermediate- and poor-risk patients[1] after orchiectomy. Partial responders with normal or normalized serum tumor markers (α-fetoprotein [AFP], human chorionic gonadotropin [hCG], and lactate dehydrogenase [LDH]) are candidates for elective surgical removal of any residual mass whereas marker-positive partial responders, nonresponders, and patients who relapse after complete remission are candidates for salvage chemotherapy. All patients with technically resectable chemorefractory masses that remain after salvage chemotherapy should potentially undergo salvage surgery, independently of serum tumor marker (STM) status.[2–4]

POSTCHEMOTHERAPY HISTOLOGY

The histology of a residual mass after initial chemotherapy varies substantially in different series. Steyerberg and colleagues[5] reviewed 996 postchemotherapy resections from 19 studies published between 1983 and 1990. Residual cancer was present in an average of 16% of cases, mature teratoma was in 36% of cases, and fibrotic and/or necrotic tissue was in 48%. In resected lung lesions, necrosis was found more often (57% of cases) and teratoma was found less frequently (27% of cases). The same author[6] reviewed six studies published between 1986 and 1993 that included a total of 556 patients undergoing postchemotherapy retroperitoneal lymph node dissection (RPLND); 13% of patients had residual cancer, 42% had mature teratoma, and 45% had fibrosis-necrosis. Steyerberg and colleagues[7] also found a higher frequency of residual necrosis in patients treated with regimens containing etoposide (as I and my colleagues had predicted in 1985).[8] Last, but not least, about 50% of patients undergoing surgery following salvage chemotherapy do have persistent cancer in the resected specimen.[9,10]*

The point is that it is difficult to predict histology of postchemotherapy residual masses. Fossa and colleagues[11] reported that 13 of 37 patients with normal postchemotherapy STMs and normal computed tomography (CT) scans (ie, no lymph nodes > 10 mm) had teratoma or viable tumor in the resected lymph node specimens. Similarly, Toner and colleagues[12] reported residual retroperitoneal tumor in 8 of 39 patients who had normal CT scans (ie, residual masses < 1.5 cm in largest diameter) after chemotherapy. It has also been recently concluded, in an Italian radiologic study,[13] that neither the density nor the character of the residual mass as manifested

---

*Editor's note: In my experience, the tailoring of chemotherapy to address the risk factors defined by the International Consensus Classification, with the use of more intensive regimens for poor-risk metastatic disease, has reduced the proportion of postchemotherapy resection specimens that contain viable tumor from around 20% in the 1980s to approximately 10% or less in the present era.

on CT or by T1- and T2-weighted magnetic resonance imaging (MRI) can reliably predict the ultimate effect of chemotherapy on metastatic NSGCT of the testis.

Donohue and colleagues[14] identified a combination of different variables (including normal postchemotherapy STMs, a 90% or greater decrease in the volume of the retroperitoneal mass, and the absence of teratomatous elements in the orchiectomy specimen) as a means to reliably identify the patients for whom postchemotherapy RPLND could be safely omitted, but these results were not universally confirmed. Steyerberg and colleagues[5] conducted a meta-analysis on 996 postchemotherapy resections from 19 studies in order to quantify predictors of the histology of residual masses. They then collected an international data set comprising 556 patients from six study groups, and logistic regression analysis was used to estimate the probability of necrosis and the ratio of cancer and mature teratoma in the retroperitoneal nodes after first-line cisplatin-based chemotherapy.[6] In this report, patients with elevated STMs at the time of surgery, extragonadal primaries, pure seminoma, or relapse after initial chemotherapy were excluded. The resulting predictors of histology of the residual retroperitoneal masses after initial chemotherapy (teratomatous elements in the primary tumor; prechemotherapy levels of AFP, hCG, and LDH; and the size of the residual mass and the percentage of its shrinkage) were compared to the previously published logistic regression formulas. The results validated the predicted probabilities of necrosis (45%), but residual cancer (13%) could not be reliably predicted or adequately discriminated from mature teratoma (42%).[7] When this validated European prediction model was used to provide predictions for 276 patients treated with chemotherapy before RPLND at Indiana University Medical Center between 1985 and 1999 (with the necessary modifications to fit this patient population), the predicted probabilities for benign tissue were generally too high due to the low prevalence (28%) of fibrosis necrosis in the Indiana population, even if the modified model had good discriminative ability (concordance statistic, 0.79). In particular, residual cancer was present at the Indiana center in 13% of cases, as in the European series, but mature teratoma was found in 59%[15] instead of 42%.[6,7]

INDICATIONS FOR RESECTION OF RESIDUAL MASSES

Reports by Fossa[11] and Toner[12] and their respective colleagues indicate that there is no minimal size of residual mass that identifies complete remission (CR) after chemotherapy for advanced NSGCT of the testis. An acceptable definition of clinical CR is "normal or normalized STM, with no evidence of any residual mass after chemotherapy."[16] In my experience, the relapse rate following chemotherapy alone is 3% for this category of patients.[16] In my opinion, this is the only category of patients for whom postchemotherapy surgery can be omitted.

On the other hand, every patient with an obvious residual mass is a candidate for postchemotherapy surgery, including those with normal STMs after first-line chemotherapy, all patients (regardless of STM titers) following salvage chemotherapy, and those with a resectable relapsed tumor after salvage therapy. The uncertain zone is represented by a small residual mass with the following good prognostic indicators: normal postchemotherapy STMs (normal AFP and hCG before chemotherapy with elevated LDH), minimal size and $\geq$ 90% shrinkage, and no teratoma in the primary tumor. The risk of leaving behind residual tumor foci in these patients is less than 10%, with a 3:1 ratio of residual teratoma to residual viable cancer.[5–7] On the other hand, a major complication rate of 5 to 10% has been reported in some large series of postchemotherapy RPLNDs.[17,18] In particular, these patients had a significantly increased risk for the development of pulmonary complications as a result of bleomycin-induced pulmonary toxicity.[19] The key for decision making in regard to these patients is the possibility of following them up meticulously; if adequate follow-up cannot be guaranteed, surgery is strongly recommended. If patients can be followed-up very carefully, an expectant policy can be applied, with delayed surgery in the case of documented progression of the residual mass and with salvage chemotherapy preceding surgery in the event of STM relapse.[20] It must be remembered that the risk of late relapse after chemotherapy alone for patients with NSGCTs is approximately 3% and that the key for success in treating these patients is the inclusion of surgery.[21]

Particular indications for postchemotherapy surgery include: (1) no change or even enlargement of the tumor mass during chemotherapy, with normalization of STMs[22] and (2) resectable chemo-refractory NSGCT, with elevated STMs.[23] In the first instance, the tumor masses are usually teratomatous; in the second case, surgery may provide salvage in itself, and complete resection is the only possibility for a favorable outcome.[22,23]

EXTENT OF POSTCHEMOTHERAPY SURGERY

The most frequent site of a postchemotherapy residual mass is the retroperitoneum.[5–7] Other sites are lungs, mediastinal and supraclavicular nodes, liver, brain, and bone, in decreasing order.[16] Furthermore, extra-retroperitoneal metastases are more frequent in the salvage setting than after primary chemotherapy.[9,10] (The treatment of brain metastases and extragonadal tumors is not considered here. They are covered in detail in Chapters 17 and 21, respectively.)

Two important questions must be answered in planning postchemotherapy surgery. First, is an extended radical operation required, or is complete resection of the residual mass sufficient? Second, in the case of multiple organ site metastases, in which order should they be resected and in which cases is it appropriate to remove them at a single operation?

Early in his very large experience, Donohue[24] found residual tumor in the para-aortic and right and left suprahilar nodes in patients with a right-sided primary tumor and in the right and left suprahilar, right iliac, and interiliac nodes in patients with left-sided primaries (15 cases). Therefore, due to an obvious risk for the presence of residual tumor in lymph node groups located outside the boundaries of a limited template dissection, a modified retroperitoneal lymphadenectomy was considered an unacceptable compromise for patients with advanced-stage disease after chemotherapy. On the other hand, a significant number of intra- and postoperative complications have been reported in patients undergoing extended postchemotherapy RPLND.[17–19,25] Therefore, several investigators have tried to identify the optimal extent of limited postchemotherapy RPLND. Hendry and colleagues[26] evaluated the outcome of the excision of

para-aortic tumor masses alone (lumpectomy) in 231 patients after primary chemotherapy, electively for 182 patients and for relapse after chemotherapy for 49 patients. The 5-year retroperitoneal relapse rate was 8%, and the variables of prognostic importance for overall survival were (1) complete versus incomplete resection, (2) the histology of the resected specimen, (3) elective versus salvage surgery, and (4) titers of preoperative STMs. The extent of postchemotherapy RPLND was also studied in detail at Memorial Sloan-Kettering Cancer Center in New York.[27–29] Wood and colleagues[27] reported that only 2 of 40 patients with left-sided primary tumors had lymph node metastases beyond the confines of the residual mass in a modified RPLND, and that no tumor was found beyond the boundaries of a modified-template RPLND in the 39 patients with right-sided primaries. Herr[28] reported 62 patients who underwent complete resection of retroperitoneal masses after chemotherapy. A limited-template RPLND was performed if frozen sections of the mass showed necrosis (37 patients) whereas a bilateral extended RPLND was carried out if the frozen sections indicated residual tumor (25 patients). Of the 37 patients whose masses showed necrosis on frozen sections, 4 patients had residual tumor on final histology, which was confined in the resected mass in all four cases. Only 1 of these 37 patients experienced relapse (teratoma) in the retroperitoneum after a median follow-up of 6 years. Rabbani and colleagues[29] reported that only 1 of 39 patients undergoing a routine bilateral dissection had tumor (teratoma) outside the boundaries of the modified template whereas 1 of 2 patients undergoing resection of the residual mass alone (lumpectomy) had two recurrences arising from incomplete resection. In conclusion, extended bilateral RPLND for all postchemotherapy residual retroperitoneal masses is not mandatory, and lumpectomy as the sole procedure cannot be recommended. The key for success seems to be complete removal of the residual mass[26] with a modified-template dissection.[27,28]

Full bilateral-template and operative RPLNDs are shown in Figure 11–1 for the right side and in Figure 11–2 for the left side. The modified bilateral RPLND avoids the contralateral dissection below the level of the origin of the inferior mesenteric artery, in order to try to preserve ejaculation (Figure 11–3). Unilateral

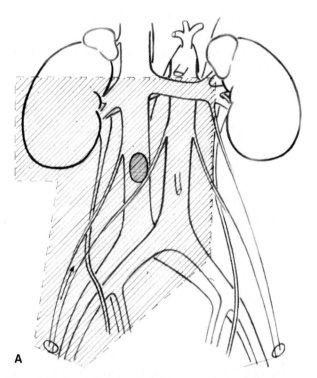

Figure 11–1. *A,* Template for bilateral retroperitoneal lymph node dissection for retroperitoneal metastases from the right testis. *B,* The operative field at the end of dissection; no nerves are spared.

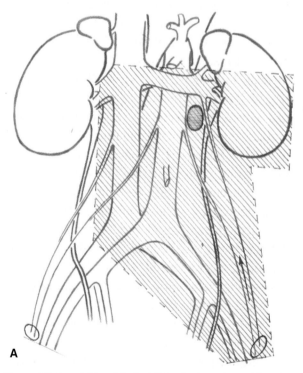

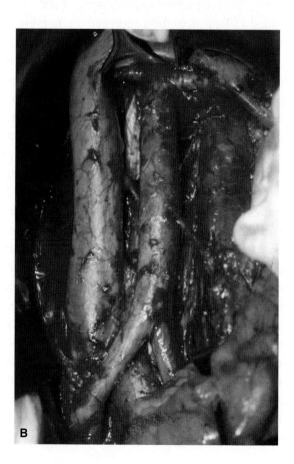

Figure 11–2. *A,* Template for bilateral retroperitoneal lymph node dissection for retroperitoneal metastases from the left testis. *B,* The operative field at the end of dissection; no nerves are spared. The inferior mesenteric artery was not divided.

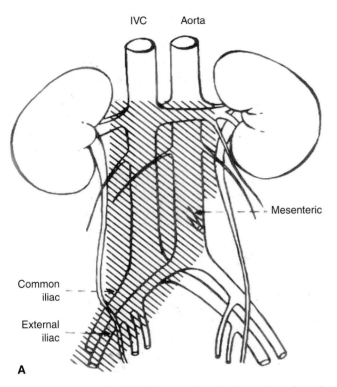

Figure 11–3. *A,* Modified bilateral template for retroperitoneal lymph node dissection for tumors of the right testis; the contralateral dissection below the level of the inferior mesenteric artery was avoided. (IVC = inferior vena cava.) *B,* The operative field at the end of the operation. Contralateral L3 branch of the sympathetic chain has probably been spared.

dissection can be performed when there is no contralateral involvement. As it is the aorta that divides the left-sided from the right-sided para-aortic nodes, the unilateral-template RPLND ends on the contralateral border of aorta above the mesenteric artery and just on the midline below, in order to preserve the contralateral sympathetic nerves (Figure 11–4).

Nerve-sparing RPLND can also be performed after chemotherapy. During the removal of a huge left preaortic mass, both superior hypogastric nerves are identified at the crossing of the common iliac arteries; the left one is cut, the right one is preserved, and the inferior mesenteric artery is divided (Figure 11–5, *A* and *B*). The operative field at the end of the operation illustrates a complete dissection around the great vessels, with complete preservation of the right branches of the hypogastric nerve (see Figure 11–5, *C*). In the case of high bilateral para-aortic metastases, a full radical bilateral dissection can be performed, preserving both L3 branches of the sympathetic chain together with the superior hypogastric plexus (Figure 11–6). In

addition, for a unilateral dissection, it is convenient to preserve L3 where there is only a high residual teratomatous metastasis (Figure 11–7). Major vascular surgery is rarely necessary, but minor vascular surgery is often performed when removing residual precaval or hilar metastases after chemotherapy.[25] Precaval residual masses seem to be very adherent to the inferior vena cava as seen by CT and during surgery (Figure 11–8, *A* and *B*), but they can often be detached with a very careful dissection (see Figure 11–8, *C* and *D*).

Sometimes, a precaval metastasis invades the inferior vena cava and it becomes necessary to resect the vein, with a patch repair, during RPLND (Figure 11–9). Also, the left renal vein may be adherent to residual disease or scar tissue at the point of entry of the spermatic vein; a wedge resection is usually sufficient (Figure 11–10). Last, but not least, a laparoscopic RPLND can also be performed in selected cases of residual teratoma.[30]

In regard to the first question posed above (ie, is an extended radical operation required, or is complete resection of the residual mass sufficient?), the National Cancer Institute (NCI) in Milan reported its published experience of surgery following first-line chemotherapy in 221 consecutive cases treated between 1980 and 1991. The disease-free and overall 5-year survival rates among 201 radically resected patients (surgical margins defined in obvious healthy tissue) were, respectively, 92% and 94% for fibrosis

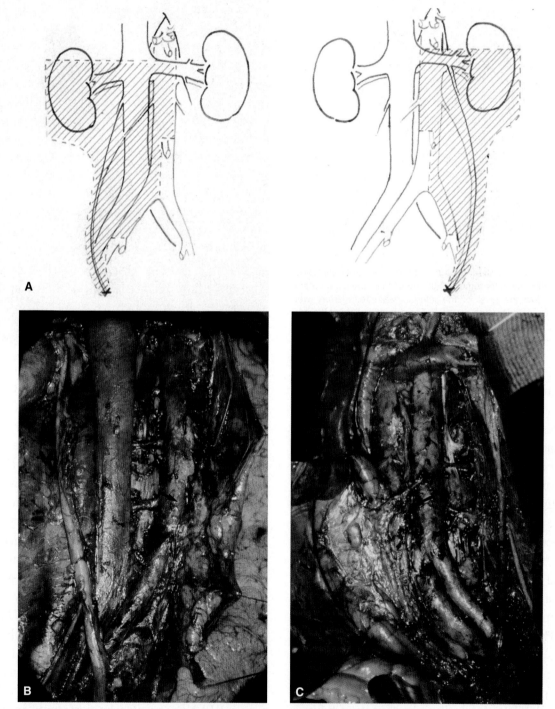

Figure 11–4. *A,* Templates for right and left unilateral retroperitoneal lymph node dissection (RPLND) for stage I nonseminomatous germ cell tumor of the testis. In order to preserve the contralateral sympathetic nerves, there is no dissection on the other side of the aorta. *B,* Operative field of a right unilateral RPLND; the superior left hypogastric nerve (*arrow*) can be seen on the left border of the dissection. *C,* Operative field of a left unilateral RPLND; the right superior hypogastric nerve (*arrow*) is seen at the right margin of the dissection.

and/or necrosis, 85% and 92% for teratoma, and 67% and 72% for residual cancer. The overall 5-year survival rates for the 20 patients who did not have resections with macroscopically healthy margins were

67% for fibrosis-necrosis, 50% for teratoma, and 20% for residual cancer. Furthermore, to get clear margins in all 221 postchemotherapy RPLNDs, it was necessary to perform 8 nephrectomies, 4 inferior vena cava resections, 3 aorta substitutions, and 2 bowel resections (17 patients [8%]).

STRATEGIC PLANNING

Postchemotherapy surgery should be planned strategically in the case of multiple-site residual masses. At the very beginning of the cisplatin era, Merrin[31] proposed a heroic operation: contemporary median laparotomy and sternal split to remove, in a single operation, the abdominal, thoracic, and (eventually) supraclavicular metastases. This very heavy surgery had too many complications and has been practically abandoned.

Usually, RPLND is performed first, with the contemporaneous removal of the testis that harbors the initial tumor if the patient has not previously undergone orchiectomy.[32] Figure 11–11 shows an en bloc specimen of fibrous necrotic para-aortic tissue that was adherent to the left renal vein (see Figure 11–10, *A*), with spermatic vessels, spermatic cord, and the left testis, which contained residual cancer. Hepatic and supraclavicular metastases[33] can also be resected at the same time as the RPLND is performed. Figure 11–12 shows the resection of a fifth-segment liver metastasis with the argon beam; Figure 11–13 shows the intraoperative ultrasonographically guided high intensity focused ultrasound (HIFU) destruction

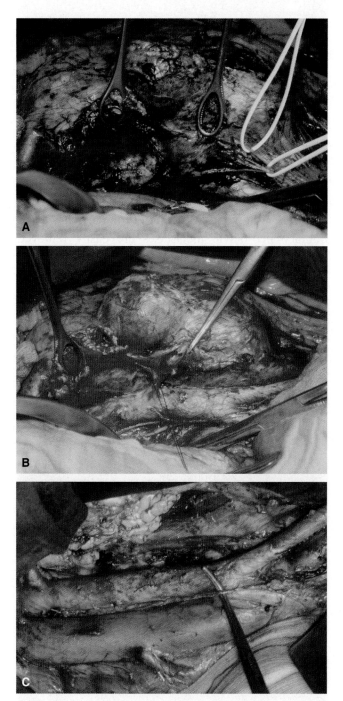

Figure 11–5. Dissection of a large preaortic mass. *A,* Both superior hypogastric nerves are identified at the beginning of the dissection. *B,* The left hypogastric nerve has been cut because it is entering the mass; the right hypogastric nerve is isolated and preserved. The inferior mesenteric artery is about to be divided. *C,* The operative field at the end of the dissection with prospective right-side nerve sparing.

Figure 11–6. For upper bilateral retroperitoneal metastases, it is possible to do a complete bilateral retroperitoneal lymph node dissection with prospective sparing of both L3 nerves and the superior hypogastric plexus.

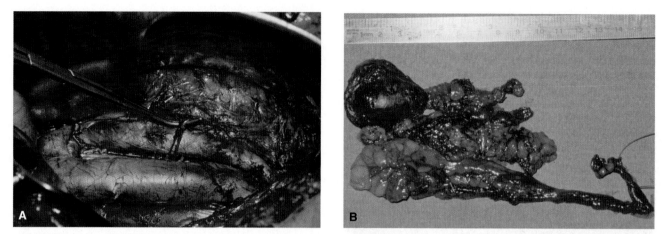

Figure 11–7. *A,* Prospective nerve sparing of L3 can be performed during a unilateral retroperitoneal lymph node dissection for a solitary upper residual metastasis. *B,* The resected residual metastasis.

of a small deep lesion. The special needle is also shown in the closed and open position. Figure 11–14 shows large left supraclavicular metastases, the operative field following supraclavicular node dissection, the teratomatous specimen, and the supraclavicular incision, along with the position of the patient's neck. Solitary ileo-pelvic metastases are easily removed with an extraperitoneal iliac incision (Figure 11–15).

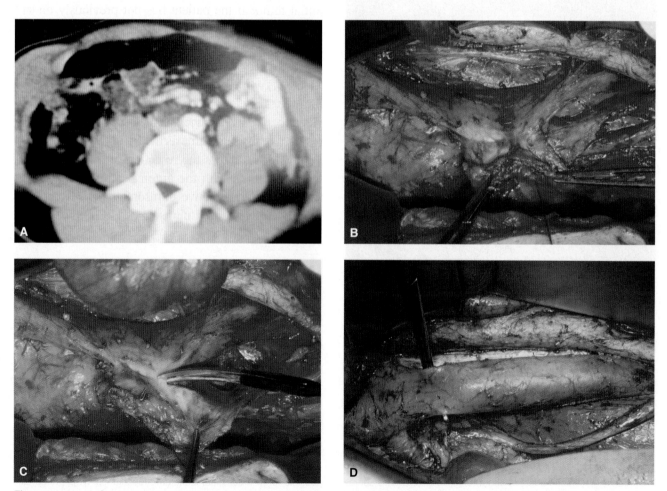

Figure 11–8. *A,* Computed tomography scan shows residual tumor compressing the inferior vena cava (IVC). *B* and *C,* The tumor appears to be extensively attached to the IVC (*B*); however, it can be dissected carefully (*C*). *D,* The operative field at the end of the dissection.

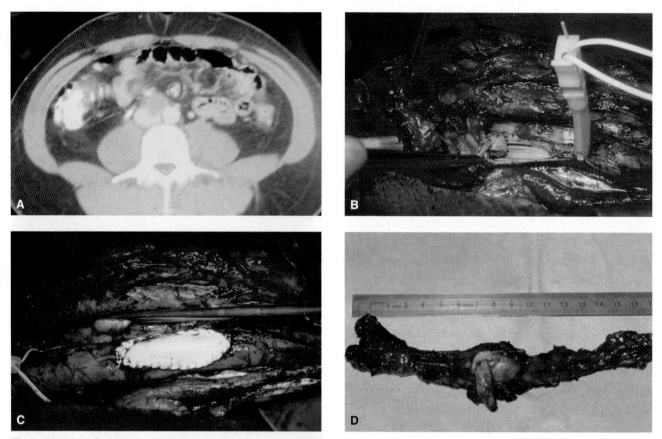

Figure 11–9. *A,* Computed tomography scan shows a small residual tumor entering the inferior vena cava (IVC). *B,* During retroperitoneal lymph node dissection, the IVC is opened, following distal and proximal control, and a partial resection of the vein is performed. *C,* The defect is repaired with a Goretex patch. *D,* The pre-aortocaval and interaortocaval specimen, with the resected IVC and the protruding tumor thrombus.

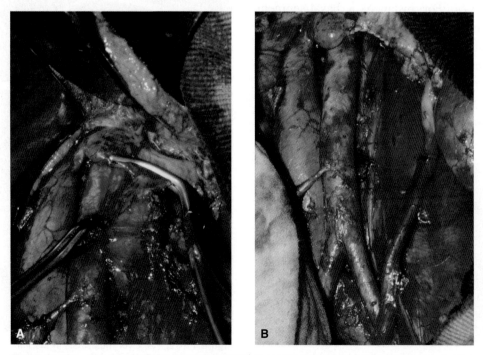

Figure 11–10. The left renal vein is often adherent to scar or residual tumor close to the confluence of the spermatic vein (*A*). In this case, a wedge resection can easily be done (*B*).

Intrathoracic masses are usually removed at a subsequent operation.[34] In particular, intrathoracic access may vary in relation to disease localization. Lower mediastinal metastases, which are posterolateral to the descending aorta, are easily removed through a posterolateral approach, just dividing only the dorsal and intercostal muscles (Figure 11–16, A and B); the sympathetic chain is separated from the teratomatous mass, which is detached from the costovertebral angle and descending aorta (see Figure 11–16, C and D). Anterior mediastinal or bilateral lung metastases are best removed through a median sternal split (Figure 11–17). Large solitary upper-lobe (Figure 11–18) or para-tracheal metastases (Figure 11–19) are best approached through an anterolateral thoracotomy (Figure 11–20). Unilateral lung metastases can be approached through an axillary thoracotomy, separating the anterior serratus muscle and dividing only the intercostal muscles (Figure 11–21). Nevertheless, relatively small retrocrural masses can be removed at laparotomy during a RPLND, vertically dividing the diaphragmatic crus laterally to the aorta[35] (Figure 11–22), and large upper retroperitoneal and lower thoracic metastases can be contemporaneously resected with a thoracoabdominal approach[36] (Figure 11–23). It is clear that different clinical situations may require different surgical strategies. For instance, a basal-segment right pulmonary metastasis and an upper-eighth-segment liver metastasis could be removed through a low posterolateral thoracotomy combined with a limited phrenotomy (Figure 11–24). So far, complex situations will need a multidisciplinary surgical approach, discussed and organized by the team leader. In particular, when dealing with mediastinal and supraclavicular metastases, it is important to remember that para-aortic lymphatics at the level of the renal arteries drain into the posterior medi-

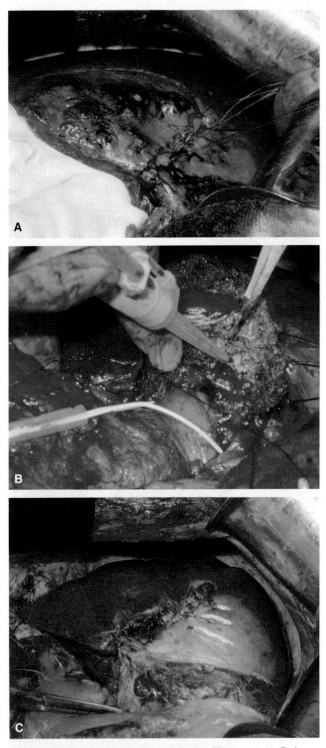

Figure 11–12. *A,* Liver metastasis in the fifth segment. *B,* Argon beam resection. *C,* The liver is sutured, following resection of the metastasis.

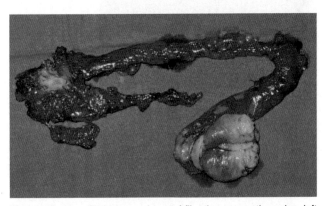

Figure 11–11. En bloc specimen of fibrotic para-aortic nodes, left spermatic vessels and cord, and left testis with residual cancer.

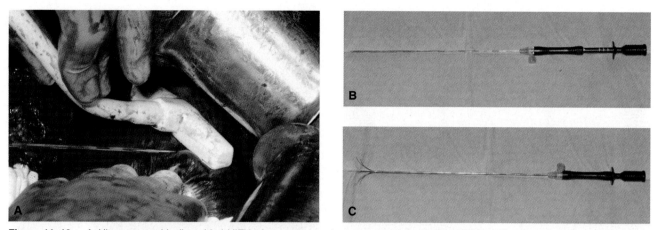

Figure 11–13. *A,* Ultrasonographically guided HIFU of a small deep hepatic metastasis. *B,* The HIFU needle, closed. *C,* The HIFU needle, opened.

astinum, passing behind the diaphragmatic crura on both sides of the aorta (Figure 11–25). They then course laterally and posterior to the descending thoracic aorta to reach the subcarinal nodes and then the anterosuperior mediastinum (Figure 11–26), ending in the left supraclavicular nodes, where the thoracic duct enters the left supraclavicular vein at the confluence with the internal jugular vein (Figure 11–27).

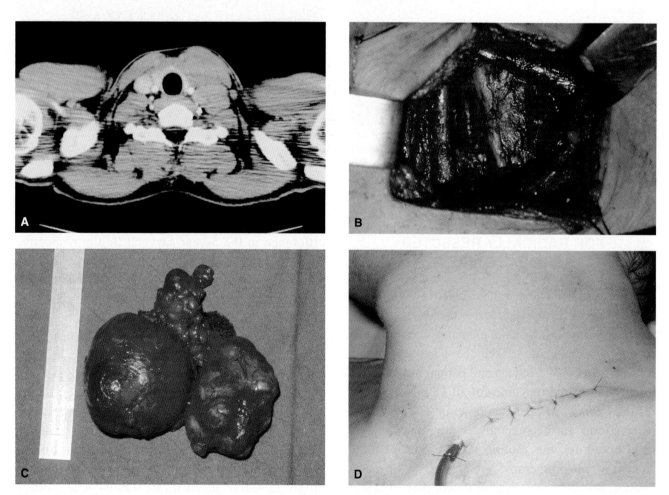

Figure 11–14. *A,* Computed tomography scan of the neck, showing two large left supraclavicular nodes. *B,* The operative field following supraclavicular lymphadenectomy, showing (from left to right) the internal jugular vein, the phrenic nerve, the scalene muscle, and the digastric muscle. *C,* The specimen with two large teratomatous masses. *D,* The supraclavicular incision and the position of the head and neck.

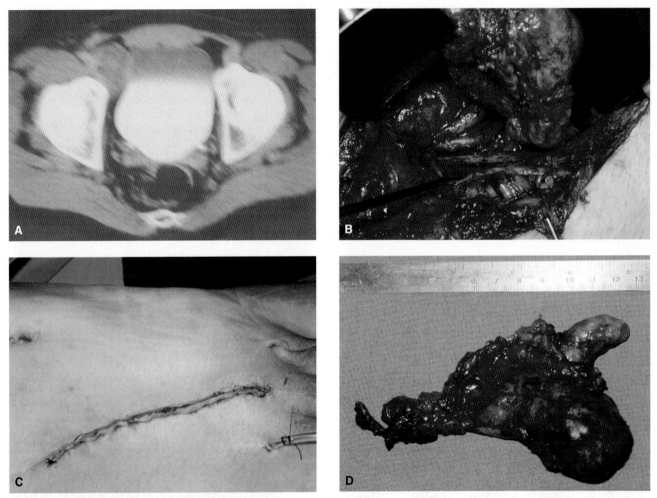

Figure 11–15. *A,* Computed tomography scan showing a residual right ileo-pelvic teratomatous mass. *B,* From bottom to top, the iliac vessels, the obturator nerve, the ureter, and the vesical artery can be seen in this photograph. *C,* The skin suture after resection. *D,* The specimen, with the extension into the obturator fossa.

FURTHER CHEMOTHERAPY FOR RADICALLY RESECTED RESIDUAL CANCER

The presence of viable cancer cells in completely resected residual masses carries the worst prognosis when compared with the presence of mature teratoma or necrosis alone (see also Chapter 16).[26,33] Since the study by Einhorn and colleagues,[37] which reported a dismal outcome for all 18 patients with residual cancer at postchemotherapy surgery who received no further therapy, many investigators have opted for the routine use of postoperative "adjuvant chemotherapy."[2,5,9,11,12,24,26,33] No compelling evidence has existed to confirm whether adjuvant chemotherapy for consolidation is justified in this setting. Thus, my colleagues and I

recently challenged this approach as we found no difference in the 5-year survival in a retrospective study of 49 evaluable patients who were treated (24 patients) or not treated (25 patients) with "adjuvant" chemotherapy following complete resection of residual cancer after first-line (30 patients) or salvage (19 patients) chemotherapy.[38,39] An international retrospective cooperative study was then undertaken to assess the value of postsurgery chemotherapy in patients with disseminated NSGCT and viable residual cancer after first-line chemotherapy.[40] The outcomes of 238 patients were reviewed, and a multivariate analysis of survival was performed for 146 patients. The 5-year progression-free survival rate was 64%, and the 5-year overall survival rate was 72%. Three factors were independently associated with both progres-

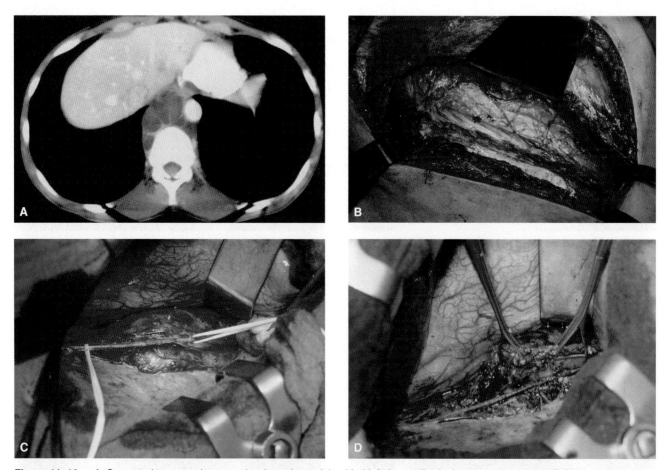

Figure 11–16. *A,* Computed tomography scan showing a large right-sided inferior mediastinal teratomatous mass. *B,* Posterolateral thoracotomy, with division of the latissimus dorsi muscle only. *C,* The sympathetic chain is detached from the retrocrural mass. *D,* Medial dissection of the mass begins with detachment from the costovertebral angle.

sion-free and overall survival: (1) complete resection (*p* < .001), (2) less than 10% viable malignant cells in the residual mass (*p* = .001), and (3) a good prognostic group[1] (*p* = .01). No significant difference was detected in the 5-year overall survival rate in postoperative chemotherapy recipients when compared to those who did not receive chemotherapy. In particular, patients in the favorable risk group had a 100% 5-year overall survival rate, with or without postoperative chemotherapy.

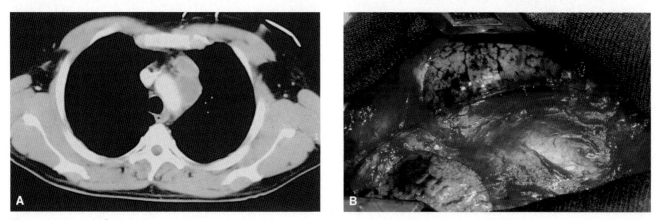

Figure 11–17. *A,* Computed tomography scan showing an anterior mediastinal residual teratoma. *B,* Divarication of the sternal split; the mass is between the two lungs.

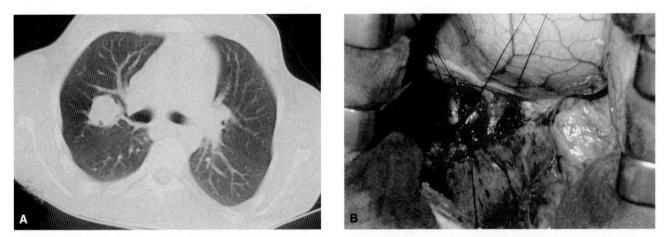

Figure 11–18. *A,* Large metastasis in the right upper lobe of the lung. *B,* Hilar dissection through an anterolateral thoracotomy to perform an upper right lobectomy.

CONCLUSION

Surgery of metastatic disease after chemotherapy is indicated for the majority of patients with a residual mass; normal STMs are mandatory only following first-line chemotherapy whereas every mass should be resected in the salvage setting every time it is technically feasible. Only patients with no evidence of a residual postchemotherapy mass and with normal or normalized markers do not need postchemo-

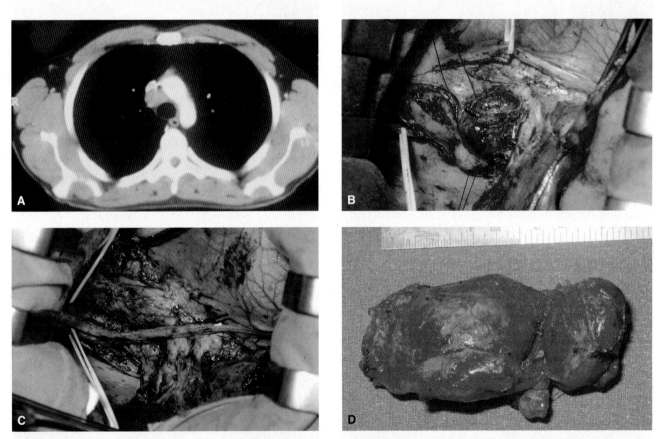

Figure 11–19. *A,* Computed tomography scan showing a right para-tracheal residual tumor (desperation surgery following surgery following third line chemotherapy). *B,* The mass adherent to the superior vena cava, the trachea, and the origin of the right bronchus encircling the azygos vein; the phrenic and vagus nerves have been isolated. *C,* The operative field after removal of the mass. *D,* The resected mass, with the sulcus of the azygos vein.

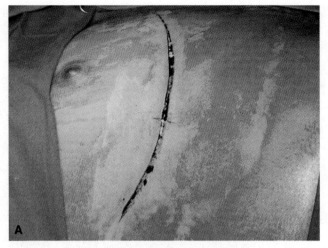

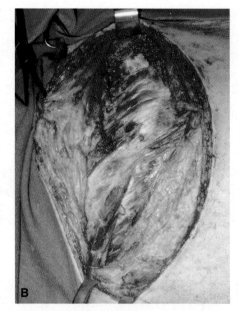

Figure 11–20. *A,* Anterolateral thoracotomy along the submammillary line. *B,* Separation of the serratus anterior and division of the pectoralis major and of the cartilage of the fourth rib to get a wide opening of the fourth intercostal space.

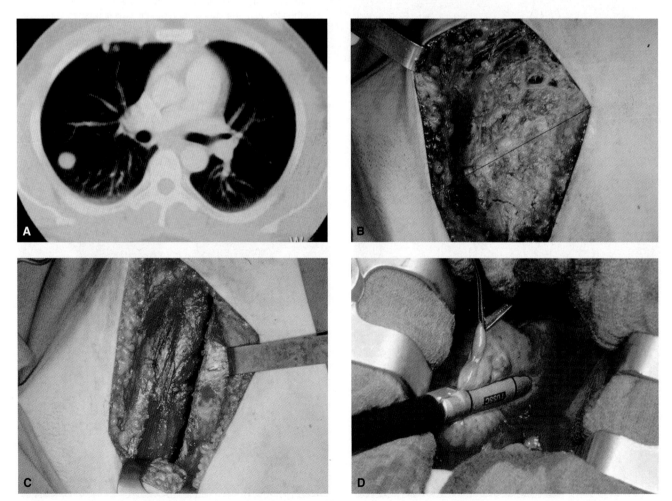

Figure 11–21. *A,* Computed tomography scan showing several lung metastases on the right side only. *B,* Vertical skin incision along the midaxillary line and skin dissection anteriorly to the pectoralis major and posteriorly to the dorsal vessels and nerve. *C,* Following separation of the serratus anterior, the intercostal muscles are divided in the sixth intercostal space. *D,* Stapler resection of lung metastases.

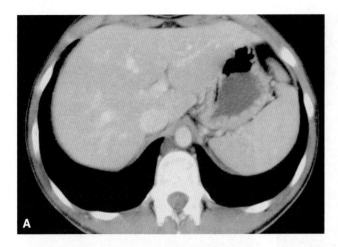

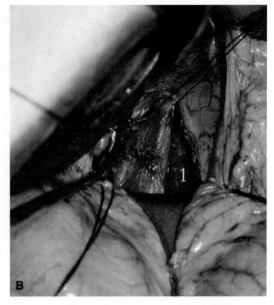

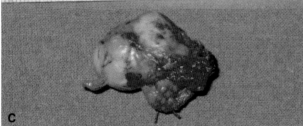

Figure 11–22.   *A,* Computed tomography scan showing a small right retrocrural residual teratoma. *B,* After opening the epiploon retrocavity between the liver and the stomach, the right diaphragmatic crus is opened vertically, and the right para-aortic tissue is dissected from the aorta (left). *C,* The resected small right retrocrural teratoma (the operation is easier on the left side).

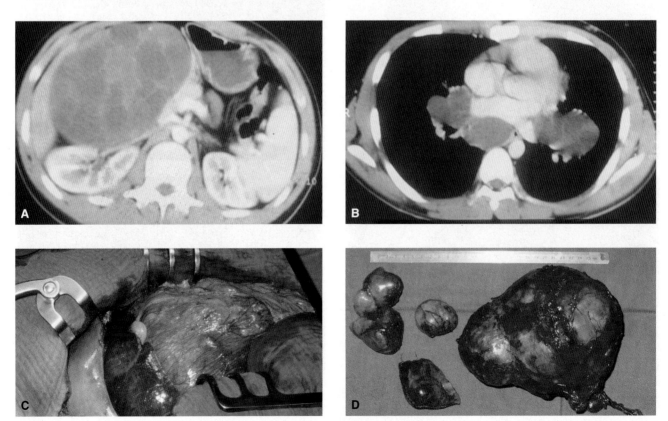

Figure 11–23.   *A,* Computed tomography showing a huge right retroperitoneal teratomatous mass. *B,* Multiple bilateral hilar and mediastinal masses. *C,* Right laparo-phreno-thoracotomy interrupting the costal arcade. From right to left can be seen the omentum covering the intestine and the mass, the liver, and the opened diaphragm. The lung cannot be seen. *D,* The resected retroperitoneal mass, with the spermatic vessel, a lung metastasis, and posterior mediastinal, subcarenal, and parahilar cystic masses of the right side.

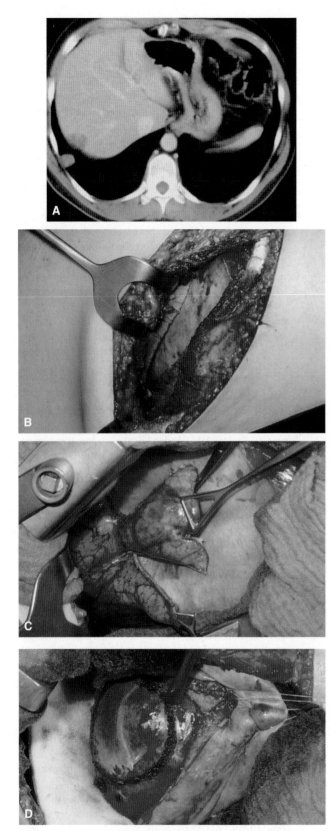

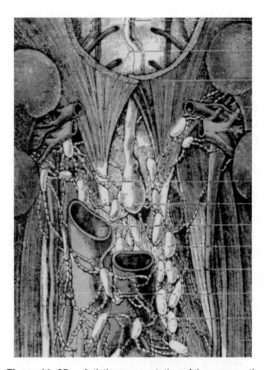

Figure 11–25. Artistic representation of the para-aortic nodes, cisterna chyli, great and renal vessels, and diaphragmatic crura; the right para-aortic nodes encircle the inferior vena cava, and the left para-aortic nodes are on the left side of the aorta. Retroperitoneal lymphatic drainage goes up into the thorax, passing behind the renal vessels and beneath the diaphragmatic crura.

therapy surgery; patients with low-risk parameters (very small residual mass with ≥ 90% shrinkage, no teratoma in the primary tumor, normal postchemotherapy marker levels) can undergo an expectant policy only if a very careful follow-up can be guaranteed. Fibrosis and/or necrosis can be predicted

Figure 11–24. *A,* Computed tomography scan showing adjacent lung and liver solitary metastases. *B,* Posterolateral thoracotomy in the ninth intercostal space. *C,* Stapler resection of the basal lung metastasis. *D,* Opened diaphragm and encircled liver metastasis in the eighth segment.

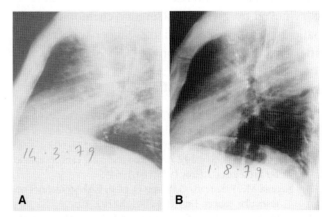

Figure 11–26. Old lymphangiography shows lymphatic drainage from the retroperitoneum to the posterior lower mediastinum, up to the carinal bifurcation, and then further upwards to the anterior mediastinum, before chemotherapy (*A*) and after chemotherapy (*B*).

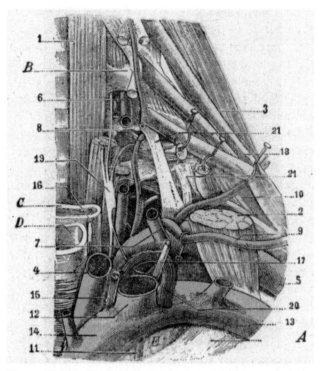

Figure 11–27. The thoracic duct ends in the left supraclavicular vein, very close to the confluence with the internal jugular vein. The testicular lymphatic drainage ends there.

with greater than 80% accuracy, but it is impossible to predict either teratoma or viable cancer. Their proportion, however, is approximately 3:1 after first-line chemotherapy whereas residual cancer is present in approximately 50% of cases in the salvage setting. The key to success is complete resection with obvious healthy or tumor-free margins; the resection of multiple residual masses at different organ sites should be planned rationally. In my experience, no documented advantage in overall survival is achieved by giving postsurgery chemotherapy to patients whose residual viable cancer was resected after first line chemotherapy.

REFERENCES

1. International Germ Cell Cancer Collaborative Group. A prognostic factor–based staging system for metastatic germ cell cancers. J Clin Oncol 1997;15:594–603.
2. Einhorn LH, Donohue JP. Advanced testicular cancer: update for urologists. J Urol 1998;160:1964–9.
3. Laguna MP, Pizzocaro G, Klepp O, et al. EAU guidelines on testicular cancer. Eur Urol 2001;40:102–10.
4. Krege S, Souchon R, Schmoll HJ. Interdisciplinary consensus on diagnosis and treatment of testicular germ cell tumors. Results of an update conference on evidence-based medicine. Eur Urol 2001;40:372–91.
5. Steyerberg EW, Keizer HJ, Stoter G, Habbema JDF. Predictors of residual mass histology following chemotherapy for metastatic non-seminomatous testicular cancer: a quantitative overview of 996 resections. Eur J Cancer 1994;30A(9):1231–9.
6. Steyerberg EW, Keizer HJ, Fossa SD, et al. Prediction of residual retroperitoneal mass histology after chemotherapy for metastatic non-seminomatous germ cell tumor: multivariate analysis of individual patient data from six study groups. J Clin Oncol 1995;13:1177–87.
7. Steyerberg EW, Ger A, Fossa SD, et al. Validity of predictions of residual retroperitoneal mass histology in non-seminomatous testicular cancer. J Clin Oncol 1988;16:269–74.
8. Pizzocaro G, Piva L, Salvioni R, et al. Cisplatin, etoposide, bleomycin first line chemotherapy and early resection of residual tumor for advanced germinal testis cancer. Cancer 1985;56:2411–5.
9. Donohue JP, Fox EP, Williams SD, et al. Persistent cancer in postchemotherapy retroperitoneal lymph-node dissection: outcome analysis. World J Urol 1994;12:190–5.
10. Pizzocaro G, Salvioni R, Piva L, et al. Modified cisplatin, etoposide (or vinblastine) and ifosfamide salvage therapy for male germ-cell tumors: long term results. Ann Oncol 1992;3:211–6.
11. Fossa SD, Ous S, Lien HH, et al. Post-chemotherapy lymph node histology in radiologically normal patients with metastatic non-seminomatous testicular cancer. J Urol 1989;141:557–9.
12. Toner GC, Panicek DM, Heelan RT, et al. Adjunctive surgery after chemotherapy for non seminomatous germ cell tumors: recommendations for patient selection. J Clin Oncol 1990;8:1683–94.
13. Gualdi GF, Petta S, Liberti M, et al. Radiologic staging after surgical, chemical and radiation treatment of non-seminomatous tumors of the testis. Arch Ital Urol Androl 1997;69(1):9–14.
14. Donohue JP, Rowland RG, Kopecky K, et al. Correlation of computed tomographic changes and histology finding in 80 patients having radical retroperitoneal lymph node dissection after chemotherapy for testis cancer. J Urol 1987;137:1176–9.
15. Vergouwe Y, Steyerberg W, Foster RS, et al. Validation of a prediction model and its predictors for the histology of residual masses in non seminomatous testicular cancer. J Urol 2001;165:84–8.
16. Pizzocaro G, Salvioni R, Nicolai N. Surgery in non-seminomatous germ cell tumors of the testis. Advances in the biosciences. Germ cell tumors III. 1994;91:311–7.
17. Gels ME, Nijboer AP, Hoekstra HJ, et al. Complications of the post-chemotherapy resection of retroperitoneal residual tumor mass in patients with non-seminomatous testicular germ cell tumors. Br J Urol 1997;79:263–8.
18. Baniel J, Foster RS, Rowland RG, et al. Complications of post-chemotherapy retroperitoneal lymph-node dissection. J Urol 1995;153:976–80.
19. Donat SM, Levy DA. Bleomycin associated pulmonary toxicity: is perioperative oxygen restriction necessary? J Urol 1998;160:1347–52.
20. Kuczyk M, Machtens S, Stief C, Jonas U. Management of the

post chemotherapy residual mass in patients with advanced stage non-seminomatous germ cell tumors. Int J Cancer 1999;83:852–5.

21. Baniel J, Foster RS, Gonin R, et al. Late relapse of testicular cancer. J Clin Oncol 1995;13:1170–6.

22. Tonkin KS, Rustin GJ, Wignall B, et al. Successful treatment of patients in whom germ cell tumor masses enlarged on chemotherapy while their serum tumor markers decreased. Eur J Cancer Clin Oncol 1989;25:139–43.

23. Albers P, Ganz A, Hannig E, et al. Salvage surgery of chemo refractory germ cell tumors with elevated tumor markers. J Urol 2000;164:381–4.

24. Donohue JP, Roth LM, Zachary JM, et al. Cytoreductive surgery for metastatic testicular cancer: tissue analysis of retroperitoneal masses after chemotherapy. J Urol 1982; 127:1111–4.

25. Christmas TJ, Smith GC, Kooner R. Vascular interventions during post chemotherapy retroperitoneal lymph node dissection for metastatic testis cancer. Eur J Surg Oncol 1998;24:292–7.

26. Hendry WF, A'Hern RP, Hetherington JW, et al. Para-aortic lymphadenectomy after chemotherapy for metastatic non seminomatous germ cell tumors: prognostic value and therapeutic benefit. Br J Cancer 1993;71:208–13.

27. Wood DP Jr, Herr HW, Heller G, et al. Distribution of retroperitoneal metastases after chemotherapy in patients with non seminomatous germ cell tumors. J Urol 1992; 148:1812–6.

28. Herr HW. Does necrosis on frozen section analysis of a mass after chemotherapy jusify limited retroperitoneal resection in patients with advanced testis cancer? Br J Urol 1997;80:653–7.

29. Rabbani F, Goldenberg SL, Gleave ME, et al. Retroperitoneal lymphadenectomy for post chemotherapy residual masses: is a modified dissection and resection of residual mass sifficient? Br J Urol 1998;81:295–300.

30. Janetschek G. Laparoscopic retroperitoneal lymph node dissection. Urol Clin North Am 2001;28(1):107–14.

31. Merrin CE, Takita H. Cancer reductive surgery: report of the simultaneous excision of abdominal and thoracic metastases from wide spread testicular cancer. Cancer 1978;42: 495–501.

32. Leibovitch I, Little JS Jr, Foster RS, et al. Delayed orchiectomy after chemotherapy for metastatic non seminomatous germ cell tumors. J Urol 1996;155:952–4.

33. See WA, Laurenzo JF, Dreicer R, Hoffman HT. Incidence and management of testicular carcinoma metastatic to the neck. J Urol 1996;155:590–2.

34. Gerl A, Clemm C, Schmeller N, et al. Sequential resection of residual abdominal and thoracic masses after chemotherapy for metastatic non seminomatous germ cell tumors. Br J Cancer 1994;70:960–5.

35. Fadel E, Court B, Chapelier AR, et al. One stage approach for retroperitoneal and mediastinal metastatic testicular tumor resection. Ann Thorac Surg 2000;69:1717–21.

36. Skinner DG, Melamud A, Lieskovsky G. Complications of thoraco-abdominal retroperitoneal lymph node dissection. J Urol 1982;127:1107–10.

37. Einhorn L, Williams SD, Mandelbaum I, et al. Surgical resection in disseminated testicular cancer following chemotherapeutic cytoreduction. Cancer 1981;48:904–8.

38. Pizzocaro G, Nicolai N, Milani A, et al. Is further chemotherapy necessary in radically resected residual cancer in non-seminomatous germ cell tumors (NSGCT) of the testis following induction chemotherapy? Proc Am Soc Clin Oncol 1998;17:309a.

39. Pizzocaro G, Nicolai N, Milani A, et al. Adjuvant post operative chemotherapy in radically resected residual cancer in non-seminomatous germ cell tumors of the testis. In: Jones WG, Appleyard I, Harnden P, Joffe JK, editors. Germ cell tumors IV. London: John Libbey & Co. Ltd; 1998. p. 293–7.

40. Fizazi K, Tjulandin S, Salvioni R, et al. Viable malignant cells after primary chemotherapy for disseminated non-seminomatous germ cell tumors: prognostic factors and role of post surgery chemotherapy: results from an international study group. J Clin Oncol 2001;19:2647–57.

12

Active Surveillance for Stage I Nonseminomatous Germ Cell Tumors

GEDSKE DAUGAARD, MD

MIKAEL RØRTH, MD

The stage distribution of nonseminomatous germ cell tumor (NSGCT) has changed over the last two decades, apparently as the result of a shift of patients with low-volume disseminated disease to patients with stage I disease.[1] About one-half of patients with NSGCT have clinical stage I disease at first presentation. The management of such patients has generated considerable interest and some controversy over the last 20 years. Adjuvant abdominal irradiation and retroperitoneal lymph node dissection (RPLND) after orchiectomy have both been commonly practiced in the past, and the latter is still popular in North America (Table 12–1). Both of these management policies do, however, have disadvantages, including a 10 to 15% failure rate in patients with subclinical thoracic disease and also including specific toxicities, such as bone marrow suppression after radiotherapy and failure of ejaculation after surgery.

Management options were increased when Peckham and colleagues[2] published the results of their study of orchiectomy and surveillance in patients with clinical stage I disease. At the same time, a study was conducted in Denmark[3] in which 156 patients were randomly assigned to surveillance versus periaortic-iliac radiation therapy for stage I NSGCT. Radiotherapy completely prevented retroperitoneal relapse, resulting in an overall reduction of relapse rate (30% vs 11%). There were only two tumor deaths, both occurring in patients who had received radiation therapy. These equivalent survival figures and the morbidity associated with radiotherapy resulted in a recommendation of surveillance policy for this group of patients in preference to adjuvant radiotherapy for stage I NSGCT.

SURVEILLANCE STRATEGY

When computed tomography (CT) of the abdomen, reliable tumor markers, and effective chemotherapy became available, many clinicians felt that orchiectomy followed by surveillance and chemotherapy at relapse was a valid management option.

The basis of this surveillance policy is as follows. If CT of the abdomen, radiography of the lungs, and tumor markers show no disease, approximately 10 to 20% of patients will have micrometastases in their lymph nodes at RPLND. Another 10 to 15% of patients will experience relapse in the lung after retroperitoneal lymphadenectomy or external irradiation and thus would not benefit from therapy directed to the retroperitoneal lymph nodes. For the 70 to 80% of patients who in fact have no disease at lymph nodes, further treatment beyond inguinal orchiectomy is not necessary. A second consideration is the case of early detection of relapse by close and accurate follow-up and the high probability of cure for early-relapse patients by modern cisplatin-

Table 12–1. TREATMENT MODALITIES FOR NONSEMINOMATOUS GERM CELL TUMOR
Nerve-sparing retroperitoneal lymph node dissection
Surveillance
Adjuvant chemotherapy (for high-risk patients)

based combination chemotherapy. Finally, there is the desire to avoid unnecessary treatment.

The argument against subjecting all patients with clinical stage I NSGCT to nerve-sparing RPLND is that only 10 to 25% of patients[4] at surgery have disease in their retroperitoneal lymph nodes. Thus, 75 to 90% undergo an invasive procedure for no immediately apparent benefit. Furthermore, nerve-sparing RPLND does not guarantee that a patient will not relapse. Conservation of fertility obviously depends on the skill and experience of the surgeon. There is no doubt that at specialized centers, the impact on the fertility rate is very low; however, this is not a standardized finding. After RPLND, patients still require further follow-up surveillance for relapse.

FOLLOW-UP

A surveillance policy is ideally suited to patients with stage I NSGCT because most tumors produce circulating tumor markers and because the majority of relapses occur within the first 2 years after orchiectomy. However, the fact that the most frequent sites of relapse are the retroperitoneal lymph nodes and that only two-thirds of the patients have elevated serum markers at relapse makes visualization of the retroperitoneal area of key importance in follow-up. Even with recent technical improvements, the false-positive and (especially) false-negative evaluation rates of CT are significant. In most cases in which the results of CT are ambiguous, ultrasonography with biopsy or repeated CT at monthly intervals can resolve the diagnostic problem without jeopardizing the treatment results. The ideal frequency of CT scanning is debatable, and the optimal follow-up scheme has not been defined. Magnetic resonance scanning of the abdomen and pelvis does not yield any additional diagnostic benefit.[5,6]

Because of the lower rate of relapse in the chest, there is some question as to whether patients need chest imaging during surveillance. In the report by Gels and colleagues,[7] 42 of 154 surveillance patients relapsed, but none of these relapses were initially detectable by chest radiography. Furthermore, for the 13 patients with lung metastases, chest radiography resulted in false-negative evaluations in all but 2 cases. Fosså and colleagues[8] described 4 of 102 surveillance patients with lung recurrence; in 3 of these 4 patients, the chest CT scan was abnormal but the chest radiograph was normal. In the study by Sharir and colleagues,[9] chest radiography was not the sole sign of relapse in any of the patients. Thus, chest radiography may be a modality that contributes relatively little, if at all, in the follow-up of patients on surveillance.

For accurate evaluation of the lung and the mediastinum, chest CT is more sensitive than chest radiography.[10] On the other hand, elimination of chest CT did not compromise the outcome in a study by Harvey and colleagues.[11] It should also be noted that pulmonary/pleural nodular structures of < 1 cm may lead to incorrect findings that are interpreted as spread of germ cell cancer.[10,12]

Positron emission tomography (PET) permits functional characterization and visualization of biologic processes and can determine regional metabolic activity, thereby refining the staging of germ cell tumors. With PET, Müller-Mattheis and colleagues[13] found that in 7 patients with stage I NSGCT, 2 patients had an abnormal PET scan and a normal CT scan. Four patients had micrometastases that were not detected by PET. In a study by Lassen and colleagues,[14] PET with 18-fluoro-2-deoxyglucose (FDG-PET) was used for 46 patients with stage I NSGCT, after staging with normal CT and tumor markers. To exclude diagnostic test bias and work-up bias, all patients had routine follow-up with repeated CT and tumor marker evaluation, even in the face of a positive finding on initial PET-FDG scanning. Thirty-six patients have remained disease free with a median follow-up of 36 months (range, 12–64 months). Ten patients (25%) relapsed after a median of 2 months (range, 1–15 months), and of these, 7 had a true-positive finding on initial PET, with an increased uptake of FDG in the retroperitoneum, indicating metastatic disease. Three patients had false-negative findings on PET (two with relapse in the inguinal lymph nodes), and one patient with an initially abnormal finding on PET relapsed after 4 months, with an elevated human chorionic gonadotropin (hCG) level but a negative finding on CT. The PET scan had then become abnormal. There were no false-positive findings on PET. Albers and colleagues[15] reported correct staging by PET results in 34 of 37 patients with stage I or II testicular cancer, compared with 29 of 37 patients by CT.

In conclusion, CT of the abdomen is the most important radiologic investigation in patients on surveillance, so far. The need for chest radiography is debatable, and there is still no consensus on the role of PET in testicular cancer cases.

RISK FACTORS

In 1987, the UK Medical Research Group reported on a retrospective study of risk factors for predicting relapse in patients with clinical stage I nonseminomatous tumors. The group found that invasion of testicular blood vessels, invasion of testicular lymphatics, the presence of embryonal carcinoma cells, and the absence of yolk sac elements were significantly important in this respect.[16] Freedman and colleagues[16] reported the following incidences of these poor-risk factors: lymphatic invasion, 19%; vascular invasion, 50%; absence of yolk sac, 32%; and presence of embryonal carcinoma, 87%.

Subsequently, a prospective study of surveillance in 366 patients supported the use of a prognostic index based on these four factors. The study's results indicated that patients with at least three of the factors had a 46% risk of relapse, compared to 21% for those with two factors and 16% for for those with one factor; there were no relapses in the nine patients who had no risk factors.[17] It is likely that the good prognostic influence of yolk sac elements within the primary may relate to an association with a raised serum concentration of AFP. The long physiologic half-life of this protein in serum leads to a longer delay between orchiectomy and registration for surveillance. In the prospective Medical Research Council (MRC) surveillance study, a period of more than 3 weeks between orchiectomy and normalization of markers was associated with a lower 2-year recurrence rate.[17] A second problem was that many pathologists felt there was difficulty in truly distinguishing venous from lymphatic invasion in the testis.

Many other groups have investigated risk factors in stage I NSGCT and have reached similar conclusions with some variations, but there is overwhelming agreement that vascular invasion in the primary tumor is the most important factor.[18–22]

Of patients with stage I NSGCT, 20 to 25% have vascular invasion in their tumor.[23] However, with the present definition of a high-risk group, it is possible to identify only around half of those destined for relapse.

Patients with no vascular invasion in their primary tumor carry only a 15% chance of relapse. In these low-risk patients, the duration of symptoms before orchiectomy does not influence the probability of relapse.[24]

A histopathologic examination of 149 patients with clinical stage I disease after RPLND found that in 91.5% of the cases, those patients with less than 45% embryonal cell carcinoma and no vascular invasion in their primary tumor had pathologic stage I disease.[25]

In a multivariate analysis by Alexandre and colleagues,[26] only two factors were independently correlated with relapse-free survival: vascular invasion, which was associated with a higher probability of relapse (relative risk [RR] = 3.8; 95% confidence interval [CI], 1.4–10.4), and the presence of mature teratoma, which was associated with a lower probability of relapse (RR = 0.2; 95% CI, 0.1–0.6).

Finally, several studies have assessed the usefulness of cell proliferation markers[27] such as deoxyribonucleic acid (DNA) index, proliferating cell nuclear antigen, and Ki67. These studies have suffered from small size, lack of multivariate testing, and conflicting results. The use of molecular genetic markers for staging and prognosis in testicular cancer is now emerging. Concerning oncogenes,[27] a low incidence of *ras* mutation has been observed, and no clinical correlation is evident. Data for *hst*-1 oncogene, the *myc* family oncogenes, and the *bcl*-2 oncogene in stage I patients are not available. de Riese and colleagues [28] performed a study to determine whether the tumor suppressor gene *p53* could be used as a marker for occult disease in stage I nonseminoma and concluded that *p53* was not useful for this purpose. The role of adhesion molecules (cadherin-catenin complex) has been investigated by Spermon and colleagues,[29] but this also provides no additional information, compared to standard risk markers. However, Fukuda and colleagues[30] found that a high expression of vascular endothelial growth factor (VEGF) in the primary tumor was an indicator of metastatic disease in NSGCT patients.

More work is necessary to determine whether proliferative and molecular markers will aid in the care of patients with clinical stage I nonseminoma. The different risk factors are shown in Table 12–2.

The identification of a subgroup of patients with stage I NSGCT with lymphovascular invasion at a high risk of relapse has led to recent trials of two courses of adjuvant cisplatin, etoposide, and bleomycin, with the aim of reducing recurrence. The early evidence shows that this does appear to be effective and that it may reduce the rate of recurrence from 50% to 5 to 8%.[19,31,32] However, because of the development of chemoresistance, salvage treatment may be more difficult for those patients whose disease recurs. The salvage rates in the current studies are variable, and it is too early to interpret the data on account of the very small numbers. Again, there is the problem of overtreating 50% of patients with chemotherapy, the long-term toxicities of which are not yet fully known. So, sparing morbidity of adjuvant treatment by a surveillance protocol remains a feasible option, even with these patients.

RESULTS OF WAIT-AND-SEE POLICY

The results of 29 studies of wait-and-see policy, (including unpublished Daugaard results)[2,3,7–9,16–18, 26,33–51] which included 3,008 patients, have been noted. In some of the studies, high-risk patients have been excluded. The total number of relapses seen in these studies is 841 (28.1%), and the overall survival rate is 98%. The median time to relapse has been between 3 and 13 months, most often between 4 and 6 months. The median follow-up was between 24 and 132 months.

The characteristics of the relapse were available in 17 studies.[3,7–9,16,26,36–38,40–42,46–50] Relapse in the abdomen was seen in 46% of patients, relapse in the lungs in 24%, and relapse in both lung and abdomen in 6%. Increased markers were found in 68% of patients. Two percent of the patients had a relapse in the inguinal region, 2 patients (0.4%) had scrotal metastases (both had undergone scrotal orchiectomy), and 1 patient relapsed with liver metastasis. At relapse, 81% of patients had stage II disease and 19% had stage III disease (10% of these patients had mediastinal disease). The sites of relapse are shown in Figure 12–1. When relapses were treated with chemotherapy, the rate for no evidence of disease was 98%.

Discrepancies between the studies are often related to the inclusion criteria used. Those centers that exclude patients who have factors believed to be predictive of disease progression from surveillance will have a lower progression rate and a greater number of patients with no evidence of disease at lymphadenectomy, as a result of clinical overstaging. Conversely, centers that exclude only patients with obvious stage II or stage III disease from surveillance will have a higher proportion of patients who subsequently progress and require additional treatment, as a result of understaging.

MAJOR CRITICISMS

There have been three major criticisms of the policy of orchiectomy and surveillance only for patients with clinical stage I NSGCT:

1. Lack of compliance, which may result in inadequate surveillance
2. Occurrence of late relapses
3. High costs

Compliance

Patient compliance becomes the crucial element in surveillance studies and significantly determines the quality and feasibility of this approach. However, noncompliance is a common finding in a proportion

Table 12–2. RISK FACTORS FOR RELAPSE OF PATIENTS WITH CLINICAL STAGE I NONSEMINOMATOUS GERM CELL TUMOR	
Risk Factor	Level of Risk
Vascular invasion	+++
Lymphatic invasion	+++
Presence of embryonal carcinoma	+++
Absence of yolk sac	?
Ras mutation	–
p53	–
VEGF expression	+

VEGF = vascular endothelial growth factor.
+++ = High risk; ? = Not clear; – = No increased risk; + = Increased risk

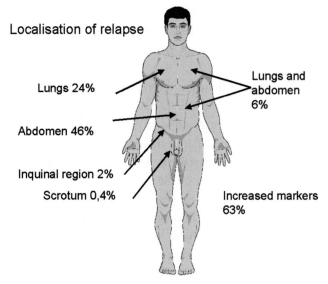

Localisation of relapse

Lungs 24%

Lungs and abdomen 6%

Abdomen 46%

Inquinal region 2%

Scrotum 0,4%

Increased markers 63%

Figure 12–1. Localization of relapse in patients with stage I non-seminomatous germ cell tumors.

of patients with any illness; it would be surprising if all patients with NSGCT did comply as they are generally young men who are often socially mobile. Noncompliance is also seen with patients who are offered, are receiving, or have had chemotherapy and is a reflection of the complex psychosocial situation in which these young men find themselves.

Patients' preference of surveillance versus adjuvant chemotherapy has been investigated in two studies.[52,53] Adjuvant chemotherapy was preferred at projected relapse rates above 50% in the study by Stiggelbout and colleagues.[52] In the study by Cullen and colleagues,[53] a group of patients undergoing surveillance preferred to undergo surveillance again if the relapse rate was less than 30 to 40%; the same group preferred chemotherapy if the relapse rate was around 70%. For patients who had been initially treated with adjuvant chemotherapy, the limiting criterion for starting a surveillance program was a relapse rate of less than 10%; there was a preference for adjuvant chemotherapy if the relapse rate was greater than 25%. A high percentage of patients (33–64%) opted for the physician to decide the treatment.

Late Relapse

The phenomenon of late relapse has led critics to state that RPLND is the primary treatment of choice immediately after orchiectomy. As it removes the major risk of relapse at a site that is most difficult and costly to monitor. We do not agree that RPLND is a superior treatment since late relapses also occur in those who have undergone RPLND as the initial treatment. Baniel and colleagues[54] reported 81 late relapses (at > 2 years), 35 of which occurred in patients who had originally had clinical stage I disease; of these, 2 were followed with surveillance after orchiectomy, 31 were treated with primary RPLND, 1 was treated with radiotherapy, and 1 was treated with chemotherapy. The other 46 late relapses occurred in patients who had presented with stage II or III disease. The report would suggest that there will be late relapses irrespective of the primary mode of treatment. The first evidence of relapse is most commonly the elevation of serum tumor markers, either alone or in combination with an abnormality seen on abdominal CT. However, the tumor markers are often inconsistent between presentation and relapse. Thus, the measurement of tumor markers is important, irrespective of whether or not they were originally abnormal.

Time to relapse is mentioned in eight studies.[7–9,36,47,48,50,55] These studies include 1,169 stage I NSGCT patients on surveillance, with a relapse rate of 28.7%. The majority of the relapses were seen within the first 2 years (95.5%); 1.8% were observed in the third year, 0.6% in the fourth, 0.3% in the fifth, 0.9% in the sixth, and 0.3% in the seventh. There was one relapse (0.3%) after more than 10 years (Figure 12–2). All patients on surveillance are followed for at least 5 years, and 98.5% of the relapses would be diagnosed within this period. Also, in our experience, patients who are re-admitted with relapse after 5 years of follow-up can be cured with chemotherapy. Against this background, it can be concluded that late relapses in patients on surveillance are not a major problem.*

---

*Editor's note: In many centers, particular concern is held for the phenomenon of late relapse among patients with immature teratoma in the primary tumor; in many of the series cited, late relapses occurred among patients with a dominance of this histologic pattern in the primary tumor. At the University of Southern California, we do not believe that it is safe to discharge patients from surveillance within a period of less than 10 years; ideally, patients should be monitored indefinitely, especially if immature teratoma is present in the primary tumor.

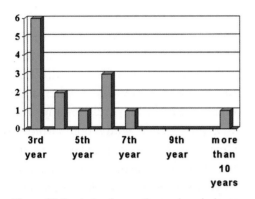

Figure 12–2. Late relapses: the number of relapses after the second year in 1,169 patients with stage I nonseminomatous germ cell tumors.

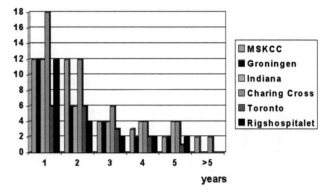

Figure 12–3. The number of clinical controls, including tumor markers, for patients with stage I nonseminomatous germ cell tumors at six centers. (MSKCC = Memorial Sloan-Kettering Cancer Center.)

Cost

Baniel and colleagues[56] found that the choice of nerve-sparing RPLND or surveillance for patients with clinical stage I NSGCT could not be made on the basis of cost as a discriminator. The program for surveillance used in their study included a larger number of control visits and investigations than are seen in most surveillance programs. A cost analysis performed by Francis and colleagues[50] showed that a surveillance policy is certainly not more expensive than the other treatment strategies and may in fact be more cost-effective.

FOLLOW-UP PROGRAMS

Schedules of follow-up programs for patients with stage I NSGCT at six different centers are shown in Figures 12–3 to 12–5. There is no consensus as to how these patients should be followed, assuming a high survival rate and no unnecessary investigations. At our institution, a follow-up program consisting of 12 clinical visits (including marker assessment) for the first year, four assessments during the second year, and two follow-up visits from years 3 to 5; CT of the abdomen every 4 months at the first year and once at 5 years of follow-up; four chest radiographs the first year; and two yearly examinations from years 2 to 5 works without major problems.

CARCINOMA IN SITU

The view in Denmark is that the contralateral testis should be explored at orchiectomy. The contralateral testis harbors carcinoma in situ (CIS) in approximately 5% of cases.[57] This condition will lead to testicular cancer in the years following orchiectomy, and it is conceivable that some "late relapses" are caused by this lesion.

It has not been the policy in the United States to perform a contralateral biopsy at the initial orchiectomy, probably because the development of a secondary testicular tumor is not a survival issue and because of a concern that 96% of patients would undergo unnecessary morbidity from a contralateral surgical procedure. That a secondary testicular tumor is not a survival issue may not always be true. Of patients with bilateral testicular germ cell tumors, 30 to 50% had disseminated tumor at the time of diagnosis of the second tumor, and 10 to 20% of the patients died of their secondary tumor.[58–60] Although these data include data from patients from the precisplatin era, the development of a second testicular cancer is not

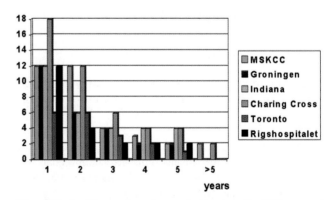

Figure 12–4. The number of computed tomography (CT) scans of the abdomen performed in patients with stage I nonseminomatous germ cell tumors at six centers (numbers from Groningen and Charing Cross include CT scans of the chest). (MSKCC = Memorial Sloan-Kettering Cancer Center.)

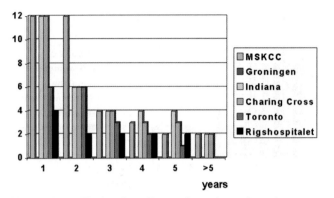

Figure 12–5. The number of lung radiographs made at six centers during follow-up of patients with stage I nonseminomatous germ cell tumors. (MSKCC = Memorial Sloan-Kettering Cancer Center.)

without risk. The policy of surveillance and no biopsy of the contralateral testis will almost inevitably lead to the development of a second cancer in 5% of patients, with total castration as the only possible treatment.[57] The patient will lose his endogenous androgen production, a loss that will have a serious negative impact on his quality of life, even with androgen replacement. Therefore, localized irradiation has been introduced as treatment of CIS in this group of patients.[61] Initially, a dose of 20 Gy in 10 daily fractions was effectively shown to eradicate CIS and thereby prevent subsequent cancer development.[62,63] However, Leydig's cell function is affected by this treatment as evidenced by a rise in luteinizing hormone (LH) level and a decline in the hCG-stimulated testosterone concentration.[62,63] Therefore, the irradiation dose has subsequently been decreased to 18 Gy and 16 Gy, but there is still some effect on hormone production.[64]*

ADVERSE EFFECTS

Effects on Fertility

Most treatment options for NSGCT carry potential deleterious effects on the fertility of the patient.

---

*Editor's note: This area remains somewhat controversial. The 20-year safety of the contralateral irradiation has not been proven, with the possibility of low-dose exposure of pelvic organs, such as the prostate and bladder via internal scatter, remaining a theoretical possibility. The approach of contralateral prophylactic irradiation, while predicated on very sound concepts, will require further long-term follow-up in my view.

However, there is a growing body of evidence to suggest preexisting infertility in these patients. Using predetermined minimum criteria for sperm banking (40 million/mL and 60% motility), Bracken and Smith[65] found that only 4% of patients met minimum requirements after orchiectomy for testis tumor. In a prospective study comparing patients who had testicular tumors, untreated or treated only with orchiectomy, to controls, a significant decrease in sperm density was noted in the patients who had testicular tumors.[66]

Insights into the causes of subfertility in patients with testicular tumors were provided by Berthelsen and Skakkebæk.[67] In 63 patients with stage I NSGCT who underwent biopsy of the contralateral testis, spermatogenic arrest was found in 5 patients, Sertoli's cell only in 8, hyalinized tubules in 5, and CIS in 1 patient. Thus, 19 (30%) of the 63 patients had histologic evidence of sterility. Lange and colleagues[68] have suggested that, based on initial fertility status, testicular tumor patients fall into three categories: (1) patients who are are fertile at diagnosis (40% of patients), (2) patients who are temporarily subfertile, and (3) patients who are sterile (approximately 25%). Carroll and colleagues[69] studied the fertility status of 22 patients with stage I NSGCT who were entered in a surveillance protocol at Memorial Sloan-Kettering Cancer Center. Eleven patients had a normal sperm study. Of the remaining 11 patients with abnormal spermatogenesis, 3 were found to have recovered normal spermatogenesis within 4 to 19 months.

Herr and colleagues[70] investigated paternity in men with stage I testicular tumors on surveillance. They entered 105 patients with clinical stage I NSGCT into a surveillance protocol and followed them up for more than 10 years. Fertility potential was assessed by pregnancy. Of the 105 patients, 41 (39%) had fathered children; these 41 patients included 36 (46%) of 78 patients on active surveillance and 5 (19%) of 27 patients who had completed treatment for relapse. Of 63 couples who attempted a pregnancy on surveillance or were presumed to be capable of impregnation (whether they tried or not), 41 (65%) were successful.

The linkage between infertility and testicular cancer has been reinforced by a major study in the

Danish population. The study examined the Danish population of males born between 1945 and 1980 and their biologic children.[71] The men who developed testicular cancer (identified by the cancer registry) had a lower standardized fertility ratio (0.93) and a lower proportion of sons than did the general population (48.9% vs 51.3%). The same group of investigators also undertook a linkage study of a cohort of men who had their semen examined for infertility. Men with sperm counts of $< 20 \times 10^6$ spermatozoa per milliliter had a standardized incidence ratio of 2.3 for testicular cancer.[72]

Psychological Effects

There are reports of the psychological effects that cancer and its treatment have in young patients.[53,73] Proponents of RPLND and selective adjuvant chemotherapy for high-risk cases postulate that their management protocols minimize follow-up visits, thus avoiding such psychological trauma. We question this; relapse is still possible, and patients treated by either of these techniques require a relatively intense follow-up. Indeed, the follow-up schedule recommended by the MRC group[32] for those patients who have had adjuvant chemotherapy is almost identical with the schedule recommended for surveillance patients. It is unlikely that follow-up for patients who have undergone adjuvant chemotherapy would be any less stressful psychologically than that imposed on patients undergoing surveillance.

Fosså and colleagues[8] interviewed patients who were on a surveillance program, at 1 and 3 years after orchiectomy. About 50% of the relapse-free patients had no psychological problems and were satisfied with the surveillance program whereas 46% reported minor psychological distress and 4% reported major psychological distress. A pilot study investigating the perceptions of patients and doctors in regard to long-term morbidity in patients with testicular cancer and clinical stage I disease has been undertaken.[74] The most significant discrepancy in that study was found in psychological functioning, especially in the case of patients on the surveillance program. The doctors tended to overestimate the patients' emotional problems. The prevalence and degree of psychological morbidity, in general, did not differ between treatment groups.

SURVIVAL

Orchiectomy with surveillance and treatment of relapse produces survival figures that are comparable to those achieved by orchiectomy plus RPLND. As the outcomes in terms of survival appear to be equal across the three management techniques, the adverse effects of these treatments should be compared. RPLND has the disadvantage that patients are hospitalized for 10 to 14 days (less, in US contemporary practice—see Chapter 10), and full recovery usually takes several weeks. Virtually all patients lose ejaculatory function after traditional bilateral suprahilar node dissection.[75] Nerve-sparing node dissection may evade this problem but may be less useful in preventing relapse.[76] As noted previously, some of these patients will relapse and will need to undergo chemotherapy.[54] This group of patients will need to be observed closely for a few years after the operation. (A contrasting view of surgery is summarized in Chapter 10.)

Other patients are treated with orchiectomy and adjuvant chemotherapy. Those patients who are selected for adjuvant chemotherapy because of their high risk of relapse require two to three cycles of combination chemotherapy. Only one-half of these patients can benefit as only this proportion would, in fact, have relapsed (depending on the selection criteria for chemotherapy). Thus, up to one-half of these patients would be unnecessarily exposed to the toxicities of cytotoxic drugs, which is undesirable. The adjuvant cytotoxic treatment usually recommended is two cycles of bleomycin, etoposide, and cisplatin (BEP).[32] Although careful management should preclude most short-term problems, impaired hearing due to auditory toxicity may still reduce the patient's quality of life, and even single doses of bleomycin can precipitate pulmonary fibrosis.

CONCLUSION

The primary goal of any treatment for low-stage testicular cancer is to cure the patient, at the lowest possible risk. Active surveillance is a useful and safe strategy in the management of patients with stage I disease. This policy satisfies the dual requirements of maintaining a high cure rate and minimizing the toxicity of treatment for these patients.

Germ cell tumors of the testis are rare complex neoplasms of young adulthood. Dramatic changes in management have occurred in the last two decades, predominantly as a result of trial collaboration. Patients with these cancers require a comprehensive treatment approach that should routinely encompass all aspects of specialized oncologic care. This should include pathology and radiology review, sperm banking, assessment of the contralateral testis, and effective medical and surgical treatment managed by a limited subspecialist group. Entry into trials, when available, is strongly recommended and is probably advantageous.

In conclusion, we believe that orchiectomy and surveillance with combination chemotherapy at relapse has the fewest overall adverse effects on this cohort of patients and is the optimal treatment.*

REFERENCES

1. Sonneveld DJ, Hoekstra O, Van Der Graaf, et al. The changing distribution of stage in nonseminomatous testicular germ cell tumours from 1977 to 1996. Br J Urol 1999;84:68–74.
2. Peckham MJ, Barrett A, Husband JE, et al. Orchidectomy alone in testicular stage I non-seminomatous germ cell tumours. Lancet 1982;2:678–80.
3. Rørth M, Jacobsen GK, von der Maase H, et al. Surveillance alone versus radiotherapy after orchidectomy for clinical stage I nonseminomatous testicular cancer. J Clin Oncol 1991;9:1543–8.
4. Foster RS, Donohue JP. Surgical treatment of stage a nonseminomatous testis cancer. Semin Oncol 1992;19:166–70.
5. Bellin M, Roy C, Kinkel K, et al. Lymph node metastases: safety and effectiveness of MR imaging with ultrasmall superparamagnetic iron oxide particles—initial clinical experience. Radiology 1998;207:799–808.
6. Hogeboom WR, Hoekstra HJ, Mooyart EL, et al. Magnetic resonance imaging of retroperitoneal lymph node metastases of non-seminomatous germ cell tumors of the testis. Eur J Surg Oncol 1993;207:429–37.

*Editor's note: The issue of active surveillance remains controversial. This chapter (written by experts in the field) presents the very reasonable view that active surveillance, when applied by experts, is an appropriate choice for patients with clinical stage A (or I) testicular germ cell tumors. However, many experts in this field would not agree that this is the optimal treatment, and primary orchiectomy with RPLND in appropriately selected and informed patients remains a very appropriate alternative (see Chapter 10).

7. Gels ME, Hoekstra HJ, Sleijfer DTH, et al. Detection of recurrence in patients with clinical stage I nonseminomatous testicular germ cell tumors and consequences for further follow-up: a single-center 10-year experience. J Clin Oncol 1995;13(5):1188–94.
8. Fosså SD, Jacobsen AB, Aass N, et al. How safe is surveillance in patients with histologically low-risk non-seminomatous testicular cancer in a geographically extended country with limited computerised tomographic resources? Br J Cancer 1994;70:1156–60.
9. Sharir S, Foster RS, Jewett MAS, et al. Optimizing follow-up for early stage nonseminomatous testicular cancer. J Urol 1996;155:327a.
10. White PM, Adamson DJA, Howard GCW, et al. Imaging of the thorax in the management of germ cell testicular tumours. Clin Radiol 1999;54:207–11.
11. Harvey ML, Geldart TR, Duell R, et al. Routine computerized tomographic scans of thorax in surveillance of stage I testicular non-seminomatous germ-cell cancer—a necessary risk? Ann Oncol 2002;13:237–42.
12. See WA, Hoxie L. Chest staging in testis cancer patients: imaging modality selection based upon risk assessment as determined by abdominal computerized tomography scan results. J Urol 1993;150:874–8.
13. Müller-Mattheis V, Reinhardt M, Gerharz CD, et al. Die Posititronenemissionstomographie mit (18F)-2-fluoro-2-deoxy-D-glucose (^{18}FDG-PET) bei der Diagnostik retroperitonealer Lymphknotenmetastasen von Hodentumoren. Urologe 1998;37:609–20.
14. Lassen U, Daugaard G, Eigtued A, et al. Whole body positron emission tomography (PET) with FDG, in patients with Stage I nonseminatomatous germ cell tumors (NSGCT). Eur J Nucl Med. [In press]
15. Albers P, Bender H, Yilmas H, et al. Positron emission tomography in the clinical staging of patients with stage I and II testicular germ cell tumors. Urology 1999;53:808–11.
16. Freedman LS, Parkinson MC, Jones WG, et al. Histopathology in the prediction of relapse in patients with stage I testicular teratoma treated by orchidectomy alone. Lancet 1987;2:294–8.
17. Read G, Stenning SP, Cullem MH, et al. Medical Research Council prospective study of surveillance for stage I testicular teratoma. J Clin Oncol 1992;10:1762–8.
18. Colls BM, Harvey VJ, Skelton L, et al. Results of the surveillance policy of stage I non-seminomatous germ cell testicular tumours. Br J Urol 1992;70:423–8.
19. Pont J, Albrecht W, Postner G, et al. Adjuvant chemotherapy for high-risk clinical stage I nonseminomatous testicular germ cell tumours: long term results of a prospective trial. J Clin Oncol 1996;14:441–8.
20. Horwich A. Current issues in the management of clinical stage I testicular teratoma. Eur J Cancer 1993;29A:933–4.
21. Klepp O, Dahl O, Flodgren P, et al. Risk-adapted treatment of clinical stage I non-seminoma testis cancer. Eur J Cancer 1997;33:1038–44.
22. Sesterhenn IA, Weiss RB, Mostofi F, et al. Prognosis and other clinical correlates of pathologic review in stage I and II testicular carcinoma: a report from the testicular intergroup study. J Clin Oncol 1992;10:69–78.
23. Stephenson RA. Surveillance for clinical stage I nonsemino-

matous testis carcinoma: rationale and results. Urol Int 1991;46:290–3.

24. Napier MP, Rustin GJS. Diagnostic delay and risk of relapse in patients with stage I nonseminomatous germ cell tumour followed on active surveillance. Br J Urol 2000; 86:486–90.

25. Heidenreich A, Sesterhenn IA, Mostofi FK, et al. Prognostic risk factors that identify patients with clinical stage I non-seminomatous germ cell tumors at low risk and high risk for metastasis. Cancer 1998;83:1002–11.

26. Alexandre J, Fizazi K, Mahé C, et al. Stage I non-seminomatous germ-cell tumours of the testis: identification of a subgroup of patients with a very low risk of relapse. Eur J Cancer 2001;37:576–82.

27. Moul JW, Heidenreich A. Prognostic factors in low-stage non-seminomatous testicular cancer. Oncology 1996;10(9): 1359–74.

28. De Riese WTW, Orazi A, Foster RS, et al. The clinical relevance of p53 expression in early stage non-seminomatous germ cell tumour [abstract]. J Urol 1993;149:311A.

29. Spermon JR, de Wilde PC, Hanselaard AGJM, et al. Alpha-catenin expression pattern and DNA image-analysis cytometry have no additional value over primary histology in clinical stage I nonseminomatous testicular cancer. BJU Int 2002;89:278–84.

30. Fukuda S, Shirahama T, Imazono Y, et al. Expression of vascular endothelial growth factor in patients with testicular germ cell tumors as an indicator of metastatic disease. Cancer 1999;85:1323–30.

31. Oliver RTD, Raja MA, Ong J, Gallager CJ. Pilot study to evaluate impact of a policy of adjuvant chemotherapy for high risk stage I malignant teratoma on overall relapse rate of stage I cancer patients. J Urol 1992;148:1453–6.

32. Cullen MH, Stenning SP, Parkinson MC, et al. Short-course adjuvant chemotherapy in high-risk stage I nonseminomatous germ cell tumours of the testis: a Medical Research Council report. J Clin Oncol 1996;14:1106–13.

33. Hoskin P, Dilly S, Easton D, et al. Prognostic factors in stage I nonseminomatous germ-cell testicular tumors managed by orchiectomy and surveillance: implications for adjuvant chemotherapy. J Clin Oncol 1986;4:1031–6.

34. Sturgeon JFG, Jewett MAS, Alison RE, et al. Surveillance after orchidectomy for patients with clinical stage I nonseminomatous testis tumors. J Clin Oncol 1992;10:564–8.

35. Swanson D, Johnson DE. M. D. Anderson experience with surveillance for clinical stage I disease. In: Johnson DE, Logothetis CJ, Von Eschenbach AC, editors. Systemic therapy for genitourinary cancers. Chicago: Year Book Medical Publishers; 1989. p. 304–11.

36. Nicolai N, Pizzocaro G. A surveillance study of clinical stage I nonseminomatous germ cell tumors of the testis: 10-year followup. J Urol 1995;154:1045–9.

37. Raghavan D, Colls B, Levi J, et al. Surveillance for stage I nonseminomatous germ cell tumours of the testis: the optimal protocol has not yet been defined. Br J Urol 1988;61:522–6.

38. Gelderman WAH, Schraffordt Koops H, Sleijfer DTH, et al. Orchidectomy alone in stage I nonseminomatous testicular germ cell tumors. Cancer 1987;59:578–80.

39. Crawford SM, Rustin GJS, Begent RHJ, et al. Safety of sur-

40. Germa Lluch JR, Climent MA, Villavicencio H, et al. Treatment of stage I testicular tumours. Br J Urol 1993;71:473–7.

41. Thompson PI, Nixon J, Harvey VJ. Disease relapse in patients with stage I non-seminomatous germ cell tumor of the testis on active surveillance. J Clin Oncol 1988; 6:1597–603.

42. Johnson DE, Lo RK, von Eschenbach AC, Swanson DA. Surveillance alone for patients with clinical stage I nonseminomatous germ cell tumors of the testis: preliminary results. J Urol 1984;131:491–3.

43. Patel SR, Richardson RL, Kvols L, Zincke H. Observation after orchiectomy in clinical stage I nonseminomatous germ cell tumor of testis. Am J Clin Oncol 1990;13:379–81.

44. Sujka SK, Huben RP. Clinical stage I nonseminomatous germ cell tumors of testis. Urology 1991;38:29–31.

45. Gez E, Wygoda M, Nussbaum N, et al. Surveillance in patients with stage I testicular nonseminomatous germ cell tumors. Cancer Invest 1993;11:10–4.

46. Sogani PC. Evolution of the management of stage I non-seminomatous germ-cell tumor of the testis. Urol Clin 1991;18:561–73.

47. Ondrus D, Hornak M. Orchiectomy alone for clinical stage I nonseminomatous germ cell tumors of the testis (NSGCTT): a minimum follow-up period of 5 years. Tumori 1994;80:362–4.

48. Boyer MJ, Tattersall MH, Findlay MP, et al. Active surveillance after orchiectomy for non-seminomatous testicular germ cell tumors: late relapse may occur. Urology 1997; 50:588–92.

49. Pizzocaro G, Zanoni F, Milani A, et al. Orchiectomy alone in clinical stage I nonseminomatous testis cancer: a critical appraisal. J Clin Oncol 1986;4:35–40.

50. Francis R, Bower M, Brunström L, et al. Surveillance for stage I testicular germ cell tumours: results and cost benefit analysis of management options. Eur J Cancer 2000; 36:1925–32.

51. Roeleveld TA, Horenblas S, Meinhardt W, et al. Surveillance can be standard care for stage I nonseminomatous testicular tumors and even high risk patients. J Urol 2001; 166:2166–70.

52. Stiggelbout AM, Kiebert GM, de Haes JCJM, et al. Surveillance versus adjuvant chemotherapy in stage I non-seminomatous testicular cancer: a decision analysis. Eur J Cancer 1996;32A(13):2267–74.

53. Cullen MH, Billingham LJ, Cook J, Woodroffe CM. Management preferences in stage I non-seminomatous germ cell tumours of the testis: an investigation among patients, controls and oncologists. Br J Cancer 1996;74:1487–91.

54. Baniel J, Foster RS, Gonin R, et al. Late relapse of testicular cancer. J Clin Oncol 1995;13:1170–5.

55. Sogani PC, Perrotti M, Herr HW, et al. Clinical stage I testis cancer: long-term outcome of patients on surveillance. J Urol 1998;159:855–8.

56. Baniel J, Roth BJ, Foster RS, Donohue JP. Cost- and risk-benefit considerations in the management of clinical stage I nonseminomatous testicular tumors. Ann Surg Oncol 1996;3(1):86–93.

57. von der Maase H, Rørth M, Walbom-Jørgensen S, et al. Car-

cinoma in situ of the contralateral testis in patients with testicular germ cell cancer: study of 27 cases in 500 patients. BMJ 1986;293:1398–401.

58. Scheiber K, Ackermann D, Studer UE. Bilateral testicular germ cell tumors: a report of 20 cases. J Urol 1987;138:73–6.

59. Dieckmann KP, Brockmann W, Brosig W, et al: Bilateral testicular germ cell tumors. Report of nine cases and review of the literature. Cancer 1986;57:1254–8.

60. Østerlind A, Berthelsen JG, Abildgaard N, et al. Risk of bilateral testicular germ cell cancer in Denmark 1960–1984. J Natl Cancer Inst 1991;83:1391–5.

61. von der Maase H, Giwercman A, Skakkebæk NE. Radiation treatment of carcinoma-in-situ of testis. Lancet 1986;i: 624–5.

62. von der Maase H, Giwercman A, Møller J, et al: Management of carcinoma in situ of the testis. Int J Androl 1987;10:209–20.

63. Giwercman A, von der Maase H, Berthelsen J, et al: Localized irradiation of testis with carcinoma-in-situ: effects on Leydig cell function and erradication of malignant germ cells in 20 patients. J Clin Endocrinol Metab 1991;73:596–603.

64. Petersen PM, Giwercman A, Daugaard G, et al. Effect of graded testicular doses of radiotherapy in patients treated for carcinoma in situ. J Clin Oncol 2002;20:1537–43.

65. Bracken RB, Smith KD. Is semen cryopreservation helpful in testicular cancer. Urology 1980;15:581–3.

66. Tachil JV, Jewett MAS, Rider WD. The effects of cancer and cancer therapy on male fertility. J Urol 1981;126:141–5.

67. Berthelsen JG, Skakkebæk NE. Gonadal function in men with testicular cancer. Fertil Steril 1983;39:68–75.

68. Lange PH, Narayan P, Fraley EE. Fertility issues following therapy for testicular cancer. Semin Urol 1984;2:264–73.

69. Carroll PR, Morse MJ, Whitmore WF Jr, et al. Fertility status of patients with clinical stage I testis tumors on observation alone protocol. J Urol 1987;138:70–2.

70. Herr HW, Bar-Chama N, O'Sullivan M, Sogani PC. Paternity in men with stage I testis tumors on surveillance. J Clin Oncol 1998;16:733–4.

71. Jacobsen R, Bostofte E, Skakkebæk NE, et al. Offspring sex ratio of subfertile men and men with abnormal sperm characteristics. Hum Reprod 2000;15:2369–70.

72. Jacobsen R, Bostofte E, Engholm G, et al. Risk of testicular cancer in men with abnormal semen characteristics: cohort study. BMJ 2000;301:789–92.

73. Moynihan C. Testicular cancer: the psychosocial problems of patients and their relatives. Cancer Surv 1987;6:477–510.

74. Fosså SD, Moynihan C, Serbouti S. Patients' and doctors' perception of long-term morbidity in patients with testicular cancer clinical stage I. Support Care Cancer 1996;4: 118–28.

75. Skinner DG, Leadbetter WF. The surgical management of testis tumours. J Urol 1971;106:84–93.

76. Droz JP, Oosterom AT. Treatment options in clinical stage I non-seminomatous germ cell tumours of the testis: a wager on the future? A review. Eur J Cancer 1993;29A:1038–44.

13

Management of Nonseminomatous Germ Cell Tumors: Chemotherapy for Patients with a Good Prognosis

GUY C. TONER, MD, FRACP

The development of curative therapy for patients with metastatic germ cell tumors is one of the great successes of the discipline of oncology. It is the result of drug discovery efforts, intelligent implementation of oncologic principles and multidisciplinary care, rational application of clinical trials, and international communication and cooperation. In less than 40 years, oncologists have transformed this disease from a fatal condition into one with well-defined management principles in which cure is the expected outcome.[1-4] Despite these dramatic advances, any complacency is misplaced as there remain important opportunities to improve outcomes and reduce the burden of therapy.

Factors that are important in determining the management of germ cell tumors include the potential for rapid growth, a generally predictable pattern of metastatic spread (Figures 13–1 and 13–2), the finding of teratoma at metastatic sites, and sensitivity to treatment modalities, including surgery, cytotoxic chemotherapy, and radiation therapy. This malignancy was the first that was found to have highly sensitive and specific tumor markers that contribute to all phases of management. The frequent finding of a histologically benign tumor (mature teratoma) at sites of metastatic disease after chemotherapy is an important contributor to management principles and has prompted the study of differentiation as a potential mechanism of treatment success.

Many of the management principles used for these tumors vary considerably from those commonly used for other malignancies. The use of tumor markers to determine, monitor, and modify treatment is more advanced and complex in the management of nonseminomatous germ cell tumor (NSGCT) than in that of other malignancies. The aggressive use of surgery to resect residual masses at sites of metastatic disease is peculiar to NSGCT treatment. Conventional assessment of response to chemotherapy by measurement of changes in tumor size is less important than the pattern of response of the tumor markers. For example, when a metastatic mass increases in size during chemotherapy for most other malignancies, the chemotherapy is deemed to have failed, and second-line or salvage chemotherapy is usually recommended. If a mass in a patient with NSGCT enlarges during chemotherapy but the tumor markers fall to normal levels, the mass almost always is composed of teratoma, chemotherapy is deemed to have been successful, and the appropriate next step is surgical resection.[5]

DEVELOPMENT OF EFFECTIVE CHEMOTHERAPY

The development of effective management strategies for patients with germ cell tumors has been the result of work undertaken by investigators from around the world. Much of the credit belongs to

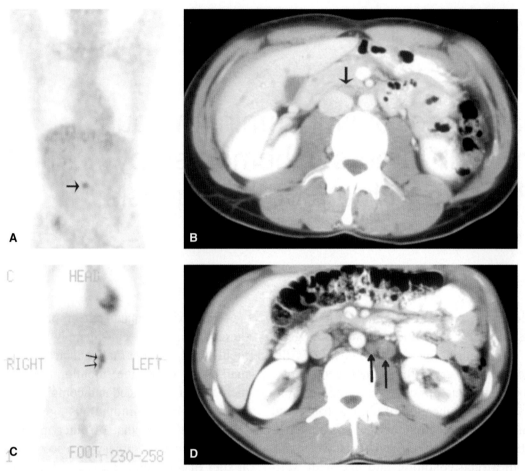

Figure 13–1. Typical site of first metastases. *A* and *B,* Right testicular primary. Fluorodeoxyglucose positron emission tomography (FDG-PET) scan (*A*) of a patient with nonseminomatous germ cell tumor of the right testis demonstrates increased metabolic activity (*arrow*) at the typical location of first lymphatic spread of a right testis tumor, namely, the interaortocaval nodes just below the renal hila. This scan identified early metastatic spread in a patient with elevated tumor markers and a computed tomography (CT) scan reported as normal (*B*). In retrospect, a suspicious abnormality (*arrow*) can be seen on the CT scan. *C* and *D,* Left testicular primary. FDG-PET scan (*C*) and CT scan (*D*) demonstrate the typical site of early spread of left testis lesions in the left para-aortic nodes (*arrows*) just below the renal hila, with subsequent spread in cephalad and caudad directions along the lymph node chain.

Einhorn and colleagues at Indiana University for the initial identification of a highly effective combination chemotherapy regimen and for a series of clinical trials that have been at the forefront of subsequent developments. The regimen of cisplatin, etoposide, and bleomycin reported on by them in 1984 remains the standard of care for most patients with NSGCTs.[6,7] However, the contributions of many other individuals and groups have been important, particularly those from other centers in North America and from centers in Britain, Europe, Scandinavia, Australia, and New Zealand. A sense of competition has existed between many of the major centers, but the results of new therapies have been

openly available and debated freely. This debate has aided the development and prompt dissemination of changing optimal management strategies.

Cytotoxic chemotherapy is the foundation of successful treatment strategies for advanced NSGCTs. Germ cell tumors have a unique sensitivity to cytotoxic chemotherapy, and numerous active agents were identified between 1950 and the early 1970s. Early experience with single-agent chemotherapy showed responses with alkylating agents, antimetabolites, and antitumor antibiotics.[8] However, responses were brief in duration, and there were few long-term survivors. Responses were more frequent in seminoma and in female choriocarcinoma, compared to NSGCT. Attempts to improve results led to the early introduction of combinations of drugs. Early combination therapy produced greater toxicity and a modest increase in the frequency of responses.[9]

Bleomycin was developed in the mid-1960s[10] and was quickly shown to have activity in testicular cancer, with little hematologic toxicity.[11] Samuels and colleagues at M D Anderson Cancer Center combined bleomycin with vinblastine, based on their single-agent activities, nonoverlapping toxicity, and potential synergy.[12,13] A series of studies performed with variations of dose and schedule demonstrated responses in up to 95% of cases, with complete responses in up to 65% of cases.[12,13] Similar results were achieved by other investigators using this combination.[14,15]

In 1965, Rosenberg and colleagues first reported the ability of platinum coordination compounds to inhibit cell growth.[16] Investigation of several of these compounds led to the discovery of the significant cytotoxic activity of cisplatin.[17] Clinical trials with cisplatin rapidly demonstrated an impressive proportion of responses against germ cell tumors.[18–21] Responses were observed in up to 70% of cases with single-agent therapy, suggesting that cisplatin was the most active agent yet identified.

Einhorn and Donohue combined cisplatin with the best existing combination of agents against germ cell tumors of that era, vinblastine and bleomycin.[22] This combination of three drugs was attractive in view of the impressive activity of each agent against germ cell tumors and that their respective toxicities generally did not overlap. The results obtained represented a major breakthrough in the treatment of testicular cancer and a milestone in the development of medical oncology. In the initial cohort of 57 patients, 56% of the patients were alive and disease free at the time of the report.[22] A retrospective analysis of the first 229 patients treated with this regimen (with or without doxorubicin) revealed that 65% of the patients were alive 12 years after treatment and that 83.5% remained relapse free after achieving a complete response.[23] The dramatic effectiveness of the combination of cisplatin, vinblastine, and bleomycin was soon confirmed by other investigators at a number of North American and European

centers.[24–29] Subsequent studies at Indiana University included a small randomized three-arm trial that lowered the dose of vinblastine.[30] Initially, maintenance therapy was used routinely, modeled on therapy for leukemia. However, another prospective trial performed by Einhorn and colleagues failed to show an advantage with maintenance vinblastine, and maintenance therapy was subsequently omitted from treatment regimens at Indiana University.[31]

Investigators at Memorial Sloan-Kettering Cancer Center (MSKCC) also added cisplatin to combination chemotherapy at about the same time that combination was introduced at Indiana University. However, their efforts were less successful, at least

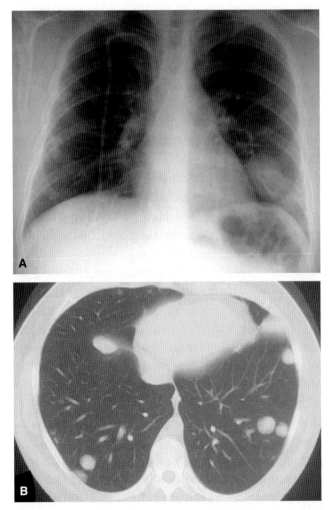

Figure 13–2. Lung metastases. Chest radiograph (*A*) and computed tomography scan (*B*) of the lungs show multiple pulmonary metastases from a testicular nonseminoma. Nonseminomatous tumors spread hematogenously to the lungs, most commonly in a subpleural location. Lung metastases may occur in association with or in the absence of retroperitoneal nodal metastases. Spread to other sites is rare if the lungs and retroperitoneal lymph nodes are not involved.

initially. They had attempted to improve on the activity of vinblastine and bleomycin by the addition of actinomycin D; the resulting combination was called the VAB regimen.[32] Between 1974 and 1976, the VAB-2 regimen was used and represented the introduction of cisplatin for this malignancy at MSKCC.[33] This complicated regimen, including maintenance therapy for 2 to 3 years, did produce improved proportions of complete responses and prolonged survival. The VAB-3 and VAB-4 regimens were used between 1975 and 1978 and added cyclophosphamide in the induction phase of a complex treatment program based on concepts developed in the management of acute leukemia.[34,35] The VAB-5 regimen was a more intensive approach that was evaluated simultaneously with the VAB-4 regimen, but its use was restricted to patients with a poor prognosis.[36] The identification and treatment of a poor-prognosis group with a more intensive regimen were innovative and have been copied in many subsequent studies. Each of the VAB regimens had produced some potential improvements, but the therapy was prolonged, had significant toxicity, and did not achieve the same dose intensity of cisplatin that had been demonstrated to be effective by Einhorn and others. The VAB-6 regimen was used from 1979 until 1982 and used full doses of cisplatin every 3 to 4 weeks, initially with maintenance therapy.[37] Subsequently, this regimen was used without a maintenance component.[38,39] This five-drug regimen appeared to be as effective as other cisplatin-based regimens but was likely to be more toxic, but not directly compared.

The importance of cisplatin dose intensity in treatment was suggested by the lower proportion of long-term survivors in the early VAB programs at MSKCC. However, this issue was more directly addressed by a Southwest Oncology Group (SWOG) trial that compared bleomycin and vinblastine with cisplatin either at a dose of 75 mg/m^2 per cycle or 120 mg/m^2 per cycle.[40] The higher-dose cisplatin regimen resulted in a significant improvement in the proportion of complete response (63% vs 43%, $p = .03$) and in overall survival ($p = .009$). Subsequently, a minimum cisplatin dose of 100 mg/m^2 per cycle has been employed by all of the major trial groups.

Etoposide, whose activity was first reported by Newlands and Bagshawe,[41] has become a key compo-nent of therapy for germ cell tumors. Etoposide initially was shown to be effective in patients who had relapsed after therapy.[41–44] Peckham and colleagues reported its efficacy as part of first-line therapy for germ cell tumors, in place of vinblastine.[45] In this small phase II study, all 18 patients who were treated with bleomycin, etoposide, and cisplatin achieved complete remission and remained disease free.[45]

At Indiana University, etoposide was studied in the salvage setting, either as a single agent or in combination with cisplatin.[44,46] Its activity and favorable toxicity profile subsequently led to its comparison to vinblastine as first-line therapy in a prospective randomized trial.[7] Of the 261 randomized patients, 244 were evaluable for response. Of these, 74% were rendered disease free with chemotherapy including vinblastine (with or without surgery), compared to 83% in the etoposide-containing arm. There was no significant difference in overall survival for the entire group. However, when a prospectively stratified subgroup of patients with more advanced disease was examined, the improved response rate and overall survival with etoposide therapy were statistically significant. The regimen of bleomycin, etoposide, and cisplatin (BEP) described in this trial remains the standard of care 15 years later.

PROGNOSTIC CLASSIFICATION

The expectation of cure for the majority of patients with germ cell tumors (often with therapy that may cause death or major long-term morbidity) mandates a careful assessment of prognosis to allow appropriate tailoring of management to the individual. An understanding of the variation in the use of prognostic factors is also essential to the interpretation of the published literature. Until the mid-1990s, the lack of accepted definitions of good and poor prognoses prevented the accurate comparison of clinical trials that used a variety of criteria to assess prognosis, and delayed the identification of optimal therapy for poor-prognosis patients.

The use of pretreatment characteristics to determine the most appropriate treatment program was proposed early in the development of effective chemotherapy.[36,47,48] Factors reported to have prognostic value included tumor bulk, tumor extent or number of metastatic sites, pretreatment serum tumor marker levels, primary site, visceral organ involvement, pure seminoma versus NSGCT, histologic subtypes, delay in treatment, age, and performance status. A number of reports considering reasonable numbers of patients receiving cisplatin-based chemotherapy and assessing some or all of these factors in multivariate statistical analyses have been published.[49–54] Although most analyses were in general agreement, many trial groups or individual centers developed and used their own prognostic classification systems exclusively. Bajorin and colleagues demonstrated that the use of different criteria to assign prognostic categories has clinically important effects on patient selection for therapy and on the results of treatment trials.[55]

In the early 1990s, an international group of investigators was brought together by the Medical Research Council (MRC) to develop a prognostic classification system for all germ cell tumors through shared data and a consensus process. The resulting classification was published in 1997[56] and has been widely accepted and implemented. This classification should be used in clinical practice to select treatment and in all reports of treatment trials in order to improve interpretation and the comparability of the achieved outcomes (it is described in greater detail in Chapter 8). The definition of a good-prognosis nonseminomatous tumor is shown in Table 13–1. Of the 5,202 cases of nonseminoma considered in the original analysis, 56% were classified in the good-prognosis group. This group achieved an 89% 5-year progression-free survival rate and an overall survival rate of 92%. Given the recognized pattern, over time, of more frequent presentation with earlier-stage disease,[57,58] both the proportion of patients classified in the good-prognosis category and the proportion of survivors are likely to have improved since the data used in this analysis were collected.

RANDOMIZED TRIALS OF THERAPIES FOR GOOD-PROGNOSIS GERM CELL TUMORS

The main aim of clinical trials of therapies for good-prognosis germ cell tumors has been to reduce the toxicity and complexity of therapy without jeopardizing the chance of cure. Earlier trials, described above, had already demonstrated that a brief course of chemotherapy only was required and that cisplatin, etoposide, and bleomycin were the most effective agents. Table 13–2 summarizes selected randomized clinical trials that have defined optimal management. The trials have been grouped into categories based on the questions addressed and as a result are not listed in temporal sequence. The categories of trials considered are the following:

1. Can cisplatin be replaced by the potentially less toxic analogue carboplatin?
2. What is the optimal duration of therapy: three or four cycles?
3. What is the best dose and schedule for each of the drugs?
4. Can bleomycin be omitted from the treatment regimen without compromising efficacy?

Cisplatin or Carboplatin

Each of the first two questions of the above list has been addressed in two clinical trials, and the conclusions are widely accepted. Despite promising results in single-arm studies and nonrandomized comparisons,[59] carboplatin has clearly been shown to be inferior to cisplatin in the management of good-prognosis nonseminoma. Carboplatin was substituted for cisplatin as a component of therapy in a trial performed by MSKCC and SWOG [60] and in a second trial undertaken by the MRC and the European Organization for Research and Treatment of Cancer (EORTC)[61] groups. In both studies, the outcome of

Table 13–1. INTERNATIONAL GERM CELL CANCER CONSENSUS PROGNOSTIC CLASSIFICATION FOR PATIENTS RECEIVING CHEMOTHERAPY	
	Good-Prognosis Nonseminoma*
Primary site	Testis or retroperitoneum
Sites of metastases	No nonpulmonary visceral metastases (ie, lymph node and pulmonary metastases only)
Serum tumor marker levels prior to chemotherapy	AFP < 1,000 ng/mL and hCG < 5,000 IU/L and LDH < 1.5 × upper limit of normal

Adapted from International Germ Cell Cancer Collaborative Group.[56]
AFP = α-fetoprotein; hCG = human chorionic gonadotropin; LDH = lactate dehydrogenase.
*All five criteria must be met.

therapy was worse in the carboplatin arm. The MSKCC/SWOG trial, published first, was criticized because the carboplatin was given at a dose determined by body surface area and because the carboplatin was administered once, each 4 weeks.[62] Neither of these issues affected the MRC/EORTC trial, in which the carboplatin dose was calculated according to renal function and the carboplatin was administered once, every 3 weeks. As a result of these studies, carboplatin has no role in current management strategies for the initial therapy of good-prognosis nonseminoma. The salutary lesson from these studies is that despite phase II results that led experienced investigators to claim the therapeutic equivalence of carboplatin and cisplatin,[59,63] randomized comparisons demonstrated clear differences in the efficacy of these agents. Once again, this demonstrated the importance of appropriately designed and conducted phase III clinical trials, especially when effective treatment is being considered for modification.

Number of Cycles of BEP

Two randomized trials have compared three versus four cycles of chemotherapy with BEP administered according to the dose and schedule recommended by Indiana University investigators. The first trial, initiated at Indiana University, was performed in conjunction with the Southeastern Cancer Study Group (SECSG) and reported no statistically significant difference in outcome.[64] The investigators concluded that three cycles of this regimen should be considered the standard treatment for this group of patients with good prognosis NSGCT. This program has remained the standard approach at Indiana University since that time.[65] The conclusions were criticized because the number of patients who were entered (184 total) was inadequate to determine equivalence and because the follow-up at the time of initial reporting was brief.[66] Longer follow-up was available only for the subgroup that received treatment at Indiana University.[67]

Table 13–2. RANDOMIZED CLINICAL TRIALS IN GOOD-PROGNOSIS GERM CELL TUMORS				
Issue Addressed/ Study (Reference)	Good-Prognosis Criteria (Reference)	Treatment Arms	No. of Patients	Conclusions
Cisplatin or carboplatin				
Bajorin et al, 1993 (60)	MSKCC (49)	EP × 4	134	Carboplatin inferior
		EC × 4	131	
Horwich et al, 1997 (61)	MRC (52)	BEP × 4	268	Carboplatin inferior
		CEB × 4	260	
Number of cycles				
Einhorn et al, 1989 (64)	Indiana (50)	BEP × 4	96	No difference, 3 cycles preferred
		BEP × 3	88	Study underpowered to assess equivalence
De Wit et al, 2001 (66)	IGCCC (56)	BEP × 3, EP × 1	406	Equivalent efficacy
		BEP × 3	406	3 cycles preferred
Dose and Schedule				
Toner at al, 2001 (70)	MSKCC (49)	$B_{90}E_{500}P \times 3$	83	Inferior survival with less dose-intense regimen
		$B_{30}E_{360}P \times 4$	83	
De Wit et al, 2001 (66)	IGCCC (56)	$BE_{100 \times 5}P_{20 \times 5}$	342	Equivalent efficacy
		$BE_{165 \times 3}P_{50 \times 2}$	339	Both 3- and 5-day regimens appropriate
Omission of Bleomycin				
Bosl et al, 1987 (76)	MSKCC (49)	VAB-6 × 3	82	No difference in efficacy
		$E_{500}P \times 4$	82	EP preferred as less toxic
Loehrer et al, 1995 (77)	Indiana (50)	$BE_{500}P \times 3$	86	Inferior overall and failure-free survivals in EP arm
		$E_{500}P \times 3$	85	
De Wit et al, 1997 (69)	EORTC (53)	$BE_{360}P \times 4$	200	Inferior response proportion in EP arm
		$E_{360}P \times 4$	195	BEP preferred despite greater toxicity
Culine et al, 1999 (81)	IGV (54)	$BE^{500}P \times 3$	250	No difference at preliminary analysis
		$E^{500}P \times 4$	Total	Published only in abstract form

B = bleomycin; C = carboplatin; E = etoposide; P = cisplatin;
MSKCC = Memorial Sloan-Kettering Cancer Center; MRC = Medical Research Council; Indiana = Indiana University; IGCCC = International Germ Cell Cancer Consensus Classification; EORTC = European Organization for Research and Treatment of Cancer; IGV = Institut Gustave Roussy.
*Subscript numerals refer to dose and schedule (eg, $E_{100 \times 5}$ = etoposide 100 mg/m^2 days 1 to 5; B_{90} = bleomycin 90 kU/cycle).

The question was more definitively answered by the recently published results of a four-arm trial conducted by the EORTC and MRC groups.[66] This study compared three cycles of BEP versus four cycles of treatment, with bleomycin omitted from the fourth cycle to avoid cumulative toxicity. This trial was correctly designed to assess equivalency, defined prospectively as less than a 5% difference in the 2-year progression-free survival rate. The final result was that the 80% confidence interval for any difference was less than 1.8% worse outcome for the three-cycle arm. As a result of these trials, three cycles are considered the optimal duration for the therapy regimen developed at Indiana University, providing excellent efficacy and avoiding the toxicity of an additional cycle.

Optimal Dose and Schedule

The choice of the three most effective drugs—cisplatin, etoposide, and bleomycin—was evident in the early 1980s. However, the optimal dose and schedule of administration of each drug have been less clear. In particular, the dose and schedule of etoposide traditionally used in Great Britain were quite different from those used in North America. The original British BEP regimen incorporated etoposide as 120 mg/m^2 on days 1, 2, and 3 of each cycle. This results in a dose intensity that is 28% less than that of the North American regimen of 100 mg/m^2 administered on days 1, 2, 3, 4, and 5 of each cycle. The 3- and 5-day schedule, in addition to the dose issue, might also be important, given the schedule-dependency of this drug.[68] Published trials conducted by the MRC and the EORTC using the lower dose of etoposide show response and survival proportions similar to those of North American trials.[61,69] However, the variation in patient selection criteria, which tended to be more selective for a better prognosis in these trials (favoring a better outcome), and problems of cross-trial comparison render this observation invalid.

Cisplatin has been administered at doses of 100 to 120 mg/m^2 on a single day[39,70] or in divided doses over 2 to 5 days.[6,66] The schedule of cisplatin does not appear to have an impact on the efficacy of therapy. The optimal schedule and mode of the administration of bleomycin also remains uncertain, with

suggestions that administration by infusion (or the intramuscular route) might produce less toxicity.[71,72] The control arm of the MRC/EORTC trial assessing carboplatin used bleomycin given once per cycle rather than weekly.[61] The lower dose and dose intensity of the bleomycin did not appear to have a dramatic negative impact on the outcome in the control arm, which produced 3-year failure-free and overall survival rates of 90% and 97%, respectively.[61]

Some of these issues were addressed by two recently published trials performed by the Australian and New Zealand Germ Cell Trial Group (AGCTG)[70] and the EORTC and MRC groups.[66] The AGCTG study compared a regimen (based on the Indiana University approach) consisting of three cycles of BEP with full-dose etoposide (500 mg/m^2/cycle) and weekly bleomycin to a regimen similar to that used in the control arm of the MRC/EORTC carboplatin trial[61] and including four cycles of cisplatin administered on a single day, etoposide at the conventional British dose, and bleomycin only once per cycle.[70] The trial demonstrated inferior survival in the less dose-intense latter arm (Figure 13–3), and, despite the many differences in the two arms, the authors concluded that the lower dose intensity of etoposide was the most likely cause.[70]

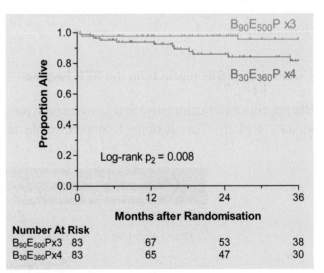

Figure 13–3. Overall survival curves from the Australian and New Zealand Germ Cell Trial Group randomized comparison of two regimens of bleomycin, etoposide, and cisplatin (BEP) chemotherapy. (Subscript numerals refer to dose per cycle in mg/m^2; ×3 and ×4 refer to the number of cycles.) This phase III trial demonstrated the superiority of the more dose-intense regimen, which was based on treatment recommendations developed at Indiana University. (B = bleomycin; E = etoposide; P = cisplatin.)

The EORTC/MRC trial used a 2×2 factorial design to compare three or four cycles of BEP administered over 3 or 5 days.[66] The investigators decided to use the higher dose of etoposide in all arms, and this led to a change in practice at most European centers, prior to the availability of the Australian study results. The study demonstrated equivalence for both of the study questions. These events have led to a recommendation that the lower dose of etoposide should no longer be used in the treatment of good-prognosis nonseminoma.

The AGCTG and EORTC/MRC trials have also shed some light on other scheduling issues. Cisplatin, when administered on a single day in the AGCTG study or over 2 days in the EORTC/MRC trial, produced increased nausea and vomiting when compared to a 5-day schedule.[66,70] The EORTC/MRC comparison also demonstrated increased ototoxicity with the 2-day schedule in both the physician-reported toxicity data[66] and the separately published patient-reported quality-of-life data.[73] However, this difference was predominantly seen in those patients who received four cycles of therapy. Thus, the additional toxicity seen with the shorter schedule seems to be limited to a modest increase in short-term nausea and vomiting if only three cycles of treatment are administered. The details and current status of several published regimens incorporating BEP and their current status are shown in Table 13–3.

Omission of Bleomycin from the BEP Regimen

Bleomycin causes cumulative and idiosyncratic pulmonary toxicity. This toxicity is unpredictable in severity and can cause death in patients who have been cured of their underlying malignancy. Variable mortality rates have been reported, with rates as high as 4% of cases.[74,75] Other toxicities resulting from the inclusion of bleomycin in the treatment regimen include increased myelosuppression, Raynaud's phenomenon, and cutaneous toxicity. As bleomycin appears to be the least important of the three drugs in a standard BEP regimen, many investigators and trial groups have questioned whether omitting bleomycin from the regimen is feasible without compromising outcomes for those patients with a good prognosis. A number of clinical trials have addressed this question and are listed in Table 13–3.

Bosl and colleagues at MSKCC compared three cycles of the VAB-6 regimen with four cycles of cisplatin and etoposide alone in patients with a good prognosis, between 1982 and 1986. The two-drug regimen was as effective but was less toxic.[76] Subsequently, four cycles of cisplatin and etoposide have been considered standard therapy at MSKCC for patients with a good prognosis. The results of this trial have been used to argue that bleomycin is not required as part of treatment. However, the trial is only an indirect comparison as the control arm was a five-drug regimen that did not incorporate etoposide. Three other trials have assessed this issue more directly by including or omitting bleomycin as the only variable in a randomized comparison. In summary, these trials have demonstrated a reduced antitumor efficacy when bleomycin was omitted from the following regimens:

1. Three cycles of Indiana University BEP (etoposide, 500 mg/m^2/cycle)[77]
2. Four cycles of BEP with the traditional British

Table 13–3. CURRENT STATUS OF SELECTED PUBLISHED REGIMENS CONTAINING BLEOMYCIN, ETOPOSIDE, AND CISPLATIN		
Study (Reference No.)	Regimen	Status*
Williams et al, 1987 (7)	Cisplatin 100 mg/m^2/cycle Etoposide 500 mg/m^2/cycle Bleomycin 90 kU/cycle	Recommended
De Wit et al, 1997 (69)	Cisplatin 100 mg/m^2/cycle Etoposide 360 mg/m^2/cycle Bleomycin 90 kU/cycle	Not recommended (etoposide dose intensity probably inadequate)
Horwich et al, 1997 (61) Toner et al, 2001 (70)	Cisplatin 100 mg/m^2/cycle Etoposide 360 mg/m^2/cycle Bleomycin 30 kU/cycle	Definitely contraindicated; inferior survival in a randomized comparison

*See text for explanation of comments.

dose of etoposide (360 mg/m^2/cycle), administered to patients in Europe[69]

3. Four cycles of cisplatin, vinblastine, and bleomycin (PVB), administered to an unselected population of germ cell tumor patients in Australia and New Zealand [78]

Despite these results, there remains some uncertainty about this issue. The EORTC study, which was the largest study performed, showed a lower response rate with etoposide and cisplatin (EP), but disease-free and overall survivals were not statistically significantly different despite a median follow-up of 7.3 years.[69] The bleomycin-containing arm had greater late neurotoxicity and pulmonary toxicity, and two patients (1%) died from bleomycin pulmonary toxicity.

Investigators at MSKCC have argued that if cisplatin and etoposide are given at full dose (etoposide at 500 mg/m^2/cycle) and for four cycles rather than three cycles, the results are equivalent to those of three cycles of Indiana University BEP, and the toxicity profile is preferable.[4,79] They published the results of long-term follow-up of patients treated with four cycles of cisplatin and etoposide and found no late relapses, with 87% of patients remaining disease free.[80] A randomized comparison of the MSKCC and Indiana University approaches has been performed by the Genitourinary Group of the French Federation of Cancer Centers, with accrual of 250 cases.[81] A preliminary analysis (to date, presented only in abstract form) concluded that there were no significant differences between the regimens. Most clinicians have accepted that four cycles of cisplatin and etoposide (with an etoposide dose of 500 mg/m^2/cycle) is a reasonable alternative to the Indiana University regimen of three cycles of BEP.

SELECTION OF PATIENTS FOR GOOD-PROGNOSIS THERAPY

The recommendations discussed in this chapter are derived from published results and clinical trials describing the treatment of patients with metastatic nonseminoma and a good prognosis. In the current era, the recommendations should be applied to those patients who fulfill the criteria defined by the Inter-

national Germ Cell Consensus Classification (IGCCC) criteria (see Table 13–1).[56]

However, there are differences in international practice that need to be understood by the clinician attempting to interpret the medical literature. The standard management of nonbulky stage II nonseminoma (generally a solitary lymph node < 3 cm in diameter) in most North American centers is with retroperitoneal lymph node dissection. Selected patients will receive adjuvant chemotherapy or chemotherapy at the time of relapse. Outside North America, many clinicians treat this group of patients with initial chemotherapy and reserve surgical resection for the minority of patients left with residual masses. The divergence of practices is due to differences in the perception of toxicity and long-term morbidity between the two approaches and is also possibly due to a relative lack of highly specialized surgical expertise and experience outside major US centers. The resultant variation in patients included in treatment results for "good-prognosis nonseminoma" is also likely to have some impact on the reported results of therapy.

The final group of patients who may be treated with the same choice of chemotherapy consists of patients with elevated serum tumor marker levels in the absence of demonstrable metastatic disease (stage 15). The rationale for chemotherapeutic treatment in this group is described elsewhere and essentially relates to the substantial chemosensitivity of small-volume NSGCTs, accompanied by the lack of certainty that retroperitoneal lymph node dissection will identify the sites of disease in all such cases.[82] These three groups of nonseminoma patients who are eligible for good-prognosis therapy are summarized in Table 13–4.

RECOMMENDATIONS FOR CHEMOTHERAPY

The chemotherapy regimen developed at Indiana University should be considered the standard of care for patients with good-prognosis NSGCT. This recommendation is based on successful results with this program in a number of randomized clinical trials comparing it to other treatment programs.[7,64,66,70,77,81] The regimen has been used successfully in centers

Table 13–4. PATIENT GROUPS WITH NONSEMINOMA ELIGIBLE FOR GOOD-PROGNOSIS CHEMOTHERAPY REGIMENS
1. Patients with metastatic disease fulfilling all of the International Germ Cell Consensus Classification (IGCCC) criteria as described in Table 13–1.
2. Patients with low-bulk stage II disease managed in centers (generally outside North America) that select primary chemotherapy rather than retroperitoneal lymph node dissection for this group. These patients should also fulfill the IGCCC criteria for good prognosis.
3. Patients with persistent and unexplained tumor marker elevation with no evidence of metastatic disease on appropriate diagnostic imaging studies (stage 15)

with considerable expertise but also in cooperative group studies including a diverse range of treating centers and clinicians.

The recent MRC/EORTC trial demonstrated that the same doses of chemotherapy could be delivered over 3 days without compromising efficacy.[66] Toxicity and quality-of-life data indicate little difference between the 3- and 5-day schedule, with increased nausea and vomiting constituting the main issue.[66,73] Greater short- and long-term ototoxicity was found with the 3-day regimen, but this appeared predominantly in those patients who were receiving four cycles of therapy. Despite this, given the substantial cost reduction and reduced attendance requirements for patients associated with a 3-day regimen, it may be reasonable to use the shorter administration program as a valid alternative, based on the results of this carefully performed trial.

Many investigators consider the regimen developed at MSKCC, comprising four cycles of cisplatin and etoposide (500 mg/m²/cycle), also to be a valid alternative to the Indiana University BEP regimen. This regimen results in a higher cumulative dose of cisplatin and etoposide but avoids bleomycin and its potential short- and long-term toxicity. The conclusion that this regimen is as effective as the Indiana University program is based on the excellent results achieved at MSKCC and a preliminary analysis of a randomized comparison with a regimen similar to the Indiana University program.[81] There are important caveats on this conclusion. Results achieved at MSKCC may not be reproducible elsewhere. For example, a high rate of retroperitoneal lymph node dissection is performed at MSKCC in comparison to other centers, particularly centers outside North America. In the series demonstrating long-term outcomes from MSKCC, 56% of patients had postchemotherapy node dissections.[80] In

other series, the rate of postchemotherapy surgery has been as low as 20%.[66] The results achieved at MSKCC have not yet been duplicated in large trials performed by cooperative groups. The issue of equivalence of the MSKCC and Indiana University approaches may be addressed by the randomized comparison undertaken by the French group. The final results are awaited with interest. Unfortunately, to date, the available results are from a preliminary analysis and have been presented only in abstract form.[81] Most important, total accrual to the trial was only 250 patients, and this number is unlikely to be adequate to determine equivalency.

Given our present knowledge, it is appropriate to use the MSKCC approach of four cycles of cisplatin and etoposide when bleomycin is contraindicated. Bleomycin is contraindicated in patients with underlying respiratory disease or possibly in those at greater risk of bleomycin toxicity, such as older patients (eg > 40 years) or patients with renal impairment.[75] Additional factors, such as the effect on long-term quality of life, and patient preference might also need to be considered. Table 13–5 summarizes the regimens currently considered to be options for chemotherapy for patients with good-prognosis nonseminoma.

MANAGEMENT ISSUES AND PATIENT CARE

This chapter has focused on the choice of an optimal chemotherapy regimen for patients with nonseminoma and a good prognosis; however, it is essential to recognize that chemotherapy is only part of an integrated care plan. Prior to chemotherapy, it is essential to carefully explain the diagnosis, the prognosis, the treatment plan, the logistics of therapy,

Table 13–5.   RECOMMENDED CHEMOTHERAPY REGIMENS FOR PATIENTS WITH GOOD-PROGNOSIS NONSEMINOMA

Status*	Regimen	Cycle Length	Number of Cycles
Standard of care	Cisplatin 20 mg/m² days 1, 2, 3, 4, 5 Etoposide 100 mg/m² days 1, 2, 3, 4, 5 Bleomycin 30 kU weekly†	21 days	3
Alternative schedule‡	Cisplatin 50 mg/m² days 1, 2 Etoposide 165 mg/m² days 1, 2, 3 Bleomycin 30 kU weekly†	21 days	3
Consider if bleomycin is contraindicated	Cisplatin 20 mg/m² days 1, 2, 3, 4, 5 Etoposide 100 mg/m² days 1, 2, 3, 4, 5	21 days	4

*See text for caveats and explanation.
†Maximum of nine doses of bleomycin.
‡Increased late toxicity if this schedule is used for more than three cycles.

and the potential side effects of treatment to the patient. (See Chapters 27 and 28 for discussion of the short- and long-term toxicities of this therapy.)

The potential need for postchemotherapy surgery should be discussed at this early stage. Evaluation prior to chemotherapy should include computed tomography (CT) of the chest, abdomen, and pelvis; serum tumor marker monitoring; and consideration of semen analysis and storage.

Chemotherapy doses should be calculated by using actual body weight to calculate the body surface area (BSA), except possibly when the patient is morbidly obese (eg, body mass index > 35 kg/m²). Young men with testicular cancer often have large BSA measurements, without being obese. The BSA should not be capped at an arbitrary level. There should rarely be a need to modify or reduce the dose of cisplatin or etoposide during therapy. There is no consensus as to how best to manage leukopenia or thrombocytopenia at day 22 of the treatment cycle. Recent trials have allowed delaying the next cycle of therapy for up to 1 week without apparent deterioration in outcome.[66,70] Investigators at MSKCC studied the effect of delays of 1 week and did not observe a negative impact.[83] Recommendations from Indiana University have suggested that treatment be on time at day 22, irrespective of leukopenia, with omission of the day 5 dose of etoposide if neutropenia is still present at day 26. The availability of hematopoietic growth factors offers an alternative solution for managing neutropenia complicating this potentially curative chemotherapy. The author's practice when neutropenia interferes with the administration of treatment is to continue with therapy without delay or dose reduction and to add growth factor support. Delaying therapy for more

than 7 days is certainly not acceptable and has the potential to compromise the chance of achieving cure.

The administration of bleomycin should be stopped if significant signs of pulmonary or other severe toxicity develop (Figure 13–4). (Monitoring for bleomycin toxicity and indications to cease administering this agent are considered in Chapter 27). When bleomycin administration has been stopped early, it is reasonable practice to give a fourth cycle of cisplatin and etoposide if an inadequate amount of bleomycin has been delivered.[66] What constitutes an "inadequate" dose of bleomycin in this setting is unclear. In the recent EORTC/MRC trial, the median delivered dose intensity of bleomycin was 100% of the planned dose intensity, but 26% of patients received less than 90% of the planned dose.[66] In the AGCTG trial, strict criteria were specified to stop bleomycin if the vital capacity or diffusion capacity fell by 15% from baseline. The median delivered total bleomycin dose was 240 kU (the planned dose was 270 kU), 52% of patients received less than 90% of the planned total dose, and 25% of patients received less than six doses (180 kU).[70] My practice is to recommend a fourth cycle of cisplatin and etoposide if bleomycin administration is stopped before six doses are administered.

During the course of chemotherapy, patients should be monitored closely for toxicity, and serum tumor markers should be checked regularly. Serum

---

*Editor's note: I remain cautious about the use of colony-stimulating factors in potentially cured patients with germ cell tumors, given the absence of long-term follow-up information regarding the frequency of iatrogenic leukemia among patients treated with etoposide-containing regimens.

tumor marker levels should be measured at least weekly while they remain abnormal, then once per cycle and at the completion of therapy. Multiple studies have assessed the interpretation of marker levels during chemotherapy (Figure 13–5). There is increas-

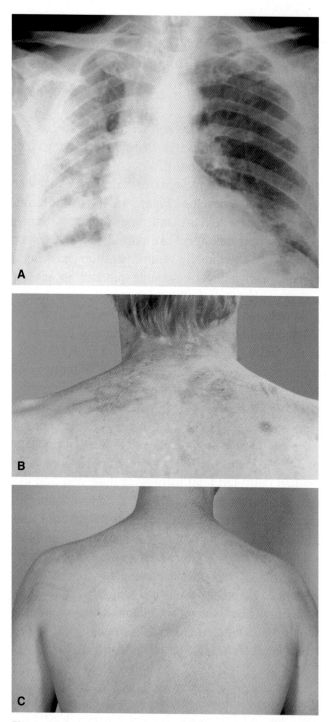

Figure 13–4. Bleomycin toxicity. *A,* Chest radiograph showing evidence of severe bleomycin pulmonary toxicity. *B,* Effects of acute bleomycin skin toxicity. *C,* Pigmented scratch marks still visible 16 months after completing chemotherapy.

ing evidence that the rate of fall of marker levels may predict outcome.[84-94] However, there is no consensus in regard to the optimal methodology. The assessment of overall response to therapy is best judged by the response in tumor markers. Patients require careful reassessment if their marker levels fail to reach the normal range or start to rise again. If no spurious cause for marker elevation is identified,[95] the chemotherapy has failed, and the patient is considered to have refractory disease with its attendant poor prognosis.[96] CT of the chest, abdomen, and pelvis should be repeated at the completion of chemotherapy. The degree of shrinkage of tumor masses cannot be used as the sole criterion to assess response and is an imperfect predictor of the histologic makeup of postchemotherapy residual masses.[97] When the tumor mass enlarges during chemotherapy but the markers return to normal levels, the mass usually consists of mature teratoma without malignant elements.[5] Teratoma may also result in a residual mass of substantial size, often with central necrosis (Figure 13–6). In each of these cases, complete surgical resection is required, not further chemotherapy.

When tumor marker levels are normal at the completion of chemotherapy, surgical resection of residual masses at metastatic sites is an integral and essential part of the treatment plan.[4,98] As a general rule, all residual masses should be resected (Figures 13–7, 13–8, and 13–9). In cases of nonseminoma, 40 to 50% of residual masses contain teratoma (see Figure 13–7), which is refractory to chemotherapy or radiation therapy and which may lead to complications, including local progression, dedifferentiation to a malignant germ cell tumor, development of nongerm cell malignancies such as sarcoma, and late relapse.[97,99,100] (Issues of case selection for surgery, the type and extent of surgery, and pathologic findings in resected specimens are discussed in greater detail in Chapter 11.)

Follow-up after chemotherapy, with or without postchemotherapy surgery, should be planned with the knowledge of subsequent risks. Approximately 5 to 10% of good-prognosis cases relapse after treatment, and the majority of relapses occur within the first 2 years.[66,80] Salvage therapy is expected to cure only up to 40% of relapsed patients.[101] Late relapses (up to 17 years after treatment) have been reported

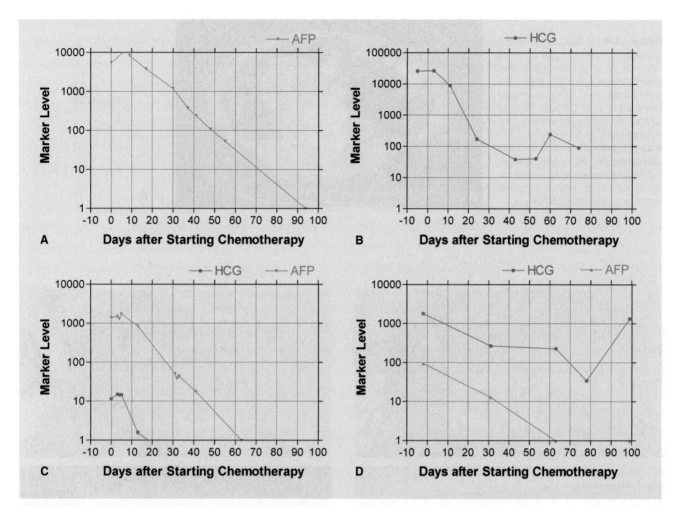

Figure 13–5. The monitoring of serum tumor marker levels during chemotherapy provides valuable information. *A* demonstrates the expected fall in α-fetoprotein (AFP) during chemotherapy, with a half-life of approximately 7 days. Note the early rise in the first 10 days of chemotherapy, which is common. Note also that the AFP level takes a long time to reach normal levels, but this does not indicate a failure of therapy in this case. This patient was free of disease after resection of a residual mass and achieved long-term disease-free survival. *B* demonstrates a typical pattern of failure of chemotherapy. This patient had refractory disease and died 14 months after starting chemotherapy. *C* shows appropriate fall in both AFP and human chorionic gonadotropin (hCG) levels. The expected half-life for hCG is 3 to 4 days. This patient achieved a complete response and prolonged disease-free survival. *D* shows a discordant response in the two markers: AFP fell as expected, but the hCG levels indicate refractory malignancy. This patient died 6 months after starting chemotherapy.

and are usually associated with the presence of teratoma in the primary tumor or in masses resected after chemotherapy (see also Chapter 16).[102,103] The risk of relapse in the abdomen after surgery depends on the histology of the residual mass, the completeness of the resection, and (probably) the extent of surgery (template dissection vs less extensive surgery) and the experience of the surgeon.[104] There is no standard or consensus approach to follow-up, and there is considerable variation in clinical practice internationally.[105] One reasonable approach to follow-up after chemotherapy for good-prognosis nonseminoma is as follows:

1. Clinical review and assessment of serum tumor marker levels every 3 months in the first year, every 4 months in the second year, every 6 months to year 5, and then annually.
2. Chest radiography or CT of the chest at 6 months and at 1, 2, 3, 5, and 10 years.
3. CT of the abdomen and pelvis at the same intervals as chest imaging. Reduced surveillance of the abdomen may be warranted in those cases in which a template dissection of retroperitoneal nodes has been performed by an experienced surgeon, particularly if no teratoma was identified in the orchiectomy or retroperitoneal specimens.

Figure 13–6. Characteristic cystic appearance seen in some cases of teratoma in a residual mass after chemotherapy. In this case, the appearance on the computed tomography scan (*A*) was complemented by the appearance on the positron emission tomography (PET) scan (*B*), which showed a metabolically active rim. PET scans indicate increased glucose uptake in a minority of cases of teratoma in the absence of malignant elements.

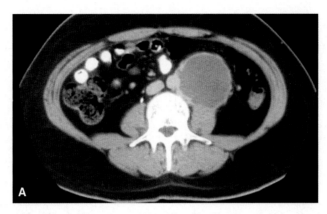
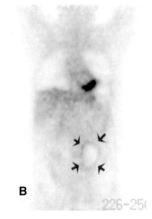

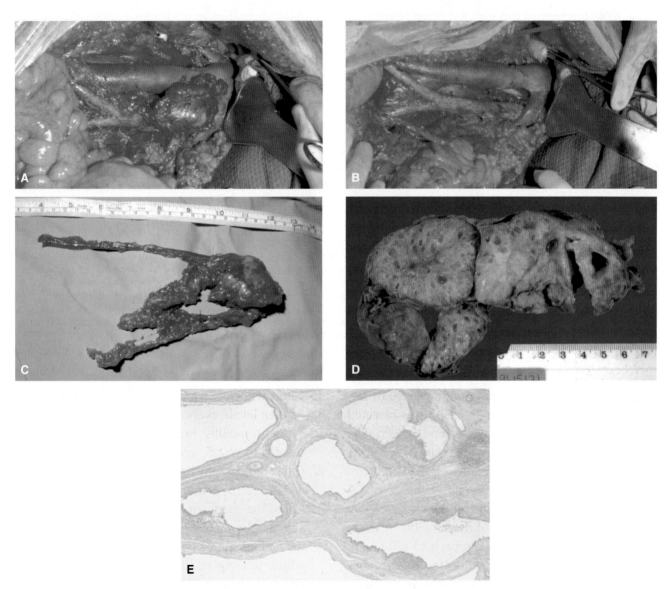

Figure 13–7.   Resection of a residual mass of teratoma from the retroperitoneum. *A,* Residual mass in situ at completion of dissection. *B,* The retroperitoneum after completion of template dissection. *C,* Surgical specimen. *D,* Cross section of the specimen after storage in formalin, showing cystic spaces. *E,* Morphology of the mass. (All images courtesy of Laurence Cleeve.)

The duration of follow-up at major centers is also variable. At some centers, no follow-up is performed after 5 years; at other centers, indefinite annual review is planned. Given the risks of late toxicity[106] (some of which are only recently being recognized) and the small risk of late relapse, follow-up for a minimum of 10 years appears appropriate.

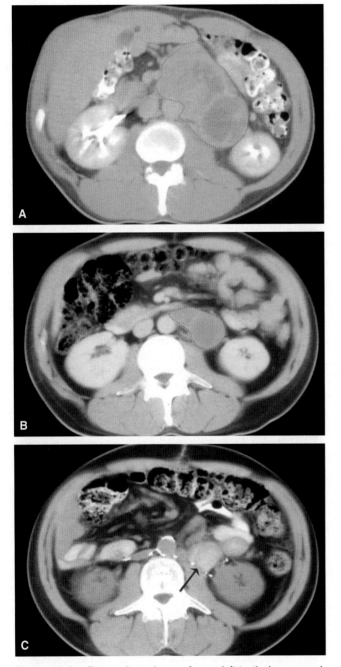

Figure 13–8. Retroperitoneal mass from a left testicular nonseminoma. *A,* Computed tomography (CT) prior to chemotherapy shows a large heterogeneous retroperitoneal mass. The largest mass is outlined (*dotted line*). *B,* CT scan of the same patient, after chemotherapy. The mass (*dotted outline*) has shrunk considerably. *C,* CT scan taken after retroperitoneal lymph node dissection in the same patient. Note the small bowel in the surgical bed (*arrow*); this can be mistaken for recurrent tumor, particularly if adequate oral contrast is not given prior to the examination. The resected specimen showed necrotic debris only, with no teratoma or residual malignancy identified.

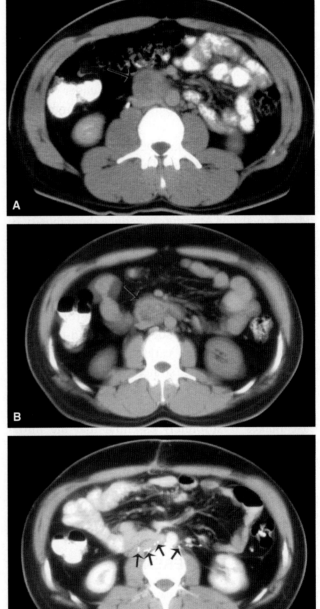

Figure 13–9. Retroperitoneal mass from a right testicular nonseminoma. *A,* Computed tomography (CT) before chemotherapy shows a retroperitoneal mass (*arrow*). *B,* CT scan of the same patient, after chemotherapy. The mass (*arrow*) has changed little in size but has become more heterogeneous in appearance on CT. *C,* CT scan after retroperitoneal lymph node dissection in the same patient. Note the multiple surgical clips (*arrows*). The resected specimen showed mature teratoma.

CONCLUSION

The emphasis of clinical research efforts in the last two decades has been on identifying more clearly those patients with a good prognosis and on minimizing the toxicity of therapy in this group without compromising the chance of cure. This has largely been achieved with an internationally developed and widely accepted classification of prognosis and with clearly defined chemotherapy and treatment programs. This success is reflected by the fact that no major clinical trials are currently under way for patients with good-prognosis nonseminomatous germ cell tumors.

Important lessons have been learned throughout the development process. The value of randomized clinical trials has once again been demonstrated by at least two trials unexpectedly demonstrating inferior survival.[61,70] Attempts to reduce the intensity of therapy have essentially reached the limit of safety, given currently available cytotoxic agents. There is little margin for error as dose reductions or modifications of proven treatment strategies threaten to reduce the chance of cure. The proven role of less-toxic therapy for those patients with good-prognosis disease mandates both careful and timely surveillance and diagnostic strategies that ensure that treatment is initiated when the extent of malignancy is minimal. The relative resistance of recurrent disease makes it absolutely essential that the initial choice for treatment be correct and that it is implemented appropriately. Treatment should be undertaken only by clinicians who have a detailed knowledge of this uncommon malignancy and its unique treatment paradigms.

REFERENCES

1. Einhorn LH. Testicular cancer as a model for a curable neoplasm: The Richard and Hinda Rosenthal Foundation Award Lecture. Cancer Res 1981;41:3275–80.
2. Einhorn LH. Treatment of testicular cancer: a new and improved model. J Clin Oncol 1990;8:1777–81.
3. Einhorn LH. Testicular cancer: an oncological success story. Clin Cancer Res 1997;3:2630–2.
4. Bosl GJ, Motzer RJ. Testicular germ-cell cancer. N Engl J Med 1997;337:242–53.
5. Panicek DM, Toner GC, Heelan RT, Bosl GJ. Nonseminomatous germ cell tumors: enlarging masses despite chemotherapy. Radiology 1990;175:499–502.
6. Williams SD, Birch R, Greco FA, Einhorn LH. Comparison of cisplatin + bleomycin + either vinblastine or VP-16 in disseminated testicular cancer: a preliminary report. Prog Clin Biol Res 1984;153:219–23.
7. Williams SD, Birch R, Einhorn LH, et al. Treatment of disseminated germ-cell tumors with cisplatin, bleomycin, and either vinblastine or etoposide. N Engl J Med 1987;316:1435–40.
8. Nichols CR, Roth BJ. Chemotherapy for metastatic non-seminoma. In: Horwich A, editor. Testicular cancer: investigation and management. 2nd ed. London: Chapman & Hall; 1996. p. 227–49.
9. Li MC, Whitmore WF, Golbey R, Grabstald H. Effects of combined drug therapy on metastatic cancer of the testis. JAMA 1960;74:1291–9.
10. Umezawa H, Suhara Y, Takita T, Maeda K. Purification of bleomycins. J Antibiot (Tokyo) 1966;19:210–5.
11. Clinical Screening Co-operative Group of the EORTC. Study of the clinical efficiency of bleomycin in human cancer. BMJ 1970;2:643–5.
12. Samuels ML, Holoye PY, Johnson DE. Bleomycin combination chemotherapy in the management of testicular neoplasia. Cancer 1975;36:318–26.
13. Samuels ML, Lanzotti VJ, Holoye PY, et al. Combination chemotherapy in germinal cell tumors. Cancer Treat Rev 1976;3:185–204.
14. Spigel SC, Coltman CA Jr. Vinblastine (NSC-49842) and bleomycin (NSC-125066) therapy for disseminated testicular tumors. Cancer Chemother Rep 1974;58:213–6.
15. Spigel SC, Stephens RL, Haas CD, et al. Chemotherapy of disseminated germinal tumors of the testis—comparison of vinblastine and bleomycin with vincristine, bleomycin, and actinomycin D. Cancer Treat Rep 1978;62:129–30.
16. Rosenberg B, Van Camp L, Krigas T. Inhibition of cell division in E. coli by electrolysis products from a platinum electrode. Nature 1965;205:698–9.
17. Drobnik J. Antitumor activity of platinum complexes. Cancer Chemother Pharmacol 1983;10:145–9.
18. Rossof AH, Slayton RE, Perlia CP. Preliminary clinical experience with cis-diamminedichloroplatinum (II) (NSC 119875, CACP). Cancer 1972;30:1451–6.
19. Higby DJ, Wallace HJ Jr, Holland JF. Cis-diamminedichloroplatinum (NSC-119875): a phase I study. Cancer Chemother Rep 1973;57:459–63.
20. Higby DJ, Wallace HJ Jr, Albert D, Holland JF. Diamminodichloroplatinum in the chemotherapy of testicular tumors. J Urol 1974;112:100–4.
21. Higby DJ, Wallace HJ Jr, Albert DJ, Holland JF. Diamino-dichloroplatinum: a phase I study showing responses in testicular and other tumors. Cancer 1974;33:1219–5.
22. Einhorn LH, Donohue J. Cis-diamminedichloroplatinum, vinblastine, and bleomycin combination chemotherapy in disseminated testicular cancer. Ann Intern Med 1977;87:293–8.
23. Roth BJ, Greist A, Kubilis PS, et al. Cisplatin-based combination chemotherapy for disseminated germ cell tumors: long-term follow-up. J Clin Oncol 1988;6:1239–47.
24. Krikorian JG, Daniels JR, Brown BW Jr, Hu MS. Variables for predicting serious toxicity (vinblastine dose, performance status, and prior therapeutic experience): chemotherapy for metastatic testicular cancer with cis-dichlorodiammineplat-

inum(II), vinblastine, and bleomycin. Cancer Treat Rep 1978;62:1455–63.

25. Stoter G, Sleijfer DT, Vendrik CP, et al. Combination chemotherapy with cis-diammine-dichloro-platinum, vinblastine, and bleomycin in advanced testicular non-seminoma. Lancet 1979;1:941–5.

26. Garnick MB, Canellos GP, Richie JP, Stark JJ. Sequential combination chemotherapy and surgery for disseminated testicular cancer: cis-dichlorodiammineplatinum(II), vinblastine, and bleomycin remission-induction therapy followed by cyclophosphamide and adriamycin. Cancer Treat Rep 1979;63:1681–6.

27. Wilkinson P, Gibb R, Read G. Combination chemotherapy for metastatic malignant teratoma of testis [letter]. Lancet 1979;1:1185.

28. Bosl GJ, Lange PH, Fraley EE, et al. Vinblastine, bleomycin and cis-diamminedichloroplatinum in the treatment of advanced testicular carcinoma. Possible importance of longer induction and shorter maintenance schedules. Am J Med 1980;68:492–6.

29. Ramsey EW, Bowman DM, Weinerman B. The management of disseminated testicular cancer. Br J Urol 1980;52:45–9.

30. Einhorn LH, Williams SD. Chemotherapy of disseminated testicular cancer. A random prospective study. Cancer 1980;46:1339–44.

31. Einhorn LH, Williams SD, Troner M, et al. The role of maintenance therapy in disseminated testicular cancer. N Engl J Med 1981;305:727–31.

32. Wittes RE, Yagoda A, Silvay O, et al. Chemotherapy of germ cell tumors of the testis. I. Induction of remissions with vinblastine, actinomycin D, and bleomycin. Cancer 1976;37:637–45.

33. Cheng E, Cvitkovic E, Wittes RE, Golbey RB. Germ cell tumors (II): VAB II in metastatic testicular cancer. Cancer 1978;42:2162–8.

34. Reynolds TF, Vugrin D, Cvitkovic E, et al. VAB-3 combination chemotherapy of metastatic testicular cancer. Cancer 1981;48:888–98.

35. Vugrin D, Cvitkovic E, Whitmore WF Jr, et al. VAB-4 combination chemotherapy in the treatment of metastatic testis tumors. Cancer 1981;47:833–9.

36. Vugrin D, Whitmore WF Jr, Golbey RB. VAB-5 combination chemotherapy in prognostically poor risk patients with germ cell tumors. Cancer 1983;51:1072–5.

37. Vugrin D, Herr HW, Whitmore WF Jr, et al. VAB-6 combination chemotherapy in disseminated cancer of the testis. Ann Intern Med 1981;95:59–61.

38. Vugrin D, Whitmore WF Jr, Golbey RB. VAB-6 combination chemotherapy without maintenance in treatment of disseminated cancer of the testis. Cancer 1983;51:211–5.

39. Bosl GJ, Gluckman R, Geller NL, et al. VAB-6: an effective chemotherapy regimen for patients with germ-cell tumors. J Clin Oncol 1986;4:1493–9.

40. Samson MK, Rivkin SE, Jones SE, et al. Dose-response and dose-survival advantage for high versus low-dose cisplatin combined with vinblastine and bleomycin in disseminated testicular cancer. A Southwest Oncology Group study. Cancer 1984;53:1029–35.

41. Newlands ES, Bagshawe KD. Epipodophylin derivative (VP

16-23) in malignant teratomas and chonocarcinomas [letter]. Lancet 1977;2:87.

42. Fitzharris BM, Kaye SB, Saverymuttu S, et al. VP16-213 as a single agent in advanced testicular tumors. Eur J Cancer 1980;16:1193–7.

43. Cavalli F, Klepp O, Renard J, et al. A phase II study of oral VP-16-213 in non-seminomatous testicular cancer. Eur J Cancer 1981;17:245–9.

44. Williams SD, Einhorn LH, Greco FA, et al. VP-16-213 salvage therapy for refractory germinal neoplasms. Cancer 1980;46:2154–8.

45. Peckham MJ, Barrett A, Liew KH, et al. The treatment of metastatic germ-cell testicular tumours with bleomycin, etoposide and cis-platin (BEP). Br J Cancer 1983;47:613–9.

46. Williams SD, Einhorn LH. Etoposide salvage therapy for refractory germ cell tumors: an update. Cancer Treat Rev 1982;9 Suppl:67–71.

47. Peckham MJ, Barrett A, McElwain TJ, et al. Non-seminoma germ cell tumours (malignant teratoma) of the testis. Results of treatment and an analysis of prognostic factors. Br J Urol 1981;53:162–72.

48. Germa-Lluch JR, Begent RH, Bagshawe KD. Tumour-marker levels and prognosis in malignant teratoma of the testis. Br J Cancer 1980;42:850–5.

49. Bosl GJ, Geller NL, Cirrincione C, et al. Multivariate analysis of prognostic variables in patients with metastatic testicular cancer. Cancer Res 1983;43:3403–7.

50. Birch R, Williams S, Cone A, et al. Prognostic factors for favorable outcome in disseminated germ cell tumors. J Clin Oncol 1986;4:400–7.

51. Prognostic factors in advanced non-seminomatous germ-cell testicular tumours: results of a multicentre study. Report from the Medical Research Council Working Party on Testicular Tumours. Lancet 1985;1:8–11.

52. Mead GM, Stenning SP, Parkinson MC, et al. The second Medical Research Council study of prognostic factors in nonseminomatous germ cell tumors. Medical Research Council Testicular Tumour Working Party. J Clin Oncol 1992;10:85–94.

53. Stoter G, Sylvester R, Sleijfer DT, et al. Multivariate analysis of prognostic factors in patients with disseminated nonseminomatous testicular cancer: results from a European Organization for Research on Treatment of Cancer multiinstitutional phase III study. Cancer Res 1987;47:2714–8.

54. Droz JP, Kramar A, Ghosn M, et al. Prognostic factors in advanced nonseminomatous testicular cancer. A multivariate logistic regression analysis. Cancer 1988;62:564–8.

55. Bajorin D, Katz A, Chan E, et al. Comparison of criteria for assigning germ cell tumor patients to "good risk" and "poor risk" studies. J Clin Oncol 1988;6:786–92.

56. International Germ Cell Cancer Collaborative Group. International Germ Cell Consensus Classification: a prognostic factor-based staging system for metastatic germ cell cancers. J Clin Oncol 1997;15:594–603.

57. Bosl GJ, Geller NL, Chan EY. Stage migration and the increasing proportion of complete responders in patients with advanced germ cell tumors. Cancer Res 1988;48:3524–7.

58. Toner GC, Neerhut GJ, Schwarz MA, et al. The management of testicular cancer in Victoria, 1988-1993. Urology Study Committee of the Victorian Co-operative Oncology Group. Med J Aust 2001;174:328–31.

59. Horwich A, Dearnaley DP, Nicholls J, et al. Effectiveness of carboplatin, etoposide, and bleomycin combination chemotherapy in good-prognosis metastatic testicular non-seminomatous germ cell tumors. J Clin Oncol 1991;9:62–9.

60. Bajorin DF, Sarosdy MF, Pfister DG, et al. Randomized trial of etoposide and cisplatin versus etoposide and carboplatin in patients with good-risk germ cell tumors: a multiinstitutional study. J Clin Oncol 1993;11:598–606.

61. Horwich A, Sleijfer DT, Fossa SD, et al. Randomized trial of bleomycin, etoposide, and cisplatin compared with bleomycin, etoposide, and carboplatin in good-prognosis metastatic nonseminomatous germ cell cancer: a multi-institutional Medical Research Council/European Organization for Research and Treatment of Cancer trial. J Clin Oncol 1997;15:1844–52.

62. Childs WJ, Nicholls EJ, Horwich A. The optimisation of carboplatin dose in carboplatin, etoposide and bleomycin combination chemotherapy for good prognosis metastatic nonseminomatous germ cell tumours of the testis. Ann Oncol 1992;3:291–6.

63. Horwich A, Mason M, Dearnaley DP. Use of carboplatin in germ cell tumors of the testis. Semin Oncol 1992;19:72–7.

64. Einhorn LH, Williams SD, Loehrer PJ, et al. Evaluation of optimal duration of chemotherapy in favorable-prognosis disseminated germ cell tumors: a Southeastern Cancer Study Group protocol. J Clin Oncol 1989;7:387–91.

65. Einhorn LH. Curing metastatic testicular cancer. Proc Natl Acad Sci U S A 2002;99:4592–5.

66. de Wit R, Roberts JT, Wilkinson PM, et al. Equivalence of three or four cycles of bleomycin, etoposide, and cisplatin chemotherapy and of a 3- or 5-day schedule in good-prognosis germ cell cancer: a randomized study of the European Organization for Research and Treatment of Cancer Genitourinary Tract Cancer Cooperative Group and the Medical Research Council. J Clin Oncol 2001;19:1629–40.

67. Saxman SB, Finch D, Gonin R, Einhorn LH. Long-term follow-up of a phase III study of three versus four cycles of bleomycin, etoposide, and cisplatin in favorable-prognosis germ-cell tumors: the Indiana University experience. J Clin Oncol 1998;16:702–6.

68. Slevin ML, Clark PI, Joel SP, et al. A randomized trial to evaluate the effect of schedule on the activity of etoposide in small-cell lung cancer. J Clin Oncol 1989;7:1333–40.

69. de Wit R, Stoter G, Kaye SB, et al. Importance of bleomycin in combination chemotherapy for good-prognosis testicular nonseminoma: a randomized study of the European Organization for Research and Treatment of Cancer Genitourinary Tract Cancer Cooperative Group. J Clin Oncol 1997;15:1837–43.

70. Toner GC, Stockler MR, Boyer MJ, et al. Comparison of two standard chemotherapy regimens for good-prognosis germ-cell tumours: a randomised trial. Australian and New Zealand Germ Cell Trial Group. Lancet 2001;357:739–45.

71. Oliver RT, Dhaliwal HS, Hope-Stone HF, Blandy JP. Short-course etoposide, bleomycin and cisplatin in the treatment of metastatic germ cell tumours. Appraisal of its potential as adjuvant chemotherapy for stage 1 testis tumours. Br J Urol 1988;61:53–8.

72. Chisholm RA, Dixon AK, Williams MV, Oliver RT. Bleomycin lung: the effect of different chemotherapeutic regimens. Cancer Chemother Pharmacol 1992;30:158–60.

73. Fossa SD, Collette L, Aaronson N, et al. Quality of life in patients with good prognosis metastatic germ cell tumours: comparison of four chemotherapy schedules. In: Harnden P, Joffe JK, Jones WG, editors. Germ cell tumours V. London: Springer-Verlag; 2002. p. 183–95.

74. Levi JA, Thomson D, Bishop J, et al. Dose intensity and outcome with combination chemotherapy for germ cell carcinoma. Australasian Germ Cell Trial Group. Eur J Cancer Clin Oncol 1989;25:1073–7.

75. Simpson AB, Paul J, Graham J, Kaye SB. Fatal bleomycin pulmonary toxicity in the west of Scotland 1991–95: a review of patients with germ cell tumours. Br J Cancer 1998;78:1061–6.

76. Bosl GJ, Geller NL, Bajorin D, et al. A randomized trial of etoposide + cisplatin versus vinblastine + bleomycin + cisplatin + cyclophosphamide + dactinomycin in patients with good-prognosis germ cell tumors. J Clin Oncol 1988;6:1231–8.

77. Loehrer PJ Sr, Johnson D, Elson P, et al. Importance of bleomycin in favorable-prognosis disseminated germ cell tumors: an Eastern Cooperative Oncology Group trial. J Clin Oncol 1995;13:470–6.

78. Levi JA, Raghavan D, Harvey V, et al. The importance of bleomycin in combination chemotherapy for good- prognosis germ cell carcinoma. Australasian Germ Cell Trial Group. J Clin Oncol 1993;11:1300–5.

79. Bajorin DF, Bosl GJ. Bleomycin in germ cell tumor therapy: not all regimens are created equal. J Clin Oncol 1997;15:1717–9.

80. Bajorin DF, Geller NL, Weisen SF, Bosl GJ. Two-drug therapy in patients with metastatic germ cell tumors. Cancer 1991;67:28–32.

81. Culine S, Kerbrat P, Bouzy J, et al. Are 3 cycles of bleomycin, etoposide and cisplatin (3BEP) or 4 cycles of etoposide and cisplatin (4EP) equivalent regimens for patients with good-risk metastatic non seminomatous germ cell tumours? Preliminary results of a randomized trial. Proc Am Soc Clin Oncol 1999;18:A1188.

82. Saxman SB, Nichols CR, Foster RS, et al. The management of patients with clinical stage I nonseminomatous testicular tumors and persistently elevated serologic markers. J Urol 1996;155:587–9.

83. Motzer RJ, Geller NL, Bosl GJ. The effect of a 7-day delay in chemotherapy cycles on complete response and event-free survival in good-risk disseminated germ cell tumor patients. Cancer 1990;66:857–61.

84. Lange PH, Vogelzang NJ, Goldman A, et al. Marker half-life analysis as a prognostic tool in testicular cancer. J Urol 1982;128:708–11.

85. Toner GC, Geller NL, Tan C, et al. Serum tumor marker half-life during chemotherapy allows early prediction of complete response and survival in nonseminomatous germ cell tumors. Cancer Res 1990;50:5904–10.

86. See WA, Cohen MB, Hoxie LD. Alpha-fetoprotein half-life as a predictor of residual testicular tumor. Effect of the analytic strategy on test sensitivity and specificity. Cancer 1993;71:2048–54.

87. Murphy BA, Motzer RJ, Mazumdar M, et al. Serum tumor marker decline is an early predictor of treatment outcome in germ cell tumor patients treated with cisplatin and ifosfamide salvage chemotherapy. Cancer 1994;73:2520–6.

88. Bosl GJ, Head MD. Serum tumor marker half-life during chemotherapy in patients with germ cell tumors. Int J Biol Markers 1994;9:25–8.

89. Stevens MJ, Norman AR, Dearnaley DP, Horwich A. Prognostic significance of early serum tumor marker half-life in metastatic testicular teratoma. J Clin Oncol 1995;13:87–92.

90. de Wit R, Sylvester R, Tsitsa C, et al. Tumour marker concentration at the start of chemotherapy is a stronger predictor of treatment failure than marker half-life: a study in patients with disseminated non-seminomatous testicular cancer. Br J Cancer 1997;75:432–5.

91. Gerl A, Lamerz R, Clemm C, et al. Does serum tumor marker half-life complement pretreatment risk stratification in metastatic nonseminomatous germ cell tumors? Clin Cancer Res 1996;2:1565–70.

92. Gerl A, Lamerz R, Mann K, et al. Is serum tumor marker half-life a guide to prognosis in metastatic nonseminomatous germ cell tumors? Anticancer Res 1997;17:3047–9.

93. Inanc SE, Meral R, Darendeliler E, et al. Prognostic significance of marker half-life during chemotherapy in nonseminomatous germ cell testicular tumors. Acta Oncol 1999;38:505–9.

94. Mazumdar M, Bajorin DF, Bacik J, et al. Predicting outcome to chemotherapy in patients with germ cell tumors: the value of the rate of decline of human chorionic gonadotrophin and alpha-fetoprotein during therapy. J Clin Oncol 2001;19:2534–41.

95. Morris MJ, Bosl GJ. Recognizing abnormal marker results that do not reflect disease in patients with germ cell tumors. J Urol 2000;163:796–801.

96. Broun ER, Nichols CR, Kneebone P, et al. Long-term outcome of patients with relapsed and refractory germ cell tumors treated with high-dose chemotherapy and autologous bone marrow rescue. Ann Intern Med 1992;117:124–8.

97. Toner GC, Panicek DM, Heelan RT, et al. Adjunctive surgery after chemotherapy for nonseminomatous germ cell tumors: recommendations for patient selection. J Clin Oncol 1990;8:1683–94.

98. Reddel RR, Thompson JF, Raghavan D, et al. Surgery in patients with advanced germ cell malignancy following a clinical partial response to chemotherapy. J Surg Oncol 1983;23:223–7.

99. Michael H, Lucia J, Foster RS, Ulbright TM. The pathology of late recurrence of testicular germ cell tumors. Am J Surg Pathol 2000;24:257–73.

100. Ulbright TM, Loehrer PJ, Roth LM, et al. The development of non-germ cell malignancies within germ cell tumors. A clinicopathologic study of 11 cases. Cancer 1984;54: 1824–33.

101. McCaffrey JA, Mazumdar M, Bajorin DF, et al. Ifosfamide- and cisplatin-containing chemotherapy as first-line salvage therapy in germ cell tumors: response and survival. J Clin Oncol 1997;15:2559–63.

102. Baniel J, Foster RS, Gonin R, et al. Late relapse of testicular cancer. J Clin Oncol 1995;13:1170–6.

103. Michael H, Lucia J, Foster RS, Ulbright TM. The pathology of late recurrence of testicular germ cell tumors. Am J Surg Pathol 2000;24:257–73.

104. Tait D, Peckham MJ, Hendry WF, Goldstraw P. Post-chemotherapy surgery in advanced non-seminomatous germ-cell testicular tumours: the significance of histology with particular reference to differentiated (mature) teratoma. Br J Cancer 1984;50:601–9.

105. Joffe JK. Risks and benefits of follow-up of early germ cell tumours—a survey of current practice. In: Harnden P, Joffe JK, Jones WG, editors. Germ cell tumours V. London: Springer-Verlag; 2002. p. 275–6.

106. Kollmannsberger C, Kuzcyk M, Mayer F, et al. Late toxicity following curative treatment of testicular cancer. Semin Surg Oncol 1999;17:275–81.

14

Management of Nonseminomatous Testicular Cancer Chemotherapy for Poor-Risk Patients: Standard-Dose Therapy

EDWARD S. NEWLANDS, MD, PhD, FRCP

The survival of patients with metastatic nonseminomatous germ cell tumors (NSGCTs) was poor prior to the introduction of cisplatin and etoposide in the mid-1970s. Only about 10% of these patients achieved durable remission with drugs such as the vinca alkaloids, methotrexate, actinomycin D, cyclophosphamide, doxorubicin, and bleomycin. In a phase I trial of cisplatin, Higby and colleagues[1] noted the initial responses in patients with NSGCTs, as well as the nephrotoxicity of the drug if the patients were not hydrated. This study was rapidly followed up with the introduction of the combination of cisplatin, vinblastine, and bleomycin (PVB) by Einhorn and colleagues.[2] In their initial cohort, approximately 50% of patients achieved durable remission. It became apparent that patients with advanced disease did worse than those with small volume metastatic disease.

Etoposide was introduced at the Charing Cross Hospital in 1977[3] as an additional active agent in heavily pretreated patients with NSGCTs. It was clear at this time that the potential for radically altering the survival of patients with metastatic NSGCT was dramatic. The question was how to maximize the complete and durable remission rates in these young patients. Although the PVB regimen was clearly a dramatic advance over previous therapeutic approaches, its results in patients with advanced disease were much less satisfactory. In the United Kingdom at that time, patients with NSGCTs tended

to present very late, with a long history of testicular swelling for 6 to 12 months before their orchiectomy, and the majority of the patients at the Charing Cross Hospital at that time had large-volume metastatic disease. In addition, at the Charing Cross Hospital, Bagshawe and colleagues had developed the routine monitoring of these patients with serial human chorionic gonadotropin (hCG) and α-fetoprotein (AFP) tumor markers. The early use of these clinically dynamic monitors of treatment allowed both the confirmation of the dramatic activity of cisplatin and etoposide in treating patients with this disease and the identification of complete remission in relation to the two most lethal elements within NSGCTs: (1) the choriocarcinoma cells producing hCG and (2) the yolk sac cells producing AFP. The use of tumor markers had significant advantages over the relatively primitive radiologic tests that were available at that time.

It also became rapidly apparent that patients with large-volume disease were frequently left with residual masses that needed to be removed surgically (1) to determine whether they contained active tumor or simply differentiated teratoma or necrosis and (2) to maximize the patient's chance of achieving durable remissions. It was clear that it was important to introduce etoposide and cisplatin into patients' primary treatment.

The schedule for the combination of cisplatin, vincristine, methotrexate, and bleomycin (POMB) and actinomycin D, cyclophosphamide, and etoposide (ACE) was devised in 1977.[4] The concept behind this essentially alternating schedule of chemotherapy was to alternate the POMB schedule, which was less myelosuppressive than the ACE schedule, and to increase the dose intensity by having a schedule of every two weeks rather than the more commonly used schedule of every three weeks of chemotherapy. Although the POMB/ACE schedule contains seven drugs, the total cumulative dose of each individual drug is less than that in schedules such as PVB and such as bleomycin, etoposide, and cisplatin (BEP)[5] because the component schedules essentially alternate. The experience of the past 25 years of treating these patients is that durable remissions are maximized if the chemotherapy contains a minimum of 300 mg/m^2 of cisplatin and that the proportion of remissions probably increases with the total dose of etoposide administered.*

Over the last 25 years, there have been major changes in the pattern of presentation of patients with NSGCT in the United Kingdom. With better diagnostic equipment and medical education together with the awareness of the curability of this disease, the pattern of referral has changed dramatically. Currently, we are seeing over 80% of patients referred with stage I disease. These patients are monitored on a program of surveillance that was introduced at Charing Cross Hospital in 1979[6] (see also Chapter 10). This is in contrast to the invasive histologic staging of these patients by retroperitoneal lymph node dissection. Only a small number of patients now present with advanced disease, and this is usually when the primary tumor has not been clinically evident and the patient presents with symptoms of metastatic spread.

---

*Editor's note: To date the cooperative groups have chosen not to test the POMB/ACE regimen against the current standard of care, preferring (at least in North America) to test the impact of high-dose therapy. One must simply note that the POMB/ACE regimen, in very experienced hands, yields highly impressive response and cure rates for patients with poor risk disease, as defined by the IGCCC. In my own experience, I have not found POMB/ACE to be a panacea of extragonadal germ cell tumors or relapsed malignancy, but have certainly been able to duplicate the Charing Cross experience with first presentations of IGCCC poor risk, metastatic testis cancer.

STAGING INVESTIGATIONS AND PROGNOSTIC FACTORS

At Charing Cross Hospital, the routine staging investigation performed on these patients after their initial orchiectomy is computed tomography (CT) of the thorax and abdomen (usually omitting the pelvis, except in patients who have had a previous orchiopexy), to minimize the radiation to these patients. Patients are all routinely monitored with the three serum tumor markers hCG, AFP, and lactate dehydrogenase (LDH). Patients with pulmonary metastases routinely have a magnetic resonance imaging (MRI) brain scan performed. Baseline renal function is measured by ethylenediaminetetraacetic acid (EDTA) clearance. In patients with poor-prognosis NSGCTs, initial organ failure can be a problem at the initiation of treatment. Renal failure from ureteric obstruction, liver failure, and severely compromised pulmonary function can all be problems that need addressing at the start of treatment.

A variety of staging and prognostic classifications have been used over the years, but since the international consensus by the International Germ Cell Cancer Collaborative Group (IGCCCG) was published,[7] most centers have been routinely using this classification (Table 14–1). Key components of poor-risk disease are a mediastinal primary, nonpulmonary metastases (such as liver and brain metastases), and high tumor marker levels as defined in Table 14–1.

PRIMARY CHEMOTHERAPY FOR PATIENTS WITH POOR-RISK NSGCT

The two schedules most commonly used in treating patients with poor-risk NSGCT are shown in Table 14–2. Einhorn and colleagues confirmed that BEP was superior to PVB[8] in a randomized trial in 1987. Since then, BEP has been the most widely used schedule in the initial therapy for this disease. The results of the major randomized trials in patients with poor-risk disease that have reported the proportion of durable remissions are shown in Table 14–3.[9–12] While the rate of complete response in this group of patients varies between 38 and 74%, the rates of durable remissions are less satisfactory and range from 50 to 73% (the 73% rate came from a small ran-

Table 14–1.   INTERNATIONAL GERM CELL CONSENSUS CLASSIFICATION PROGNOSIS CRITERIA

	Nonseminoma	Seminoma
Good Prognosis*†	Testicular/retroperitoneal primary and No nonpulmonary visceral metastases and Good markers (all): AFP < 1,000 ng/mL, hCG < 5,000 IU/L (1,000 ng/mL), and LDH < 1.5 × upper limit of N	Any primary site and No nonpulmonary visceral metastases and Normal AFP, any hCG, any LDH
Intermediate Prognosis‡§	Testicular/retroperitoneal primary and No nonpulmonary visceral metastases and Intermediate markers (any 1): AFP ≥ 1,000 ng/mL and ≤ 10,000 ng/mL, or hCG ≥ 5,000 IU/L and ≤ 50,000 IU/L, or LDH ≥ 1.5 × N and ≤ 10 × N	Any primary site and Nonpulmonary visceral metastases and Normal AFP, any hCG, any LDH
Poor Prognosis‖	Mediastinal primary or Nonpulmonary visceral metastases or Poor markers (any 1): AFP > 10,000 ng/mL, or hCG > 50,000 IU/L (10,000 ng/mL), or LDH > 10 × N	(No patients classified as poor prognosis)

Adapted from International Germ Cell Cancer Collaborative Group.[7]
AFP = α-fetoprotein; hCG = human chorionic gonadotropin; LDH = lactate dehydrogenase; N = normal; PFS = progression-free survival.
*58% of nonseminomas; 5-year PFS, 89%; 5-year survival, 92%.
†90% of seminomas; 5-year PFS, 82%; 5-year survival, 86%.
‡28% of nonseminomas; 5-year PFS, 75%; 5-year survival, 80%.
§10% of seminomas; 5-year PFS, 67%; 5-year survival, 72%.
‖16% of nonseminomas; 5-year PFS, 41%; 5-year survival; 48%.

domized trial performed at the National Cancer Institute). It is clear from these data that patients with poor-risk disease still need further improvements in therapy. The philosophy at the Charing Cross Hospital has been to try to maximize the initial complete responses and durable remissions since it has always been difficult to salvage cases after the induction of drug resistance or after relapse.

The role of high-dose chemotherapy with autologous bone marrow support (HD/ABMT) for patients with poor-risk NSGCT is under current evaluation (see Chapter 15). At the Charing Cross Hospital, this approach has been used primarily for patients who have relapsed after their primary treatment and occasionally for patients whose disease relapses through their primary chemotherapy.[13]

The schedule we continue to use for patients with metastatic germ cell tumors is the POMB/ACE schedule,[14–16] which is shown in Table 14–4. Patients with good- and intermediate-risk disease receive a total of five courses of chemotherapy at 2-week intervals of two weeks (ie, POMB ×3 and ACE ×2). For patients with poor-risk disease, we have used the rate of response in serum tumor markers as a guide

Table 14–2.   COMMONLY USED CHEMOTHERAPY REGIMENS FOR METASTATIC GERM CELL TUMOR

Patient Status	Regimen	Cycles Administered
Previously untreated (poor risk)	Etoposide, 100mg/m² IV daily × 5 days Cisplatin, 20 mg/m² IV daily × 5 days Bleomycin, 30 U IV weekly on days 2, 9, and 16	4 cycles administered at 21-day intervals

Previously treated
(first-line salvage therapy)
	Ifosfamide, 1.2 mg/m² IV daily × 5 days
	Mesna, 400 mg/m² IV every 8 hours × 5 days
	Cisplatin, 20 mg/m² IV daily × 5 days
	   plus either
	Vinblastine, 0.11 mg/kg IV on days 1 and 2,
	   or
	etoposide, 75 mg/m² IV daily × 5 days
		—

Table 14–3.   RESULTS OF RANDOMIZED TRIALS IN PATIENTS WITH POOR-RISK GERM CELL TUMORS

Reference	Organization	Treatment	No. of Patients	Complete Responses (%)	Durable Remissions (%)
9	Indiana U.	PEB	77	73	61
		P(200)EB	76	68	63
10	NCI	PVB	18	67	50
		P(200)BE	34	88	73
11	Indiana U.	PEB	141	60	57
		VIP	145	63	56
12	EORTC/MRC	BEP/EP	185	57	55
		BOP/VIP-B	186	54	53

B = bleomycin; E = etoposide; EORTC = European Organization for the Research and Treatment of Cancer; I = ifosfamide; MRC = Medical Research Council; NCI = National Cancer Institute; O = vincristine; P = cisplatin, 100 mg/m^2; P(200) = cisplatin, 200 mg/m^2; V = vinblastine.

for the duration of therapy. We try for normalization of the main two serum tumor markers hCG and AFP and continue alternating POMB and ACE until the patient has been in tumor marker remission for approximately 4 weeks (Figure 14–1). In common with other centers, as confidence in the stability of the complete remissions obtained with chemotherapy has increased, we have shortened the total duration of treatment. It should be noted that we have modified our current approach to this regimen, shortening the duration of treatment by omitting the second 24-hour infusion of bleomycin.

In patients with initial organ failure (lung, liver, and kidney), we have used an induction schedule of etoposide and cisplatin (EP), as shown in Table 14–5. This can be repeated 1 week later, and one or two courses usually are sufficient to reduce the organ failure so that the full POMB/ACE schedule can be started as described above. This approach allows chemotherapy to be delivered to patients who would otherwise get major toxicity if they received either BEP in full dose or POMB in full dose.

In our last analysis of the patients treated with POMB/ACE chemotherapy for metastatic NSGCT between 1977 and 1995,[16] there were 339 men, including 42 patients who had received prior treatment (30 with irradiation, 6 with chemotherapy, and 6 with both). Forty-one patients (12%) had an extragonadal primary, 54 (16%) had nonpulmonary visceral metastases, and 80 (24%) had high-risk levels of serum tumor markers (AFP > 10,000 mg/mL or hCG > 50,000 IU/L). This analysis reclassified

Table 14–4.   SCHEDULE FOR POMB/ACE REGIMEN

Day	Agent	Dose*
POMB		
1	Vincristine	1 mg/m^2 (max 2 mg) IV bolus
	Methotrexate	300 mg/m^2 IV infusion
2	Bleomycin	30 mg IV infusion over 24 h
	Folinic acid	15 mg at 24, 36, 48, and 60 h
3	Cisplatin	120 mg/m^2 IV infusion over 12 h
ACE		
1	Etoposide	100 mg/m^2 IV infusion
	Actinomycin D	0.5 mg IV bolus
2	Etoposide	100 mg/m^2 IV infusion
	Actinomycin D	0.5 mg IV bolus
3	Etoposide	100 mg/m^2 IV infusion
	Actinomycin D	0.5 mg IV bolus
	Cyclophosphamide	500 mg/m^2 in 250 mL NS over 30 min

Adapted from Bower M et al.[16]
ACE = actinomycin D, cyclophosphamide, and etoposide; max = maximum; NS = normal saline; POMB = cisplatin, vincristine, methotrexate, and bleomycin.
*The POMB/ACE schedule is administered fortnightly and alternates between POMB and ACE regimens after the first two cycles, which are both with POMB.

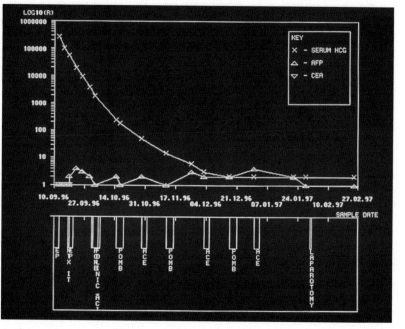

Figure 14–1. Graph of tumor marker levels in a patient with poor-prognosis disease according to the International Germ Cell Cancer Collaborative Group classification. The patient presented with inferior vena caval thrombosis and renal failure. His initial treatment was with etoposide and cisplatin (EP) followed by chemotherapy with cisplatin/vincristine/methotrexate/bleomycin and actinomycin D/cyclophosphamide/etoposide (POMB/ACE). His treatment was completed by the removal of the para-aortic nodes via the retroperitoneal approach. (AFP = α-fetoprotein; hCG = human chorionic gonadotropin; THRCTMY = thoracotomy; EPPT(L) = etoposide and cisplatinum.) (Reproduced with permission from Christmas TJ et al.[18])

the previously untreated patients into the three prognostic groups of the IGCCCG classification (see Table 14–1). Patients were identified as having poor-prognosis disease on account of mediastinal primaries (14 patients), nonpulmonary visceral metastases (50 patients), and/or high-risk tumor markers (74 patients). There were 41 patients in the intermediate prognostic group according to Table 14–1. Sixty-five patients (19%) presented with respiratory, renal, hepatic, or cerebral metastases and needed initial treatment with EP (see Table 14–5) before starting POMB/ACE chemotherapy. The majority of our patients with cerebral metastases have been treated with the EP/OMB schedule (this has been reported separately).[17] Ninety-eight patients required surgical resection of residual masses at the end of chemotherapy[18] (Figure 14–2).

The overall survival rate of the 339 patients is 82% (95% confidence interval [CI], 78–85%) at 5 years and 79% (95% CI, 75–84%) at 10 years (Figure 14–3).

Not surprisingly, patients who had received prior radiotherapy/chemotherapy had worse survival rates than did the untreated patients ($p = .039$). Comparing our results with the 3-year survival rates initially published in the IGCCCG prognostic classification, the survival rate for patients in the good-risk group was 97% (95% CI, 94–99%), the rate for the intermediate-risk group was 88% (95% CI, 77–98%), and the rate in the poor-risk group was 75% (95% CI, 65–84%). These figures compare with the IGCCCG groups of

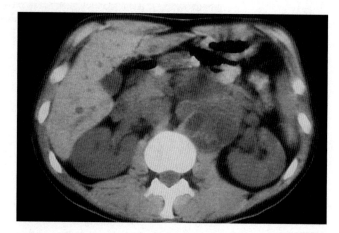

Figure 14–2. Computed tomography (CT) scan of the patient whose resected specimen is shown in Figure 14–7 and who presented with massive liver disease at the start of treatment. This CT scan was made after the completion of treatment that included cisplatin/vincristine/methotrexate/bleomycin and actinomycin D/cyclophosphamide/etoposide (POMB/ACE) chemotherapy followed by high-dose chemotherapy.

Table 14–5.	ETOPOSIDE/CISPLATIN INDUCTION SCHEDULE FOR PATIENTS WITH INITIAL ORGAN FAILURE	
Day	Drug	Dosage
1	Etoposide	100 mg/m²
	Cisplatin	20 mg/m²
2	Etoposide	100 mg/m²
	Cisplatin	20 mg/m²

92%, 81%, and 50% survival rates at 3 years (Table 14–6). The prognosis for patients with extragonadal germ cell tumors was inferior to that for patients with primary testicular tumors, with 5-year overall survival rates of 63% (95% CI, 38–87%) for primary retroperitoneal tumors and 60% (95% CI, 40–80%) for primary mediastinal germ cell tumors ($p \leq .0001$) (Figures 14–4, 14–5, and 14–6).[19] The survival of the patients treated with POMB/ACE, classified into the three IGCCCG groups, is shown in Figure 14–7. Of particular interest is the poor-prognosis group, in which the survival rate drops from 75% at 3 years to just greater than 60% with a maximum follow-up of 20 years. Late relapses continue to be a problem for a minority in this group of patients, and studies reporting results after 3- to 5-year periods of follow-up should be interpreted with caution (see Table 14–3).

Toxicity: Experience and Studies

Ten men died within 2 months of starting POMB/ACE chemotherapy: 3 from progressive disease, 1 from a pulmonary embolus, 1 from a ruptured aorta, 3 from neutropenic sepsis, 1 from pulmonary edema, and 1 from methotrexate-induced hepatotoxicity.

Late toxicity is important in these young patients. Over the period of 1977 to 1995, we had five patients who subsequently developed acute myeloid leukemia. One of these patients also had a primary mediastinal germ cell tumor, and this is a known association in this subgroup of patients.[20] Over that 25-year period, the policy has been one of gradually shortening the duration of chemotherapy, and there have been no new cases of acute myeloid leukemia in the last 12 years. An analysis of 679 patients treated in London between 1979 and 1992 showed that there was approximately the same incidence of acute myeloid leukemia in patients treated with POMB/ACE (343 patients) as there was in patients treated with PVB and/or BEP (336 patients).[21] There were three cases of acute myeloid leukemia in the POMB/ACE group and three cases in the PVB and/or BEP group. Of note, there was only one death from pulmonary failure (a patient who had completed treatment 5 months previously). This is in sharp contrast to the incidence of pneumonitis reported among patients on the BEP schedule, in which the bleomycin is frequently administered as an intravenous bolus. In a recent randomized trial comparing two different schedules of BEP, the incidence of pneumonitis among patients using the 5-day and most widely used version (see Table 14–3) was 12%.[22] One of our patients developed adenocarcinoma of the lung 5 years after completing treatment. Three patients died of cerebro- or cardiovascular disease 3.7, 8.5, and 10.3 years, respectively, after completing chemotherapy.

Other Series Involving POMB/ACE

To my knowledge, the POMB/ACE regimen has been tested in two other reported case series. Investigators at Queen Elizabeth Hospital in Birmingham and at Guy's Hospital in London collaborated on a study of 55 patients with advanced malignant germ cell tumors and 5 patients with large-volume

Table 14–6. SURVIVAL RATES FOR PATIENTS WITH METASTATIC NONSEMINOMATOUS GERM CELL CANCER		
	3-Year Overall Survival (%)	
Patient Status	POMB/ACE*	IGCCCG Cohort
Good prognosis	97	92
Intermediate prognosis	88	81
Poor prognosis	75	50

ACE = actinomycin D, cyclophosphamide, and etoposide; IGCCCG = International Germ Cell Cancer Collaborative Group; POMB = cisplatin, vincristine, methotrexate, and bleomycin.
*339 patients treated with POMB/ACE chemotherapy; analyzed by the Kaplan-Meier method.

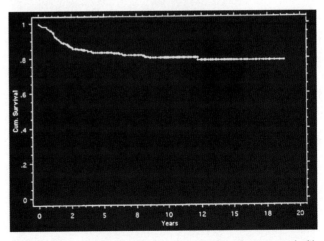

Figure 14–3. Overall survival curve for all 339 patients treated with POMB/ACE chemotherapy, as analyzed by the Kaplan-Meier method. (Reproduced with permission of the editor of *Annals of Oncology*.)

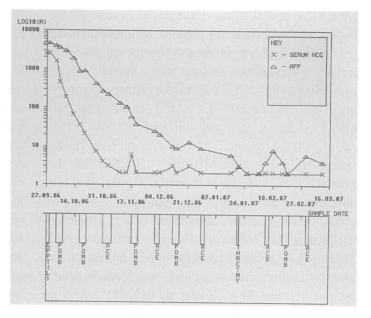

Figure 14–4. Tumor markers in a patient treated with chemotherapy with cisplatin/vincristine/methotrexate/bleomycin and actinomycin D/cyclophosphamide/etoposide (POMB/ACE). The patient presented with breathlessness and chest pain from a massive α-fetoprotein (AFP) and human chorionic gonadotropin (hCG)-producing mediastinal germ cell tumor. Following eight courses of POMB/ACE chemotherapy, tumor markers were falling; his overall chest mass had decreased in size and was completely resected surgically. As large masses frequently contain some residual active tumor, the patient received several postoperative courses of chemotherapy.

metastatic seminomas.[23] This series included 21 previously untreated patients with very large-volume disease (including 4 patients with hepatic involvement and 4 patients with central nervous system [CNS] metastases) and 16 previously untreated patients with extragonadal NSGCTs. The long-term survival rate was approximately 70% although it is noted that there were four treatment-related deaths (6%). For those patients with disease of very high volume and very high tumor marker levels, the long-term survival rate was only around 50% although the authors acknowledged that they abbreviated the duration of therapy, compared to the Charing Cross Hospital experience.

Husband and Green reported the experience from Clatterbridge Hospital, in Liverpool, United Kingdom, in 53 patients who were treated between 1983 and 1989.[24] The series included a mixed group of

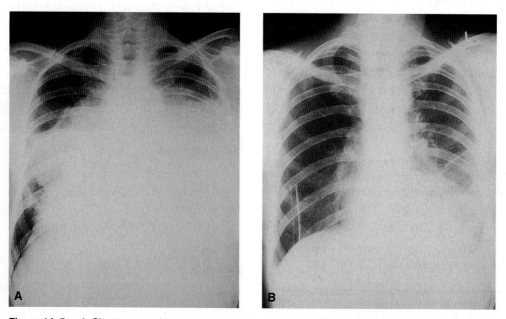

Figure 14–5. *A,* Chest x-ray at the start of treatment for a mediastinal germ cell tumor in the patient whose tumor markers are graphed in Figure 14–4. *B,* Chest x-ray of the same patient at the end of treatment. (Reproduced with permission of the editor of *Annals of Oncology.*)

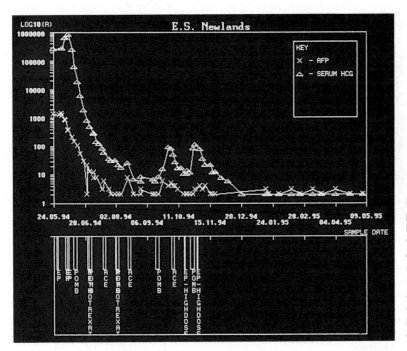

Figure 14–6. Tumor marker response in a patient who presented with metastatic testicular germ cell tumor and hepatic failure at the start of chemotherapeutic treatment with etoposide and cisplatin (EP) followed by cisplatin/vincristine/methotrexate/bleomycin and actinomycin D/cyclophosphamide/etoposide (POMB/ACE). Resistance to POMB/ACE chemotherapy became apparent with rising levels of human chorionic gonadotropin later in his treatment, and he underwent bone marrow harvest and high-dose chemotherapy with carboplatin, etoposide, and cyclophosphamide.

patients, including 24 patients with very large-volume disease (including liver, CNS, or bone metastases or L3 disease [bulky, in the Medical Research Council classification]) and others with less extensive tumor. A median of five courses of POMB (range, three to eight courses) was delivered, with a median of four courses of ACE (range, two to seven courses). There were no toxic deaths although there were 16 episodes of neutropenic fever. The overall complete response rate was 62%, with a long-term survival rate (maximum follow-up of 20 years) of around 65%. Of the 12 patients with poor prognostic sites (liver, bone, CNS, and mediastinal primary), 6 died of progressive tumor. This study suggested that the dose intensity of cisplatin had no prognostic significance but that the dose intensity of etoposide was associated with a survival benefit.

It is hard to compare these two small series with the results generated from the Charing Cross Hospital. We believe that dose intensity is an important factor in the efficacy of the POMB/ACE regimen and that the duration of treatment may also be important. As discussed by the authors of these two series, the POMB/ACE regimen is a complex and demanding schedule, and we believe strongly that experience in its delivery is an important component of success. No randomized trial has tested the utility

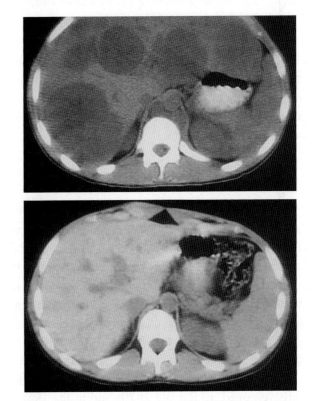

Figure 14–7. Computed tomography (CT) scans showing differentiated cystic teratoma in a patient presenting with large-volume disease and large residual masses in the para-aortic region and lower thorax. CT shows the mixed density of lesions, suggesting differentiated cystic teratoma. The left and right intra-abdominal and intrathoracic differentiated teratoma was removed through a surgical resection via the retroperitoneal approach. (Reproduced with permission from Christmas TJ et al.[18])

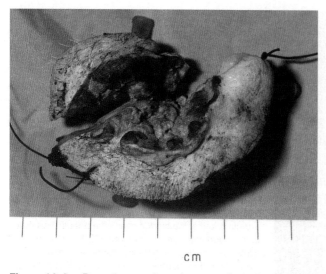

cm

Figure 14–8. Resection specimen from a patient who presented with metastatic testicular germ cell tumor and hepatic failure at the start of chemotherapeutic treatment with etoposide and cisplatin (EP) followed by cisplatin/vincristine/methotrexate/bleomycin and actinomycin D/cyclophosphamide/etoposide (POMB/ACE). Resistance to POMB/ACE chemotherapy became apparent with rising levels of human chorionic gonadotropin later in his treatment, and he underwent bone marrow harvest and high-dose chemotherapy with carboplatin, etoposide, and cyclophosphamide.

of POMB/ACE against that of any commonly used schedules, but as the 20-year results show, in our hands it produces a high cure rate for patients with poor-risk metastatic germ cell tumors, when classified by IGCCCG criteria.

SALVAGE THERAPY

In the POMB/ACE series reported, 40 patients relapsed after the completion of treatment, at a mean of 1.4 years (range, 0.4 to 9.8 years), and 25 (60%) of these men have died. This emphasizes the need to maximize the durable complete remission rate in patients' primary therapy. Salvage treatment has always been difficult. The chances of successful salvage are greater if the tumor remains sensitive to cisplatin-based chemotherapy and particularly if the main site of active disease is known and can be surgically removed. In the late 1970s and in the 1980s, we managed to salvage approximately 40% of cases with this approach.

In the last decade, it has become clearer that there is a role for high-dose chemotherapy with autologous bone marrow transplantation (ABMT) in two contexts: (1) patients with extreme poor-prognosis dis-

ease that does not go into complete remission on primary chemotherapy (Figures 14–7 and 14–8) and (2) patients who relapse after primary chemotherapy; such cases may be salvaged with this approach. We reported our previous result of using a combination of carboplatin, etoposide, and cyclophosphamide, which was that approximately 30 to 40% of cases were salvaged with this approach.[13] Recently, we have added paclitaxel to the other three drugs, and the preliminary results indicate that salvage rates may be superior with this approach.[25]

Our results, in common with a number of other reporting centers, are that the patients who are most likely to achieve durable remission on high-dose chemotherapy are those with cisplatin-sensitive disease. In our most recent analysis, the survival of patients with cisplatin-sensitive disease prior to their receiving high-dose chemotherapy was 75%, in contrast to 15% for those whose disease was not clearly sensitive to re-induction chemotherapy containing cisplatin.

FERTILITY

We routinely arrange for sperm storage prior to starting chemotherapy. We have recently analyzed long-term post-treatment fertility in these patients. Of those patients who wanted to father children, 72% have been successful. Only two patients used their stored sperm. The infertility rate was 12%, and infertility was associated with prior radiotherapy, an atrophic contralateral testis, and a low sperm count prior to treatment. A few cases were unexplained.

FUTURE DIRECTIONS

Clearly, the main two future directions in treating these young patients are (1) improving survival and (2) reducing toxicity. The main two new drugs with activity against NSGCT that have been introduced over the last decade are paclitaxel and gemcitabine (see also Chapter 16). We have achieved a high response rate by combining paclitaxel (Taxol) with cisplatin, alternating with Taxol and etoposide, to re-induce remissions in patients who have relapsed prior to their high-dose chemotherapy. The combination of gemcitabine and cisplatin is clearly active in a wide range of tumors. It may be that a future successor to the widely used BEP chemotherapy will be the combination of gemcitabine, etoposide, and cisplatin although this concept will require testing in well-designed clinical trials.

ACKNOWLEDGMENTS

I would like to thank all of my colleagues at Hammersmith Hospitals NHS Trust for excellent support.

REFERENCES

1. Higby DJ, Wallace HJ, Albert DJ, Holland JF. Diamminodichloroplatinum: a phase I study showing responses in testicular and other tumors. Cancer 1974;33:1219–25.
2. Einhorn LH, Donohue JP. Cis-diamminedichloroplatinum, vinblastine, and bleomycin combination chemotherapy in disseminated testicular cancer. Ann Intern Med 1977; 87:293–8.
3. Newlands ES, Bagshawe KD. Epipodophyllin derivative (VP.16-213) in malignant teratomas and choriocarcinomas. Lancet 1977;ii:87.
4. Newlands ES, Begent RHJ, Kaye SB, et al. Chemotherapy in advanced malignant teratomas. Br J Cancer 1980;42: 378–84.
5. Peckham MJ, Barrett, A, Liew KH, et al. The treatment of metastatic germ-cell testicular tumours with bleomycin, etoposide and cisplatin (BEP). Br J Cancer 1983;47:613–9.
6. Francis R, Bower M, Brunstrom G, et al. Surveillance for stage I testicular germ cell tumours: results and cost benefit of management options. Eur J Cancer 2000;36:1925–32.
7. International Germ Cell Cancer Collaborative Group. International Germ Cell Consensus Classification: a prognostic factor-based staging system for metastatic germ cell cancers. J Clin Oncol 1997;15:594–603.
8. Williams SD, Birch R, Einhorn LH. Treatment of disseminated germ cell tumors with cisplatin, bleomycin, and either vinblastine or etoposide. N Engl J Med 1987;316:1435–40.
9. Nichols CR, Wiliams SD, Loehre PJ, et al. Randomized study of cisplatin dose intensity in poor-risk germ-cell tumors: a Southeastern Cancer Study Group and Southwest Oncology Group protocol. J Clin Oncol 1991;9:1163–72.
10. Ozols RF, Ihde DC, Linehan WM, et al. A randomized trial of standard chemotherapy vs. a high dose chemotherapy regimen in the treatment of poor prognosis nonseminomatous germ-cell tumours. J Clin Oncol 1988;6:1031–40.
11. Nichols CR, Loehrer PJ, Einhorn LH, et al. Phase III study of cisplatin, etoposide and bleomycin (PVP16B) or etoposide,
12. ifosfamide and cisplatin (VIP) in advanced stage germ-cell tumours: an intergroup trial [abstract 632]. Proc ASW 1995.
13. Kaye SB, Mead GM, Fossa S, et al. Intensive induction-sequential chemotherapy with BOP/VIP-B compared with treatment with BEP/EP for poor prognosis metastatic non-seminomatous germ cell tumor: a randomised Medical Research Council/European Organisation for Research and Treatment of Cancer study. J Clin Oncol 1998;16:692–701.
13. Lyttelton MPA, Newlands ES, Giles C, et al. High-dose therapy including carboplatin adjusted for renal function in patients with relapsed or refractory germ cell tumour: outcome and prognostic factors. Br J Cancer 1998;77:1672–6.
14. Newlands ES, Begent RH, Rustin GJ, et al. Further advances in the management of malignant teratomas of the testis and other sites. Lancet 1983;1:948–51.
15. Hitchins RN, Newlands ES, Smith DB, et al. Long-term outcome in patients with germ cell tumours treated with POMB/ACE chemotherapy: comparison of commonly used classification systems of good and poor prognosis. Br J Cancer 1989;59:236–42.
16. Bower M, Newlands ES, Holden L, et al. Treatment of men with metastatic non-seminomatous germ cell tumours with cyclical POMB/ACE chemotherapy. Ann Oncol 1997;8: 477–83.
17. Rustin GJ, Newlands ES, Bagshawe KD, et al. Successful management of metastatic and primary germ cell tumors in the brain. Cancer 1986;57:2108–13.
18. Christmas TJ, Doherty AP, Rustin GJ, et al. Excision of residual masses of metastatic germ cell tumours after chemotherapy: the role of extraperitoneal surgical approaches. Br J Urol 1998;81:301–8.
19. Bower M, Brock C, Holden L. POMB/ACE chemotherapy for mediastinal germ cell tumours. Eur J Cancer 1997;33: 838–42.
20. Nichols CR. Mediastinal germ cell tumors. Semin Thorac Cardiovasc Surg 1992;4:45–50.
21. Boshoff C, Begent RHJ, Oliver RTD, et al. Secondary tumours following etoposide containing therapy for germ cell cancer. Ann Oncol 1995;6:35–40.
22. Toner GC, Stockler MR, Boyer MJ, et al. Comparison of two standard chemotherapy regimens for good-prognosis germ-cell tumours: a randomized trial. Lancet 2001;357:739–45.
23. Cullen MH, Harper PG, Woodroffe CM, et al. Chemotherapy for poor risk germ cell tumours. An independent evaluation of the POMB/ACE regimen. Br J Urol 1988;62:454–60.
24. Husband DJ, Green JA. POMB/ACE chemotherapy in non-seminomatous germ cell tumours: outcome and importance of dose intensity. Eur J Cancer 1992;28:86–91.
25. McNeish IA, Kanfer EJ, Haynes R, et al. Paclitaxel-containing high-dose chemotherapy for relapsed or refractory germ cell tumours [abstract 41, #3870]. Proc Am Assoc Cancer Res 2000;41:608.

15

High-Dose Chemotherapy and Stem Cell Support in the Treatment of Poor-Risk Germ Cell Cancer

KIM MARGOLIN, MD

One of the greatest therapeutic triumphs of modern chemotherapy was the application of cisplatin-containing chemotherapy to the treatment of advanced germ cell cancer.[1] For the small percentage of patients who failed to achieve initial remission or who relapsed following a response to chemotherapy with or without surgery, newer agents that emerged in the 1980s, such as etoposide and ifosfamide, were found to be active in second-line therapy, providing remissions and some cures in a fraction of patients who relapsed after initial therapy.[2–4] Because of synergy between cisplatin and many other chemotherapeutic agents, chemotherapy combinations for first and second relapse have included cisplatin with one or two other agents, and reports of the activity of other single agents have been limited. Resistance to standard-dose chemotherapies occurs in a fraction of patients with advanced germ cell tumors (GCTs) who either fail to achieve complete remission with first-line therapy or relapse following an initial complete remission to chemotherapy with or without surgery. In some instances, drug resistance may be overcome by high doses of drugs that have a steep dose-response relationship and tolerable extramedullary toxicities when used with autologous stem cell support.

"Poor-risk" patients are defined by two different systems, depending on whether the classifications are applied at the time of initial diagnosis or at the time of relapse. Patients who fulfill the criteria established by the International Germ Cell Cancer Collaborative Group (IGCCCG)[5] at the time of initial diagnosis have less than a 50% probability of cure from standard-dose chemotherapy with or without surgery. The risk categories for patients at the time of initial diagnosis were developed and validated on a data set on over 5,000 patients from centers in the United States and Europe, and this IGCCCG system (Table 15–1) is now widely used to select and stratify patients in current clinical trials (see below).

Patients in relapse have also been classified into three prognostic categories for outcome following high-dose chemotherapy with autologous peripheral blood stem cell transplantation (aPSCT). In a multivariate analysis by a collaborative group of international investigators, five factors emerged as statistically significant: (1) tumor progression immediately before aPSCT, (2) mediastinal primary, (3) tumor refractory to chemotherapy (progression within 4 weeks of the last cisplatin-based regimen after an initial response) prior to aPSCT, (4) tumor absolutely refractory (progression *during* a cisplatin-based regimen), and (5) beta subunit of human chorionic gonadotropin (β-hCG) > 1,000 U/L just prior to aPSCT. The application of this system to patients undergoing aPSCT showed patients with no poor-risk features to have a 77% response rate (complete clinical response, complete pathologic response, or partial clinical/radiographic response with negative serum tumor markers); those with one or two risk factors had a 59% response rate, and patients with three or more unfavorable features had only a 22%

Table 15–1. INTERNATIONAL GERM CELL CANCER COLLABORATIVE GROUP PROGNOSTIC SYSTEM

	Nonseminoma	Seminoma
Good Prognosis	Testis/retroperitoneal primary and No nonpulmonary visceral metastases and Good markers (all): AFP < 1,000 ng/mL, hCG < 5,000 IU/L (1,000 ng/mL), and LDH < 1.5 × upper limit of N	Any primary site and No nonpulmonary visceral metastases and Normal AFP, any hCG, any LDH
Intermediate Prognosis	Testicular/retroperitoneal primary and No nonpulmonary visceral metastases and Intermediate markers (any): AFP ≥ 1,000 and ≤ 10,000 ng/mL; or hCG ≥ 5,000 IU/L and ≤ 50,000 IU/L; or LDH ≥ 1.5 × N and ≤ 10 × N	Any primary site and Nonpulmonary visceral metastases and Normal AFP, any hCG, any LDH
Poor Prognosis	Mediastinal primary or Nonpulmonary visceral metastases or Poor markers (any): AFP > 10,000 ng/mL, or hCG > 50,000 IU/L (10,000 ng/mL), or LDH > 10 × upper limit of N	(No patients classified as poor–prognosis)

Adapted from International Germ Cell Consensus Classification.[5]

likelihood of response.[6] The latter database contained only 310 patients and has not been formally adapted for use but is a valuable tool for clinical decision making about the potential role of aPSCT for individual patients. It may also serve as a useful system for the prestratification of patients undergoing prospective phase II and randomized phase III trials of aPSCT in the relapse setting.

Another group of patients who may benefit from aPSCT is the small cohort of patients who have residual viable tumor at the time of postchemotherapy surgical resection for marker-negative radiologic partial response (radiologic partial response with achievement of negative serum tumor markers). Although about half of these patients remain disease free after brief additional therapy with the same agents used to induce their remission, the remainder of these individuals relapse with disease that is presumably resistant to standard chemotherapy but may be responsive to dose-intense therapy.

Partly on the basis of a series of investigations (described later in this chapter) that incorporated the presenting prognostic features with a set of predictive factors during first-line chemotherapy (the rate of decline of tumor markers proved to be the most important predictive parameter), investigators at Memorial Sloan-Kettering Cancer Center (MSKCC) designed a phase III prospective randomized trial of standard-dose chemotherapy alone versus standard-dose chemotherapy augmented with aPSCT for patients in the poor- and intermediate-risk categories at presentation. Because of the relatively low numbers of patients with this disease who are in the poor- and intermediate-risk categories (14% and 26%, respectively, of all patients with advanced GCT, based on the IGCCCG database), all of the cooperative groups in the United States are participating in this important trial, the results of which are expected in late 2003. This trial has also been designed to validate the predictive value of treatment-related factors—in particular, the rate of decline of serum tumor markers during initial chemotherapy—on the complete response rate and on the effect of incorporating aPSCT as part of first-line chemotherapy.

GENERAL PRINCIPLES OF aPSCT FOR GERM CELL CANCER PATIENTS

In early studies, published predominantly in the 1980s, germ cell cancer patients were often included with other solid tumor and lymphoma patients in autologous bone marrow transplantation trials. The drugs were chosen for their relative lack of severe dose-limiting extramedullary toxicities, and in some cases, they had shown a dose-response relationship in preclinical models. In general, clinical successes for these drugs had been demonstrated in the allogeneic and autologous transplant settings for hematologic malignancies. Thus, the first regimens tested in GCT cases lacked a strong preclinical and pharmacologic rationale for use in this disease. Thus, it is not surprising that only a small fraction of the heavily pretreated patients enrolled in these trials achieved long-term benefit.[7] Several developments in the early and mid-1990s led to a renewed enthusiasm for this modality, including experience with the use of high-dose etoposide in myeloablative regimens[8] and the demonstration that carboplatin and ifosfamide had substantial single-agent activity in GCTs. All of these drugs possess favorable characteristics for dose escalation (in particular, the lack of major extramedullary toxicity at doses up to six times higher than could be administered without hematopoietic cell rescue) and have shown synergy with one or more of the other agents used in this setting.[9-13] More recently, paclitaxel has been investigated at high doses and has been shown to be tolerable, in combination with these and other drugs, at high doses with stem cell rescue.[14,15] Regimens containing paclitaxel in combination with carboplatin, ifosfamide, and etoposide are currently under active investigation for treatment of GCT.[16]

Over the same time interval, improvements in the supportive care for dose-intense chemotherapy—from the collection and storage of the stem cell product to the availability of hematopoietic growth factors and better antibiotics—provided an improved safety profile that permitted its use in patients with a better prognosis who could potentially benefit more from this intervention (see Figure 15–1).[17]

The series of studies reported from MSKCC, reviewed in detail below, demonstrated the safety and efficacy of tandem cycles of aPSCT in patients with relapsed GCT. Predictive factors (developed from the patient database) for the success and failure of standard therapy were used to select patients at high risk of first-line treatment failure. These data were used in support of the ongoing United States Intergroup phase III protocol that is comparing standard therapy alone to initial standard therapy augmented by aPSCT. The study is also designed to provide statistical validation of the rate of decline of the serum tumor markers β-hCG and α-fetoprotein (AFP) during therapy, as a predictive parameter that may be of value in future studies to select patients for new regimens. Although the formal primary end point of the Intergroup study is to compare the percentage of patients with durable complete responses at 1 year from the initiation of therapy, the true goal is to determine whether the incorporation of aPSCT in frontline therapy provides a higher cure rate than does treatment without aPSCT. Since a substantial fraction of relapsing patients in the non-aPSCT arm will be offered second-line therapy with regimens that include aPSCT using the same drugs that are used for the frontline aPSCT cohort, there is a possibility that this study will answer the question of "transplant early or transplant later?" more accurately. The argument has often been raised that a difference in a definitive end point such as overall survival (cure) may be obscured by using a study design that allows crossover from one treatment arm to the other. Nevertheless, it is reasonable to expect that a regimen with sufficient activity to improve on 1-year disease-free survival will also improve overall survival and that the introduction of aPSCT as treatment for relapse will not provide the same benefit it provides when included in initial therapy. For patients with unfavorable characteristics at the time of relapse, the optimal therapy remains unknown due to the lack of any prospectively randomized controlled clinical trial comparing regimens that have appeared promising in phase II trials. A large number of patients have been enrolled in phase II trials in the United States and Europe that suggest a benefit for aPSCT over the published results from series of relapse patients treated with standard-dose therapy. However, the limitations of interpreting these data are emphasized by the fact that (1) the data are based on historical controls, and (2) in some cases, the data on aPSCT outcomes were derived from retrospective reviews of patients treated in "standard regimens" used for aPSCT, rather than from prospective phase II trials. Even a comparison of sequential phase II trials is suboptimal as illustrated by the results of a recent review of nearly 300 patients treated at a single institution in a series of trials over 20 years. The authors found improvements in survival during the second decade (1987 to 1996) in comparison with the first (1977 to 1986),[18] and when patients were classified according to the IGCCCG system for their presenting prognostic features, patients in the most unfavorable prognostic groups had the greatest improvement in therapeutic outcomes between first and second time intervals. Since none of these patients was treated with aPSCT, the data in this study are a sharp reminder of the importance of randomized controlled trials in determining the benefit of new therapies over standard regimens. The combination of a rare tumor with limited numbers of patients for phase III studies, together with rapid improvements in supportive care and the continuing emergence of new agents, makes it nearly impossible to answer this question for GCT patients in relapse. Nevertheless, these patients should continue to be the focus of vigorous efforts to test and prove the ultimate value of new regimens in carefully designed randomized controlled trials.

MECHANISMS OF RESISTANCE AND BIOLOGY OF HIGH-RISK GCTS

It has long been known that patients with nonseminomatous GCTs (NSGCTs) arising in the mediastinum have an unfavorable prognosis with standard therapy and that for patients with mediastinal primary NSGCT in who relapse after chemotherapy, second-line therapy, even with aggressive tandem aPSCT, is rarely if ever curative.[19–22] Retroperitoneal primary NSGCT was originally believed to be an unfavorable prognostic feature as well,[23] but the data used to develop the IGCCCG risk scoring system did not confirm this to be an independent factor.[5] The intriguing observation has been made that the unusual hematologic malignancies that arise in about 2% of patients with mediastinal GCTs and rarely in patients with a testicular primary GCT[24–27] share a chromosomal marker (isochromosome 12p) with GCTs of testicular origin; unfortunately, the precise molecular characterization of this chromosomal abnormality and its relationship to the

biologic behavior of these malignancies (particularly the inferior response to chemotherapy that cure most patients with nonmediastinal primary GCTs) have impeded efforts to improve outcomes for that subset of patients. The results of further studies to correlate the epidemiologic, molecular, and treatment outcome data from GCT patients will be of great interest to the designing of future regimens so that curative therapy can be considered a realistic goal for all patients with advanced GCT.

CURRENT STATUS OF aPSCT FOR GCT

For the purposes of this chapter, a simple distinction will be made between poor-risk patients at the time of presentation and those who relapse with characteristics associated with an unfavorable outcome. The latter group has not been as precisely defined, and a system analogous to the IGCCCG prognostic index that is based on a large patient database does not exist. Furthermore, many of the factors that have been associated with an unfavorable outcome following relapse are linked to the initial poor prognostic features. The published literature has not provided an adequate distinction between the impact of the presenting risk factors, predictive factors during therapy (such as the rate of fall of serum tumor markers), and patient characteristics at the time of relapse that are associated with the failure of second-line therapy. Thus, most of the earlier publications either do not provide precise descriptions of the patients in terms of their risk category at relapse or simply divide them by the degree of cisplatin refractoriness (ie, resistant = relapse at any time; refractory = relapse within 4 weeks of exposure to cisplatin, with a previous response; absolutely refractory = progression while on a cisplatin-based regimen [eg, failure to respond]). The report of Beyer and colleagues described a database of 310 patients who underwent aPSCT for relapsed GCT at centers in the United States and Europe. The prognostic factors that demonstrated significance in multivariate analysis—progressive disease before aPASCT, mediastinal primary nonseminoma, refractory or absolutely refractory disease—were used to classify patients into three categories with 2 year failure-free survival rates of 51%, 27%, and 5%. Although it has not been formalized for prospective use, this system should be considered for use in future trials of second-line therapy in NSGCT[6] provides a system for classifying patients in relapse that is now being applied to many prospective protocols for descriptive (in phase II) and stratification (in phase III) purposes.

aPSCT for Relapsed Germ Cell Cancer

Table 15–2[16,17,28–38] summarizes the published studies of aPSCT for refractory or relapsed germ cell cancer that have been reported since the subject was thoroughly reviewed by Motzer and Bosl in 1992.[7]

The data summarized in the table indicate that the earlier regimens were generally based on a regimen of high-dose etoposide and carboplatin that was developed at Indiana University,[28] and later regimens added a high-dose alkylating agent such as thiotepa, cyclophosamide, or ifosfamide (see Table 15–2). Although cyclophoshamide/ifosfamide had not been studied in randomized trials, it appeared that its addition and the use of tandem cycles (double-cycle) of chemotherapy and rescue were associated with the highest durable response rates and tolerable toxicity, so most investigators currently

Table 15–2. STUDIES OF HIGH-DOSE CHEMOTHERAPY WITH AUTOLOGOUS STEM CELL SUPPORT FOR RELAPSED GERM CELL TUMOR, 1992 TO 2001						
Author, institution (Reference)	Agents	Cycles	Patients	Status at High-Dose Rx*	Durable CR*†	Comment
Broun, Indiana U, 1992 (28)	Carbo, VP-16 (3 with IFX)	2	40	2nd relapse or refractory	15%	Retro review
Nichols, ECOG, 1992 (30)	Carbo, VP-16	2	40	2nd relapse or refractory	12%	
Barnett, UBC, 1993 (31)	Carbo, VP-16, IFX Carbo, VP-16, CTX	1 1	6 15	(a) 4 with refractory relapse; (b) 17 with incomplete response of "high-burden" disease	(a) None; (b) 67%	
Lotz, Hospital Tenon, 1994 (29)	Carbo, VP-16, IFX	2	31	(a) 22 testicular, 18 refractory; (b) 9 extragonadal, 7 refractory	(a) 39%; (b) 0%	
Rodenhuis Netherlands CA Institute, 1995 (32)	Carbo, CTX, thiotepa	1	18	(a) 7 refractory; (b) 11 responsive relapse	(a) 1/7; (b) 73%	
Lampe, Royal Marsden, 1995(33)	Carbo, VP-16	2	23	8 progressed after cycle 1	35%	
Motzer, MSKCC, 1996 (34)	Carbo, VP-16, CTX	2	58	(a) 10 in 1st incomplete response; (b) 48 beyond 1st relapse	21% (not reported by status)	
Margolin, City of Hope, 1996 (35)	Carbo, VP-16, IFX	2	20	(a) 13 IGCCCG poor-risk in incomplete response or relapse; (b) 7 int-, good-risk or unknown, beyond first relapse	(a) 62%; (b) 2/7	
Mandanas, U Oklahoma, 1998 (36)	CDDP or Carbo, VP-16, CTX	1	21	8 refractory	52% overall; 1/8 refractory	
Bhatia, Indiana U, 2000 (17)	VP-16, carbo	2	65	(a) 51 sensitive; (b) 14 refractory	(a) 68%; (b) 40%	Retro review; no extragonadal
Ayash, U Michigan, 2000 (37)	VP-16, carbo	2	29	Heterogeneous presenting and relapsing features	28% (1/10 abs refractory‡)	
Rick, Berlin (multicenter), 2001 (38)	VP-16, carbo, thiotepa	1	62	(a) 40 initial good-risk; (b) 13 initial int-risk; (c) 10 initial poor-risk	(a) 45%; (b) 1/13; (c) 1/10	
Margolin, City of Hope, 2002 (16)	Taxol, VP-16, carbo; Taxol, IFX, carbo	2	28	21 initial poor-risk	8/21	

abs = absolute; carbo = carboplatin; CDDP = cisplatin; CR = complete response; ECOG = Eastern Cooperative Oncology Group; IFX = ifosfamide; IGCCCG = International Germ Cell Consensus Collaborative Group; int = intermediate; MSKCC = Memorial Sloan-Kettering Cancer Center; retro = retrospective; Rx = therapy; UBC = University of British Columbia; VP-16 = etoposide.
*Refractory = responsive or stable disease with tumor progression within 4 weeks of exposure to cisplatin-containing chemotherapy.
†Absolute refractory = disease progression during cisplatin-containing chemotherapy.

include cyclophosphamide or ifosfamide and administer tandem cycles of high-dose therapy.[7,29]

Several points about the data in this summary table merit further discussion. In the earliest trials, patients with a poor prognosis (second relapse or "platinum refractory," defined as progression within 4 weeks of prior exposure) were treated with only carboplatin and etoposide. The size of the studies was modest (40 patients), and the durable (> 2 years) complete response (CR) rate was only 12 to 15%. With advances in the supportive care of patients who are undergoing aPSCT and with the emergence of safety and efficacy data supporting the addition of high-dose ifosfamide to the regimen, the risk-to-benefit ratio of aPSCT for patients with germ cell cancer became more favorable, supporting the use of this modality in less heavily pretreated patients with a lower likelihood of chemotherapy-refractory disease. Thus, the apparent improvements in outcomes indicated by the later entries in Table 15–2 probably represent both improvements in therapy and the selection of patients who were more likely to realize a benefit from aPSCT.

Whenever it could be determined from the original report, the patients whose data are summarized in Table 15–2 were divided into risk groups based on how the authors reported the data, predominantly by the degree of refractoriness to the prior cisplatin-based chemotherapy. Most investigators in this field have recognized that on the basis of these outcome data, it is nearly impossible to identify patients with GCT who are so refractory to standard therapy that they have no meaningful possibility of benefiting from aPSCT. Patients with a mediastinal primary site may be exceptions because the available data indicate that patients with a relapsed mediastinal primary GCT are practically never cured by aPSCT.[19–23]

aPSCT as First-Line Therapy

The pioneering studies from MSKCC have provided a foundation for the current United States Intergroup study that will define the role of aPSCT in the initial treatment of patients with poor-risk GCT. In the first of these studies, Motzer and colleagues reported on a phase II trial of 28 patients with poor-risk features

at diagnosis, based on a system derived at MSKCC from a multivariate analysis of their large patient database.[39] The VAB-6 regimen (consisting of vinblastine, bleomycin, actinomycin, cisplatin, and cyclophosphamide) was used. Patients who responded optimally (ie, with a half-life of < 7 days for AFP and < 3 days for β-hCG)[40,41] to the first two cycles received one additional cycle of VAB-6. After the first two cycles of VAB-6, those who demonstrated a prolonged half-life of either marker were switched to tandem cycles of aPSCT, using high-dose etoposide and carboplatin. Twenty-two of the 27 study patients fell into the latter category; among them, 8 patients had durable complete remissions. These data suggested that switching patients with a suboptimal response to standard therapy onto a more intensive regimen could produce a superior outcome, compared with that of the historical group of similar high-risk patients treated with standard-dose chemotherapy.[42]

In the second trial, 30 patients with poor-risk features similar to those of the patients reported in the prior trial were initially treated with the combination of etoposide, ifosfamide/mesna, and cisplatin (VIP). Sixteen patients whose tumor markers declined at the predicted half-life completed therapy with two more cycles of VIP while 14 patients with delayed clearance of one or both tumor markers were switched, after two cycles of VIP, to tandem cycles of aPSCT that included cyclophosphamide with etoposide and carboplatin (CEC). Again, the results for event-free and overall survivals of both subsets in this study appeared superior to the overall expected outcome from similar regimens without aPSCT.[43] In view of the concurrent result of a large randomized intergroup trial (Southwest Oncology Group and Eastern Cooperative Oncology Group), demonstrating a VIP outcome equivalent to that of the standard first-line regimen of bleomycin, etoposide, and cisplatin (BEP) developed at Indiana University,[44] investigators at MSKCC adopted BEP as their standard therapy and used CEC as the aPSCT regimen in a phase III trial to answer definitively the question of whether aPSCT has a role in frontline therapy for GCTs. The IGCCCG prognostic system was used to select poor-risk patients for enrollment, based on an expected 5-year survival rate of 48%. These patients were expected to have an absolute improvement in outcome comparable to that of the poor-risk group, despite a higher chance of cure (79%) with standard therapy.[5] This change in the protocol also provided for more timely completion of the study, which included as important secondary end points the validation of predictive factors such as rate of decline of serum tumor markers during therapy and prognostic factors based on the IGCCCG system,[5] as well as further assessment of the risks and toxicities of both treatment regimens in the cooperative group setting. Until more data regarding the benefit of intensifying first-line therapy with aPSCT become available from this trial, it is difficult to recommend a switch to aPSCT for any category of patients undergoing first-line standard-dose chemotherapy, except for those who fail to achieve a complete marker response after four cycles of standard therapy. For these patients, the choice remains limited to the consideration of surgery (in the presence of elevated markers, only selected patients with limited foci of tumor amenable to complete excision should be considered) or second-line chemotherapy in an attempt to achieve complete marker remission. The challenge of selecting patients for optimal management, including aPSCT, is illustrated by the cases represented in Figures 15–2 and 15–3.

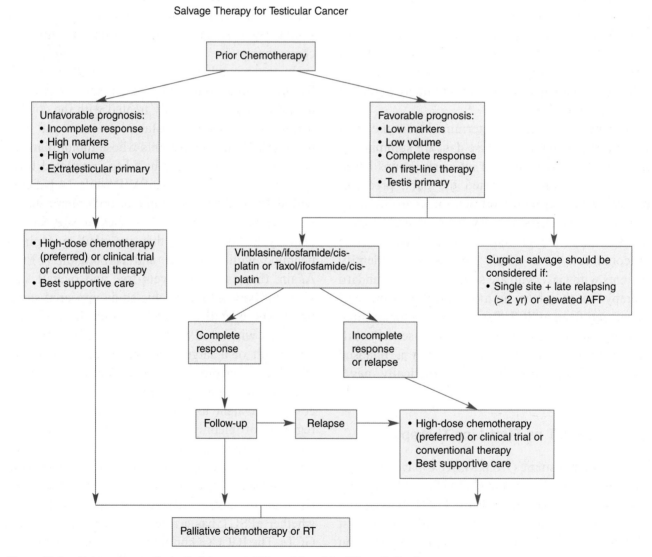

Figure 15–1.   Salvage therapy for testicular cancer. AFP = α-fetoprotein; RT = radiation therapy.

CURRENT ISSUES IN THE TREATMENT OF HIGH-RISK GERM CELL CANCER WITH aPSCT

The choice of a regimen remains one of the major unresolved issues in the treatment of poor-risk germ cell cancer with high-dose chemotherapy and stem cell support. Elements of regimen design include (1) the safety of each agent at the dose and schedule and in the combination selected for study, (2) the timing of this modality and the use of alternative regimens such as multicycle high-dose therapy, (3) tandem cycles using different agents in each cycle, and (4) the incorporation of new pharmacologic agents. Each of these aspects

of high-dose chemotherapy for germ cell tumors are discussed.

Safety and Tolerability

Are the drugs safe and tolerable for the majority of patients being considered for treatment? Since the major drugs used at standard doses for germ cell cancer are the same agents used at high doses with stem cell support, the concern is about both acute and chronic/cumulative toxicities affecting the same organ systems. While the potential cumulative toxicities of prior exposure to these drugs could be an obstacle to their safe use at high doses, this risk is mitigated by the relatively limited overall drug expo-

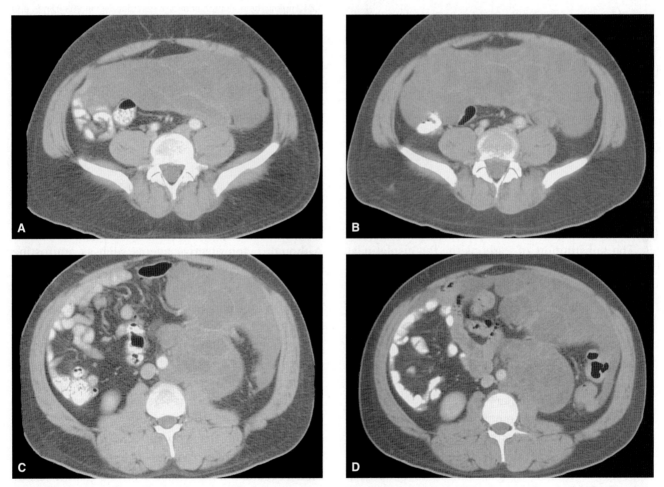

Figure 15–2. A computed tomography of 34-year-old man was referred for autologous peripheral blood stem cell transplantation for refractory germ cell cancer. He had presented with massive retroperitoneal metastasis from a mixed germ cell cancer in the left testis. Serum tumor markers were α-fetoprotein (AFP) at 255 ng/mL and beta–human chorionic gonadotropin at 1,300 IU/mL. After three cycles of bleomycin, etoposide, and cisplatin, the patient had a persistent mass that had not diminished in size despite normalization of his markers. Because the mass was considered unresectable (*A* and *B*), he received salvage therapy with VeIP, with no change in the masses (*C* and *D*) and a modest rise in the AFP level, to 42 ng/mL. He then underwent resection of the mass. Pathologic findings were mature teratoma with no evidence of viable cancer. The patient remained well and disease free at 12+ months following surgery.

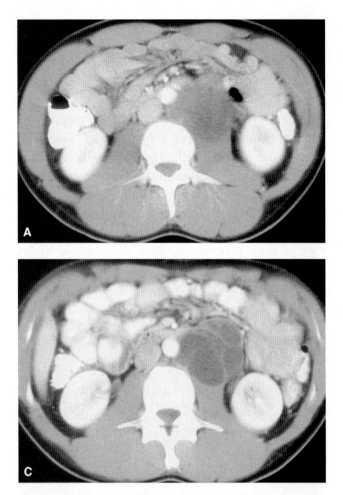

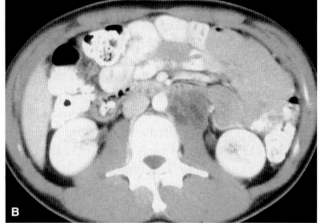

Figure 15–3. Computed tomography (CT) scans from a 21-year-old man with stage III mixed germ cell cancer who was referred for autologous peripheral blood stem cell transplantation. His original presentation was of intermediate risk, with a testicular primary mixed nonseminomatous germ cell tumor, α-fetoprotein elevated at 4,643 ng/mL, beta–human chorionic gonadotropin at 903 IU/mL, and a 5 cm retroperitoneal tumor mass (*A*). After two cycles of bleomycin, etoposide, and cisplatin, the patient's serum tumor markers were normal, and there was a partial regression of the retroperitoneal mass (*B*). After two additional cycles, the tumor markers remained normal, and the mass had grown to 5 cm in diameter and had a cystic appearance on the CT scan (*C*). Surgical excision confirmed the mass to be a mature teratoma with cystic elements and multiple histologically negative lymph nodes.

sure of patients currently referred for high-dose therapy regimens for germ cell cancer and by the use of high-dose carboplatin rather than cisplatin in aPSCT.

The substitution of carboplatin for cisplatin at standard doses resulted in inferior therapeutic outcomes in phase III trials of first-line therapy,[45,46] presumably because the dose-limiting myelosuppression of carboplatin is associated with a narrower therapeutic index than is the dose-limiting nephrotoxicity (and prolonged neuro- and ototoxicity) of cisplatin. Nevertheless, high dose carboplatin, more limited in its extramedullary toxicities by hepatotoxicity than by nephro- or ototoxicity,[47] is highly active and synergistic with the other agents in the treatment of resistant germ cell cancer. The dose intensity of etoposide is limited by gastrointestinal toxicity, a side effect that rarely occurs at standard doses and that is generally reversible without permanent sequelae when given at high doses in combinations supported by aPSCT.[8] The dose escalation of both ifosfamide and paclitaxel is limited by toxicities that

may be intolerable in the setting of prior therapy with cisplatin, including nephrotoxicity from ifosfamide.[48,49] and neurotoxicity due to paclitaxel.[14,15] Although cytoprotective agents such as amifostine have shown some evidence of protection against the nephrotoxicity of cisplatin and the neurotoxicity of both cisplatin and paclitaxel,[50] the reversibility of these toxicities and the possibility that the cytoprotective agent will also reduce antitumor activity has limited the use of agents other than mesna for essential uroprotection. Mesna is included in all ifosfamide regimens and has generally been added to high-dose cyclophosphamide regimens, which can also cause hemorrhagic cystitis. Several new agents have been developed to reduce stomatitis beyond the modest reduction associated with the routine use of acyclovir for herpes prophylaxis; these include the investigational agent recombinant human keratinocyte growth factor[51] and topical antibacterial agents that are still under investigation. It is hoped that the results of ongoing randomized controlled trials will identify an agent that can reduce this toxicity and associated risks such as airway compromise and viral and bacterial infection.

The most devastating late complication of successful therapy for malignancy is the development of secondary malignancies due to the chromosomal damage caused by the drugs used to cure the original disease. Although a slightly increased risk of secondary leukemia was recently reported in a large series of seminoma patients who had been cured with radiotherapy, patients with NSGCTs have not been reported to have an excessive risk of second malignancies, probably because these patients are cured with a brief exposure to drugs that are rarely associated with such a complication. Etoposide, generally in high doses, has been implicated in the development of the "topoisomerase inhibitor" type of leukemia that involves abnormalities of chromosome 11q23, and regimens that contain *cis*-diamminedichloroplatinum (CDDP) (ie, cisplatin) also appear to contribute to secondary leukemia in rare instances and at high cumulative doses.[52–54] Data regarding the risk of secondary malignancies in patients whose curative treatment for NSGCT included high-dose chemotherapy with aPSCT have not been reported, but such risk is likely to be lower than that which has been associated with aPSCT for patients with lymphoma (in the range of 10–15%), presumably due to the greater exposure of patients with lymphoma to repetitive cycles and high doses of alkylating agents.[55] While the risk-to-benefit ratio for aPSCT in selected patients with GCTs remains favorable, it will be necessary to keep this risk in mind as newer regimens are developed that increase the proportion of patients enjoying long-term survival and potentially running the risk of late treatment-related complications.

Therapeutic Efficacy and Alternatives to Traditional aPSCT

Many regimens used for high-dose therapy for germ cell cancer contain cyclophosphamide in lieu of ifosfamide. Cyclophosphamide has a lower risk of renal, bladder, and central nervous system toxicity and has been used extensively at high doses in conditioning and therapeutic regimens for autologous

and allogeneic stem cell transplantation. In pooled data from nonrandomized trials, the inclusion of either of these agents in the regimen appears to enhance its activity; since the two agents have never been formally compared in patients with germ cell cancer, the choice remains empiric. Etoposide and carboplatin, which are used in almost every regimen (see Table 15–2), can generally be given at their individual maximum-tolerated doses even in the presence of cyclophosphamide or ifosfamide, because of mainly nonoverlapping dose-limiting toxicities. Thus, it is recommended that one of these three-drug regimens be used for patients with this disease when they are treated outside of a clinical trial.[5]

Some of the remaining issues concerning the components of the regimen include the following: (1) the value of incorporating newer agents shown to be active in germ cell cancer and to be associated with manageable toxicities in the high-dose setting (eg, paclitaxel)[14–16]; (2) the replacement of single or tandem cycles of aPSCT with multiple (generally four) cycles of dose-intense therapy, each supported by autologous stem cells collected following mobilization by a prior chemotherapy regimen[56]; and (3) the relative value of using different "noncross-resistant" drug regimens in the two or more cycles of stem cell–supported therapy administered in this setting.[16] While it is not feasible to perform phase III trials to answer each of these questions, it may be possible to apply findings from other high-dose therapy trials to the design of optimal regimens for treating germ cell cancer.

At the present time, one of the most important unanswered questions is that of the role of dose intensification for treatment of patients in first relapse. Only a fraction of patients with favorable characteristics (25–33% of unselected relapse patients in early published series)[57,58] may be cured with standard-dose regimens containing one or two drugs not included in the first-line regimen (in most cases, BEP as first-line therapy and VeIP [vinblastine, ifosfamide, cisplatin, or CDDP] as therapy for first relapse) whereas the remaining patients either fail to achieve another complete response or relapse again. Although tandem cycles of high-dose chemotherapy with aPSCT may even cure a small fraction of unselected patients when administered as a third-line regimen,[7] this approach, which involves waiting until the patient has relapsed twice to introduce the dose-intensive treatment, is likely to result in a loss of the opportunity for cure in some patients.*

Investigators at MSKCC have developed two regimens for relapse that take advantage of the salvage activity of paclitaxel and the feasibility and potential synergy of its combination with other active drugs[59] such as cisplatin and ifosfamide. When standard-dose paclitaxel was combined with cisplatin and ifosfamide for relapse patients with favorable prognostic characteristics, a CR or PR/marker negative response rate of 80% was reported among 30 patients, pathologic complete responses were documented in all 11 patients who underwent postchemotherapy resection, and 73% of all study patients were still in complete response at nearly 3 years' median follow-up.[60]

For patients with unfavorable prognostic characteristics at relapse (a group for which the role of aPSCT is strongly suggested by data from the studies listed in Table 15–2), the optimal method for dose-intensification remains unresolved. Applying the principles of Norton and Simon,[61] the MSKCC group studied a regimen of sequential dose-intensive chemotherapy containing all of the most active agents that was administered to 37 patients with unfavorable characteristics at relapse. Two cycles of paclitaxel and ifosfamide were used for both therapeutic and stem cell mobilization purposes, followed by three cycles of high-dose carboplatin and etoposide, each supported by the previously collected stem cells. Sixty-two percent of patients experienced a favorable response, and 41% of patients had maintained their response at a median follow-up time of 2.5 years.[56] Based on these encouraging outcomes and the potential bias associated with patient selec-

tion factors and the single-institution nature of these studies, the group at MSKCC has proposed a cooperative-group phase III trial to directly compare the two regimens described above for patients in first relapse. Selection factors for trial participation include testicular primary site and first relapse with initial therapy limited to EP with or without bleomycin. Patients who responded to initial therapy and subsequently relapsed and patients who did not have a marker complete response to first-line therapy are eligible; patients with refractory or absolutely refractory disease and patients with mediastinal primary tumors are excluded because of their extremely low likelihood of attaining a durable complete remission with these regimens.

New Directions

In addition to testing new drugs for their potential efficacy and possible dose escalation for germ cell cancers, it is essential to continue to study tumor-related prognostic factors that aid in the understanding of cancer biology and in the identification of new therapeutic targets. One such example was the recent report, by Bokemeyer and colleagues, of the clinical impact of circulating cancer cells from germ cell cancer patients undergoing stem cell collections for aPSCT. Among 57 patients whose apheresis specimens were analyzed by polymerase chain reaction (PCR) methods to detect sequences from seven different genes associated with germ cell cancer, 29 (58%) were positive for one or more markers. Nevertheless, the presence of circulating tumor cells (or contaminating PCR-positive products of transcription from noncirculating tumor cells) did not emerge as an independent variable with a negative impact on clinical outcome.[62]

CONCLUSION

Most patients with germ cell tumors enjoy an excellent prognosis, so therapeutic investigations focus on the reduction of short- and long-term toxicities; however, the treatment and cure of high-risk and relapsing patients remains the goal of new therapeutic strategies. It is likely that novel agents with promising activity in these diseases will be selected on the

---

*Editor's note: The fraction of patients who will be permanently cured in the salvage setting, even when dose-intensive therapy is delivered at first relapse, remains controversial; some clinicians believe it to be appropriate to investigate salvage regimens that are not dose intensive but that involve novel cytotoxic compounds in this setting. What is clear is that standard regimens with conventional agents rarely achieve cure for relapsed testicular cancer and that the correct selection of initial chemotherapy, based on attribution of potential risk, is critically important in maximizing cure rates.

basis of improvements in our precise understanding of the molecular biology of germ cell malignancies, as were the disease-specific molecularly targeted therapies for diseases like chronic myelogenous leukemia. Until that time, it will be necessary to continue refining existing techniques (which includes the study of new agents, doses, schedules, and cytoprotective agents) in order to improve the safety and efficacy of high-dose chemotherapy with autologous stem cell support for patients with poor-prognosis germ cell malignancies.

REFERENCES

1. Einhorn LH, Donahue J: Cis-diamminedichloroplatinum, vinblastine, and bleomycin combination chemotherapy in disseminated testicular cancer. Ann Intern Med 1977;87: 293–8.

2. Bosl GJ, Yagoda A, Golbey RB, et al. Role of etoposide-based chemotherapy in the treatment of patients with refractory or relapsing germ cell tumors. Am J Med 1985; 78:423–8.

3. Loehrer PJ, Lauer R, Roth BJ, et al. Salvage therapy in recurrent germ cell cancer: ifosfamide and cisplatin plus either vinblastine or etoposide. Ann Intern Med 1988;109:540–6.

4. Motzer RJ, Cooper K, Geller NL, et al. The role of ifosfamide plus cisplatin-based chemotherapy as salvage therapy for patients with refractory germ cell tumors. Cancer 1990;66:2476–81.

5. International Germ Cell Cancer Collaborative Group. International germ cell consensus classification: a prognostic factor-based staging system for metastatic germ cell cancers. J Clin Oncol 1997;15:594–603.

6. Beyer J, Kramar A, Mandanas R, et al. High-dose chemotherapy as salvage treatment in germ cell tumors: a multivariate analysis of prognostic variables. J Clin Oncol 1996; 14:2638–45.

7. Motzer RJ, Bosl GJ. High-dose chemotherapy for resistant germ cell tumors: recent advances and future directions [review]. J Natl Cancer Inst 1992;84:1703–9.

8. Blume KG, Forman SJ, O'Donnell MR, et al. Total body irradiation and high-dose etoposide: a new preparatory regimen for bone marrow transplantation in patients with advanced hematologic malignancies. Blood 1987;69: 1015–20.

9. Durand RE, Goldie JH. Interaction of etoposide and cisplatin in an in vitro tumor model. Cancer Treat Rep 1987;71:673–9.

10. Schabel FM, Trader MW, Laster WR, et al. Cis-dichlorodiammineplatinum (II): combination chemotherapy and crossresistance studies with tumors of mice. Cancer Treat Rep 1979;63:1459–73.

11. Wilson WH, Jain V, Bryant G, et al. Phase I and II study of high-dose ifosfamide, carboplatin, and etoposide with autologous bone marrow rescue in lymphomas and solid tumors. J Clin Oncol 1992;10:1712–22.

12. Elias AD, Ayash LJ, Wheeler C, et al. Phase I study of high-dose ifosfamide, carboplatin and etoposide with autologous hematopoietic stem cell support. Bone Marrow Transplant 1995;15:373–9.

13. Fields KK, Elfenbein GJ, Lazarus HM, et al. Maximum-tolerated doses of ifosfamide, carboplatin, and etoposide given over 6 days followed by autologous stem-cell rescue: toxicity profile. J Clin Oncol 1995;13:323–32.

14. Stemmer SM, Cagnoni PJ, Shpall EJ, et al. High-dose paclitaxel, cyclophosphamide and cisplatin with autologous hematopoietic progenitor-cell support: a phase I trial. J Clin Oncol 1996;14:1463–72.

15. Somlo G, Doroshow JH, Synold T, et al. High-dose paclitaxel in combination with doxorubicin, cyclophosphamide and peripheral blood progenitor cell rescue in patients with high-risk primary and responding metastatic breast carcinoma: toxicity profile, relationship to paclitaxel pharmacokinetics and short-term outcome. Br J Cancer 2001;84: 1591–8.

16. Doroshow JH, Margolin K, Chow W, et al. High-dose chemotherapy with autologous stem cell rescue (PSCT) for relapsed nonseminomatous germ cell cancer (NSGCT): effective salvage for poor-risk patients (pts) in first relapse. Proc Amer Soc Clin Oncol 2002.

17. Bhatia S, Abonour R, Porcu P, et al. High-dose chemotherapy as initial salvage chemotherapy in patients with relapsed testicular cancer. J Clin Oncol 2000;18:3346–51.

18. Sonneveld DJA, Hoekstra HJ, van der Graaf, et al. Improved long term survival of patients with metastatic nonseminomatous testicular germ cell carcinoma in relation to prognostic classification systems during the cisplatin era. Cancer 2001;91:1304–15.

19. Broun ER, Nichols CR, Einhorn LH, et al. Salvage therapy with high-dose chemotherapy and autologous bone marrow support in treatment of primary nonseminomatous mediastinal germ cell tumors. Cancer 1991;7:1513–5.

20. Hartmann JT, Einhorn L, Nichols CR, et al. Second-line chemotherapy in patients with relapsed extragonadal nonseminomatous germ cell tumors: results of an international multicenter analysis. J Clin Oncol 2001;19:1641–8.

21. Dulmet EM, Macchiarini P, Suc B, et al. Germ cell tumors of the mediastinum. Cancer 1993;72:1894–901.

22. Bokemeyer C, Nichols CR, Droz JP, et al. Extragonadal germ cell tumors of the mediastinum and retroperitoneum: results from an international analysis. J Clin Oncol 2002; 20:1864–73.

23. Saxman SB, Nichols CR, Einhorn LH. Salvage chemotherapy in patients with extragonadal nonseminomatous germ cell tumors: the Indiana University experience. J Clin Oncol 1994;12:1390–3.

24. Nichols CR, Hoffman R, Einhorn LH, et al. Hematological malignancies associated with primary mediastinal germ cell tumors. Ann Intern Med 1985;102:603–9.

25. DeMent SH. Association between mediastinal germ cell tumors and hematological malignancies: an update. Hum Pathol 1990;21:699–703.

26. Hartmann JT, Nichols CR, Droz JP, et al. Hematologic disorders associated with primary mediastinal nonseminomatous germ cell tumors. J Natl Cancer Inst 2000;92: 54–61.

27. Margolin K, Traweek T. The unique association of malignant

histiocytosis and a primary gonadal germ cell tumor. Med Pediatr Oncol 1992;20:162–4.

28. Broun ER, Nichols CR, Kneebone P, et al. Long-term outcome of patients with relapsed and refractory germ cell tumors treated with high-dose chemotherapy and autologous bone marrow rescue. Ann Intern Med 1992;117:124–8.

29. Lotz JP, Thierry A, Donsimoni R, et al. High dose chemotherapy with ifosfamide, carboplatin, and etoposide combined with autologous bone marrow transplantation for the treatment of poor-prognosis germ cell tumors and metastatic trophoblastic disease in adults. Cancer 1995;75:874–85.

30. Nichols CR, Andersen J, Lazarus HM, et al. High-dose carboplatin and etoposide with autologous bone marrow transplantation in refractory germ cell cancer: an Eastern Cooperative Oncology Group protocol. J Clin Oncol 1992; 10:558–63.

31. Barnett MJ, Coppin CML, Murray N, et al. High-dose chemotherapy and autologous bone marrow transplantation for patients with poor prognosis nonseminomatous germ cell tumours. Br J Cancer 1993;68:594–8.

32. Rodenhuis S, van der Wall E, ten Bokkel Huinink WW, et al. Pilot study of a high-dose carboplatin-based salvage strategy for relapsing or refractory germ cell cancer. Cancer Invest 1995;13:355–62.

33. Lampe H, Dearnaley DP, Price A, et al. High-dose carboplatin and etoposide for salvage chemotherapy of germ cell tumours. Eur J Cancer 1995;31A:717–23.

34. Motzer RJ, Mazumdar M, Bosl GJ, et al. High-dose carboplatin, etoposide, and cyclophosphamide for patients with refractory germ cell tumors: treatment results and prognostic factors for survival and toxicity. J Clin Oncol 1996;14:1098–105.

35. Margolin K, Doroshow JH, Ahn C, et al. Treatment of germ cell cancer with two cycles of high-dose ifosfamide, carboplatin, and etoposide with autologous stem-cell support. J Clin Oncol 1996;14:2631–7.

36. Mandanas RA, Saez RA, Epstein RB, et al. Long-term results of autologous marrow transplantation for relapsed or refractory male or female germ cell tumors. Bone Marrow Transplant 1998;21:569–76.

37. Ayash LJ, Clarke M, Silver SM, et al. Double dose-intensive chemotherapy with autologous stem cell support for relapsed and refractory testicular cancer: the University of Michigan experience and literature review. Bone Marrow Transplant 2001;27:939–47.

38. Rick O, Bokemeyer C, Beyer J, et al. Salvage treatment with paclitaxel, ifosfamide, and cisplatin plus high-dose carboplatin, etoposide, and thiotepa followed by autologous stem-cell rescue in patients with relapsed or refractory germ cell cancer. J Clin Oncol 2001;19:81–8.

39. Bosl GJ, Geller NL, Cirrincione C, et al. Multivariate analysis of prognostic variables in patients with metastatic testicular cancer. Cancer Res 1983;43:3403–7.

40. Toner GC, Geller NL, Tan C, et al. Serum tumor marker half-life during chemotherapy allows early prediction of complete response and survival in nonseminomatous germ cell tumors. Cancer Res 1990;50:5904–10.

41. Mazumdar M, Bajorin DF, Bacik J, et al. Predicting outcome to chemotherapy in patients with germ cell tumors: the value of the rate of decline of human chorionic gonadotrophin and alpha-fetoprotein during therapy. J Clin Oncol 2001;19:2534–41.

42. Motzer RJ, Mazumdar M, Subhash C, et al. Phase II trial of high-dose carboplatin and etoposide with autologous bone marrow transplantation in first-line therapy for patients with poor-risk germ cell tumors. J Natl Cancer Inst 1993;85:1828–35.

43. Motzer RJ, Mazumdar M, Bajorin DF, et al. High-dose carboplatin, etoposide, and cyclophosphamide with autologous bone marrow transplantation in first-line therapy for patients with poor-risk germ cell tumors. J Clin Oncol 1997;15:2546–52.

44. Nichols CR, Catalano PJ, Crawford ED, et al. Randomized comparison of cisplatin and etoposide and either bleomycin or ifosfamide in treatment of advanced disseminated germ cell tumors: an Eastern Cooperative Oncology Group, Southwest Oncology Group, and Cancer and Leukemia Group B study. J Clin Oncol 1998;16:1287–93.

45. Bajorin DF, Sarosdy MF, Pfister DG, et al. Randomized trial of etoposide and cisplatin versus etoposide and carboplatin in patients with good-risk germ cell tumors: a multi-institutional study. J Clin Oncol 1993;11:598–606.

46. Horwich A, Sleijfer D, Fossa S, et al. Randomized trial of bleomycin, etoposide, and cisplatin compared with bleomycin, etoposide, and carboplatin in good-prognosis metastatic nonseminomatous germ cell cancer: a multi-institutional medical research council/European Organization for Research and Treatment of Cancer trial. J Clin Oncol 1997;15:1844–52.

47. Shea TC, Flaherty M, Elias A, et al. A phase I clinical and pharmacokinetic study of carboplatin and autologous bone marrow support. J Clin Oncol 1989;7:651–61.

48. Elias AD, Eder JP, Shea T, et al. High-dose ifosfamide with mesna uroprotection: a phase I study. J Clin Oncol 1990; 8:170–8.

49. Elias AD, Ayash LJ, Eder JP, et al. A phase I study of high-dose ifosfamide and escalating doses of carboplatin with autologous bone marrow support. J Clin Oncol 1991;9: 320–7.

50. Hensley ML, Schuchter LM, Lindley C, et al. American Society of Clinical Oncology clinical practice guidelines for the use of chemotherapy and radiotherapy protectants. J Clin Oncol 1999;17:3333–55.

51. Spielberger RT, Stiff P, Emmanouilides C, et al. Efficacy of recombinant human keratinocyte growth factor (rHuKGF) in reducing mucositis in patients with hematologic malignancies undergoing autologous peripheral blood progenitor cell transplantation (auto-PBPCT) after radiation-based conditioning—results of a phase 2 trial. Proc Am Soc Clin Oncol 2001;20:25.

52. Whitlock J, Greer J, Lukens J. Epipodophyllotoxin-related leukemia. Cancer 1991;68:600–4.

53. Travis LB, Andersson M, Gospodarowicz M, et al. Treatment-associated leukemia following testicular cancer. J Natl Cancer Inst 2000;92:1165–71.

54. Kollmannsberger C, Beyer, J, Droz JP, et al. Secondary leukemia following high cumulative doses of etoposide in patients treated for advanced germ cell tumors. J Clin Oncol 1998;16:3386–91.

55. Deeg HJ. Delayed complications after hematopoietic cell transplantation. In: Thomas ED, Blume KG, Forman SJ, editors. Hematopoietic cell transplantation. 2nd ed. Malden (MA): Blackwell Science, Inc.; 1999. p. 783–7.

56. Motzer RJ, Mazumdar M, Sheinfeld J, et al. Sequential dose-intensive paclitaxel, ifosfamide, carboplatin, and etoposide salvage therapy for germ cell tumor patients. J Clin Oncol 2000;18:1173–80.

57. Loehrer PJ, Gonin R, Nichols CR, et al. Vinblastine plus ifosfamide plus cisplatin as initial salvage therapy in recurrent germ cell tumor. J Clin Oncol 1998;16:2500–4.

58. McCaffrey JA, Mazumdar M, Bajorin DF, et al. Ifosfamide and cisplatin containing chemotherapy as first-line salvage therapy in germ cell tumors: response and survival. J Clin Oncol 1997;15:2559–63.

59. Chou T, Motzer RJ, Tong Y, et al. Computerized quantification of synergism and antagonism of Taxol, topotecan, and cisplatin against human teratocarcinoma cell growth: a rational approach to clinical protocol design. J Natl Cancer Inst 1994;86:1517–24.

60. Motzer RJ, Sheinfeld J, Mazumdar M, et al. Paclitaxel, ifosfamide, and cisplatin second-line therapy for patients with relapsed testicular germ cell cancer. J Clin Oncol 2000; 18:2413–8.

61. Norton L, Simon R. The Norton-Simon hypothesis revisited. Cancer Treat Rep 1986;70:163–9.

62. Bokemeyer C, Gillis AJM, Pompe K, et al. Clinical impact of germ cell tumor cells in apheresis products of patients receiving high-dose chemotherapy. J Clin Oncol 2001;19: 3029–36.

16

Salvage Chemotherapy and New Drugs

IRENE PANAGIOTOU, MD
TOMASZ M. BEER, MD

Germ cell tumors are among the most chemotherapy-sensitive solid tumors. The expectation for cure exceeds 95% for those patients presenting with testicular cancer.[1] In the subset of patients with disseminated disease, cure with chemotherapy is slightly less reliable, despite dramatic advances since the introduction of cisplatin-based combination chemotherapy.[1,2] Depending on presenting prognostic features, 40 to 90% of patients are cured with primary chemotherapy with or without postchemotherapy surgery.[1–4] For those patients who do not achieve disease-free status after first-line treatment or for those who relapse after primary chemotherapy, the outlook is considerably less hopeful. Conventional-dose salvage chemotherapy in combination with resection of residual masses produces second complete remissions in 30 to 60% of patients, but less than half of these remissions are durable.[5] Overall, approximately 25% of patients are cured with second-line standard therapy, and 15% are cured with third-line therapy using high-dose chemotherapy and stem cell transplantation. Certain prognostic factors predict exceedingly poor outcomes with salvage therapies; these factors include cisplatin-refractory disease, extragonadal primary, and failure of two or more lines of chemotherapy.[6–8] Patients with these prognostic features, who have little hope of durable response to the currently available salvage therapies, are candidates for trials of novel agents.

PATIENT SELECTION

Syndromes That Mimic Recurrence

Recognition of syndromes that can mimic tumor recurrence or progression is the first critical step in the evaluation of a patient suspected of having recurrent, persistent, or progressive germ cell tumor. Recognition of several special situations is also essential for the proper management of recurrent germ cell neoplasms. Figure 16–1 illustrates an unusual case of "pseudorecurrence" of germ cell cancer.

Growing Teratoma

One clinical situation frequently mistaken for progressive disease is the syndrome of growing teratoma.[9] This should be suspected when lesions slowly progress radiographically during chemotherapy, despite an appropriate serologic response with declining tumor markers (Figure 16–2). Slowly enlarging lesions after the termination of chemotherapy, despite normal levels of tumor markers, are also likely to represent teratomatous elements. The appropriate management of such patients includes the completion of induction chemotherapy and subsequent surgical resection of the masses associated with the residual radiographic abnormalities. Such patients are not candidates for aggressive salvage chemotherapy.

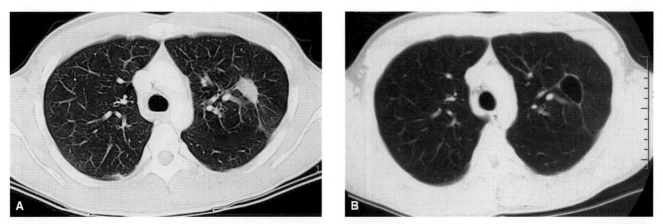

Figure 16–1. *A*, Computed tomography (CT) scan showing a suspected pulmonary recurrence of germ cell tumor. *B*, Review of earlier CT scan indicates that a pneumatocele is present and confirms the diagnosis of a fluid-filled pneumatocele and not recurrent germ cell tumor.

Pulmonary Nodules Due to Bleomycin

The development of pulmonary nodules during or after bleomycin-containing chemotherapy in a patient who responds serologically or radiographically at other tumor sites may represent bleomycin-induced pulmonary injury and not progressive cancer.[10] Other nonmalignant pulmonary conditions should also be considered when the diagnosis of a marker-negative pulmonary recurrence is being considered. Figure 16–3 shows pulmonary histoplasmosis, another condition that may be confused with metastatic germ cell tumor.

False-Positive Tumor Marker Elevations

Modest elevations of circulating human chorionic gonadotropin (hCG) can be nonspecific, and fluctuations that do not progressively increase may be difficult to interpret. False-positive elevations can occasionally be seen owing to radioimmunoassay cross reactivity with luteinizing hormone (LH)[11] or in association with marijuana use[12] although these phenomena are much less frequent since the introduction of the beta-subunit assay into routine clinical practice. In hypogonadal patients, administration of exogenous testosterone can lower circulating LH levels by feedback inhibition when cross reactivity is suspected.[13] Restaging and further evaluation should be considered if hCG levels remain high despite the approaches mentioned above.[14,15]

Patients with massively elevated hCG values at diagnosis may have persistently elevated hCG at the completion of initial chemotherapy, and hCG normalization may be extremely slow, despite tumor eradication.[16*] A well-documented rise in tumor markers should be observed in such patients before salvage therapy is contemplated.[14–16]

False-positive elevation of α-fetoprotein (AFP) is uncommon. Laboratory errors,[17] a second primary neoplasm (mainly hepatocellular carcinoma), or liver diseases (including cirrhosis, hepatitis, and liver inflammation from drug abuse) can cause AFP elevation.[18]

Special Situations

Sanctuary Sites

Evaluation of sanctuary sites of persistent disease, such as the central nervous system (CNS) or the testis, is also crucial in patients with complete systemic remission and persistent or elevated serum tumor markers.[14,15] All sanctuary sites should be investigated before initiating salvage treatment, even in the absence of clinical signs or symptoms. Early recognition of isolated brain metastases is essential as multimodality treatment (including surgery and radiotherapy) may be curative.[19,20]

---

*Editor's note: This phenomenon is uncommon as the majority of cases show a steady decline of circulating levels of hCG, according to standard half-life clearance values; in some instances, minute releases of hCG by dying tumor cells may not have been identified due to inadequate frequency of measurement, thus explaining an artifact of slowly declining circulating hCG.

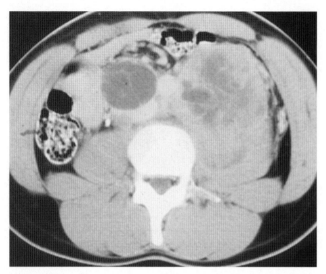

Figure 16–2. Computed tomography scan showing a large intra-abdominal teratoma.

Late Relapse

Most patients who relapse after initial therapy for disseminated germ cell tumors relapse within 1 year of therapy, and the overwhelming majority of relapses occur within 2 years. Relapse after more than 24 months is considered a late relapse.[21] A late-relapse rate of 2 to 4% at 10 years has been consistently described, and recurrences as late as 32 years after the attainment of complete remission have been reported.[22,23]

Surgery plays an important role in the management of such patients.[22,23] Surgical excision is recommended for patients with localized completely resectable disease.[22] Patients with pure teratoma at surgical excision have a significantly more favorable outcome compared to those with carcinoma.[22–24] Baniel and colleagues[23] reviewed 81 patients who experienced late relapse (median, 6.2 years). Of 65 patients who were managed with primary chemotherapy, 17 (26.2%) had complete responses, but only 2 patients remained continuously disease free with chemotherapy alone; both were patients who had previously never received chemotherapy. Among the 15 patients who experienced recurrence with mature teratoma, 12 (80%), after one or more surgeries, were disease free in the long term. In contrast, only 19 (32%) of 59 patients with viable germ cell cancer at late relapse remained disease free, despite the fact that aggressive surgery was performed in almost all. Seven of the patients who relapsed with cancer had sarcomatous elements in their tumor; of those 7 patients, 4 (58%) remained disease free for the long term.

Standard Salvage Patient Population

Patients who experience a relapse after achieving a complete remission with standard initial therapy (with or without resection of residual masses) are candidates for salvage chemotherapy.[25] Similarly, those who fail to achieve a complete remission after standard initial therapy (patients who progress during induction chemotherapy or after achieving an unresectable partial remission) may benefit from salvage chemotherapy.[25] Among these patients, those who do not achieve a complete remission after standard induction chemotherapy have a worse prognosis.[6,8] Overall, approximately 25% of patients are cured with second-line standard therapy, and 15% are cured with third-line therapy using high-dose chemotherapy and stem cell transplantation.

Patients with "cisplatin-refractory" disease (defined as disease that progresses during cisplatin-containing therapy or within 4 weeks of the last cisplatin dose) and patients with "absolute cisplatin–refractory" (defined as disease that shows no response to cisplatin-based therapy)[26,27] have a dismal prognosis.[6,8] Patients who relapse from a nonseminomatous mediastinal primary also have a grave prognosis.[6–8,28] The ability of currently available therapies to induce durable remissions in these patients remains in question, and such patients are thus suitable candidates for experimental therapies.

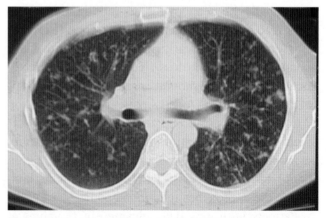

Figure 16–3. Computed tomography (CT) scan showing pulmonary histoplasmosis.

SINGLE AGENTS WITH ACTIVITY IN THE SALVAGE SETTING

Etoposide

Given its routine incorporation into initial chemotherapy of germ cell tumors, etoposide is no longer viewed as a "salvage agent." The development of etoposide, from its initial demonstration of activity in the cisplatin-refractory setting to its evaluation in combination with cisplatin in frontline therapy, remains a paradigm for the development of a new agent today. Etoposide, a type II topoisomerase inhibitor, was the first cytotoxic agent to have significant activity in patients with cisplatin-refractory testicular cancer and is one of the most active agents to be investigated in the treatment of germ cell cancer.[2,29,30]

Newlands and Bagshawe first reported responses to single-agent etoposide in four of five patients with refractory disease.[31] Overall, pooled data suggested a response rate of approximately 25% although only 3% of patients achieved complete responses.[29] Oral etoposide is also active in patients with cisplatin-refractory disease, including patients who have had prior etoposide-containing combination chemotherapy[32] and patients who are relapsing after high-dose salvage regimens.[33]

Ifosfamide

Ifosfamide is another active agent that has been investigated in the treatment of germ cell cancer. An initial prospective evaluation of single-agent ifosfamide for patients with refractory germ cell tumors who had received prior cisplatin was reported by Scheulen and colleagues.[34] A confirmatory study was conducted at Indiana University.[35] In this phase II trial, ifosfamide at 2 $g/m^2/d$ for 5 consecutive days every 3 weeks was administered to a heavily pretreated poor-prognosis population. (Twenty-eight of 30 patients received ifosfamide as third-line or further therapy after the failure of at least two previous cisplatin-based regimens; 7 patients had extragonadal primaries.) Seven objective responses, including one complete remission, were reported. Of the 7 responders, 1 patient had a primary retroperitoneal germ cell tumor, 3 were cisplatin refractory, and 2 were refractory to etoposide, having progressed during or within 1 month of treatment with these agents. None of these responses was durable, and the median response duration was 3.5 months.

Overall, of patients previously treated with cisplatin, single-agent ifosfamide produces responses in 20% and produces complete responses in 1%.[35–37] The subsequent success of ifosfamide in multiagent salvage regimens suggests that a 20% response rate in cisplatin-refractory patients denotes an important level of activity.

Carboplatin

At conventional doses, carboplatin has modest activity after cisplatin chemotherapy. In one series, 2 (10%) of 20 evaluable patients achieved a partial response.[38] The principal use of this agent in the salvage setting has been as a component of high-dose regimens.

Paclitaxel

Paclitaxel is another agent with demonstrable activity against relapsed or resistant germ cell tumors. Its mechanisms of activity and resistance patterns differ from those of deoxyribonucleic acid (DNA)-damaging agents such as cisplatin and ifosfamide.[39,40] In one study, no cross-resistance in cisplatin-resistant cell lines was demonstrated.[39] Furthermore, in preclinical studies, paclitaxel showed significant cytotoxicity against teratocarcinoma cell lines, particularly those that were relatively resistant to cisplatin.[41,42]

A number of investigators have examined paclitaxel in refractory germ cell cancer.[43–47] The German Testicular Cancer Study Group treated 24 patients who had multiply relapsed nonseminomatous germ cell tumors, 75% of whom had cisplatin-refractory disease, with paclitaxel at 225 mg/m^2 over a 3-hour infusion, every 3 weeks.[44] This group reported an overall response rate of 25%, with 8% complete responses (4% aided by surgery). Many of the responders who had cisplatin-refractory disease had relapsed after high-dose chemotherapy or had a mediastinal primary. The median response duration was 8 months, and 17% of patients remained alive or progression free after a median follow-up of 10 months. Similar activity was seen with paclitaxel at 250 mg/m^2, administered by continuous infusion over 24 hours, every 21 days.[45] Overall, responses to paclitaxel in the salvage setting ranged from 11 to 30% (with an average of 21%), demonstrating important activity for this agent.

Gemcitabine

Gemcitabine (2′,2′-difluorodeoxycytidine) is a nucleoside analogue that inhibits DNA synthesis.[48] Initial interest in this agent was partly stimulated by a report of a response in a female patient with cisplatin- and paclitaxel-refractory ovarian germ cell cancer.[49]

Two phase II trials evaluated this agent in patients with relapsed or refractory germ cell cancer.[50,51] Bokemeyer and colleagues[50] reported a 19% partial reponse rate for patients with tumor progression after conventional salvage chemotherapy, cisplatin-refractory disease, or relapse after high-dose chemotherapy when treated with gemcitabine at 1,000 mg/m^2 administered weekly for 3 consecutive weeks and repeated in a 4-week cycle. Similar activity was seen in patients relapsing after high-dose therapy (17%), patients who had previously undergone salvage therapy with a paclitaxel-containing regimen (16%), and patients with mediastinal germ cell tumors (25%). No patient with absolute cisplatin-refractory disease responded. The median progression-free survival was 4 months. Investigators at Indiana University[51] reported 1 complete response and 2 partial responses among 20 evaluable similar patients (15%) treated with gemcitabine at 1,200 mg/m^2 on a similar schedule. In both trials, gemcitabine was generally well tolerated and demonstrated an important level of activity in a population of patients who are typically unresponsive to treatment, suggesting that this agent may be an excellent candidate for incorporation into multiagent salvage regimens.[52]

Agents with Limited Activity

A number of agents have little demonstrable activity in recurrent or refractory germ cell cancer. No activity was reported for mitoxantrone,[53] vinorelbine,[54] suramin,[55] topotecan,[56] and all-*trans* retinoic acid.[57] Minimal acitivity was seen with methotrexate,[58] vindesine,[59] iproplatin,[60,61] mitomycin-C,[62] bendamustine,[63] and high-dose epirubicin.[64,65]

COMBINATION CHEMOTHERAPY

Standard Salvage: Vinblastine/Ifosfamide/Cisplatin

Several studies from Indiana University, Memorial Sloan-Kettering Cancer Center, and European institutions have shown the activity of the combination of cisplatin, ifosfamide, and vinblastine as salvage therapy for patients for whom treatment with the standard combination of cisplatin, etoposide, and bleomycin has failed.[66–73] A typical schedule is the following: cisplatin at 20 mg/m^2 daily for 5 days, ifosfamide at 1.2 g/m^2 daily for 5 days, and vinblastine at 0.11 mg/kg on days 1 and 2, every 21 days, for 4 consecutive cycles. This regimen, known as VeIP, has become a standard regimen in this context. The outcomes of 135 patients treated at Indiana University were encouraging: 67 patients (50%) achieved a disease-free status with either chemotherapy alone or resection of teratoma or viable carcinoma; 32 (24%) of these patients were continuously disease free, and 42 (31%) were free of disease after a minimum follow-up of 6 years.[72,73] Nevertheless, long-term disease-free survival was not seen in those patients who had extragonadal nonseminomatous germ cell tumors.[28] Toxicity was significant. Seventy-three percent of these patients developed neutropenic fevers. Transfusions of platelets (27%) and red blood cells (49%) were common. Renal insufficiency (serum creatinine > 4 mg/dL) was seen in 8 patients, and 3 treatment-related deaths were reported. In contrast to the results in nonseminoma cases, results in recurrent seminoma cases were more impressive although in a much smaller cohort of patients: 83% of patients had complete responses, and 54% remained in continuous complete remission.[71]

Contemporary Studies of New Combination Regimens

Paclitaxel/Cisplatin

The combination of paclitaxel and cisplatin has been studied for patients who have previously received platinum-based chemotherapy.[74] One complete response (6%) and 3 partial responses (19%) were seen among 16 patients with nonseminomatous germ cell tumors who had failed to achieve a complete remission after platinum-based induction chemotherapy and cytoreductive surgery. These patients were treated with paclitaxel at 175 to 225 mg/m^2 over 3 hours and cisplatin at 100 mg/m^2, every 3 weeks, for up to 4 cycles. The 25% overall response rate was similar to that previously reported from the use of paclitaxel alone,[43–45] including paclitaxel used for an equivalently difficult tumor population.[45]

Paclitaxel/Ifosfamide/Cisplatin

Motzer and colleagues[75–77] reported a phase I/II trial in patients with previously treated germ cell tumors but relatively favorable prognostic features (ie, a gonadal primary tumor site, relapsed after complete response to first-line therapy). In their study, the phase II paclitaxel dose was 250 mg/m^2 over 24 hours while the ifosfamide and cisplatin doses were identical to those of the VeIP regimen. In this highly select group of patients, 80% responded (77% achieving a complete response to chemotherapy alone and 3% achieving a durable partial response with tumor marker normalization). Seventy-three percent of responders were living event free after a median follow-up of approximately 3 years. Because of the patient selection and the single-arm design, the efficacy of the regimen cannot be compared to that of the standard VeIP regimen. An ongoing European trial (EU-99012) is currently evaluating the regimen in a patient population similar to the VeIP population from Indiana University.

Paclitaxel plus Gemcitabine

In a trial conducted by the Eastern Cooperative Oncology Group,[78] patients with a metastatic gonadal or extragonadal primary who had cisplatin-refractory disease or who had relapsed after salvage conventional- or high-dose chemotherapy regimens were treated with paclitaxel at 110 mg/m^2 over 1 hour and gemcitabine at 1,000 mg/m^2 over 30 minutes on days 1, 8, and 15 of a 4-week cycle for a maximum of 6 cycles. Of 28 eligible patients, 6 (21%) responded, including 3 patients (12%) with complete responses. The median response duration was 10 months. Two of the complete responders remained continuously free of disease after 15 and 25 months,

respectively. Responders included patients with cisplatin-refractory disease and patients relapsing after high-dose chemotherapy. These results suggest a significant usefulness for this regimen, given the difficult tumor population studied.

Standard-Dose Salvage Chemotherapy: Summary

Approximately 50% of recurrent testicular cancer patients will achieve a disease-free status when VeIP is administered as second-line therapy.[72,73] Half of the patients who achieve complete remission on VeIP eventually relapse; therefore, approximately 25% of patients with recurrent germ cell tumors can have the expectation of long-term disease-free survival with standard salvage chemotherapy. The substitution of paclitaxel for vinblastine has yielded impressive results in a patient population with favorable prognostic features. However, a direct comparison to VeIP is needed to determine its true worth in this setting.

Prognostic factors need to be considered in the interpretation of all salvage data and may partly explain the observed differences in outcomes reported in different phase II trials. Patients with recurrent seminomas have a better prognosis than those with recurrent nonseminomatous germ cell tumors.[71,79] Response to first-line treatment, duration of response, and serum tumor marker levels have prognostic value in the salvage setting.[6,8] Patients who do not have a complete response to first-line treatment, patients with absolute cisplatin-refractory disease, and patients with recurrent primary mediastinal nonseminomatous tumors have a particularly poor prognosis.[6,72,73] A scoring system based on a multivariate analysis of prognostic factors has been developed (Table 16–1).[8]

HIGH-DOSE CHEMOTHERAPY FOR RELAPSED OR REFRACTORY GERM CELL TUMORS

The role of high-dose chemotherapy and bone marrow or stem cell support has been discussed elsewhere in this volume (see Chapter 15). However, for completeness, the role of this treatment strategy in the management of relapsed germ cell tumors will be briefly reviewed here.

Rationale

A steep dose-response curve has been demonstrated for cisplatin and/or carboplatin, as well as for etoposide, in a variety of preclinical systems.[80–82]

As they are typically young and unencumbered by multiple comorbid conditions, patients with relapsed or refractory germ cell tumors are often able to tolerate high-dose chemotherapy.[25,83] Although early clinical trials exploring dose escalations of standard agents (such as cisplatin and etoposide) without stem cell support yielded encouraging results,[84–88] a randomized study failed to show an improvement in outcome with doubling of the cisplatin dose.[89] Therefore, further attempts to exploit the chemotherapeutic dose-response relationship focused on chemotherapy doses that were high enough to require bone marrow or stem cell support.

Carboplatin, active as a single agent in the salvage setting,[38] proved to be more amenable to substantial dose escalation than did cisplatin. With the principal dose-limiting toxicity of myelosuppression and fewer nonhematologic toxicities than cisplatin, carboplatin could be escalated to a maximum tolerated dose of 2,000 mg/m^2.[90] Carboplatin thus became the backbone of high-dose chemotherapy regimens for germ cell tumors. Salvage regimens incorporating carboplatin plus etoposide[91–94] and carboplatin/etoposide plus ifosfamide[95–105] or cyclophosphamide[106–110] have been developed for patients with germ cell tumors.

One of the most important series describing carboplatin/etoposide/ifosfamide was reported in Germany.[101,102] Seventy-four patients with multiply relapsed/refractory germ cell tumors were administered the regimen following conventional salvage treatment. Patients with an incomplete response to first-line treatment and patients at first relapse were also eligible for the trial. Forty-three percent of patients were heavily pretreated with three or more chemotherapy regimens, 49% had received two previous conventional-dose regimens, 8% were in first relapse, and 32% had cisplatin-refractory disease. The maximum tolerated dose for the three-drug combination was 1,500 mg/m^2, 2,400 mg/m^2, and 10 g/m^2 for carboplatin, etoposide, and ifosfamide, respectively. Severe nephrotoxicity limited the carboplatin dose. Only 3% of patients died as a result of treatment. Of 64 patients initially assessable for response, 51% responded and 31% achieved a complete response. After a median follow-up of 12 months, 39% of patients remained in complete remission or inoperable partial remission with tumor marker normalization. Of the cisplatin-sensitive patients, 44% were continuously event free as compared to only 4% of the patients with cisplatin-refractory disease. After a median follow-up of 4 years, 28 (38%) of 74 patients were alive and free of disease. Fifty-three percent of patients with cisplatin-sensitive disease became long-term survivors, in contrast to 4% of those with refractory disease. Similarly, 82% of the long-term survivors were cisplatin-sensitive patients who received high-dose therapy as early intensification of first salvage treatment, compared to only 22% of patients for whom one or more salvage attempts had failed.[102] Because of nonuniform patient entry criteria, it has been difficult to draw conclusions about the relative efficacy of high-dose regimens with ifosfamide and those without ifosfamide.[15,96,103–105]

Peripherally collected stem cells have replaced bone marrow in contemporary high-dose therapy and have reduced the duration of leukopenia and thrombocytopenia.[111,112]

New drug combinations[113,114] that incorporate conventional- and/or intermediate-dose chemother-

Table 16–1. PROGNOSTIC SCORING FOR OVERALL SURVIVAL AND FAILURE-FREE SURVIVAL OF PATIENTS RECEIVING CONVENTIONAL-DOSE CHEMOTHERAPY FOR RELAPSED OR REFRACTORY GERM CELL TUMORS				
	Scoring Scheme		Risk Estimate	
Factor	Points	Sum of Points	Risk Group	OS
Progression-free interval of < 2 yr	1	< 3	Good	47% at 5 yr
Lack of CR to induction therapy	1	3	Poor	0% at 3 yr
AFP > 100 kU/L or hCG > 100 IU/L at relapse	1			

Adapted from Fossa SD et al.[8]

AFP = α-fetoprotein; CR = complete response; hCG = human chorionic gonadotropin; OS = overall survival.

apy with ifosfamide plus etoposide or carboplatin plus etoposide followed by two courses of high-dose therapy with cyclophosphamide, carboplatin, and thiotepa have recently been reported. While these studies demonstrate the feasibility of these regimens, the inclusion of heterogenous groups of patients, including patients in first relapse, makes efficacy comparison to prior regimens impossible.

Study Results and Summary

The published experience indicates that approximately 15% of patients with multiply relapsed germ cell tumors can achieve long-term disease-free status with high-dose chemotherapy, but at a price of significant treatment-related toxicity. With the routine use of growth factors, the incorporation of peripherally collected progenitor cells,[111,112] and advances in supportive care, the morbidity and mortality associated with high-dose chemotherapy are less today than in the initial studies. Patients with overtly cisplatin-refractory disease or with recurrent mediastinal non-seminomatous germ cell cancer fare very poorly even with salvage high-dose treatment[7] and should be enrolled in clinical trials of new agents instead. In a multivariate model, Beyer examined predictors for outcome with salvage high-dose therapy and developed a readily usable scoring system (Table 16–2).[7]

The optimal high-dose chemotherapy regimen remains to be defined. While it is generally agreed that the backbone of the regimen is carboplatin and etoposide, the benefits of adding a third drug—be it ifosfamide, cyclophosphamide, or thiotepa—remain uncertain. The inclusion of patients with a more favorable prognosis in trials of new regimens makes comparisons to the historical data particularly challenging.

The optimal number of high-dose chemotherapy cycles also remains a matter of controversy. While some investigators point to the occasional conversion of partial response to complete remission with a second high dose of chemotherapy, in support of two-cycle regimens,[96] others note that overall similar results are reported with one or two cycles of high-dose chemotherapy.[15,103]

HIGH-DOSE CHEMOTHERAPY AT FIRST RELAPSE

High-dose chemotherapy as the first salvage treatment of relapsed germ cell tumors has been less extensively investigated.[115] Unlike patients with multiply recurrent germ cell cancer, patients in first relapse can expect a 50% likelihood of complete remission and a 25% chance of long-term freedom from disease with conventional-dose salvage chemotherapy. The goal, therefore, is not the salvage of otherwise doomed patients but improvement in the efficacy of salvage therapy. Demonstrating efficacy in this setting is thus more challenging.

The typical approach employed to date has included one or two cycles of conventional-dose chemotherapy followed by one or two courses of high-dose chemotherapy with carboplatin/etoposide, with or without an alkylating agent.[116–119] Less commonly, high-dose therapy has been administered alone, without a prior conventional-dose salvage regimen.[120,121] Investigators at Indiana University

	Scoring Scheme		Risk Estimate		
Factor*	Points	Sum of Points	Risk Group	2-yr FFS (%)	2-yr OS (%)
Progressive disease	1	0	Good	51	61
Primary mediastinal tumor	1	1–2	Intermediate	27	34
Cisplatin-refractory disease	1	>2	Poor	5	8
Absolute cisplatin-refractory disease	2				
hCG > 1,000 IU/L	2				

Table 16–2. PROGNOSTIC SCORING FOR OVERALL SURVIVAL AND FAILURE-FREE SURVIVAL OF PATIENTS RECEIVING HIGH-DOSE CHEMOTHERAPY FOR RELAPSED OR REFRACTORY GERM CELL TUMORS

Adapted from Beyer J et al.[7]
FFS = failure-free survival; hCG = human chorionic gonadotropin; OS = overall survival.
*Prior to transplantation.

have reported a continuous disease-free status in 40 to 52% of patients treated with two cycles of conventional-dose cisplatin-based chemotherapy followed by one or two courses of high-dose carboplatin and etoposide.[116–118] After a median follow-up period of 39 months for patients in both studies, a 57% rate of long-term disease-free survival was reported.[119]

Motzer and colleagues[122] investigated sequential dose-intensive treatment of two cycles of paclitaxel (200 mg/m^2) and ifosfamide (6 g/m^2) given 2 weeks apart, followed by three cycles of high-dose carboplatin (target area under the concentration curve [AUC] ranged from 12 to 32 mg/mL × min) and etoposide (1,200 mg/m^2) given 14 to 21 days apart with peripheral stem cell re-infusion, administered to patients with unfavorable prognostic features (ie, extragonadal primary site, progressive disease after an incomplete response to first-line treatment, poor response or lack of response to prior treatment with cisplatin plus ifosfamide–containing conventional-dose therapy). Sixty-two percent of patients responded, 57% achieved a complete remission, and 49% remained alive and progression free after a median follow-up of 31 months—an encouraging result in a difficult patient population.

Rick and colleagues[123] explored a treatment strategy that combined intensive conventional-dose salvage with paclitaxel (175 mg/m^2), ifosfamide (5 times 1.2 g/m^2), and cisplatin (5 times 20 mg/m^2), followed by a single cycle of high-dose chemotherapy with carboplatin (3 times 500 mg/m^2), etoposide (4 times 600 mg/m^2), and thiotepa (3 times 150 to 250 mg/m^2). Sixty-seven percent of patients were in first relapse, and the rest of the patients were in second or subsequent relapses; 16% of patients had an extragonadal primary, and 24% had cisplatin-refractory disease. Seventy-eight percent of patients proceeded to high-dose therapy; of those, 66% responded and 45% achieved a complete remission. Overall, after a median follow-up of 36 months, 33% of the initial patient population remained alive, and 26% were continuously disease free. Peripheral neurotoxicity was common.

While the results of high-dose chemotherapy in first-line salvage treatment appear encouraging, it is difficult to know the actual contribution of high-dose therapy to the long-term disease-free survival of patients who are in a disease state with a measurable cure rate achieved by conventional therapy. A matched-pair analysis suggested that high-dose therapy might improve survival by 10%,[124] but the limitations of such analytical approaches are well known from the breast cancer literature. Randomized studies will answer this question. Currently, a European randomized phase III trial[125] is comparing four cycles of conventional-dose cisplatin-based salvage chemotherapy to three cycles of the same regimen, followed by one cycle of high-dose chemotherapy with carboplatin/etoposide plus cyclophosphamide.

EMERGING DRUGS

Arsenic Trioxide

Initial trials of arsenic trioxide in both China and the United States have demonstrated substantial activity in promyelocytic leukemia.[126–130] In preclinical systems, arsenic trioxide has a broad spectrum of activity, not only in hematologic malignancies but also in a variety of solid tumors.[131–143] The dominant mechanism of activity appears to be the induction of apoptosis[131,132,144–147] although some evidence also supports anti-angiogenic properties[134,148–150] and cell cycle arrest associated with p21 induction.[151] Preliminary results in phase I studies suggested that arsenic trioxide has clinical activity against several solid tumors.[152] Motivated by preclinical and early clinical evidence of a broad spectrum of activity, the Southwest Oncology Group has initiated a trial of arsenic trioxide in refractory germ cell malignancies.

Imatinib Mesylate and Other Tyrosine Kinase Inhibitors

Imatinib mesylate (STI-571) is an inhibitor developed to target the BCR-ABL tyrosine kinase, the critical defect in chronic myelogenous leukemia.[153,154] Imatinib mesylate inhibits several other tyrosine kinases, including c-Kit, a 145 kD transmembrane glycoprotein and a member of the receptor tyrosine kinase subclass family III.[155] Activating *c-kit* mutations have been described in the majority of gastrointestinal stromal tumors, and imatinib mesylate has demonstrated remarkable activity in that uniformly chemotherapy-resistant disease.[156]

Several investigators have reported c-Kit expression in germ cell tumors.[157–159] A recent report that examined 46 seminoma specimens and 36 nonseminomatous germ cell tumor specimens found activating *c-kit* mutations in 26% of seminomas but in none of the nonseminomatous tumors. Unfortunately, the majority of these activating mutations result in dysregulated tyrosine kinase activity that is not inhibited by imatinib mesylate. Overall, fewer than 5% of seminomas were found to have mutant *c-kit* that is susceptible to inhibition by imatinib mesylate.[160] Mutant *c-kit* remains a promising target in the treatment of seminoma, but tyrosine kinase inhibitors with a different spectrum of activity will be needed to adequately target *c-kit* in seminoma.

Oxaliplatin

In vitro studies of oxaliplatin (*trans*-1-diaminocyclohexane oxaliplatin, a platinum analogue) have demonstrated incomplete cross-resistance with cisplatin in nonseminomatous germ cell tumor cell lines.[161] The German Testicular Cancer Study Group recently reported the initial results in 32 patients whose disease progressed after at least two cisplatin-containing regimens, after high-dose therapy, or during initial induction or salvage treatment.[162] Treatment included oxaliplatin at 60 mg/m^2 on days 1, 8, and 15, every 4 weeks ($n = 16$), or 130 mg/m^2 on days 1 and 15, every 4 weeks ($n = 16$). Overall, 4 (13%) of the patients achieved a partial remission, all with cisplatin-refractory disease.

ONGOING TRIALS AND FUTURE DIRECTIONS

Current investigations are focused on several areas. Patients with refractory or multiply recurrent germ cell cancer who currently have no hope for durable remission with any standard therapy are candidates for trials of new agents. The paradigm of identifying promising new agents in this patient population and then incorporating them in first salvage and ultimately front-line regimens is a proven pathway to progress. This approach has led to the incorporation of etoposide into initial therapy and the development of ifosfamide-based salvage regimens. Paclitaxel and gemcitabine have recently established activity in this setting. Paclitaxel is under investigation in the first-salvage setting; gemcitabine and oxaliplatin are likely to be examined there as well. Arsenic trioxide and (perhaps) tyrosine kinase inhibitors are earlier in their development in this setting.

Preclinical activity in human testicular xenografts was also seen with the type I topoisomerase inhibitor irinotecan.[163] No data regarding single-agent activity in humans are yet available.

Immunohistochemical analysis suggests that approximately 20% of patients (2 of 10) with relapsed nonseminomatous germ cell cancer may overexpress the Her2/neu oncoprotein,[164] perhaps identifying another potential therapeutic target in refractory germ cell cancer.[165]

A number of questions remain to be answered regarding high-dose therapy. The optimal regimen and number of cycles, as well as the value of high-dose therapy in the first salvage setting, remain to be defined. This last question is being addressed by the ongoing European trial.[125] Another ongoing German trial is tackling the question of the optimal number of cycles of high-dose therapy.[5] If high-dose therapy is adopted into the front-line salvage setting, its long-term toxicity, including secondary neoplasms, will require further evaluation, particularly in patients with a more favorable prognosis, who may have done well with conventional salvage therapy.[103] Selected ongoing trials are summarized in Table 16–3.

"DESPERATION" SURGERY

The role of salvage surgery in the treatment of germ cell tumors is discussed in greater detail elsewhere in this textbook. It is important to note that there is substantial literature support for attempts at complete resection of residual tumor, even after the most extensive efforts at chemotherapy and in patients with persistently elevated tumor markers.[166–173] Long-term disease-free survival is reported for such patients who have a solitary resectable recurrent or persistant mass.

SPECIAL SITUATIONS

Central Nervous System Recurrence

Rarely, a patient is found (either by symptoms or in a work-up of elevated serum tumor markers) to have central nervous system (CNS) recurrence.[15]

Recurrence that is limited to the CNS is potentially curable with resection and whole brain radiation,[19,20,174] often with the addition of abbreviated chemotherapy.[15,19,175]

In contrast, patients experiencing CNS recurrence with simultaneous extracerebral disease activity have a very poor prognosis and can be salvaged only very rarely. Most investigators recommend that such patients should be treated only with palliative measures or in clinical trials.[15,19,20,175]

Primary Extragonadal Germ Cell Tumors

Primary extragonadal germ cell tumors make up only 1 to 5% of all germ cell malignancies[176] (see Chapter 21). They usually arise from the mediastinum or the retroperitoneum and have a histology similar to that of gonadal primaries (seminoma and nonseminoma).[176] Nonseminomatous extragonadal germ cell tumors have an inferior outcome with initial therapy and an exceedingly poor prognosis if they recur, and therefore represent a distinct clinical and biologic entity.[177] Neither conventional salvage chemotherapy[5,6,72,73] nor high-dose chemotherapy[7,15,23,28,103,178] have been able

to substantially affect the outcome with recurrent extragonadal germ cell tumors. An overview of 142 patients with relapsed extragonadal nonseminomatous germ cell tumors treated at multiple institutions[179] reported a 19% long-term disease-free survival rate. Survival was similar for patients receiving conventional-dose and high-dose salvage therapy. The most important adverse prognostic factors in this group were a primary mediastinal location and cisplatin-refractory disease. Thirty percent of patients with a retroperitoneal primary and 10% of those with a mediastinal primary were long-term survivors after first relapse. Desperation surgery should be considered for patients in this population who have solitary resectable lesions.[180,181] Extragonadal seminoma does not share the poor prognosis associated with extragonadal nonseminomatous germ cell tumors.[4,182]

Relapse after High-Dose Chemotherapy

Patients relapsing after high-dose chemotherapy and autologous bone marrow transplantation have a dismal prognosis. Paclitaxel and ifosfamide have produced nondurable responses in this setting,[33,183] as have oral etoposide[33] and gemcitabine.[33,50–52,184] For selected patients, salvage surgery should be considered.[33,173] Finally, clinical trials of novel agents should be strongly considered in this patient population.

TREATMENT RECOMMENDATIONS

The approach to a patient with a suspected recurrence of germ cell cancer is complex and nuanced. Initial evaluation should focus on ensuring that the

Table 16–3. ACTIVE MULTI-INSTITUTIONAL CLINICAL TRIALS OF SALVAGE CHEMOTHERAPY FOR GERM CELL NEOPLASMS			
Regimen	Trial Type	Organization and Trial ID	Patient Population
Cisplatin/etoposide/ifosfamide or VeIP for 4 cycles vs same regimen for 3 cycles followed by high-dose chemotherapy with carboplatin/etoposide/cyclophosphamide	Randomized phase III	FRE-FNCLCC-IT-94	Relapse after complete remission or progression after partial remission with cisplatin-based first-line therapy
Arsenic trioxide	Phase II	SWOG 0207	Cisplatin-refractory disease or relapse after at least 2 regimens, one of which must include high-dose chemotherapy†

ID = identification; FNCLCC-IT = Federation Nationale des Centres de Lutte Contre le Cancer Intergroup Trial; SWOG = Southwest Oncology Group.
*Cisplatin-refractory patients excluded.
†Unless patient is ineligible for high-dose chemotherapy.

patient indeed has relapsed or persistent cancer. Sanctuary sites should be examined next and treated appropriately if involved.

Conventional salvage therapy with VeIP is recommended for patients with good prognostic features such as seminoma, relapse after complete response to induction chemotherapy, and cisplatin-sensitive disease. Resection of residual masses is an important component of salvage chemotherapy. Regimens that incorporate newer agents, (ie, paclitaxel or high-dose chemotherapy) remain experimental for this population of patients. Approximately 15% of patients relapsing after first-salvage treatment, can still be cured with high-dose chemotherapy and autologous progenitor cell support.

All patients with a relapsed mediastinal non-seminomatous primary should be considered for experimental treatments, particularly treatments that involve novel approaches. The impact of conventional salvage treatments, with or without transplantation, is meager and should be considered only for those patients for whom clinical investigations are not suitable. Patients with cisplatin-refractory cancer or those who relapse after high-dose therapy and who are not cured with desperation surgery have no realistic chance of cure with current medical therapy and can be offered either transient palliation with additional chemotherapy or enrollment in clinical trials that are examining novel agents.

REFERENCES

1. Einhorn LH. Treatment of testicular cancer: a new and improved model. J Clin Oncol 1990;8:1777–81.
2. Williams SD, Birch R, Einhorn LH, et al. Treatment of disseminated germ-cell tumors with cisplatin, bleomycin, and either vinblastine or etoposide. N Engl J Med 1987;316:1435–40.
3. Bosl GJ, Motzer RJ. Testicular germ-cell cancer. N Engl J Med 1997;337:242–53.
4. International Germ Cell Consensus Classification. A prognostic factor-based staging system for metastatic germ cell cancers. International Germ Cell Cancer Collaborative Group. J Clin Oncol 1997;15:594–603.
5. Rick O, Siegert W, Beyer J. Chemotherapy in patients with metastatic or relapsed germ-cell tumours. Cancer Treat Rev 2001;27:283–8.
6. Motzer RJ, Geller NL, Tan CC, et al. Salvage chemotherapy for patients with germ cell tumors. The Memorial Sloan-Kettering Cancer Center experience (1979-1989). Cancer 1991;67:1305–10.
7. Beyer J, Kramar A, Mandanas R, et al. High-dose chemotherapy as salvage treatment in germ cell tumors. A multivariate analysis of prognostic variables. J Clin Oncol 1996;14:2638–45.
8. Fossa SD, Stenning SP, Gerl A, et al. Prognostic factors in patients progressing after cisplatin-based chemotherapy for malignant non-seminomatous germ cell tumours. Br J Cancer 1999;80:1392–9.
9. Logothetis CJ, Samuels ML, Trindade A, et al. The growing teratoma syndrome. Cancer 1982;50:1629–35.
10. Bellamy EA, Husband JE, Blaquiere RM, et al. Bleomycin-related lung damage. CT evidence. Radiology 1985;156:155–8.
11. Fowler JE Jr, Platoff GE, Kubrock CA, et al. Commercial radioimmunoassay for beta subunit of human chorionic gonadotropin: falsely positive determinations due to elevated serum luteinizing hormone. Cancer 1982;49:136–9.
12. Garnick MB. Spurious rise in human chorionic gonadotropin induced by marihuana in patients with testicular cancer. N Engl J Med 1980;303:1177.
13. Catalona WJ, Vaitukaitis JL, Fair WR. Falsely positive specific human chorionic gonadotropin assays in patients with testicular tumors: conversion to negative with testosterone administration. J Urol 1979;122:126–8.
14. Nichols CR, Saxman S. Primary salvage treatment of recurrent germ cell tumors: experience at Indiana University. Semin Oncol 1998;25:210–4.
15. Nichols CR. Treatment of recurrent germ cell tumors. Semin Surg Oncol 1999;17:268–74.
16. Zon RT, Nichols C, Einhorn LH, et al. Management strategies and outcomes of germ cell tumor patients with very high human chorionic gonadotropin levels. J Clin Oncol 1998;16:1294–7.
17. Dahlmann N, Hartlapp JH. False positivity with one-step monoclonal assay for alpha-fetoprotein. Lancet 1988;1:1172–3.
18. Germa JR, Llanos M, Tabernero JM, et al. False elevations of alpha-fetoprotein associated with liver dysfunction in germ cell tumors. Cancer 1993;72:2491–4.
19. Spears WT, Morphis JG 2nd, Lester SG, et al. Brain metastases and testicular tumors: long-term survival. Int J Radiat Oncol Biol Phys 1992;22:17–22.
20. Fossa SD, Bokemeyer C, Gerl A, et al. Treatment outcome of patients with brain metastases from malignant germ cell tumors. Cancer 1999;85:988–97.
21. Terebelo HR, Taylor HG, Brown A, et al. Late relapse of testicular cancer. J Clin Oncol 1983;1:566–71.
22. Gerl A, Clemm C, Schmeller N, et al. Late relapse of germ cell tumors after cisplatin-based chemotherapy. Ann Oncol 1997;8:41–7.
23. Baniel J, Foster RS, Gonin R, et al. Late relapse of testicular cancer. J Clin Oncol 1995;13:1170–6.
24. Gelderman WA, Scraffordt Koops H, Sleijfer DT, et al. Late recurrence of mature teratoma in nonseminomatous testicular tumors after PVB chemotherapy and surgery. Urology 1989;33:10–4.
25. Einhorn LH. Salvage therapy for germ cell tumors. Semin Oncol 1994;21:47–51.
26. Nichols CR, Tricot G, Williams SD, et al. Dose-intensive chemotherapy in refractory germ cell cancer—a phase I/II

trial of high-dose carboplatin and etoposide with autologous bone marrow transplantation. J Clin Oncol 1989;7: 932–9.

27. Linkesch W, Greinix H, Hocker P, et al. Long-term follow-up of phase I/II trial of ultra-high carboplatin, VP-16 cyclophosphamide with ABMT in refractory or relapsed NSGCT [abstract]. Proc Am Soc Clin Oncol 1993;12:232.

28. Saxman SB, Nichols CR, Einhorn LH. Salvage chemotherapy in patients with extragonadal nonseminomatous germ cell tumors: the Indiana University experience. J Clin Oncol 1994;12:1390–3.

29. Nichols CR. The role of etoposide therapy in germ cell cancer. Semin Oncol 1992;19:67–71.

30. Loehrer PJ Sr. Etoposide therapy for testicular cancer. Cancer 1991;67:220–4.

31. Newlands ES, Bagshawe KD. Epipodophylin derivative (VP 16-23) in malignant teratomas and choriocarcinomas. Lancet 1977;2:87.

32. Miller JC, Einhorn LH. Phase II study of daily oral etoposide in refractory germ cell tumors. Semin Oncol 1990;17: 36–9.

33. Porcu P, Bhatia S, Sharma M, et al. Results of treatment after relapse from high-dose chemotherapy in germ cell tumors. J Clin Oncol 2000;18:1181–6.

34. Scheulen ME, Niederle N, Bremer K, et al. Efficacy of ifosfamide in refractory malignant diseases and uroprotection by mesna: results of a clinical phase II-study with 151 patients. Cancer Treat Rev 1983;10 Suppl A:93–101.

35. Wheeler BM, Loehrer PJ, Williams SD, et al. Ifosfamide in refractory male germ cell tumors. J Clin Oncol 1986; 4:28–34.

36. Nichols CR. Ifosfamide in the treatment of germ cell tumors. Semin Oncol 1996;23:65–73.

37. Roth BJ. The role of ifosfamide in the treatment of testicular and urothelial malignancies. Semin Oncol 1996;23:19–27.

38. Motzer RJ, Bosl GJ, Tauer K, et al. Phase II trial of carboplatin in patients with advanced germ cell tumors refractory to cisplatin. Cancer Treat Rep 1987;71:197–8.

39. Spencer CM, Faulds D. Paclitaxel. A review of its pharmacodynamic and pharmacokinetic properties and therapeutic potential in the treatment of cancer. Drugs 1994;48: 794–847.

40. Belotti D, Vergani V, Drudis T, et al. The microtubule-affecting drug paclitaxel has antiangiogenic activity. Clin Cancer Res 1996;2:1843–9.

41. Motzer RJ, Chou TC, Schwartz L, et al. Paclitaxel in germ cell cancer. Semin Oncol 1995;22:12–5.

42. Dunn TA, Grunwald V, Bokemeyer C, et al. Pre-clinical activity of taxol in non-seminomatous germ cell tumor cell lines and nude mouse xenografts. Invest New Drugs 1997;15:91–8.

43. Bokemeyer C, Schmoll HJ, Natt F, et al. Preliminary results of a phase I/II trial of paclitaxel in patients with relapsed or cisplatin-refractory testicular cancer. J Cancer Res Clin Oncol 1994;120:754–7.

44. Bokemeyer C, Beyer J, Metzner B, et al. Phase II study of paclitaxel in patients with relapsed or cisplatin-refractory testicular cancer. Ann Oncol 1996;7:31–4.

45. Motzer RJ, Bajorin DF, Schwartz LH, et al. Phase II trial of paclitaxel shows antitumor activity in patients with previ-

ously treated germ cell tumors. J Clin Oncol 1994;12: 2277–83.

46. Sandler AB, Cristou A, Fox S, et al. A phase II trial of paclitaxel in refractory germ cell tumors. Cancer 1998;82:1381–6.

47. Nazario A, Amato R, Hutchinson L, et al. Paclitaxel in extensively pretreated nonseminomatous germ cell tumors. Urol Oncol 1995;1:184–7.

48. Plunkett W, Huang P, Xu YZ, et al. Gemcitabine: metabolism, mechanisms of action, and self-potentiation. Semin Oncol 1995;22:3–10.

49. Maas K, Daikeler T, Kanz L, et al. Activity of gemcitabine in platinum-resistant ovarian germ cell cancer. Eur J Cancer 1996;32A:1437–8.

50. Bokemeyer C, Gerl A, Schoffski P, et al. Gemcitabine in patients with relapsed or cisplatin-refractory testicular cancer. J Clin Oncol 1999;17:512–6.

51. Einhorn LH, Stender MJ, Williams SD. Phase II trial of gemcitabine in refractory germ cell tumors. J Clin Oncol 1999;17:509–11.

52. Bokemeyer C, Kollmannsberger C, Harstrick A, et al. Treatment of patients with cisplatin-refractory testicular germ-cell cancer. German Testicular Cancer Study Group (GTCSG). Int J Cancer 1999;83:848–51.

53. Williams SD, Birch R, Gams R, et al. Phase II trial of mitoxantrone in refractory germ cell tumors: a trial of the Southeastern Cancer Study Group. Cancer Treat Rep 1985;69: 1455–6.

54. Bokemeyer C, Droz J, Hanauske A, et al. Treatment of relapsed nonseminoma germ cell tumors with vinorelbine: a trial of the phase I/II study group of the Association of Medical Oncology of the German Cancer Society. Onkologie 1993;16:29–31.

55. Motzer RJ, Dmitrovsky E, Miller WH Jr, et al. Suramin for germ cell tumors. In vitro growth inhibition and results of a phase II trial. Cancer 1993;72:3313–7.

56. Puc HS, Bajorin DF, Bosl GJ, et al. Phase II trial of topotecan in patients with cisplatin-refractory germ cell tumors. Invest New Drugs 1995;13:163–5.

57. Moasser MM, Motzer RJ, Khoo KS, et al. all-trans retinoic acid for treating germ cell tumors. In vitro activity and results of a phase II trial. Cancer 1995;76:680–6.

58. Atkinson CH, Horwich A, Peckham MJ. Methotrexate for relapse of metastatic non-seminomatous germ-cell tumours. Med Oncol Tumor Pharmacother 1987;4:33–7.

59. Reynolds TF, Vugrin D, Cvitkovic E, et al. Phase II trial of vindesine in patients with germ-cell tumors. Cancer Treat Rep 1979;63:1399–401.

60. Drasga RE, Williams SD, Einhorn LH, et al. Phase II evaluation of iproplatin in refractory germ cell tumors: a Southeastern Cancer Study Group trial. Cancer Treat Rep 1987;71:863–4.

61. Murphy BA, Motzer RJ, Bosl GJ. Phase II study of iproplatin (CHIP) in patients with cisplatin-refractory germ cell tumors; the need for alternative strategies in the investigation of new agents in GCT. Invest New Drugs 1992;10: 327–30.

62. Hoskins P, Coppin CM, Murray N. Mitomycin is active against refractory germ-cell tumors. A phase II study. Am J Clin Oncol 1990;13:35–8.

63. Kollmannsberger C, Gerl A, Schleucher N, et al. Phase II

study of bendamustine in patients with relapsed or cis-platin-refractory germ cell cancer. Anticancer Drugs 2000;11:535–9.

64. Harstrick A, Schmoll HJ, Wilke H, et al. High dose epirubicin in refractory or relapsed non-seminomatous testicular cancer: a phase II study. Ann Oncol 1990;1:375–6.

65. Stoter G, Akdas A, Fossa SD, et al. High-dose epirubicin in chemotherapy refractory non-seminomatous germ cell cancer: a phase II study. EORTC Genito-Urinary Tract Cancer Co-operative Group. EORTC Early Clinical Trials Group. Ann Oncol 1992;3:577–8.

66. Loehrer PJ Sr, Lauer R, Roth BJ, et al. Salvage therapy in recurrent germ cell cancer. Ifosfamide and cisplatin plus either vinblastine or etoposide. Ann Intern Med 1988;109:540–6.

67. Motzer RJ, Bajorin DF, Vlamis V, et al. Ifosfamide-based chemotherapy for patients with resistant germ cell tumors: the Memorial Sloan-Kettering Cancer Center experience. Semin Oncol 1992;19:8–11.

68. Pizzocaro G, Salvioni R, Piva L, et al. Modified cisplatin, etoposide (or vinblastine) and ifosfamide salvage therapy for male germ-cell tumors. Long-term results. Ann Oncol 1992;3:211–6.

69. Farhat F, Culine S, Theodore C, et al. Cisplatin and ifosfamide with either vinblastine or etoposide as salvage therapy for refractory or relapsing germ cell tumor patients: the Institut Gustave Roussy experience. Cancer 1996;77:1193–7.

70. McCaffrey JA, Mazumdar M, Bajorin DF, et al. Ifosfamide- and cisplatin-containing chemotherapy as first-line salvage therapy in germ cell tumors: response and survival. J Clin Oncol 1997;15:2559–63.

71. Miller KD, Loehrer PJ, Gonin R, et al. Salvage chemotherapy with vinblastine, ifosfamide, and cisplatin in recurrent seminoma. J Clin Oncol 1997;15:1427–31.

72. Loehrer PJ Sr, Gonin R, Nichols CR, et al. Vinblastine plus ifosfamide plus cisplatin as initial salvage therapy in recurrent germ cell tumor. J Clin Oncol 1998;16:2500–4.

73. Einhorn L, Weathers T, Loehrer P, et al. Second line chemotherapy with vinblastine, ifosfamide, and cisplatin after initial chemotherapy with cisplatin, VP-16 and bleomycin (PVC-16B) in disseminated germ cell tumors (GCT) [abstract]. Proc Am Soc Clin Oncol 1992;11:196.

74. Tjulandin SA, Titov DA, Breder VV, et al. Paclitaxel and cisplatin as salvage treatment in patients with non-seminomatous germ cell tumour who failed to achieve a complete remission on induction chemotherapy. Clin Oncol 1998;10:297–300.

75. Motzer RJ, Sheinfeld J, Mazumdar M, et al. Paclitaxel, ifosfamide, and cisplatin second-line therapy for patients with relapsed testicular germ cell cancer. J Clin Oncol 2000; 18:2413–8.

76. Motzer RJ. Paclitaxel in salvage therapy for germ cell tumors. Semin Oncol 1997;24(5 Suppl 15):S15-83–S15-85.

77. Motzer RJ. Paclitaxel (Taxol) combination therapy for resistant germ cell tumors. Semin Oncol 2000;27:33–5.

78. Hinton S, Catalano P, Einhorn LH, et al. Phase II study of paclitaxel plus gemcitabine in refractory germ cell tumors (E9897): a trial of the Eastern Cooperative Oncology Group. J Clin Oncol 2002;20:1859–63.

79. Vuky J, Tickoo SK, Sheinfeld J, et al. Salvage chemotherapy for patients with advanced pure seminoma. J Clin Oncol 2002;20:297–301.

80. Frei E 3rd, Antman K, Teicher B, et al. Bone marrow autotransplantation for solid tumors—prospects. J Clin Oncol 1989;7:515–26.

81. Ozols RF, Behrens BC, Ostchega Y, et al. High dose cisplatin and high dose carboplatin in refractory ovarian cancer. Cancer Treat Rev 1985;12 Suppl A:59–65.

82. Colombo T, Broggini M, Torti L, et al. Pharmacokinetics of VP16-213 in Lewis lung carcinoma bearing mice. Cancer Chemother Pharmacol 1982;7:127–31.

83. Sobecks RM, Vogelzang NJ. High-dose chemotherapy with autologous stem-cell support for germ cell tumors: a critical review. Semin Oncol 1999;26:106–18.

84. Ghosn M, Droz JP, Theodore C, et al. Salvage chemotherapy in refractory germ cell tumors with etoposide (VP-16) plus ifosfamide plus high-dose cisplatin. A VIhP regimen. Cancer 1988;62:24–7.

85. Droz JP, Pico JL, Ghosn M, et al. Long-term survivors after salvage high dose chemotherapy with bone marrow rescue in refractory germ cell cancer. Eur J Cancer 1991;27:831–5.

86. Ozols RF, Ihde DC, Linehan WM, et al. A randomized trial of standard chemotherapy vs. a high-dose chemotherapy regimen in the treatment of poor prognosis nonseminomatous germ-cell tumors. J Clin Oncol 1988;6:1031–40.

87. Samson MK, Rivkin SE, Jones SE, et al. Dose-response and dose-survival advantage for high versus low-dose cisplatin combined with vinblastine and bleomycin in disseminated testicular cancer. A Southwest Oncology Group study. Cancer 1984;53:1029–35.

88. Daugaard G, Rorth M. High-dose cisplatin and VP-16 with bleomycin, in the management of advanced metastatic germ cell tumors. Eur J Cancer Clin Oncol 1986;22:477–85.

89. Nichols CR, Williams SD, Loehrer PJ, et al. Randomized study of cisplatin dose intensity in poor-risk germ cell tumors: a Southeastern Cancer Study Group and Southwest Oncology Group protocol. J Clin Oncol 1991;9:1163–72.

90. Shea TC, Flaherty M, Elias A, et al. A phase I clinical and pharmacokinetic study of carboplatin and autologous bone marrow support. J Clin Oncol 1989;7:651–61.

91. Nichols CR, Andersen J, Lazarus HM, et al. High-dose carboplatin and etoposide with autologous bone marrow transplantation in refractory germ cell cancer: an Eastern Cooperative Oncology Group protocol. J Clin Oncol 1992;10:558–63.

92. Broun ER, Nichols CR, Kneebone P, et al. Long-term outcome of patients with relapsed and refractory germ cell tumors treated with high-dose chemotherapy and autologous bone marrow rescue. Ann Intern Med 1992;117:124–8.

93. Broun ER, Nichols CR, Mandanas R, et al. Dose escalation study of high-dose carboplatin and etoposide with autologous bone marrow support in patients with recurrent and refractory germ cell tumors. Bone Marrow Transplant 1995;16:353–8.

94. Ayash LJ, Clarke M, Silver SM, et al. Double dose-intensive chemotherapy with autologous stem cell support for relapsed and refractory testicular cancer: the University of Michigan experience and literature review. Bone Marrow Transplant 2001;27:939–47.

95. Broun ER, Nichols CR, Tricot G, et al. High dose carbo-

platin/VP-16 plus ifosfamide with autologous bone marrow support in the treatment of refractory germ cell tumors. Bone Marrow Transplant 1991;7:53–6.

96. Siegert W, Beyer J. Germ cell tumors: dose-intensive therapy. Semin Oncol 1998;25:215–23.

97. Lotz JP, Machover D, Malassagne B, et al. Phase I-II study of two consecutive courses of high-dose epipodophyllotoxin, ifosfamide, and carboplatin with autologous bone marrow transplantation for treatment of adult patients with solid tumors. J Clin Oncol 1991;9:1860–70.

98. Lotz JP, Andre T, Donsimoni R, et al. High dose chemotherapy with ifosfamide, carboplatin, and etoposide combined with autologous bone marrow transplantation for the treatment of poor-prognosis germ cell tumors and metastatic trophoblastic disease in adults. Cancer 1995; 75:874–85.

99. Rosti G, Albertazzi L, Salvioni R, et al. High dose chemotherapy with carboplatin, VP 16 +/– ifosfamide in germ cell tumors: the Italian experience. Bone Marrow Transplant 1991;7:94.

100. Rosti G, Albertazzi L, Salvioni R, et al. High-dose chemotherapy supported with autologous bone marrow transplantation (ABMT) in germ cell tumors: a phase two study. Ann Oncol 1992;3:809–12.

101. Siegert W, Beyer J, Strohscheer I, et al. High-dose treatment with carboplatin, etoposide, and ifosfamide followed by autologous stem-cell transplantation in relapsed or refractory germ cell cancer: a phase I/II study. The German Testicular Cancer Cooperative Study Group. J Clin Oncol 1994;12:1223–31.

102. Beyer J, Kingreen D, Krause M, et al. Long-term survival of patients with recurrent or refractory germ cell tumors after high dose chemotherapy. Cancer 1997;79:161–8.

103. Nichols CR, Roth BJ, Loehrer PJ, et al. Salvage chemotherapy for recurrent germ cell cancer. Semin Oncol 1994; 21:102–8.

104. Bokemeyer C. Current trends in chemotherapy for metastatic nonseminomatous testicular germ cell tumors. Oncology 1998;55:177–88.

105. Bokemeyer C, Harstrick A, Beyer J, et al. The use of dose-intensified chemotherapy in the treatment of metastatic nonseminomatous testicular germ cell tumors. German Testicular Cancer Study Group. Semin Oncol 1998;25:24–32; discussion 45–8.

106. Motzer RJ, Gulati SC, Crown JP, et al. High-dose chemotherapy and autologous bone marrow rescue for patients with refractory germ cell tumors. Early intervention is better tolerated. Cancer 1992;69:550–6.

107. Motzer RJ, Mazumdar M, Bosl GJ, et al. High-dose carboplatin, etoposide, and cyclophosphamide for patients with refractory germ cell tumors: treatment results and prognostic factors for survival and toxicity. J Clin Oncol 1996; 14:1098–105.

108. Ibrahim A, Zambon E, Bourhis JH, et al. High-dose chemotherapy with etoposide, cyclophosphamide and escalating dose of carboplatin followed by autologous bone marrow transplantation in cancer patients. A pilot study. Eur J Cancer 1993;10:1398–403.

109. Linkesch W, Krainer M, Wagner A. Phase I/II trial of ultra-high carboplatin, etopside and cyclophosphamide with

110. Linkesch W, Greinix H, Kalhs P. Long-term results of phase I/II trial of Carbo-PEC with ABMT in refractory or relapsed NSGCT. Bone Marrow Transplant [abstract] 1994;14(Suppl 1):S41.

111. Beyer J, Schwella N, Zingsem J, et al. Hematopoietic rescue after high-dose chemotherapy using autologous peripheral-blood progenitor cells or bone marrow: a randomized comparison. J Clin Oncol 1995;13:1328–35.

112. Schwella N, Beyer J, Schwaner I, et al. Impact of preleukapheresis cell counts on collection results and correlation of progenitor-cell dose with engraftment after high-dose chemotherapy in patients with germ cell cancer. J Clin Oncol 1996;14:1114–21.

113. Rodenhuis S, van der Wall E, ten Bokkel Huinink WW, et al. Pilot study of a high-dose carboplatin-based salvage strategy for relapsing or refractory germ cell cancer. Cancer Invest 1995;13:355–62.

114. Rodenhuis S, de Wit R, de Mulder PH, et al. A multi-center prospective phase II study of high-dose chemotherapy in germ-cell cancer patients relapsing from complete remission. Ann Oncol 1999;10:1467–73.

115. Flechon A, Culine S, Droz JP. Intensive and timely chemotherapy, the key of success in testicular cancer. Crit Rev Oncol Hematol 2001;37:35–46.

116. Broun ER, Nichols CR, Turns M, et al. Early salvage therapy for germ cell cancer using high dose chemotherapy with autologous bone marrow support. Cancer 1994;73: 1716–20.

117. Barnett MJ, Coppin CM, Murray N, et al. High-dose chemotherapy and autologous bone marrow transplantation for patients with poor prognosis nonseminomatous germ cell tumours. Br J Cancer 1993;68:594–8.

118. Broun ER, Nichols CR, Gize G, et al. Tandem high dose chemotherapy with autologous bone marrow transplantation for initial relapse of testicular germ cell cancer. Cancer 1997;79:1605–10.

119. Bhatia S, Abonour R, Porcu P, et al. High-dose chemotherapy as initial salvage chemotherapy in patients with relapsed testicular cancer. J Clin Oncol 2000;18:3346–51.

120. Rodenhuis S, Vlasveld LT, Dubbelman R, et al. Feasibility study of high-dose carboplatin and etoposide in the salvage treatment of testicular cancer. Ann Oncol 1992;3:463–7.

121. Margolin BK, Doroshow JH, Ahn C, et al. Treatment of germ cell cancer with two cycles of high-dose ifosfamide, carboplatin, and etoposide with autologous stem-cell support. J Clin Oncol 1996;14:2631–7.

122. Motzer RJ, Mazumdar M, Sheinfeld J, et al. Sequential dose-intensive paclitaxel, ifosfamide, carboplatin, and etoposide salvage therapy for germ cell tumor patients. J Clin Oncol 2000;18:1173–80.

123. Rick O, Bokemeyer C, Beyer J, et al. Salvage treatment with paclitaxel, ifosfamide, and cisplatin plus high-dose carboplatin, etoposide, and thiotepa followed by autologous stem-cell rescue in patients with relapsed or refractory germ cell cancer. J Clin Oncol 2001;19:81–8.

124. Beyer J, Stenning S, Gerl A, et al. High-dose versus conventional dose first salvage treatment in nonseminomatous

ABMT in refractory or relapsed non-seminomatous germ cell tumors. Bone Marrow Transplant [abstract]. Proc Am Soc Oncol 1992;11:196.

germ cell tumors: a matched pair-analysis [abstract]. Proc Am Soc Clin Oncol 1999;18:326.

125. Pico JL, Castagna L, Kramar A, et al. High-dose chemotherapy as salvage treatment for germ cell tumors. The ongoing IT94 study. Bone Marrow Transplant 1996;18 Suppl 1: S63–6.

126. Shen ZX, Chen GQ, Ni JH, et al. Use of arsenic trioxide (As2O3) in the treatment of acute promyelocytic leukemia (APL). II. Clinical efficacy and pharmacokinetics in relapsed patients. Blood 1997;89:3354–60.

127. Sun HD, Na L, Hu XC, et al. Treatment of acute promyelocytic leukemia by Ailing-1 therapy with use of syndrome differentiation of traditional Chinese medicine. Chin J Comb Trad Chin Med West Med 1992;12:170–1.

128. Zhang P, Wang SY, Hu XH. Arsenic trioxide treated 72 cases of acute promyelocytic leukemia. Chin J Hematol 1996; 17:58–62.

129. Soignet SL, Maslak P, Wang ZG, et al. Complete remission after treatment of acute promyelocytic leukemia with arsenic trioxide. N Engl J Med 1998;339:1341–8.

130. Soignet S, Frankel S, Tallman M, et al. U.S. multicenter trial of arsenic trioxide (AT) in acute promyelocytic leukemia (APL) [abstract]. Proc Am Soc Hem 1999;94:3084.

131. Akao Y, Yamada H, Nakagawa Y. Arsenic-induced apoptosis in malignant cells in vitro. Leuk Lymphoma 2000;37:53–63.

132. Shen ZY, Tan LJ, Cai WJ, et al. Arsenic trioxide induces apoptosis of oesophageal carcinoma in vitro. Int J Mol Med 1999;4:33–7.

133. Zhang TC, Cao EH, Li JF, et al. Induction of apoptosis and inhibition of human gastric cancer MGC-803 cell growth by arsenic trioxide. Eur J Cancer 1999;35:1258–63.

134. Lew YS, Brown SL, Griffin RJ, et al. Arsenic trioxide causes selective necrosis in solid murine tumors by vascular shutdown. Cancer Res 1999;59:6033–7.

135. Ma Y, Yuan R, Meng Q, et al. P53 status as a determinant of response to arsenic trioxide in human Burkitt's lymphoma, prostate and breast cancer cells [abstract]. Proc Am Assoc Cancer Res 2000;41:753.

136. Dai J, Jing Y, Hellinger N, et al. Mechanism of arsenic trioxide induced growth inhibition and apoptosis in malignant cells [abstract]. Proc Am Assoc Cancer Res 1998;39:68.

137. Nagourney RA, Danskin JW, Chou C, et al. Arsenic trioxide (AS2O3) activity spectrum in human tumors [abstract]. Proc Am Assoc Cancer Res 1999;397.

138. Uslu R, Sezgin C, Karabulut B, et al. Arsenic trioxide-mediated cytotoxicity in prostate and ovarian carcinoma lines [abstract]. Clin Cancer Res 1999;5:271.

139. Zhou DC, Gao M, Ferrari AC, et al. Arsenic trioxide is an equipotent inducer of apoptosis in androgen-dependent and androgen-independent LNCaP prostate cancer cell sublines [abstract]. Proc Am Assoc Cancer Res 1998;39:588.

140. Akao Y, Nagakawa Y. Arsenic-induced apoptosis in solid tumor cells [abstract]. Proc Am Assoc Cancer Res 2000;41:416.

141. Seol JG, Park WH, Kim ES, et al. Induction of apoptosis by APAF-1 and cytochrome C-dependent activation of caspace after treatment with arsenic trioxide (AS2O3) in head and neck cancer cell PCI-1 [abstract]. Proc Am Assoc Cancer Res 2000;41:155.

142. Seol JG, Park WH, Kim ES, et al. Effect of arsenic trioxide on cell cycle arrest in head and neck cancer cell line PCI-1. Biochem Biophys Res Commun 1999;265:400–4.

143. Yang CH, Wang TY, Chen YC. Cytotoxicity of arsenic trioxide in cancer cell lines. Proc Am Assoc Cancer Res 1998;227.

144. Huang C, Ma WY, Li J, et al. Arsenic induces apoptosis through a c-Jun NH2-terminal kinase-dependent, p53-independent pathway. Cancer Res 1999;59:3053–8.

145. Chen GQ, Zhu J, Shi XG, et al. In vitro studies on cellular and molecular mechanisms of arsenic trioxide (As2O3) in the treatment of acute promyelocytic leukemia. As2O3 induces NB4 cell apoptosis with downregulation of Bcl-2 expression and modulation of PML-RAR alpha/PML proteins. Blood 1996;88:1052–61.

146. Akao Y, Mizoguchi H, Kojima S, et al. Arsenic induces apoptosis in B-cell leukaemic cell lines in vitro: activation of caspases and down-regulation of Bcl-2 protein. Br J Haematol 1998;102:1055–60.

147. Shen L, Chen TX, Wang YP, et al. As2O3 induces apoptosis of the human B lymphoma cell line MBC-1. J Biol Regul Homeost Agents 2000;14:116–9.

148. Roboz GJ, Dias S, Lam G, et al. Arsenic trioxide induces dose- and time-dependent apoptosis of endothelium and may exert an antileukemic effect via inhibition of angiogenesis. Blood 2000;96:1525–30.

149. Lew YS, Kolozsvary A, Brown SL, et al. Arsenic trioxide: anti-vascular effect and radiosensitization [abstract].. Proc Am Assoc Cancer Res 2000;41:294.

150. Griffin RJ, Lee SH, Rood KL, et al. Arsenic trioxide reduces tumor flow, inhibits endothelial cell growth and selectively kills hypoxic cells [abstract]. Proc Am Assoc Cancer Res 2000;41:650.

151. Park WH, Seol JG, Kim ES, et al. Arsenic trioxide-mediated growth inhibition in MC/CAR myeloma cells via cell cycle arrest in association with induction of cyclin-dependent kinase inhibitor, p21, and apoptosis. Cancer Res 2000;60:3065–71.

152. Soignet S, Bienvenu B, Cheung N, et al. Clinical and pharmacologic study of arsenic trioxide (As2O3) in patients with solid tumors. Proc Am Soc Clin Oncol 2000;19:201a.

153. Druker BJ, Tamura S, Buchdunger E, et al. Effects of a selective inhibitor of the Abl tyrosine kinase on the growth of Bcr-Abl positive cells. Nat Med 1996;2:561–6.

154. Druker BJ, Talpaz M, Resta DJ, et al. Efficacy and safety of a specific inhibitor of the BCR-ABL tyrosine kinase in chronic myeloid leukemia. N Engl J Med 2001;344: 1031–7.

155. Heinrich MC, Griffith DJ, Druker BJ, et al. Inhibition of c-kit receptor tyrosine kinase activity by STI 571, a selective tyrosine kinase inhibitor. Blood 2000;96:925–32.

156. Blanke C, Mehren MV, Joensuu H, et al. Evaluation of the safety and efficacy of an oral molecularly-targeted therapy, STI-571, in patients with unresectable or metastatic gastrointestinal stromal tumors (GISTs) expressing c-kit (CD 117) [abstract]. Proc Am Soc Clin Oncol 2001;20:1a.

157. Tian Q, Frierson HF Jr, Krystal GW, et al. Activating c-kit gene mutations in human germ cell tumors. Am J Pathol 1999;154:1643–7.

158. Bokemeyer C, Kuczyk MA, Dunn T, et al. Expression of stem-cell factor and its receptor c-kit protein in normal testicular tissue and malignant germ-cell tumours. J Cancer Res Clin Oncol 1996;122:301–6.

159. Rajpert-De M, Skakkebaek N. Expression of the c-kit protein product in carcinoma-in-situ and invasive testicular germ cell tumors. Int J Androl 1994;17:85–92.

160. Kemmer K, Corless C, McGreevey L, et al. Characterization of c-kit mutations in seminomas [abstract]. Proc Am Assoc Cancer Res 2002;43:831.

161. Dunn TA, Schmoll HJ, Grunwald V, et al. Comparative cytotoxicity of oxaliplatin and cisplatin in non-seminomatous germ cell cancer cell lines. Invest New Drugs 1997; 15:109–14.

162. Kollmannsberger C, Rick O, Derigs HG, et al. Activity of oxaliplatin in patients with relapsed or cisplatin-refractory germ cell cancer: a study of the German Testicular Cancer Study Group. J Clin Oncol 2002;20:2031–7.

163. Miki T, Sawada M, Nonomura N, et al. Antitumor effect of CPT-11, a camptothecin derivative, on human testicular tumor xenografts in nude mice. Eur Urol 1997;31:92–6.

164. Henley J, Einhorn L. C-ERBB-2 (HER-2-NEU) overexpression in recurrent germ cell tumors. Proc Am Soc Clin Oncol 1999;18:341a.

165. Kollmannsberger C, Pressler H, Mayer F, et al. Cisplatin-refractory, HER2/neu-expressing germ-cell cancer: induction of remission by the monoclonal antibody trastuzumab. Ann Oncol 1999;10:1393–4.

166. Toner GC, Panicek DM, Heelan RT, et al. Adjunctive surgery after chemotherapy for nonseminomatous germ cell tumors: recommendations for patient selection. J Clin Oncol 1990; 8:1683–94.

167. Ravi R, Ong J, Oliver RT, et al. Surgery as salvage therapy in chemotherapy-resistant nonseminomatous germ cell tumours. Br J Urol 1998;81:884–8.

168. Albers P, Ganz A, Hannig E, et al. Salvage surgery of chemorefractory germ cell tumors with elevated tumor markers. J Urol 2000;164:381–4.

169. Fox EP, Weathers TD, Williams SD, et al. Outcome analysis for patients with persistent nonteratomatous germ cell tumor in postchemotherapy retroperitoneal lymph node dissections. J Clin Oncol 1993;11:1294–9.

170. Murphy BR, Breeden ES, Donohue JP, et al. Surgical salvage of chemorefractory germ cell tumors. J Clin Oncol 1993; 11:324–9.

171. Wood DP Jr, Herr HW, Motzer RJ, et al. Surgical resection of solitary metastases after chemotherapy in patients with nonseminomatous germ cell tumors and elevated serum tumor markers. Cancer 1992;70:2354–7.

172. Eastham JA, Wilson TG, Russell C, et al. Surgical resection in patients with nonseminomatous germ cell tumor who fail to normalize serum tumor markers after chemotherapy. Urology 1994;43:74–80.

173. Flechon A, Rivoire M, Biron P, et al. Importance of surgery as salvage treatment after high dose chemotherapy failure in germ cell tumors. J Urol 2001;165:1920–6.

174. Raghavan D, Mackintosh JF, Fox RM, et al. Improved survival after brain metastases in non-seminomatous germ cell tumours with combined modality treatment. Br J Urol 1987;60:364–7.

175. Bokemeyer C, Nowak P, Haupt A, et al. Treatment of brain metastases in patients with testicular cancer. J Clin Oncol 1997;15:1449–54.

176. Hainsworth JD, Greco FA. Extragonadal germ cell tumors and unrecognized germ cell tumors. Semin Oncol 1992;19: 119–27.

177. Fizazi K, Culine S, Droz JP, et al. Primary mediastinal non-seminomatous germ cell tumors: results of modern therapy including cisplatin-based chemotherapy. J Clin Oncol 1998;16:725–32.

178. Broun ER, Nichols CR, Einhorn LH, et al. Salvage therapy with high-dose chemotherapy and autologous bone marrow support in the treatment of primary nonseminomatous mediastinal germ cell tumors. Cancer 1991;68:1513–5.

179. Hartmann JT, Einhorn L, Nichols CR, et al. Second-line chemotherapy in patients with relapsed extragonadal nonseminomatous germ cell tumors: results of an international multicenter analysis. J Clin Oncol 2001;19: 1641–8.

180. Vuky J, Bains M, Bacik J, et al. Role of postchemotherapy adjunctive surgery in the management of patients with nonseminoma arising from the mediastinum. J Clin Oncol 2001;19:682–8.

181. Rivoire M, Voiglio E, Kaemmerlen P, et al. Salvage resection of a chemorefractory mediastinal germ cell tumor. J Thorac Cardiovasc Surg 1996;112:1124–6.

182. Bokemeyer C, Droz JP, Horwich A, et al. Extragonadal seminoma: an international multicenter analysis of prognostic factors and long term treatment outcome. Cancer 2001; 91:1394–401.

183. Pont J, Bokemeyer C, Harstrick A, et al. Chemotherapy for germ cell tumors relapsing after high-dose chemotherapy and stem cell support: a retrospective multicenter study of the Austrian Study Group on Urologic Oncology. Ann Oncol 1997;8:1229–34.

184. Kollmannsberger C, Mayer F, Kuczyk M, et al. Treatment of patients with metastatic germ cell tumors relapsing after high-dose chemotherapy. World J Urol 2001;19:120–5.

17

Central Nervous System Metastases

DAVID I. QUINN, MBBS, PhD, FRACP
OMID HAMID, MD
OSCAR E. STREETER JR, MD
THOMAS C. CHEN, MD

Central nervous system (CNS) metastases represent a relatively uncommon but difficult management issue in patients with testicular (and extracranial nongonadal) germ cell tumors. Their presentation varies from being an incidental finding on imaging studies at diagnosis or during the course of treatment to the catastrophic clinical consequences of acute raised intracranial pressure and/or cerebral hemorrhage. CNS metastases are an adverse prognostic and predictive factor in patients with germ cell tumors of both testicular and extragonadal origin. Despite this, early aggressive surgical and radiation therapy management of these metastases, in combination with systemic chemotherapy, can facilitate cure in 30 to 80% of patients. This chapter will describe the demographics, presentation, clinical outcome, and therapeutic management of patients with brain metastases from extracranial germ cell tumors. (Pineal germ cell tumors are discussed and illustrated in Chapter 21.)

INCIDENCE

The incidence of CNS metastases in patients with extracranial germ cell tumors varies, depending on the cell type and primary site of the tumor (Tables 17–1 and 17–2). Brain metastases are associated most commonly with the following clinical situations:

1. Nonseminomatous germ cell tumor (NSGCT) arising in the testis or retroperitoneum (versus tumor in the mediastinum)

2. Choriocarcinoma

3. High levels of serum human chorionic gonadotropin

4. Pulmonary metastases

5. NSGCT (versus seminoma)

In reported autopsy series, brain metastases from germ cell tumors are surprisingly common although it should be noted that many of these series antedated the availability of curative treatment strategies for most patients. Earle[1] found cerebral metastases in 32.1% of 27 cases of testicular cancer in a series of 3,946 necropsies undertaken at the Los Angeles Department of Veterans Affairs between 1948 and 1952. Bredael and colleagues[2–4] reported on autopsy experience in 154 of approximately 1,300 cases of germ cell tumor treated at Memorial Sloan-Kettering Cancer Center between 1949 and 1978. Of these, 120 cases included postmortem examination of the CNS, and cerebral metastases were found in 38 (31%) of these cases. In contrast, Cox reported on a series of 24 patients with mediastinal germ cell tumors (GCTs) treated at Walter Reed Hospital between 1949 and 1971 and found no cases with CNS metastases.[5]

Within case series of extracranial GCTs when the predominant definition of CNS involvement is based on clinical and radiologic diagnosis, CNS metastases occur in 2.5 to 12.5% of cases[6–13] Kaye and colleagues[6] reported the first sizable clinical series of this type (see Table 17–1). Their findings included the following:

Table 17–1. CENTRAL NERVOUS SYSTEM METASTASES IN CASE SERIES OF GERM CELL TUMORS

Series Location, Era	Primary Site	Diagnostic Basis	Total Cases*	Cases with Brain Involvement	%	Therapy	Prognostic Effect
LA DVA, United States, 1948–1952[1]	Testis	Autopsy	27	8	32.1	NA	NA
MSKCC, United States, 1949–1978[2,4]	All	Autopsy	120	38	31	NA	NA
Walter Reed Hosp., United States, 1949–1971[5]	Mediastinal	Autopsy	24	0	0	NA	NA
Indiana, United States, 1986–1987[9]	All	Radiologic	299	20	6.7	Not stated	NR
MSKCC, United States, 1972–1977[3]	Testis	Clinical, radiologic, autopsy	242	38	15.7	Chemo (VAB) and WBRT	Worse; mean survival 6.5 mo for embryonal (compared to 1 mo for choriocarcinoma)
United Kingdom, 1973–1977[6]	All	Clinical, radiologic	274	17	6.2	Variety of combination chemo; WBRT	Mean survival 1.5 mo
Germany, 1974–1979[58]	Testis	Clinical, radiologic	344	16	1.7	Not stated	NR
M.D. Anderson Hosp., United States, 1977–1979[10]	All	Clinical, radiologic	104	12	12.5	Chemo, WBRT	Brain metastases correlated with poorer outcome; MS > 12 mo
United Kingdom, 1976–1982[59]	Testis	Clinical, radiologic	458	NR	—	Not stated	L3 disease† correlated with poorer outcome
Australia, 1980–1984[7]	All	Clinical, radiologic	101	4	4	Surgery, cisplatin based chemo, WBRT	MS > 12 mo
Charing Cross Hosp., United Kingdom, 1977–1984[11,12]	All	Clinical, radiologic	147	7 (10)‡	4.8	POMB/ACE + WBRT	8/10 alive with MS 32 mo
Norway and Sweden, 1981–1986[60]	Testis	Clinical, radiologic	200	NR	NR	Not stated	L3 disease† correlated with poorer outcome
United Kingdom, 1982–1986[14]	Testis	Clinical, radiologic	795	16	2	Not stated	Brain metastases patients had 37% 3-yr survival (compared to 86% for those without), L3 disease† correlated with poorer outcome in multivariate analysis (p < .0001; HR, 3.13; 95% CI, 2.06–4.77)
United Kingdom, 1977–1995[34]	All	Clinical, radiologic	339	15	4.4	POMB/ACE + WBRT and/or surgery	75% 3-yr OS for poor-risk patients, including those with brain metastases

Continued

Table 17–1. CONTINUED

Series Location, Era	Primary Site	Diagnostic Basis	Total Cases*	Cases with Brain Involvement	%	Therapy	Prognostic Effect
International, 1976–1995[15]	NSGCT, all	Clinical, radiologic	4,944	63	1.3	Not stated	27% 5-yr PFS with brain metastases (vs 76% without) (p < .01); 5 year OS, with brain metastases 33% (vs 88% without) (p < .01)
International, 1976–1995[15]	Seminoma, all	Clinical, radiologic	926	7	0.8	Not stated	5-yr PFS with brain metastasis, 57% (vs 81% without) (p < .01); OS, 57% (vs 85% without) (p < .01)
Turkey, 1990–1996[13]	All	Clinical, radiologic	167	11	6.6	Cisplatin-based chemo	NR
Indiana, 1973–1978[19]	Poor-risk GCT, all	Clinical, radiologic	139	21	15.1	Mixed chemo regimens, WBRT	No effect on OS because associated with progressive systemic disease
United Kingdom, 1978–1985[16]	Refractory and poor-risk GCT, all	Clinical, radiologic	55	4	7.3	POMB/ACE	—
MSKCC, United States, 1975–1988[20]	Poor-risk GCT, all	Clinical, radiologic	149	9	6	Chemo: VAB 52%, VAB/EP 28%, EBC 22%	Brain and/or bone metastasis was dominant factor in predicting relapse and death in multivariate analysis (p <.0001)
Indiana, 1993–1994[18]	Refractory GCT, all	Clinical, radiologic	18	5	27	Cisplatin-based chemo	NR
ECOG,‡ United States, 1999–2000[17]	Refractory GCT, all	Clinical, radiologic	28	3	11	Paclitaxel and gemcitabine	NR
MSKCC, United States, 1949–1971[61]	Mediastinal	Clinical, radiologic	30	4	7.5	Vinblastine, bleomycin, methotrexate combinations	1.5 mo MS from diagnosis or brain metastases
France, 1960–1990[62]	Mediastinal	Clinical, radiologic	48	0	0	Not stated	NA
Norway, 1979–1994[63]	Mediastinal	Clinical, radiologic	48	2	2.4	Cisplatin-based chemo	NR
International, 1975–1996[22,64]	Extragonadal, all histologies	Clinical, radiologic	635	22	4	Not stated	24% OS at 5 yr (vs 53% without CNS metastases). CNS metastases were an independent predictor of survival in multivariate analysis (p = .002)
International, 1975–1996[65]	Extragonadal seminoma	Clinical, radiologic	104	0	0	Not stated	NA

chemo = chemotherapy; CNS = central nervous system; EBC = etoposide, bleomycin, carboplatin; ECOG = Eastern Cooperative Oncology Group; EP = etoposide and cisplatin; GCT = germ cell tumor; HR = hazard ratio; LA DVA = Los Angeles Department of Veterans Affairs; MS = median survival; MSKCC = Memorial Sloan-Kettering Cancer Center; NA = not applicable; NR = not reported; NSGCT = nonseminomatous germ cell tumor; OS = overall survival; PFS = progression-free survival; POMB/ACE = cisplatin/vincristine/methotrexate/bleomycin + actinomycin D/cyclophosphamide/etoposide; VAB = vinblastine, actinomycin D, bleomycin; WBRT = whole-brain radiation therapy.

*Testicular tumor cases.

†Brain, bone, liver metastases.

‡Three patients added in subsequent reports of patients with CNS metastases.

Table 17–2. RELATIVE INCIDENCE OF BRAIN METASTASES IN GCT, BY PREDOMINANT CELL TYPE

	Case Series	Incidence Rate (%)
Histopathology	MSKCC*	Indiana†
Choriocarcinoma	83	30.8
Embryonal	20	10.1
Teratocarcinoma	20	12.5
Mixed choriocarcinoma with other histologies	32	NR
Seminoma	25	18.2
Yolk sac tumor	NR	50

Adapted from Bredael JJ et al[2]; Williams SD, Einhorn LH.[19]
MSKCC = Memorial Sloan-Kettering Cancer Center; NR = Not reported.
*Autopsy was diagnostic basis.
†Clinical and radiologic diagnostic basis.

1. The incidence rises from 2% in those without pulmonary metastases to approximately 10% in patients with pulmonary metastases.
2. Patients staged as high risk according to Indiana University or International Germ Cell Consensus Classification criteria have a greater than 15% chance of cerebral metastases.
3. Patients with a serum beta–human chorionic gonadotropin (β-hCG level > 10,000 IU/mL have a reported 26% rate of incidence (compared with 1.8% for those with lower levels).

The salient findings based on the Indiana University classification have been confirmed in subsequent larger compilations used to formulate prognostic classifications, such as the Medical Research Council Testicular Cancer Working Party[14] and the International Germ Cell Consensus Group.[15]

In subsequent series of patients with poor risk characteristics or of patients with chemorefractory GCTs, the risk of brain metastases ranges from 6 to 27% (see Table 17–1). In each series reported, the risk of brain metastases in these groups exceeds the risk of brain metastases in patients with a better prognosis who were treated at the same institution or in the same cooperative trial group.[16–20] Patients with extragonadal GCTs, particularly those tumors arising from the mediastinum, have a lower incidence of brain metastases, compared to participants in contemporaneous series of patients with testicular GCTs, with a reported incidence of 0 to 7.5% (see Table 17–1). The reasons for this are unclear, but the lower incidence may be due to a lower incidence of choriocarcinoma

at this site, coupled with the fact that mediastinal GCTs are often resistant to chemotherapy and may cause early death from local progression.[20–22] Thus, there is a lower biologic preponderance for CNS metastases based on cell type (see below) and less time for such metastases to develop.

HISTOPATHOLOGY

The different histopathologic patterns seen in GCTs are described in Chapter 4 and reviewed elsewhere.[23] The germ cell types included within the GCT are important as predictors of the incidence of brain metastases. While any subtype of testicular cancer can be present within brain metastases, embryonal and choriocarcinoma histologies are disproportionately represented[2,3,19] (Table 17–3). The brain metastases from these two histologic subtypes of GCTs tend to have different patterns of distribution within the brain. Embryonal carcinomas and malignant teratomas tend to produce single metastases that involve the supratentorial brain whereas choriocarcinoma tends to produce multiple metastases with a propensity to involve the cerebellum (Figures 17–1 and 17–2; see also Table 17–3).[2,3,10] In addition, choriocarcinoma has a tendency to undergo internal infarction and hemorrhage within the brain because of its high vascularity[24,25] although this complication can occur in metastases of any histologic subtype (Figures 17–3 and 17–4). The appearance of multiple hemorrhagic metastases as a clinical presentation in a young man raises the differential diagnosis of choriocarcinoma against metastases from other vascular tumors such as melanoma and renal cell carcinoma (which can have the same radiologic appearance).

CLINICAL PRESENTATION AND DIAGNOSTIC EVALUATION

Patients may present with a variety of manifestations of their CNS metastases, including headache, focal neurologic deficit, focal or nonspecific visual changes, confusion, vomiting, and/or seizures. Alternatively, they may be asymptomatic and may be diagnosed only when CNS imaging is undertaken.[9] The intensity of diagnostic evaluation of the CNS in patients with testicular germ cell cancer is based on individual risk stratification. Patients with higher-risk

Table 17–3. CORRELATION BETWEEN GERM CELL HISTOPATHOLOGY AND DISTRIBUTION OF INTRACRANIAL METASTASES

Histopathology	Distribution of Metastases		
	≤ 2 Intracerebral Metastases	≥ 3 Intracerebral Metastases	Cerebellar Metastases
Choriocarcinoma predominant*	1/11 (9%)	10/11 (91%)	7/11 (64%)
Embryonal, with or without others elements	10/11 (91%)	1/11 (9%)	0/11 (0%)

Adapted from Bredael JJ et al.[2]
*In addition Logothetis and colleagues[10] found that 1 of 6 patients with a single brain metastasis from a germ cell tumor had choriocarcinoma whereas 3 of 6 patients with multiple brain metastases had choriocarcinoma.

extracranial disease merit more intensive investigation. The evaluation of the CNS for involvement should include a detailed clinical neurologic assessment and magnetic resonance imaging of the brain, with additional imaging of the spine as required clinically. This should be undertaken for any patients with tumors classified as poor risk on the basis of International Germ Cell Consensus Classification criteria[15] (see Chapter 8), particularly those patients with high serum β-hCG levels as well as multiple or bulky pulmonary metastases, because of the increased risk of CNS metastases.[6] The International Germ Cell Consensus Classification criteria do not attribute classification as poor risk solely for large-volume disease per se; however, because of the association between large-volume pulmonary metastases and brain metastases, such patients warrant close evaluation even if they do not satisfy the criteria for being "poor risk."

CNS Imaging

In an acute setting in which the patient has a rapidly progressive neurologic deficit or a fluctuating level of consciousness, initial computerized tomography

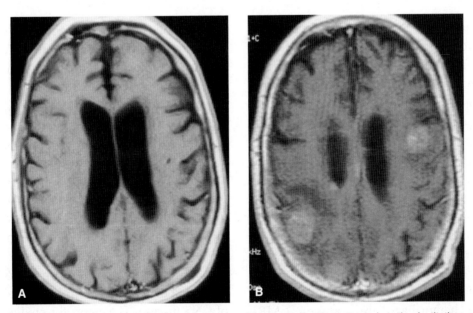

Figure 17–1. Metastatic choriocarcinoma. The patient was a 38-year-old man who had been treated at other institutions over a 4-year period for metastatic germ cell tumor with multiple recurrences despite retroperitoneal lymph node dissection, standard cisplatin-based chemotherapy (bleomycin/etoposide/cisplatin [BEP]), ifosfamide-based salvage therapy, two autologous stem cell transplantations, and radiation therapy to the axilla and retroperitoneum. At presentation to our facility in December 2000, he had disseminated disease involving lung and multiple lymph node sites, with a serum beta–human chorionic gonadotropin (β-hCG) level of 493,000 U/L. A computed tomography (CT) scan of the brain at that time (*A*) was evaluated as negative for metastatic disease. Chemotherapy with paclitaxel and gemcitabine was commenced, and the patient improved over 9 weeks, with a fall in serum β-hCG (to 136,000 U/L), less pain, and a decrease in the size of palpable disease. After 9 weeks, therapy was stopped due to malaise and cytopenia. The patient re-presented 4 weeks later with fluctuating levels of consciousness after several hours of geographic disorientation in his home. His CT scan (*B*) demonstrated three large intracerebral lesions, with impression of the right ventricle by tumor and surrounding edema. His serum β-hCG had risen to 484,000 U/L, and physical examination showed an increase in the size of lymph nodes in the cervical and axillary regions. The patient and his family chose to have no further treatment, and he lapsed into coma and died 4 days after his GCT brain metastasis diagnosis.

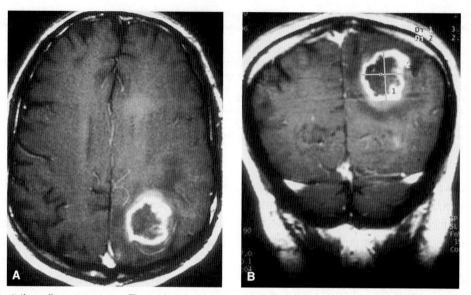

Figure 17–2.   Metastatic malignant teratoma. The patient was a 29-year-old man with recurrent malignant teratoma in the retroperitoneum and lungs. He was originally treated with left orchiectomy and three cycles of bleomycin/etoposide/cisplatin (BEP) chemotherapy for a serum marker–negative high-risk stage I mixed nonseminomatous germ cell tumor of the right testis from August 1998. The orchiectomy specimen demonstrated elements of malignant teratoma. A computed tomography (CT) scan of the abdomen was normal at that time. The patient declined retroperitoneal lymph node dissection. Seventeen months later, the patient re-presented with abdominal and back pain as well as morning headaches and visual field changes. CT of the abdomen demonstrated a retroperitoneal mass 11 cm in maximal diameter. Chest radiography demonstrated as many as 100 small nodules consistent with metastases. Magnetic resonance imaging of the brain (A and B) demonstrated a single large metastasis. The patient was started on dexamethasone, with a plan for surgery, chemotherapy, and radiation, but opted to leave the hospital against medical advice. He was not seen again at our facility.

may be preferable to magnetic resonance imaging (MRI) because of its rapidity and accessibility. Once the patient's condition has stabilized, whether by way of surgical intervention, corticosteroid therapy, or other treatment modalities, MRI can be undertaken to provide a more detailed survey of sites of CNS metastases.

CT findings for brain metastases usually include iso- or hyperdense masses on noncontrast studies; when contrast is given, these masses exhibit strong uniform or ring enhancement. MRI usually shows isointense to slightly hypointense lesions on T1-weighted images and hyperintense lesions on T2-weighted images. There are multiple lesions in almost 50% of cases of GCT, and small areas of intra-metastatic hemorrhage are common.[26] MRI needs to be performed with and without gadolinium, to visualize the tumor fully and to detect evidence of smaller metastases that are not detectable by non-contrast scanning.[27,28] As GCTs are often surrounded by edema, a large portion of a patient's functional impairment may simply be secondary to edema, not caused by the tumor itself. In such patients, preoperative functional MRI to determine

the location of the motor strip relative to the tumor will help the surgeon in determining the risk of open surgery in terms of potential postoperative disability.

Cerebrospinal Fluid Marker Concentrations

The evaluation of cerebrospinal fluid (CSF) for β-hCG can be a valuable tool in the diagnosis of CNS metastases from GCTs. In patients in whom β-hCG is the predominant marker, measurement of CSF β-hCG may detect patients with CNS involvement with metastatic disease that is below the limits of detection by CT.[6] The original work undertaken by Bagshawe and colleagues[29,30] (in the era prior to CT and MRI) suggested that a high CSF β-hCG level was predictive of CNS disease. The cutoff for prediction of the presence of CNS metastases was where the CSF concentration exceeded 2% of the serum concentration. In confirmation of this finding, investigators at Memorial Sloan-Kettering Cancer Center reported that a CSF concentration greater than 2% of the serum concentration was of positive predictive value for CNS metastases at autopsy or on imaging studies (Table 17–4).[4] Similarly, Kaye and colleagues found that a CSF β-

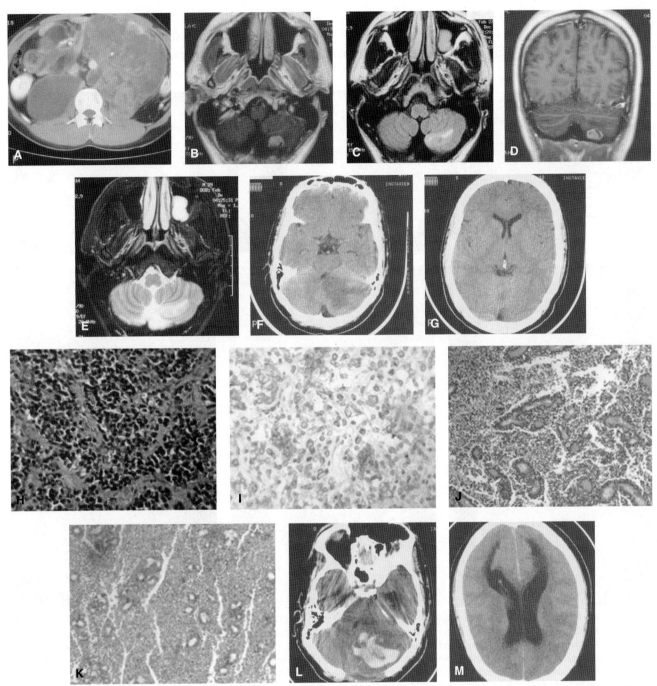

Figure 17–3. Metastatic mixed nonseminomatous germ cell tumor. The patient was a 24-year-old man who presented with testicular pain and abdominal bloating. Examination revealed right testicular induration and an upper abdominal mass on the right side. His abdominal computed tomography (CT) scan (*A*) demonstrated a large retroperitoneal mass. There were no lung metastases seen on chest CT. The preoperative serum α-fetoprotein (AFP) level was 18,345 ng/mL, the serum beta–human chorionic gonadotropin (β-hCG) level was 302 ng/mL, and the lactate dehydrogenase (LDH) level was 704 U/L. Inguinal orchiectomy was undertaken, and histopathologic study showed a mixed pattern including major elements of embryonal malignant teratoma and seminoma as well as a small element of choriocarcinoma. Postoperative serum AFP was 7,435 ng/mL, serum β-hCG was 76 ng/mL, and the LDH was 673 U/L. The patient then commenced his first cycle of POMB/ACE chemotherapy. Midway through the first cycle of chemotherapy, the patient complained of headache and difficulty with balance. Magnetic resonance imaging scans of the brain (*B to E*) demonstrated a single right cerebellar metastasis adjacent to the midline. The metastasis was removed at craniotomy (*F and G*). The histopathologic differential diagnosis of the brain lesion included primitive neuroectodermal tumor . However, it was only when the case was reviewed at a multidisciplinary case conference that it became clear that the brain lesion was a metastasis derived from one of the elements of the retroperitoneal cancer. (The retroperitoneal mass is shown in *H;* the cerebellar mass is shown in *I*). Immunohistochemistry for a variety of molecules including myoglobin provided further evidence for common tumor derivation (*J,* retroperitoneal mass; *K,* cerebellar mass). Postoperatively, the patient was scheduled for further chemotherapy and radiation therapy. Unfortunately, he failed to attend follow-up appointments. Six weeks after his craniotomy he was taken by his family to the emergency room because of an inability to walk and a decreased level of consciousness. CT scans of the brain (*L and M*) showed intracerebellar hemorrhage with secondary hydrocephalus. Despite ventriculo-peritoneal shunting, the patient deteriorated and died several days later.

hCG concentration greater than 2.5% of the serum β-hCG concentration was highly predictive of CNS involvement with GCT.[6] CSF β-hCG values lower than the described cutoff of about 2% are of little value because they do not exclude the presence of CNS metastases.[4,6] Measurement of CSF α-fetoprotein has

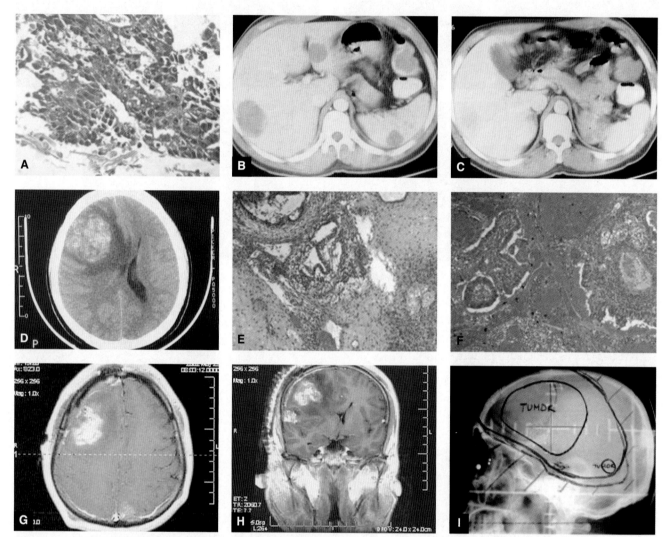

Figure 17–4. Metastatic yolk sac tumor. The patient is a 28-year-old man. In November 1998, he presented to another hospital with a left-side testicular mass 8 cm in diameter. He underwent orchiectomy, but details on histopathology, marker status, and postoperative therapy are not available. In November 2001, he presented to our medical center with cough and shortness of breath. Chest radiography demonstrated multiple pulmonary metastases and a mediastinal mass. A transbronchial biopsy specimen showed an undifferentiated malignancy consistent with yolk sac tumor, as well as elements suggestive of teratoma (*A*). The serum α-fetoprotein (AFP) concentration was 8,967 ng/mL, the human chorionic gonadotropin level was 7 mIU/mL, and lactate dehydrogenase was 197 U/L. Computed tomography (CT) of the chest, abdomen, and pelvis confirmed the presence of bilateral lung metastases and a mediastinal mass and demonstrated metastases to the liver, spleen, and right adrenal gland (*B and C*). Magnetic resonance imaging (MRI) of the brain was ordered, but the patient failed to attend on two occasions. Neurologic examination was normal. The decision was made to start the patient on POMB/ACE chemotherapy in January 2002. He tolerated therapy well, and the serum AFP fell to a level of < 100 ng/mL by April 2002. During this time, he failed to attend further appointments for cerebral MRI, and his serum AFP level plateaued at around 20 ng/mL and then rose to 297 ng/mL. He was started on gemcitabine and paclitaxel, and his serum AFP stabilized at around 200. In May 2002, the patient developed the sudden onset of a right-sided frontal headache, vomiting, and blurring of vision and was taken to the emergency room. A cerebral CT scan (*D*) demonstrated a right frontal mass lesion, 4 cm in diameter, with intralesion hemorrhage, surrounding edema, and midline shift. While undergoing CT, the patient's affect became altered, and his level of consciousness declined. He was administered dexamethasone intravenously and was taken to the operating room. A right frontal craniotomy was performed, and evacuation of intracranial hematoma was undertaken. Given the clinical condition of the patient, excision of the metastasis was not attempted. Histopathologic examination demonstrated 90% yolk sac tumor and 10% teratoma, with elements of glandular epithelium, cartilage, and immature brain as well as surrounding hemorrhage (*E and F*). The patient recovered well. Postoperative MRI scans (*G and H*) showed the previously identified frontal lesion and a small adjacent lesion. The patient was planned for radiation therapy with bilateral subtotal brain fields (50 Gy in 25 fractions over 5 weeks) and a 10 Gy boost to the right frontal lobe (*I*). After radiation therapy, the patient was functionally well, and restaging before consideration of further systemic therapy was planned.

no clinical usefulness.[4] The value of routine CSF examination in patients with normal MRI scans has not been prospectively evaluated because most of the data available come from studies that were done prior to the use of MRI and in which CT was infrequently performed. In contemporary practice, many clinicians reserve quantification of CSF β-hCG for patients who have equivocal MRI findings or who have normal scans but garner a high index of suspicion based on serum β-hCG level and/or bulky pulmonary disease.

INTERDISCIPLINARY MANAGEMENT

The outcomes for patients with CNS metastases from GCTs have improved significantly since the 1970s, when the average survival from time of diagnosis was less than 6 months.[6] This improvement has occurred in the context of better efficacy of systemic chemotherapy for GCT and improved local management of CNS metastases[7,31] Recent reports of results from multimodal therapy demonstrate disease-free survival greater than 2 years from diagnosis in up to 80% of patients presenting with cerebral metastases.[11,32–34] The therapy for patients with CNS involvement from testicular GCTs requires an integrated approach incorporating surgery, irradiation, and chemotherapy (Figure 17–5).

Once the diagnosis of brain metastasis is suspected, the patient is admitted for observation and treatment, which includes commencement of dexamethasone at a dose of 4 mg every 6 hours or an equivalent dosing regimen of another corticosteroid.[35] In the intensive care setting, the patient is positioned with the head of the bed elevated 30° and, if ventilated, has ventilator settings directed at producing mild alkalosis to minimize cerebral edema.

The diagnostic and therapeutic management of germ cell testicular cancer metastatic to the CNS is predicated by necessity on an interdisciplinary approach. With respect to diagnosis, interaction between the pathologist, radiologist, neurosurgeon, and oncologist is paramount. The pathologic and clinical diagnosis of highly mitotic CNS neoplasms in young patients can be very difficult. An integrated review involving clinical, radiologic, and pathologic correlation of extra- and intracranial disease concurrently may be extremely helpful. Such an approach can help distinguish between differential diagnoses such as brain abscess, metastases from a range of extracranial malignancies, or primary cerebral neoplasms. Given the potentially diffuse range of pathologic appearances seen in GCTs (see Chapter 4), a comparison of extracranial (eg, testicular) histopathology with that seen in an intracranial lesion may be diagnostic in itself.

Cerebral metastases in patients with testicular germ cell cancer may present in the following settings:

- As part of the initial presentation, before the administration of combination chemotherapy
- As an isolated recurrence in the brain after response of disease elsewhere in the body
- In concert with the development of recurrence or chemotherapy-refractory disease in other areas of the body

Patients in the first two groups may be curable with aggressive combined-modality therapy.[32,36] Patients in the last group generally do poorly, especially in the presence of extracranial chemorefractory disease.[32,36]

In addition, patients with metastatic germ cell tumors may develop spinal cord metastases, epidural deposits (Figure 17–5), and leptomeningeal involvement (Figure 17–6),[37–41] but these events are less common than those that may develop in patients with parenchymal cerebral metastases. It should be noted

		β-hCG Concentration		
	No. of Patients	Plasma or Serum (ng/mg)	CSF (ng/mg)	CSF to Plasma or Serum Ratio (%)
No CNS metastases	10	63–25,900	0–316	0.12 (0.10–0.50)
CNS metastases	5	26–20,800	6–2,220	214 (8.1–672)

Table 17–4. CORRELATION OF BETA–HUMAN CHORIONIC GONADOTROPIN CONCENTRATIONS IN CEREBROSPINAL FLUID AND PLASMA OR SERUM WITH THE PRESENCE OF CENTRAL NERVOUS SYSTEM METASTASES

Adapted from Schold SC et al.[4]
β-hCG = human chorionic gonadotropin; CNS = central nervous system; CSF = cerebrospinal fluid.

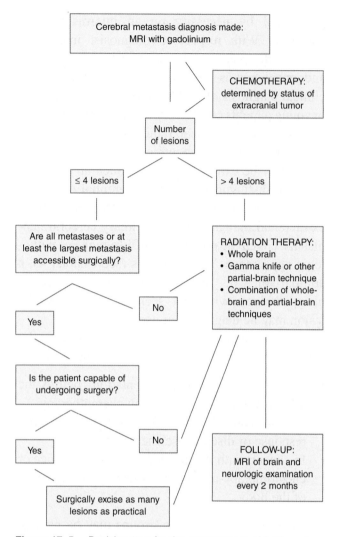

Figure 17–5. Decision tree for the management of brain metastases in patients with germ cell tumors.

that with the use of modern systemic chemotherapy regimens, concurrent or subsequent intrathecal chemotherapy does not appear to have an incremental beneficial impact. Intrathecal therapy should be reserved for those rare patients with demonstrated leptomeningeal involvement from a GCT.*

The CNS is a potential sanctuary site for germ cell cancer treated with systemic chemotherapy.[3,8] This is because the agents that were first used in successful and durable combination chemotherapy for testicular cancer (ie, cisplatin, vinblastine, and bleomycin) are not actively transported into the CNS from the serum and may not readily diffuse passively across the blood-brain barrier.[42] Consequently, these agents may not attain cytotoxic concentrations within the CNS. Most current regimens that are used to treat

testicular cancer contain one or more agents capable of therapeutic efficacy in the CNS. Examples of such regimens are the substitution of etoposide for vinblastine in standard chemotherapy[43,44] and regimens for poor-risk disease that incorporate moderate- to high-dose methotrexate with folinic acid rescue, actinomycin D, and etoposide, such as the cisplatin/vincristine/methotrexate/bleomycin plus actinomycin D/cyclophosphamide/etoposide (POMB/ACE) regimen.[11,12,16,34] The result is that these regimens now form a cornerstone of management of GCT patients with brain and spinal involvement.

It needs to be emphasized that patients with disseminated disease have a prognosis that is often independent of any CNS involvement that may be present.[19] If, for example, the extracranial metastases are refractory to initial chemotherapy, the response of the disease in these areas to further therapy will predict outcome. The important issue in attaining cure is that cerebral metastases will require both effective systemic and effective local therapies. If these therapies are not optimally delivered, the lack of disease control in the CNS may compromise any opportunity for long-term survival.

The selection and order of therapies depend on the clinical setting with which the patient presents. In the case of patients who are chemotherapy naive or in whom the CNS is the only site of disease recurrence, aggressive intervention is essential.

Three major groups of patients require management. The first group consists of patients with a single surgically accessible site of metastasis either at initial presentation of an NSGCT or as a single site of recurrence. These patients should undergo surgery.[45,46] The risk of surgery in these cases is lower than the risk of hemorrhage or the risk incurred by radiation therapy as the sole local therapy. However, if there are multiple lesions (ie, two to four lesions), we generally reserve the craniotomy for resection of one or two of the largest and most accessible lesions; the rest of the lesions are treated

*Editor's note: There is little evidence that intrathecal chemotherapy for leptomeningeal metastases of germ cell cancer gives a result superior to that of modern systemic chemotherapy. Most published studies that have addressed intrathecal chemotherapy have been confounded by the use of other modalities, including radiotherapy and the use of systemic cytotoxic agents.

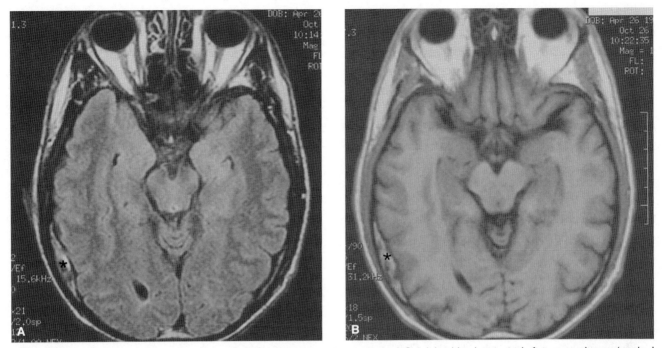

Figure 17–6.   *A and B,* Cerebral MRI scan (*A* horizontal view, and *B* coronal view) Cranial epidural metastasis from a seminoma (marked by asterisk).

by radiosurgery ("gamma knife" therapy). At the University of Southern California, we generally treat both the surgically excised tumor bed and the unresected tumors with radiosurgery. Whole-brain irradiation is reserved for patients who develop further intracranial metastasis on follow-up examination. Surgical excision is offered to patients who initially received radio surgery for a small lesion that has been subsequently found to progress. Following radiation therapy, systemic chemotherapy is usually administered. It should be emphasized, however, that this approach has not been addressed in clinical trials of patients with germ cell tumor CNS metastases; rather, this treatment paradigm is based on published and unpublished experience with this strategy.[7,47] In part, early surgery is recommended to avoid the complication of hemorrhagic rupture of metastases. The predisposing factor for this is rapid regression and necrosis in response to chemotherapy, with a resultant friable blood vessel network. This may be exacerbated by the presence of chemotherapy-induced thrombocytopenia.[25] Emergency excision of metastases that bleed acutely can also save some patients who would quickly die from this complication.[25] However, the salvage yield is low in our experience, even with a carefully con-

ceived contingency plan. The initial use of surgery where feasible, followed by radiation therapy, is predicated on experience with surgery and irradiation compared to radiation therapy alone for single metastases from a range of different primary sites; these studies demonstrated better survival and functional outcome with excision.[48–50] In contrast, studies on brain metastases from a number of primary sites suggest that there is no benefit from surgery once the patient has multiple brain metastases.[50]

The second group of patients who require management are patients whose clinical scenarios involve multiple (ie, greater than four) cerebral metastases or have seminoma without other elements. For these patients, whole-brain radiation therapy concurrently administered with chemotherapy is the treatment of choice.[47,51] Surgery is then reserved for acute hemorrhage or (more profitably) for any residual masses after combined-modality therapy is complete, provided that the extracranial disease has responded to chemotherapy and that serum markers are appropriately declining or are no longer elevated. Overall, the outcomes described for patients treated with such multimodality approaches suggest a long-term survival with good function for at least 30% of patients.[11,32,34]

The third group requiring management consists of patients with brain metastases that are not easily accessible surgically, such as metastasis in the subcortical, midbrain, or brainstem regions. For these patients, standard therapy would involve a combination of whole-brain radiation therapy (WBRT) and chemotherapy. One potential option for patients with a limited number of small metastases (< 2.5 cm^3) that are not surgically accessible is the use of focused radiation therapy techniques such as gamma knife radiosurgery.[52,53] There are limited published data on the use of these techniques for treating GCTs, but the experience at the University of Southern California has been that radiosurgery treatment induces regression in most patients and has a low complication rate. Issues related to this technique, such as optimal delivery and dosing and their effect on outcome, require further prospective evaluation.[54]

Unfortunately, patients who develop CNS metastases as part of recurrence or progressive disease that is refractory to chemotherapy have a much poorer outlook. While long-term survivors from this group are described, such patients have generally been identified by a complete response to subsequent salvage chemotherapy. Hence, for patients with this clinical scenario it is usual to give whole-brain radiation therapy and systemic chemotherapy while reserving surgery for patients who are having a major response to chemotherapy and who have a residual intracranial mass.

SPECIFIC TREATMENT MODALITIES

Chemotherapy

The selection of a specific chemotherapeutic combination for use in patients with brain metastases from testicular GCTs is dependent on a number of factors. One factor is the presence of adequate renal, pulmonary, and hepatic function and other potential intercurrent illnesses. Another is prior drug exposure and the length of the time interval since that exposure (see further discussion in Chapters 13,14, and 16).

For patients with an initial presentation and with adequate renal and hepatic function, there are two regimens that have been reported on extensively in combination with whole-brain radiation therapy and/or surgery. The first regimen, favored in the United States and many other parts of the world, is a combination of bleomycin, etoposide, and cisplatin (BEP), given every 3 weeks for four cycles.[19,43] The second regimen, favored in the United Kingdom for selected poor-risk cases, is the POMB/ACE regimen (see Chapter 14)—cisplatin, vincristine (Oncovin), methotrexate, and bleomycin, alternating with actinomycin D, cyclophosphamide, and etoposide.[11,12,16,34] This regimen involves the use of more rapid cycling of agents on a treatment schedule that repeats every 2 weeks. The two regimens have never been compared to each other in a structured or randomized trial setting. Such comparisons are unlikely to happen, given the relatively low incidence of testicular cancer and cerebral metastasis, with even large centers seeing only a few cases per year. The BEP regimen has the advantage of being familiar to most medical oncologists and is associated with less unpredictable toxicity. However, it contains two drugs, cisplatin and bleomycin, that have variable penetration of the CNS. POMB/ACE is a more intense regimen with more toxicity than the BEP regimen in some hands, especially when administered infrequently at the treating center. It has the advantage of cycling a series of drugs that have better CNS penetration, in the form of moderate-dose methotrexate, actinomycin D, and etoposide. Reports from Charing Cross Hospital of using multimodal therapy incorporating POMB/ACE describe complete brain and systemic responses in 80% of patients, with intermediate- to long-term disease-free survival in most of these patients. Both BEP and POMB/ACE combinations require significant resources and skill to administer them safely with concurrent radiation and are optimally given in a center with significant experience in GCT management. Support with blood products and judicious assessment and treatment of infections and hemorrhagic problems is mandatory. Initial admission to an intensive care service for close monitoring is optimal. The availability of rapid access to ventilatory and inotropic support and neurosurgical intervention is also essential.

For patients presenting with chemorefractory disease, there is no defined optimal regimen. Many large centers maintain cisplatin in the regimen and add ifosfamide and etoposide or vinblastine, similar to standard salvage regimens such as the etoposide/

ifosfamide/cisplatin (VIP) or vinblastine/ifosfamide/cisplatin (VeIP) regimen (see Chapters 14 and 16).[21,46] Precautions similar to those discussed above need to be exercised in following these cases, despite the fact that the prognosis of these patients is worse. Among the newer drugs, the taxanes and gemcitabine have activity against the disease,[17,55] but their place in therapy and in combination or salvage therapy for patients with brain metastases has not been determined. There is some experience in a few centers with combined high-dose chemotherapy and concurrent radiation therapy with stem cell rescue.[33] The initial results of this approach appear promising but must be placed in the context of the facts that high-dose chemotherapy protocols have not demonstrated a sustained survival advantage in refractory patients and that the role of such therapy in GCT management is yet to be determined.

Radiation Therapy

Radiation therapy is a standard component of treatment for brain metastases from GCTs. It may be used either in the setting of primary local therapy for patients who have seminoma, are unstable for surgery, or for whom resection is not feasible. Radiation therapy may also be given as adjuvant therapy after surgical resection. The method of administration of radiation therapy varies, depending on the clinical status of the patient and the distribution of metastases in the CNS. WBRT still represents a reliable standard as part of both primary and adjuvant therapy. However, in certain circumstances, partial-brain or gamma knife irradiation (also called radiosurgery) can be used.[56] Partial-brain irradiation requires delineation of all lesions on MRI, and in an acute setting, CT may be the initial imaging modality of choice. In addition, partial-brain irradiation techniques are generally limited to patients with two or fewer metastases or with lesions < 20 mm in diameter.[56] When gamma knife radiosurgery is used, subsequent whole-brain irradiation can be given if there is intracranial progression that requires palliation. For whole-brain radiation therapy, the usual dose is between 30 and 50 Gy in 180 to 200 cGy fractions in 20 to 30 treatment sessions administered through two laterally opposed fields[36] (Figure 17–7).

Gamma knife radiosurgery involves high-dose radiation, usually a minimum of 1,600 cGy, delivered in one or two treatment sessions (Figure 17–8). In patients treated with surgical excision, either WBRT or radiosurgery is used to sterilize the area around the surgical field and reduce local recurrence. This is usually started 1 week after surgery and after initial chemotherapy delivery is complete.

During radiotherapy for nonseminomatous germ cell malignancies metastatic to the brain, the levels of β-hCG and α-fetoprotein may continue to rise. This may be due to a marker release phenomenon from the destruction of tumor cells and should not be interpreted as meaning early systemic progressive disease.[35] Concurrent WBRT and chemotherapy carry an increased risk of myelosuppression compared with that carried by either modality when given alone, and this needs to be observed and proactively treated with transfusion, growth factors, and antibiotic intervention as required. In the longer-term context, local radionecrosis of brain substance may occur, especially in areas that have received supplemental radiation therapy or a "boost" after WBRT (Figure 17–9).

Surgery

The decision to perform surgery for intracranial metastasis of a germ cell tumor needs to be based on the patient's overall medical condition, the number and size of intracranial metastases, and the feasibility of gamma knife radiosurgical treatment. Given the chemosensitivity of GCTs, chemotherapy should be used in the perioperative setting and can be commenced either just prior to or immediately after surgery, without compromising the safety of the patient. Indeed, delay in the commencement of either therapy may represent the greatest danger to the patient who presents with symptomatic brain metastases from GCT. Early surgery may contribute significantly to eventual cure by providing control of CNS disease while chemotherapy takes effect. The ideal candidate for surgery is the patient with a large single metastasis, good performance status, and a tumor located in a region of the brain that is feasible for resection. Patients with multiple intracranial metastases, a poor prognosis or intercurrent poor medical condition, or metastatic GCT in surgically inaccessible

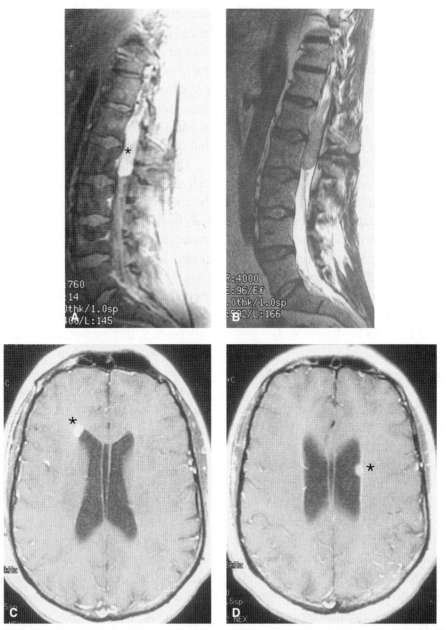

Figure 17–7. Seminoma of the conus medullaris with intraventricular metastases. The lesion can be seen as an increased attenuation lesion (*A*) and with corresponding low attenuation (*B*). Two small exophytic nodules are seen within the ventricles, in the anterior horn of the right ventricle (*C*) and mid left ventricle (*D*). (Reproduced with permission from Horvath L et al.[41]).

regions of the brain should be considered for either gamma knife radiosurgery or whole-brain irradiation. In patients who do not have a response to chemotherapy, surgery should also be considered since some patients may present with cerebral metastasis that represents the sole site of disease recurrence.[57]

No reports of large series on the surgical management of brain metastases from GCTs have been published. However, the basic principles regarding prognosis and surgical resection need to be discussed with each patient on the basis of the predicted natural history and response of the tumor to surgery and other modalities of treatment.

At the University of Southern California, we generally perform our craniotomies using a neuro-navigational system (Stealth, Medtronic Inc.) to help tailor the craniotomy flap and to localize the tumor intraoperatively (Figure 17–11, *A*). The surgery is

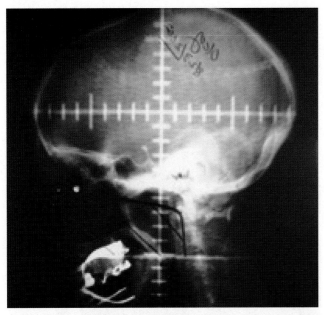

Figure 17–8. Simulation film used for whole-brain radiation therapy, demonstrating a lateral field contour to cover the meninges as well as the brain itself (the so-called German-helmet field).

carried out with the use of an operating microscope, and a microscopic excision of the tumor is performed (Figure 17–11). One helpful feature of metastatic tumors (as opposed to intrinsic brain tumors such as gliomas) is the fact that the tumor does not arise from the neural structures themselves. Therefore, a pseudocapsule can usually be identified and dissected between the brain and the tumor, with resec-

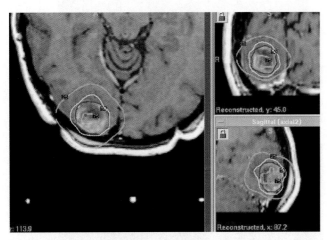

Figure 17–9. Local radiation field generated for "gamma knife" radiosurgery. The simulation shows targeting in three dimensions (axial, coronal, and sagittal) of a single right occipital lobe metastasis. Isolines demonstrate the percentage of dose delivered to the surrounding brain tissue compared to that delivered to the epicenter of the lesion. (Courtesy of Dr. Z. Petrovich and Dr. C. Yu, University of Southern California, Department of Radiation Oncology.)

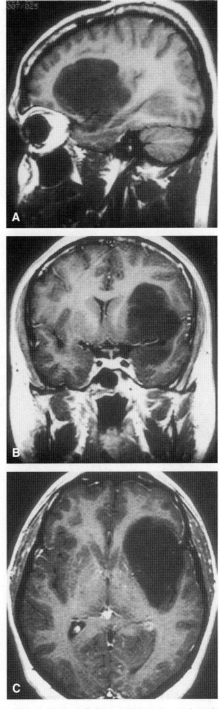

Figure 17–10. *A, B,* and *C,* Magnetic resonance imaging (MRI) of the brain: *A* sagittal view, *B* coronal view, and *C* horizontal view: radionecrosis in the left temporal lobe. The patient is a 44-year-old man with a history of embryonal predominantly mixed nonseminomatous germ cell tumor who presented with a single cerebral metastasis measuring 40 mm in diameter in the left temporal lobe. He was treated with combination surgery, POMB/ACE chemotherapy, and radiation therapy consisting of whole-brain irradiation to 50 Gy, with a 10 Gy "boost" to the site of the metastasis. The patient remained clinically well throughout treatment but developed progressive radiation necrosis in the maximally irradiated area. This had no clinical correlates, and the patient remains in remission after 4 years of follow-up, with no detectable neurologic deficit.

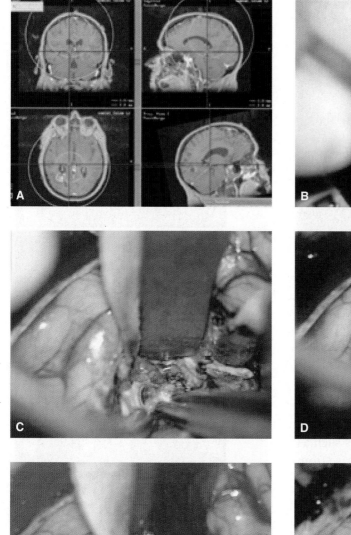

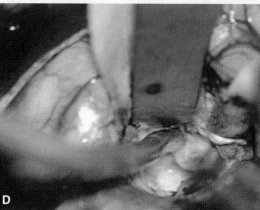

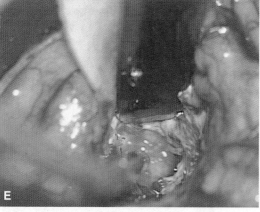

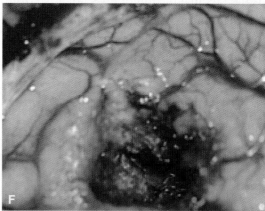

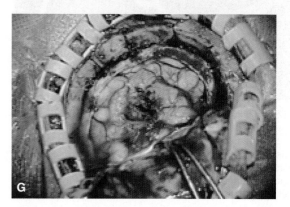

Figure 17–11.   *A,* Excision of an intracranial metastasis. Alignment of a right midbrain metastasis, using the Medtronic Stealth neuro-navigational system. The system identifies the ideal path to the tumor through overlying brain (*blue path* in bottom right panel). *B,* Incision of the cerebral cortex overlying the tumor mass. *C,* Dissection to the mass. *D and E,* Dissection of the mass. *F and G,* Appearance of the cortex after removal of the metastasis and before closure of the overlying dura.

tion of the tumor itself. The chance of a postoperative neurologic deficit can be minimized, even in functionally important regions of the brain, if care is taken to make the initial corticectomy and incision in a functionally non-eloquent region, with careful dissection toward the tumor. GCTs are often easily distinguished from the adjacent brain via the operating microscope. They are often vascular and tend to be soft in consistency. Lesions that have been previously treated with radiosurgery are yellowish and are often firm. One week after surgery, it is our standard practice to "sterilize" the tumor bed using gamma knife radiosurgery or larger-field radiation therapy.

CONCLUSION

Central nervous system metastases represent a unique challenge in patients with germ cell tumors. With an aggressive multidisciplinary approach, between 30 and 80% of patients can have long-term survival and the potential for cure.

REFERENCES

1. Earle KM. Metastatic and primary intracranial tumors of the adult male. J Neuropathol Exp Neurosurg 1954;13:448–54.
2. Bredael JJ, Vugrin D, Whitmore WF Jr. Autopsy findings in 154 patients with germ cell tumors of the testis. Cancer 1982;50:548–51.
3. Vugrin D, Cvitkovic E, Posner J, et al. Neurological complications of malignant germ cell tumors of testis: biology of brain metastases (I). Cancer 1979;44:2349–53.
4. Schold SC, Vurgrin D, Golbey RB, Posner JB. Central nervous system metastases from germ cell carcinoma of testis. Semin Oncol 1979;6:102–8.
5. Cox JD. Primary malignant germinal tumors of the mediastinum. A study of 24 cases. Cancer 1975;36:1162–8.
6. Kaye SB, Bagshawe KD, McElwain TJ, Peckham MJ. Brain metastases in malignant teratoma: a review of four years' experience and an assessment of the role of tumour markers. Br J Cancer 1979;39:217–23.
7. Raghavan D, Mackintosh JF, Fox RM, et al. Improved survival after brain metastases in non-seminomatous germ cell tumours with combined modality treatment. Br J Urol 1987;60:364–7.
8. Gerl A, Clemm C, Kohl P, et al. Central nervous system as sanctuary site of relapse in patients treated with chemotherapy for metastatic testicular cancer. Clin Exp Metastasis 1994;12:226–30.
9. Mathews VP, Broome DR, Smith RR, et al. Neuroimaging of disseminated germ cell neoplasms. AJNR Am J Neuroradiol 1990;11:319–24.
10. Logothetis CJ, Samuels ML, Trindade A. The management of brain metastases in germ cell tumors. Cancer 1982;49:12–8.
11. Rustin GJ, Newlands ES, Bagshawe KD, et al. Successful

12. Newlands ES, Bagshawe KD, Begent RH, et al. Current optimum management of anaplastic germ cell tumours of the testis and other sites. Br J Urol 1986;58:307–14.
13. Mahalati K, Bilen CY, Ozen H, et al. The management of brain metastasis in nonseminomatous germ cell tumours. BJU Int 1999;83:457–61.
14. Mead GM, Stenning SP, Parkinson MC, et al. The Second Medical Research Council study of prognostic factors in nonseminomatous germ cell tumors. Medical Research Council Testicular Tumour Working Party. J Clin Oncol 1992;10:85–94.
15. International Germ Cell Consensus Classification: a prognostic factor-based staging system for metastatic germ cell cancers. International Germ Cell Cancer Collaborative Group. J Clin Oncol 1997;15:594–603.
16. Cullen MH, Harper PG, Woodroffe CM, et al. Chemotherapy for poor risk germ cell tumours. An independent evaluation of the POMB/ACE regime. Br J Urol 1988;62:454–60.
17. Hinton S, Catalano P, Einhorn LH, et al. Phase II study of paclitaxel plus gemcitabine in refractory germ cell tumors (E9897): a trial of the Eastern Cooperative Oncology Group. J Clin Oncol 2002;20:1859–63.
18. Sandler AB, Cristou A, Fox S, et al. A phase II trial of paclitaxel in refractory germ cell tumors. Cancer 1998;82:1381–6.
19. Williams SD, Einhorn LH. Brain metastases in disseminated germinal neoplasms: incidence and clinical course. Cancer 1979;44:1514–6.
20. Toner GC, Geller NL, Lin SY, Bosl GJ. Extragonadal and poor risk nonseminomatous germ cell tumors. Survival and prognostic features. Cancer 1991;67:2049–57.
21. McCaffrey JA, Mazumdar M, Bajorin DF, et al. Ifosfamide- and cisplatin-containing chemotherapy as first-line salvage therapy in germ cell tumors: response and survival. J Clin Oncol 1997;15:2559–63.
22. Bokemeyer C, Nichols CR, Droz JP, et al. Extragonadal germ cell tumors of the mediastinum and retroperitoneum: results from an international analysis. J Clin Oncol 2002; 20:1864–73.
23. Ulbright TM. Germ cell neoplasms of the testis. Am J Surg Pathol 1993;17:1075–91.
24. Guest PJ, Guy R, Wilkins PR, Byrne JV. Haemorrhagic cerebral metastases from malignant testicular teratoma. Clin Radiol 1992;45:190–4.
25. Motzer RJ, Bosl GJ. Hemorrhage: a complication of metastatic testicular choriocarcinoma. Urology 1987;30:119–22.
26. Osborn AG, Blaser SI, Salzman KL. Germinoma. In: Osborn AG, editor. Pocket radiologist: brain 100 top diagnoses. Salt Lake City: Amirsys; 2001. p. 162–4.
27. Yuh WT, Tali ET, Nguyen HD, et al. The effect of contrast dose, imaging time, and lesion size in the MR detection of intracerebral metastasis. AJNR Am J Neuroradiol 1995; 16:373–80.
28. Yuh WT, Fisher DJ, Engelken JD, et al. MR evaluation of CNS tumors: dose comparison study with gadopentetate dimeglumine and gadoteridol. Radiology 1991;180:485–91.
29. Bagshawe KD, Orr AH, Rushworth AG. Relationship between concentrations of human chorionic gonadotrophin in plasma and cerebrospinal fluid. Nature 1968; 217:950–1.

30. Bagshawe KD, Harland S. Immunodiagnosis and monitoring of gonadotrophin-producing metastases in the central nervous system. Cancer 1976;38:112–8.

31. Kaye SB, Begent RH, Newlands ES, Bagshawe KD. Successful treatment of malignant testicular teratoma with brain metastases. BMJ 1979;1:233–4.

32. Bokemeyer C, Nowak P, Haupt A, et al. Treatment of brain metastases in patients with testicular cancer. J Clin Oncol 1997;15:1449–54.

33. Bamberg M, Beyer J, Bokemeyer C, et al. First-line high-dose chemotherapy plus radiation therapy in patients with CNS metastases of non-seminomatous germ cell tumors. Proceedings of the American Society of Clinical Oncology: 1999 May 15–18; Atlanta, Georgia. Proc Am Soc Clin Oncol, 1999.

34. Bower M, Newlands ES, Holden L, et al. Treatment of men with metastatic non-seminomatous germ cell tumours with cyclical POMB/ACE chemotherapy. Ann Oncol 1997;8:477–83.

35. Israel VK, Russell CA, Dolkar D, Streeter O. Recurrent mediastinal nonseminomatous germ cell malignancy. In: Winchester DP, Brennan MF, Dodd GD, et al, editors. Tumor board case management. Philadelphia: Lippincott-Raven; 1997. p. 301–6.

36. Lester SG, Morphis JG 2nd, Hornback NB, et al. Brain metastases and testicular tumors: need for aggressive therapy. J Clin Oncol 1984;2:1397–403.

37. Colak A, Benli K, Berker M, Onol B. Epidural metastasis of testicular yolk sac tumor: an unusual cause of spinal cord compression. Case report. Pediatr Neurosurg 1991;17:139–41.

38. Cooper K, Bajorin D, Shapiro W, et al. Decompression of epidural metastases from germ cell tumors with chemotherapy. J Neurooncol 1990;8:275–80.

39. Arnold PM, Morgan CJ, Morantz RA, et al. Metastatic testicular cancer presenting as spinal cord compression: report of two cases. Surg Neurol 2000;54:27–33.

40. Wassenaar HA, Roos RA, Spaander PJ, van Oosterom AT. Unusual metastatic pattern in testicular malignant teratoma. Med Pediatr Oncol 1983;11:8–11.

41. Horvath L, McDowell D, Stevens G, et al. Unusual presentations of germ cell tumors. Case 2. Seminoma of the conus medullaris. J Clin Oncol 2001;19:911–5.

42. Pardridge WM. Targeting neurotherapeutic agents through the blood-brain barrier. Arch Neurol 2002;59:35–40.

43. Williams SD, Birch R, Einhorn LH, et al. Treatment of disseminated germ-cell tumors with cisplatin, bleomycin, and either vinblastine or etoposide. N Engl J Med 1987;316:1435–40.

44. Newlands ES, Reynolds KW. The role of surgery in metastatic testicular germ cell tumours (GCT). Br J Cancer 1989;59:837–9.

45. Raina V, Singh SP, Kamble N, et al. Brain metastasis as the site of relapse in germ cell tumor of testis. Cancer 1993;72:2182–5.

46. Simmonds PD, Mead GM, Whitehouse JM. A complicated case of metastatic teratoma. Growing teratoma syndrome and cerebral metastasis. Ann Oncol 1995;6:181–5.

47. Spears WT, Morphis JG 2nd, Lester SG, et al. Brain metastases and testicular tumors: long-term survival. Int J Radiat Oncol Biol Phys 1992;22:17–22.

48. Patchell RA, Tibbs PA, Walsh JW, et al. A randomized trial of surgery in the treatment of single metastases to the brain. N Engl J Med 1990;322:494–500.

49. Patchell RA, Tibbs PA, Regine WF, et al. Postoperative radiotherapy in the treatment of single metastases to the brain: a randomized trial. JAMA 1998;280:1485–9.

50. Nussbaum ES, Djalilian HR, Cho KH, Hall WA. Brain metastases. Histology, multiplicity, surgery, and survival. Cancer 1996;78:1781–8.

51. Mackey JR, Venner P. Seminoma with isolated central nervous system relapse, and salvage with craniospinal irradiation. Urology 1998;51:1043–5.

52. Breneman JC, Warnick RE, Albright RE Jr, et al. Stereotactic radiosurgery for the treatment of brain metastases. Results of a single institution series. Cancer 1997;79:551–7.

53. Muacevic A, Kreth FW, Horstmann GA, et al. Surgery and radiotherapy compared with gamma knife radiosurgery in the treatment of solitary cerebral metastasis of small diameter. J Neurosurg 1999;91:35–43.

54. Pirzkall A, Debus J, Lohr F, et al. Radiosurgery alone or in combination with whole-brain radiotherapy for brain metastases. J Clin Oncol 1998;16:3563–9.

55. Motzer RJ, Sheinfeld J, Mazumdar M, et al. Paclitaxel, ifosfamide, and cisplatin second-line therapy for patients with relapsed testicular germ cell cancer. J Clin Oncol 2000;18:2413–8.

56. Auchter RM, Lamond JP, Alexander E, et al. A multiinstitutional outcome and prognostic factor analysis of radiosurgery for resectable single brain metastasis. Int J Radiat Oncol Biol Phys 1996;35:27–35.

57. Flechon A, Culine S, Theodore C, Droz J-P. Pattern of relapse after non-evolutive disease status in advanced stage germ cell tumor treated by chemotherapy and surgery: consequence for follow-up procedures. Proceedings of the American Society of Clinical Oncology: 2001 May 12–15; San Francisco, California. Proc Am Soc Clin Oncol 2001;A714.

58. Higi M, Scheulen ME, Schmidt CG, Seeber S. Brain metastases in malignant testicular teratomas. Onkologie 1981;4:84–6.

59. Prognostic factors in advanced non-seminomatous germ-cell testicular tumours: results of a multicentre study. Report from the Medical Research Council Working Party on Testicular Tumours. Lancet 1985;1:8–11.

60. Aass N, Klepp O, Cavallin-Stahl E, et al. Prognostic factors in unselected patients with nonseminomatous metastatic testicular cancer: a multicenter experience, J Clin Oncol 1991;9:818–26.

61. Martini N, Golbey RB, Hajdu SI, et al. Primary mediastinal germ cell tumors. Cancer 1974;33:763–9.

62. Dulmet EM, Macchiarini P, Suc B, Verley JM. Germ cell tumors of the mediastinum. A 30-year experience. Cancer 1993;72:1894–901.

63. Dueland S, Stenwig AE, Heilo A, et al. Treatment and outcome of patients with extragonadal germ cell tumours—the Norwegian Radium Hospital's experience 1979-94. Br J Cancer 1998;77:329–35.

64. Hartmann JT, Nichols CR, Droz JP, et al. Prognostic variables for response and outcome in patients with extragonadal germ-cell tumors. Ann Oncol 2002;13:1017–28.

65. Bokemeyer C, Droz JP, Horwich A, et al. Extragonadal seminoma: an international multicenter analysis of prognostic factors and long term treatment outcome. Cancer 2001;91:1394–401.

18

Approach to the Management of Stage I Seminoma

MARY K. GOSPODAROWICZ, MD, FRCPC, FRCR (HON)
PADRAIG R. WARDE, MB, MRCPI, FRCPC

The majority (more than 75%) of patients with seminoma present with clinical stage I disease; that is, no apparent involvement is found outside the testis.[1,2] The classic presentation of stage I disease is painless testicular enlargement although up to 30% of patients can have some pain at presentation. The traditional management of patients with stage I seminoma involves inguinal orchiectomy, which provides detailed information on tumor pathology, information on the extent of primary disease, and local tumor control. Local recurrence in the scrotum following surgery is exceedingly uncommon, at least in the case of surgery performed (and presentation with small- to moderate-sized tumors) in the developed world. The current management options for patients with stage I seminoma include (1) adjuvant postoperative external beam radiotherapy directed to para-aortic lymph nodes alone or to para-aortic and pelvic lymph nodes, (2) surveillance, and (3) adjuvant chemotherapy. The usual approach to management involves adjuvant external beam radiotherapy to the regional lymph nodes; to date, this remains the treatment of choice in most centers. The prognosis of stage I seminoma is excellent, with an overall disease-specific survival rate approximating 100%. The choice of treatment depends on local expertise and patient preference.

CLINICAL PRESENTATION

The most common presentation of seminoma is painless testicular swelling although pain may be a feature of malignancy. A common perception that testicular tumors are painless is dangerous as it may lead to dismissal of a painful mass and a delay in diagnosis. However, data suggest that testicular pain may be a presenting symptom in approximately 30% of patients with seminoma. Testicular pain may be due to other, nonmalignant conditions such as torsion of the tumor, infarction or bleeding, or coexistent epididymitis. Classic signs and symptoms of acute epididymitis may be present in patients with seminoma. A physical examination of the testis involves inspection and palpation. A finding of a firm to hard mass is usual. In addition to tumor, the differential diagnosis of a testicular mass includes testicular torsion, hydrocele, varicocele, spermatocele, and epididymitis. Hydroceles can be transilluminated and are therefore rarely confused with tumor; however, a small percentage of tumors may coexist with hydroceles. On palpation, varicoceles in the venous plexus of the spermatic cord give the characteristic finding of a "bag of worms." Tumors are most often mistaken for epididymitis although a swollen and tender testicle along with fever is more characteristic of infection. Delays in treatment of testicular cancer may occur while patients are being treated for epididymitis. Therefore, a follow-up examination, with aggressive investigation in the absence of response to antibiotics, is recommended. Testicular ultrasonography is a sensitive and specific imaging modality useful in the differential diagnosis of testicular torsion, hydrocele, varicocele, spermatocele, epididymitis, and tumor. The demonstration of hypoechoic areas or masses on ultrasound examination should prompt further investigation.

ASSESSMENT OF PROGNOSIS

Pure seminoma is exquisitely sensitive to radiation therapy and chemotherapy.[3] Therefore, there is no need for prognostic factors in stage I seminoma cases to predict survival. However, depending on the management approach, prognostic factors can be used to identify the risk of disease recurrence.[4–15] In other testicular germ cell tumors, serum markers are of great prognostic significance. In seminoma, markers may help to identify nonseminomatous tumor elements by an elevated α-fetoprotein (AFP) level, even when histologic diagnosis reveals pure seminoma. In addition, 10% of patients with pure seminoma will have an elevated beta–human chorionic gonadotropin (β-hCG) level. However, following a radical orchiectomy, the β-hCG level should return to normal. An elevated β-hCG level following orchiectomy is a sign of occult metastatic disease, and such patients should receive additional treatment.

MANAGEMENT OPTIONS

Surgery

The initial treatment of seminoma always involves orchiectomy.[2,3,5,16] Surgery allows accurate pathologic diagnosis and provides local tumor control. Although a needle biopsy may indicate the diagnosis, it may not identify mixed seminoma and nonseminomatous tumors.* The classic approach to the management of stage I seminoma following orchiectomy involves adjuvant retroperitoneal irradiation (Table 18–1).

In the past two decades, alternative management strategies have emerged as viable options for patients with stage I seminoma. As in the management of stage I nonseminoma, postorchiectomy observation strategy (ie, surveillance) is now a viable option. In

---

*Editor's note: It should be noted that in most cases, needle biopsy of a suspected testicular mass should be avoided because of the risk of local tumor seeding or altering the normal patterns of spread. This, in turn, may require a modification of radiotherapy, with the need for a scrotal field (which usually leads to sterility).

addition, the recognition of the exquisite chemosensitivity of seminoma has led to trials of adjuvant single-agent adjuvant chemotherapy.

Radiation Therapy

For the past half-century, the traditional management of stage I seminoma patients after an orchiectomy has consisted of radiation therapy (RT) to the para-aortic and pelvic lymph nodes.[2,3,14] Such management resulted in an overall survival rate in excess of 95% and a very low relapse rate (see Table 18–1). In the absence of reliable retroperitoneal imaging, adjuvant RT resulted in unprecedented success. Recent surveillance studies have shown that occult para-aortic lymph node metastasis is present in at least 15% of patients with clinical stage I seminoma (based on the relapse rate without radiation).[4,9,13,17]

The lymphatic drainage of the testis is directly to the para-aortic lymph nodes (see Chapter 3).[18] Minor differences are noted in the distribution of metastases from left- versus right-sided testicular tumors. The left side drains to the left testicular vein, then to the left renal vein, with lymphatic drainage primarily to the lymph nodes located around the left renal hilum. On the right side, the testicular vein drains into the inferior vena cava below the level of the renal vein. In right-sided tumors, paracaval and interaortocaval lymph nodes are the first to be involved. Pelvic and

---

Table 18–1. MANAGEMENT OPTIONS IN STAGE I SEMINOMA

Adjuvant retroperitoneal RT
  Relapse rate: < 5%
  Relapse pattern: supradiaphragmatic sites
  Effective salvage: cisplatin and VP-16 chemotherapy
  Disease-specific survival: 99–100%

Surveillance
  Relapse rate: 15%
  Relapse pattern: para-aortic lymph nodes
  Effective salvage: retroperitoneal RT
  Second-relapse rate: 10–20%
  Effective second-relapse salvage: cisplatin and VP-16
    chemotherapy
  Disease-specific survival: 99–100%

Adjuvant carboplatin chemotherapy
  Relapse rate: < 5%
  Relapse pattern: para-aortic lymph nodes
  Effective salvage: retroperitoneal RT; cisplatin and VP-16
    chemotherapy
  Disease-specific survival: not determined (limited data)

RT = radiation therapy; VP-16 = etoposide.

inguinal lymph node involvement is rare and is usually limited to patients with factors leading to altered lymphatic drainage of the testis.[19] These factors include a past history of scrotal or inguinal surgery, a prior history of cryptorchid testis, a prior scrotal orchiectomy with incision of the tunica albuginea, and tumor invading the tunica vaginalis and lower third of the epididymis. A disruption of the lymphatic vessels in the spermatic cord during inguinal surgery induces anastomosis between testicular lymphatic vessels and regional lymphatics draining to the inguinal and pelvic lymph nodes. A connection with the contralateral inguinal lymph nodes may be established, but this is extremely rare. Occasionally, patients with inguinal or pelvic lymph node relapse have no apparent predisposing factors.

The conventional radiation fields for clinical stage I seminoma are designed to treat the para-aortic lymph nodes from the level of the diaphragm at the level of the T10–11 vertebral body to the lower border of the L4 vertebral body and include the ipsilateral common iliac and external iliac lymph nodes.[15] If patients are at risk of occult pelvic lymph node involvement, the field is often extended to include the ipsilateral inguino-femoral lymph nodes. The usually quoted risk factors for increased risk of an abnormal lymph node drainage pattern include a history of prior inguinal or scrotal surgery, and the presence of a cryptorchid testis located in the groin or pelvis. Extensive involvement of the spermatic cord can necessitate a radiation field to cover the inguinal region whereas scrotal skin involvement mandates irradiation to the hemiscrotum.

The usual irradiation technique involves treatment with parallel-opposed anteroposterior fields treated with 6 to 18 MeV linear accelerator photons. The clinical target volume includes the para-aortic and ipsilateral pelvic lymph nodes and is defined with the help of information obtained from CT scans of the abdomen and pelvis, to avoid irradiation of renal parenchyma. This classic plan was called "hockey stick" in North America and "dog leg" in the United Kingdom and Europe (Figure 18–1). Typically, the radiation fields extended from the T10–11 vertebral body to the inguinal ligament and were typically 8 to 10 cm wide. No attempt was made to treat the hypogastric and contralateral pelvic lymph

nodes. With this technique, it is important to ensure that the penis is moved out of the field; in addition, place the contralateral testis in a scrotal shield to protect fertility and hormonal function. Verification, simulator, and port fields are routine.

It is important to realize that in a routine "dog leg" or "hockey stick" field arrangement, the inguinal lymph nodes may not be fully covered. The inguinal lymph nodes should be treated in patients with risk factors for inguinal lymph node involvement, either by extending the radiation field inferiorly or by adding a direct anterior field to cover the inguinal lymph nodes. In general, scrotal irradiation is avoided even in patients with scrotal violation. The only instance in which scrotal irradiation may be recommended is when patients have very extensive local disease, incomplete surgery, and gross scrotal contamination prior to surgery. In some centers, the radiation field is divided into two separate fields, one treating para-aortic lymph nodes and one directed to

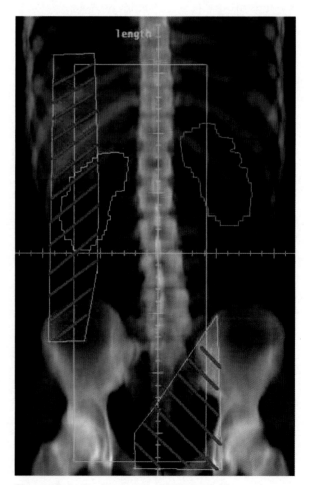

Figure 18–1. The "hockey stick" radiation field.

the pelvis. This is done where local conditions do not permit the design of wide field irradiation.

The low incidence of pelvic lymph node involvement in stage I seminoma has led to the investigation of adjuvant RT directed to the para-aortic lymph nodes alone.[20] Reports from phase II trials and retrospective experience have shown excellent results, with no pelvic treatment failures. The Medical Research Council Testicular Study Group in the United Kingdom has conducted a prospective randomized trial of the traditional para-aortic and pelvic irradiation versus para-aortic irradiation alone (Figure 18–2).[21] The results of this study, which included 478 patients, showed a 96% relapse-free survival rate for patients treated with para-aortic RT alone versus a 96.6% relapse-free survival rate for those treated with irradiation to the para-aortic and pelvic lymph nodes. All patients who received para-aortic and pelvic RT experienced relapse in supradiaphragmatic sites, but four patients in the para-aortic RT group

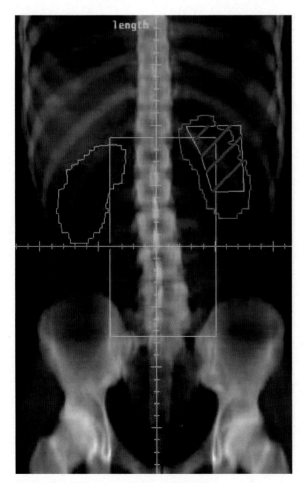

Figure 18–2. The para-aortic radiation field.

had relapsed disease in the pelvis. This trial showed that reduced RT volume yields excellent results but that a small risk of pelvic failure remains with its use. The experience of Christie Hospital in Manchester with the use of para-aortic RT alone revealed 10 recurrences in 339 patients, with 6 of these being in nodes in the pelvis or groin.[22] Those who recommend the use of smaller radiation fields do not recommend a routine follow-up with pelvic CT and accept a small pelvic failure rate even if patients relapse with large-volume disease; the median size of nodes at relapse in the Christie Hospital experience was 7.3 cm. A number of patients who had recurrence after adjuvant para-aortic RT recurred with elevated markers only (both β-hCG and AFP) or with distant metastasis in lung or bone. If one accepts that all failures after adjuvant RT should be treated with chemotherapy, the overall disease-specific survival rate is expected to remain in excess of 99%.[22]

The in-field control rate after retroperitoneal radiotherapy is close to 100%, and no in-field failures were seen in a cohort of 282 patients with stage I seminoma treated at Princess Margaret Hospital in Toronto between 1981 and 1999. The minimum dose of radiation required to control occult retroperitoneal disease has not been defined. There is variation in the dose prescribed for adjuvant external beam radiotherapy for seminoma. At Princess Margaret Hospital, a dose of 2,500 cGy prescribed at midline and delivered in 20 daily fractions has been used for over 25 years, with no in-field recurrences observed.[11] In the literature, the RT dose used varies between 2,000 and 3,500 cGy. While it is apparent from our experience that a dose of > 2,500 cGy is unnecessary, the issue of whether a dose of < 2,000 cGy is sufficient has not been determined. Published reports include radiation doses ranging from 2,500 to 4,000 cGy. Isolated local treatment failures have been reported at 1,500 cGy and 2,100 cGy.[11,14,23] Read and Johnson described 91 patients who underwent treatment to the para-aortic area only, with a radiation dose of 2,000 cGy in 8 fractions and with a median follow-up of 34 months; no local failures were reported.[24] The updated Christie Hospital results published by Livsey and colleagues showed no abdominal relapses in a series of 409 patients treated to the dose of 2,000 cGy in 8 fractions.[22]

Approximately 3 to 5% of patients with stage I seminoma who received adjuvant retroperitoneal radiation had a relapse outside the treated area (Table 18–2).[2,3,10,15,20,22–30] Relapse is most common in the first 18 months after diagnosis of seminoma, but it has been reported to occur as late as 6 years after diagnosis. The pattern of relapse following adjuvant radiation is well documented. The majority of relapses occur in the supraclavicular lymph nodes and in the mediastinum; few are seen in the lungs or in bone. Failure with elevated AFP, indicating the presence of non-seminomatous elements, has also been reported. Uncommon sites of isolated metastasis (such as brain and tonsil) have also been noted. In the Princess Margaret Hospital experience, 13 of 14 relapses occurred at 6 to 24 months from diagnosis, and one patient experienced a relapse at 72 months. A small proportion of patients, usually with predisposing factors, had a relapse in the inguinal lymph nodes.[31]

The disease-specific survival rate in stage I seminoma approaches 100%. The overall survival rate ranges between 92 and 99% at 5 to 10 years.[3,11,15,16,30,32] Most deaths are due to intercurrent illness, but there is a concern that premature death may be occurring from radiation-induced cancer (see Chapter 28). With such excellent results, the prognostic factors for relapse are difficult to establish. One of the potential factors predicting relapse is the occurrence of anaplastic seminoma. In the Princess Margaret Hospital experience, 8 of 55 patients with anaplastic seminoma had relapses, compared to 2 of 116 patients with classic seminoma (14.5% vs 1.7%).[3,11,15,16,30,32] The World Health Organization (WHO) criteria for the diagnosis of anaplastic seminoma (three or more mitoses per high-power field) are not uniformly used, and other series indicate that the prognosis for patients with anaplastic seminoma is similar to that for patients with classic seminoma. Other factors reported to be associated with higher risk of relapse include tumor invasion of the tunica albuginea, invasion of the epididymis, and spermatic cord involvement.

Isolated recurrences may respond well to RT although most radiation failures are now salvaged with systemic chemotherapy since the observation of the exquisite sensitivity of seminoma to cisplatin-based chemotherapy. In the past, prophylactic mediastinal and supraclavicular RT has been used as a means of reducing relapses in these regions, but this approach has not been shown to confer a survival advantage. Consequently, at present, extended field RT is not recommended (see Chapter 19).

The side effects of the low doses of radiotherapy required for the treatment of stage I seminoma are mild and include mild nausea, transient oligospermia, and a modest but measurable increase in the risk of subsequent (secondary) malignancies.

Surveillance

The possibility of reducing both early and late radiation-associated toxicity, coupled with the availability of salvage therapy with excellent results, is the impetus behind the evaluation of surveillance as a therapeutic option in clinical stage I seminoma (Table 18–3).[4,7,9,12,13,15,33–40] By and large, surveillance programs have included clinical assessments, including laboratory and imaging studies, every 2 months for the first year after diagnosis, every 3

Table 18–2. RESULTS OF STUDIES OF RETROPERITONEAL RADIATION THERAPY IN STAGE I SEMINOMA			
Author, Date	No. of Cases	Survival Rate (%)	Relapse Rate (%)
Bauman et al, 1998	169	100	3
Duncan et al, 1987	103	96	5
Dosmann et al, 1993	282	97.2	3
Fosså et al, 1989	365	99	4
Giacchetti et al, 1993	184	96	2
Kellokumpu-Lehtinen et al, 1990	129	95	6
Sommer et al, 1990	133	100	0
Willan et al, 1985	149	98	7
Warde et al, 2002	282	100	5

		Table 18–3. RESULTS OF SERIES OF SURVEILLANCE PROGRAMS IN STAGE I SEMINOMA		
Series Author	No. of Patients	Median Follow-Up (mo)	No. of Relapses	Survival Rate* (%)
Warde	345	113	55	99.8
von der Masse	261	48	49	98.9
Horwich	103	62	17	100
Ramakrishnan	72	44	13	100
Oliver	67	61	18	97
Germa Lluch	45	34	5	100
Alhoff	33	—	3	100
Miki	23	43	2	—
Yonese	22	—	5	100
Charig	15	31	5	100

*Disease-specific survival.

months in the second year, every 4 months in the third year, every 6 months in the fourth year, and then annually. Three large studies have evaluated the role of surveillance in patients with stage I seminoma, with similar results. The risk of relapse within the first year is 5 to 10% and rises to 15 to 20% by the third year. These data have allowed an estimation of the frequency of occult nodal metastases in clinical stage I seminoma. The most common site of relapse has been the para-aortic lymph nodes, with rare intrathoracic relapses. Despite these relapses, salvage therapy with either radiation or systemic therapy has been extremely successful, resulting in a cause-specific survival identical to that historically experienced with conventional radiotherapy.

Between January 1981 and December 1999, 627 patients with stage I seminoma were seen at Princess Margaret Hospital.[31] Of those, 345 were managed on a surveillance protocol and 282 patients received adjuvant RT. Patient preferences determined the management approach. Follow-up was according to a standardized protocol and included visits every 4 months for 3 years, every 6 months for 4 years, and yearly thereafter. Abdominal and pelvic CT was done at each visit of the patients managed by surveillance. The median age for both surveillance and adjuvant RT patients was 34 years. The median follow-up was 9.4 years for the surveillance cohort. Of 345 patients on surveillance, 55 had relapses, which gave a 5-year relapse-free rate of 85%. Forty-nine of these patients had relapses in para-aortic lymph nodes; 6 of the patients had relapses at other sites. Of the 55 relapses, 40 were managed with retroperi-

toneal RT, 13 with chemotherapy, and 2 with surgery. Of 40 patients managed with RT for first relapse, 5 developed a second relapse and were salvaged with chemotherapy. For patients managed on the surveillance protocol, the actuarial probability of requiring chemotherapy for treatment of first or second relapse was 5.1%.*

Prognostic factors for relapse have been studied in a number of the surveillance studies. In the Princess Margaret Hospital series, multivariate analysis showed patient age and tumor size to be predictive of relapse whereas the presence of small-vessel invasion (SVI) did not reach statistical significance.[41] In the Danish Testicular Cancer Study Group (DATECA), reported tumor size was the only significant predictive factor for relapse on multivariate analysis.[13] In the Royal Marsden Hospital series of 103 patients managed with surveillance, the only significant factor predicting relapse was the presence of lymphatic and/or vascular invasion (9% vs 17% relapse rate).[9] To more accurately determine prognostic factors for relapse in patients with stage I

*Editor's note: It is emphasized that to ensure safety, a surveillance protocol requires meticulous attention by the clinician and the patient. This is not a good approach for the inexperienced clinician or for a patient who appears likely to be unreliable or to default from follow-up. In my clinical practice, I have seen several patients who have required chemotherapy for extensive initial relapse when the patients have been inappropriately entered into surveillance (when retroperitoneal adenopathy was missed clinically) or when a poorly defined program of surveillance was attempted (eg, with the first follow-up visit occurring as late as 6 months after orchiectomy).

testicular seminoma managed by surveillance, a pooled analysis of the four large surveillance series, using individual patient data, has recently been published. Data on 638 patients was obtained from four centers: the Royal Marsden Hospital, the Danish Testicular Cancer Study Group, Princess Margaret Hospital, and the Royal London Hospital.[42] On multivariate analysis, tumor size and rete testis invasion predicted for relapse. The hazard ratio for relapse with a tumor size $\geq$ 4 cm was 2.0 (95% CI, 1.3, 3.2) relative to baseline (tumor size < 4 cm and no rete testis invasion). The hazard ratio for rete testis involvement was 1.7 (95% CI, 1.1, 2.6), and with both adverse prognostic factors present, the hazard ratio for relapse was 3.4 (95% CI, 2.0, 6.1).

A surveillance policy for stage I seminoma allows 85% of patients to avoid unnecessary exposure to radiation. No significant increase in the proportion of patients who require chemotherapy has been observed. With these results, surveillance should remain a treatment option and should be offered to all patients with stage I seminoma.

Adjuvant Chemotherapy

The use of one or two courses of adjuvant carboplatin for patients with stage I seminoma has been reported by a number of investigators over the past decade (see Chapter 19).[6,12,43–45] Oliver and colleagues, who treated stage I seminoma with one to two courses of adjuvant carboplatin chemotherapy, pioneered this approach. Dieckmann and colleagues, with a median follow-up of 48 months, reported no relapses among 32 patients treated with two courses of carboplatin and reported 8 relapses in 93 patients given only one course. Steiner and colleagues reported their institutional experience over 10 years using two courses of carboplatin in 99 patients.[45] With a median follow-up of 60 months, 2 patients (1.85) developed recurrence; both relapses occurred within the first year and were successfully salvaged with cisplatin-based regimens. Reiter and colleagues reported on their 12-year experience with 107 patients treated with two courses of carboplatin. No recurrences or deaths from seminoma were noted at a median follow-up of 74 months.[44]

While adjuvant carboplatin may well be an effective treatment strategy for patients with stage I seminoma, such an approach is less likely to be widely accepted if two courses of treatment are necessary. If indeed the relapse rate for patients with stage I seminoma treated with one course of adjuvant carboplatin is 10% or greater, as the data from Dieckmann and colleagues would suggest, this strategy is unlikely to be adopted in practice. If, however, the relapse rate is 5% or less, as Oliver and colleagues have reported, then this approach is likely to replace the use of adjuvant RT for stage I seminoma. A possible explanation for the difference in relapse rates in the various studies is that the dose of carboplatin administered to patients was not uniform. In the study by Oliver and colleagues, carboplatin dose was based on the area under the curve (AUC) formula of Calvert and colleagues whereas in the report of Dieckmann and colleagues, the dosage of carboplatin was 400 mg/m^2. Basing the dose on body surface area rather than AUC can lead to administration of a significantly lower dose. For example, a 34-year-old man with normal renal function, a glomerular filtration rate of 110 mL/min based on ethylenediaminetetraacetic acid (EDTA) clearance, and a body surface area of 1.787 m^2 would receive 715 mg under the body surface area approach but 945 mg using the formula of Calvert and colleagues.

Preliminary data indicate that there is minimal gonadal toxicity with this adjuvant carboplatin, and Oliver and colleagues have suggested that patients treated with this strategy have fewer side effects and return to work earlier than those treated with adjuvant RT. Dieckmann evaluated the gonadal toxicity of this regimen by serially determining levels of follicle-stimulating hormone in a subset of his cohort. Only mild elevations were noted, and six patients were able to father children. There is insufficient follow-up to assess the risk of second malignancy in patients treated with this approach. The Medical Research Council in the United Kingdom is presently conducting a phase III study comparing adjuvant carboplatin therapy to standard retroperitoneal RT in patients with stage I seminoma. It is hoped that this trial will address the issue of the efficacy of adjuvant carboplatin in this setting as well as compare the different toxicities of the two strategies.

Management of Stage I Seminoma Patients with Horseshoe Kidney

Horseshoe kidney occurs in approximately 1 of 400 persons in the general population. Patients with horseshoe kidneys are at an increased risk of testicular tumors as there is an association between renal fusion abnormalities and cryptorchidism, a major risk factor for testicular germ cell tumors. There are two main problems in the management of patients with stage I seminoma and horseshoe kidney.[46] The first is the difficulty in delivering RT to the retroperitoneal nodes, as a large part of the renal parenchyma often directly overlies the regional lymph nodes and lies within the standard radiation volume; the delivery of RT would be associated with an unacceptable risk of radiation nephritis. In addition, because of the possible abnormalities in lymphatic drainage of the testis in these patients, it is difficult to determine the lymphatic pathways. For these reasons, in patients with stage I seminoma, postorchiectomy surveillance is recommended. However, retroperitoneal lymph node dissection or adjuvant chemotherapy are the other options available to patients unwilling to follow the surveillance program.

FOLLOW-UP

The risk of disease recurrence following treatment of stage I seminoma varies with the choice of adjuvant treatment after orchiectomy.[47] The risk of recurrence is highest in unselected patients who have received no adjuvant treatment and is approximately 15%. The risk of recurrence after adjuvant radiotherapy is less than 5%, and after adjuvant single-agent carboplatin chemotherapy, recurrence is very rare. However, because recurrent disease is curable with further treatment, follow-up is important.

The methods of follow-up vary, depending on the pattern of failure following the initial treatment. In patients who receive adjuvant retroperitoneal radiotherapy, failure in the para-aortic lymph nodes is extremely rare; failure usually occurs in the supraclavicular, mediastinal, or inguinal lymph nodes. Therefore, routine abdominal imaging is not required. In patients treated only with orchiectomy, the most common site of recurrence is the para-aortic lymph nodes; therefore, abdominal imaging is crucial if recurrence is to be detected early. In cases in which all recurrence has been managed with chemotherapy and the extent of recurrence has been of less concern, abdominal imaging has been omitted by some investigators.[22] There are not enough data and sufficiently mature follow-up to establish the pattern of failure for patients treated with adjuvant chemotherapy. Most patients should be included in prospective trials and their pattern of failure reported in the literature. Unlike in the case of nonseminomatous germ cell testicular tumors, the time to relapse in seminoma cases may be prolonged. Recurrence as late as 9 years after orchiectomy has been reported.[31] Currently, we recommend a follow-up schedule of examinations every 4 months in the first 2 to 3 years following treatment, biannual follow-up visits until the 5-year anniversary, and annual follow-ups until the 10-year anniversary.[31] The patients should be educated about a very small risk of late recurrence and about the risk of a second testicular tumor. Contralateral testicular tumors have been reported to occur as late as 18 years after treatment of the original tumor.

RECURRENT DISEASE

Recurrent disease in seminoma cases is still a highly curable situation.[47] Therefore, aggressive investigation of disease extent and treatment is warranted. Recurrence in the para-aortic lymph nodes after orchiectomy and surveillance may be treated with retroperitoneal RT or with chemotherapy. Local tumor control approximates 100%, and second relapse is uncommon but has been documented, especially in patients with large tumors at relapse. For patients with recurrence following RT and for patients with bulky or extensive recurrence on surveillance, four cycles of cisplatin and VP-16 chemotherapy are usually sufficient to obtain a complete remission rate of 96% or more. Recurrence after cisplatin-based chemotherapy is rare.

SUMMARY

The prognosis of patients with stage I seminoma is excellent, regardless of the approach being used.

Data suggest that management with orchiectomy and adjuvant radiotherapy is the most popular strategy at present.[48,49] However, the data also suggest that late toxicity is not negligible.[50,51] The newer approaches with surveillance or adjuvant single-agent chemotherapy with carboplatin do not compromise treatment results and offer management without exposure to unnecessary radiation therapy. These forms of management are sure to result in lower rates of late morbidity. The reluctance of physicians to adopt these newer approaches reflects the slow adoption curve of newer forms of management, especially when the classic approach results in excellent long-term outcomes.

REFERENCES

1. Union Internationale Contre le Cancer. TNM Classification of malignant tumours. 6th ed. New York: Wiley–Liss, 2002.

2. Steele GS, Richie JP, Stewart AK, et al. The National Cancer Data Base report on patterns of care for testicular carcinoma, 1985–1996. Cancer 1999;86:2171–83.

3. Milosevic MF, Gospodarowicz M, Warde P. Management of testicular seminoma. Semin Surg Oncol 1999;17:240–9.

4. Bayley A, Warde P, Milosevic M, et al. Surveillance for stage I testicular seminoma. A review. Urol Oncol 2001;6:139–43.

5. Classen J, Souchon R, Hehr T, et al. Treatment of early stage testicular seminoma. J Cancer Res Clin Oncol 2001;127: 475–81.

6. Dieckmann KP, Bruggeboes B, Pichlmeier U, et al. Adjuvant treatment of clinical stage I seminoma: is a single course of carboplatin sufficient? Urology 2000;55:102–6.

7. Duchesne GM, Horwich A, Dearnaley DP, et al. Orchidectomy alone for stage I seminoma of the testis. Cancer 1990;65:1115–8.

8. Duncan W, Munro AJ. The management of testicular seminoma: Edinburgh 1970–1981. Br J Cancer 1987;55:443–8.

9. Horwich A, Alsanjari N, A'Hern R, et al. Surveillance following orchidectomy for stage I testicular seminoma. Br J Cancer 1992;65:775–8.

10. Kellokumpu-Lehtinen P, Halme A. Results of treatment in irradiated testicular seminoma patients. Radiother Oncol 1990;18:1–7.

11. Gospodarowicz MK, Sturgeon JF, Jewett MA. Early stage and advanced seminoma: role of radiation therapy, surgery, and chemotherapy. Semin Oncol 1998;25:160–73.

12. Oliver RT, Lore S, Ong J. Alternatives to radiotherapy in the management of seminoma. Br J Urol 1990;65:61–7.

13. von der Maase H, Specht L, Jacobsen GK, et al. Surveillance following orchidectomy for stage I seminoma of the testis. Eur J Cancer 1993;14:1931–4.

14. Thomas GM, Rider WD, Dembo AJ, et al. Seminoma of the testis: results of treatment and patterns of failure after radiation therapy. Int J Radiat Oncol Biol Phys 1982;8:165–74.

15. Warde P, Gospodarowicz M, Panzarella T, et al. Results of adjuvant radiation therapy and surveillance in stage I seminoma [abstract 1144]. Br J Urol 1997;8 Suppl 2:291.

16. Bauman GS, Venkatesan VM, Ago CT, et al. Postoperative radiotherapy for stage I/II seminoma: results for 212 patients. Int J Radiat Oncol Biol Phys 1998;42:313–7.

17. Warde P, Gospodarowicz M. Surveillance in stage I testicular seminoma: an overview. In: Jones W, Appleyard I, Harnden P, et al, editors. Germ cell tumours IV. The Proceedings of the Fourth Germ Cell Tumour Conference. Leeds, November 1997. London: John Libbey & Company Ltd.; 1998. p 115–20.

18. Ohyama C, Chiba Y, Yamazaki T, et al. Lymphatic mapping and gamma probe guided laparoscopic biopsy of sentinel lymph node in patients with clinical stage I testicular tumor. J Urol 2002;168:1390–5.

19. Gauwitz MD, Zagars GK. Treatment of seminoma arising in cryptorchid testes. Int J Radiat Oncol Biol Phys 1992;24: 153–9.

20. Kiricuta IC, Sauer J, Bohndorf W. Omission of the pelvic irradiation in stage I testicular seminoma: a study of postorchiectomy paraaortic radiotherapy. Int J Radiat Oncol Biol Phys 1996;35:293–8.

21. Fossa SD, Horwich A, Russell JM, et al. Optimal planning target volume for stage I testicular seminoma: a Medical Research Council randomized trial. Medical Research Council Testicular Tumor Working Group. J Clin Oncol 1999;17:1146.

22. Livsey JE, Taylor B, Mobarek N, et al. Patterns of relapse following radiotherapy for stage I seminoma of the testis: implications for follow-up. Clin Oncol (R Coll Radiol) 2001;13:296–300.

23. Warde P, Gospodarowicz MK, Panzarella T, et al. Stage I testicular seminoma: results of adjuvant irradiation and surveillance. J Clin Oncol 1995;13:2255–62.

24. Read G, Johnston RJ. Short duration radiotherapy in stage I seminoma of the testis: preliminary results of a prospective study. Clin Oncol (R Coll Radiol) 1993;5:364–6.

25. Thomas GM. Over 20 years of progress in radiation oncology: seminoma. Semin Radiat Oncol 1997;7:135–45.

26. Taylor MB, Carrington BM, Livsey JE, et al. The effect of radiotherapy treatment changes on sites of relapse in stage I testicular seminoma. Clin Radiol 2001;56:116–9.

27. Thomas GM. Is "optimal" radiation for stage I seminoma yet defined? J Clin Oncol 1999;17:3004–5.

28. Jacobsen KD, Olsen DR, Fossa K, et al. External beam abdominal radiotherapy in patients with seminoma stage I: field type, testicular dose, and spermatogenesis. Int J Radiat Oncol Biol Phys 1997;38:95–102.

29. Lederman GS, Herman TS, Jochelson M, et al. Radiation therapy of seminoma: 17-year experience at the Joint Center for Radiation Therapy. Radiother Oncol 1989;14:203–8.

30. Fossa SD, Aass N, Kaalhus O. Radiotherapy for testicular seminoma stage I: treatment results and long-term postirradiation morbidity in 365 patients. Int J Radiat Oncol Biol Phys 1989;16:383–8.

31. Warde P, Gospodarowicz M, Panzarella T, et al. Surveillance is an appropriate management strategy in patients with stage I seminoma. Int J Radiat Oncol Biol Phys 2002;54:61.

32. Melchior D, Hammer P, Fimmers R, et al. Long term results

and morbidity of paraaortic compared with paraaortic and iliac adjuvant radiation in clinical stage I seminoma. Anticancer Res 2001;21:2989–93.

33. Warde PR, Gospodarowicz MK, Goodman PJ, et al. Results of a policy of surveillance in stage I testicular seminoma. Int J Radiat Oncol Biol Phys 1993;27:11–5.

34. Warde P, Jewett MA. Surveillance for stage I testicular seminoma. Is it a good option? Urol Clin North Am 1998;25:425–33.

35. Allhoff EP, Liedke S, de Riese W, et al. Stage I seminoma of the testis. Adjuvant radiotherapy or surveillance? Br J Urol 1991;68:190–4.

36. Germa Lluch JR, Climent MA, Villavicencio H, et al. Treatment of stage I testicular tumours. Br J Urol 1993;71:473–7.

37. Miki T, Nonomura N, Saiki S, et al. Long-term results of adjuvant irradiation or surveillance in stage I testicular seminoma. Int J Urol 1998;5:357–60.

38. Yonese J, Kawai T, Yamauchi T, et al. Surveillance following orchiectomy for stage I testicular tumor. Nippon Hinyokika Gakkai Zasshi 1993;84:1804–10.

39. Ramakrishnan S, Champion AE, Dorreen MS, et al. Stage I seminoma of the testis: is post-orchidectomy surveillance a safe alternative to routine postoperative radiotherapy? Clin Oncol 1992;4:284–6.

40. Charig MJ, Hindley AC, Lloyd K, et al. "Watch policy" in patients with suspected stage I testicular seminoma: CT as a sole staging and surveillance technique. Clin Radiol 1990;42:40–1.

41. Warde P, Gospodarowicz MK, Banerjee D, et al. Prognostic factors for relapse in stage I testicular seminoma treated with surveillance. J Urol 1997;157:1705–10.

42. Warde P, Specht L, Horwich A, et al. Prognostic factors for relapse in stage I seminoma managed by surveillance: a pooled analysis. J Clin Oncol 2002;20:4448–52.

43. Dieckmann KP, Krain J, Kuster J, et al. Adjuvant carboplatin treatment for seminoma clinical stage I. J Cancer Res Clin Oncol 1996;122:63–6.

44. Reiter WJ, Brodowicz T, Alavi S, et al. Twelve-year experience with two courses of adjuvant single-agent carboplatin therapy for clinical stage I seminoma. J Clin Oncol 2001;19:101–4.

45. Steiner H, Holtl L, Wirtenberger W, et al. Long-term experience with carboplatin monotherapy for clinical stage I seminoma: a retrospective single-center study. Urology 2002;60:324–8.

46. Elyan SA, Reed DH, Ostrowski MJ, et al. Problems in the management of testicular seminoma associated with a horseshoe kidney. Clin Oncol (R Coll Radiol) 1990;2:163–7.

47. ESMO minimum clinical recommendations for diagnosis, treatment and follow-up of testicular seminoma. Ann Oncol 2001;12:1217–8.

48. Choo R, Sandler H, Warde P, et al. Survey of radiation oncologists: practice patterns of the management of stage I seminoma of testis in Canada and a selected group in the United States. Can J Urol 2002;9:1479–8.

49. Hruby G, Choo R, Jackson M, et al. Management preferences following radical inguinal orchidectomy for stage I testicular seminoma in Australasia. Australas Radiol 2002;46:280–4.

50. Travis LB, Andersson M, Gospodarowicz M, et al. Treatment-associated leukemia following testicular cancer. J Natl Cancer Inst 2000;92:1165–71.

51. Travis LB, Curtis RE, Storm H, et al. Risk of second malignant neoplasms among long-term survivors of testicular cancer. J Natl Cancer Inst 1997;89:1429–39.

19

Irradiation for Seminoma

A. ROBERT KAGAN, MD

Patients with early and advanced seminoma have at least a 95% and an 80% chance of cure, respectively. Since the mid-1970s, radiation therapy for early seminoma and chemotherapy for advanced seminoma have usually achieved cure. The confidence engendered by this success has led to the exploration of less intensive strategies of treatment for stage I seminoma (see Chapter 18). However, the relatively standard treatment approaches mentioned above remain the most widely used strategies for the treatment of most patients with this disease.

A radiobiologic doctrine is that oxygenation and active cell division are prerequisites for radiosensitivity. Although seminoma of the testicle is neither very vascular nor rapidly growing, it is most radiosensitive and radiocurable at a relatively low dose of 25 to 30 Gy in fractions of 160 to 180 cGy, using 5 fractions per week.

Many tumors are staged by the size of the primary or the extent of histopathologic invasion. However, the size of seminomas has not been a strong predictor for survival. A unique characteristic of seminoma is its ability to reach sizes greater than 2 cm without metastasizing. It is often not a locally invasive cancer as it may grow to a large size without extending through the tunica albuginea. Spread occurs along lymphatics that follow the spermatic cord to end in the aortocaval lymph nodes alongside of lumbar vertebrae 1 to 3 for the right testicle and lumbar vertebrae 1 to 2 for the left testicle (see Chapter 3). Bipedal lymphography has been definitive in showing these nodes, but the primary drainage from seminoma of the left testicle, located at the level of the left renal vein, near the renal hilus, is often not opacified (unless the testicle has been injected with dye). However, the discomfort of this technique and the difficulties of reproducing high-quality films after each procedure have led to its replacement by less invasive strategies. Computerized tomography (CT) of this region has solved this disparity and may even show lateral deviation of the left ureter when this left "renal vein" node is enlarged (Figures 19–1 and 19–2).

Before the advent of curative chemotherapy, radiation was used to treat all patients with seminomas. Palpable abdominal masses were given abdominal irradiation, and the portal size was reduced after tumor shrinkage. The goal was to limit the dose to

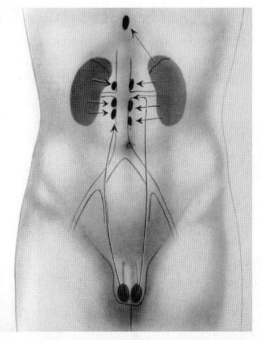

Figure 19–1. Common diagram showing para-aortic drainage. Note the absence of the left renal-gonadal vein lymph node, which is the sentinel node from the left testicle.

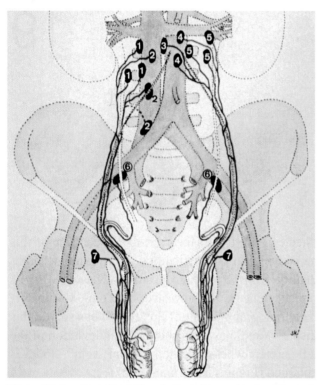

Figure 19–2. Illustration of lymphatic drainage, showing left renal-gonadal vein sentinel lymph nodes, from the left testicle.

the kidneys to 20 Gy and to deliver 30 Gy to the para-aortic nodes (Figure 19–3). Modifications of this "shrinking-field" technique were also used to treat para-aortic nodes larger than 5 cm, which often overlay one-half of the kidney or kidneys (Figures 19–4 and 19–5). In addition, mediastinal and left supraclavicular ports were added. Clinicians knew that extensive infradiaphragmatic disease meant a

higher probability of undetectable supradiaphragmatic disease (Table 19–1). Although the cisterna chyli drains mainly to the left supraclavicular nodes, the right supraclavicular node may be a drainage site in 10% of patients.[1]

Currently, most advanced presentations (nodes ≥ 5 cm) are often referred for treatment with chemotherapy. The practice of irradiating the bilateral iliac lymph node regions (common plus external iliac) and/or the homolateral hemiscrotum has decreased.[2] The iliac nodes are rarely involved unless large para-aortic nodes are present. The 2–3% risk of local recurrence in the hemiscrotum that housed the primary tumor has been exaggerated.[3,4] The practice of irradiating the iliac nodes after a herniorrhaphy or orchiopexy is justified although the probability of these nodes having disease is low (10–13%), despite the altered lymphatics[5] (Figure 19–6). The stratagem of irradiating the contralateral testicle (to 20 Gy) to prevent a second primary seminoma has been successful at the Christie Hospital in Manchester, England, but has not been a common practice,[6] predominantly because of the relatively low rate (4–5%) of second testicular malignancies without added therapy.

ASSESSMENT OF PATIENTS

Seminoma is usually found in patients aged 25 to 40 years. In general, younger patients (less than 30 years of age) presenting with a testicular mass will have testicular nonseminomatous germ cell tumors

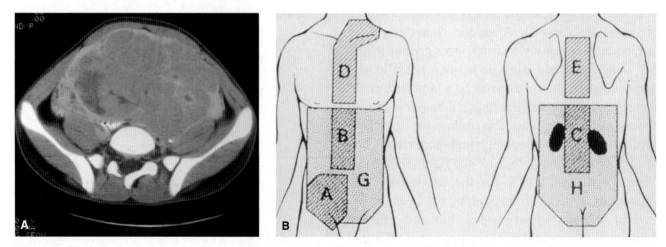

Figure 19–3. *A,* Seminoma. Computed tomography shows a large abdominal mass. *B,* Total abdominal radiation to 15 Gy. 15Gy is delivered to the entire abdomen. Kidney blocks are placed in the path of radiation for an addition 10 Gy. The para-aortic region (and the right iliac region) is given an additional 10 Gy. The total dose to the iliac and para-aortic region is 35Gy. The total dose to the rest of the abdomen is 25 Gy.

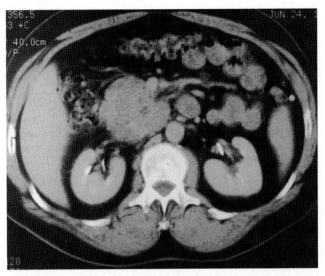

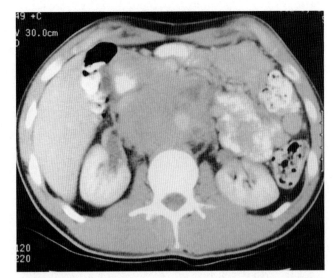

Figure 19–4. Computed tomography scan in a patient with stage II seminoma. Note para-aortic node overlying the kidney. The patient is a candidate for chemotherapy.

Figure 19–5. Computed tomography scan in a patient with stage II seminoma. Note paraortic node overlying both kidneys. The patient is a candidate for chemotherapy.

(NSGCTs) whereas older patients (more than 50 years of age) more commonly have lymphomas. Sarcomas of the spermatic cord and other uncommon tumors of the testis are rarely diagnosed preoperatively. At operation, the gross seminoma specimen is usually smooth and often homogeneous; areas of necrosis and hemorrhage suggest the presence of nonseminomatous malignancy or the uncommon anaplastic seminoma. Stage for stage, an anaplastic seminoma has the same patient survival as a seminoma but often presents as higher than stage I. A detailed history and physical examination may indicate whether a tumor is likely to be clinically localized or to be more extensive. For example, the presence of back pain, abdominal pain, cough, or dyspnea may suggest the presence of more extensive disease. Careful staging should be implemented (see Chapter 5). In brief, for patients with seminoma, routine blood work and biochemistry analysis are usually normal, as are circulating levels of

the beta subunit of human chorionic gonadotropin (β-hCG) and α-fetoprotein (AFP). In 10 to 30% of reported series, the β-hCG level may be slightly elevated (usually up to around 40 IU/L) in patients with seminoma. The circulating level of lactic acid dehydrogenase may be elevated in patients with seminoma. However, by definition, any patient with raised serum levels of AFP has an NSGCT as seminoma cannot produce this marker (see Chapter 7). The staging of seminoma depends on the extent of secondary lymph node metastases, not the size or focal invasiveness of the primary tumor (see Chapter 5). The majority of patients presenting with seminoma have stage I disease (no spread beyond the testis) or stage II disease (involvement of para-aortic nodes). Patients with stage III, IV, or IIC (ie, large para-aortic nodes) should be suspected of having a nonseminomatous malignancy or anaplastic seminoma although occasional cases of pure seminoma will present in this way.

	Recurrences/ Total Patients	Supraclavicular/ Mediastinal	Region of Recurrence			
			Para-aortic	Groin	Lung	Other
Nonpalpable aortic nodes	33/448	20	—	1	6	6
Palpable aortic nodes	37/67	24	5	—	7	3
Stage I*	11/194	5	—	3	2	1

Table 19–1. RELAPSE IN INFRADIAPHRAGMATIC-IRRADIATED PATIENTS

Adapted from Read G et al[21]; Warde P et al.[22]
*Modified to fit table.

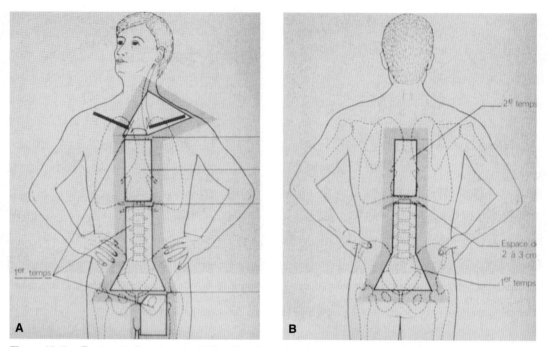

Figure 19–6. Treatment of seminoma with "total" node irradiation. Note the inclusion of the scrotum and the supraclavicular regions by anterior fields. Deeper lymph node regions are managed by anterior-posterior (*A*) and posterior-anterior (*B*) fields.

TREATMENT PLANNING

The hila of the left and right kidneys are 5 cm from the midline, the left at the L1-to-L2 interspace and the right opposite L2 (see also Chapter 3). The kidneys usually lie at an angle so that the superior pole is 1 cm closer and the inferior pole is 1 cm further away, relative to each hilum. This can be easily confirmed by CT. The left renal vein is longer than the right as it has to cross the aorta to reach the inferior vena cava. The lymphatics follow the gonadal venous system: the left enters the renal vein, and the right enters the inferior vena cava. To accommodate this anatomic variation, an extended window is designed for the left hilum when the seminoma presents in the left testicle (Figures 19–7 and 19–8). As there are enough glomeruli in the outer third of the kidney to preserve adequate function, it is safe to include the inner third of the kidney in the 30 Gy treatment volume. Only 20 Gy is tolerated by the whole kidney. Port reduction to protect the entire kidney from the full 30 Gy treatment volume, as was practiced before effective chemotherapy for large para-aortic nodes, is not recommended because patients with nodes > 5 cm are also at risk for distant metastasis. Thus, at many centers, chemotherapy is used as the initial therapy for patients with large para-aortic masses (stage IIC).

After treatment of only the para-aortic port for stage I seminoma (ie, with no radiation directed to the pelvis), the recurrence rate in the iliac region is less than 5%; therefore, only para-aortic irradiation is recommended in current clinical practice.[7] Fossa and colleagues found that radiation of iliac nodes did not reduce overall relapse rate.[7] The advantage of treating only the para-aortic port is that it reduces the irradiated volume, thus decreasing the incidence of a second nontesticular malignancy, and that it eliminates irradiation as a cause for infertility since the contralateral testicle will receive less than 1% of the given 30 Gy.[8,9]

The common and external iliac nodes should be irradiated if the seminoma occurs in a cryptorchid testicle or if the para-aortic nodes are multiple or > 5 cm. Often the common external iliac and/or inguinal nodes are treated when there is a history of a scrotal incision, orchiopexy, or herniorrhaphy, but the evidence to support this practice is weak. It is rare for a seminoma to extend through the tunica albuginea to invade the tunica vaginalis and penetrate the

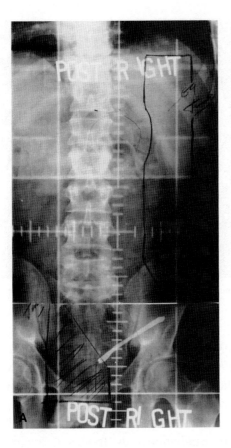

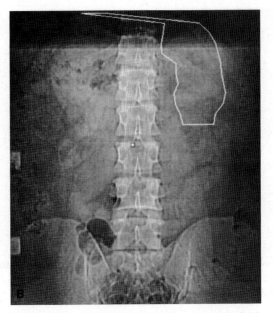

Figure 19–7. *A,* Simulation film of a para-aortic field. *B,* The exact kidney hilum position can be established by computed tomography.

scrotum, but if this occurs, then the inguinal nodes are at risk. Although supradiaphragmatic irradiation and prophylactic supraclavicular irradiation for stage II disease has been recommended in the past,[10] trials conducted toward the end of the twentieth century showed clearly that this added only toxicity without survival benefit, and adjuvant supradiaphragmatic irradiation is rarely used today.[11]*

Depending on the sites of tumor, the para-aortic field has often extended from T10–T11 to L5–S1. At the superior level, unnecessary heart irradiation occurs. One might question the need for this suprarenal volume or the need to irradiate inferior to L4. At most, the superior margin should stop at the diaphragm. Its width varies from 8 to 12 cm, and protection of the outer two-thirds of the kidneys is recommended. It is unlikely that all of the para-aortic and precaval nodes must be irradiated to effect a cure.[12] When an "iliac" treatment volume is added, it should stop at the pubic symphysis, sparing the contralateral testicle. Why some clinicians routinely include the inguinal incision is a mystery. The spermatic cord is clamped at the internal ring, and the testicle is delivered through the inguinal incision and removed. Thus, there is no contamination of the wound by tumor spill. Irradiation of the hemiscrotum and inguinal area is not advised unless the tumor extends to the tunica vaginalis, which almost never happens in patients with seminoma. Occasionally, lymphatic disturbance by previous surgical events will be so severe that "para-aortic" and bilateral iliac irradiation should be considered because the lymphatic drainage will be unpredictable.

CONTRAINDICATIONS

Although radiotherapy is frequently used as adjuvant therapy after orchiectomy for stage I disease or used in the active treatment of small-volume stage II (A to B) seminoma, there are situations in which there may be absolute or relative contraindications

---

*Editor's note: In fact, if the metastatic seminoma is sufficiently extensive to lead to the consideration of prophylactic mediastinal or supraclavicular irradiation, chemotherapy should usually be used as first-line treatment.

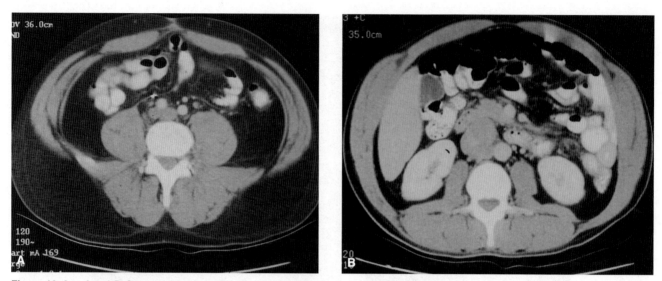

Figure 19–8.   *A* and *B*, Computed tomography scans showing stage II seminoma para-aortic nodes of < 5 cm. The patient was a candidate for irradiation of 25 to 30 Gy to the para-aortic region.

to its use. Contraindications to radiotherapy may occur with the following:

1. A displaced or rotated position of the left kidney, which may alter the lymphatic drainage
2. Inflammatory diseases of the abdomen (regional ileitis, pancreatitis, gastroduodenal ulcer, diverticulitis, hepatitis)
3. Morbid obesity
4. Abdomino-pelvic adhesions
5. Acquired immunodeficiency syndrome (AIDS) with a low CD4 count
6. Extragonadal seminoma (large size)
7. Horseshoe or pelvic kidney (in the field of irradiation)
8. Patient refusal

In these situations, the clinician should discuss the treatment options with the patient, and the clinical setting will govern whether adjuvant radiotherapy is used or whether (for defined lymph node metastases) chemotherapy is administered as an alternative. The situation for the patient with AIDS and a low CD4 count is particularly difficult, and once again, the clinical situation will usually govern the decision process.

RESULTS OF STUDIES

A review of 2,558 patients irradiated for stage I seminoma revealed a long-term survival rate of 96 to 100%, with a 0 to 10% relapse rate. Surveillance of 727 patients with stage I disease showed a median relapse rate of 13%, with a 100% survival rate[13] (see Chapter 18 for a detailed discussion). A review of survival rates in 469 patients with stage II disease treated with irradiation only (nodes ≤ 5 cm in diameter) demonstrated a survival rate of 85 to 100%; for 189 patients with stage II disease with nodes > 5 cm, the survival rate was 60 to 80%.[14] In this series, mediastinal and supraclavicular irradiation was commonly employed in these patients with stage II seminoma. Relapse rates in patients treated with and without retroperitoneal irradiation from Christie Hospital, Princess Margaret Hospital, and Aarhus University Hospital are shown in Tables 19–1 and 19–2. In general, when patients treated with radiotherapy experience recurrence, it is usually in the mediastinum; by contrast, in unirradiated patients, relapses that occur are usually found in the para-aortic region. In 49 irradiated patients with stage II disease, the relapse rate was 4% for those with para-aortic nodes < 5 cm and 33% for those with nodes > 10 cm. In a review of 148 patients with seminomatous bulk ≥ 10 cm, treated with irradiation only, the survival rates ranged from 33 to 70% whereas the rates were 80 to 100% for patients with bulk < 10 cm.[15] As the size of the para-aortic mass increases, the ability to control it with radiation decreases.

Before the era of precise tumor markers, an autopsy review of 154 patients with pure seminoma

Stage	Recurrences/ Total Patients	Supraclavicular/ Mediastinal	Region of Recurrence			
			Para-aortic	Groin	Lung	Other
I*	27/148	1	24	1	—	1
I	48/261	—	46[†]	2	1	—

Table 19–2. RELAPSE IN STAGE I PATIENTS UNDERGOING SURVEILLANCE

Adapted from von der Maase et al.[23]
*Modified to fit table.
[†]Includes 5 patients with relapse pelvic lymph nodes.

showed nonseminomatous metastases in 44% of patients.[16,17] More recently, with the use of tumor markers for routine diagnosis, the few seminomatous patients who die from cancer do so most often from seminoma; but exceptions do occur. Retroperitoneal masses are expected to shrink over time. It may take months for this shrinkage to occur. In the past, some investigators viewed patients with residual masses ≥ 3 cm as being candidates for retroperitoneal lymphadenectomy although such surgery is especially difficult in patients with seminoma. Two of the six patients with stage II disease who relapsed at Princess Margaret Hospital had embryonal carcinoma. The slim possibility of carcinoma or teratoma must be weighed against the morbidity of the dissection, which can involve injury to the aorta, the inferior vena cava, the small bowel, and the ureter.[18] In one report, 302 patients (from 10 centers) with metastatic seminoma treated by chemotherapy were analyzed; of these, 34 patients had resected masses. The histology results indicated seminoma in 4 patients, teratoma in 2 patients, NSGCTs in 2 patients, and necrosis/fibrosis in 26 patients. Eighteen of these 34 patients had only a residual retroperitoneal mass: 15 with necrosis, 1 with seminoma, 1 with teratoma, and 1 with teratocarcinoma. Most of these 302 patients with abdominal masses did *not* undergo resection. The 3-year survival rate of this group approached 85%, whether radiation was given (67 patients) or not given (105 patients) post chemotherapy. To conclude, in most instances, resection of a residal mass in a patient with seminoma after irradiation (or platinum-containing chemotherapy) will be of little benefit since finding persistent seminoma, teratoma, or carcinoma is highly unlikely, and the morbidity of the procedure is likely to be substantial.[19]

SURVEILLANCE

The application of the strategy of active surveillance for patients with stage I seminoma has been discussed in detail in Chapter 18. It is always best to treat only the patients who need to be treated and to spare the patients who do not need to be treated. At my institution, most patients with stage I seminoma, after inguinal orchiectomy, are given the choice of active surveillance or adjuvant radiotherapy at a recommended dose of 25–30 Gy, to the para-aortic nodes. The center's approach to surveillance involves quarterly follow-up for tumor markers, CT of para-aortic nodes, and chest radiography. The risk for these patients is that a change in insurance coverage or their moving to outside the institution's area may lessen their chance of adequate follow-up. Some patients who have chosen surveillance are noncompliant, missing their follow-up visits and returning with large-volume recurrences. It has also been suggested that, for the patient with stage I seminoma, adjuvant management with a platinum-containing regimen may be more beneficial than surveillance,[20] and this concept is currently being tested in a randomized trial in the United Kingdom.

COMPLICATIONS

The incidence of infertility after irradiation varies greatly because it depends on multiple factors. In addition, the measured end points that are used to define infertility differ from one series to another. Parameters that have been recorded include levels of follicle stimulating hormone (FSH), sperm count, and progeny.[20] About 50% of measured patients with testicular malignancies have sperm counts below the reference value, prior to treatment.[21] With a "hockey stick" port, the remaining testicle receives 3 to 5% of the "tumor" dose. Added shielding against the direct beam and a testicular clamshell to reduce scatter from the thighs can reduce the contralateral testicular dose to less than 1%. This 1% represents *internal* scatter and can be diminished only by distance or by decreasing the tumor dose. The use of only a para-aortic field supplies this distance. With the hockey stick port, reversible azoospermia is induced in all men whose contralateral testicle is exposed to 1 to 6 Gy, but this recovery takes 1 to 5 years, depending on the dose.[22] The para-aortic field stopping at L5 allows less than 0.01 Gy to the contralateral testicle. In my opinion, loss of libido and sexual potency is underrated in men who have undergone post-orchiectomy irradiation.

Cardiopulmonary deaths associated with mediastinal irradiation should cease to be a problem since the results of current practice has shown that there is no need for mediastinal irradiation for most patients with stage II seminoma.[23] However, there is still a cohort of living patients who were treated in the latter part of the twentieth century with mediastinal irradiation and who remain at risk for cardiac ischemia.

Second primary tumors have been reported after radiotherapy for seminoma.[8] The most common of these is malignancy in the remaining testicle although it should be noted that this is part of the natural history of testicular cancer and that it will occur in patients who have undergone only active surveillance. The incidence is 4 to 5%, which translates to an increased risk of 40 times the normal risk. Other solid tumors have a threefold increased risk of malignancy (see Chapter 28). The patient and physician should discuss the risks and significance of the second primary, especially in the context of adjuvant radiotherapy. From a practical viewpoint, the incidence of secondary malignancy from irradiation alone is relatively small and should not be an important factor in decision making for the patient with known para-aortic disease. Also, it should not be forgotten that chemotherapy drugs are also associated with a risk of second malignancies (see Chapter 28).

CONCLUSION

In the historical context, radiation for all patients with seminoma was advocated in a world that described oncologic management in terms of surgery or irradiation. The adoption of chemotherapy for advanced disease followed the recognition that chemotherapy was curative treatment for regional distant malignant deposits. Whether radiation can be avoided altogether is a subject of future investigation. Caution is advised, however, since patients with chemotherapy have a shorter follow-up relative to those treated with radiotherapy, and the final prevalence of second malignancies has not been defined. (For example, it is only relatively recently that etoposide was implicated in increasing the risk of developing acute monocytic leukemia.) Utimately, patterns of practice in this area will be heavily influenced by the outcomes of current randomized trials.

ACKNOWLEDGMENT

The author is grateful to Dr. Brace Hintz, for his additions.

REFERENCES

1. Viamonte M, Ruttimann A, editors Atlas of lymphography. New York: Georg Thieme Verlag, Stuttgart; 1980.
2. Schmidberger H, Bamberg M, Meisner C, et al. Radiotherapy in stage IIA and IIB testicular seminoma with reduced portals: a prospective multicenter study. Int J Radiat Oncol Biol Phys 1997;39:321–6.
3. Boileau MA, Steers WD. Testis tumors: the clinical significance of the tumor-contaminated scrotum. J Urol 1984;132:51–4.
4. Capelouto CC, Clark PE, Ransil BJ, Loughlin KR. A review of scrotal violation in testicular cancer: is adjuvant local therapy necessary? J Urol 1995;153:981–5.
5. Li Y-X, Coucke PA, Qian T-N, et al. Seminoma arising in corrected and uncorrected inguinal cryptorchidism: treatment and prognosis in 66 patients. Int J Radiat Oncol Biol Phys 1997;38(2):343–50.
6. Giwercman A, von der Maase H, Rorth M, Skakkebaek NE. Current concepts of radiation treatment of carcinoma in situ of the testis. World J Urol 1994;12:125–30.
7. Fossa SD, Horwich A, Russell, JM, et al. Optimal planning target volume for stage I testicular seminoma: a Medical Research Council randomized trial. J Clin Oncol 1999; 17:1146.
8. Bokemeyer C, Schmoll H-J. Treatment of testicular cancer and the development of secondary malignancies. J Clin Oncol 1995;13:283–92.

9. Jacobsen KD, Olsen DR, Fossa K, Fossa SD. External beam abdominal radiotherapy in patients with seminoma stage I: field type, testicular dose, and spermatogenesis. Int J Radiat Oncol Biol Phys 1997;38:95–102.

10. Zagars GK, Pollack A. Radiotherapy for stage II testicular seminoma. Int J Radiat Oncol Biol Phys 2001;51:643–9.

11. Loehrer PJ Sr, Birch R, Williams SD, et al. Chemotherapy of metastatic seminoma: the Southeastern Cancer Study group experience. J Clin Oncol 1987;5(8):1212–20.

12. Pearcey RG, Griffiths SE. The impact of treatment errors on post-operative radiotherapy for testicular tumours. Br J Radiol 1985;58:1003–5.

13. Gospodarowicz MK, Warde PR. Management of stage I-II seminoma. In: Raghavan D, Scher HI, Liebel SA, Lange PH, editors. Principles and practice of genitourinary oncology. Philadelphia: Lippincott; 1997.

14. Whipple GL, Sagerman RH, van Rooy EM. Long-term evaluation of postorchiectomy radiotherapy for stage II seminoma. Am J Clin Oncol 1997;20:196–201.

15. Mason BR, Kearsley JH. Radiotherapy for stage 2 testicular seminoma: the prognostic influence of tumor bulk. J Clin Oncol 1988;6(12):1856–62.

16. Bredael JJ, Vugrin D, Whitmore WF Jr. Autopsy findings in 154 patients with germ cell tumors of the testis. Cancer 1982;50(3):548–51.

17. McCrystal MR, Zwi LJ, Harvey VJ. Late seminomatous relapse of a mixed germ cell tumor of the testis on intensive surveillance. J Urol 1995;153:1057–9.

18. Baniel J, Foster RS, Rowland RG, et al. Complications of post-chemotherapy retroperitoneal lymph node dissection. J Urol 1995;153:976.

19. Duchesne GM, Stenning SP, Aass N, et al. Radiotherapy after chemotherapy for metastatic seminoma—a diminishing role. Eur J Cancer 1997;33:829–35.

20. Kagan AR, Steckel RJ. Uniformity, conformity and change in management of seminomas. Int J Radiat Oncol Biol Phys 1994;29:197–9.

21. Gordon W Jr, Siegmund K, Stanisic TH, et al. A study of reproductive function in patients with seminoma treated with radiotherapy and orchidectomy: (SWOG-8711). Int J Radiol Oncol Biol Phys 1997;381:83–94.

22. Hansen PV, Trykker H, Svennekjaer IL, Hvolby J. Long-term recovery of spermatogenesis after radiotherapy in patients with testicular cancer. Radiother Oncol 1990;18:117–25.

23. Hanks GE, Peters T, Owen J. Seminoma of the testis: long-term beneficial and deleterious results of radiation. Int J Radiol Oncol Biol Phys 1992;24:913–9.

24. Read G, Robertson AG, Blair V. Radiotherapy in seminoma of the testis. Clin Radiol 1983;34:469–73.

25. Warde P, Gospodarowicz MK, Panzarella T, et al. Stage I testicular seminoma: results of adjuvant irradiation and surveillance. J Clin Oncol 1995;13:2255.

26. von der Maase H, Specht L, Jacobsen GK, et al. Surveillance following orchiedectomy for stage I seminoma of the testis. Eur J Cancer 1993;29A:1931–4.

27. Kagan AR. Bladder, testicle, and prostate irradiation injury. Front Radiat Ther Oncol 1989;23:323–37.

20

Chemotherapy for Metastatic Seminoma

ALAN HORWICH, PhD, FRCR, FRCP

Seminomatous germ cell tumors represent a relatively infrequent indication for chemotherapy. The majority of presentations are at an early stage and are managed currently by adjuvant radiotherapy or by surveillance. Since relapse from these stages is uncommon and the presentation of seminoma with disseminated metastases is also uncommon, the chemotherapy for seminoma has developed mainly in parallel with chemotherapy for nonseminomatous germ cell tumors. However, there are important differences, including the extreme sensitivity of seminoma to platinum drugs and the lack of clear evidence of benefit from the incorporation of bleomycin. There are also differences in regard to the assessment and management of residual masses and the potential for salvage (in some cases) with radiotherapy.

Prior to the introduction of cisplatin into the management of germ cell tumors, seminomas were widely treated with alkylating agents.[1,2] Although complete responses were seen, they were usually of short duration. The combination of vinblastine and bleomycin was unsuccessful in patients with seminoma. However, the derivative regimen of bleomycin, cyclophosphamide, vincristine, methotrexate, and 5-fluorouracil achieved five prolonged remissions in 18 treated patients.[3,4] The modern era of chemotherapy for advanced seminoma was heralded by the report of the dramatic efficacy of cisplatin, vinblastine, and bleomycin.[5] This and other chemotherapeutic approaches will be discussed below.

PATTERNS OF PRESENTATION OF ADVANCED SEMINOMA

As described elsewhere in this volume, there is considerable overlap in the biology and natural history of testicular seminoma and nonseminomatous germ cell tumors (NSGCTs). This is hardly surprising in view of the common germ cell origin of both histologic types, the shared expression of the i(12p) chromosome, and their shared responsiveness to chemotherapy. Notable differences between seminoma and NSGCT cases include an older age of presentation, a more dramatic sensitivity to radiation, and a substantially improved therapeutic response for extragonadal primary tumors.

Seminomas most commonly present as early-stage (I–II) disease (see Chapters 18 and 19). Within the spectrum of stage II disease, involving retroperitoneal lymphadenopathy, seminomas may present as small-volume disease, measuring < 5 cm in diameter, and may be virtually asymptomatic. In this setting, stage II seminoma is usually identified by a series of staging investigations (eg, in a program of active surveillance for stage I seminoma). Occasionally, back or flank pain may be associated with surprisingly small tumor deposits in the retroperitoneum.

More advanced presentations of stage II disease, with extensive retroperitoneal lymph node involvement, may be associated with tumor masses > 20 cm in diameter. Characteristically, patients with such disease present with severe pain in the back, flank, or abdomen; this may be associated with gastrointestinal features including nausea, vomiting, anorexia, or irregularity of bowel function. With extensive stage II seminoma, the ureters may be obstructed, causing pain or evidence of acute renal failure. The larger the tumor mass, the more likely the association of nonspecific constitutional features such as asthenia, anorexia, malaise, weakness, and weight loss. While this is a relatively uncommon pattern for initial presentation, it is sometimes seen after the failure of radiotherapy or in a failed program of active surveillance.

In addition to retroperitoneal lymph node presentations, seminoma may present initially or at the time of relapse as disease involving the supradiaphragmatic lymphatic tissue (mediastinal, supraclavicular, or cervical nodes) or with distant metastases. Although uncommon in the present era (in which patients with testicular cancer tend to present at an earlier stage than did patients 50 years ago), seminoma will occasionally present initially with metastases of the bone, lung, brain, or liver, with clinical features reflecting the sites of metastasis and the extent of tumor involvement. However, extranodal metastases at first presentation are more characteristic of NSGCTs.

INDICATIONS FOR CHEMOTHERAPY

It is now generally accepted that patients with bulky abdominal nodal metastases from testicular seminoma, patients with supradiaphragmatic metastases, and patients with extranodal metastases should be treated with chemotherapy. There is some controversy over the treatment of patients with small-volume retroperitoneal node metastases since in the past, these patients have been treated with radiotherapy, reserving chemotherapy for those 10 to 20% who experience recurrence. However, with abdominal node metastases that are greater than about 5 cm in diameter (see Figure 20–1), there is a risk of renal damage from the radiation fields, and the risk of recurrence after radiotherapy becomes higher.[6] Also, in most centers, abdominal node metastases > 5 cm in cross-sectional diameter would provide an indication for chemotherapy rather than radiotherapy. The efficacy of chemotherapy is such that many centers would administer chemotherapy for abdominal node metastases of smaller volume. There are relatively little outcome data on this. Similarly, the efficacy of chemotherapy in the treatment of metastatic seminoma is such that its role is now being explored in the adjuvant treatment of patients presenting with stage I disease, and currently the outcome of a prospective randomized trial of radiotherapy versus single-dose single-agent carboplatin in this context is awaited.

For pure seminoma, extragonadal presentations appear to have the same chemosensitivity as testicular presentations.[7,8] Since these tumors usually present in the retroperitoneum or in the mediastinum with bulky disease, they are also treated with chemotherapy.

PROGNOSIS AFTER CHEMOTHERAPY

In a prognostic factor analysis of chemotherapy results in germ cell tumors, the International Germ Cell Cancer Collaborative Group (IGCCCG) reviewed 637 patients treated for advanced seminoma. The 3-year survival rate was 82%.[9] However, the majority of patients were in a good prognostic subgroup, with metastasis confined to either lymph nodes or lung fields, and in this group, the 5-year survival rate was 86%. Those with nonpulmonary visceral metastases had a 5-year survival rate of 72%. In an analysis of a subset of 236 of these patients treated with cisplatin-based chemotherapy at 1 of 10 European oncology units, a very-good-prognosis group was identified; this group comprised patients who had not had previous radiotherapy and who either had abdominal node metastases with any level of serum lactate dehydrogenase (LDH) or were stage C patients without nonpulmonary visceral metastases and whose serum LDH was less than twice the upper limit of normal. These patients had a 94% 3-year progression-free survival rate whereas the remainder of patients comprising a poor prognostic group had a 56% 3-year progression-free survival.[10] A retrospective single-institution analysis of 142

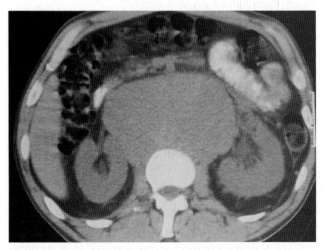

Figure 20–1. Moderately bulky retroperitoneal metastasis from testicular seminoma.

patients treated in New York was consistent with these prognostic conclusions but also suggested that an elevated pretreatment human chorionic gonadotropin (hCG) level may indicate a poorer outcome.[11] However, there is the possibility that a high serum hCG level may indicate the presence of an occult nonseminomatous component of the tumor.

COMBINATION CHEMOTHERAPY

There are relatively few prospective randomized trials of different chemotherapy regimens for advanced seminoma. When interpreting reports of uncontrolled trials, it should be remembered that over the last two decades there have been considerable changes in staging classifications, in the use of radiotherapy for metastatic seminoma, and in the definition of response. The modern era of successful chemotherapy for seminoma was heralded by the introduction of cisplatin. As early as 1974, there was a reported case of a complete response of stage C seminoma to cisplatin despite relapse after previous treatment with radiotherapy and with actinomycin D.[12]

It was rapidly recognized that the combination of cisplatin, vinblastine, and bleomycin, so successful in the treatment of patients with NSGCTs, was also effective in the treatment of seminoma.[5] This observation (from Indiana University) was soon complemented by a large multicenter collaborative report from Europe[13] and by a report of the efficacy of the vinblastine/actinomycin D/bleomycin/cisplatin/cyclophosphamide (VAB-6) regimen at Memorial Sloan-Kettering Cancer Center.[14]

At the same time, at the M. D. Anderson Hospital, less aggressive chemotherapy that also appeared to be effective had been evaluated. This treatment was based on sequential weekly pulse cisplatin combined (in most patients) with cyclophosphamide. The report on 52 patients included 8 patients treated only with cisplatin; 85% of patients achieved a complete response, and 48 of the 52 patients remained progression free.[15]

More recently, most centers have replaced vinblastine in the cisplatin/vinblastine/bleomycin (PVB) schedule with etoposide in an attempt to reduce toxicity. The seminal prospective randomized trial comparing these regimens in patients with metastatic germ

cell tumors contained only a small number of patients with pure seminoma.[16] However, equivalent or better results appeared with the use of bleomycin, etoposide, and cisplatin (BEP), and toxicity was reduced.

A further modification based on results from Memorial Sloan-Kettering Cancer Center questions the role of bleomycin. The convention at that center was to treat patients with the combination of etoposide and cisplatin (EP). In a report on 60 patients, 55 achieved long-term progression-free survival.[17] The durable response rates were 79% for 43 patients treated with VAB-6, 92% for 62 patients treated with EP, and 83% for 35 patients treated with etoposide and carboplatin (EC). This was not a randomized trial, and the differences in outcomes with these regimens could easily reflect case selection bias or other confounding factors. Of relevance, several studies of advanced NSGCT have questioned the safety of omitting bleomycin (see Chapter 13).

Finally, in another attempt to reduce the risk of lung toxicity and to improve efficacy against seminoma, an alkylating agent has been introduced via the combination of vinblastine, ifosfamide, and cisplatin (VIP).[18] Subsequently, vinblastine was replaced by etoposide in this regimen. Fossa and colleagues[19] reported a multicenter experience of the combination of ifosfamide, cisplatin, and vincristine (the holoxan, oncovin, cisplatin [HOP] regimen), which resulted in a 90% long-term disease-free survival rate for 42% of patients.

These combination chemotherapy approaches are summarized in Table 20–1, where it can be seen that modern cisplatin-based combination chemotherapy achieved long-term progression-free survival rates of between 80 and 90% in the majority of represented series.

Recent approaches to reducing the toxicity of treatment have included an assessment of the use of carboplatin rather than cisplatin in combinations, following the demonstration of the efficacy of this drug as a single agent.[20] For example, at the M. D. Anderson Hospital, Amato and colleagues[21] conducted a study of the combination of carboplatin and cyclophosphamide, given in a 28-day cycle, with myelosuppression abrogated by hemopoietic growth factors. Forty-six patients were treated, 30 with chemotherapy alone and the remainder with some

Table 20–1. CISPLATIN-BASED COMBINATION CHEMOTHERAPY FOR ADVANCED SEMINOMA

Series	Regimen	Patients	Continuous DFS (%)
Peckham et al, 1985[37]	PVB or BEP	39	90
Van Oosterom et al, 1986[13]	PVB (A)	80	71
Logothetis et al, 1987[38]	CyP	42	92
Clemm et al, 1989[39]	VIP	24	83
Mencel et al, 1994[17]	EP	60	92
Fossa et al, 1995[19]	HOP	42	90
Horwich et al, 2000[27]	EP	66	81
Arranz Arija et al, 2001[40]	EP	64*	89

A = doxorubicin; B = bleomycin; Cy = cyclophosphamide; DFS = diesease-free survival; E = etoposide; H = holoxan; I = ifosfamide; O = vincristine; P = cisplatin; V = vinblastine.
*Good-prognosis patients.

consolidation to a residual mass (usually by radiotherapy). The long-term continuous disease-free survival rate was 93%.

With regard to the number of cycles of chemotherapy, the standard approach with EP has been to administer four cycles, with etoposide at 360 to 500 mg/m^2 per cycle and cisplatin at 100 mg/m^2 per cycle. For BEP, a trial in 812 patients with all histologies of testicular germ cell tumor compared three versus four cycles and showed no significant differences in outcomes[22]; 23% of patients had pure seminoma, 93 randomized to three cycles and 89 randomized to four cycles. Patients with seminoma were stratified at randomization. It can be concluded that for bleomycin at 30,000 IU per week, etoposide at 500 mg/m^2, and cisplatin at 100 mg/m^2 per cycle, three cycles of BEP are sufficient for patients with good-prognosis seminoma.

SALVAGE CHEMOTHERAPY

In patients in whom BEP-type chemotherapy has failed, there is good evidence for the benefit of salvage with an ifosfamide-containing regimen. Miller and colleagues[23] reported on 24 patients with seminoma that recurred after cisplatin-based chemotherapy; 54% were long-term survivors after treatment with vinblastine, ifosfamide, and cisplatin. There is some evidence that this approach is as effective as high-dose chemotherapy.[24]

SINGLE-AGENT PLATINUM DRUGS

When the extreme sensitivity of seminoma to chemotherapy became apparent, single-agent carbo-platin and single-agent cisplatin were investigated. There has been particularly extensive investigation of single-agent carboplatin because of the toxicity advantages, thought to be especially important for older patients. The pilot studies were carried out at the Royal Marsden Hospital (United Kingdom) with single-agent carboplatin at a dose of 400 mg/m^2 every 3 to 4 weeks. Between 1982 and 1990, 70 patients were treated.[25] No patients suffered neurotoxicity, ototoxicity, or significant renal damage, and there was only one episode of neutropenic sepsis. With a median follow-up of 3 years, the actuarial 3-year relapse-free survival rate was 77% and the cause-specific survival rate was 94%. Of the 16 patients who relapsed, 12 were successfully salvaged with combination chemotherapy, leading to an overall level of survival equivalent to that achieved with cisplatin-based combination chemotherapy. These results were supported by a phase II study from Germany[26] and led to the launch of a prospective randomized trial by the UK Medical Research Council. A total of 130 patients with advanced seminoma were randomized between EP or single-agent carboplatin. The estimated progression-free survival rate at 3 years was 71% in those randomized to carboplatin and 81% in those randomized to EP. The difference was not statistically significant, and there was also no significant difference in overall survival (see Figure 20–2). However, it was recognized that this may be a consequence of the relatively small size of the trial, and it was therefore concluded that the standard approach should continue to be the combination of etoposide and cisplatin.[27] A similar concept was evaluated in a multicenter trial in Germany and has been

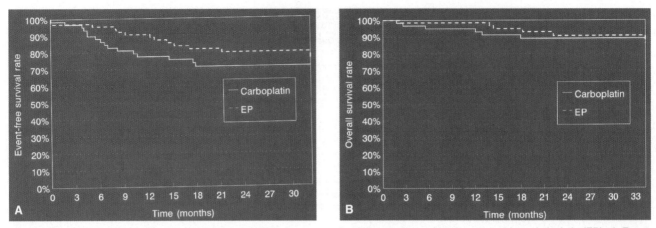

Figure 20–2. Survival results from a randomized trial of single-agent carboplatin versus combination etoposide and cisplatin (EP). *A*, Event-free survival. *B*, Overall survival. (Reproduced with permission from Horwich A et al.[26])

reported in an abstract.[28] This trial was a comparison in 251 patients treated with either single-agent carboplatin or the combination of cisplatin, etoposide, and ifosfamide (PEI). Again, there was a nonsignificant higher relapse-free survival rate with the combination as compared to the single agent, and there was no difference in overall survival.

There are also limited data on single-agent cisplatin in patients with advanced seminoma. In a report on 27 previously untreated patients, the continuous disease-free survival rate was 77%.[29]

RESIDUAL MASSES AND POSTCHEMOTHERAPY RADIATION

Especially with cases of large-volume seminoma, it is common to find a residual mass on scanning the patient after a course of chemotherapy. However, approximately 90% of these masses do not contain residual malignancies and appear to be fibrotic remnants (Figure 20–3).[30,31] Attempted resection can be hazardous because of extensive dense scar tissue involving the great vessels and retroperitoneal tissues. The analysis from the Memorial Sloan-Kettering Cancer Center suggested that there was a higher risk of residual malignancy if the residual mass was > 3 cm in diameter.[32] This suggestion has led, at some centers, to a policy of particularly close surveillance or adjuvant radiotherapy for this subset of patients.[33] However, other investigators have not found that recurrence was more likely when the residual mass was 3 cm in diameter.[34] Furthermore,

retrospective data from 302 patients treated in 10 European centers with chemotherapy for metastatic seminoma indicated that 174 of those patients had residual disease at the completion of chemotherapy.[35] Approximately half of these patients had been treated with postchemotherapy radiotherapy, with selection based mainly on institutional practice. Outcome analysis revealed no significant difference in progression-free survival whether or not adjuvant radiotherapy was employed. Thus, most centers would now follow a policy of close observation after chemotherapy for seminoma, considering the use of adjuvant radiotherapy only in those for whom the response is uncertain, or when there is radiologic or marker evidence of progression. Positron emission tomography results may be an indicator of persisting malignancy (see Chapter 6).[36]

LATE EFFECTS OF TREATMENT

At present, there are no clear data to indicate whether advanced seminoma is associated with different patterns of late complications from NSGCT. The fact that up to 50% of the patients who require chemotherapy for seminoma will have been previously treated with radiotherapy is potentially important. Extensive data gleaned from patients with lymphoma and other curable malignancies suggest that higher second malignancy rates will occur in patients who are treated with a combination of chemotherapy and radiotherapy. Similar findings have been identified in long-term follow-up series of patients treated for advanced germ cell tumors although a specific histologic breakdown has not yet been defined (see Chapter 28). Nonetheless, patients with advanced seminoma, treated with chemotherapy (with or without radiation), will need to be followed in long-term surveillance programs to discern the presence of late complications, including second malignancies.

CONCLUSION

Advanced seminoma is extremely sensitive to modern combination chemotherapy. The high cure rates and the relatively young age of the patients make it important to consider long-term toxicity issues when constructing a treatment plan. Fortunately, data produced over the last 20 years have provided a sound basis for curing the majority of patients, with minimal long-term compromise of their health.

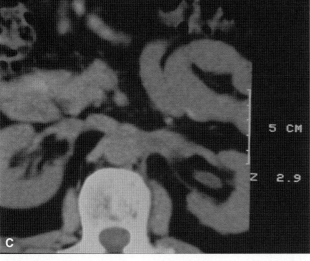

Figure 20–3. Sequence of photographs showing a pre-chemotherapy mass (*A*), response 1 month following cisplatin-based chemotherapy (*B*), and further shrinkage of residual mass 1 year later (*C*).

REFERENCES

1. Golbey RB. The place of chemotherapy in the treatment of testicular tumors. JAMA 1970;213:101–3.
2. Calman FMB, Peckham MJ, Hendry WF. The pattern of spread and treatment of metastases in testicular seminoma. Br J Urol 1979;51:154–60.
3. Samuels ML, Lanzotti VJ, Holoye PT, et al. Combination chemotherapy in germinal cell tumour. Cancer Treat Rev 1976;3:185–204.
4. Samuels ML, Logothetis CJ. Follow up study of sequential weekly pulse cisplatinum for advanced seminoma. Proc Am Soc Clin Oncol 1983;2:137.
5. Einhorn LH, Williams SD. Chemotherapy of disseminated seminoma. Cancer Clin Trials 1980;3:307–13.
6. Gregory C, Peckham MJ. Results of radiotherapy for stage II testicular seminoma. Radiother Oncol 1986;6:285–92.
7. Childs WJ, Goldstraw P, Nicholls JE, et al. Primary malignant mediastinal germ cell tumors: improved prognosis with platinum-based chemotherapy and surgery. Br J Cancer 1993;67:1098–101.
8. Bokemeyer C, Droz JP, Horwich A, et al. Extragonadal seminoma. An international multicenter analysis of prognostic factors and long term treatment outcome. Cancer 2001; 91:1394–401.
9. International Germ Cell Consensus Classification: a prognostic factor based staging system for metastatic germ cell cancers. International Germ Cell Cancer Collaborative Group. J Clin Oncol 1997;15:594–603.
10. Fossa SD, Horwich A. Current status of chemotherapy in advanced seminoma. Eur J Cancer 1997;33(2):181–3.
11. Mencel PJ, Motzer RJ, Mazumdar M, et al. Advanced seminoma: treatment results, survival and prognostic factors in 142 patients. J Clin Oncol 1994;12:120–6.
12. Higby DJ, Wallace HJ, Albert DJ, Holland JF. Diammino-dichloroplatinum: a phase I study showing responses in testicular and other tumors. Cancer 1974;33:1219–25.
13. Van Oosterom A, Williams SD, Cortes Funs H, et al. The treatment of metastatic seminoma with combination

chemotherapy. In: Jones WG, Ward AM, Anderson CK, editors. Germ cell tumors. Part II. Oxford: Pergamon Press; 1986. p. 229–33.

14. Stanton GF, Bosl FJ, Whitmore WF, et al. VAB-6 as initial treatment of patients with advanced seminoma. J Clin Oncol 1985;3:336–9.

15. Logothetis CJ, Samuels ML, Ogden SL, et al. Cyclophosphamide and sequential cisplatin for advanced seminoma: long term follow up in 52 patients. J Urol 1989;138:789–94.

16. Williams SD, Birch R, Einhorn LH, et al. Treatment of disseminated germ-cell tumors with cisplatin, bleomycin, and either vinblastine or etoposide. N Engl J Med 1987; 316:1435–40.

17. Mencel PJ, Motzer RJ, Mazumdar M, et al. Advanced seminoma: treatment results, survival and prognostic factors in 142 patients. J Clin Oncol 1994;12:120–6.

18. Clemm CH, Hartenstein R, Willich N, et al. Vinblastine, ifosfamide, cisplatin treatment of bulky seminoma. Cancer 1986;58:2203–7.

19. Fossa SD, Droz JP, Stoter G, et al. Cisplatin, vincristine and ifosphamide combination chemotherapy of metastatic seminoma: results of EORTC trial 30874. Br J Cancer 1995;71:619–24.

20. Horwich A, Dearnaley DP, Duchesne GM, et al. Simple non toxic treatment of advanced metastatic seminoma with carboplatin. J Clin Oncol 1989;7:1150–6.

21. Amato RJ, Millikan R, Daliani D, et al. Cyclophosphamide and carboplatin and selective consolidation in advanced seminoma. Clin Cancer Res 2000;6(1):72–7.

22. de Wit R, Roberts T, Wilkinson P, et al. Equivalence of 3 or 4 cycles of bleomycin, etoposide, and cisplatin chemotherapy and of a 3- or 5-day schedule in good prognosis germ cell cancer: a randomised study of the European Organisation for Research and Treatment of Cancer Genitourinary Tract Cancer Cooperative Group and the Medical Research Council. J Clin Oncol 2001;19(6):1629–40.

23. Miller KD, Loehrer PJ, Gonin R, Einhorn LH. Salvage chemotherapy with vinblastine, ifosfamide, and cisplatin in recurrence seminoma. J Clin Oncol 1997;15(4):1427–31.

24. Vuky J, Tickoo SK, Sheinfeld J, et al. Salvage chemotherapy for patients with advanced pure seminoma. J Clin Oncol 2002;20(1):297–301.

25. Horwich A, Huddart R, Dearnaley DP. Markers and management of germ cell tumors of the testes. Lancet 1989;352: 1535–8.

26. Schmoll HJ, Bokemeyer C, Harstrick A, et al. Single agent carboplatinum (CBDCA) for advanced seminoma: a phase II study. Proc Am Soc Clin Oncol 1991;10:181.

27. Horwich A, Oliver RTD, Wilkinson PM, et al. A Medical Research Council randomised trial of single agent carbo-

platin versus etoposide and cisplatin for advanced metastatic seminoma. Br J Cancer 2000;83(12):1623–9.

28. Clemm C, Bokemeyer A, Gerl D, et al. Randomised trial comparing cisplatin/etoposide/ifosfamide with carboplatin monochemotherapy in patients with advanced metastatic seminoma [abstract]. Proc Am Soc Clin Oncol 2000;19:1283.

29. Oliver RT, Love S. Alternatives to radiotherapy in the management of seminoma. Br J Urol 1990;65:61–7.

30. Schultz SM, Einhorn LH, Conces DJ Jr, et al. Management of postchemotherapy residual mass in patients with advanced seminoma. Indiana University Experience. J Clin Oncol 1989;7:1497–503.

31. Fossa SD, Kullman G, Lien HH, et al. Chemotherapy of advanced seminoma: clinical significance of radiological findings before and after treatment. Br J Urol 1989; 64:530–4.

32. Puc HS, Heelan R, Mazumdar M, et al. Management of residual mass in advanced seminoma: results and recommendations from the Memorial Sloan-Kettering Cancer Center. J Clin Oncol 1996;14:454–60.

33. Amato RJ, Millikan R, Daliani D, et al. Cyclophosphamide and carboplatin and selective consolidation in advanced seminoma. Clin Cancer Res 2000;6(1):72–7.

34. Horwich A, Paluchowska B, Norman A, et al. Residual mass following chemotherapy of seminoma. Ann Oncol 1997; 8:37–40.

35. Duchesne G, Stenning S, Aass N, et al. Radiotherapy after chemotherapy for metastatic seminoma—a diminishing role. Eur J Cancer 1997;33(6):829–35.

36. De Santis M, Bokemeyer C, Becherer A, et al. Predictive impact of 2-18fluoro-2-deoxy-D-glucose positron emission tomography for residual postchemotherapy masses in patients with bulky seminoma [published erratum appears in J Clin Oncol 2001;19(23):4355]. J Clin Oncol 2001; 19(17):3740–4.

37. Peckham MJ, Horwich A, Hendry WF. Advanced seminoma: treatment with cisplatinum-based combination chemotherapy or carboplatin (JM8). Br J Cancer 1985;52:7–13.

38. Logothetis CJ, Samuels ML, Ogden SL, et al. Cyclophosphamide and sequential cisplatin for advanced seminoma: long term follow up in 52 patients. J Urol 1987;138:789–94.

39. Clemm C, Hartenstein R, Willich N, et al. Combination chemotherapy with vinblastine, ifosfamide and cisplatin in bulky seminoma. Acta Oncol 1989;28:231–5.

40. Arranz Arija JA, Garcia del Muro X, Guma J, et al. E400P in advanced seminoma of good prognosis according to the International Germ Cell Cancer Collaborative Group (IGCCCG) classification: the Spanish Germ Cell Cancer Group experience. Ann Oncol 2001;12(4):487–91.

21

Management of Extragonadal Germ Cell Tumors

STACEY B. LEIBOWITZ, MD

RAMESH A. SHIVDASANI, MD, PhD

PHILIP W. KANTOFF, MD

Although more than 90% of germ cell tumors in males arise in the testis, a distinct group of such tumors originates outside of the testes; these tumors are known as primary extragonadal germ cell tumors (EGGCTs). EGGCTs account for approximately 1 to 5% of germ cell neoplasms and are histologically identical to primary gonadal germ cell tumors (GCTs). They are typically found in the retroperitoneum, the mediastinum, and the central nervous system, with no associated clinical abnormality of the testes detectable.

GENERAL CHARACTERISTICS

Etiology and Pathogenesis

Historically, cases of EGGCTs have been described in the literature at least since the 1930s.[1] Through the years, there has been a debate as to whether these EGGCTs represent true primary lesions originating outside the gonads or are secondary metastases from occult testicular lesions. In 1961, Azzopardi and Hoffbrand published histologic evidence of testicular scars in 17 patients with presumed EGGCTs and hypothesized that these scars represented regression of primary testicular neoplasms.[2] The argument that EGGCTs represent metastases is based on numerous case reports of microscopic intratesticular tumors or burnt-out scars discovered on histologic examination of testes from patients with presumed primary EGGCTs and normal testes on palpation.[3–7] The majority of these

patients had primary retroperitoneal germ cell tumors (RPGCTs).

One line of evidence to support the notion that EGGCTs are primary tumors is that they occur at sites where GCT metastases are extremely uncommon. The best example of this is the primary intracranial germ cell tumor. Given the usual pattern of metastasis for GCTs, it would be highly unusual to have isolated central nervous system (CNS) metastases with sparing of the retroperitoneum and mediastinum. Another example is the primary mediastinal germ cell tumor. Isolated mediastinal metastases occur in less than 1% of patients with GCTs.[8] When these tumors do metastasize to the mediastinum, they are found in all regions of the mediastinum whereas primary mediastinal EGGCTs are found almost exclusively in an anterior superior distribution.[9]

A second line of evidence is that many patients with disease limited to the mediastinum or retroperitoneum have been cured after local therapy alone.[10] Only rarely are testicular recurrences reported, and most of these are in patients who had RPGCTs. Furthermore, the majority of patients with presumed EGGCTs whose testes were serially sectioned had neither small primary tumors nor scars.[8] Finally, there is an association between primary mediastinal nonseminomatous germ cell tumor (MNSGCT) and Klinefelter's syndrome[11] as well as with the development of hematologic neoplasia,[12] suggesting that this group of tumors represents a distinct clinical and biologic entity.

Based on this evidence, it is now widely accepted that a subset of GCTs do indeed originate in extragonadal locations. However, RPGCTs represent a diverse group that likely includes some primary EGGCTs as well as some cases of secondary metastases from occult GCTs, and it remains difficult to separate these two entities. RPGCTs behave clinically like disseminated GCTs.[13,14] Because of these factors, the International Germ Cell Cancer Collaborative Group, which developed the prognostic classification for metastatic GCTs in 1997, grouped RPGCTs together with GCTs.[15] Management recommendations for RPGCTs are the same as for disseminated GCTs and will not be further addressed in this chapter, which will focus on the characteristics and management of primary mediastinal and intracranial GCTs.

The exact cell of origin in EGGCTs remains unknown. In 1946, Schlumberger proposed that EGGCTs develop from primitive rests of totipotential cells that dislocate from the urogenital ridge during the blastula or morula stage of embryogenesis and are left behind to attach to other organs.[16] More popular is the idea that, later in embryogenesis, some primordial germ cells from the entoderm of the yolk sac fail to migrate completely into the scrotum, leaving behind remnants that then transform into malignant GCTs.[17] Since embryonic germ cells migrate to the scrotum along a midline course, this theory helps explain the presence of EGGCTs in midline locations such as the retroperitoneum and mediastinum.

As with GCTs, the histologic type of each tumor is determined by the degree of further differentiation of these presumptive precursor cells either (1) down a gametic lineage (seminoma) or (2) with embryonic (embryonal carcinoma) or extraembryonic (yolk sac tumor or choriocarcinoma) differentiation.

Explaining the origin of intracranial GCTs is a bit more difficult since no direct evidence exists to support the presence of primordial germ cells in this region. Of interest, there are reports of intracranial GCTs that have an isochromosome for the short arm of chromosome 12.[18] This i(12p) abnormality is found in approximately 80% of GCTs in adults, as well as in some EGGCTs, and is highly specific for GCTs.[19,20] The presence of this abnormality in intracranial tumors is the best indirect evidence that these tumors originate from the same primordial germ cells as do GCTs in other locations.

Epidemiology

The proportion of EGGCTs is estimated at 1 to 5% of all GCTs.[8] The American Cancer Society estimated that 7,500 new cases of testicular cancer would be diagnosed in the United States in 2002. Accordingly, it could be estimated that 75 to 375 new cases of EGGCT would be diagnosed in the United States in 2002, illustrating the rarity of these tumors.

Rare cases of EGGCTs have been reported in a variety of locations, including the prostate,[21] the seminal vesicle,[22] the iliac fossa,[23] and the liver.[24] However, the majority of cases occur in midline locations, including the mediastinum, the sacrococcyx, and the pineal gland. While true primary EGGCTs occur in the retroperitoneum as well, many investigators (for the reasons discussed above) consider this group as originating from gonadal primary tumors.

In adults, more than 90% of malignant EGGCTs occur in men, and the most common primary site is the mediastinum, followed by the retroperitoneum. In contrast, EGGCTs account for two-thirds of the GCTs diagnosed in children, and in this population, there is a higher incidence among girls than among boys. This difference is due to the contribution of sacrococcygeal teratomas, which account for 42% of pediatric GCTs[10] and which occur in girls two to four times more often than in boys.[25,26]

Intracranial GCTs are exceedingly rare and account for only 0.4 to 3.4% of all primary CNS tumors diagnosed in Western countries.[27] Interestingly, the incidence of intracranial GCTs in Japan and other countries of the Far East is five to eight times greater than in Western countries.[28] The reason for this difference remains unknown.

Most EGGCTs in adults occur between the ages of 20 and 35 years although there are documented cases in patients older than 60 years.[10] The average age at presentation varies according to the primary site. For example, most intracranial GCTs present in patients who are between the ages of 10 and 21 years[28] whereas the majority of sacrococcygeal teratomas are diagnosed and removed during the neonatal period.[26] The most common histologic type of

EGGCT seen in adults is seminoma; teratoma is the most common pediatric GCT.

Histopathology

All histologic subtypes seen with GCTs are reported in EGGCTs as well. Most investigators believe that both groups of tumors arise from primordial germ cells. The histologic patterns reflect the normal stages of embryonic and fetal development that these totipotential cells undergo. When primordial germ cells undergo malignant transformation, they can differentiate along a gamete lineage or anywhere along the spectrum of embryonic and extraembryonic differentiation. Tumor histologic type is determined by the degree of differentiation.

In a series of unselected retrospective studies of adult EGGCTs, the most common histology reported was pure seminoma, which accounted for approximately one-third of cases.[8] Also referred to as germinomas, these tumors represent differentiation along a spermatocytic lineage (Figure 21–1). In order for the lesion to be classified as pure seminoma, there must be no nonseminomatous elements present (just as with GCTs of gonadal origin). Serum tumor markers are not usually elevated in seminomas although low-level elevation of beta–human chorionic gonadotropin (β-hCG) can be seen. An elevated α-fetoprotein (AFP) level is diagnostic of the presence of nonseminomatous elements. Because the treatment and prognosis of pure seminomas differ considerably from the treatment and prognosis of nonseminomatous GCTs, obtaining an appropriate specimen for histologic review is crucial to establishing an accurate diagnosis.

The remaining cases, including yolk sac (endodermal sinus) tumor, embryonal carcinoma, choriocarcinoma, and mature and immature teratoma, contain nonseminomatous elements (Figure 21–2). Although any of these histologies can present in pure form, most nonseminomatous GCTs are of mixed composition.

The presence of teratoma requires brief discussion. Mature teratoma, sometimes referred to as benign teratoma, is composed of well-differentiated tissue derived from one or more of the three germinal layers (Figure 21–3). Unlike malignant EGGCTs, the

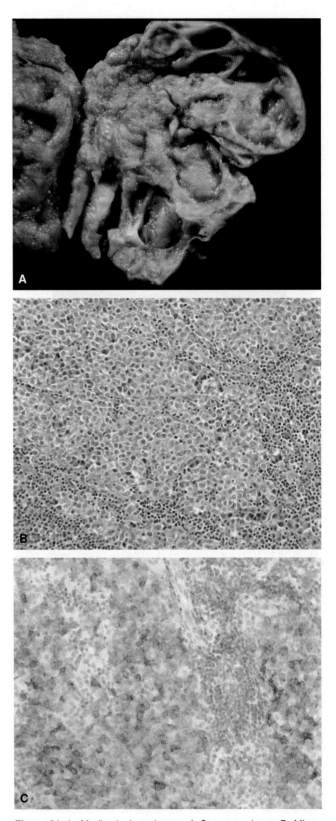

Figure 21–1. Mediastinal seminoma. *A,* Gross specimen. *B,*. Microscopic specimen stained with hematoxylin and eosin. Note numerous lymphocytes in close association. *C,* Immunohistochemical stain for placenta-like alkaline phosphatase. Tumor cells stain strongly positive whereas the lymphocytes are negative. (Courtesy of Dr. Michael H. Weinstein, Brigham and Women's Hospital, Boston, MA.)

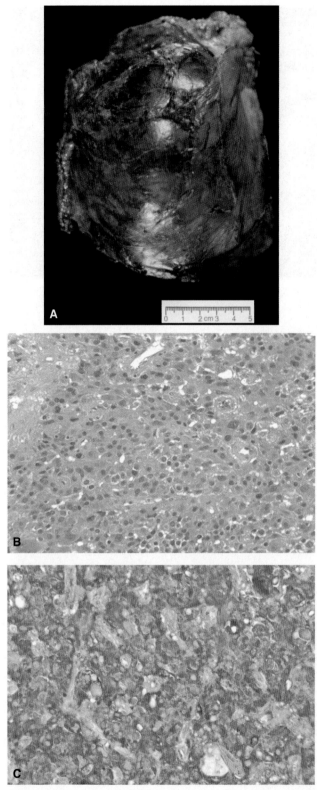

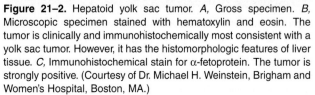

Figure 21–2. Hepatoid yolk sac tumor. *A,* Gross specimen. *B,* Microscopic specimen stained with hematoxylin and eosin. The tumor is clinically and immunohistochemically most consistent with a yolk sac tumor. However, it has the histomorphologic features of liver tissue. *C,* Immunohistochemical stain for α-fetoprotein. The tumor is strongly positive. (Courtesy of Dr. Michael H. Weinstein, Brigham and Women's Hospital, Boston, TMA.)

Figure 21–3. Mediastinal teratoma. *A,* Gross specimen. *B,* Radiography reveals areas of calcification within the specimen. (Courtesy of Dr. Gilbert Brodsky, Brigham and Women's Hospital, Boston, MA.)

distribution of mature teratomas of the anterior mediastinum is the same in both men and women.[29] If left behind, these tumors can grow and undergo malignant transformation. "Immature teratoma" refers to the presence of foci of poorly differentiated cells or mitotic figures together with the mature elements; this tumor tends to have an even higher incidence of malignant transformation. Teratoma is unique in that the only curative therapy is surgery. In cases in which histologic examination reveals pure teratoma and in which the serum tumor markers are normal, surgery remains the primary treatment. However, in cases in which histologic examination reveals pure teratoma and in which the serum tumor markers are elevated, chemotherapy is often given initially, based on the assumption that nonseminomatous elements are present. Surgical resection is then reserved for any residual masses that are present once serum tumor markers normalize after chemotherapy.

It is important to recognize a subset of patients with poorly differentiated or undifferentiated carcinoma who may actually have histologically atypical EGGCTs. Patients diagnosed with poorly differentiated carcinoma of an unknown primary site have tumors that are very difficult to classify by light microscopy and that have varied clinical characteristics. This diagnosis is applied to a very heterogeneous group that tends to have a grim prognosis and a poor response to therapy. However, some of these patients have dramatic responses to cisplatin-based chemo-

therapy, and some are even cured.[30] Based on clinical characteristics such as age, gender, tumor location, and serum tumor markers, many in this group of responders are thought to have atypical EGGCTs. Because of these patients, the term "unrecognized extragonadal germ cell cancer syndrome" was coined to refer to the following constellation of features: age less than 50 years; tumor involving primarily midline structures (such as the mediastinum or retroperitoneum), lungs, or lymph nodes; elevated levels of serum β-hCG or AFP; clinical evidence of rapid tumor growth; and previous responsiveness to prior radiotherapy or chemotherapy.[31] It must be noted that this diagnosis of atypical EGGCT is based entirely on clinical features, and the true origin of these neoplasms remains obscure in most of these cases. Also, this broad constellation of features certainly encompasses patients who do not have atypical EGGCTs and who will not respond to cisplatin-based chemotherapy. Because of the dismal prognosis for patients with poorly differentiated or undifferentiated carcinoma, anyone with this histologic diagnosis and at least one clinical feature of the unrecognized extragonadal germ cell syndrome should be considered for empiric treatment with cisplatin-based chemotherapy.[30,31]

In addition to being identical histologically, EGGCTs and GCTs are also similar cytogenetically. Both GCTs and EGGCTs share the i(12p) chromosomal abnormality (Figure 21–4). In approximately 80% of GCTs, the long arm of chromosome 12 is lost

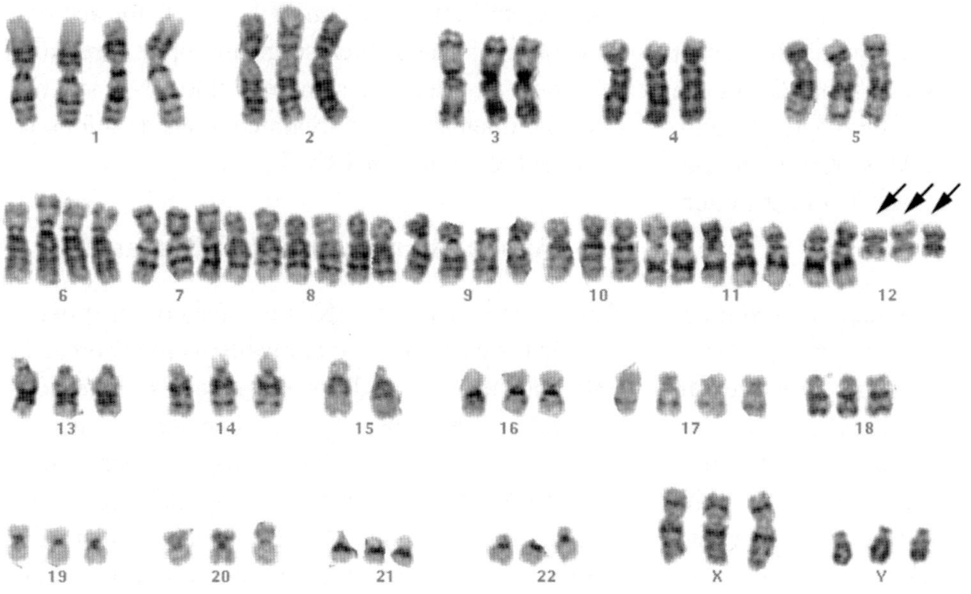

Figure 21–4. Malignant germ cell tumor karyotype showing hyperdiploidy with three copies of characteristic isochromosome 12p (*arrows*). (Courtesy of Dr. Jonathan A. Fletcher, Brigham and Women's Hospital, Boston, MA.)

and the short arm is duplicated, with symmetry around the centromere.[19,32] This abnormality is found in both seminomas and nonseminomas and is highly specific for GCTs. However, i(12p) has been identified rarely in other solid tumors[33] and is therefore not pathognomic for GCTs. i(12p) has been identified in many EGGCTs as well, including tumors arising in the mediastinum and the pineal gland.[18,20,32,34] How this genetic alteration is related to the neoplastic transformation of germ cells remains unknown.

Since i(12p) is highly specific for germ cell tumors, the detection of this cytogenetic abnormality has been used as a tumor marker to help identify the population of poorly differentiated carcinomas that may actually represent atypical EGGCTs. Motzer and colleagues performed genetic analysis on tissue from eight patients with poorly differentiated carcinoma of unknown primary and found that two specimens had evidence of i(12p) and that two others had other abnormalities of chromosome 12. These four patients were treated with cisplatin-based chemotherapy, based on the diagnosis of EGGCT, and three patients achieved a complete response.[33] This example illustrates how genetic studies can be used as a diagnostic tool to better define who in this population will benefit from cisplatin-based chemotherapy.

PRIMARY MEDIASTINAL GERM CELL TUMORS

Presentation

Although EGGCTs in adults most commonly present in the mediastinum, primary mediastinal GCTs are still quite rare. In a study of 1,064 patients with mediastinal tumors seen at the Mayo Clinic, malignant GCTs accounted for less than 1% of the tumors in this location while mature teratomas accounted for approximately 8% of cases.[35]

The majority of patients are symptomatic at diagnosis, with nonspecific symptoms frequently due to a large mass compressing surrounding structures. In one retrospective study of 56 patients, 86% were symptomatic at diagnosis.[36] The most common presenting symptoms in this study were chest pain, cough, weight loss, dyspnea, and superior vena cava obstruction. Other series reported similar findings.[9,37,38] Hemoptysis suggests the presence of embryonal carcinoma or choriocarcinoma.[36,37] Often these cases are very advanced at presentation because symptoms do not develop until a large mass is present. In those who are asymptomatic, a mass is often detected incidentally by chest radiography.

Once a primary mediastinal GCT is suspected, staging should include a physical examination, a computed tomography (CT) of the thorax and abdomen, and the measurement of serum tumor markers, including β-hCG, AFP, and lactate dehydrogenase (LDH). Careful examination of the testes is imperative, and testicular ultrasonography is also recommended. CT of the thorax complements chest radiography by helping to define the extent of disease for invasion of crucial structures (Figures 21–5 and 21–6). The presence of elevated levels of serum tumor markers depends on the histology. By definition, pure mature teratoma is marker negative. Although 7 to 10% of seminomas can produce low levels of β-hCG, high levels are highly suggestive of the presence of nonseminomatous elements.[39] Elevation of AFP is diagnostic for the presence of nonseminomatous elements and is the tumor marker that is most often elevated in patients with MNSGCTs.[10]

Although serum tumor markers can sometimes be helpful, diagnosis is ultimately based on histologic review of a tissue sample. Histology is of the utmost importance as both treatment and prognosis vary widely for seminomas and nonseminomas. Often a tumor may contain many histologic types; therefore, a sufficient biopsy specimen is crucial for accurate diagnosis. At times, open surgical biopsy is required to obtain an adequate sample. Table 21–1 summarizes the diagnostic and treatment considerations for a suspected mediastinal GCT.

Associations with Other Diseases

Klinefelter's syndrome (KS) is a genetic disorder of men that is characterized clinically by gynecomastia, testicular atrophy, and increased levels of follicle-stimulating hormone[40] and is characterized genetically by the 47,XXY karyotype. An association between MNSGCT and KS exists. At Indiana University, 22 consecutive MNSGCT patients had chromosome studies performed on blood or a bone marrow aspirate; 18% (4 of 22) of the patients were diagnosed with KS by karyotype, and a fifth patient clinically appeared to have KS.[11] This rate is much higher than expected when compared to the expected 0.2% incidence of KS in the general male population[11] Although there are single case reports of KS

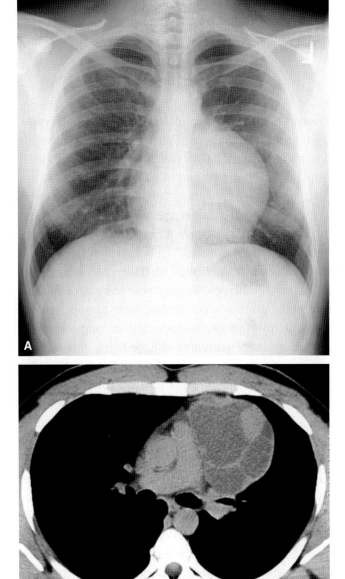

Figure 21–5. A 26-year-old patient presented with chest pain, weight loss, fatigue, and night sweats. Examination of a biopsy specimen revealed a pure mediastinal seminoma. *A,* Posterioranterior chest radiograph reveals a large anterior mediastinal mass projecting to the left, with loss of the left heart border. *B,* Computed tomography scan of the chest shows a complex solid and cystic mass with septations compressing the main pulmonary artery. (Courtesy of Dr. Kitt Shaffer, Dana-Farber Cancer Institute, Boston, MA.)

associated with retroperitoneal or intracranial EGGCTs, the vast majority of EGGCTs in KS patients are MNSGCTs.[41] In a retrospective study of 455 GCT patients treated at M. D. Anderson Hospital from 1977 to 1985, 49 patients had EGGCTs, including 15 patients with MNSGCTs. Four (27%) of the fifteen MNSGCT patients were diagnosed with KS while none of the remaining 440 patients were found to have KS. The pathogenesis of this association remains unknown. Although the median age at diagnosis of MNSGCT in the KS patients was almost a decade younger than in the non-KS patients (16 years vs 27 years),[41] survival and response to treatment did not differ between these two groups.

An association between MNSGCTs and hematologic disorders has been recognized for many years as well. Since the original recognition of this association in 1985,[42] more than 70 cases have been identified.[43] The most common hematologic diagnosis reported in this patient group is acute megakaryocytic leukemia.[43] In addition, many other disorders of megakaryocyte lineage have been reported, including essential thrombocytosis, myelodysplastic syndrome with abnormal megakaryocytes,[12] and idiopathic thrombocytopenia.[44,45] Although less commonly seen, there have also been recorded cases of acute lymphoblastic leukemia, acute myeloid leukemia, malignant mastocytosis, and malignant histiocytosis.[43]

Table 21–1. EVALUATION OF SUSPECTED MEDIASTINAL GERM CELL TUMOR
I. Suspect mediastinal GCT if
Presence of an isolated midline mass (especially in anterior mediastinum)
Male gender
Age of 20 to 35 years
II. Work-up for suspected mediastinal GCT
Testicular examination and ultrasonography
Serum tumor markers (β-hCG, AFP, LDH)
CT of thorax and abdomen
Biopsy for definitive histologic diagnosis
III. Factors influencing treatment choice
Histology (seminoma vs nonseminoma)
Extent of disease*
IGCCCG prognostic classification†
Good-risk vs intermediate-risk for seminoma
All nonseminomas are poor-risk

AFP = α–fetoprotein; β-hCG = human chorionic gonadotropin; CT = computed tomography; GCT = germ cell tumor; IGCCCG = International Germ Cell Cancer Collaborative Group; LDH = lactate dehydrogenase.
*Consideration of local treatment only for small seminomas.
†International Germ Cell Consensus Classification.[15]

This association is unique to MNSGCT. In a retrospective review of 635 patients with EGGCTs, 17 (6%) of 287 patients with MNSGCTs developed hematologic disorders whereas none of the remaining 348 patients with other types of EGGCTs did.[43] The median time from diagnosis of the MNSGCT to the development of the hematologic disorder was 6 months, and two patients presented with both disorders simultaneously.[43] Unfortunately, these hematologic malignancies tend to be extremely virulent and do not respond well to therapy. In the previous study, the median overall survival from the time of diagnosis of the hematologic disorder was 5 months, and all 17 patients died within 2 years of the diagnosis.[43]

There is considerable evidence that these rare hematologic disorders are not related to prior therapy but rather to the specific biology of MNSGCTs. Many of the MNSGCT patients developed the hematologic disorder prior to receiving any radiation or cytotoxic therapy.[12] In addition, both the timing and type of the hematologic disorders seen are different than those of the typical treatment-related leukemias. Acute leukemia associated with alkylating agents typically presents at an average of 5 to 7 years after treatment and with a prodrome of myelodysplastic syndrome. Type II topoisomerase inhibitor–related leukemia occurs an average of 2 to 3 years after treatment and is typically an acute myeloid leukemia. Treatment-related leukemias have characteristic chromosomal alterations that are not commonly seen in the leukemias in the MNSGCT population.

In the above study, cytogenetic studies were performed on the leukemic cells of 13 patients; 38% demonstrated the i(12p) abnormality characteristic of GCTs.[12] These findings lend support to the theory that the hematologic malignancies and the MNSGCTs arise from a common progenitor cell. It has been proposed that the leukemic cells develop from a population of neoplastic progenitor cells that are within the yolk sac tumor component of the MNSGCT and that undergo hematopoietic differentiation.[46,47] Further research is needed to better understand the pathogenesis behind this interesting disease association.

The presence of teratomatous elements within EGGCTs raises the possibility of an increased risk for these patients to develop nongerm cell malignancies. Theoretically, these teratomatous elements could undergo somatic differentiation into other types of solid tumors. In fact, the finding of sarcomatous elements (such as rhabdomyosarcoma and angiosarcoma) in MNSGCT specimens lends some credence to this theory.[48] Recently, however, Hartmann and colleagues reviewed the records of 635 EGGCT patients, including 287 patients with MNSGCTs, and found that the incidence of second solid malignancies in this group is not increased when compared with that of age-matched controls.[49]

Management of Primary Mediastinal Seminoma

Prior to the advent of cisplatin-based chemotherapy, the traditional treatment of primary mediastinal seminoma was surgery and/or radiation therapy. Although surgical resection was curative in some patients in the past, the tumor is not amenable to complete resection in the majority of cases as a result of extramediastinal or extensive local disease. Given the potential morbidity of extensive debulking surgery and the sensitivity of seminoma to other modalities such as radiation or chemotherapy, surgery now has a very limited role in the primary treatment of these tumors.

Radiation therapy has resulted in long-term survival for many patients with primary mediastinal seminomas. In one review of 82 patients from nine reported studies of patients receiving radiation therapy, 49 patients (60%) achieved long-term disease-free survival, with survival rates from these studies ranging from 38 to 100%.[8] In these studies, many patients had also undergone either partial or complete surgical resection. In 1998, Fizazi and colleagues conducted a similar review of the published literature, which revealed that 62% of patients treated with radiation were alive and free of disease at 2 years follow-up.[50] These results clearly demonstrate the exquisite radiosensitivity of these tumors and show that primary mediastinal seminoma patients can be cured with radiation therapy alone. However, many patients have extensive local disease, and despite radiation therapy, almost half of these patients will either experience local relapse or develop metastatic disease.

Cisplatin-based chemotherapy has now essentially replaced radiation therapy as the primary treatment modality for patients with primary mediastinal seminoma. With the arrival of cisplatin-based chemotherapy, the ability to cure advanced testicular seminoma greatly improved. In patients with bulky stage II disease (retroperitoneal lymphadenopathy > 5 cm) or stage III seminoma, cisplatin-based chemotherapy induces complete responses in more than 85% of patients.[51] As shown in Table 21–2, cisplatin-based chemotherapy is highly effective against primary mediastinal seminoma as well.[50–63] In these select series, 104 patients were treated with primary cisplatin-based chemotherapy; 88% of patients achieved a complete remission, with the majority attaining long-term disease-free survival. These studies are limited by a number of factors. Given the relative rarity of primary mediastinal seminoma, most studies contain very few patients and include cases of both primary mediastinal and primary retroperitoneal seminoma. In addition, almost all the reports are retrospective and include cases of seminoma as well as nonseminoma (cases of the latter have been excluded in Table 21–2). Despite these shortcomings, these studies clearly illustrate the efficacy of cisplatin-based chemotherapy in treating extragonadal seminomas. Complete response rates seen in extragonadal seminoma patients treated with cisplatin-based chemotherapy are essentially equivalent to those seen in patients with advanced testicular seminomas.

Some studies further suggested that chemotherapy used as salvage treatment after radiation therapy is less effective than chemotherapy used as primary treatment. Loehrer and colleagues retrospectively reviewed 62 patients with advanced testicular seminomas or extragonadal seminomas who were treated with cisplatin-based therapy.[57] Fifteen percent of the patients included had primary mediastinal seminomas. Of the 62 patients reviewed, 75% of those who had never received radiation or had received only limited field radiation attained a complete response.

Table 21–2. RESULTS OF STUDIES OF TREATMENTS OF MEDIASTINAL SEMINOMAS*

Investigators	Study Type	Pts	Chemotherapy	CR (%)	Comment
Feun et al, 1980[52]	P	2	PVB, maintenance actinomyin D, chlorambucil, vinblastine	0 (0)	Doses of cisplatin used were lower than those considered standard.
Hainsworth et al, 1982[53]	R	6†	PVB ± doxorubicin	4 (66)	
Jain et al, 1984[54]	R	7	VAB, CTX/Cis	7 (100)	NED 19+ to 46+ mo
Logothetis et al, 1985[55]	R	18†	CISCA, CTX/Cis	16 (89)	
Israel et al, 1985[56]	R	8†	VAB	8 (100)	100% NED
Loehrer et al, 1987[57]	R	9	PVB, PVB + doxorubicin, BEP	7 (78)	
Motzer et al, 1988[58]	P	17†	VAB, VAB/EP, EP	NS	4-yr survival: 88%
Bukowski et al, 1993[59]	P	8	PVB, BEP + doxorubicin	5 (63)	CRs obtained with chemo + surgery
Childs et al, 1993[60]	R	7	PVB, BEP, carbo alone	7 (100)	100% OS, median follow-up 41 mo
Goss et al, 1994[61]	R	8	Various	8 (100)	NED at median 45 mo (range, 4–132 mo)
Mencel et al, 1994[51]	R	19†	VAB, EP, VAB/EP, carbo/etoposide	19 (100)	95% long-term survival
Gerl et al, 1996[62]	R	3	VIP, VeIP, carbo alone	3 (100)	
Fizazi et al, 1998[50]	R	9	VAB, PVB, EP	8 (89)	Long-term NED, 89%; 2 required postchemo surgery
Bokemeyer et al, 2001[63]	R	51	Various	NS	5-year OS: 88%; 3 received radiation therapy only
Total		104		92 (88)	

BEP = bleomycin/etopside/cisplatin; carbo = carboplatin; chemo = chemotherapy; CISCA = cyclophosphamide/cisplatin/doxorubicin; CR = complete response; CTX/Cis = cyclophosphamide/cisplatin; EP = etoposide/cisplatin; NED = no evidence of disease; NS = not stated; OS = overall survival rate; P = prospective; Pts = patients; PVB = cisplatin/vinblastine/bleomycin; R = retrospective; VAB = vinblastine/actinomycin/bleomycin; VeIP = vinblastine/ifosfamide/cisplatin; VIP = etoposide/ifosfamide/cisplatin.
*Includes only patients who were treated with cisplatin-based chemotherapy.
†Includes some patients with primary retroperitoneal tumors.

Of those who had received extended field (chest plus abdomen) radiation, only 42% achieved a complete response. Logistic regression analysis revealed that prior extended field radiation was an adverse prognostic factor for response to chemotherapy. Similar studies of patients with advanced seminomas that have included patients with extragonadal seminomas also found trends toward inferior survival for those treated with chemotherapy after radiation therapy.[51,54,58] However, due to small numbers, these studies lack the power required to show a statistically significant difference between these groups. Some studies found an increase in myelotoxicity in patients who had received prior radiation therapy, a finding that makes it difficult to administer full doses of chemotherapy to this group.[51,58] While radiation therapy may still have a role as primary treatment of patients with small tumors, chemotherapy is now considered the primary treatment of choice for most extragonadal seminomas. If a patient has good-risk disease, the standard therapy is three cycles of a cisplatin-based chemotherapy regimen such as bleomycin/etoposide/cisplatin (BEP); a patient with intermediate-risk disease should receive four cycles.

The role of surgical resection of a residual mass after chemotherapy remains controversial for patients with extragonadal seminomas. Surgery following chemotherapy for seminoma can be difficult due to underlying fibrosis, and early studies reported significant surgical mortality in this group of patients.[64] The risk of mortality, coupled with the fact that there was often no evidence of viable tumor on histologic review of these masses, led many to believe that surgical resection of residual masses might not be warranted. In an attempt to better define who would benefit from surgery, Motzer and colleagues did a retrospective review of 41 patients with advanced seminoma who were treated at the Memorial Sloan-Kettering Cancer Center (MSKCC) and who had achieved either a complete response or a partial response with normal serum tumor markers after cisplatin-based chemotherapy.[65] Nine of the included patients had primary mediastinal seminomas. Of 6 patients with a residual mass < 3 cm in diameter, 5 underwent surgery and none had residual viable tumor. Of the 14 patients with a residual mass ≥ 3 cm, 6 (42%) had evidence of viable tumor

(5 with seminoma and 1 with mature teratoma.) There was no surgical mortality in this series. Based on these findings, some practitioners advocate observing any patient whose imaging is normal or in whom CT shows a residual mass < 3 cm. These patients are followed-up closely with serial imaging studies, and salvage treatment with chemotherapy or radiation therapy is instituted only if any relapse occurs. For patients with a residual mass ≥ 3 cm, either surgical exploration or multiple biopsies may be performed to determine if viable tumor remains.

Puc and colleagues published an update of the MSKCC experience. In this study, 2 (3%) of 74 patients with residual masses < 3 cm were considered site failures, compared to 8 (27%) of 30 patients with residual masses ≥ 3 cm.[66] The only factor that was found to be a significant independent variable predictive of site failure in this study was the size of the residual mass on the CT scan. However, other investigators have failed to find a significant relationship between the size of residual disease and the risk of recurrence.[67–69] While radiation therapy to any residual mass ≥ 3 cm has been considered by some practitioners as an alternative to surgery, this treatment plan is not recommended by most. Even if a residual mass ≥ 3 cm is present, the majority of patients will not have evidence of viable tumor at surgery.[70] Thus, many would be unnecessarily exposed to radiation.

Management of Primary Mediastinal Nonseminomatous Tumors

Prior to the advent of cisplatin-based chemotherapy, the prognosis for patients with MNSGCTs was dismal. Economou and colleagues summarized the published experience in this group of patients from 1964 to 1978.[71] Treatment for these patients included surgery, radiation therapy, and noncisplatin-containing combination chemotherapy; only 3% (2 of 63) of these patients survived past 16 months.

With the arrival of cisplatin, the ability to achieve long-term survival in this group improved. Table 21–3 summarizes the results from a selection of studies of MNSGCT patients treated with cisplatin-based regimens.[14,52,53,55,56,59–62,71–76] In the 271 patients included in these studies, 51% achieved a complete response (range, 20–82%), and 45% were reported as having no evidence of disease. Most of these studies are retrospective and contain very few patients (including some who had primary retroperitoneal nonseminomatous GCTs). It is difficult to determine how many patients received prior surgery or radiation therapy, and the number of patients with extramediastinal disease is not always reported. Last, certain histologies, such as choriocarcinoma and yolk sac tumor, are thought to portend a worse prognosis, and each study includes a different proportion of patients with these entities.

Two prospective studies have been published since 1990 and are included in Table 21–3. In the Indiana University experience from 1976 to 1988,[74] among 31 patients with MNSGCTs treated with cisplatin-based chemotherapy regimens, 35% (11 of 31)

achieved complete resonse (CR) with chemotherapy alone. An additional 7 patients required adjunctive surgery to attain CR, bringing the total CR rate to 58%. Of these 18 patients, 83% remained alive and disease free with a median follow-up of 55 months. The second prospective study was performed by the Southwest Oncology Group[59] and included both patients with seminomas and patients with nonseminomatous tumors. Sixteen patients with MNSGCTs took part in this study. Patients received cisplatin, vinblastine, and bleomycin (PVB), alternating with etoposide, bleomycin, cisplatin, and doxorubicin (EBPA). Of the MNSGCT patients, 25% achieved CR with chemotherapy alone, and an additional 56% achieved CR with surgery following chemotherapy, for a total CR rate of 81%. The authors state that

Table 21–3. RESULTS OF STUDIES OF TREATMENT OF MEDIASTINAL NONSEMINOMATOUS GERM CELL TUMORS*)

Investigators	Study Type	Pts	Chemo	CR (Chemo Only)	CR (Chemo + Surgery)	Total CR # (%)	Pts with NED	Comment
Feun et al, 1980[52]	P	10[†]	PVB, maintenance ACV	0	0	0 (0)	0	Lower-than-standard cisplatin doses used
Vogelzang et al, 1982[72]	R	8	PVB, VAB	0	3	3 (37.5)	3	NED: 12+ to 30+ mo Others: MS of 6 mo
Hainsworth et al, 1982[53]	R	31[†]	PVB, PVB + doxorubicin	15	6	21 (68)	19	Excluded all yolk sac tumor histology; 5-yr OS: 64%
Economou et al, 1982[71]	R	10	PVB, VAB	0	2	2 (20)	NS	MS: 14 mo
Logothetis et al, 1985[55]	R	11	CISCA, CISCA/VB	2	2	4 (36)	4	NED: 27.5–296+ mo
Israel et al, 1985[56]	R	29[†]	VAB	NS	NS	12 (41)	5	
Kay et al, 1987[73]	R	12	PVB, BEP	1	5	6 (50)	5	NED: 4–7 yr
Nichols et al, 1990[74]	P	31	PVB, PVB + doxorubicin, BEP	11	7	18 (58)	15	5-yr OS: 48%
Toner et al, 1991[14]	R	32	Various	6	6	12 (37.5)	NS	MS: 12.2 mo
Bukowski et al, 1993[59]	P	16	BEP, PVB/EBAP	4	9	13 (81)	12	Long-term NED: 74%; duration of follow-up NS
Childs et al, 1993[60]	R	11	Various	2	7	9 (82)	8	Median NED: 55 mo
Dulmet et al, 1993[75]	R	14	PVB	2	2	4 (28.5)	NS	MS: 38.5 mo
Goss et al, 1994[61]	R	15	Various	NS	NS	8 (53)	7	Median NED: 70 mo
Gerl et al, 1996[62]	R	12	PVB, BEP, BEP + CTX, VIP	6	2	8 (67)	6	Median NED: 96 mo; 5-yr OS: 58%
Fizazi et al, 1998[76]	R	29	VAB, PVB, BEP	4	15	19 (66)	13	2-yr OS: 45%
Total		271		53	66	139 (51)	97	

ACV = actinomycin D/chlorambucil/vinblastine; BEP = bleomycin/etopside/cisplatin; chemo = chemotherapy; CISCA = cyclophosphamide/cisplatin/doxorubicin; CISCA/VB = CISCA alternating with vinblastine/bleomycin; CR = complete response; CTX = cyclophosphamide; EBAP = etoposide/bleomycin/doxorubicin/cisplatin; EP = etoposide/cisplatin; MS = median survival; NED = no evidence of disease; NS = not stated; OS = overall survival rate; P = prospective; Pts = patients; PVB = cisplatin/vinblastine/bleomycin; R = retrospective; VAB = vinblastine/actinomycin/bleomycin/cyclophosphamide/cisplatin; VIP = etoposide/ifosfamide/cisplatin.
*Includes only patients treated with cisplatin-based chemotherapy.
[†]Includes some patients with primary retroperitoneal tumors.

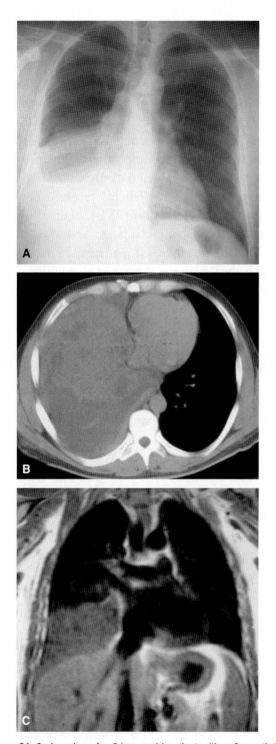

Figure 21–6. Imaging of a 34-year-old patient with a 2-month history of chest pain and dyspnea on exertion. *A,* Posterioranterior chest radiograph shows a right-sided pleural effusion and mass with a partial collapse of the right lower lobe. *B,* Computed tomography scan of the chest shows a heterogeneous mass over the dome of the right diaphragm, with dependent pleural fluid and indentation of the right atrium. *C,* T1-weighted coronal magnetic resonance image confirms the presence of a heterogeneous mass filling the right base from the costophrenic angle to the mediastinum abutting the right atrium. Examination of a biopsy specimen revealed a nonseminomatous germ cell tumor. (Courtesy of Dr. Kitt Shaffer, Dana-Farber Cancer Institute, Boston, MA.)

74% were alive and free of disease, but the duration of follow-up is not specified. This trial represents one of the largest prospective series of patients with MNSGCTs treated with a standard chemotherapy regimen, and the results are among the best published for this group of patients.

Recently, some studies have used high-dose chemotherapy (HDCT) as first-line therapy for patients with poor-risk nonseminomatous GCTs, including some MNSGCTs. The rationale for using HDCT as first-line therapy rather than as salvage therapy is that patients who are less heavily pre-treated will have less toxicity and shorter recovery times after HDCT. Also, further dose intensification might be feasible in this population. Physicians at MSKCC performed two studies that included the use of first-line HDCT for patients with poor-risk GCTs.[77,78] Fifty-eight patients were included, and all patients were given two cycles of conventional-dose chemotherapy (vinblastine/actinomycin D/bleomycin/ cisplatin/cyclophosphmide [VAB-6 regimen][77] or etoposide/ifosfamide/cisplatin [VIP][78]). Patients with an appropriate decline in marker levels received two additional cycles of conventional-dose chemotherapy while those with a slow marker level decline received two cycles of high-dose carboplatin/etoposide (CE) or cyclophosphamide/etoposide/carboplatin (CEC), each followed by autologous bone marrow transplantation. Included in both of these studies were some patients with EGGCTs although the exact number is not stated. The patients in these two studies had significantly better overall and event-free survivals when compared to a group of patients treated in an earlier study at MSKCC that used only conventional-dose chemotherapy.[78,79] Decatris and colleagues published a similar single-institution experience from the United Kingdom that included 20 patients with poor-risk nonseminomatous GCTs. These patients received three to four cycles of BEP followed by high-dose CEC with stem cell rescue. Of the study's 5 patients with MNSGCTs, 2 achieved CR; one subsequently relapsed and was salvaged with radiation therapy, and both remain alive, with no evidence of disease.[80]

A phase III trial is currently under way, using HDCT as first-line therapy in intermediate- and poor-risk patients as defined by the International Germ Cell Cancer Collaborative Group, which includes

MNSGCT patients.[15] In this study, patients have been randomized to receive either four cycles of BEP or two cycles of BEP followed by two cycles of high-dose CEC with peripheral blood stem cell support. The results from this large randomized study should help shed some light on the exact role that first-line HDCT will play in the treatment of this patient group.

The role of surgical resection of residual disease after chemotherapy for MNSGCT has been universally accepted. As can be seen from the data of the studies noted in Table 21–3, the total CR rate attained with the addition of radical resection of all residual masses is double that achieved with chemotherapy alone. As with advanced testicular nonseminoma, excision of all residual masses should be performed in any patient who has normal tumor markers and abnormal findings on imaging studies post chemotherapy. Unlike in patients with seminoma, surgical resection of these residual masses in this patient group will usually reveal either viable GCT or teratoma.[81] If residual viable carcinoma is found, additional adjuvant chemotherapy should be administered. While some practitioners favor giving two cycles of the induction regimen,[74] others recommend using a regimen that contains different drugs because of the theoretical concern of drug resistance in these residual cells.[76] Given the poor outcome of patients in whom residual carcinoma is found, a more aggressive approach seems reasonable.

Primary surgical resection in not recommended for patients with MNSGCTs for two reasons. First, by giving chemotherapy first, one can avoid performing unnecessary surgery in the group of nonresponders. Second, primary surgery will result in a delay in initiating chemotherapy. The one exception to the rule is patients with mature teratoma. Pure mature teratoma is unresponsive to chemotherapy and radiation therapy. Although patients with these tumors have an excellent prognosis, a percentage will undergo malignant degeneration; thus, these tumors should be removed. Dulmet and colleagues reported on a series of 50 patients with mature teratoma who underwent radical resection.[75] At 15 years, 93% of these individuals are alive and free of disease, demonstrating the high curability of these tumors with surgery alone. Complete resection should be done if possible. It is important to note that a patient who carries the diagnosis of pure teratoma and has elevated serum tumor markers should be treated as if he or she has an MNSGCT. Chemotherapy should be given as primary therapy, and surgery should be performed after serum tumor markers return to normal.

Patients with MNSGCTs who relapse after first-line cisplatin-based chemotherapy have a very poor prognosis, even with salvage chemotherapy. Motzer and colleagues reviewed the experience at MSKCC with salvage chemotherapy for GCTs. Of the 14 patients included who had EGGCTs, none were alive at 2 years.[82] Similarly, at the Institut Gustave-Roussy, 20 patients with MNSGCTs were treated with salvage chemotherapy between 1976 and 1993; all but one have died, and the final living patient has progressive disease.[76] One large retrospective study that looked at salvage therapy exclusively in patients with EGGCTs was published by Saxman and colleagues. At Indiana University between 1976 and 1993, 73 patients with EGGCTs that relapsed after primary cisplatin-based chemotherapy were treated with salvage therapy. Of the 42 patients who had MNSGCTs, only 2 (5%) are alive without evidence of disease. The median survival for this entire cohort of 73 patients was 9 months (range, 1 to 147 months) from the start of salvage treatment.[83] Most recently, Bokemeyer and colleagues published a retrospective review of 635 patients with EGGCTs treated at 11 cancer centers around the world. Of 79 patients with mediastinal GCTs who received salvage chemotherapy, only 8% are alive and free of disease.[70] These results are in contrast to those of patients with advanced GCTs, for whom the long-term disease-free survival rate with salvage chemotherapy is approximately 30%.

The results of HDCT as salvage therapy are similar to those of conventional-dose salvage therapy and are quite dismal. Broun and colleagues reported on a group of 12 patients with either recurrent or refractory MNSGCTs after first-line cisplatin-based chemotherapy who were treated with high-dose carboplatin and etoposide (ifosfamide was added in two patients). No complete responses were obtained. Six patients had partial responses, but none lasted for more than 6 months. The median survival was 107 days from bone marrow infusion (range, 14–347days), but one-third of the patients died of transplant-related complications.[84] Results from other studies of HDCT as salvage therapy in patients with EGGCTs have been equally poor.[85,86] In a multivariate analysis of 310 patients treated with HDCT for relapsed and refractory GCTs, one of the factors identified as an independent adverse prognostic variable for failure-free survival post HDCT was the presence of an MNSGCT.[87] Given these poor results, the use of HDCT as salvage therapy for patients with MNSGCTs should probably be limited to the clinical trial setting at this time.

Prognosis

There have been many debates in the past over whether EGGCTs inherently carry a worse prognosis or whether more patients with this diagnosis fare poorly due to an increased number of patients who present with bulky disease. Some studies have found that EGGCTs as a group respond worse to treatment than do testicular GCTs.[14,52,88] Other studies have found no difference in prognosis between these two groups.[53,63,89] However, these reports are limited by the small number of patients included.

The International Germ Cell Cancer Collaborative Group (IGCCCG), which was formed to create a unifying staging classification for metastatic GCTs, published its prognostic factor–based staging system in 1997.[15] This classification was based on a retrospective review of 660 cases of seminoma and 5,202 patients with nonseminomatous tumors that was compiled from collaborative groups from 10 countries.

Of the 660 patients with seminoma, 6% had primary mediastinal tumors and 7% had primary retroperitoneal tumors. The 5-year progression-free survival rate was 80% for the primary mediastinal group, 88% for the primary retroperitoneal group, and 80% for the primary testicular group. The 5-year overall survival rates were essentially equivalent. Based on these results, it was concluded that in the case of seminomas, a primary extragonadal site does not impact negatively on prognosis in any way. In a multivariate analysis, the single most important factor that influenced prognosis in this group was the presence of nonpulmonary visceral metastases. As such, the classification for seminomas is divided into good- and intermediate-prognosis tumors, based solely on the presence or absence of this finding.

The results in the patients with nonseminomatous tumor were quite different. Of the cohort of 5,202 patients, 3% of the patients had MNSGCTs. The 5-year progression-free survival rate in this group was 35%, compared to 77% for the patients with GCTs. The 5-year overall survival rate was also much better in the GCT group than in the MNSGCT group (82% vs 40%). Although the number of MNSGCT patients included is relatively small, these results are striking. In a multivariate analysis, primary mediastinal site was identified as a major adverse prognostic factor affecting both progression and survival. These findings clearly suggest that MNSGCT is a unique clinical entity with an inherently worse prognosis than other germ cell entities and within the IGCCCG classification, all MNSGCTs are classified as poor-prognosis tumors.

INTRACRANIAL GERM CELL TUMORS

Presentation

Ninety-five percent of intracranial germ cell tumors (ICGCTs) arise in the region of the third ventricle, along an axis from the suprasellar cistern to the pineal gland. The most common site involved is the pineal gland, followed closely by the suprasellar region. Rarely, these tumors present within the third ventricle, basal ganglia, thalamus, or other ventricular sites.[27] Germinomas (a term used for intracranial seminoma) preferentially involve the suprasellar region whereas nonseminomatous tumors tend to involve the pineal gland. Approximately 5 to 10% of cases will present in both locations, and these are usually germinomas.[28]

The ratio of ICGCTs in males to ICGCTs in females is 2:1,[28] and the majority of these tumors are diagnosed in children and young adults between the ages of 10 and 21 years. All of the types of histologies seen in GCTs are also found in ICGCTs. Approximately two-thirds of ICGCTs are germinomas, and the rest contain nonseminomatous elements.[27]

Clinical symptoms are based mostly on the size of the tumor and on its primary location. Pineal gland tumors most commonly present with symptoms due to increased intracranial pressure caused by obstruction of the third ventricle; these symptoms include hydrocephalus, Parinaud's syndrome (upward-gaze paralysis, pupillary areflexia, and lack of convergence), obtundation, pyramidal signs, and ataxia.[27,28] Tumors in the suprasellar region tend to present with visual field defects, diabetes insipidus, and other signs of hypothalamic-pituitary dysfunction and are more often asymptomatic when compared with pineal gland tumors.[27,28]

Neuroradiologic imaging, including both CT and magnetic resonance imaging (MRI), is extremely sensitive in detecting intracranial masses, but one cannot determine a tumor's histology by images alone (Figures 21–7 and 21–8). Although each type

of tumor histology has its own characteristic radiologic findings to some extent, it is still impossible to determine a histologic diagnosis on the basis of these studies alone.[90] Levels of cerebrospinal tumor markers, if high enough, are highly suggestive of the presence of a mixed GCT, but biopsy is often required to obtain a definitive diagnosis.

Prior to 1970, surgical biopsy and resection of these intracranial masses carried significant risks of morbidity and mortality. Because of these risks, many of these patients were treated empirically with 20 Gy of radiation. If the mass shrank, a presumptive diagnosis of germinoma was made.[91] With the devel-

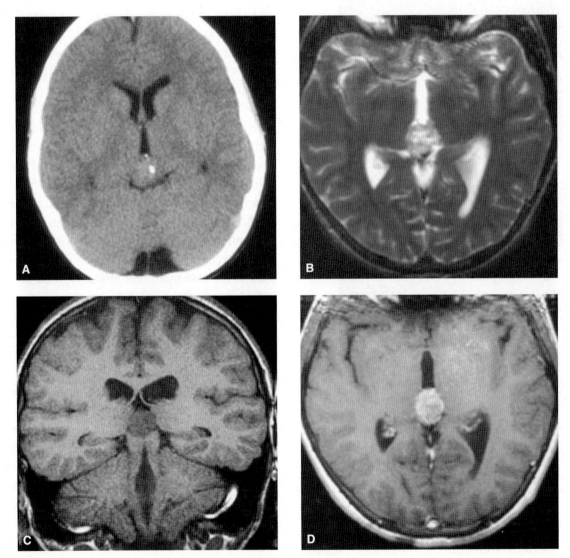

Figure 21–7. Pineal gland germinoma. *A,* Noncontrast computed tomography image shows an isodense mass in the region of the pineal gland. *B,.* Coronal T1-weighted magnetic resonance (MR) image shows a low-signal mass in the region of the pineal gland. *C,* Axial T2-weighted MR image shows a mixed signal within the pineal mass. *D,* Axial T1-weighted MR image after the administration of intravenous gadolinium shows bright enhancement of the pineal mass. (Courtesy of Dr. Kitt Shaffer, Dana-Farber Cancer Institute, Boston, MA.)

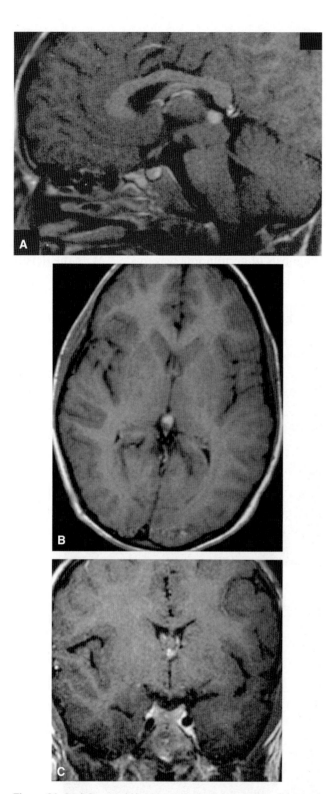

Figure 21–8. A 6-year-old boy presented with precocious puberty. *A and B,* Sagittal (*A*) and axial T1-weighted (*B*) magnetic resonance (MR) images after administration of intravenous gadolinium show a small enhancing lesion in the region of the pineal gland. *C,* Coronal T1-weighted MR image at the level of the foramen of Monro after administration of intravenous gadolinium demonstrates a heterogeneous signal within the mass. Examination of a biopsy specimen revealed a mixed germ cell tumor. (Courtesy of Dr. Kitt Shaffer, Dana-Farber Cancer Institute, Boston, MA.)

opment of new surgical techniques, biopsy of these masses can now be performed safely. Presently, the general consensus is that surgery is required for diagnosis unless a patient clearly has characteristic tumor marker elevations.[92]

Intracranial Germinoma

Given the exquisite sensitivity of intracranial germinomas (ICGs) to both radiation and chemotherapy, the role for radical surgery is questionable. Sawamura and colleagues retrospectively reviewed the experience of 29 patients who underwent surgery for germinoma and found that radical resection offered no benefit in either response rate or overall survival when compared to biopsy alone.[93] Because of the potential risks of radical surgery (including seeding of the cerebrospinal fluid), once a diagnosis of germinoma is confirmed, further surgical resection should not be undertaken.

Radiation therapy is considered the standard treatment of ICG. Based on small retrospective studies, 5-year survival rates ranging from 70 to 100% with radiation therapy alone have been reported.[94–97] It must be noted that many of the patients included in these studies did not have histologically confirmed germinomas.

Both the appropriate radiation dose and treatment volume remain topics of debate. When radiation is used as the sole treatment modality, total doses of 45 to 50 Gy are often used. Some authors feel that doses of < 40 Gy to the primary tumor result in an increased rate of failure[97] whereas others have found that reduced doses of radiation are just as effective.[98,99] Some advocate the use of partial-brain radiation. Recently, Haddock and colleagues found that the risk of postradiation relapse locally in the brain is significantly less if whole-brain or craniospinal radiation is given rather than partial-brain radiation.[97] The authors retrospectively reviewed 31 patients who had been treated since 1973 and found that the actuarial 5-year and 10-year disease-free survival rates were 29% and 0%, respectively, for those treated with partial-brain irradiation and 94% for those who received whole-brain or craniospinal irradiation.[97]

Approximately 10 to 15% of patients will have disseminated disease throughout the cerebrospinal axis.[27] It is universally accepted that these patients need radiation treatment to the entire craniospinal axis as well as to the primary tumor site. High rates of long-term disease-free survival can be achieved in this group of patients when the entire neuraxis is appropriately treated.[99] However, the role for prophylactic spinal irradiation (PSI) in patients in whom there is no evidence of disseminated disease is questionable. In the above-mentioned study by Haddock and colleagues, the spinal axis failure rate was 49% in patients treated with partial-brain irradiation and 0% for those who received either whole-brain or craniospinal irradiation.[97] The authors conclude that as long as an adequate cranial volume is treated, there appears to be no need for PSI. Other small and older retrospective studies also support the avoidance of PSI[91,95] but again are limited in that many patients in these studies did not have confirmed histologic diagnoses. Most authors agree that if MRI and cerebrospinal fluid cytology show no evidence of spinal metastases and if there are no clinical signs of neurologic compromise, PSI is not needed.

There is much concern over the toxicities of whole-brain and craniospinal irradiation. Both may lead to significant neuro-cognitive and endocrinologic sequelae, and may cause growth retardation in prepubescent children. Because of these concerns, attempts have been made to find alternative treatments, such as chemotherapy, that retain the efficacy of radiation therapy but decrease toxicity. The First International Central Nervous System Germ Cell Tumor Study assessed the role of chemotherapy as primary treatment of intracranial germ cell tumors. Forty-five patients with germinomas were included and were treated with four cycles of carboplatin, etoposide, and bleomycin. Overall, the complete response rate was 82%. However, 57% of those who achieved CR subsequently relapsed at a median of 18 months after diagnosis.[100] Many of these cases were then successfully salvaged with the use of chemoradiotherapy.[101] Compared with the results achieved with radiation therapy alone, primary chemotherapy as a single modality resulted in fewer and less durable CRs. As such, most practitioners agree that radiation therapy should be included as part of a patient's primary treatment for ICG. Conceivably, more durable CRs might be obtained with more optimal chemotherapy, such as a cisplatin-based regimen. However, it is difficult to address this question as studies pertaining to it have not been done.

Recently, chemotherapy has been used in combination with radiation therapy in an attempt to lower the radiation treatment doses needed. The Société Française d'Oncologie Pédiatrique (SFOP) conducted a multicenter prospective study using alternating courses of etoposide/carboplatin and etoposide/ifosfamide followed by 40 Gy of focal irradiation to the initial tumor volume in children with ICGs. Fifty-seven patients were treated from January 1990 to December 1996. After four cycles of chemotherapy, information on response to chemotherapy was reported for 38 patients; all responded (47% with CR and 53% with partial response), and the 3-year event-free survival was 96.4%.[92] Sawamura and colleagues treated 17 ICG patients with chemotherapy (cisplatin and etoposide with or without ifosfamide) followed by 24 Gy of local irradiation; 94% (16 of 17) were alive and free of recurrence at a median follow-up of 24 months.[102] A third study, by Buckner and colleagues, showed similar results.[103] The encouraging results of these trials confirm that it is feasible to use chemotherapy prior to radiation therapy, to reduce the dose and volume of radiation used.

The incidence of long-term complications (such as secondary leukemia) from chemotherapy cannot be accurately assessed at this time because the follow-up time is so short. It remains to be seen whether adding chemotherapy to smaller doses of radiation will reduce overall toxicity and improve quality of life or will merely replace radiation-induced toxicities with chemotherapy-induced toxicities.

In summary, patients with ICGs have an excellent overall prognosis, and the 5-year survival rate today exceeds 90%. Radiation therapy remains the "gold standard." However, many questions remain, such as (1) what is the optimum radiation volume and radiation dose to use? (2) is there a role for PSI? and (3) what is the role of chemotherapy? Additional randomized controlled trials are needed to define the most effective yet least toxic treatment for this highly curable tumor.

Intracranial Nonseminomatous GCTs

As with other types of nonseminomatous GCTs, intracranial nonseminomatous germ cell tumors

(ICNSGCTs) do not respond as well to treatment and carry a worse prognosis than that carried by ICGs. There are many fewer cases of ICNSGCT than there are cases of ICG, so much of what is published is based on a very small number of patients.

The role of surgery remains undefined. One study suggests that survival is dependent on the extent of surgical resection performed. In a retrospective study of 57 patients with ICNSGCTs, the 3-year survival rates were 0% for patients who underwent biopsies only, 32% for patients who had subtotal resections, and 73% for those who underwent gross total resection.[104] However, other studies have shown no correlation between extent of surgery and survival.[105] For patients with mature or immature teratoma, the treatment of choice is gross total resection as neither chemotherapy nor radiation therapy tends to be effective in these cases.

Unlike ICGs, ICNSGCTs do not respond very well to external beam radiotherapy. Prior to the advent of cisplatin-based chemotherapy, long-term disease-free survival rates for individuals with ICNSGCTs were less than 25%.[27] Dearnaley and colleagues published a report reviewing all of the patients who were treated for intracranial germ cell tumors at the Royal Marsden Hospital between 1962 and 1987. Of the 12 patients with ICNSGCTs, the 5- and 10-year overall actuarial survival rate was 18.2% for both 5- and 10-year survival rates.[96]

Chemotherapy, both alone and in combination with radiation therapy, appears to improve the rate of response and the duration of survival in these patients. In the First International Central Nervous System Germ Cell Tumor Study, 26 patients with ICNSGCTs were included.[100] Treatment consisted of four cycles of carboplatin, etoposide, and bleomycin. If CR was obtained, two additional cycles were administered. In those who did not achieve CR, either a second surgery or two additional cycles of chemotherapy intensified with cyclophosphamide were given. In the ICNSGCT patients, 81% achieved CR, and the estimated 2-year survival rate was 62% at a median follow-up of 35 months.[100] Recently, smaller series have used aggressive multimodality therapy, including combined chemotherapy, radical surgical resection, and irradiation, with promising results.[103,105–107] There has even been an attempt to incorporate high-dose chemother-

apy to treat this tumor. Tada and colleagues treated six ICNSGCT patients with consolidation high-dose cisplatin, etoposide, and ACNU followed by autologous stem cell rescue. All six patients were in complete remission following surgical resection, radiation therapy, and induction chemotherapy. There was no treatment-related mortality in this group, and all six patients are alive and disease free with a follow-up range of 9 to 95 months.[108]

Because of the rarity of ICNSCGTs, the available data are very limited, and it is difficult to conduct prospective trials with these patients. Historically, the prognosis for these patients was dismal. However, recent studies suggest that the prognosis can be improved with a combination of chemotherapy, radiation therapy, and surgical resection. Further clinical trials are necessary to better define the roles of each of these therapeutic modalities.

CONCLUSION

EGGCTs are a rare entity, representing 1 to 5% of all germ cell neoplasms. They occur predominantly in midline locations, including the retroperitoneum, mediastinum, sacrococcyx, and pineal gland region.

Regardless of the site of origin, all extragonadal seminomas have an overall excellent prognosis due to their exquisite sensitivity to both radiation therapy and cisplatin-based chemotherapy. Patients with mediastinal seminomas or intracranial germinomas have equivalent long-term survivals compared to patients with seminomas of gonadal origin. The current standard treatment of mediastinal seminoma consists of 3 to 4 cycles of a standard cisplatin-based chemotherapy regimen. The role for postchemotherapy surgery remains debatable. The current standard treatment of intracranial germinoma is radiation therapy. A role for the addition of chemotherapy is under investigation.

When compared to other GCTs, mediastinal non-seminomatous GCTs (MNSGCTs) appear to represent a distinct clinical and biologic entity. This group of tumors has a unique association with Klinefelter's syndrome and with the development of hematologic neoplasia. In addition, patients with these tumors respond less well to cisplatin-based chemotherapy when it is administered either as first-line therapy or in the salvage setting. Presently, the standard therapy for these patients is four cycles of cisplatin-based chemotherapy followed by aggressive surgical resection of any residual masses if the serum tumor markers normalize. The use of high-dose chemotherapy with stem cell support as salvage therapy has been very disappointing. Currently, the use of high-dose chemotherapy as first-line treatment in this group of patients is under investigation.

Given the significant differences between the treatment and prognosis of seminomas and the treatment and prognosis of nonseminomatous tumors, it is imperative that an adequate tissue sample is obtained from each patient so that an accurate histologic diagnosis can be made. Future research will be aimed at developing more effective treatments for patients with nonseminomatous tumors and at discovering treatments that minimize toxicity and maximize efficacy for patients with seminomas. Given the poor prognosis of both MNSGCT and ICNS-GCT, patients with these tumors should be considered for enrollment in clinical trials.

ACKNOWLEDGMENT

We greatly appreciate the contributions of Dr. Gilbert Brodsky, Dr. Jonathan A. Fletcher, Dr. Kitt Shaffer, Dr. Michael H. Weinstein, and Minou Modabber in helping to illustrate this chapter.

REFERENCES

1. Meares EM Jr, Briggs EM. Occult seminoma of the testis masquerading as primary extragonadal germinal neoplasms. Cancer 1972;30(1):300–6.
2. Azzopardi J, Mostofi FK, Theiss EA. Lesions of testes observed in certain patients with widespread choriocarcinoma and related tumors. The significance and genesis of hematoxylin staining bodies in human testis. Am J Pathol 1961;38:207–25.
3. Powell S, Hendry WF, Peckham MJ. Occult germ-cell testicular tumours. Br J Urol 1983;55(4):440–4.
4. Bohle A, Studer UE, Sonntag RW, et al. Primary or secondary extragonadal germ cell tumors? J Urol 1986;135(5):939–43.
5. Montague DK. Retroperitoneal germ cell tumors with no apparent testicular involvement. J Urol 1975;113(4):505–8.
6. Saltzman B, Pitts WR, Vaughan ED Jr. Extragonadal retroperitoneal germ cell tumors without apparent testicular involvement. A search for the source. Urology 1986;27(6):504–7.
7. Daugaard G, von der Maase H, Olsen J, et al. Carcinoma-in-situ testis in patients with assumed extragonadal germ-cell tumours. Lancet 1987;2(8558):528–30.
8. Hainsworth JD, Greco FA. Extragonadal germ cell tumors and unrecognized germ cell tumors. Semin Oncol 1992;19(2):119–27.
9. Kiffer JD, Sandeman TF. Primary malignant mediastinal germ cell tumors: a study of eleven cases and a review of the literature. Int J Radiat Oncol Biol Phys 1989;17(4):835–41.
10. Nichols CR, Fox EP. Extragonadal and pediatric germ cell tumors. Hematol Oncol Clin North Am 1991;5(6):1189–209.
11. Nichols CR, Heerema NA, Palmer C, et al. Klinefelter's syndrome associated with mediastinal germ cell neoplasms. J Clin Oncol 1987;5(8):1290–4.
12. Nichols CR, Roth BJ, Heerema N, et al. Hematologic neoplasia associated with primary mediastinal germ-cell tumors. N Engl J Med 1990;322(20):1425–9.
13. McAleer JJ, Nicholls J, Horwich A. Does extragonadal presentation impart a worse prognosis to abdominal germ-cell tumours? Eur J Cancer 1992;28A(4-5):825–8.
14. Toner GC, Geller NL, Lin SY, et al. Extragonadal and poor risk nonseminomatous germ cell tumors. Survival and prognostic features. Cancer 1991;67(8):2049–57.
15. International Germ Cell Consensus Classification: a prognostic factor-based staging system for metastatic germ cell cancers. International Germ Cell Cancer Collaborative Group. J Clin Oncol 1997;15(2):594–603.
16. Schlumberger HG. Teratoma of anterior mediastinum in a group of military age: study of 16 cases and review of theories of genesis. Arch Pathol Lab Med 1946;41:398–444.
17. Utz DC, Buscemi MF. Extragonadal testicular tumors. J Urol 1971;105(2):271–4.
18. de Bruin TW, Slater RM, Defferrari R, et al. Isochromosome 12p-positive pineal germ cell tumor. Cancer Res 1994;54(6):1542–4.
19. Atkin NB, Baker MC. Specific chromosome change, i(12p), in testicular tumours? Lancet 1982;2(8311):1349.
20. Suijkerbuijk RF, Looijenga L, de Jong B, et al. Verification of isochromosome 12p and identification of other chromosome 12 aberrations in gonadal and extragonadal human germ cell tumors by bicolor double fluorescence in situ hybridization. Cancer Genet Cytogenet 1992;63(1):8–16.
21. Tay HP, Bidair M, Shabaik A, et al. Primary yolk sac tumor of the prostate in a patient with Klinefelter's syndrome. J Urol 1995;153(3 Pt 2):1066–9.
22. Adachi Y, Rokujyo M, Kojima H, et al. Primary seminoma of the seminal vesicle: report of a case. J Urol 1991;146(3):857–9.
23. Steiner MS, Goldman SM, Smith DP, et al. Extragonadal germ cell tumor originating in iliac fossa. Urology 1993;41(6):575–8.
24. Hart WR. Primary endodermal sinus (yolk sac) tumor of the liver. First reported case. Cancer 1975;35(5):1453–8.
25. Raney RB Jr, Chatten J, Littman P, et al. Treatment strategies for infants with malignant sacrococcygeal teratoma. J Pediatr Surg 1981;16(4 Suppl 1):573–7.
26. Noseworthy J, Lack EE, Kozakewich HP, et al. Sacrococcygeal germ cell tumors in childhood: an updated experience with 118 patients. J Pediatr Surg 1981;16(3):358–64.

27. Jennings MT, Gelman R, Hochberg F. Intracranial germ-cell tumors: natural history and pathogenesis. J Neurosurg 1985;63(2):155–67.

28. Packer RJ, Cohen BH, Cooney K. Intracranial germ cell tumors. Oncologist 2000;5(4):312–20.

29. Lewis BD, Hurt RD, Payne WS, et al. Benign teratomas of the mediastinum. J Thorac Cardiovasc Surg 1983;86(5): 727–31.

30. Richardson RL, Schoumacher RA, Fer MF, et al. The unrecognized extragonadal germ cell cancer syndrome. Ann Intern Med 1981;94(2):181–6.

31. Greco FA, Vaughn WK, Hainsworth JD. Advanced poorly differentiated carcinoma of unknown primary site: recognition of a treatable syndrome. Ann Intern Med 1986;104(4):547–53.

32. Chaganti RS, Rodriguez E, Mathew S. Origin of adult male mediastinal germ-cell tumours. Lancet 1994;343(8906): 1130–2.

33. Motzer RJ, Rodriguez E, Reuter VE, et al. Genetic analysis as an aid in diagnosis for patients with midline carcinomas of uncertain histologies. J Natl Cancer Inst 1991; 83(5):341–6.

34. Dal Cin P, Drochmans A, Moerman P, et al. Isochromosome 12p in mediastinal germ cell tumor. Cancer Genet Cytogenet 1989;42(2):243–51.

35. Wychulis AR, Payne WS, Clagett OT, et al. Surgical treatment of mediastinal tumors: a 40 year experience. J Thorac Cardiovasc Surg 1971;62(3):379–92.

36. Knapp RH, Hurt RD, Payne WS, et al. Malignant germ cell tumors of the mediastinum. J Thorac Cardiovasc Surg 1985;89(1):82–9.

37. Cox JD. Primary malignant germinal tumors of the mediastinum. A study of 24 cases. Cancer 1975;36(3):1162–8.

38. Truong LD, Harris L, Mattioli C, et al. Endodermal sinus tumor of the mediastinum. A report of seven cases and review of the literature. Cancer 1986;58(3):730–9.

39. Clamon GH. Management of primary mediastinal seminoma. Chest 1983;83(2):263–7.

40. Klinefelter HFJ, Reifenstein ECJ, Albright F. Syndrome characterized by gynecomastia, aspermatogenesis without a-leydigism and increased excretion of follicle-stimulating hormone. J Clin Endocrinol 1942;2:615–27.

41. Dexeus FH, Logothetis CJ, Chong C, et al. Genetic abnormalities in men with germ cell tumors. J Urol 1988; 140(1):80–4.

42. Nichols CR, Hoffman R, Einhorn LH, et al. Hematologic malignancies associated with primary mediastinal germ-cell tumors. Ann Intern Med 1985;102(5):603–9.

43. Hartmann JT, Nichols CR, Droz JP, et al. Hematologic disorders associated with primary mediastinal nonseminomatous germ cell tumors. J Natl Cancer Inst 2000;92(1):54–61.

44. Garnick MB, Griffin JD. Idiopathic thrombocytopenia in association with extragonadal germ cell cancer. Ann Intern Med 1983;98(6):926–7.

45. Helman LJ, Ozols RF, Longo DL. Thrombocytopenia and extragonadal germ-cell neoplasm. Ann Intern Med 1984;101(2):280.

46. Ladanyi M, Samaniego F, Reuter VE, et al. Cytogenetic and immunohistochemical evidence for the germ cell origin of a subset of acute leukemias associated with mediastinal germ cell tumors. J Natl Cancer Inst 1990;82(3):221–7.

47. Orazi A, Neiman RS, Ulbright TM, et al. Hematopoietic precursor cells within the yolk sac tumor component are the source of secondary hematopoietic malignancies in patients with mediastinal germ cell tumors. Cancer 1993;71(12):3873–81.

48. Manivel C, Wick MR, Abenoza P, et al. The occurrence of sarcomatous components in primary mediastinal germ cell tumors. Am J Surg Pathol 1986;10(10):711–7.

49. Hartmann JT, Nichols CR, Droz JP, et al. The relative risk of second nongerminal malignancies in patients with extragonadal germ cell tumors. Cancer 2000;88(11):2629–35.

50. Fizazi K, Culine S, Droz JP, et al. Initial management of primary mediastinal seminoma: radiotherapy or cisplatin-based chemotherapy? Eur J Cancer 1998;34(3):347–52.

51. Mencel PJ, Motzer RJ, Mazumdar M, et al. Advanced seminoma: treatment results, survival, and prognostic factors in 142 patients. J Clin Oncol 1994;12(1):120–6.

52. Feun LG, Samson MK, Stephens RL. Vinblastine (VLB), bleomycin (BLEO), cis-diamminedichloroplatinum (DDP) in disseminated extragonadal germ cell tumors. A Southwest Oncology Group study. Cancer 1980;45(10):2543–9.

53. Hainsworth JD, Einhorn LH, Williams SD, et al. Advanced extragonadal germ-cell tumors. Successful treatment with combination chemotherapy. Ann Intern Med 1982;97(1): 7–11.

54. Jain KK, Bosl GJ, Bains MS, et al. The treatment of extragonadal seminoma. J Clin Oncol 1984;2(7):820–7.

55. Logothetis CJ, Samuels ML, Selig DE, et al. Chemotherapy of extragonadal germ cell tumors. J Clin Oncol 1985; 3(3):316–25.

56. Israel A, Bosl GJ, Golbey RB, et al. The results of chemotherapy for extragonadal germ-cell tumors in the cisplatin era: the Memorial Sloan-Kettering Cancer Center experience (1975 to 1982). J Clin Oncol 1985;3(8):1073–8.

57. Loehrer PJ Sr, Birch R, Williams SD, et al. Chemotherapy of metastatic seminoma: the Southeastern Cancer Study Group experience. J Clin Oncol 1987;5(8):1212–20.

58. Motzer RJ, Bosl GJ, Geller NL, et al. Advanced seminoma: the role of chemotherapy and adjunctive surgery. Ann Intern Med 1988;108(4):513–8.

59. Bukowski RM, Wolf M, Kulander BG, et al. Alternating combination chemotherapy in patients with extragonadal germ cell tumors. A Southwest Oncology Group study. Cancer 1993;71(8):2631–8.

60. Childs WJ, Goldstraw P, Nicholls JE, et al. Primary malignant mediastinal germ cell tumours: improved prognosis with platinum-based chemotherapy and surgery. Br J Cancer 1993;67(5):1098–101.

61. Goss PE, Schwertfeger L, Blackstein ME, et al. Extragonadal germ cell tumors. A 14-year Toronto experience. Cancer 1994;73(7):1971–9.

62. Gerl A, Clemm C, Lamerz R, et al. Cisplatin-based chemotherapy of primary extragonadal germ cell tumors. A single institution experience. Cancer 1996;77(3):526–32.

63. Bokemeyer C, Droz JP, Horwich A, et al. Extragonadal seminoma: an international multicenter analysis of prognostic factors and long term treatment outcome. Cancer 2001;91(7):1394–401.

64. Friedman EL, Garnick MB, Stomper PC, et al. Therapeutic guidelines and results in advanced seminoma. J Clin Oncol 1985;3(10):1325–32.

65. Motzer R, Bosl G, Heelan R, et al. Residual mass: an indication for further therapy in patients with advanced seminoma following systemic chemotherapy. J Clin Oncol 1987;5(7):1064–70.

66. Puc HS, Heelan R, Mazumdar M, et al. Management of residual mass in advanced seminoma: results and recommendations from the Memorial Sloan-Kettering Cancer Center. J Clin Oncol 1996;14(2):454–60.

67. Schultz SM, Einhorn LH, Conces DJ Jr, et al. Management of postchemotherapy residual mass in patients with advanced seminoma: Indiana University experience. J Clin Oncol 1989;7(10):1497–503.

68. Horwich A, Dearnaley DP, A'Hern R, et al. The activity of single-agent carboplatin in advanced seminoma. Eur J Cancer 1992;28A(8-9):1307–10.

69. Horwich A, Paluchowska B, Norman A, et al. Residual mass following chemotherapy of seminoma. Ann Oncol 1997; 8(1):37–40.

70. Bokemeyer C, Nichols CR, Droz JP, et al. Extragonadal germ cell tumors of the mediastinum and retroperitoneum: results from an international analysis. J Clin Oncol 2002; 20(7):1864–73.

71. Economou JS, Trump DL, Holmes EC, et al. Management of primary germ cell tumors of the mediastinum. J Thorac Cardiovasc Surg 1982;83(5):643–9.

72. Vogelzang NJ, Raghavan D, Anderson RW, et al. Mediastinal nonseminomatous germ cell tumors: the role of combined modality therapy. Ann Thorac Surg 1982;33(4):333–9.

73. Kay PH, Wells FC, Goldstraw P. A multidisciplinary approach to primary nonseminomatous germ cell tumors of the mediastinum. Ann Thorac Surg 1987;44(6):578–82.

74. Nichols CR, Saxman S, Williams SD, et al. Primary mediastinal nonseminomatous germ cell tumors. A modern single institution experience. Cancer 1990;65(7):1641–6.

75. Dulmet EM, Macchiarini P, Suc B, et al. Germ cell tumors of the mediastinum. A 30-year experience. Cancer 1993; 72(6):1894–901.

76. Fizazi K, Culine S, Droz JP, et al. Primary mediastinal nonseminomatous germ cell tumors: results of modern therapy including cisplatin-based chemotherapy. J Clin Oncol 1998;16(2):725–32.

77. Motzer RJ, Mazumdar M, Gulati SC, et al. Phase II trial of high-dose carboplatin and etoposide with autologous bone marrow transplantation in first-line therapy for patients with poor-risk germ cell tumors. J Natl Cancer Inst 1993;85(22):1828–35.

78. Motzer RJ, Mazumdar M, Bajorin DF, et al. High-dose carboplatin, etoposide, and cyclophosphamide with autologous bone marrow transplantation in first-line therapy for patients with poor-risk germ cell tumors. J Clin Oncol 1997;15(7):2546–52.

79. Bosl GJ, Geller NL, Vogelzang NJ, et al. Alternating cycles of etoposide plus cisplatin and VAB-6 in the treatment of poor-risk patients with germ cell tumors. J Clin Oncol 1987;5(3):436–40.

80. Decatris MP, Wilkinson PM, Welch RS, et al. High-dose chemotherapy and autologous haematopoietic support in poor risk non-seminomatous germ-cell tumours: an effective first-line therapy with minimal toxicity. Ann Oncol 2000;11(4):427–34.

81. Vuky J, Bains M, Bacik J, et al. Role of postchemotherapy adjunctive surgery in the management of patients with nonseminoma arising from the mediastinum. J Clin Oncol 2001;19(3):682–8.

82. Motzer RJ, Geller NL, Tan CC, et al. Salvage chemotherapy for patients with germ cell tumors. The Memorial Sloan-Kettering Cancer Center experience (1979-1989). Cancer 1991;67(5):1305–10.

83. Saxman SB, Nichols CR, Einhorn LH. Salvage chemotherapy in patients with extragonadal nonseminomatous germ cell tumors: the Indiana University experience. J Clin Oncol 1994;12(7):1390–3.

84. Broun ER, Nichols CR, Einhorn LH, et al. Salvage therapy with high-dose chemotherapy and autologous bone marrow support in the treatment of primary nonseminomatous mediastinal germ cell tumors. Cancer 1991;68(7):1513–5.

85. Lotz JP, Andre T, Donsimoni R, et al. High dose chemotherapy with ifosfamide, carboplatin, and etoposide combined with autologous bone marrow transplantation for the treatment of poor-prognosis germ cell tumors and metastatic trophoblastic disease in adults. Cancer 1995;75(3):874–85.

86. Motzer RJ, Mazumdar M, Sheinfeld J, et al. Sequential dose-intensive paclitaxel, ifosfamide, carboplatin, and etoposide salvage therapy for germ cell tumor patients. J Clin Oncol 2000;18(6):1173–80.

87. Beyer J, Kramar A, Mandanas R, et al. High-dose chemotherapy as salvage treatment in germ cell tumors: a multivariate analysis of prognostic variables. J Clin Oncol 1996; 14(10):2638–45.

88. Nichols CR, Catalano PJ, Crawford ED, et al. Randomized comparison of cisplatin and etoposide and either bleomycin or ifosfamide in treatment of advanced disseminated germ cell tumors: an Eastern Cooperative Oncology Group, Southwest Oncology Group, and Cancer and Leukemia Group B study. J Clin Oncol 1998; 16(4):1287–93.

89. Birch R, Williams S, Cone A, et al. Prognostic factors for favorable outcome in disseminated germ cell tumors. J Clin Oncol 1986;4(3):400–7.

90. Fujimaki T, Matsutani M, Funada N, et al. CT and MRI features of intracranial germ cell tumors. J Neurooncol 1994;19(3):217–26.

91. Wara WM, Jenkin RD, Evans A, et al. Tumors of the pineal and suprasellar region: Childrens Cancer Study Group treatment results 1960–1975: a report from Childrens Cancer Study Group. Cancer 1979;43(2):698–701.

92. Bouffet E, Baranzelli MC, Patte C, et al. Combined treatment modality for intracranial germinomas: results of a multicentre SFOP experience. Societe Francaise d'Oncologie Pediatrique. Br J Cancer 1999;79(7-8):1199–204.

93. Sawamura Y, de Tribolet N, Ishii N, et al. Management of primary intracranial germinomas: diagnostic surgery or radical resection? J Neurosurg 1997;87(2):262–6.

94. Shibamoto Y, Abe M, Yamashita J, et al. Treatment results of intracranial germinoma as a function of the irradiated volume. Int J Radiat Oncol Biol Phys 1988;15(2):285–90.

95. Linstadt D, Wara WM, Edwards MS, et al. Radiotherapy of primary intracranial germinomas: the case against routine craniospinal irradiation. Int J Radiat Oncol Biol Phys 1988;15(2):291–7.

96. Dearnaley DP, A'Hern RP, Whittaker S, et al. Pineal and CNS germ cell tumors: Royal Marsden Hospital experience 1962-1987. Int J Radiat Oncol Biol Phys 1990;18(4):773–81.

97. Haddock MG, Schild SE, Scheithauer BW, et al. Radiation therapy for histologically confirmed primary central nervous system germinoma. Int J Radiat Oncol Biol Phys 1997;38(5):915–23.

98. Bamberg M, Kortmann RD, Calaminus G, et al. Radiation therapy for intracranial germinoma: results of the German cooperative prospective trials MAKEI 83/86/89. J Clin Oncol 1999;17(8):2585–92.

99. Hardenbergh PH, Golden J, Billet A, et al. Intracranial germinoma: the case for lower dose radiation therapy. Int J Radiat Oncol Biol Phys 1997;39(2):419–26.

100. Balmaceda C, Heller G, Rosenblum M, et al. Chemotherapy without irradiation—a novel approach for newly diagnosed CNS germ cell tumors: results of an international cooperative trial. The First International Central Nervous System Germ Cell Tumor Study. J Clin Oncol 1996;14(11):2908–15.

101. Merchant TE, Davis BJ, Sheldon JM, et al. Radiation therapy for relapsed CNS germinoma after primary chemotherapy. J Clin Oncol 1998;16(1):204–9.

102. Sawamura Y, Shirato H, Ikeda J, et al. Induction chemotherapy followed by reduced-volume radiation therapy for newly diagnosed central nervous system germinoma. J Neurosurg 1998;88(1):66–72.

103. Buckner JC, Peethambaram PP, Smithson WA, et al. Phase II trial of primary chemotherapy followed by reduced-dose radiation for CNS germ cell tumors. J Clin Oncol 1999;17(3):933–40.

104. Schild SE, Haddock MG, Scheithauer BW, et al. Nongerminomatous germ cell tumors of the brain. Int J Radiat Oncol Biol Phys 1996;36(3):557–63.

105. Robertson PL, DaRosso RC, Allen JC. Improved prognosis of intracranial non-germinoma germ cell tumors with multimodality therapy. J Neurooncol 1997;32(1):71–80.

106. Knappe UJ, Bentele K, Horstmann M, et al. Treatment and long-term outcome of pineal nongerminomatous germ cell tumors. Pediatr Neurosurg 1998;28(5):241–5.

107. Herrmann HD, Westphal M, Winkler K, et al. Treatment of nongerminomatous germ-cell tumors of the pineal region. Neurosurgery 1994;34(3):524–9.

108. Tada T, Takizawa T, Nakazato F, et al. Treatment of intracranial nongerminomatous germ-cell tumor by high-dose chemotherapy and autologous stem-cell rescue. J Neurooncol 1999;44(1):71–6.

22

Pediatric Germ Cell Tumors

MARCIO H. MALOGOLOWKIN, MD
HECTOR L. MONFORTE, MD
ARZU KOVANLIKAYA, MD
STUART E. SIEGEL, MD

INCIDENCE

Germ cell tumors are uncommon in children and are presumed to originate from primordial germ cells. These tumors occur at varied primary sites, both gonadal and extragonadal, and manifest in a variety of different histologies. Germ cell tumors represent approximately 7% of all cases of cancer in children and in adolescents less than 20 years of age. They account for 2 to 4% of all cancers in children younger than 15 years of age and approximately 14% for those between 15 and 19 years of age.[1,2] The incidence for males younger than 20 years of age is slightly higher than that for females (12 vs 11.1 per million).

Unlike in adults, the incidence of extragonadal tumors exceeds that of gonadal tumors in children less than 15 years of age. However, in the population aged 15 to 19 years, the testicles and ovaries are the most common sites of tumor origin. Several large pediatric series show that approximately 59% of these tumors originate in extragonadal sites and that 41% originate in the gonads.[3]

The incidence of germ cell tumors peaks at two distinct ages. The first peak occurs before 2 years of age, reflecting the high incidence of sacrococcygeal tumors.[4,5] The incidence then declines to very low levels before increasing again between 8 and 12 years of age for females and between 11 and 14 years of age for males. This later peak represents an increase in the incidence of both testicular and ovarian tumors in older children and adolescents.

According to data from the National Cancer Institute's Surveillance, Epidemiology and End Results (SEER) program, the incidence of germ cell tumors has increased from 3.4 per million between 1975 and 1979 to 5.1 per million between 1990 and 1995 for children less than 15 years of age. For infants and younger children, the increase resulted from higher rates of extragonadal tumors. However, this increase must be interpreted with caution since it may represent the improved recognition by pathologists of malignant tissue foci in mature and immature sacrococcygeal teratomas.[6,7] For adolescent males, the increase in incidence is attributed to central nervous system (CNS) and testicular germ cell tumors whereas for females, it is attributable to ovarian germ cell tumors.

The incidence of germ cell tumors is lower in black children (7 per million) when compared with white children (10.7 per million). This difference reflects the lower rate of gonadal germ cell tumors among black children than among white children (3.2 per million and 12.3 per million, respectively).

To understand more clearly the incidence patterns of germ cell tumors in children, one needs to recognize that the biologic behavior of these tumors in infancy and early childhood is significantly different from their biologic behavior in older children and adolescents.[1,4,8] Table 22–1 describes the clinical behavior and biologic characteristics of pediatric germ cell tumors. In the pediatric population, approximately 56% of all germ cell tumors are mature teratomas, 11% have immature tissues with

Table 22–1. BIOLOGIC CHARACTERISTICS OF PEDIATRIC GERM CELL TUMORS				
Site	Age Group	Histology	Symptoms	Characteristics
Extragonadal Sacrococcygeal	Infants, young children	50–65% mature, 5–15% immature, 10–30% malignant	Presence of mass, constipation, urinary symptoms, lower back pain, lower-extremity weakness/sensory disturbance	About 35% of all GCTs; more common in females. Degree of externally visible mass and intrapelvic extension varies, as well as frequency of malignant histology. Rate of malignant tumors is higher in older patients with larger intrapelvic component.
Mediastinal	Adolescents, older children	60% mature, 40% malignant	Cough, wheezing, shortness of breath, superior vena cava syndrome	About 4% of all GCTs; more common in males; frequently associated with Klinefelter's syndrome
Intracranial	Adolescents, older children	50–60% germinomas, 20–40% nongerminomas	Visual disturbances, diabetes insipidus, hypopituitarism, Parinaud's syndrome	About 5% of all GCTs; more common in males; found most frequently in pineal and suprasellar region, rarely intraspinal.
Other	Infants, young children	50–60% mature, 20–30% immature, 10–20% malignant	Presence of a mass, pain, abdominal distention	About 10% of all GCTs. Sites are head and neck, abdominal wall, retroperitoneum, vagina
Gonadal Ovary	Early teens, adolescents, young adults	50–65% mature, 5–10% immature, 15–30% malignant	Abdominal pain (chronic, acute), abdominal mass, amenorrhea, vaginal bleeding	About 25% of all GCTs; unusual in children younger than 2 years: associated with gonadal dysgenesis
Testicle	Infants, adolescents, young adults	15–20% mature, 80–85% malignant	Nontender mass, pain with torsion, abdominal distention; precocious puberty	About 15% of all GCTs; associated with cryptorchidism and gonadal dysgenesis; may be associated with hydrocele

GCT = germ cell tumor.

or without mature elements, and 33% contain frankly malignant components.[4,5,9]

TUMOR MARKERS

Serum tumor markers are very useful in the diagnosis and management of germ cell tumors. They have been used in predicting response and determining the presence of residual disease or progressive tumor. α-Fetoprotein (AFP) and beta–human chorionic gonadotropin (β-hCG) are the most valuable tumor markers. Different types of germ cell tumors secrete these markers: yolk sac tumors produce AFP, choriocarcinoma produces β-hCG, embryonal carcinomas can elaborate small amounts of AFP and/or β-hCG, and germinomas can have detectable levels

of β-hCG. The serum half-life of AFP is 5 to 7 days in children older than 1 year; that of β-hCG is 24 to 36 hours.[10] AFP levels are normally high at birth and slowly decline to adult levels by 8 months of age. Because the half-life of AFP has a wide variability at different ages during the first year of life, the decay of serum AFP levels with therapy in infants less than 1 year of age is difficult to interpret. Normal ranges have been established to address this problem.[11]

PATHOLOGY

The pathologist plays an integral and crucial role in every step of the management of patients with germ cell tumors. Precise, definitive, and conclusive determination of tumor morphology and integration of gross and microscopic findings as well as clinical, physical, imaging, and serologic findings are all key elements in the adequate diagnosis and management of children and adolescents with these tumors.

This review of the pathology of germ cell tumors in children and adolescents is abbreviated since an excellent general oversight precedes this chapter (see Chapter 4). It is meant to complement that overview with a discussion of the pathology of the most important aspects of these conditions from a pediatric perspective.

Intraoperative Consultation

The initial assessment of patients with neoplastic disease should include, in all cases, intraoperative consultation by the surgical pathologist. Whether at initial biopsy, tumor resection, or follow-up, valuable information for diagnosis, management, and prognosis can be obtained by gross assessment and/or microscopic examination by frozen section. In most instances, frozen-section examination on biopsy specimens allows the recognition of germ cell neoplasia and the exclusion of potential differential diagnoses. This practice is of great importance with patients in whom malignancy is not initially suspected, namely, (1) patients with ovarian or testicular tumors felt to represent teratomas and who are undergoing tumorectomy only, (2) patients presenting with metastatic tumors of an unrecognized gonadal or extragonadal primary, (3) adolescent patients with retroperitoneal metastases of an unrecognized occult or regressed testicular primary, and (4) patients in whom germ cell neoplasia has not been specifically considered as a possible diagnosis. When a working or definitive diagnosis of germ cell malignancy is established, then specific prognostic and therapeutic issues can be addressed at the same operative time.

Surgical Pathology Specimen

Great responsibility falls upon the surgical pathologist for the careful, methodical, and structured evaluation of germ cell tumor specimens. Important decisions are made at the time of gross or frozen-section assessment that affect the establishment of all relevant criteria for adequate patient staging and management.

If the specimen is from a biopsy, depending on the working diagnosis, anticipating the required immunohistochemical stains or group protocol compliance requirements makes the need for additional unstained slides likely. Thus, it is essential to preserve as much of the biopsy specimen as possible. Frozen-section blocks should remain frozen as their usefulness for light microscopy is suboptimal unless a particular specimen is the only documentation of the neoplasm. Archived frozen tissue can be used later, for molecular genetic studies. Thus far, cytogenetics has a limited role in the diagnosis and prognosis of germ cell tumors, but the advent of new modalities within conventional cytogenetics and fluorescence in situ hybridization makes tissue imprints or cell culture a possible ancillary study in clinical practice in the near future.

Resection specimens should be received intact from the operating room, in a fresh state and (when applicable) adequately oriented. Orchiectomy specimens should be enclosed by the tunica vaginalis. Specific issues of handling and sampling have been the subject of thorough reviews.[12,13] For all sites in general, the more complex the gross appearance of a tumor is, the more likely it is to harbor subtle or conspicuous malignant germ cell components; this is particularly true for teratomas. Extensive sampling and careful microscopic examination is the best way to avoid under-diagnosing malignancy. Of particular importance is the fact that the subtle presence of endodermal sinus tumor has wide spectrum of morphologic features, in many instances mimicking immature somatic teratoma elements, particularly enteric or glandular structures.

Surgical margins should be marked with ink. Various colored inks can be used for large tumors, depending on orientation. The initial sectioning of specimens must be in a plane that offers the most acceptable and informative results. Examples of informative planes of section are planes where anatomic structures that are present with or within the specimen are exposed and planes that lead to anatomic correlation with imaging studies. A knowledge of current classification schemes and staging criteria on the part of the surgical pathologist is of paramount importance and usually dictates the features that are to be documented and the components of the diagnosis, descriptions, and comments in the final surgical pathology report.

Postchemotherapy resection of residual tumor specimens from all sites may show confluent necrosis of tumor, isolated pleomorphic cells, fibrosis, maturation into mature-appearing teratomatous structures with atypia, or (more often) a combination of all of these elements. It is important not to interpret these teratoid elements as indolent structures since they have matured under therapy; they also may retain dedifferentiation or metastatic potential.

GONADAL GERM CELL TUMORS

Testicular Tumors

In infants and prepubertal children, the vast majority of testicular germ cell tumors consist of pure endodermal sinus tumor and, less frequently, teratoma.[14] Testicular germ cell tumors in adolescent patients represent a rare but broader spectrum similar to that seen in adults. It behooves the pediatric surgical pathologist to maintain a broad differential diagnosis either in primary or in metastatic sites for these neoplasms.

Teratoma

The gross appearance of mature testicular teratomas in infancy and early childhood is that of a predominantly cystic mass, confined to the testicle and, by definition, devoid of any incipient or overt germ cell malignancy (Figure 22–1, *A*). Ultrasonographic evidence or gross appearance of macroscopic cysts and mesenchymal derivatives including bone and cartilage suggest the diagnosis (see Figure 22–1, *B*). Many of these tumors are diagnosed by ultrasonography and are amenable to intraoperative tumorectomy.[15]

In postpubertal patients, there is a greater incidence of teratomas that show coexisting intratubular germ cell neoplasia or overt malignant germ cell components. When careful gross evaluation discloses solid or hemorrhagic areas, these should be extensively sampled (Figure 22–2). Microscopic examination of tumors in infants and young children usually reveals maturity in all embryonic layers.

Pure testicular teratomas in postpubertal patients are clearly a different neoplasm. While they may show "mature" elements, they may also exhibit some degree of cytologic atypia. This feature should be interpreted with great caution since it correlates with the plasticity of so-called mature teratomas, which may recur or metastasize as overt malignancies. This concept of not equating maturity in postpubertal teratomas or postchemotherapy maturation with benignity is valid for all sites.[16]

Endodermal Sinus Tumor (Yolk Sac Carcinoma)

In its pure form, the endodermal sinus tumor (EST) is the most common germ cell tumor of the testicle

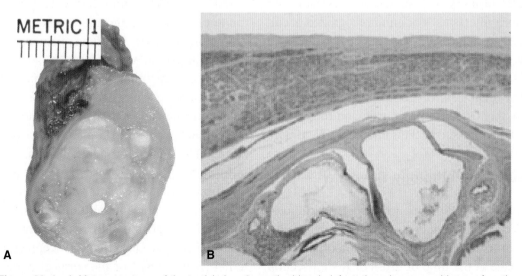

Figure 22–1. *A*, Mature teratoma of the testicle in a 6-month-old male infant; there is gross evidence of cartilage, and cysts are distinctly circumscribed from the adjacent testicle stroma. *B*, Microscopic appearance of circumscribed mature teratoma in testicle; all germlines are represented (original magnification × 20).

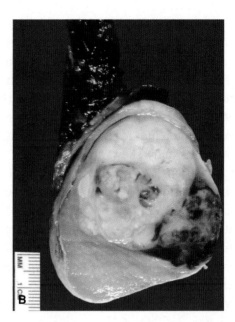

Figure 22–2. *A*, Heterogeneous testicular mass composed of teratoma and other solid tumor tissue, with evidence of hemorrhage and necrosis. *B*, Malignant mixed germ cell tumor of the testicle (seminoma, embryonal carcinoma, and choriocarcinoma and immature teratoma).

in children and can also present in the neonatal period.[14] This tumor represents more than 60% of testicular germ cell tumors in childhood.[17,18] The typical gross features are those of a firm granular homogeneous tumor replacing the testicular parenchyma (Figure 22–3) These tumors show no defined borders, unlike pure seminoma, which has the gross appearance of a more compact tumor with glossy surfaces. The presence of necrosis or hemorrhage should be carefully noted and sampled. Sectioning of the spermatic cord and evaluation of its margin, separately identified, are necessary for staging purposes. Samples of any grossly identifiable residual testicular parenchyma and the relationship of the tumor to the tunica albuginea, testicular hilus, and epididymis should be examined. Pure EST has a bewildering spectrum of microscopic features. It is important to recognize all patterns, particularly solid and parietal morphologic patterns, so that misinterpretation as seminoma or embryonal carcinoma does not result in an over-diagnosis of mixed malignant germ cell neoplasm.[16] The evaluation of the extent of tumor and the presence or absence of vascular invasion is important in assessing the biologic potential of the tumor.

Intratubular Germ Cell Neoplasia-Unclassified

Cryptorchid testicles are at increased risk of development of malignancy, even after orchiopexy.

Malignant disease seldom occurs before puberty.[19] Some authors advocate close follow-up and screening and biopsy at age 18 to 20 years for men with a history of cryptorchidism.[20]

Several reports document the absence of intratubular germ cell neoplasia-unclassified (ITGCNU) adjacent to testicular germ cell neoplasia in infancy and childhood (Figure 22–4).[21,22] A large study from the Pediatric Oncology Group and Children's Cancer Study Group specifically addressed the issue of

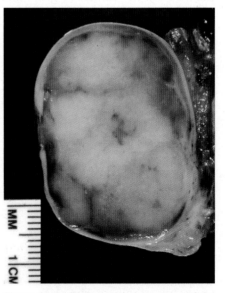

Figure 22–3. Endodermal sinus tumor of the infantile testis. Note the homogeneous granular appearance of tumor replacing the testicle.

ITGCN in prepubertal children. These authors concluded that the atypical cells seen in the seminiferous tubules adjacent to tumors are proliferative and not neoplastic. They advocate the use of immunohistochemistry for placental alkaline phosphatase (PLAP) and *c-kit* proto-oncogene in children older than 1 year who have cryptorchid testes or gonadal dysgenesis.[23,24] Another study shows that even when PLAP-positive germ cells were identified with features of ITGCNU in postorchiopexy biopsy specimens, no testicular cancer developed after 20 years' follow-up in 15 patients.[25] The finding of ITGCN adjacent to testicular tumors in postpubertal patients or ITGCN in patients with retroperitoneal or mediastinal malignant germ cell tumors warrants close follow-up to exclude the early development of invasive testicular germ cell tumor (Figure 22–5). ITGCN may also spread into the rete testis, mimicking invasive germ cell tumor.[26]

Seminoma, Embryonal Carcinoma, Choriocarcinoma, and Regressed Testicular Primary

Examples of pure seminoma or embryonal carcinoma of the testicle are only rarely reported in the pediatric age population[27] but are seen relatively frequently in adolescence and early adulthood.[28] Seminoma has a homogeneous, smooth, and lobulated appearance and bulges from the cut surface of the testis (Figure 22–6); its distinctive gross and micro-

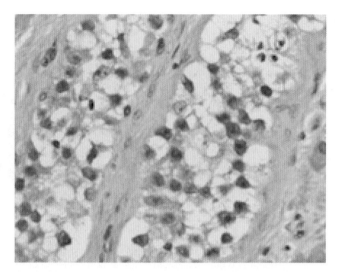

Figure 22–5. Intratubular germ cell neoplasia-unclassified (ITGCNU) and intratubular seminoma in an adolescent testicle, adjacent to a malignant germ cell tumor (original magnification ×100).

scopic morphology allows its recognition during intraoperative consultation with frozen section, even in extragonadal sites (Figure 22–7). Seminoma, embryonal carcinoma, and choriocarcinoma are all seen as a component of mixed malignant germ cell neoplasia at primary or metastatic sites. It is important to remember that intermediate trophoblast in seminomatous tumors may be responsible for subtle elevations of β-hCG.[29]

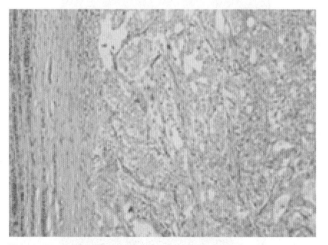

Figure 22–4. Absent intratubular germ cell neoplasia adjacent to an endodermal sinus tumor of an infant testicle; tubules are lined by Sertoli's cells and isolated germ cells devoid of atypia or solid growth (original magnification ×400).

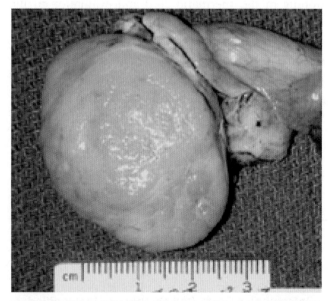

Figure 22–6. A testicle with a homogeneous-appearing tumor with a lobulated outline and a bulging surface. This is the typical gross appearance of seminoma (germinoma, when extragonadal). (Courtesy of Dr. D. Schofield, CHLA Pathology.)

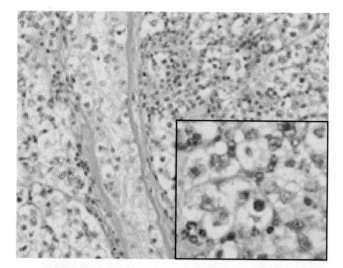

Figure 22–7. Photomicrograph of a seminoma, showing a conspicuous lymphocytic infiltrate amidst monotonous cells of seminoma; note the entrapped seminiferous tubule showing intratubular germ cell neoplasia-unclassified (ITGCNU). The insert shows seminoma tumor cells at a higher magnification. The patient is a 16-year-old male. These features may be compared with those of dysgerminoma and germinoma (Figures 22–11, B and 22–12, B) (original magnification ×20; insert, original magnification ×400).

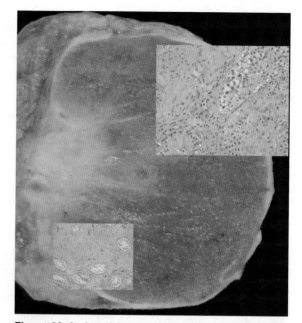

Figure 22–8. An adolescent male testicle with regressed primary germ cell tumor; the patient had metastasis to the retroperitoneum, which was the primary manifestation. Note focal area of scar. The insert shows scar and tubules; the peripheral section shows intratubular germ cell neoplasia-unclassified (left lower insert, original magnification ×40; upper right insert ×200).

With male adolescent patients with retroperitoneal or metastatic germ cell tumors, it is imperative that testicular ultrasonography be performed to evaluate the possibility of an occult or partially regressed testicular primary (Figure 22–8).[30] Choriocarcinoma in infancy and childhood has been reported as an extragonadal neoplasm (see below).

Ovarian Tumors

Teratoma with Malignant Germ Cell Neoplasm

Overall, the ovary is the second most common site (after the sacrococcygeal region) for teratomas with malignant germ cell neoplasm in children.[31] These tumors are also frequent in the first and second decades of life. They are classified as mature, immature (as graded on the amount of immature tissue present), and malignant.

Mature teratoma of the ovary tends to be cystic and is readily recognizable by imaging studies (Figure 22–9, A); grossly, they are frequently solidified, with apparent sebaceous and hair material, keratinous debris, cartilage, mature convoluted neural elements and bones, cartilage, or teeth structures (see Figure 22–9, B and C). Many of these tumors are amenable to tumorectomy with sparing of the underlying ovarian stroma.

Immature teratomas tend to be more complex and show extensive glandular and solid areas. As in all other sites, any area of necrosis or hemorrhage warrants careful sectioning (Figure 22–10, A and B). Surgical surfaces and margins should be addressed and inked when appropriate; of more critical importance is any evidence of adherent omental or regional pelvic soft tissues invaded by neoplasm.

Microscopic examination shows limited representation of ectoderm, neuroectoderm, and mesodermal derivatives, with few endodermal components in the more mature examples. Immature teratomas show a spectacular spectrum of tissues and structures from all somatic layers in different degrees of maturation and organization. Clear examples of zoning and migration mechanisms such as hematopoietic elements within bone marrow and liver or ganglion cells within organized gut myenteric zones are frequently observed (see Figure 22–10, C and D).

Careful examination of solid areas may disclose subtle or overt elements of EST or other malignancy.

Figure 22–9. Bilateral ovarian teratoma. *A,* Transverse computed tomography images at two different levels reveal a large complex cystic mass with calcifications and fat component. The ovaries cannot be identified separately, and the uterus is deviated to the left. *B,* Gross specimen example of mature teratoma, grade 0, showing lobular cerebriform tissue; microscopically, this corresponded to mature central nervous system tissues. *C,* Hair, fat, sebaceous material, and cartilage are recognizable in this grade 0 mature teratoma of the ovary.

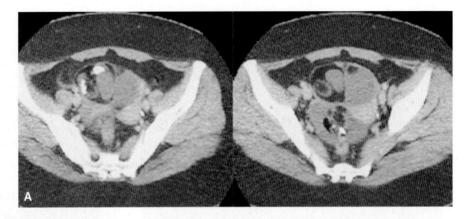

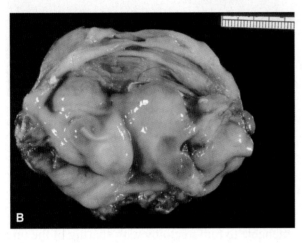

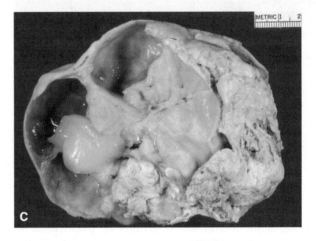

Many of these are in contiguity with true enteric somatic formations, so cytologic and architectural criteria are of paramount importance (Figure 22–11, A and B).[32] Gliomatosis peritonei and more unusual forms of nodal gliomatosis usually have a favorable outcome as long as they remain mature (grade 0).

Dysgerminoma

Dysgerminoma is the most common malignant germ cell tumor of the ovary. Seventy-five percent of patients with dysgerminoma are within the ages of 10 and 30 years.[33]

On gross assesment, these are large, fleshy, and firm tumors with smooth surfaces (Figure 22–12, A); usually, no hemorrhage or necrosis is seen within the tumor.

Microscopically, dysgerminomas are strikingly uniform tumors composed of large polygonal cells with abundant cytoplasm (see Figure 22–12, B). Frequently, the tumor is punctuated by a conspicuous lymphocytic and/or granulomatous reaction,

occasional giant cells or intermediate trophoblastic cells. Rarely, pseudoglandular spaces may be identified, inviting confusion with EST or sex cord–stromal tumors of the ovary.[34] True transformation of dysgerminoma into EST is now a well-recognized phenomenon.[35,36]

Endodermal Sinus Tumor

A review of 71 patients with EST, the second most frequent malignant germ cell tumor of the ovary, demonstrated an age range of 14 months to 45 years, the median age being 19 years.[37] Typically, EST is associated with highly elevated serum AFP levels.

Gross assessment shows large solid-to-cystic tumors with a mucoid appearance and focal areas of hemorrhage and necrosis. Microscopic features range from the typical polyvesicular appearance, with papillary formations and rare Schiller-Duval bodies, to solid, parietal, hepatoid, endometrioid, and enteric patterns of differentiation (Figure 22–13, A and C).

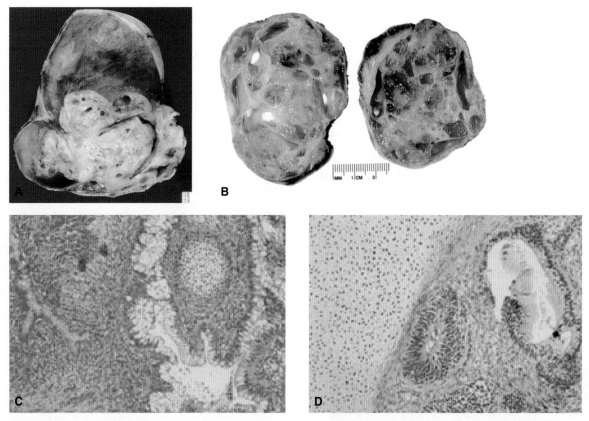

Figure 22–10. Examples of immature teratoma of the ovary, showing increasing complexity of gross characteristics. *A* shows solid cystic tumor (grade 2); *B* shows predominantly small cysts and solid areas (grade 3). *C* and *D* show microscopic appearance of immature teratoma areas (immaturity of endoderm-, mesoderm-, and ectoderm-derived elements. Original magnification ×200).

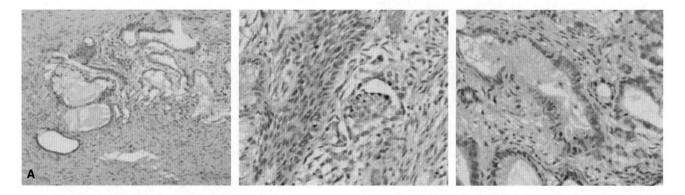

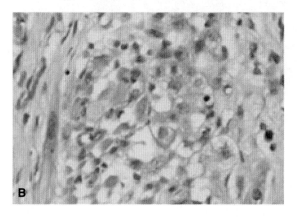

Figure 22–11. Photomicrographs of subtle examples of malignant germ cell neoplasms. *A*, Endodermal sinus tumor amidst teratomatous elements, some in contiguity with enteric-type structures (mucin-producing lining). *B*, Subtle component of germinoma amidst skeletal muscle in extragonadal teratoma. (Original magnifications: *A*, ×100; *B*, ×200; *C*, ×400.)

Malignant Mixed Germ Cell Tumor

Malignant mixed germ cell tumors constitute a significant number of ovarian malignancies representing 50% of ovarian germ cell tumors and 30% of malignant germ cell tumors in children and adolescents.[13] They are usually composed of teratoid elements with dysgerminoma, EST, embryonal carcinoma, and choriocarcinoma in different proportions (Figure 22–14). Documentation of all tumor types determines the types of chemotherapeutic agents to be used.

Gonadoblastoma and Germ Cell Tumors in Intersex Syndromes

The term "gonadoblastoma" refers to a tumorlike lesion that recapitulates the development of gonads by incorporating germ cell clusters or cords and sex cord–stromal components surrounding these elements. It usually originates in dysgenetic gonads in genotypes in which a Y chromosome exists. Most gonadoblastomas arise in streak gonads, a testis, or an indeterminate gonad. Rare instances in which they arise in the ovaries of normal genotypic females

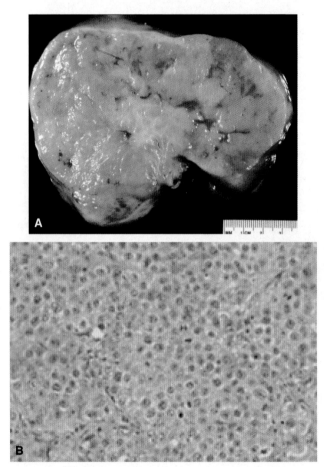

Figure 22–12. *A*, Dysgerminoma of the ovary, a large lobulated firm tumor with a homogeneous appearance; note the absence of teratoid elements, necrosis, or hemorrhage. *B*, Photomicrograph showing the typical appearance of dysgerminoma or germinoma, large cells with big nuclei and distinct nucleoli (original magnification ×200).

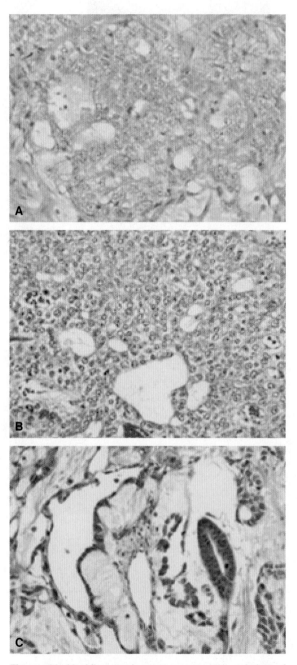

Figure 22–13. Microscopic appearance and variation of endodermal sinus tumor. *A*, Conventional polyvesicular areas with α-fetoprotein globules. *B*, Solid and pseudoglandular morphology. *C*, Myxoid vesicular and enteric differentiation. (Original magnification ×200.)

Figure 22–14. Mixed germ cell neoplasm of the ovary, with grossly recognizable teratomatous elements and overwhelming replacement by solid growth of endodermal sinus tumor extending beyond the ovary and into adherent omental fat (left edge).

are increasingly recognized.[38] They may be bilateral[39] and may be associated with androgen secretion and ataxia-telangiectasia. Microscopically, they are characterized by discrete aggregates of germ cells and immature cells reminiscent of Sertoli's cells and granulosa cells as cords or Call-Exner formations, defined by connective-tissue stroma. There are frequent calcifications (Figure 22–15). The most common malignancy arising in gonadoblastomas is germinoma, but teratoma, EST, and all other germ cell malignancies have been described.[39,40]

The intersex syndromes make up a complex and difficult group of disorders with distinctive clinicopathologic implications for diagnosis and treatment. This group includes the following: defects in testicular differentiation, such as (1) Denys-Drash syndrome; (2) the syndrome of Wilms' tumor, aniridia, genitourinary abnormalities or gonadoblastoma, and mental retardation (WAGR syndrome); (3) camptomelic syndrome; (4) XY pure gonadal dysgenesis; and (5) XY gonadal agenesis; defects in testicular hormone synthesis, such as Leydig cell aplasia, congenital adrenal hyperplasia (various forms), persistent müllerian duct syndrome; and defects in androgen action, such as 5α-reductase deficiency and androgen insensitivity syndromes.[41] Androgen insensitivity syndrome has been associated with the development of ITGCN, germinoma, other germ cell tumors, and Sertoli cell lesions.[41] Persistent müllerian duct syndrome has been associated with a broad spectrum of germ cell tumors. Gonadal dysgenesis is associated with gonadoblastoma, ITCGN, and stromal tumors.[43]

Germ Cell Tumors with Embryonal Neoplasia or Somatic Differentiated Malignancy

Occasional development of somatic malignancy in the form of embryonic tumors or adult-type sarcoma has been found in gonadal and extragonadal sites (Figure 22–16).[44–46] The recognition and confirmation of such malignancy may require immunohistochemistry and other ancillary techniques. Modification of treatment modalities is warranted, depending on the type of tumor.[48]

EXTRAGONADAL GERM CELL TUMORS

Sacrococcygeal Teratoma

The sacrococcygeal region is the most common location for germ cell neoplasms of childhood, accounting for 40% of all germ cell tumors and for up to 78% of those in extragonadal locations.[13] The largest single compilation, of 371 cases by survey, divides these tumors into four types, depending on topography: type I, which is predominantly external with a minor sacral component; type II, a dumbbell-shaped tumor with nearly equal internal and external components; type

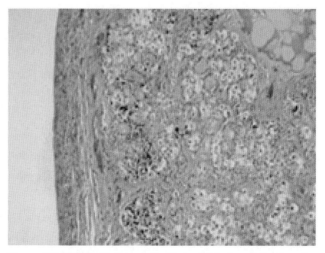

Figure 22–15. Photomicrograph of gonadoblastoma, showing distinctive characteristics of germ cell clusters defined by cords of sex cord–stromal cells and calcification (original magnification ×40).

III, of predominantly internal components; and type IV, an internalized pre-sacral tumor with no external evidence of disease.[49] Seventy-four percent of the patients were female; 90% were delivered at term. The majority of these tumors are recognized at birth (Figure 22–17). Early complete resection with coccygectomy is the key to successful management, along with close follow-up. The presence of malignancy increases dramatically when diagnosis is delayed beyond 2 months of age. The vast majority of those tumors that are recognized and resected in early infancy exhibit a benign behavior; a small percentage have malignant components at the time of diagnosis at this age. These tumors, like all other teratomas, may be cystic, cystic and solid, or predominantly solid. Malignant components (usually EST) may be present in all types but primarily in type IV tumors; this may be a subtle finding, requiring extensive sampling and careful analysis (Figure 22–18).[6] The fact that these are complex and heterogeneous tumors makes surgical margins difficult to evaluate for clearance. Extensive gross sampling for microscopy of solid areas and of margins are the best policy. It is therefore important to examine the entire gross specimen carefully, and to examine histologically as many solid areas of the tumor and margins as is feasible.

Mediastinal Tumors

Germ cell tumors always figure in the differential diagnosis of mediastinal neoplasms at any age. From the larger series, we can conclude that the whole spectrum of teratoma and germ cell malignancy occurs in the mediastinum of children and adolescents.[50–53] Approximately half of mediastinal germ cell tumors are represented by pure teratomatous tumors, and the other half is represented by malignant mixed germ cell tumors that may include teratomatous tumors. Mature teratomas usually behave in a benign fashion, as reported in two large series.[31,52] At least one series suggests a relationship between age greater than 15 years and recurrences with immature teratoma, emphasizing the careful exclusion of subtle components of EST and other germ cell tumor malignancy.[52]

These tumors are usually bulky with extensive areas of fibrosis, degenerative changes, and necrosis (Figure 22–19); aggressive tumor may invade other mediastinal organs or structures and even the lungs (Figure 22–20).

Retroperitoneal Tumors

The retroperitoneum is an unusual site for germ cell tumors. Germ cell tumors in the retroperitoneum represent 4% of all gonadal and extragonadal germ cell tumors in this pediatric age group. In respect to age, they occur in a wide range of individuals, from newborns to persons in the sixth decade of life. Approximately 7% of these tumors are malignant.[54,55] The spectrum of gross and microscopic morphology is very similar to that seen in all other sites. Most arise in

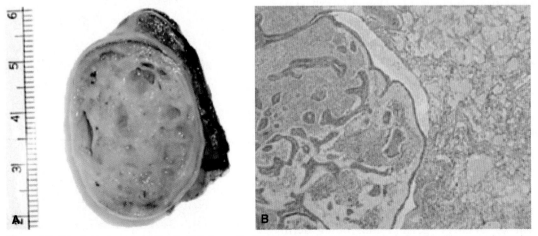

Figure 22–16. *A*, Replacement of a testicle by multicystic teratoid-appearing tumor confined to the parenchyma by intact tunica. *B*, Microscopic appearance, showing endodermal sinus tumor (*right*) and embryonic tumor reminiscent of blastoma with immature teratoma (*left*) (original magnification ×40).

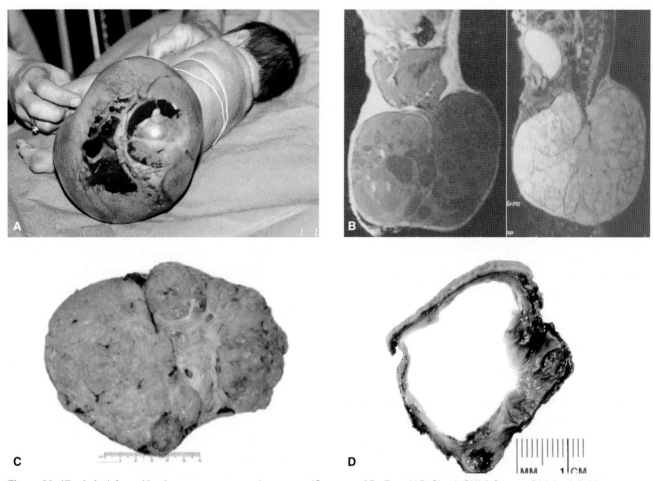

Figure 22–17. *A,* An infant with a large sacrococcygeal teratoma. (Courtesy of Dr. Donald B. Shaul, CHLA Surgery Division.) *B,* Magnetic resonance images of a patient with sacrococcygeal teratoma (T1-weighted image at left, T2-weighted image at right); sagittal views demonstrate a large mass extending from the sacrococcygeal region. Within the mass, there are necrotic regions that are hypointense on T1-weighted images and hyperintense on T2-weighted images. The hyperintense foci on T1-weighted images most likely represent calcifications. The sacrum is dysplastic. *C,* Gross cut surface of the same sacrococcygeal teratoma after resection shows complex multicystic areas and solid uniform firm areas; these solid areas contained grade 3 immature teratoma and endodermal sinus tumor elements throughout. *D,* Another example of mature cystic sacrococcygeal teratoma; this was composed of all mature tissues and was filled with seromucinous fluid.

the retroperitoneal soft tissue, but rarely, adrenal and renal teratomas are encountered (Figure 22–21). This is a frequent location for metastatic testicular germ cell tumors (Figure 22–22). Biopsies should be performed on unresectable tumors, and measurements of serum markers should be obtained, in an attempt to find malignant elements that will require systemic therapy to shrink the mass and make it resectable.

Tumors of the Viscera and Other Sites

Teratomatous neoplasms have been reported in virtually every anatomic region and organ. Visceral teratomas vary, from incipient small lesions to massive disfiguring tumors.[55] Most visceral mature ter-

atomas of childhood behave in a benign fashion and prognosis is linked to resectability.[31] One distinctive condition that frequently becomes manifest in the liver or lungs but that may affect other organs (including the brain) is infantile choriocarcinoma syndrome.[56] Originally described by Witzleben,[57] it includes presentation within the first days to weeks of life, anemia and/or pallor, hepatomegaly, melena, hematuria, occasional precocious puberty, and consistently elevated levels of β-hCG. When choriocarcinoma occurs in an infant as multiple visceral or cutaneous lesions, it usually represents metastases from gestational trophoblastic disease.[58] The placental primary may be diminutive.[56] Prompt recognition and treatment represent the only hope for survival.

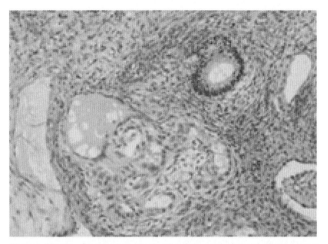

Figure 22–18. Photomicrograph of subtle endodermal sinus tumor in sacrococcygeal teratoma. Areas like these can be misinterpreted as immature somatic gut or glandular tissues. Note the nuclear atypicality and lack of distinct organization into a teratomatous structure (original magnification ×100).

ASSOCIATED ANOMALIES AND SYNDROMES

Other than the intersex disorders discussed above, a variety of paraneoplastic manifestations of endocrine dysfunction have been associated with germ cell tumors.[34] Klinefelter's syndrome remains the most common association of mediastinal and intracranial germ cell tumors.[59–63] Among the most intriguing associations of germ cell tumors of the mediastinum and other sites are associations with myelodysplastic disorders, non-lymphoblastic leukemias, and mast cell disease.[64]

CYTOGENETICS AND MOLECULAR BIOLOGY

Recent investigations into the cytogenetics and molecular genetics of pediatric germ cell neoplasia have disclosed interesting and challenging findings as the foundation for future research endeavors.[65–67] Two broad groups of germ cell tumors must be recognized in the pediatric population: (1) those that present perinatally and in early childhood and (2) those that form a group analogous to adult germ cell tumors and that present in the postpubertal period.

Cytogenetic studies of EST in infancy and early childhood have not shown any evidence of i(12p) or any other abnormality of chromosome 12.[68] Perlman and colleagues found various abnormalities involving chromosome arms 1p, 6q, and 3q[68]; further analysis identified deletion of 1p36 in these tumors in 80% of cases.[69]

The largest study of the cytogenetics of germ cell tumors of childhood[65] attempted to categorize germ cell tumors into six groups by sex, age, site, and histology, based on similar cytogenetic alterations: (1) gonadal and extragonadal teratomas of infants and young children, (2) malignant germ cell tumors of infants and young children, (3) ovarian teratomas, (4) malignant ovarian germ cell tumors, (5) pubertal and postpubertal testicular tumors, and (6) extragonadal tumors of older and adolescent boys. The investigators concluded that the pathogenesis of germ cell tumors in prepubertal males is different

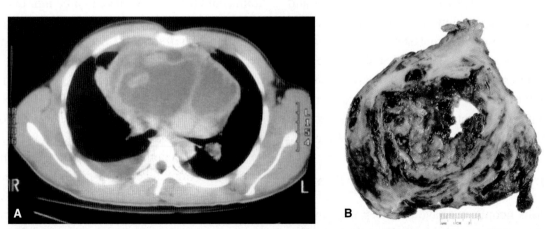

Figure 22–19. *A*, Axial computed tomography scan of chest shows a large multicystic anterior and middle mediastinum mass. There is also a right-sided pleural effusion. *B*, Cut surface of the mediastinal tumor shows fibrosis, cystic degeneration, hemorrhage, and necrosis; despite its worrisome appearance, this was a mature teratoma in a 13-year-old male. The pathogenesis of degenerative changes are ischemia and the presence of pancreatic tissue.

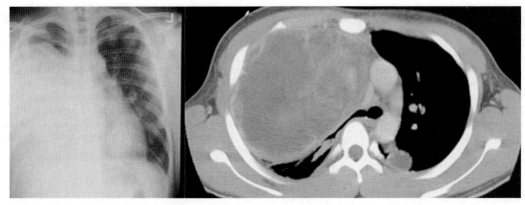

Figure 22–20. Chest radiograph (*left*) and computed tomography scan (*right*) of malignant mediastinal germ cell tumor involving the midthoracic anterior mediastinum, with metastatic nodules in the lung parenchyma.

than that in postpubertal and adult males. Another large series of pediatric mediastinal nonseminomatous germ cell tumors in children and adolescents identified differences in genetic profiles in patients older versus younger than 8 years of age.[66] Schneider and colleagues[66] analyzed 35 mediastinal germ cell tumors by comparative genomic hybridization and found that all of the pure teratomas had normal profiles. Malignant germ cell tumors in children younger than 8 years had no isochromosome 12 but showed gains of 1q, 3, and 20q and loss of 1p, 4q, and 6q. Patients older than 8 years commonly showed gains in chromosome 12p. Various candidate genes have been identified.[70]

Thus far, the clinical and morphologic complexity of germ cell tumors extends into the molecular characteristics as well. Future ancillary studies to probe for loss and overexpression of genes appear justified.

STAGING

Currently, the staging system used for childhood germ cell tumors differs from the ones used for adults tumors (Table 22–2). This system is based on the known differences between the respective natural histories of these tumors in children and in adults. The system adopted by the Children's Oncology Group trials includes the incorporation of the serial determination of serum tumor markers for all sites. For testicular tumors, this system uses tumor marker status as an alternative for findings of retroperitoneal lymph node dissection and up-stages those patients who undergo transscrotal surgery. In the case of ovarian tumors, the presence of gliomatosis peritonei (nodule of mature teratomatous tissue) does not change the stage of the tumor whereas the finding of positive peritoneal washings up-stages the tumor.

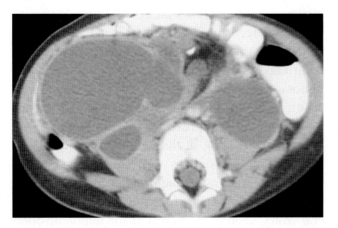

Figure 22–21. Retroperitoneal teratoma. Transverse computed tomography shows a large septated multicystic mass with calcifications and fat tissue within.

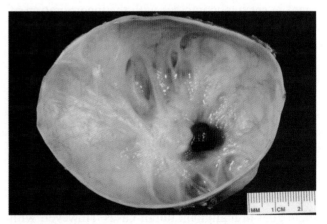

Figure 22–22. A rare example of an adrenal cystic mature teratoma, with residual adrenal cortex at upper right. The wall was composed predominantly of connective tissue and mature neuroglia.

Stage	Ovarian Tumors	Testicular Tumors	Extragonadal Tumors
	Table 22–2. CHILDREN'S ONCOLOGY GROUP STAGING OF PEDIATRIC GERM CELL TUMORS		
I	Limited to ovary or ovaries; peritoneal washings negative for malignant cells; no clinical, radiographic, or histologic evidence of disease beyond ovaries; tumor markers normal after appropriate postsurgical half-life decline. Bilaterality does not change the stage. The presence of gliomatosis peritonei does not up-stage patient.	Limited to the testes; completely resected by high inguinal orchiectomy; no clinical, radiographic, or histologic evidence of disease beyond the testes; tumor markers normal after appropriate postsurgical half-life decline. Patients with normal or unknown markers at diagnosis must have negative ipsilateral retroperitoneal node dissection. Bilaterality does not change the stage.	Complete resection at any site (coccygectomy for sacrococcygeal site); no clinical, radiographic, or histologic evidence of disease beyond primary site; tumor markers normal after appropriate postsurgical half-life decline.
II	Microscopic residual or positive lymph nodes (< 2 cm by pathologist's measurement); peritoneal washings negative for malignant cells; tumor markers positive or negative. The presence of gliomatosis peritonei does not up-stage patient.	Transscrotal orchiectomy; microscopic disease in scrotum or high in spermatic cord (≤ 5 cm from proximal end); retroperitoneal lymph node involvement (< 2 cm by pathologist's measurement); increased tumor markers after appropriate half-life.	Microscopic residual is present. Lymph nodes are negative. Tumor markers are positive or negative.
III	Lymph node with malignant metastatic nodule (> 2 cm by pathologist's measurement); gross residual or biopsy only; contiguous visceral involvement (omentum, intestine, bladder); peritoneal washings positive for malignant cells; tumor markers positive or negative.	Retroperitoneal lymph node involvement; no visceral or extra-abdominal involvement (< 2 cm by pathologist's measurement).	Gross residual disease or biopsy only. Lymph nodes are negative or positive. Tumor markers are negative or positive.
IV	Distant metastases, including liver.	Distant metastases, including liver.	Distant metastases, including liver.

TREATMENT AND OUTCOMES

Based on data from the National Cancer Institute's SEER program, the overall 5-year survival rate for patients with germ cell tumors has increased since 1975. Currently, more than 75% of all children and adolescents with germ cell tumors will be alive and free of disease 5 years after diagnosis. This improvement in survival coincides with the incorporation of cisplatin into therapeutic combinations for the treatment of these tumors.

Surgery

In the case of mature and immature teratomas, an aggressive up-front nonmutilating surgical approach is indicated in order to avoid tumor recurrence or malignant transformation.

Complete surgical resection is always the ultimate goal in malignant tumor cases. However, with the improvements seen with chemotherapy, the use of an initial mutilating surgical procedure or debulking surgery is no longer indicated in the management of childhood germ cell tumors. Some authors feel that in some cases of sacrococcygeal and mediastinal tumors, a diagnosis can be established by imaging study and by the demonstration of elevated tumor markers, thus avoiding the need for an initial biopsy or up-front tumor resection.[1,71] Germ cell tumors arising in the sacrococcyx ultimately require the excision of the entire coccyx to avoid the recurrence of tumor, since incomplete surgery is associated with a higher risk of tumor recurrence.[71,72] During surgery of ovarian germ cell tumors, peritoneal washings and a specimen of ascitic fluid should be submitted for cytologic evaluation since the presence of malignant cells changes the staging of the tumor. Also, pelvic and retroperitoneal nodes, as well as any other tissue containing nodules suspicious for tumor involvement, should be sampled. In addition, the contralateral ovary should be inspected for tumor involvement. Testicular germ cell tumors are better approached by an inguinal excision with resection of the extra-abdominal spermatic cord, testicle, and adnexa en bloc. Transscrotal biopsy should be avoided since it is associated with a higher risk of recurrence. Patients who have trans-scrotal excision are immediately up-staged.

Some patients with malignant tumors may have a persistent residual mass after initial chemotherapy. This residual tissue may contain persistent malignant elements or may be composed of fibrosis of malignant teratoma. Therefore, second-look surgery may assist in achieving a complete response or in documenting the response to therapy.

Radiotherapy

Due to the concerns about long-term sequelae secondary to irradiation and about the efficacy of platinum-based regimens in the treatment of germ cell tumors in children, radiotherapy currently plays a limited role in the treatment of these tumors. Although intracranial germinomas have traditionally been treated with radiotherapy, recent studies have reported success in managing these tumors with carboplatin-based chemotherapeutic regimens.[73] However, since germ cell tumors are sensitive to radiation, irradiation may be helpful for the treatment of nonresectable residual disease after chemotherapy or salvage therapy or as palliative care.

Chemotherapy

Mature and Immature Teratomas

The treatment for mature teratomas is surgical resection alone; chemotherapy plays no role in the treatment of this neoplasm. However, the presence of any malignant element within these tumors requires that the tumor be treated according to the guidelines for malignant germ cell tumors. The role of chemotherapy in the treatment of immature teratomas remains controversial. In a retrospective study of females with ovarian immature teratomas treated with surgery only, the relapse rate was 70% for patients with grade 3 immature teratomas.[74] This result led to the recommendation of adjuvant chemotherapy for patients with grade 3 immature teratomas. The same relationship has not been found in immature teratomas that occur at other sites.[75]

The concern that pediatric patients with these tumors may behave differently than adults, coupled with the availability of sensitive imaging technology, more consistent pathologic interpretation, and reliable tumor markers, led to a combined Children's Cancer Group and Pediatric Oncology Group protocol designed to address this issue.[75] The hypothesis of the study was that pediatric patients with immature teratomas would have a 3-year event-free survival rate of greater than 85% when treated with surgery alone and followed up by close observation. A total of 73 patients younger than 21 years of age were entered on this study; 51 had gonadal tumors, and 22 had extragonadal tumors. Although the study was designed to exclude patients with the presence of malignant elements, upon central review, 23 patients were found to have microscopic foci of yolk sac tumor or primitive neuroectodermal tumor. The overall 3-year event-free survival rate for these patients was 93%. Only five patients (four with a presence of malignant foci) experienced disease recurrence 4 to 7 months after diagnosis. Four of the five patients who experienced recurrence are alive and without evidence of disease after platinum-based chemotherapy. This result suggests that complete surgical excision is effective treatment for children with immature teratomas with or without malignant elements.

Malignant Germ Cell Tumors

Prior to the development of platinum-based chemotherapeutic regimens, the vincristine/actinomycin D/cyclophosphamide (VAC) regimen was used; this regimen demonstrated efficacy for the treatment of localized germ cell tumors.[4,76] Although no randomized studies in children have been done, historical comparison suggests that outcome is superior with platinum-based regimens.[3] Recent regimens with a higher dose of cyclophosphamide or ifosfamide have been shown to be adequate for some pediatric germ cell tumors; however, the late sequelae of these agents (ie, infertility and cardiotoxicity) are unacceptable when high rates of cure can be achieved with platinum-based chemotherapy.

Based on the success seen in the adult trials with cisplatin-based regimens for the treatment of adult testicular germ cell tumors,[77] platinum compounds were incorporated for the treatment of children with germ cell tumors.[76,78–81] Although these studies did not use a uniform chemotherapeutic regimen, they demonstrated the substantial activity and the curative potential of platinum-based chemotherapy against pediatric germ cell tumors. As a result of these studies, the combination of cisplatin, vinblastine, and bleomycin (PVB) or that of bleomycin, etoposide, and cisplatin (BEP) became the standard treatment of pediatric germ cell tumors.

From 1990 to 1996, the Children's Cancer Group and the Pediatric Oncology Group conducted the first collaborative intergroup study for children with germ cell tumors. Patients were treated on two protocols (INT-0106 and INT-0097), according to a risk stratification schema based on primary site and stage.

Seventy-three patients with immature teratomas (ITs) and 65 patients with stage I testicular malignant germ cell tumors were treated with surgery alone, followed by close observation. Chemotherapy with BEP was given only to those patients who experienced recurrence of malignant tumor. Five patients with ITs and 11 patients with stage I testicular tumors had recurrence of malignant tumor and went on to receive chemotherapy. The 2-year event-free survival rate was 93% for patients with ITs and 82% for patients with stage I testicular tumors.[74,81] However, 4 of the 5 patients with ITs and all of the patients with stage I testicular tumors were salvaged with platinum-based chemotherapy, for a 2-year survival rate of 98% and 100%, respectively. All other patients with localized gonadal disease—stage I ovarian tumors ($n = 42$), stage II ovarian tumors ($n = 16$), and stage II testicular tumors ($n = 19$)—were treated with adjuvant chemotherapy consisting of four courses of BEP. These patients achieved a 2-year survival rate greater than 95%.[82]

Patients with stages III to IV gonadal and stages I to IV nongonadal malignant germ cell tumors were considered at higher risk for treatment failure; therefore, they were randomized to receive either 5 days of standard-dose cisplatin (BEP, 20 mg/m²/d) or high-dose cisplatin (high-dose BEP, 40 mg/m²/d). All patients also received etoposide (100 mg/m²/d for 5 days) and bleomycin (15 mg/m²/d for 1 day). The 2-year event-free survival rate was greater than 90% for patients with stages III to IV gonadal tumors and greater than 85% for those with stages I to II extragonadal tumors. No statistical difference was seen between the two doses of cisplatin for these patients.[83]

Children with stages III to IV extragonadal tumors had a 2-year event-free survival rate of 74% with standard-dose cisplatin, compared with a 2-year event-free survival rate of 84% when high-dose cisplatin was used.[84] However, patients treated with the high-dose cisplatin regimen experienced a higher rate of grade III to IV ototoxicity when compared to patients treated with the standard-dose cisplatin regimen (76% vs 19%, respectively).[85]

Analysis of the results of this collaborative intergroup study identified three distinct risk subgroups of children with germ cell tumors, based on tumor site and stage (Table 22–3). Based on these results, investigators from the Children's Oncology Group are developing therapeutic trials to improve or maintain the clinical outcomes and minimize toxicity for children with germ cell tumors. Low-risk patients will be treated with surgical resection, followed by monitoring for disease recurrence. Chemotherapy will be used only for patients whose tumor marker levels fail to return to normal or who have recurrent disease. Intermediate-risk patients will be treated with a compressed standard BEP regimen (3 days vs 5 days) aimed at minimizing toxicity and the costs associated with treatment. Children with advanced-stage (III–IV) extragonadal germ cell tumors had a

Table 22–3. RISK GROUPS OF PEDIATRIC GERM CELL TUMORS, ACCORDING TO TUMOR SITE AND STAGE					
	Tumor Type or Stage				
Site	**IT**	**Stage I**	**Stage II**	**Stage III**	**Stage IV**
Gonadal	LR	LR	IR	IR	IR
Extragonadal	LR	LR	IR	HR	HR

HR = high risk; IR = intermediate risk; IT = immature teratoma; LR = low risk.

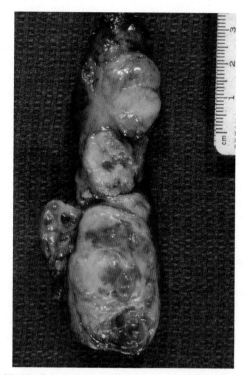

Figure 22–23. Resected retroperitoneal germ cell tumor after therapy, showing residual solid neoplastic areas and teratomatous elements. The patient had a testicular primary.

better event-free survival with more intensive therapy, at the expense of a much higher rate of ototoxicity. Therefore, future studies for these high-risk patients will explore ways to maintain the intensity of therapy while reducing long-term ototoxicity.

Undoubtedly, long-term toxicity secondary to therapy is a major concern for these children with germ cell tumors, who now have an excellent overall prognosis. Due to a high rate of pulmonary toxicity when bleomycin was given weekly and because of a high rate of deaths due to pneumopathy in the early United Kingdom Children's Cancer Study Group (UKCCSG) studies,[79] most pediatric trials give this drug once every 3 weeks. A recent Brazilian study achieved very encouraging results in patients with extragonadal tumors treated with just cisplatin and etoposide.[86] Due to concerns with long-term ototoxicity and renal toxicity, the second UKCCSG study on the treatment of children with extracranial germ cell tumors substituted carboplatin for cisplatin.[87] This approach greatly reduced the occurrence of both toxicities when compared with other reports, and the overall and event-free survivals were comparable with those obtained by other groups.

The role of drugs such as ifosfamide, doxorubicin, and topotecan continues to be unclear, as is the role of very-high-dose combination chemotherapy followed by stem cell rescue. These approaches should be further explored only in a research setting.[88]

In conclusion, continuing studies on the molecular and genetic factors of pediatric germ cell tumors will further help to determine the differences between adult and pediatric germ cell tumors, identify new prognostic factors, and identify potential new therapeutic targets. Furthermore, the development of studies to determine less toxic chemotherapy regimens, the role of chemoprotective agents, and the intensification of therapy for patients who are at a high-risk of tumor recurrence will require large national or international collaborative groups.

REFERENCES

1. Pinkerton CR. Malignant germ cell tumours in childhood. Eur J Cancer 1997;33:895–901; discussion 901–2.
2. Berstein L, Smith MA, Liu L, Deapen D, Friedman DL. Germ cell, trophoblastic and other gonadal neoplasms. Cancer incidence and survival among children and adolescents: United States SEER Program 1975-1995. Bethesda: National Cancer Institute; 1999. p. 125–37.
3. Giller R, Ablin A. Germ cell tumors. II. Clinical features and treatment. In: Pochedly C, editor. Neoplastic diseases of childhood. Vol. 2. Chur, Switzerland: Harwood Academic Publishers; 1994. p. 849–80.
4. Malogolowkin MH, Mahour GH, Krailo M, Ortega JA. Germ cell tumors in infancy and childhood: a 45-year experience. Pediatr Pathol 1990;10:231–41.
5. Hawkins EP. Germ cell tumors. Am J Clin Pathol 1998; 109:S82–8.
6. Hawkins E, Isaacs H, Cushing B, Rogers P. Occult malignancy in neonatal sacrococygeal teratomas. A report from a combined Pediatric Oncology Group and Children's Cancer Group study. Am J Pediatr Hematol Oncol 1993;15:406–9.
7. Gilcrease MZ, Brandt ML, Hawkins EP. Yolk sac tumor identified at autopsy after surgical excision of immature sacrococcygeal teratoma. J Pediatr Surg 1995;30:875–7.
8. Cushing B, Perlman EJ, Marina NM, Castleberry RP. Germ cell tumors. In: Pizzo PA, Popplack DG, editors. Principles and practice of pediatric oncology. Philadelphia: Lippincott, Williams & Wilkins; 2002. p. 1091–113.
9. Marsden HB, Birch JM, Swindell R. Germ cell tumours of childhood: a review of 137 cases. J Clin Pathol 1981;34:879–83.
10. Lange PH, Vogelzang NJ, Goldman A, et al. Marker half-life analysis as a prognostic tool in testicular cancer. J Urol 1982;128:708–11.
11. Wu JT, Book L, Sudar K. Serum alpha fetoprotein (AFP) levels in normal infants. Pediatr Res 1981;15:50–2.
12. Perlman EJ, Hawkins EP. Pediatric germ cell tumors: protocol update for pathologists. Pediatr Dev Pathol 1998;1:328–35.

13. Castleberry RP, Cushing B, Perlman EJ, Hawkins EP. Germ cell tumors. In: Pizzo P, Poplack DG, editors. Principles and practice of pediatric oncology. Philadelphia: Lippincott-Raven; 1997. p. 921–45.

14. Kay R. Prepubertal tumor registry. Urol Clin North Am 1993; 20:1–5.

15. Rushton HG, Belman AB. Testis-sparing surgery for benign lesions of the prepubertal testis. Urol Clin North Am 1993;20:27–36.

16. Ulbright TM. Germ cell neoplasms of the testis. Am J Surg Pathol 1993;17:1075–91.

17. Husain A, Selby D, Dehner LP. The male reproductive system including intersex disorders. In: Stocker JT, Dehner LP, editors. Pediatric pathology. Vol. 2. Philadelphia: Lippincott, Williams and Wilkins; 2001. p. 937–91.

18. Visfeldt J, Jorgensen N, Muller J, et al. Testicular germ cell tumours of childhood in Denmark, 1943-1989: incidence and evaluation of histology using immunohistochemical techniques. J Pathol 1994;174:39–47.

19. Rozanski T, Bloom D. The undescended testis. Theory and managmement. Urol Clin North Am 1995;22:107–18.

20. Giwercman A, Muller J, Skakkebaek NE, et al. Carcinoma in situ of the undescended testis. Semin Urol 1988;6:110.

21. Manivel JC, Reinberg Y, Niehans GA, Fraley EE. Intratubular germ cell neoplasia in testicular teratomas and epidermoid cysts. Correlation with prognosis and possible biologic significance. Cancer 1989;64:715–20.

22. Manivel JC, Simonton S, Wold LE, Dehner LP. Absence of intratubular germ cell neoplasia in testicular yolk sac tumors in children. A histochemical and immunohistochemical study. Arch Pathol Lab Med 1988;112:641–5.

23. Hawkins E, Heifetz SA, Giller R, Cushing B. The prepubertal testis (prenatal and postnatal): its relationship to intratubular germ cell neoplasia: a combined Pediatric Oncology Group and Children's Cancer Study Group. Hum Pathol 1997;28:404–10.

24. Ramani P, Yeung CK, Habeebu SS. Testicular intratubular germ cell neoplasia in children and adolescents with intersex. Am J Surg Pathol 1993;17:1124–33.

25. Engeler DS, Hosli PO, John H, et al. Early orchiopexy: prepubertal intratubular germ cell neoplasia and fertility outcome. Urology 2000;56:144–8.

26. Perry A, Wiley EL, Albores-Saavedra J. Pagetoid spread of intratubular germ cell neoplasia into rete testis: a morphologic and histochemical study of 100 orchiectomy specimens with invasive germ cell tumors. Hum Pathol 1994;25:235–9.

27. Perry C, Servadio C. Seminoma in childhood. J Urol 1980; 124:932–3.

28. Dehner LP. Pediatric surgical pathology. Baltimore (MD): Williams and Wilkins; 1987. p. 721–8.

29. Manivel JC, Niehans GA, Wick MR, Dehner LP. Intermediate trophoblast in germ cell neoplasms. Am J Surg Pathol 1987;11:693–701.

30. Hailemariam S, Engeler DS, Bannwart F, Amin MB. Primary mediastinal germ cell tumor with intratubular germ cell neoplasia of the testis—further support for germ cell origin of these tumors: a case report. Cancer 1997;79:1031–6.

31. Tapper D, Lack E. Teratomas in infancy and childhood. Ann Surg 1983;198:398–410.

32. Heifetz SA, Cushing B, Giller R, et al. Immature teratomas in children: pathologic considerations. A report from the combined POG/CCG. Am J Surg Pathol 1998;22:1115–24.

33. Kurman RJ, Norris HJ. Malignant germ cell tumors of the ovary. Hum Pathol 1977;8:551–564.

34. Young RH. New and unusual aspects of ovarian germ cell tumors. Am J Surg Pathol 1993;17:1210–24.

35. Lifschitz-Mercer B, Elliott DJ, Schreiber-Bramante L, et al. Intratubular germ cell neoplasia: associated infertility and review of the diagnostic modalities. Int J Surg Pathol 2001;9:93–8.

36. Parkash V, Carcangiu ML. Transformation of ovarian dysgerminoma to yolk sac tumor: evidence of a histogenetic continuum. Mod Pathol 1995;8:881–7.

37. Kurman RJ, Norris HJ. Endodermal sinus tumor of the ovary. Cancer 1976;38:2404–19.

38. Obata NH, Nakashima N, Kawai M, et al. Gonadoblastoma with dysgerminoma in one ovary and gonadoblastoma with dysgerminoma and yolk sac tumor in the contralateral ovary in a girl with 46XX karyotype. Gynecol Oncol 1995;58:124–8.

39. Scully RE. Gonadoblastoma. A review of 74 cases. Cancer 1970;25:1340–56.

40. Hart WR, Burrkons DM. Germ cell neoplasms arising in gonadoblastomas. Cancer 1979;43:669–78.

41. Rappaport R. Hermaphroditism (intersexuality). In: Behrman R, Kliegman R, Jenson H, editors. Nelson textbook of pediatrics. Philadelphia (PA): W.B. Saunders Company; 2000. p. 1760–5.

42. Rutgers JL, Scully RE. The androgen insensitivity syndrome (testicular feminization): a clinicopathologic study of 43 cases. Int J Gynecol Pathol 1991;10:126–44.

43. Levin HS. Tumors of the testis in intersex syndromes. Urol Clin North Am 2000;27:543–51.

44. Gonzalez-Vela JL, Savage PD, Manivel JC, et al. Poor prognosis of mediastinal germ cell cancers containing sarcomatous components. Cancer 1990;66:1114–6.

45. Ulbright TM, Loehrer PJ, Roth LM, et al. The development of non-germ cell malignancies within germ cell tumors. A clinicopathologic study of 11 cases. Cancer 1984;54:1824–33.

46. Michael H, Hull MT, Foster RS, et al. Nephroblastoma-like tumors in patients with testicular germ cell tumors. Am J Surg Pathol 1998;22:1107–14.

47. Kleinman GM, Young RH, Scully RE. Primary neuroectodermal tumors of the ovary. A report of 25 cases. Am J Surg Pathol 1993;17:764–78.

48. Manivel C, Wick MR, Abenoza P, Rosai J. The occurrence of sarcomatous components in primary mediastinal germ cell tumors. Am J Surg Pathol 1986;10:711–7.

49. Altman RP, Randolph JG, Lilly JR. Sacrococcygeal teratoma: American Academy of Pediatrics Surgical Section Survey-1973. J Pediatr Surg 1974;9:389–98.

50. Schneider DT, Calaminus G, Reinhard H, et al. Primary mediastinal germ cell tumors in children and adolescents: results of the German cooperative protocols MAKEI 83/86, 89, and 96. J Clin Oncol 2000;18:832–9.

51. Moran CA, Suster S. Primary germ cell tumors of the mediastinum. I. Analysis of 322 cases with special emphasis on teratomatous lesions and a proposal for histopathologic classification and clinical staging. Cancer 1997;80:681–90.

52. Dulmet EM, Macchiarini P, Suc B, Verley JM. Germ cell tumors of the mediastinum. A 30-year experience. Cancer 1993;72:1894–901.

53. Moran CA, Suster S, Przygodzki RM, Koss MN. Primary germ cell tumors of the mediastinum. II. Mediastinal seminomas—a clinicopathologic and immunohistochemical study of 120 cases. Cancer 1997;80:691–8.

54. Lack EE, Travis WD, Welch KJ. Retroperitoneal germ cell tumors in childhood. A clinical and pathologic study of 11 cases. Cancer 1985;56:602–8.

55. Gonzalez-Crussi F. Extragonadal teratomas. In: Hartmann WH, editor. Atlas of tumor pathology. Vol. 18. Bethesda (MD): Armed Forces Institute of Pathology; 1982.

56. Belchis DA, Moury J, Davis JH. Infantile choriocarcinoma. Cancer 1993;72:2028–32.

57. Witzleben CL, Bruninga G. Infantile choriocarcinoma: a characteristic syndrome. J Pediatr 1968;73:374–8.

58. Kim SN, Chi JG, Kim YW, et al. Neonatal choriocarcinoma of liver. Pediatr Pathol 1993;13:723–30.

59. Nichols CR, Heerema NA, Palmer C, et al. Klinefelter's syndrome associated with mediastinal germ cell neoplasms. J Clin Oncol 1987;5:1290–4.

60. Dexeus FH, Logothetis CJ, Chong C, et al. Genetic abnormalities in men with germ cell tumors. J Urol 1988;140:80–4.

61. Derenoncourt AN, Castro-Magana M, Jones KL. Mediastinal teratoma and precocious puberty in a boy with mosaic Klinefelter syndrome. Am J Med Genet 1995;55:38–42.

62. Bebb GG, Grannis FW Jr, Paz IB, et al. Mediastinal germ cell tumor in a child with precocious puberty and Klinefelter syndrome. Ann Thorac Surg 1998;66:547–8.

63. Aizenstein RI, Hibbeln JF, Sagireddy B, et al. Klinefelter's syndrome associated with testicular microlithiasis and mediastinal germ-cell neoplasm. J Clin Ultrasound 1997;25:508–10.

64. Teitell M, Rowland JM. Systemic mast cell disease associated with primary ovarian mxied malignant germ cell tumor. Hum Pathol 1998;29:1546–7.

65. Bussey KJ, Lawce HJ, Olson SB, et al. Chromosome abnormalities of eighty-one pediatric germ cell tumors: sex-, age-, site-, and histopathology-related differences—a Children's Cancer Group study. Genes Chromosomes Cancer 1999;25:134–46.

66. Schneider DT, Schuster AE, Fritsch MK, et al. Genetic analysis of mediastinal nonseminomatous germ cell tumors in children and adolescents. Genes Chromosomes Cancer 2002;34:115–25.

67. Stock C, Ambros IM, Lion T, et al. Detection of numerical and structural chromosome abnormalities in pediatric germ cell tumors by means of interphase cytogenetics. Genes Chromosomes Cancer 1994;11:40–50.

68. Perlman EJ, Cushing B, Hawkins E, Griffin CA. Cytogenetic analysis of childhood endodermal sinus tumors: a Pediatric Oncology Group study. Pediatr Pathol 1994;14:695–708.

69. Perlman EJ, Valentine MB, Griffin CA, Look AT. Deletion of 1p36 in childhood endodermal sinus tumors by two-color fluorescence in situ hybridization: a Pediatric Oncology Group study. Genes Chromosomes Cancer 1996;16:15–20.

70. Murty VV, Chaganti RS. A genetic perspective on male germ cell tumors. Semin Oncol 1998;25:133–44.

71. Gobel U, Schneider DT, Calaminus G, et al. Multimodal treatment of malignant sacrococcygeal germ cell tumors: a prospective analysis of 66 patients of the German cooperative protocols MAKEI 83/86 and 89. J Clin Oncol 2001;19:1943–50.

72. Rescorla F, Billmire D, Stolar C, et al. The effect of cisplatin dose and surgical resection in children with malignant germ cell tumors at the sacrococcygeal region: a pediatric intergroup trial (POG 9049/CCG 8882). J Pediatr Surg 2001;36:12–7.

73. Finlay J, Walker R, Balmaceda S, et al. Chemotherapy without irradiation for primary central nervous system germ cell tumors: report of an international study. Am Soc Clin Oncol 1992;11:150.

74. Norris HJ, Zirkin HJ, Benson WL. Immature (malignant) teratoma of the ovary: a clinical and pathologic study of 58 cases. Cancer 1976;37:2359–72.

75. Marina NM, Cushing B, Giller R, et al. Complete surgical excision is effective treatment for children with immature teratomas with or without malignant elements: a Pediatric Oncology Group/Children's Cancer Group Intergroup Study. J Clin Oncol 1999;17:2137–43.

76. Flamant F, Schwartz L, Delons E, et al. Nonseminomatous malignant germ cell tumors in children. Multidrug therapy in stages III and IV. Cancer 1984;54:1687–91.

77. Einhorn LH, Donohue J. Cis-diamminedichloroplatinum, vinblastine, and bleomycin combination chemotherapy in disseminated testicular cancer. Ann Intern Med 1977;87:293–8.

78. Pinkerton CR, Pritchard J, Spitz L. High complete response rate in children with advanced germ cell tumors using cis-platin-containing combination chemotherapy. J Clin Oncol 1986;4:194–9.

79. Mann JR, Pearson D, Barrett A, et al. Results of the United Kingdom Children's Cancer Study Group's malignant germ cell tumor studies. Cancer 1989;63:1657–67.

80. Gobel U, Calaminus G, Haas RJ, et al. Combination chemotherapy in malignant non-seminomatous germ-cell tumors: results of a cooperative study of the German Society of Pediatric Oncology (MAKEI 83). Cancer Chemother Pharmacol 1989;24:S34–9.

81. Ablin AR, Krailo MD, Ramsay NK, et al. Results of treatment of malignant germ cell tumors in 93 children: a report from the Children's Cancer Study Group. J Clin Oncol 1991;9:1782–92.

82. Cushing B, Giller R, Marina N, et al. Results of surgery alone or surgery plus cisplatin, etoposide and bleomycin (PEB) in children with localized gonadal malignant germ cell tumor (MGCT): a pediatric intergroup report (POG9048/CCG8891) [abstract]. Am Soc Clin Oncol 1997;16:511a.

83. Giller R, Cushing B, Lauer S, et al. Comparison of high dose or standard dose cisplatin with etoposide and bleomycin (HDPEB vs PEB) in children with stage III and IV malig-

nant germ cell tumor (MGCT) at gonadal primary sites. A Pediatric Intergoup Trial (POG9049/CCG8882) [abstract]. Am Soc Clin Oncol 1998;17:525a.

84. Cushing B, Giller R, Lauer S, et al. Comparison of high dose or standard dose cisplatin with etoposide and bleomycin (HDPEB vs PEB) in children with stage I-IV extragonadal malignant germ cell tumor (MGCT) at gonadal primary sites. A Pediatric Intergoup Trial (POG9049/CCG8882) [abstract]. Am Soc Clin Oncol 1998;17:525a.

85. Womer R. Ototoxicity of high-dose cisplatin for children with malignant germ cell tumors [personal communication].

86. Lopes LF, de Camargo B, Aguiar SS, et al. Cisplatin and etoposide regimen for germ cell tumor: preliminary results of the Brazilian germ cell study group [abstract]. Am Soc Pediatr Hematol Oncol 1999;33:216.

87. Mann JR, Raafat F, Robinson K, et al. The United Kingdom Children's Cancer Study Group's second germ cell tumor study: carboplatin, etoposide, and bleomycin are effective treatment for children with malignant extracranial germ cell tumors, with acceptable toxicity. J Clin Oncol 2000; 18:3809–18.

87. Giller R, Lauer S, Trigg M, et al. High-dose chemotherapy with autologous marrow transplant (HDC/AMT) for refractory solid tumors in children [abstract]. Am Soc Clin Oncol 1988;7:261.

23

Resources for the Patient with Testicular Cancer

STEVEN N. WOLFF, MD

Young men who are abruptly and unexpectedly diagnosed with testicular cancer face daunting circumstances. These include a life-threatening disease, distortion of body image, disruption of normal activities, substantial resource demands, unfamiliar toxic therapy, impairment of fertility, and complex treatment options, compounded by a requirement to expeditiously initiate therapy. Frequently, patients are asked to participate in clinical research that can increase their uncertainty about the appropriate therapy. It is thus quite understandable that patients and their families can feel overwhelmed by the uncertainty brought on by a serious illness. This uncertainty can be mitigated by a sound and accurate understanding of the disease and treatment alternatives.

Obtaining an accurate, comprehensive, and meaningful understanding of a complex disease can be challenging, especially for those not experienced in seeking medical information. Fortunately, there exists a number of testicular cancer resources that supply up-to-date information and provide guidance to help facilitate decision making. This chapter will highlights these resources along with key concepts that patients should understand.

WHAT PATIENTS SHOULD UNDERSTAND

Patients do have a responsibility to become informed about their disease and treatment options in addition to their trusting in physician expertise. In an attempt to gather such knowledge, patients often lose perspective by becoming overwhelmed by the encyclopedic displays of Internet information.

Patients who are attempting to understand their disease should focus on fundamental concepts, allowing the health care team to explain sophisticated details. Table 23–1 illustrates some key concepts, in the form of questions for patients and their families to consider.

RESOURCES FOR PATIENTS

Many resources are available for cancer patients and their families. These resources include local and national organizations, paper and electronic documents, local health care facilities and their personnel, and, sometimes, well-meaning patients who are having similar experiences. Some of these resources encompass all cancers, and some focus on testicular cancer, despite its low incidence. Many resources are from large well-funded organizations and institutions, and some are more modest, having been developed by motivated individuals who were themselves unable to obtain comprehensive information. Some resources are scientifically rigorous, and some are more personal and anecdotal. Table 23–2 is a list of some of the most rigorous resources that have audited and corroborated information or that offer particularly important resources or services; each is discussed in detail.

Primary Consultant Oncologist

The most available information resource for patients is their consultant medical, surgical, or radiotherapy oncologist. Specialized in the treatment of cancer,

Table 23–1. BASIC CONCEPTS FOR UNDERSTANDING TESTICULAR CANCER	
Concepts	**Questions**
Neoplastic transformation	Do I understand what testicular cancer is?
Histologic types	Do I understand my type of testicular cancer and the implications for treatment?
Staging of disease	Do I understand the concept of primary and metastatic disease?
	Do I understand the extent of my disease?
Prognostic factors	Do I understand the basis for determining my likely outcome from treatment?
Sexuality and fertility	Do I understand the effects of the diagnostic surgery and proposed therapy on fertility and sexuality?
	Do I understand my options for maintaining fertility?
	Do I understand when gamete cryopreservation must be performed?
Second opinions	Have I explored the need for a second opinion?
	Are there advantages of specialized centers of excellence?
Therapeutic interventions	Do I understand the proposed therapy?
	Do I understand the schedule of therapy?
	Do I understand the possible treatment-induced side effects?
	Have I explored options to reduce toxicity?
	Can I participate in a clinical trial?
	Are there advantages of participating in a clinical trial?
Restaging after primary therapy	Do I understand the testing required after therapy?
	Do I understand the possibility for additional surgery?
Follow-up	Do I understand the schedule for follow-up evaluation?
	Do I understand the imperatives for follow-up?
	Do I understand the time frame for likely recurrence?
Recurrence and salvage therapy	Do I understand salvage therapy options and outcomes if my disease recurs?
Survivorship	Do I understand the possibility of long-term physiologic and psychological effects of cancer and anticancer therapy?
	Do I know how I can obtain assistance if I have distress from my disease?

this physician not only provides information but also makes it relevant to each patient's particular circumstance. Each case represents a unique clinical situation that is managed from a general knowledge base. Unfortunately, because the disease is uncommon, not all physicians have extensive experience in caring for patients with testicular cancer. This may become especially problematic for unusual or advanced clinical presentations or for those patients who have recurrent disease after effective primary treatment.

The patient-physician relationship builds upon inherent trust supported by the adequate exchange of information. Patients should never be hesitant to have all of their questions addressed despite the occasional hectic pace of clinical practice. It may be helpful to acquire knowledge in a graduated process that builds on a basic foundation. A reasonable plan is to first obtain meaningful information for a basic understanding of the disease, prior to detailed discussions with consultant physicians. Supporting the need of patients to become involved in their care is a recent study about early-stage breast cancer.[1,2] This

analysis addressed the issue of whether patients were involved in their decision-making process and how their involvement matched their expectations. In a review of over 1,000 patients, it was found that most patients desired a collaboration with their surgeon but that only a minority obtained such a process. Importantly, those patients whose process matched their expectations were more satisfied with their treatment outcome. It is imperative that patients understand at least the basic fundamentals of their disease and why specific therapy is recommended.

Second Opinions

Second opinions are a standard practice of medicine, especially for uncommon or complex diseases. Health care providers are trained and required to be up-to-date in medical knowledge and frequently seek new information and advice from experts. Patients must be comfortable and at ease with their medical care and should thus never be hesitant to ask their primary consultant oncologist or urologist to

Table 23–2. RESOURCES FOR PATIENTS WITH TESTICULAR CANCER	
Resource	**Contact Information**
Primary consultant oncologist	Primary care physician or local medical society
Second opinion oncologist	Primary consultant oncologist contacting specialized cancer treatment centers
Primary-institution social worker	Local hospital or health care organization
Health care facility	Primary care physician, consultant physicians, or local medical society
American Cancer Society	http://www.cancer.org
American Society for Clinical Oncology	http://www.asco.org
Cancer BACUP series	http://www.cancerbacup.org.uk/info/testes.htm
Cancer Care, Inc.	http://www.cancercare.org
Candlelighters	http://www.candlelighters.org
Clinical cancer trial	http://www.clinicaltrials.gov/ct/gui
Coalition of National Cancer Cooperative Groups	http://www.cancertrialshelp.org
European Organization for Research and Treatment of Cancer	http://www.eortc.be/
Lance Armstrong Foundation	http://www.laf.org
National Cancer Institute	http://www.cancer.gov
National Coalition for Cancer Survivorship	http://www.cansearch.org
Oncolink	http://www.oncolink.com
Physician Data Query (PDQ)	http://www.cancer.gov/cancer_information/pdq
Testicular Cancer Resource Center	http://www.acor.org/diseases/TC/
The Wellness Community	http://www.wellness-community.org

obtain a second opinion. Patients who are uncomfortable with their medical care must seek second opinions. Sources for second opinions can vary, but second opinions may be best obtained from physicians and centers that have substantial experience or that are active in clinical research trials for testicular cancer since the disorder is uncommon as compared to most other cancers.

Second opinions can be beneficial in multiple ways. First, the opinion can support the course of action proposed by the primary consultant oncologist. Mutual agreement between consultants validates the plan of therapy and assures sound decisions. Second, concurrence on treatment helps to relieve anxiety about physician expertise and experience and strengthens the physician-patient relationship. Third, second opinions, if at variance from the proposed therapy, may suggest different approaches that could prove beneficial. The resolution of different treatment recommendations should be based on the reasoning for each approach. Last, an additional benefit is the ascertaining of whether clinical trials are available and whether the patient's specific clinical circumstances allow participation.

A simple way to obtain a second opinion is for the primary consultant oncologist to directly communicate with centers of excellence that have specialty units focused on testicular cancer management. These centers routinely provide second opinions as a part of their responsibility. Directly visiting a center of excellence can provide a useful evaluation but should be performed with complete clinical data, including the relevant pathologic tissue slides and complete laboratory and radiographic information. Generally, a second opinion is most useful prior to the initiation of treatment or at least early in the course of treatment. This allows for meaningful adjustments of therapy if necessary.*

Primary-Institution Social Worker

Most health care facilities are staffed with social workers who are specially trained in the field of oncology. Their training includes an understanding of cancer and its impact on the patient and the patient's family. Many social workers are skilled at integrating patients into programs for medical financial assistance. They may also locate other resources, such as transportation or housing assistance. Independent organizations such as Cancer Care or Candlelighters can also provide social worker assistance.

---

*Editor's note: While second opinions are very valuable, the patient should be careful to avoid embarking on a series of undirected and unfocused multiple opinions, which inevitably will lead to confusion.

Social workers may also be skilled in psychosocial evaluations and in assessing the impact of cancer therapy upon the day-to-day activities of patients and their families. If needed, they can provide individual support or group counseling, or they can refer patients if more psychosocial expertise is required. Many large institutions, in addition to social workers, have specially trained health care providers, such as advanced-practice nurses, trained to provide psychosocial assistance and counsel. If the stress of cancer is affecting a patient's well-being, resources such as these must be sought.

Health Care Facility

Many health care facilities (especially large cancer treatment centers) have dedicated educational, emotional support, and survivorship services for cancer patients. In general, patients and families who use individual or group support services adjust better to their illness, with less anxiety.

Cancer Clinical Trials

Advantages to Participants

Medical research as performed in a clinical trial is one of the most poorly understood practices of medicine.[3] A clinical trial is simply a regimented method of determining the better course of treatment. Clinical trials are required because not every treatment or state of illness has a rigidly defined treatment or because newly developed therapy needs formal evaluation. This is especially so in the case of cancer since current treatment is always being refined and new therapeutic entities are continually being developed. Clinical trials help to prevent the haphazard use of therapy by providing an organized plan for defining and determining the best outcome.

In a clinical trial, patients are treated in a predetermined and specified manner to avoid variances in care. This is the best method to ensure that treatment conclusions are valid. Noteworthy in these trials is mandated physician and scientific conduct, overseen by both the national government and by the local treatment institution.[4] Patients must be totally and clearly informed of the purpose of the study, all trial activities including additional costs, and alternative treatment. Such information helps to justify participation in the trial as opposed to alternative treatments. Participation in clinical trials is totally voluntary, and there is always the choice of not participating or of stopping participation at any time.[5] Consent from each patient must be obtained prior to participation. The process of obtaining consent includes describing in detail both the risk of participation and the justification for participation. Clinical trials are designed so that participation should not reduce the likely chances of success. However, there can never be an ensured or guaranteed outcome for treatment using newer or untested forms of therapy.

Most clinical trials compare two forms of therapy. Many times, clinical trials are performed by randomized methods in which neither the patient nor the physician can choose which treatment option will be administered; instead, a computer or some other "random" process decides which of the predefined treatments each patient receives. Despite not being able to choose the specified therapy, the patient can benefit substantially from participating in a clinical trial. Sometimes, part of the cost of care is supported by the trial.[6] Additionally, treatment in trials requires detailed patient care, including precise evaluations that could prove beneficial. Clinical trials often offer the highest standards of practice and an opportunity to receive novel or "cutting-edge" treatment that may not be routinely available. Taking all of the above into consideration, it has been demonstrated that patients entered on clinical trials can have improved outcomes when compared to patients who have similar disease but who are not treated in a clinical trial.

Pediatric oncology is very advanced in the implementation of clinical trials; the vast majority of nonadult patients are treated in formal clinical trials. On the other hand, less than 15% of adult patients participate in clinical trials. It is a current goal of the practice of adult cancer therapy to increase the number of adults treated in clinical trials. To accomplish this, more opportunities to participate in clinical trials are being offered to patients being treated in community-based practices.

All clinical trials have rigidly defined disease and patient criteria that must be met for a patient to be eligible for the trial. Thus, not every patient will qualify for participation. The physicians performing clinical trials can best ascertain a patient's qualifications for participation in a clinical trial. A decision to participate must often be made early since many clinical trials do not allow patients to have begun other forms of therapy.

Resources for Learning about Cancer Clinical Trials

The consultant oncologist is generally a satisfactory source of knowledge about clinical trials that are available but may be most knowledgeable about those in which he or she is actively participating. There are many accessible Internet resources that list a full array of cancer clinical trials. Some trials are disease specific, and some may allow the participation of patients with a range of cancers. The latter are generally trials at an earlier stage of therapeutic development that seek to develop novel or investigational chemotherapy and to determine which disease might be effectively treated by the novel treatment. These trials often seek to identify the optimal dosage of new drugs and to define patterns of side effects more clearly. Disease-specific trials may be trials on primary therapy or on therapy for recurrence.

The National Cancer Institute (NCI) has a readily searchable Internet compendium of active clinical trials (<http://clinicaltrials.gov/ct/gui>). This site also contains introductory information about participation in clinical trials. Entering "testicular cancer" will yield a listing of numerous studies for that disease. The extensive resources of the NCI can be reviewed at its link (<http://www.cancer.gov>), which includes cancer information and information about clinical trials, statistics, research programs, and research funding. The resource is quite extensive and includes material about all cancers.

Physician Data Query (PDQ), available at <http://www.cancer.gov/cancer_information/pdq>, is the NCI's comprehensive cancer database for physicians. Many patients seeking clinical trials use this database due to its complete listing of trials. PDQ contains peer-reviewed summaries on cancer treatment, screening, prevention, genetics, and supportive care; a registry of approximately 1,800 open and 12,000 closed cancer clinical trials from around

the world; and directories of physicians and other professionals who provide cancer services and organizations that provide cancer care. The American Cancer Society Web site has a clinical trials information and matching service that is available via the ACS Web site, <http://www.cancer.org> (enter "find a clinical trial" in the site's search engine) and the ACS cancer information center (1-800-ACS-2345). This application identifies clinical trials most likely to be relevant to each patient, based on clinical information entered by that patient. The database includes all trials in the PDQ system, plus additional institutional and pharmaceuical trials.

Another excellent Internet source for general and clinical trial information is Oncolink (<http://www.oncolink.com>), provided by the University of Pennsylvania. This is a more general but comprehensive source of cancer information that offers a free clinical trial-matching service to ascertain whether there are appropriate clinical trials, based on each patient's characteristics.

The Coalition of National Cancer Cooperative Groups is an organization that includes the major clinical trials organizations that are supported by the NCI. Its Web site, at <http://www.cancertrialshelp.org>, also offers detailed information to patients about all issues of participating in cancer clinical trials. Trials are searched by the "TrialCheck" tool but include only those of the participating organizations. Nonetheless, these trials represent many of the most advanced large-scale trials that are recruiting large numbers of patients.

Similarly, the European Organization for Research and Treatment of Cancer (EORTC) is the most extensive clinical trials group in Europe. Its Web site (<http://www.eortc.be/>) includes a downloadable pamphlet about clinical trials as well as a listing of all of its many active clinical trials. Each disease entity can be searched individually.

LEARNING ABOUT TESTICULAR CANCER

The Testicular Cancer Resource Center (TCRC) (<http://www.acor.org/diseases/TC/>) is a very comprehensive source of information oriented to patients and their families. This comprehensive database discusses all issues of testicular cancer and could be the first resource that patients and their families consult. It also includes links to many other sources of information. The TCRC began when one patient, diagnosed with testicular cancer, was unable to obtain comprehensive patient-oriented information. What information was obtainable was not "patient friendly," was overly technical, and did not address many personal issues. Eventually, this patient and others concluded that there was a need for a readily available source of objective and accurate patient-oriented information. Their efforts began as an E-mail support group and evolved into a complete and up-to-date Internet resource. What is excellent about this Web site is its exacting expert advice and specific information, combined with links to virtually all other resources. The TCRC has also enlisted the assistance of physician experts in testicular cancer to provide advice and guidance. The editors of the Web site are easily contacted and frequently act as patient advocates.

The TCRC Web site offers information about screening, diagnosis, therapy (surgery, radiation therapy, and chemotherapy), therapy options, survivorship, follow-up, the management of disease recurrence, and all of the day-to-day perspectives that are important to patients. Virtually any information about testicular cancer can be obtained from this site.

Another excellent information resource is Cancer BACUP, a UK cancer information service. Launched in 1985 by a patient who realized (through her own experience) that cancer patients and their families and friends had a great need for high-quality and up-to-date information, practical advice, and support. Cancer BACUP offers a free cancer information service staffed by qualified and experienced cancer nurses; publications on all aspects of cancer, written specifically for patients and their families; and a growing number of centers in UK hospitals, staffed by specialized cancer nurses. The nurses are supported by more than 200 cancer specialists to help provide the highest-quality information. The Cancer BACUP database has a comprehensive list of resources, organizations, and support groups for cancer patients in the United Kingdom. Cancer BACUP also supports health professionals by providing information, written specifically for doctors, on controversial and difficult cancer topics and by providing the most comprehensive listing of UK cancer treatment guidelines.

The Cancer BACUP Web site, at <http://www.cancerbacup.org.uk/info/testes.htm>, contains specific patient-oriented information about testicular cancer. The information is well organized and addresses all of the very important and specific issues concerning testicular cancer.

The American Cancer Society (ACS) is the largest US national organization assisting patients with cancer functioning as a nationwide community-based voluntary health organization. Headquartered in Atlanta, Georgia, the ACS has state divisions with more than 3,400 local offices. The ACS functions by (1) supporting cancer research, (2) supplying cancer information, (3) providing cancer advocacy and public policy, and (4) providing community-based programs and resources.

The ACS Web site (<http://www.cancer.org>) contains general information and specific information about testicular cancer, accessed by using the search engine of the site. Patients can review their specific treatment circumstances by using the "Cancer Profiler" tool provided by the site. The site also provides many other resources for general issues of cancer, and access to the Cancer Survivors Network, an online community created for and by cancer survivors and their loved ones. Similar information and services are also available 7 days a week 24 hours a day, through the ACS telephone information center (1-800-ACS-2345).

The American Society of Clinical Oncology (<http://www.asco.org>) is the largest full-scope organization for cancer specialists focusing on all aspects of patient care. Its 18,000 members represent all facets of cancer care, including technical, medical, and psychosocial studies as well as patient-oriented matters. The society has promoted extensive physician-oriented education projects and launched its own Web site for patients in May 2002, entitled "People Living with Cancer" (<http://www.plwc.org>). The resources on this site are comprehensive and helpful and include many of the topics that are found individually on other sites. The page contains sections for cancer overview, discussions for all types of cancers, a community center, a knowledge center, and a news center. Each chapter has many links and covers all of the technical issues of cancer therapy, clinical trials, information, advocacy, and psychosocial matters. The information on testicular cancer is not as detailed as that contained in specific testicular cancer Web sites. This site is an excellent resource for newly diagnosed patients and would establish a foundation of knowledge and resources.

The Lance Armstrong Foundation (LAF), established in 1997, supports medical research and support services for all cancer patients. Its Web site, at <http://www.laf.org>, contains links to many cancer-related resources and is an excellent reference point. The foundation was started when a world champion athlete was diagnosed with advanced testicular cancer. Despite his celebrity, he had a difficult time understanding his disease and treatment options. The LAF exists "to enhance the quality of life for those living with, through and beyond cancer." The foundation supports medical research in testicular cancer through peer-reviewed grants. It also assumes a major mission in supporting "survivorship," defined as those issues of cancer that affect patients and their families after the conclusion of active anticancer therapy. It had once been assumed that patients could return to normal day-to-day activities once anticancer therapy was concluded; now, it is realized that the diagnosis and treatment for cancer have a lifelong impact. The foundation provides survivorship services by supporting programs and helping leaders in survivorship develop better resources. The LAF wants "to continue to define, refine and improve cancer survivor services and facilitate the delivery of those services—and a large dose of hope—to the patients, their families and other loved ones touched by the disease."

ASSISTANCE FOR CANCER-RELATED PROBLEMS

Cancer Care is a national nonprofit organization whose mission is to provide free professional help to people with all cancers through counseling, education, information and referral, and direct financial assistance. Cancer Care's Web site (<http://www.cancercare.org>) offers practical assistance to all patients and not specifically to patients with testicular cancer. Since 1944, Cancer Care has been dedicated to providing emotional support, information, and practical help to people with cancer and their loved ones. As the oldest and largest national nonprofit agency devoted to offering professional services, Cancer Care has helped over two million people nationwide through its toll-free counseling telephone line (1-800-813-HOPE) and teleconference programs, its office-based services, and via the Internet. All services are provided free of charge and are available to people of all ages, with all types of cancer, at any stage of the disease. Cancer Care's reach, including its cancer awareness initiatives, also extends to family members, caregivers, and professionals, providing vital information and assistance.

The National Coalition for Cancer Survivors (NCCS) is the only patient-led advocacy organization working on behalf of people with all types of cancer and their families. It is dedicated to assuring quality cancer care for all Americans. The NCCS (whose Web site address is <http://www.canserach.org>) realizes that cancer survivors and those who care for them face many challenges. To help meet those challenges, the NCCS

1. serves as a clearinghouse for credible information about survivorship,
2. empowers cancer survivors through its publications and programs,
3. convenes other national cancer-related organizations, and
4. advocates for policy issues that affect survivors' quality of life.

The NCCS focuses on survivorship since the impact of cancer is a lifelong phenomenon. The advocacy policies of the NCCS include care of the patients and their families confronting all of the trying issues of living with cancer. The organization supplies resources such as the Cancer Survival Toolbox, a free award-winning audio program that teaches skills that can help people with cancer meet the challenges of their illness. The Toolbox includes a Basic Skills set that covers six important topics: communicating, finding information, making decisions, solving problems, negotiating, and standing up for your rights. In addition, the Toolbox includes three additional programs that cover topics for older persons, finding ways to pay for care, and caring for the caregiver.

The Wellness Community (TWC) is a national nonprofit organization that provides support, education, and hope to people with cancer and to their loved ones through professionally led support groups, educational workshops, and mind/body classes. The support groups use the "Patient Active Concept," in which people affected by cancer learn vital skills that enable them to regain control, reduce isolation, and restore hope, regardless of the stage of disease. The key concept of TWC is that patients and their families should become active participants in their cancer recovery, such that "people with cancer who participate in their fight for recovery from cancer will improve the quality of their life and may enhance the possibility of their recovery." At TWC, all local programs are free of charge and can be accessed through their Web site at <http://wellness-community.org>, which also contains a virtual "Wellness Community."

Candlelighters (<http://www.candlelighters.org>) is a national organization focusing on pediatric patients and has many local organizations that supply various resources, including support groups, social workers, and bereavement counseling.

SUMMARY

Testicular cancer is the paradigm for the curable cancer. Nonetheless, despite the success of thera-peutic interventions, patients and their families suffer through all of the myriad issues that affect all patients with cancer. There are now available numerous resources assisting patients with testicular cancer. These provide up-to-date information about the disease and the choice of therapies and offer valuable resources to help cope with the stress of the disease. Patients using these resources can now be empowered so that they can manage their disease with full knowledge and assistance.

REFERENCES

1. Keating, NL, Weeks JC, Landrum MB, et al. Discussion of treatment options for early–stage breast cancer: effect of provider specialty on type of surgery and satisfaction. Med Care 2001;39(7):681–91.
2. Keating NL, Guadagnoli E, Landrum MB, et al. Treatment decision making in early-stage breast cancer: should surgeons match patients' desired level of involvement? J Clin Oncol 2002;20(6):1473–9.
3. Daugherty C, Ratain M, Grochowski E, et al. Perceptions of cancer patients and their physicians involved in phase I trials. J Clin Oncol 1995;13:1062–72.
4. Kelch RP. Maintaining the public trust in clinical research. N Engl J Med 2002;346:285–7.
5. Jenkins V, Fallowfield L. Reasons for accepting or declining to participate in randomized clinical trials for cancer therapy. Br J Cancer 2000;82(11):1783–8.
6. Bennett C, Adams J, Knox R, et al. Clinical trials: are they a good buy? J Clin Oncol 2001;19:4330–9.

24

Psychosocial Outcomes after Testicular Cancer Treatment

DAMON J. VIDRINE, DrPH

ELLEN R. GRITZ, PhD

Although testicular cancer is relatively uncommon, representing only about 1% of all cancer incidence in males, it is the most common neoplasm in men between the ages of 15 and 35 years.[1] According to estimates from the American Cancer Society, approximately 7,500 men are diagnosed with testicular cancer each year in the United States.[2] For unknown reasons, the incidence of testicular cancer has been increasing in recent decades. Estimates suggest that the risk of testicular cancer has increased by 51% in all US males since the early 1970s.[3] This trend has been observed in both the United States and Canada, as well as in several European nations.[4–6]

The reason (or reasons) for this birth cohort effect is not known; however, several variables that are associated with a significantly increased risk have been identified, including cryptorchidism,[7] hormonal factors,[8,9] high body mass index (BMI),[10] and increased physical activity.[11] While the exact mechanisms for these relationships are not clear, it is hypothesized that exposure to androgens may be the key to these findings; exposure to androgens may decrease BMI and increase physical activity.[10,11] Other findings suggest that maternal exposure to exogenous hormones is a significant risk factor for testicular cancer.[12] Additional risk factors related to hormone levels include late onset of puberty[12] and increased body height.[11,12] Fertility problems are frequently reported as a side effect of testicular treatment, but these problems may actually be present prior to the cancer diagnosis. Evidence suggests that men with less than the expected number of children (based on their age) have a significantly increased risk of developing testicular cancer, suggesting a common mechanism for both infertility and testicular cancer.[13] Observed among Danish men, this finding remained statistically significant after controlling for cryptorchidism, age, marital status, and homosexual activity.[13] Further efforts are needed to clarify the determinants and (possibly) reduce the risk of testicular cancer as the increasing trend in incidence demonstrates no signs of waning.[6]

Fortunately, as the incidence of testicular cancer has been increasing in recent decades, tremendous advances in treatment have been made, to the point at which testicular cancer is now largely a curable disease. The overall 5-year survival rate is 95%, ranging from 99% for local disease to 76% for metastatic disease.[2] Treatment modality depends on both stage of disease and tumor histology (seminoma vs nonseminomatous germ cell tumor [NSGCT]). Patients with early-stage seminoma are typically treated with orchiectomy alone or with orchiectomy and concomitant radiation therapy. Treatment of advanced-stage seminoma usually consists of orchiectomy and radiation therapy or orchiectomy and chemotherapy.[1] The most common treatment for patients with early-stage NSGCTs is orchiectomy alone whereas treatment for advanced-stage NSGCT typically consists of orchiectomy and chemotherapy.[1] In addition, the dose of chemotherapy typically increases with the stage of disease.[14]

Because of the young age at diagnosis and the extremely high survival rates following testicular cancer treatment, survivorship issues become tremendously important. Young men are most frequently diagnosed at or near the prime of life; a time during which patients are establishing professional careers and planning families. While mortality may no longer pose the risk it did in earlier years, other important outcomes should be considered. These outcomes include toxicity of treatment, disease-related functioning (eg, body image, sexual functioning, and fertility), and overall quality of life (QOL). A better understanding of these outcomes and how they are influenced by each treatment modality (or combination of modalities) is vital for both physician and patient. Such an understanding will allow for the selection of the most appropriate treatment regimen as well as the early implementation of interventions that have the potential to minimize disease and/or treatment-related impairment.

THEORETICAL FRAMEWORK

Given the available curative treatments for testicular cancer, a thorough understanding of psychosocial outcomes, such as QOL, among patients and survivors is essential. QOL is a multidimensional concept that reflects an individual's perception of well-being. QOL measurement typically incorporates the influence of functioning domains such as physical, psychological, and social health.[15] Frequently, QOL is conceptualized as existing on a continuum, with disease onset and symptom status representing variables proximal to disease onset, and with overall (or generic) QOL as a more distal variable (Figure 24–1). An important component of this model is the distinction between disease and/or treatment–specific functioning and overall functioning. For example, the model would predict that cancer treatment would first cause treatment-related side effects (eg, gonadal toxicity). Subsequently, these side effects would adversely affect specific domains of functioning (eg, reduced fertility). Finally, reduced functional ability would lead to a reduction in overall QOL. External variables, such as personal and environmental characteristics, may exert influence throughout this continuum, further influencing QOL.[16–18] The model's

structure is useful in understanding the many factors that contribute to QOL outcomes.

PSYCHOLOGICAL FUNCTIONING

Understandably, it is common for testicular cancer patients to exhibit symptoms of psychological distress at the time of diagnosis and during treatment. However, the evidence concerning the duration of this distress is inconsistent across studies. Rieker and colleagues[19] were among the first to thoroughly assess the impact of testicular cancer treatment on the psychosocial functioning of survivors. Seventy-four men treated for either seminomatous or non-seminomatous germ cell tumors were assessed 2 to 10 years after completing therapy (median, 4 years after treatment). Overall, the findings suggested that survivors had a high level of psychological functioning. Testicular cancer survivors reported better psychological functioning than did psychiatric or male college student controls. Patients actually reported that many areas of their lives (ie, outlook on life, relationship with children, fear of death, and self-respect) had improved because of the cancer.

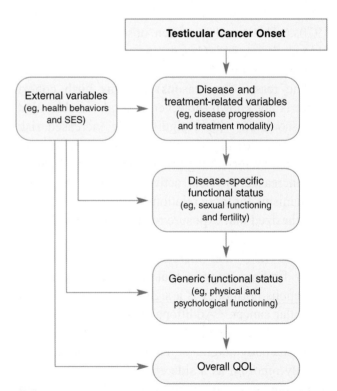

Figure 24–1. Model of quality-of-life outcomes for patients with testicular cancer. (QOL = quality of life; SES = socioeconomic status.)

Gritz and colleagues were also among the first to investigate the psychological sequelae of testicular cancer in long-term survivors. This series of papers detailed enduring psychological, sexual, and marital issues.[20–23] The sample consisted of 88 men who had been curatively treated for nonseminomatous ($n = 49$) or seminomatous ($n = 39$) germ cell tumors an average of 45 months earlier. During and following treatment, the men reported experiencing increased fear of cancer, sleep disturbance, and cognitive dysfunction.[20] At follow-up, psychological dysfunction persisted for a minority of patients. Approximately 10% reported obsessive concern about cancer, fear of recurrence, or fear of other cancer. In addition, 9% of the men reported sleep disturbance.

Interestingly, while no formal cognitive assessment was undertaken, a significant proportion of patients did report experiencing the following three problems "frequently" or "all the time" 6 months following the end of treatment ($p < .05$ compared to prior to diagnosis) and within the previous month ($p < .05$ compared to 6 months after treatment): (1) inability to concentrate (16% at 6 months; 5% in previous month), (2) inability to think clearly (14% at 6 months; 2% in previous month), and (3) inability to complete tasks (14% at 6 months; 5% in previous month).[20]

Several published reports seem to confirm the findings of Gritz and colleagues, suggesting elevated rates of anxiety among testicular cancer survivors. Stuart and colleagues[24] also performed early psychosocial research with testicular cancer survivors (mean time since treatment, 2.5 years). The authors attempted not only to describe psychosocial outcomes of testicular cancer survivors but also to compare the outcomes by treatment modality, namely, radiation therapy versus chemotherapy. Both groups reported more symptoms of anxiety and depression after treatment compared to before treatment. However, this trend was significant only for the group receiving radiation therapy. Similar findings were reported by Kaasa and colleagues.[25] The authors compared the incidence of depression and anxiety among a group of survivors (mean time since treatment, 4.5 years) to that of age-matched controls. Their findings indicated that affective disorders were significantly more common among the group of testicular cancer survivors, compared to a group of age-

matched controls. Further evidence of the relationship between psychological functioning and testicular cancer treatment was provided by Douchez and colleagues.[26] In this study, testicular cancer (nonseminomatous) survivors were assessed an average of 9 years after treatment. Symptoms of anxiety and/or depression were retrospectively reported by 60% of the patients during treatment. At the time of interview, this proportion had dropped to 30%; however, only 5% of controls reported symptoms.

More recent investigations of psychological functioning among survivors have yielded conflicting findings. For example, in a study of Japanese patients treated for testicular cancer an average of 8 years earlier, higher levels of anxiety about future health and more depression were reported after treatment than before treatment.[27] This trend was present regardless of treatment modality (ie, chemotherapy, radiation therapy, or surveillance). Psychological morbidity was most common in the men who had received chemotherapy, compared to those who had received radiation therapy or surveillance. Recent findings by Caffo and colleagues[28] suggest that a group of Italian men curatively treated for stage I testicular seminoma with radiation therapy (median time since treatment, 10 years) had good psychological functioning although 16% reported depressive symptoms and 6% reported feeling anxious since the time of their treatment. Joly and colleagues[29] examined psychological functioning in a group of French men who were long-term survivors of testicular cancer. Survivors had been treated for either seminoma ($n = 36$) or nonseminomatous germ cell tumor ($n = 34$) a mean of 11 years earlier. No significant differences in psychological functioning were observed between survivors and controls, suggesting that testicular cancer treatment (chemotherapy, radiation therapy, or surveillance) did not negatively impact the psychological functioning of long-term survivors.

PHYSICAL FUNCTIONING

Most research efforts to date have concentrated on describing the short- and long-term toxicities of testicular cancer treatment. Several clear and consistent trends have been described. For example, chemotherapy is associated with nephrotoxicity, cardiovascular toxicity, neurotoxicity, and pulmonary toxicity whereas radiation therapy is associated with gastrointestinal and cardiopulmonary toxicity.[30] The effects that these side effects and testicular cancer itself have on QOL and other psychosocial outcomes have not been as frequently studied. Moreover, there are relatively few published reports in which physical functioning is compared between treatment groups.[31] However, evidence does suggest that men receiving chemotherapy and/or radiation therapy report more long-term physical side effects than do men who are treated only with surgery[32] and that patients receiving only chemotherapy report more physical problems than do men who receive only radiation therapy.[24,33]

Long-term follow-up studies indicate that more than one-half (54%) of men treated for testicular cancer report poorer physical condition (eg, more fatigue and decreased muscle strength) 5 or more years after treatment, compared to before treatment.[34] However, findings from other studies indicate that the incidence of physical problems is low and that most men consider themselves to be in good or excellent physical health following treatment.[21,28,35] Future research efforts using a validated measure of physical functioning are needed to more definitively assess the physical functioning outcomes of testicular cancer patients and to track these outcomes as time since treatment increases.

SOCIAL FUNCTIONING

Overall, findings suggest that survivors of testicular cancer have good social functioning. While it is difficult to reach definitive conclusions (for the reasons previously discussed), when assessed, survivors generally report equal or more satisfaction with relationships after cancer treatment, compared to before treatment. For example, early efforts to describe marital satisfaction among survivors indicate that men are more likely to report improvement as opposed to deterioration in their relationship satisfaction.[19] Gritz and colleagues[36] also examined marital relationships among testicular cancer survivors by interviewing both the survivors and their wives. Results indicated that the majority of relationships were strengthened after the cancer experience. Fac-

tors identified as important for a couple's adjustment to cancer (good communication, spousal support, and marital satisfaction) all acted positively to facilitate relationship functioning. Other studies examining satisfaction with marital relationships as well as relationships with friends and family members indicate that such functioning improves among testicular cancer survivors.[27,37]

Other researchers have attempted to assess the social functioning of testicular cancer survivors by comparing them with other patient groups or healthy age-matched controls. Bloom and colleagues[23] found no differences in social functioning (ie, group participation, number of social contacts, perception of social health, and leisure time activities) between testicular cancer survivors and Hodgkin's disease survivors. Studies comparing the social functioning of testicular cancer survivors to that of healthy controls indicate that the survivors have better social functioning. For example, Kaasa and colleagues[25] report that survivors report stronger relationships with family and friends and more confidence in receiving support from their social network in the event of illness, compared to controls. Similar findings were recently reported by Joly and colleagues[29]; in this study, survivors reported fewer separations with significant others and fewer lost friends than did healthy controls.

The reasons for the improved perception of social functioning following testicular cancer treatment are not fully understood. Diagnosis and treatment of testicular cancer may fortify existing social networks as friends and family members cope with a frightening and potentially life-threatening diagnosis, resulting in improved social functioning. A diagnosis of cancer may also cause young men to reevaluate many aspects of their lives, including social relationships, leading to a perception of better social functioning, compared to healthy controls who have not had the cancer experience.

WORK-RELATED FUNCTIONING

Work-related functioning is influenced both by disease-related variables (ie, stage of disease and treatment modality) and by nondisease-related variables (ie, socioeconomic status, social-support network, and societal systems).[38] Moreover, these individual variables can interact to further affect work functional status. Based on the typically young age at diagnosis along with the high rates of survival, work-related functioning is a particularly important outcome to consider in testicular cancer patients. Men are frequently diagnosed during years that are vital to their professional development. The prospect of taking time off work for cancer treatment can pose significant obstacles and affect career advancement. Despite its importance in this patient population, work-related functioning has been examined rather infrequently. As with the other psychosocial outcomes discussed thus far, findings from the existing literature are somewhat difficult to interpret. Widely varying methods have been used to investigate work-related outcomes, and observations have been made in highly diverse samples.

While treatment side effects may adversely affect the work functioning ability of survivors, findings to date are not consistent. Several published studies suggest that testicular cancer diagnosis and treatment-related toxicities have a negative impact on work-related functioning. Stoter and colleagues[37] reported that most survivors (90%) were able to return to work (interviews were conducted 7 to 10 years after treatment); however, 23% wanted to or had to change jobs because of reduced physical ability following cancer treatment. The findings of Stuart and colleagues[24] also suggest that cancer diagnosis and treatment may negatively affect work functioning. They found that only 75% of men treated with chemotherapy were employed at an average of 2.5 years after treatment, compared to 89% being employed before treatment. In addition, 31% of men who had received chemotherapy believed that they had lost job prospects because of testicular cancer and its treatment. Other investigators have observed more job loss among patients who were receiving chemotherapy as well.[27]

In one of the first attempts to thoroughly assess work-related functioning in testicular cancer survivors (mean time of 4 years since treatment), Edbril and Rieker[39] concluded that testicular cancer did not seriously disrupt career advancement. They found that 90% of men employed prior to diagnosis were able to return to work. A majority of men (52%) reported no change in work satisfaction following treatment as compared to before treatment, 32% reported greater work satisfaction, and only 16% reported decreased satisfaction. More recent findings by Ozen and colleagues[40] seem to support this finding. Survivors reported increased work satisfaction following radiation therapy as compared to before radiation therapy. Other researchers have attempted to investigate work-related functioning by comparing the outcomes of survivors to those of age-matched controls. Using this design, Kaasa and colleagues[25] observed better functioning among men treated for testicular cancer than they observed among healthy controls. Survivors reported fewer work-related physical problems, better ability to concentrate on job activities, and better total working ability than did controls. Joly and colleagues[29] reported similar rates of employment and job change between survivors and controls. Job-related ambition, however, was lower among survivors when compared to controls. Limited evidence suggests that various treatment modalities may have differing effects on work-related functioning. Arai and colleagues[27] observed higher levels of work satisfaction, a better ability to concentrate, and higher total working ability among survivors who had received either chemotherapy or radiation therapy when compared to survivors who had received only surveillance therapy.

SEXUAL FUNCTIONING

Of all the psychosocial domains affected by testicular cancer and its treatment, sexual function, for understandable reasons, has been among the most frequently studied. Although findings generally indicate that sexual functioning is altered among survivors, careful consideration of this outcome is warranted. The reasons for altered sexual functioning among survivors are varied. Factors such as the physical sequelae of testicular cancer itself, treatment-related side effects, or psychological distress following treatment can affect sexual functioning.[38] For example, retroperitoneal lymph node dissection (RPLND), a surgical procedure commonly used in the treatment of testicular cancer, involves the resection of retroperitoneal sympathetic nerves involved in semen emission.[38] A common side effect of RPLND is dry ejaculation, which can negatively impact sexual functioning and satisfaction. Nondisease-related variables, such as age, physical or psychological comorbidity, and marital satisfaction, may also influence the relationship between testicular cancer and sexual functioning.

Schover and colleagues were among the first to describe sexual functioning among survivors of nonseminomatous ($n = 121$) and seminomatous ($n = 74$) testicular cancer.[41-43] Their findings indicated that impaired sexual functioning was common among survivors. Survivors commonly reported erectile problems, reduced orgasmic intensity, and reduced libido.[43] In addition, patients with nonseminomatous testicular cancer had less sexual activity, reduced libido, more frequent erectile dysfunction, and reduced orgasmic intensity when compared to healthy controls.[41] Rieker and colleagues[19] reported similar findings. They found that ejaculation problems were among the most commonly reported impairments of sexual functioning; 37% of survivors reported that not being able to ejaculate had been a problem more than 50% of the time in the previous 6 months. Inability to ejaculate was also highly correlated with fertility concerns and overall sexual dysfunction; and overall sexual dysfunction was related to depression and fatigue. Stoter and colleagues[37] reported a more striking decline in sexual functioning among patients who had undergone chemotherapy with cisplatin, vinblastine, and bleomycin. Ten years after treatment, 40% of survivors reported decreased sexual performance; 8% reported erection problems, and 31% reported ejaculation problems. Gritz and colleagues[20] reported that one-third of survivors reported less sexual satisfaction at the time of assessment (45 months after treatment) as compared to sexual satisfaction before cancer diagnosis. Survivors were more than twice as likely to report erectile dysfunction after cancer diagnosis than before diagnosis. The same authors further explored outcomes in sexual functioning by comparing the perceptions of survivors to those of their spouses in a subsequent analysis.[20] While both survivors and their spouses reported a decreased frequency of sexual intercourse following cancer treatment as compared to before treatment, survivors reported decreased sexual satisfaction whereas their wives reported increased satisfaction.

Other findings suggest that impaired sexual functioning among survivors of testicular cancer may not be a permanent condition. For example, the findings from a prospective analysis suggest that while patients are significantly less satisfied with their status of sexual functioning 6 months after completion of treatment, this dissatisfaction is not observed at either 12 or 36 months after the completion of treatment.[44] Similarly, a significant decrease in sexual desire and increased erectile problems were reported at 6 and 12 months after treatment when compared to baseline (prior to diagnosis). However, by 36 months post treatment, sexual desire and frequency of erectile problems were not significantly different from baseline.[44] More recently published findings by van Basten and colleagues[45] also appear to suggest that sexual functioning does recover following treatment. Their results, also from a prospective study, indicate that considerable sexual morbidity occurs during treatment but that patients tend to recover by 1 year after treatment. Ozen and colleagues[40] also observed some recovery in regard to sexual function outcomes (ie, erection problems and sexual desire) at follow-up. Sexual functioning, however, was still poorer than baseline, and the frequency of ejaculation problems continued to increase with time.

Overall, the psychosocial literature indicates that impaired sexual functioning is more enduring: approximately 15% of long-term survivors report some type of sexual dysfunction.[46] In addition, impairment of sexual functioning is not restricted to a single treatment modality. Hartmann and colleagues[33] did observe differences in the rates of sexual function problems between treatment groups, with patients who undergo RPLND (either with or without chemotherapy) reporting more problems with ejaculation, but significant problems have been reported in all treatment groups. Joly and colleagues[29] recently published findings indicating that sexual functioning was significantly modified in 49% of testicular cancer survivors (mean time of 11 years since treatment). Both sexual desire and satisfaction were significantly reduced in survivors when compared to age matched controls. Furthermore, modified sexual functioning was not significantly associated with treatment group (ie, chemotherapy or radiation with or without

RPLND). This lack of significant association between RPLND and modified sexual functioning suggests that modern nerve-sparing surgical techniques have reduced the once-common morbidities associated with this type of surgery.[47]

FERTILITY

Reduced fertility is a frequently reported adverse effect of testicular cancer treatment. In fact, estimates indicate that up to 25% of survivors may have reduced fertility.[30] It has also been reported that fertility may be reduced prior to diagnosis, suggesting a shared etiologic factor between testicular cancer and reduced fertility.[13] Reduced fertility may result from treatment side effects, such as reduced spermatogenesis following cytotoxic therapy or such as dry ejaculation following RPLND. However, modern therapeutic techniques have greatly reduced these outcomes.[38] In addition, the availability of sperm banking has further increased the ability of survivors to father children. The effects of reduced fertility on the QOL of survivors are not fully understood. Limited evidence does suggest that some survivors report an unfulfilled wish to father children[33] and more anxiety about fathering children after cancer treatment than before cancer treatment.[40]

BODY IMAGE

Another disease-specific outcome sometimes considered is body image. Gritz and colleagues[36] reported that 24% of survivors perceived themselves to be less attractive as a result of testicular cancer treatment. The perception of decreased attractiveness was significantly associated with treatment modality, with survivors who had received RPLND and/or chemotherapy being the most likely survivors to report perceived decreases in attractiveness. Patients who underwent only orchiectomy were the least likely to perceive a decrease in attractiveness. Interestingly, none of the spouses of the survivors perceived a decrease in attractiveness. Recent findings among survivors of pure seminoma who have undergone orchiectomy and radation therapy indicate that less than 5% of these survivors consider themselves to be less attractive after treatment.[48]

Gritz and colleagues[20] also investigated the impact of testicular prostheses on body image. Interestingly, only 61.8% of participants reported being offered a cosmetic replacement. While most men (57.2%) who had the option explained to them were satisfied with their body image and declined prosthetic placement, 88.9 % of the men who chose the option were happy with the result. Seventy-eight percent of men who chose to have a testicular prosthesis expressed the need to look as much as possible like they did prior to orchiectomy. These findings suggest that while the majority of testicular cancer survivors may not feel the need for a testicular prosthesis after orchiectomy, a minority may be helped by the option, emphasizing the need for health care providers to explain the option of testicular prosthesis to all testicular cancer patients.

OVERALL QUALITY OF LIFE

Several investigators have attempted to assess overall QOL of survivors of testicular cancer. Methods for assessing this outcome vary widely among studies. Overall QOL may be reported as a component summary score generated from various weighted scale scores of more specific functional status outcomes (eg, physical role limitations, emotional functioning, and social functioning). For example, the Medical Outcomes Study 36-Item Short Form (SF-36), a commonly used generic QOL measure, incorporates scores of eight different functional status constructs: physical functioning, role-physical, bodily pain, general health, vitality, social functioning, role-emotional, and mental health.[49] These eight scales can then be combined to generate two summary scores: the Physical Component Summary and the Mental Component Summary. Alternatively, overall QOL is sometimes assessed on the basis of response to a single survey item. This single item typically has the participant rate his perception of an overall sense of well-being or overall satisfaction with life. Ideally, a testicular cancer–specific scale would be used. Such a measure would incorporate the generic dimensions of functioning (ie, physical health, psychological health, and social health) as well as disease-specific dimensions. Such disease-specific dimensions would consider distress that was due to treatment side effects (eg, ototoxicity, nephrotoxicity, and Raynaud's phenomenon), as well as fertility concerns and sexual functioning. Unfortunately, such a measure with good psychometric properties is not yet widely available.

Arai and colleagues[27] used the Satisfaction with Life Scale and found overall high levels of life satisfaction among testicular survivors. Statistically significant differences, however, were observed between treatment groups. Despite the toxicities associated with cytotoxic therapy, survivors who received chemotherapy reported the highest levels of satisfaction with life, followed by patients who received radiation therapy, while patients who received only surveillance reported the lowest levels of overall life satisfaction.

Using a single item, Caffo and colleagues[28] also examined overall QOL among a group of testicular cancer survivors who had received radiation therapy. Only 8% of the survivors reported that their QOL had been negatively affected by cancer and cancer treatment, but 26% reported poor overall QOL. The only variables associated with overall QOL were information about the disease and information about the treatment. Survivors who were not satisfied with the information they received from their health care providers reported poorer overall QOL.

Joly and colleagues[29] examined overall QOL in a group of testicular cancer survivors and in a group of age-matched controls, using both the SF-36, a generic measure of QOL,[49] and the European Organization for Research and Treatment of Cancer (EORTC) Quality of Life Questionnaire (QLQ-C30), a QOL measure designed to be used with cancer patients.[50] They found no significant differences in overall QOL (as indicated by SF-36 and EORTC QLQ-C30 scores) between survivors and controls, suggesting that testicular cancer treatment does not negatively impact QOL.

Together, these findings suggest that the overall QOL of testicular cancer survivors is not significantly impaired. However, future research efforts are still warranted. A measure that is specific to testicular cancer is needed to better describe the overall QOL of testicular cancer survivors. In addition, more comparisons with appropriate controls are

needed before long-term overall QOL outcomes can be truly understood. Also, more attempts to describe potential differences in overall QOL (as well as other psychosocial outcomes) between treatment groups are needed. Such information would be valuable to both testicular cancer patients and their physicians, enabling them to select the most appropriate treatment option(s).

CONCLUSION

Limitations of the Literature

The existing psychosocial literature on testicular cancer has several clear limitations. First, the vast majority of publications to date have used a cross-sectional design. Psychosocial outcomes can only be fully assessed and interpreted with prospective data. For example, it is not possible to truly assess the effects of chemotherapy on psychosocial functioning without knowing the level of psychosocial functioning prior to the initiation of treatment. Retrospective studies, requiring participants to report functional status before their cancer diagnoses, introduce bias into any estimate of association. This recall bias obscures the true association between testicular cancer and psychosocial outcomes. Second, many previously published studies have no control group for comparison. For instance, knowing that 10% of survivors report impaired sexual functioning without knowing this proportion in an age-matched control group greatly impairs the interpretability of the findings. A third limitation is the methodology used to assess psychosocial constructs. Frequently, these outcomes were assessed by measures that are without psychometrically established properties. Such practices reduce the ability to generalize the findings and complicate comparability with other findings. A final limitation also impairing the application of findings to the broad population of patients is the composition of study samples. It is not uncommon for researchers to group all survivors together, regardless of histology, stage of disease, treatment modality, or year of treatment. Further, small sample sizes provide inadequate statistical power to examine subgroup comparisons in other than purely descriptive ways. In addition, these studies were conducted with culturally diverse (eg, American, Norwegian, French, and Japanese) populations of survivors, which further complicates comparisons. Most if not all of these limitations are understandable, considering the rarity of testicular cancer. Nonetheless, efforts to overcome these limitations are needed.

A study currently under way will attempt to provide relevant data on key remaining issues in the psychosocial literature on testicular cancer. This prospective study, Neurocognitive Function and Quality of Life after Testicular Cancer Treatment (Ellen R. Gritz, PhD, principal investigator), assesses neurocognitive function in participants with NSGCTs, using an established battery of neuropsychological tests that measure abilities such as memory, attention, concentration, oral fluency, and dexterity. Both generic and disease-specific psychosocial outcomes are also thoroughly assessed. Generic psychosocial constructs include physical functioning, social functioning, mental health, and general health perceptions. As no established measure specific to testicular cancer is available, a battery of tests and items has been compiled that assesses constructs that are likely affected by testicular cancer and its treatment. These constructs include body image, fertility, sexual function, and relationship/dating satisfaction.

The study has two major objectives: (1) to describe neurocognitive functioning and QOL in patients being treated for testicular cancer and (2) to examine prospectively the dose-response relationship between neurocognitive functioning and chemotherapy dose. Patients are assessed at three time points: (1) baseline (after orchiectomy but prior to chemotherapy), (2) immediately following the completion of chemotherapy (if the participant does not receive chemotherapy, the first follow-up assessment is performed 3 months after baseline), and (3) 12 months after the baseline assessment. Another innovative feature of this study is the sample composition. Patients are recruited from two large cancer centers, one in the Netherlands and one in the United States. Such methodology will facilitate cross-cultural comparisons. The study, which is funded by the Lance Armstrong Foundation, will not only provide a much needed prospective analysis of psychosocial outcomes and use a robust set of psychometrically validated measures (designed to assess both generic and disease-specific functioning) but will also be the first attempt to examine neurocognitive function in this patient group.

Summary

Psychosocial functioning is clearly affected by testicular cancer and testicular cancer treatment. However, questions about the magnitude and duration of these effects have not yet been definitively answered. Evidence does suggest that the majority of survivors report good psychosocial adjustment and high levels of functioning. This finding is quite encouraging, considering the ever growing population of testicular cancer survivors.

Significant problems, particularly those of impaired sexual functioning, persist even years after the completion of testicular cancer treatment. Possible impairments should be thoroughly discussed with all testicular cancer patients prior to initiating treatment, as well as during and after treatment. Fertility problems also represent a disease-specific functional impairment confronting testicular cancer survivors. Potential fertility problems should also be discussed prior to initiating treatment, and sperm banking should be offered when appropriate. Recent estimates indicate that sperm banking is not discussed with 40% of young male cancer survivors.[51] Finally, given the long life expectancy of testicular cancer survivors, it is important to assess health behaviors (eg, physical activity, diet, alcohol intake, and smoking status). Although health behaviors have not yet been thoroughly assessed among testicular cancer survivors, limited evidence suggests that survivors may be less physically active than healthy controls[26] and may smoke cigarettes at higher rates than Hodgkin's disease survivors.[23] Health care professionals should address the importance of a healthy lifestyle, and, if indicated, adequate treatment (eg, behavioral therapy and pharmacotherapy for smokers) should be offered to survivors.

ACKNOWLEDGMENT

This work was supported in part by a grant from the Lance Armstrong Foundation, Neurocognitive Function and Quality of Life after Testicular Cancer Treatment study (Ellen R. Gritz, PhD, principal investigator).

REFERENCES

1. Steele GS, Richie JP, Stewart AK, Menck HR. The National Cancer Data Base report on patterns of care for testicular carcinoma, 1985–1996. Cancer 1999;86(10):2171–83.

2. American Cancer Society. Cancer facts and figures, 2002. Atlanta (GA): American Cancer Society; 2002. p. 2, 17–18.

3. Sigurdson AJ, Cooper SJ, Burau K, Spitz M. Continued increase of testicular cancer. Cancer Bull 1994;46:452–5.

4. McKiernan JM, Goluboff ET, Liberson GL, et al. Rising risk of testicular cancer by birth cohort in the United States from 1973 to 1995. J Urol 1999;162(2):361–3.

5. Bergstrom R, Adami HO, Mohner M, et al. Increase in testicular cancer incidence in six European countries: a birth cohort phenomenon. J Natl Cancer Inst 1996;88(11):727–33.

6. Pharris-Ciurej ND, Cook LS, Weiss NS. Incidence of testicular cancer in the United States: has the epidemic begun to abate? Am J Epidemiol 1999;150(1):45–6.

7. Stang A, Ahrens W, Bromen K, et al. Undescended testis and the risk of testicular cancer: importance of source and classification of exposure information. Int J Epidemiol 2001;30(5):1050–6.

8. Gallagher RP, Huchcroft S, Phillips N, et al. Physical activity, medical history, and risk of testicular cancer (Alberta and British Columbia, Canada). Cancer Causes Control 1995;6(5):398–406.

9. Petridou E, Roukas KI, Dessypris N, et al. Baldness and other correlates of sex hormones in relation to testicular cancer. Int J Cancer 1997;71(6):982–5.

10. Akre O, Ekbom A, Sparen P, Tretli S. Body size and testicular cancer. J Natl Cancer Inst 2000;92(13):1093–6.

11. Srivastava A, Kreiger N. Relation of physical activity to risk of testicular cancer. Am J Epidemiol 2000;151(1):78–87.

12. Weir HK, Marrett LD, Kreiger N, et al. Pre-natal and peri-natal exposures and risk of testicular germ-cell cancer. Int J Cancer 2000;87(3):438–43.

13. Moller H, Skakkebaek NE. Risk of testicular cancer in subfertile men: case-control study. BMJ 1999;318(7183):559–62.

14. Benedetto P. Chemotherapy of testis cancer. Cancer Control 1999;6(6):549–59.

15. Testa MA, Simonson DC. Assesment of quality-of-life outcomes. N Engl J Med 1996;334(13):835–40.

16. Brenner MH, Curbow B, Legro MW. The proximal-distal continuum of multiple health outcome measures: the case of cataract surgery. Med Care 1995;33(4 Suppl):AS236–44.

17. Institute of Medicine (U.S.). Committee on a National Agenda for the Prevention of Disabilities. Disability in America : toward a national agenda for prevention. Washington (DC): National Academy Press; 1991. p. 1–5.

18. Wilson IB, Cleary PD. Linking clinical variables with health-related quality of life. A conceptual model of patient outcomes. JAMA 1995;273(1):59–65.

19. Rieker PP, Edbril SD, Garnick MB. Curative testis cancer therapy: psychosocial sequelae. J Clin Oncol 1985;3(8):1117–26.

20. Gritz ER, Wellisch DK, Wang HJ, et al. Long-term effects of testicular cancer on sexual functioning in married couples. Cancer 1989;64(7):1560–7.

21. Gritz ER, Wellisch DK, Landsverk JA. Psychosocial sequelae in long-term survivors of testicular cancer. J Psychosoc Oncol 1988;6(3/4):41–63.

22. Hannah MT, Gritz ER, Wellisch DK, et al. Changes in marital and sexual functioning in long-term survivors and their spouses: testicular cancer versus Hodgkin's disease. Psychooncology 1992;1:89–103.

23. Bloom JR, Fobair P, Gritz E, et al. Psychosocial outcomes of cancer: a comparative analysis of Hodgkin's disease and testicular cancer. J Clin Oncol 1993;11(5):979–88.

24. Stuart NS, Grundy R, Woodroffe CM, Cullen MH. Quality of life after treatment for testicular cancer—the patient's view. Eur J Cancer 1990;26(3):291–4.

25. Kaasa S, Aass N, Mastekaasa A, et al. Psychosocial well-being in testicular cancer patients. Eur J Cancer 1991;27(9):1091–5.

26. Douchez J, Droz JP, Desclaux B, et al. Quality of life in long-term survivors of nonseminomatous germ cell testicular tumors. J Urol 1993;149(3):498–501.

27. Arai Y, Kawakita M, Hida S, et al. Psychosocial aspects in long-term survivors of testicular cancer. J Urol 1996;155:574–8.

28. Caffo O, Amichetti M, Tomio L, Galligioni E. Quality of life after radiotherapy for early-stage testicular seminoma. Radiother Oncol 2001;59(1):13–20.

29. Joly F, Heron JF, Kalusinski L, et al. Quality of life in long-term survivors of testicular cancer: a population-based case-control study. J Clin Oncol 2002;20(1):73–80.

30. Grossfeld GD, Small EJ. Long-term side effects of treatment for testis cancer. Urol Clin North Am 1998;25(3):503–15.

31. Bertetto O, Bracada S, Tamburini M, Cortesi E. Quality of life studies and genito-urinary tumors. Ann Oncol 2001;12 Suppl 3:S43–8.

32. Fossa SD, Moynihan C, Serbouti S. Patients' and doctors' perception of long-term morbidity in patients with testicular cancer clinical stage I. A descriptive pilot study. Support Care Cancer 1996;4(2):118–28.

33. Hartmann JT, Kollmannsberger C, Kanz L, Bokemeyer C. Platinum organ toxicity and possible prevention in patients with testicular cancer. Int J Cancer 1999;83(6):866–9.

34. Gotay CC, Muraoka MY. Quality of life in long-term survivors of adult-onset cancers. J Natl Cancer Inst 1998;90(9):656–67.

35. Petersen PM, Hansen SW. The course of long-term toxicity in patients treated with cisplatin-based chemotherapy for non-seminomatous germ-cell cancer. Ann Oncol 1999;10(12):1475–83.

36. Gritz ER, Wellisch DK, Siau J, Wang HJ. Long-term effects of testicular cancer on marital relationships. Psychosomatics 1990;31(3):301–12.

37. Stoter G, Koopman A, Vendrik CP, et al. Ten-year survival and late sequelae in testicular cancer patients treated with cisplatin, vinblastine, and bleomycin. J Clin Oncol 1989;7(8):1099–104.

38. Fossa SD, Dahl AA, Haaland CF. Health-related quality of life in patients treated for testicular cancer. Curr Opin Urol 1999;9(5):425–9.

39. Edbril SD, Rieker PP. The impact of testicular cancer on the work lives of survivors. J Psychosoc Oncol 1989;7(3):17–29.

40. Ozen H, Sahin A, Toklu C, et al. Psychosocial adjustment after testicular cancer treatment. J Urol 1998;159(6):1947–50.

41. Schover LR, von Eschenbach AC. Sexual and marital relationships after treatment for nonseminomatous testicular cancer. Urology 1985;25(3):251–5.

42. Schover LR, Gonzales M, von Eschenbach AC. Sexual and marital relationships after radiotherapy for seminoma. Urology 1986;27(2):117–23.

43. Schover LR. Sexuality and fertility in urologic cancer patients. Cancer 1987;60(3 Suppl):553–8.

44. Aass N, Grunfeld B, Kaalhus O, Fossa SD. Pre- and post-treatment sexual life in testicular cancer patients: a descriptive investigation. Br J Cancer 1993;67(5):1113–7.

45. van Basten JP, van Driel MF, Hoekstra HJ, et al. Objective and subjective effects of treatment for testicular cancer on sexual function. BJU Int 1999;84(6):671–8.

46. Heidenreich A, Hofmann R. Quality-of-life issues in the treatment of testicular cancer. World J Urol 1999;17(4):230–8.

47. Turek PJ, Lowther DN, Carroll PR. Fertility issues and their management in men with testis cancer. Urol Clin North Am 1998;25(3):517–31.

48. Caffo O, Amichetti M. Evaluation of sexual life after orchidectomy followed by radiotherapy for early-stage seminoma of the testis. BJU Int 1999;83(4):462–8.

49. Ware JE Jr, Sherbourne CD. The MOS 36-item short-form health survey (SF-36). I. Conceptual framework and item selection. Med Care 1992;30(6):473–83.

50. Aaronson NK, Ahmedzai S, Bergman B, et al. The European Organization for Research and Treatment of Cancer QLQ-C30: a quality-of-life instrument for use in international clinical trials in oncology. J Natl Cancer Inst 1993;85(5):365–76.

51. Schover LR, Brey K, Lichtin A, et al. Knowledge and experience regarding cancer, infertility, and sperm banking in younger male survivors. J Clin Oncol 2002;20(7):1880–9.

25

End-of-Life Considerations for Patients with Germ Cell Tumors

ERIC A. SINGER, MA

JANE M. INGHAM, MB, BS, FRACP

Although germ cell cancer is often considered as the paradigm for curable malignancy, it remains a disease associated with a significant loss of life-years because of the youthful age group affected. While the incidence of germ cell tumors has continued to rise, ongoing research has provided patients with more effective medical and surgical treatments, resulting in a cure rate in excess of 90%. This combination of increasing incidence and survivability is producing a unique subset of cancer patients: young men and women who will live the majority of their lives post treatment. The proportion of patients with germ cell tumors in the United States who encounter progressive chemotherapy-resistant disease is small, but the general and disease-specific problems faced by these patients (those living with this disease near the end of life) and the problems of their families and health care providers have not been thoroughly examined.

This chapter addresses the epidemiology of the end-of-life experience for those patients whose germ cell tumors do not respond to curative therapy and also focuses on the spectrum of problems faced by these patients and their caregivers. The components of optimal end-of-life care will be outlined, and some approaches for optimizing this care are provided. While it must be acknowledged that the experience of cancer varies widely among countries, much of the epidemiologic data reported in this chapter relate to the experiences of cancer patients in the United States. Nonetheless, much of the discussion, particularly in regard to the components of optimal end-of-life care, has broad applicability worldwide. Finally, although there has been a recent

increase in discussion about the end-of-life components of the illness experience, both the experience itself and the interventions that may be specific to the end-of-life period have not been given a high priority in oncologic educational initiatives, health care delivery, or research. Given the paucity of data pertaining to this aspect of health care, areas that are in need of further research are highlighted throughout the chapter.

INCIDENCE

Nearly 95% of malignancies found in the testis are germ cell tumors, and these tumors account for 1% of all tumors in males.[1] In the ovary, 2 to 3% of malignancies are germ cell tumors. Germ cell tumors are the most common malignancy diagnosed in males between the ages of 15 and 34 years[1]; the peak incidence of germ cell tumors in the ovary is in the patients' early twenties. In the year 2002, approximately 7,500 new cases and 400 deaths caused by testicular germ cell tumors were anticipated in the United States.[2] Overall this incidence reflects an increase of 500 cases and 100 deaths from the estimates proposed in 2000.[3] Annually, 6,000 to 8,000 new cases of testicular germ cell tumors are diagnosed.[4]

Globally, germ cell tumor incidence rates vary, with the highest rates reported in Scandinavia, Germany, and New Zealand. Intermediate rates are seen in the United States, and the lowest rates are documented in Asia and Africa.[5] Over the past 40 years, the incidence of germ cell tumor in the United States and northern Europe has increased fourfold; during the same period, global incidence rates have doubled.[6–8] Concurrent with this increase in incidence, more-effective therapies have led to a decline in mortality.[9] The survival rate in 1963 was 63%; the 5-year survival rate for newly diagnosed germ cell tumor patients is now greater than 95%.[10] The majority of deaths that occur from this disease occur in patients under the age of 44 years. Thus, against this background (and using the common "battle" metaphor used in the oncology setting), the patient facing death due to testicular cancer will risk suffering from the added emotional burden of "losing a battle" that most other patients have "won."

MORTALITY

The initial spread of most germ cell tumors occurs to the lumbar para-aortic lymph nodes via the testicular lymphatics. Less frequently, direct lymphatic communication or hematogenous spread can occur, resulting in metastases to diverse areas. Two postmortem studies, one of 78 and the other of 154 patients with histologically confirmed germ cell tumors, found that metastatic disease often followed predictable patterns. In order of decreasing frequency, sites of metastases commonly reported were lungs (90%), retroperitoneal lymph nodes (80%), liver (70%), mediastinal lymph nodes (65%), brain (30%), kidney (30%), gastrointestinal tract (27%), bone (20–30%), adrenals (20–30%), peritoneum (20%), and spleen (10–20%).[11,12] Less frequent sites of metastases include the pancreas, pleura, heart, pericardium, and vena cava.[11,12] The diaphragm, thyroid, breasts, eyes, skin, and spinal cord are rare reported locations for germ cell tumor spread.[11,12] Despite the great impact of platinum-containing chemotherapy on the prognosis of germ cell tumors, Bredael and colleagues reported that such regimens did not alter the fundamental pattern of metastases seen in advanced disease.[12]

Most deaths related to germ cell tumors are attributable to organ failure, hemorrhage, or sepsis.[11] Iatrogenic causes, although rare, are also a risk, given the intensive manner with which primary treatment and salvage therapy are undertaken.

Thus, although death from this disease is rare, those deaths that are due to organ failure follow the patterns of metastasis outlined above, with respiratory failure and liver failure being commonly seen.[11,12] Brain metastases may also be a cause of death. Bone metastases, although not fatal in and of themselves, may be signs of advanced and resistant disease, often with multiple organ involvement. Hemorrhagic complications from hemoptysis, intrapulmonary bleeding, gastrointestinal bleeding, rupture of the inferior vena cava, intrahepatic bleeding, and cerebral hemorrhage have all been reported.[11,12] Sepsis, when it occurs, is often the result of pneumonia or obstructive uropathy.[11] Iatrogenic causes, such as pulmonary fibrosis from bleomycin toxicity, posttreatment liver failure or postirradiation pericarditis, postoperative pulmonary embolism, and sepsis, also contribute to the mortality rate of patients with germ cell tumors and accounted for 6% of deaths in one postmortem study.[12] It is important to note, however, that "iatrogenic" numbers of this magnitude were reported in only one study, which took place two decades ago; since that time, many treatment techniques have been developed to minimize the risks associated with therapy. For a more detailed discussion, readers are referred to the chapters that address short- and long-term side effects of treatment (see Chapters 27 and 28).

PURSUING A "GOOD DEATH"

Over the past several decades, Western medicine's concept of death has evolved from one viewing death as a failure of science and technology to one properly recognizing death as an experience every person must face. With this paradigm shift, educational and research projects in the United States, such as the American Medical Association's Education for Physicians on End-of-Life Care and the Robert Wood Johnson Foundation's Last Acts Campaign, have worked to focus the attention of clinicians on improving the end-of-life experience for patients.

Experts and expert groups that have published frameworks for end-of-life care include the American Geriatrics Society,[13] the Institute of Medicine,[14,15] Emanuel and Emanuel,[16] and the American Society of Clinical Oncology (ASCO) (see "Optimal Care at the End of Life" later in this chapter). Although these reports addressed the care of broad populations (and not specifically those affected by germ cell tumors), their recommendations reinforce the importance of attention to a variety of domains of patient and family care in the end-of-life setting for patients with many diseases, including those with germ cell tumors. Such domains include those of pain and symptom management, family support, caregiver support, patient preferences, care across cultures and for minority groups, systems-based barriers to care, and many other issues. Many of these are addressed in this chapter.

Researchers at the University of Toronto undertook a study that specifically examined patients' perspectives on end-of-life care. These researchers interviewed a group of 126 patients consisting of hemodialysis patients ($n = 48$), patients who were positive for human immunodeficiency virus (HIV) ($n = 40$), and residents of a long-term care facility ($n = 38$).[17] The results of this study identified five domains of quality end-of-life care that were emphasized by patients:

1. Adequate pain and symptom management
2. Avoidance of inappropriate prolongation of dying
3. Sense of control
4. Relief of burden
5. Strengthened relationships with loved ones

The domains described by the University of Toronto researchers mesh well with the components of a "good death" that were elucidated in another study, conducted in Durham, NC, by Duke University researchers who conducted focus groups consisting of physicians, nurses, social workers, chaplains, hospice volunteers, patients, and recently bereaved family members.[18] This study identified six themes believed to be critical to the end-of-life experience: (1) pain and symptom management; (2) clear decision making; (3) preparation for death by naming a medical decision maker, completing advanced directives, and putting one's financial and related affairs in order; (4) fulfillment of unfinished personal or spiritual commitments; (5) contribution to others; and (6) affirmation of the whole person.[18]

Although these studies were focused on older populations than those with germ cell tumors, the concepts raised are noteworthy. Both the University of Toronto and Duke University studies demonstrated that patients, care givers, and health care providers are concerned with much more than pain control and symptom relief. Both studies emphasize that most patients want to participate actively in decisions regarding medical interventions at the end of life and desire relief of pain and symptoms without having to sacrifice cognitive capacity. A second theme is the goal of strengthening relationships, fulfilling familial or spiritual obligations, and reflecting on the meaning of one's life. Medicine often deals poorly with these types of existential concerns, which is understandable, given their protean and subjective nature. However, it is possible to do patients a disservice by focusing on the physical aspects of their illnesses to such an extent that inadequate time is spent exploring the patients' own ultimate motivations and priorities for the time that they may have before death. Truly competent care must be committed to helping patients achieve their goals, even at the end of life.

Such care requires a broad view and a spectrum of expertise. In the United States, the Last Acts Palliative Care Task Force,[19] a group representing many constituencies that are focused on improving end-of-life care, stated, "Palliative care must focus on the comprehensive management of the physical, psychological, social, spiritual and existential needs of patients while remaining sensitive to patients' goals for medical care and their personal, cultural, and religious values, beliefs, and practices." By its nature, such care usually requires interdisciplinary input and must be available throughout the course of illness, not only at the end of life. If physicians are skilled in palliative care and can access resources that can complement their skills when needed, then regardless of whether the patient's goals are focused on life-sustaining treatments or on comfort alone, it can be feasible for the patient to hope to achieve the best possible quality of life with relief of suffering, control of symptoms, and optimization of psychological and physical functional capacity.

PHYSICAL SIGNS AND SYMPTOMS AND THE END-OF-LIFE EXPERIENCE

Symptom Distress in Patients with Advanced Cancer

Unfortunately, no studies that specifically examine the symptoms experienced by patients with germ cell tumors at the end of life have been conducted.

The numerous projects that have been completed examined patient populations with a variety of advanced malignancies, requiring readers to extrapolate a generalized "advanced-cancer" experience to the subset of patients in which they are interested. The common symptoms reported in the advanced-cancer population include fatigue, pain, anxiety, and anorexia, each with prevalence rates reported to be greater than 50%.[20-28] In addition, most patients with advanced cancer experience a multitude of symptoms simultaneously.[21,24,26]

It is important to note that the majority of studies have focused on "physical" symptoms such as pain or anorexia rather than on "psychological" symptoms such as anxiety and depression. Studies that included the examination of psychological symptoms found such symptoms to be common in patients with advanced malignancy.[24,29-33]

Pain, Dyspnea, and Anxiety/Depression in Patients with Advanced Cancer

Although entire chapters in this text are dedicated to the topics of pain management, patient support, and psychosocial issues, the regularity with which patients and their caregivers confront pain, dyspnea, and anxiety/depression at the end of life suggests that these topics merit brief discussion here as well. When interpreting the reported prevalence of symptoms, it is important to note that despite the availability of many effective treatment strategies, there is strong evidence from a multiplicity of sources that these management techniques are underused. Thus, in regard to prevalence rates, the challenge is to define both the true prevalence rates and the prevalence of undertreatment of symptoms.

Large surveys have repeatedly documented that pain is experienced by 70 to 90% of patients with advanced cancer.[34-37] The National Hospice Study ($N = 1,754$) found that pain became more prevalent in cancer patients during the last weeks of life. Of the patients enrolled in this study who could provided self-reported data, 25% indicated that persistent or severe pain was present within 2 days of death.[38] This proportion had increased from 17% in the previous 6 days. In the SUPPORT study, 40 to 46% of patients with cancer who had been conscious

during the last 3 days of life were perceived by their relatives to have had moderate to severe pain for more than half of this time period.[39,40]

Pain problems at the end of life are certainly complicated by the widely acknowledged problem of under-treatment, a problem that exists despite numerous available approaches to manage pain effectively.[41] The commonly accepted approach to cancer pain relief, outlined in the World Health Organization (WHO) cancer pain guidelines, uses a comprehensive pain assessment and a combination of opioid, non-opioid, and adjuvant drugs titrated to the individual needs of the patient according to the severity of the pain.[42,43] These guidelines have been tested in numerous studies that have confirmed that this approach can provide adequate pain relief for 70 to 90% of cancer patients who experience pain.[41,44-48] Additional strategies are available to address pain that is not responsive to the basic guideline interventions.[41] In such instances, pain specialists can be called upon to provide recommendations to help maximize the patient's alertness while providing adequate pain relief. This, as noted, was a major concern expressed by patients in the University of Toronto and Duke University studies that addressed patient preferences at the end of life.[17,18] Thus, in the setting of a wealth of data indicating that pain is undertreated,[49-51] it is not possible to ascertain the degree to which the high prevalence of pain in advanced disease reflects worsening pathology, undertreatment, or both. Nonetheless, it is apparent that in the setting of care delivery for patients with germ cell tumors (in whom pain could result from bone or visceral metastases, tumor masses adjacent to neural structures, hepatomegaly, or other causes), it is crucial that expertise in pain management be available (see also Chapter 26).

As with pain, there are now specific studies addressing the prevalence of dyspnea at the end of life for patients with germ cell tumors. Dyspnea is, however, a symptom that is commonly reported toward the end of life. Variable prevalence rates have been reported in advanced cancer cases, ranging from 20 to 78%.[52-55] Methodologic inconsistencies between studies likely account, at least in part, for this wide variation. Two studies reported that dyspnea increases at the end of life. The National Hospice Study reported that dyspnea was present in 70% of 1,754 patients during the final 6 weeks of life,[52] and a study of 86 cancer patients by Higginson and McCarthy found that in 21% of the patients, dyspnea was a severe symptom near death.[53] The SUPPORT study reported dyspnea as moderate to severe for the last few days of life in 70% and 30% of lung and colon cancer patients, respectively. Unfortunately, the methodology of studies of dyspnea has often been less than optimal, and in some studies, judgments about the presence of dyspnea have been made by caregivers (rather than patients) and may have reflected an observation of "heavy breathing" that may or may not have been distressing at the end of life. Dyspnea (when it is subjectively distressing), while not a symptom that has been as intensively studied as pain, is treatable, and there are management guidelines that describe effective strategies for minimizing patients' distress.[56] Given that lung metastases are common in the setting of advanced germ cell tumors, attention should be paid to this symptom, and clinicians should be prepared to treat it when it does occur.

Anxiety, worry, nervousness, and sadness have commonly been reported by patients with advanced cancer.[24,29–33] As with the symptoms discussed above, effective treatment guidelines have been described for these conditions.[57] In the setting of germ cell tumors, in which patients may be young and in which death is viewed as occurring at an "unnatural" time of life, these symptoms are likely to be common both in patients and in their caregivers. Many young patients have had no experiences with deaths of relatives or friends, and their fears may be focused on an array of concerns, some of which may occur and some of which are most unlikely. Some concerns may relate to the physical experience of death itself; others may relate to emotional, social, and spiritual losses and fears. Fears can be wide-ranging. For example, never having encountered death, some patients may fear worsening pain or dementia, others may fear dependence on family for long periods and loss of control, others may be focused on losses related to children or parents, and yet others may be concerned about spiritual issues. Young patients may have concerns about children, siblings, parents, finances, and other matters that are somewhat different from the concerns of older patients.

It is important for clinicians caring for patients with germ cell tumors to be aware of the spectrum of concerns that trigger anxiety and depression, including both the common concerns and concerns that may be linked to a patient's young age, and to be open to exploring these concerns. Of course, this should be undertaken in a timely manner that is respectful of the patients' culture, preferences for information, and understanding of their disease status. In addition, physicians need to be prepared to explain and implement approaches to symptom management, patient and family support, and other concerns. It is important that clinicians also are able to diagnose states of anxiety and depression that may need specific pharmacologic treatments and that they are aware of the spectrum of treatments available for such problems. In some instances, referral to specialized support may be the optimal approach. There is a risk that those clinicians who provide care for young patients (such as young patients with germ cell tumors) may assume that anxiety and depression are "natural" under such circumstances and may not recognize when such symptoms may be amenable to treatment.*

Mental Status and Consciousness

The level of consciousness near the end of life is influenced by a diverse range of factors, including the extent of disease, coexisting organ failure, and medication use. Specific germ cell tumor data are, again, not available. Clinical experience suggests that it is not uncommon for patients to harbor concerns about the "mode of death" that is likely to occur, and this can contribute to anxiety. One aspect upon which some patients focus relates to level of consciousness. Especially with patients who are young and have not been involved with others who have died, there is a risk that they may worry about losing consciousness

---

*Editor's note: In this difficult situation, another complicating variable may be the contrast between the success of therapy in other patients being treated at the same time and the failure of therapy to achieve cure in the dying patient; this may lead to an additional complexity of the depression and anxiety that characterize this phase of care of patients with advanced germ cell cancer.

or losing their ability to communicate for long periods. The data that exist for other advanced cancers suggest that the ability to communicate effectively with caregivers begins to decrease for the majority of patients only in the last few days of life. The SUPPORT study described the experiences of patients with lung cancer ($n = 409$) and documented that 80% were reported by family members to be conscious during the 3 days prior to death, with 55% reported as being able to communicate effectively at this time.[40] In the population with colon cancer ($n = 148$), these figures were 70% and 40%, respectively. A survey of patients with cancer who died at St. Christopher's Hospice in the United Kingdom described 10% of patients as alert, 67% as drowsy or semiconscious, and 23% as unarousable or unconscious during the last 24 hours of life.[58] Last, a survey of inpatient and home care cancer deaths found that one-third of patients were able to interact with others 24 hours prior to death; this group decreased to one-fifth of patients 12 hours before death and to one-tenth of patients in the hour before death.[59]

Delirium, a common condition associated with confusion, has been found to be highly prevalent in the cancer population, particularly in the days immediately prior to death. This symptom is commonly under-diagnosed and, in addition to its well known symptomatic correlates (hallucinations, confusion, and agitation), may be manifest by a myriad of "minor" symptoms, including difficulty in concentrating, anxiety, and tearfulness. As mentioned above, there is a risk that these symptoms can be viewed as normal when present in a young person who is suffering from a life-threatening disease. Without a thorough mental status examination, there is a risk that the condition (which has very specific treatment interventions, including attention to etiologic factors and specific therapies such as neuroleptics) may go untreated or may not be treated specifically. Due to the relatively small numbers of patients with germ cell tumors treated at any one institution (among other reasons), studies of prevalence rates of delirium in patients with germ cell tumors have not been reported, and data must be drawn from other more generic cancer studies.

Massie and colleagues reported that 11 (85%) of 13 terminally ill patients with cancer developed delirium prior to death and that the early symptoms were often misdiagnosed as anxiety, anger, depression, or psychosis.[60] In a survey of 140 patients with cancer who were referred for neurologic assessment of encephalopathy, a multifactorial cause of this problem was found for most patients. A single cause of the altered mental status was found in 33% of patients whereas 67% had multiple causes. Drugs (especially opioids), metabolic abnormalities, infection, and recent surgery were the most common etiologic factors.[61] In important work, Bruera and colleagues studied 66 episodes of cognitive failure in 39 patients admitted to a palliative care service and demonstrated that this condition is often reversible during the last weeks of life.[62] Drugs, sepsis, and brain metastasis were found to be the most frequently detected etiologic factors, and 22 (33%) of the 66 episodes improved, 10 spontaneously and 12 as a result of treatment. Although delirium is more commonly seen at the end of life, it can occur earlier in the course of cancer, in response to medications and infections or after surgical procedures, and is reversible in most instances. It is crucial for clinicians caring for patients with germ cell tumors to be aware of the manifestations of this important and troublesome condition and to have an understanding of the approach to its treatment.

In summary, these findings indicate that the majority of patients with cancer will be able to communicate in the days immediately prior to their deaths. This finding may be reassuring for patients or family members who harbor specific worries about this issue. Studies of mental status also point to the importance of health care providers and the patients' caregivers being watchful for changes in mental status as many causes of delirium can be remedied quickly.

Areas of Additional Research in Symptom Management

More research-based data would be optimal to quantify and improve the end-of-life experience for all patients, including those with germ cell tumors. However, it is apparent from both the hospice literature and from the clinical experience of palliative care clinicians and oncologists that even now (although functional deterioration is common at the end of life), comfort can be achieved for almost all patients. Unfortunately, despite the existence of an array of symptom-specific treatment strategies, evidence remains that these are underused and/or not optimally implemented for many symptoms.[40,49,50,63,64] Numerous aspects of palliative care could be improved through further research. Among other aspects that could be developed are instruments for the assessment of distress in cases in which self-reporting is not feasible; more effective and faster-acting treatments for delirium and anxiety/depression; interventions to minimize the distress associated with both common and less common symptoms; and approaches to eliminating the barriers to symptom relief and palliative care delivery. Readers with an interest in research in this area may be interested in the US National Institutes of Health (NIH) State-of-the-Science Statement on symptom management in cancer,[65] which focuses on pain, depression, and fatigue. This report's conclusions and recommendations, however, are broad in scope and applicability. Another helpful resource that provides a current review of the existing data and that highlights research needs in this field is an Internet-based interactive symptom research textbook recently developed through the NIH.[66]

As to specific research topics that may be helpful to illuminate and improve the symptomatic experience of the population of patients with germ cell tumors, it is unlikely that many specific studies of this population will be undertaken, due to the rarity of this disease, the small proportion of patients who have chemotherapy-resistant disease, and the fact that these patients are located in a wide array of geographic areas. Nonetheless, if such studies are not undertaken, it would be helpful to have data to illuminate the symptom-based experiences of young patients, in general, who die as a result of cancers and interventions that may be specifically applicable in such settings.

CAREGIVER BURDEN

Family Members and Friends

Although most caregivers (primarily family members) are highly motivated and are committed to providing care, caregivers involved with patients who have cancer experience substantial burdens.[67–76] Not only are caregivers called upon to provide emotional support for the patients through periods of stress, they are also increasingly being required to provide medical and nursing care in the home as a result of the shifts in care from inpatient to outpatient settings. Moreover, particularly in developing countries, the family caregiver may be the *only* caregiver toward the end of a patient's life, with little or no access to health care professionals. For patients with germ cell tumors, who are often young, caregiver issues are somewhat different from those for patients who are older. Caregivers may be parents, siblings, young spouses, or friends, and although their concerns overlap with those of caregivers of older patients, their experience is clearly also somewhat different from that of those caregivers. That stated, although there are data to quantify the general caregiver experience, there is little information to quantify the experiences of the caregivers of patients with germ cell tumors. There is a small amount of data that illuminate the experience of the caregivers of the young, and such data may point to some of the specific issues that arise in the setting of advanced disease from germ cell tumors.

In a survey of 492 caregivers involved with patients with cancer, the caregivers reported having needs in a variety of categories, including informational, household, physical, psychological, spiritual, and legal and financial categories, as well as in the areas of respite care and other concerns.[67] In this study, caregivers' greatest needs were informational and psychological, and there were significant correlations between caregivers' needs and patients' activity levels. Needs and priorities clearly changed over time, and frequent reassessment was suggested. Overall, the authors reported that their findings suggested "the urgent need" for programs and services to meet the informational and psychological needs of caregivers of patients with cancer. While caregiving is a difficult and challenging task, especially in the setting of the impending death of a loved one, many caregivers have also described the experience as a valuable one. It is apparent that in the face of adversity, sadness, and loss, great meaning can often be found in the context of the caregiving experience. That stated, most attempts at quantifying the impact of caregiving have focused on negative aspects of caregiving, and few investigators have explored ways to promote any of the positive aspects of providing care.[74] As a consequence, most of the following discussion is focused on caregiver burden.

As the gatekeepers of the health care system in most areas, physicians are in a position to observe caregiving needs, to help lessen burdens, and to promote "good health" in the context of disease. It is helpful if physicians can be attuned to noting and, at a minimum, triaging caregiver needs. Some caregiver problems may be amenable to intervention by physicians, and others may require the input of other health professionals or support resources, including social support agencies and other individuals or groups in the community.

Caregiver burden is significant in that it affects the outcomes of both patients and caregivers. Unmet patient needs occur more frequently in settings in which the burden of care on caregivers is greater, for example, in situations in which patients are severely debilitated or in which financial resources are limited.[68,69] In terms of the effects of caregiving on caregivers, there is evidence to suggest that caregiving is a significant personal and societal burden. Caregivers' health and sense of well-being can be affected negatively by the experience of living with a family member who is nearing the end of life.[72,73] Moreover, the period of bereavement after the loss of a family member can have a significant physical and psychological impact.[76]

Although the SUPPORT study did not report on data specific to the experience of patients with germ cell tumors,[70] it did provide information about the impact of caregiving on family life planning, decision making, and finances. The investigators reported that 34% of patients nearing the end of life required "considerable assistance" from a family member. In 20% of cases, the family caregiver had to quit work or make a major life change to provide care. Loss of most or all of the family savings was reported by 31% of families. In the SUPPORT study, caregivers of younger patients were in a group that was characterized as being at high risk for such burdens, and this risk is likely to apply to the families of those with germ cell tumors because of the age at which the disease is typically diagnosed. Adolescent and young adult patients will have their edu-

cational, employment, family, and other plans drastically changed. Additionally, in health care systems that lack universal access to care (including, among others, the US health care system), this patient population may be uninsured or underinsured and may have inadequate access to health care support. In the SUPPORT study, the economic concerns appeared also to be linked with decision making. When increased economic hardship was present for families, patients often expressed a preference for comfort care over life-extending care.[71] Regardless of whether or not this suggests a willingness on the part of a patient to forego treatments in order to minimize the economic impact of their illness on their families, it is important for physicians to be cognizant of the fact that caregiver burden may influence health care decisions to a greater degree than is currently appreciated. Thus, whenever feasible, physicians should explore and strive to alleviate caregiver burden, as a part of optimal patient care.

Significant burdens may affect parents, spouses, or partners, further compounding the financial impact of the disease. In the setting of disease affecting the young, there may be added concerns related to caring for the siblings, children, friends, or parents of patients. Not only are these individuals likely to be worried, anxious, and even depressed themselves, they are also likely to have responsibilities related to the delivery of medical care. Especially at the end of life and in the home, caregivers are often called upon to function in the role of health care providers, administering medications, making judgments about distress, and triaging a patient's concerns to the appropriate health professional. Carrying out such functions requires a great deal of support from health professionals.

Although further information specific to the impact of caregiving on caregivers involved with patients with germ cell tumors who are nearing the end of life may be helpful, the current body of evidence points to the importance of health care professionals being responsive to caregiver needs and being willing to both explore and implement strategies that help minimize caregiver burden.[75,76] From a policy perspective, there is a need to give greater attention to the assistance available to caregivers who are instrumental in the provision of care for patients with cancer. Such assistance is occurring in a number of countries, and in an attempt to further encourage such initiatives, the World Health Organization has made recommendations that suggest the creation of policies that address formal systems of recompense for principal family caregivers and the implementation of medical and nursing programs to back up and support home care.[43,77] Although some programs are available in the United States, they are inadequate to prevent the occurrence of the level of burden described above.

Health Care Providers

The majority of the literature concerning caregiver burden has focused on family members and friends of the patient, but an interesting subset of the literature addresses the stresses and trials experienced by members of the health care team when they care for patients with chronic and life-threatening illness. Those health professionals caring for patients with end-of-life issues in the setting of germ cell tumors are frequently caring for those who are young, and death among these individuals is most commonly considered to be "unnatural." These specific issues, combined with the stresses encountered in many health care systems today, can serve to create significant stress for health professionals.

In a study of 1,000 physician subscribers to the *Journal of Clinical Oncology*, it was reported that 56% of respondents experienced burnout in their professional lives.[78] Balfour Mount has defined burnout as the result of stress in the professional life of a physician or caregiver that results in apathy, suspicion, self-protection, disillusion, and depression.[79] Burned-out caregivers risk being emotionally exhausted, treating patients and colleagues in an unfeeling or impersonal way, and having a sense of low personal accomplishment.[80,81] Clearly, burnout is a risk that exists for the entire oncologic health care team, and its occurrence can place the provision of optimal health care at risk.

Reported causes of burnout have included dissatisfaction with the system of health care, continuous exposure to fatal illness, limited therapeutic success, reimbursement difficulties, pressure to see an ever increasing patient load, and insufficient training to handle these frustrations.[78,82,83] Of particular concern are the mention of limited therapeutic success and the exposure to fatal illness as causes of burnout since these remain two fundamental facts of oncologic care.

The low mortality rate from germ cell tumors reflects one of the tremendous advances of science and care in oncology, but when illness is clearly unresponsive to these treatment advances, physicians and other health professionals may experience both a sense of loss and a sense of frustration at the inability of medical advances to fully address this disease. As noted previously, patients with germ cell tumors comprise a small percentage of the total patient load handled by any treatment team, even at the largest of referral centers. However, given the age and historical curability of the disease, the stresses associated with this patient population may be disproportionately large. Patients with germ cell tumors and their caregivers are often young, and their lives and experiences may mirror those of the friends, brothers, sons, sisters, and daughters of health care professionals. Health care professionals may therefore be placed in a setting where they are confronted with their own mortality in a more direct and immediate manner than that to which they may be accustomed. Watching a patient in the prime of life succumb to a disease from which few patients die could place health care providers in a situation in which they may question, maybe more than in other situations, their own expertise (and whether they did all that they could), the efficacy of modern medicine, and the worth of their work in an often frustrating medical system. Furthermore, in situations (not uncommon) where health care providers have not been trained in aspects of palliative care, there is a risk that they may feel not only inadequately prepared to alleviate the suffering of their patients but also inadequately prepared to address their own stresses. These difficult aspects of working in the arena of oncology are not commonly addressed in the discourse on oncology settings and have only rarely been a part of educational initiatives.

The physicians who responded to the *Journal of Clinical Oncology* survey by Whippen and Canellos cited increased vacation or personal time as the most desirable method of preventing burnout.[78] The teaching of coping skills was ranked low by the respondents in this study. Recognizing that the physicians surveyed had already completed their training and that it was possible that new lectures or seminars could exacerbate existing time pressures, Whippen and Canellos suggested that it is the residency and fellowship programs that should better prepare trainees to cope with the reality of contemporary clinical practice.[78] This could be accomplished by increasing the time dedicated to teaching the principles of palliative care in a longitudinal manner throughout internal medicine residencies and oncology training programs and fellowships. Similar training opportunities should be available for other members of the oncology health care team. The goal of such initiatives should be to empower oncologists and other health care providers to assist with the care of patients and families dealing with life-threatening illnesses.

In the setting of care for patients with germ cell tumors, it seems logical to suggest that physicians and others in the oncology team should be attuned to their own needs and the feelings of personal loss that may arise. It is also clear that the enhancement of educational experiences related to end-of-life care is a needed part of oncologic training and may improve the care of this patient population. Finally, it is also important for health care providers in this and other end-of-life settings to become accustomed to functioning as part of an interdisciplinary team. It is untenable to believe that any individual can successfully meet all of the needs of patients and their families, even with increased training in palliative care for individual providers. The team approach to addressing the myriad needs of young patients and their families is likely to best serve the patients and their caregivers, both family and professional. This approach will also allow health care providers to set boundaries and limits and should provide each member of the health care team with important time away from clinical practice to fulfill their own personal, familial, and social obligations. Such an approach should place health professionals in a position where the care they deliver as a team is more comprehensive and effective and where they may feel more emotionally robust and thus more able to assist in the provision of optimal care for patients and families in sad and often difficult settings.

OPTIMAL END-OF-LIFE CARE

Optimal end-of-life care for patients with germ cell tumors cannot be differentiated from optimal care throughout the course of life-threatening illness. The care of these patients and their families during the patients' last phase of life requires commitments from the individual oncologists to assisting patients and families through this difficult time and a broader commitment to fostering optimal care on the part of institutions involved in care delivery and on the part of those responsible for drafting health policy. Optimal care can be broadly defined as follows: "Optimal care for each patient depends upon determination of appropriate and realistic goals of medical treatment and implementing appropriate treatment measures designed to achieve those goals."[84] Such goals can be determined only through open and ongoing communication between physicians, patients, and families.

By far, the majority of patients highly prioritize comfort as a goal throughout the course of illness. However, patients with germ cell tumors, often being young, are also likely to be willing to undergo aggressive treatment regimens, including early experimental trials with curative goals. This stance may change over time in the setting of disease progression and certainly should never be assumed. Health care providers will need to be knowledgeable about the state of developing therapies for germ cell tumors but also about how to treat symptoms, whether the symptoms occur as part of the disease or as unusual side effects of novel treatments. With a patient who chooses to consider a clinical trial, frank conversations, prior to the patient's enrollment, about the goals of care and the purpose of research with human subjects are important to ensure truly informed consent and to prevent any "therapeutic misconception" on the part of the patient and the patient's family. Physicians caring for patients with germ cell tumors should be compassionate, considerate, and skilled and knowledgeable not only in areas related to disease-specific treatment but also in other aspects of patient and family assessment and intervention options. Recognizing the myriad of physical, psychosocial, spiritual, and practical problems that may arise in the care of a young person with a life-threatening illness, and recognizing that physicians are commonly the gatekeepers of the health system, physicians should optimally be attuned to and respectful of patient preferences, cultural priorities, and family needs and should understand how to assess distress in order to facilitate appropriate referrals.

ASCO has recently published guidelines that address cancer care near the end of life.[85] These guidelines address both the components of care that are considered essential to a humane system of cancer care and the barriers that must be addressed if such a system is to be fully implemented. The following will address these elements and barriers and will provide some information about a practical approach to the assessment of patients with germ cell tumors who are experiencing increasingly burdensome illness and/or are nearing the end of life.

Elements

The ASCO statement on cancer care during the last phase of life defines the components of optimal care at the end of life.[85] The statement suggests that cancer care at the end of life should be centered on the long-standing and continuous relationship between the patient and the primary oncologist or other physician with training and interest in both the patient and end-of-life care. It states that cancer care should be responsive to the patient's wishes and based on truthful, sensitive, and empathic communication with the patient. It emphasizes that cancer care should, throughout the course of illness, focus on and optimize quality of life with "meticulous attention to the myriad of physical, spiritual, and psychosocial needs of the patient and family." Further elaborating on this, the ASCO statement supports and reiterates the American Medical Association Institute for Ethics statement defining eight elements of quality end-of-life care (Table 25–1).[85] Essentially, the ASCO statement embraces and firmly endorses the concept of integrating the principles of palliative care *throughout* the course of illness. Such a system (graphically represented in Figures 25–1 and 25–2)[86] represents a proactive approach to end-of-life distress and optimizes care though the course of cancer.

Table 25–1. AMERICAN MEDICAL ASSOCIATION INSTITUTE FOR ETHICS ELEMENTS OF QUALITY OF CARE FOR PATIENTS IN THE LAST PHASE OF LIFE

1. The opportunity to discuss and plan end-of-life care
2. Trustworthy assurance that physical and mental suffering will be carefully attended to and that comfort measures will be intently secured
3. Trustworthy assurance that preferences for withholding or withdrawing life-sustaining intervention will be honored
4. Trustworthy assurance that there will be no abandonment by the physician
5. Trustworthy assurance that dignity will be a priority
6. Trustworthy assurance that burden to family and others will be minimized
7. Attention to the personal goals related to the dying process
8. Trustworthy assurance that caregivers will assist the bereaved through the early stages of mourning and adjustment

Adapted from American Society of Clinical Oncology[85]; Ingham JM. End of life considerations in breast cancer. In: Harris J, Lippman M, Morrow M, Osborne CK, editors. Diseases of the breast. 2nd ed. Philadelphia: Lippincott Williams & Wilkins; 2000.

Practical Aspects

From a practical perspective, care for patients with germ cell tumors involves a series of assessments from which, over time, a series of care plans are developed. In nearly all cases, the "palliative care" components of such assessments will overlap with the components that are focused on the therapeutic interventions directed toward the oncologic problem. The assessments and the plan, by necessity, must therefore reflect an understanding of both of these aspects of care. At the end of life, it is not uncommon for the palliative aspects of care to become the major focus because symptoms are likely to increase in the presence of progressive disease. In parallel, other patient and family concerns in the psychosocial and spiritual realms will likely become more prominent also.

Given that palliative care assessment has often not been specifically taught in oncology training, it can be helpful for clinicians who are assessing patients to give active thought to the aspects of palliative care (for the patient and the family) that may warrant focused attention. A complete assessment (Table 25–2)[14] must include evaluations of the following:

1. Disease status and prognosis
2. Symptom distress

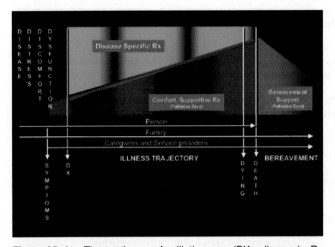

Figure 25–1. The continuum of palliative care. (DX = diagnosis; Rx = treatment.) (Reproduced with permission from Ferris F, Cummings I. In: Palliative care: Towards a consensus in standardized principle of practice. Ottawa: Canadian Hospice Palliative Care Association; 1995.)

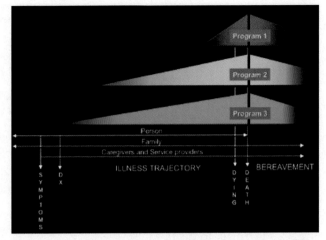

Figure 25–2. The continuum of palliative care programs. (DX = diagnoses.) (Reproduced with permission from Ferris F, Cummings I. In: Palliative care: Towards a consensus in standardized principle of practice. Ottawa: Canadian Hospice Palliative Care Association; 1995.)

3. Patient and family preferences and goals, including advanced-care plans
4. Emotional status and distress
5. Spiritual needs
6. Family functioning and needs
7. Functional status
8. Therapeutic options and their relative efficacies, benefits, and burdens
9. Available resources

The aspects of assessment noted as items 2 to 6 in the above list are the components that are often thought to be in the palliative realm. Subsequent care plans should address all of the above components and should reflect an understanding of the patient's and the family's goals, which may need to be repeatedly addressed as the disease progresses. It can be helpful for care planning if physicians actively consider the re-addressing of goals and a full assessment at times of "transition" in illness (eg, when it is clear that a treatment strategy has been ineffective, when new metastatic disease is noted, when there is a change in mental status, or when other major symptoms or complications arise). It is important to recognize that the choices made by a patient or family at times of transition and near the end of the patient's life may be different from their previously expressed preferences. In each individual case, health care professionals must be attentive to the goals and needs of

patients and families and must seek to facilitate decision making with an understanding of the available resources. An example of palliative care issues possibly influencing decision making is the case of a patient with severe pain who expresses a strong desire to be cared for at home at the end of life, yet it is clear that the home care resources are inadequate. The risks to comfort would need to be explained, along with the options and resources that are available. The ultimate goal for each patient is to develop a care plan that is medically appropriate, congruent with the patient's existential goals and values, and supportive of the patient's caregivers.

In developing the plan of care (from a practical point of view with respect to the delivery of patient care, and also from a more global care perspective), it is important to consider the patient and family (or caregivers) as the "unit" around which the care plan should be centered. In the case of young and expansive families, it should not be assumed that they are more likely to "cope" well because of their robust physical health. The stresses of caring for patients with life-threatening illnesses are great, and careful assessment of the patient's support network is prudent, particularly when home care is being considered.

Once an assessment has been completed, it may be helpful to consider some specific questions about the care plan. Most of these questions relate

Table 25–2. ASSESSMENT COMPONENTS OF A COMPREHENSIVE ONCOLOGIC CARE MANAGEMENT PLAN*

Assessment Component	Comment
1. Disease status and symptom assessment	Consider treatment options, prognosis, and anticipated symptoms. A full understanding of disease and concurrent disease is essential in planning appropriate interventions.
2. Assessment of functional status	Assessment of the patient's function should be undertaken with consideration given to the need for assistance or special assessment (eg, physical therapy assessment).
3. Emotional and spiritual assessment	Consider these issues and the role of referral to a social worker, psychological counselor, or pastoral or spiritual counselor for either assessment or intervention.
4. Assessment of patient/family goals and preferences	Initiate discussion, and consider issues related to the identification of a surrogate decision maker and the documentation of preferences.
5. Family assessment	Specific attention should be given to the family's coping, needs, understanding of the disease and likely developments, and support systems (specific providers and nonprofessional supports) that are in place.
6. Therapy review and evaluation	Regular and event-driven reviews should be planned, with assessment of medications, nonpharmacologic therapies, and the benefits and burdens of therapies.
7. Resource review and evaluation	Regular and event-driven reviews should be planned, with assessment of support systems (specific providers and nonprofessional supports) and physical supports. Consideration should be given to available resources and to whether these could be used more efficiently or effectively. Particular attention should be given to whether resources will be adequate to address any anticipated patient and/or family crises or distress.

Adapted from Field MJ, Cassel CK[14]; Ingham JM. End of life considerations in breast cancer. In: Harris J, Lippman M, Morrow M, Osborne CK, editors. Diseases of the breast. 2nd ed. Philadelphia: Lippincott Williams & Wilkins; 2000. (Reproduced with permission from Lippincott Williams & Wilkins.)
*Including palliative care assessments.

to the categories listed in Table 25–2 and include the following: (1) Are symptoms and distress being optimally addressed? (2) How could functional status be optimized? (3) Are emotional or spiritual supports adequate? (4) Are goals defined and being honored? (5) Who will the family contact if a problem arises? (6) Is increased patient or family support needed? (7) Are all available resources accessed? Other questions that can be helpful in planning care relate specifically to the system of care and raise specific questions about the role of hospice or palliative care services.

The need for care and support often intensifies near the end of life, and an expansion of the team of professional caregivers will be important if this need is to be consistently addressed. Easy access to care is imperative for both the patient and caregivers in the setting of advanced illness, regardless of the goals of care. A comfort-related intervention may require as urgent a response as a life-sustaining one. When devising a practical care plan, it is critical to recognize that while the expertise of a physician is important, patient care is likely to be optimized

through a team approach that incorporates the specialized input of a number of professionals. While team care is optimal for patients with life-threatening illnesses, it is also important for health professionals to realize the risks of team care and make active efforts to avoid such risks. The main risk is that communication may be ineffective and that patients and families may become perplexed and even distressed if messages are "mixed." To facilitate access for the patient and family, it is often helpful to have a dedicated point of entry into the system of care, such as a nurse to assist in triaging the patient's concerns and to foster mechanisms to ensure that the whole team is aware of developments. In addition to dedicated access points for patients and families in the event of crises, proactive visits with (and/or telephone calls from) a physician or nurse may detect and avert an impending crisis.

The available systems for end-of-life care vary among regions and nations. Some palliative care teams focus solely on patients who are seeking only comfort measures whereas others will participate in the delivery of care to those who are living with advanced illness and actively seeking life-sustaining therapies. The latter may be the type of team that is needed if the patient with germ cell tumor is continuing to seek life-sustaining therapies in the setting of advanced and resistant disease. If the goals, as defined by the patient and family, fit with the philosophy of care of a hospice or palliative care team, then the system of care can often be both intensified and optimized by a referral to this team. In most cases, such teams foster continued involvement by the oncologist as the primary physician and therefore truly reflect an intensification of the system of care rather than a major shift in care delivery. Many of these teams also offer specialized physician services such as specific recommendations for managing symptoms.

In summary, the practical delivery of optimal end-of-life care for patients with germ cell tumors depends on many factors. To deliver optimal care at this time, physicians, nurses, and other health care professionals need to be skilled and knowledgeable, compassionate, and humane. Communication may need to reflect an understanding of a myriad of personal and cultural factors, and a host of complex issues may arise relating to family conflicts, existential concerns, physician-assisted suicide, and euthanasia. While it is beyond the scope of this chapter to address each of these topics, specialized texts that address these and many other issues that arise in palliative care settings are now available.[87,88]

Finally, an important component of optimal end-of-life care for patients with germ cell tumors (and for patients with other diseases) is the evaluation of the care itself. Although measures have been developed to assess an array of specific symptoms and quality of life, the development of improved information systems and tools for measuring outcomes will be critical for the creation of effective and accountable systems of care and for the efficient functioning of both internal and external systems of quality monitoring and improvement.[14] While many efforts to improve the care of the dying are being made in the United States and other countries, many physicians still must contend with health care systems that are not structured to foster the provision of optimal end-of-life care. It is important that physicians and other health professionals recognize the barriers to effective end-of-life care and work with other health care professionals and civic leaders to build a system that ultimately improves the care of all of those who are living with life-threatening illnesses in their community.

Barriers to Optimal Management and Care

As with other aspects of the end-of-life experience for patients with germ cell tumors, data on the specific barriers to care in this population are few, but a great deal of insight can be obtained from a review of the broader literature that addresses end-of-life care. There are numerous barriers that hinder the delivery of optimal symptom management and end-of-life care.[14,15,85,89] By developing an understanding of these barriers, physicians and other health professionals can proceed to address and minimize these problems. In guidelines published by an ASCO task force focused on improving end-of-life care, several significant broad areas in which barriers to high-quality end-of-life care exist in the United States were defined.[85] Many of these barriers exist in other countries; therefore, a discussion of these barriers is warranted.

Clinical barriers found by the task force included attitudinal issues related to death that were viewed as "inappropriate," ineffective communication between patients and physicians, fragmentation of health care; and unavailability of (or lack of access to) high-quality end-of-life care. To address the concerns raised, the task force suggested (1) an intensified focus on education, (2) a recognition of the need to incorporate palliative care principles throughout the course of cancer treatment, (3) the broader establishment of palliative care programs, and (4) an increased focus on the patient and family dynamic within the context of cancer care. ASCO recently developed its own educational curriculum, resource book, and CD-ROM educational tool on palliative care (see Additional Readings at the end of this chapter). Research initiatives to address gaps in conventional training were recommended, and it was suggested that these initiatives should foster an increased focus on outcomes, predictors, and interventions during the last phase of life.

Economic barriers to care were highlighted in this report, and an emphasis was placed on encouraging those responsible for reimbursement systems to address policy matters that relate to many issues. Two examples of such issues of policy would be (1) disincentives that hinder optimal end-of-life care and (2) standards that would ensure more uniform coverage for the provision of opioids.

The ASCO report also addressed access to palliative care. It suggested that hospice services in the United States need to be more effectively used, and it encouraged methods of facilitating access to specialized palliative care expertise for those with more difficult problems. This is particularly important for those patients who may seek life-sustaining or experimental therapy toward the end of life. In the United States, many patients with germ cell tumors are likely to seek out such therapies, yet these patients are often ineligible for the intensive system-based patient and family support that hospices can offer in the home until they abandon such options. Furthermore, in the United States and other countries, there are many problems related to attitudinal, financial, and other limits that are impeding the development of clinical palliative care programs in cancer centers. Access to palliative care can be fostered through enhancing the capability of oncologists and oncology teams to deliver such care, but expert palliative care input is also likely to be needed from specialists in this field for some of the more difficult problems that might be encountered toward the end of life. It is incumbent on those with the capability of addressing this access barrier through policy and other changes to work to foster systems that are capable of providing access to palliative care throughout the course of illness. Of note, interfacing with this issue of access, the ASCO task force addressed the complex problem of physician-assisted suicide. While neither condoning nor condemning the practice, the task force stated that the debate in the United States over its acceptability was obscuring the underlying problem, which is that many patients fail to receive optimal end-of-life care.

From an organizational perspective, it has been suggested that end-of-life care and general care for patients with cancer will be improved through the development of cancer programs that commit to embracing four essential components of cancer treatment: the prevention of cancer, the early diagnosis of cancer, treatment to cure patients with cancer and to prolong their lives, and the prevention and treatment of suffering.[90] An extensive report produced by the Institute of Medicine (IOM) addressed concerns similar to those addressed by ASCO and made similar recommendations.[14,15] An additional recommendation by the IOM related to the need for continued public discussion in order to develop a better understanding of the modern experience of dying and the obligations communities have to those who are approaching death.

Worldwide, economic barriers and lack of access are major impediments to optimal oncologic care and optimal end-of-life care. Although populations living in poverty in developed countries such as the United States often experience access problems and many other problems as well, the most dramatic access-related disparities exist between developed nations and developing nations (where adequate resources are usually not available for palliative care).[77] Nonetheless, in all countries and for all patients (both those with curable disease and those with incurable disease), access to palliation, especially pain relief, is crucial. To begin to address these concerns, the World Health Organization has been attempting to foster an increased focus on pain relief and palliative care, both in health care education and in national health policy development.[42,43]

CONCLUSION

This chapter has reviewed some of the experiences that patients with germ cell tumors encounter at the end of life. Additionally, the critical elements of optimal end-of-life care for this population, along with some of the barriers to the provision of that care, have been discussed. Highlighted throughout this chapter are many of the questions that still need to be addressed through continued research in the realm of palliative care in general and specifically in the population impacted by germ cell tumors. Through the delivery of optimal end-of-life care, health professionals will not only relieve suffering, but will also be poised to foster positive experiences at the end of life for patients and caregivers alike.[91]

REFERENCES

1. Devesa SS, Blot WJ, Stone BJ, et al. Recent cancer trends in the United States. J Natl Cancer Inst 1995;87:175–82.

2. Jemal A, Thomas S, Murray T, Thun M. Cancer statistics 2002. CA Cancer J Clin 2002;52:23–47.

3. Greenlee R, Murray T, Bolden S, Wingo PA. Cancer statistics 2000. CA Cancer J Clin 2000;50:7.

4. American Cancer Society. Cancer facts and figures. New York: American Cancer Society; 1995.

5. Bosl GJ, Motzer RJ. Testicular germ-cell cancer. N Engl J Med 1997;337(4):242–53.

6. Hoff Wanderas, Tretli ES, Fossa S. Trends in incidence of testicular cancer in Norway. Eur J Cancer 1995;31A:2044–8.

7. Harding M, Hole D, Gillis C. The epidemiology of nonseminomatous germ-cell tumors in the west of Scotland 1975-1989. Br J Cancer 1995;72:1559–62.

8. Bosl G, Bajorin D, Sheinfeld J, Motzer R. Cancer of the testis. In: Rosenberg S, editor. Cancer: principles and practice of oncology. Philadelphia: J. B. Lippincott; 1997. p. 1397–425.

9. Forman D, Moller H., Testicular cancer. Cancer Surv 1994; 19–20:323–41.

10. Ries L, Kosary CL, Hankey BF, et al. SEER cancer statistics review 1973-1995. 1998.

11. Johnson DE, Appelt G, Samuels ML, Luna M. Metastases from testicular carcinoma. Study of 78 autopsied cases. Urology 1976;8(3):234–9.

12. Bredael JJ, Vugrin D, Whitmore WF Jr. Autopsy findings in 154 patients with germ cell tumors of the testis. Cancer 1982;50(3):548–51.

13. American Geriatrics Society. Measuring quality of care at the end of life: a statement of principles. J Am Geriatr Soc 1997;45:526–7.

14. Field MJ, Cassel CK, editors. Approaching death: improving care at the end of life. Committee on Care at the End of Life. Washington (DC): Institute of Medicine (US); 1997.

15. Foley K, Gelband H, editors. Improving palliative care for cancer. Washington (DC): National Academy Press; 2001.

16. Emanuel E, Emanuel L. The promise of a good death. Lancet 1998;351 Suppl 2:21–9.

17. Singer P, Martin D, Kelner M. Quality end-of-life care: patients' perspectives. JAMA 1999;281(2):163–8.

18. Steinhauser K, Clipp EC, McNeilly M, et al. In search of a good death: observations of patients, families, and providers. Ann Intern Med 2000;132(10):825–32.

19. Last Acts Palliative Care Task Force. Precepts of palliative care, 1997. Available at: http://www.lastacts.org (accessed February 24, 2003).

20. Brescia FJ, Adler D, Gray G, et al. Hospitalized advanced cancer patients: a profile. J Pain Symptom Manage 1990; 5(4):221–7.

21. Curtis EB, Krech R, Walsh TD. Common symptoms in patients with advanced cancer. J Palliat Care 1991;7(2):25–9.

22. Dunlop GM. A study of the relative frequency and importance of gastrointestinal symptoms and weakness in patients with far advanced cancer. Palliat Med 1989;4:37–43.

23. Grosvenor M, Bulcavage L, Chlebowski RT. Symptoms potentially influencing weight loss in a cancer population. Correlations with primary site, nutritional status, and chemotherapy administration. Cancer 1989;63(2):330–4.

24. Portenoy RK, Thaler HT, Kornblith AB, et al. Symptom prevalence, characteristics and distress in a cancer population. Qual Life Res 1994;3(3):183–9.

25. Reuben DB, Mor V, Hiris J. Clinical symptoms and length of survival in patients with terminal cancer. Arch Intern Med 1988;148(7):1586–91.

26. Coyle N, Adelhardt J, Foley KM, Portenoy RK. Character of terminal illness in the advanced cancer patient: pain and other symptoms during the last four weeks of life. J Pain Symptom Manage 1990;5(2):83–93.

27. Fainsinger R, Miller MJ, Bruera E, et al. Symptom control during the last week of life on a palliative care unit. J Palliat Care 1991;7(1):5–11.

28. Dunphy KP, Amesbury BDW. A comparison of hospice and homecare patients: patterns of referral, patient characteristics and predictors on place of death. Palliat Med 1990;4:105–11.

29. McCarthy M. Hospice patients: a pilot study in 12 services. Palliat Med 1990;4:93–104.

30. Plumb M, Holland J. Comparative studies of psychological function in patients with advanced cancer. II. Interviewer-rated current and past psychological symptoms. Psychosom Med 1981;43(3):243–54.

31. Plumb MM, Holland J. Comparative studies of psychological function in patients with advanced cancer—I. Self-reported depressive symptoms. Psychosom Med 1977;39(4):264–76.

32. Bukberg J, Penman D, Holland JC. Depression in hospitalized cancer patients. Psychosom Med 1984;46(3):199–212.

33. Holland JC, Rowland J, Plumb M. Psychological aspects of anorexia in cancer patients. Cancer Res 1977;37(7):2425–8.

34. Portenoy RK. Cancer pain. Epidemiology and syndromes. Cancer 1989;63(11 Suppl):2298–307.

35. Bonica JJI. Treatment of cancer pain: current status and future needs. In: Fields HL, Dubner R, Cervero F, editors. Advances in pain research and therapy. New York: Raven; 1985. p. 589–616.

36. Stjernsward J, Teoh N. The scope of the cancer pain problem. In: Foley KM, Bonica JJ, Ventafridda V, editors. Advances in pain research and therapy. Second International Congress on Cancer Pain. New York: Raven; 1990. p. 7–12.

37. Foley KM. The treatment of cancer pain. N Engl J Med 1985;313(2):84–95.

38. Morris JN, Mor V, Goldberg RJ, et al. The effect of treatment setting and patient characteristics on pain in terminal cancer patients: a report from the National Hospice Study. J Chronic Dis 1986;39(1):27–35.

39. The SUPPORT Principal Investigators. A controlled trial to improve care for seriously ill hospitalized patients: SUPPORT. JAMA 1995;274:1591–8.

40. Lynn J, Teno JM, Phillips RS, et al. Perceptions by family members of the dying experience of older and seriously ill patients. Ann Intern Med 1997;126(2):97–106.

41. Cherny NI. Cancer pain: principles of assessment and treatment. In: Berger A, Portenoy R, Weissman DE, editors. Principles and practice of supportive oncology. Philadelphia: Lippincott-Raven; 1998. p. 3–42.

42. World Health Organization. Cancer pain relief. Geneva: World Health Organization; 1986.

43. World Health Organization. Cancer pain relief and palliative care. Geneva: World Health Organization; 1990. p. 11.

44. Walker VA, Hoskin PJ, Hanks GW, White ID. Evaluation of

WHO analgesic guidelines for cancer pain in a hospital-based palliative care unit. J Pain Symptom Manage 1988; 3(3):145–9.

45. Ventafridda V, Tamburini M, Caraceni A, et al. A validation study of the WHO method for cancer pain relief. Cancer 1987;59(4):850–6.

46. Takeda F. Results of field-testing in Japan of WHO Draft Interim Guidelines on Relief of Cancer Pain. The Pain Clinic. 1986;1:83–9.

47. Grond S, Zech D, Lynch J, et al. Validation of World Health Organization guidelines for pain relief in head and neck cancer. A prospective study. Ann Otol Rhinol Laryngol 1993;102(5):342–8.

48. Schug SA, Zech D, Dorr U. Cancer pain management according to WHO analgesic guidelines. J Pain Symptom Manage 1990;5:27–32.

49. Cleeland CS, Gonin R, Hatfield AK, et al. Pain and its treatment in outpatients with metastatic cancer. N Engl J Med 1994;330:592–6.

50. Von Roenn JH, Cleeland CS, Gonin R, et al. Physician attitudes and practice in cancer pain management. A survey from the Eastern Cooperative Oncology Group. Ann Intern Med 1993;119(2):121–6.

51. Larue F, Colleau SM, Brasseur L, Cleeland CS. Multicentre study of cancer pain and its treatment. BMJ 1995;310: 1034–7.

52. Reuben DB, Mor V. Dyspnea in terminally ill cancer patients. Chest 1986;89(2):234–6.

53. Higginson I, McCarthy M. Measuring symptoms in terminal cancer: are pain and dyspnoea controlled? J R Soc Med 1989;82(5):264–7.

54. Heyse-Moore LH. How much of a problem is dyspnoea in advanced cancer? Palliat Med 1991;5:20–6.

55. Hockley JM, Dunlop R, Davies RJ. Survey of distressing symptoms in dying patients and their families in hospital and the response to a symptom control team. Br Med J (Clin Res Ed) 1988;296(6638):1715–7.

56. Bruera E, Ripamonti C. Dyspnea in patients with advanced cancer. In: Berger A, Portenoy R, Weissman DE, editors. Principles and practice of supportive oncology. Philadelphia: Lippincott-Raven; 1998. p. 295–309.

57. Payne D, Massie MJ. Depression and anxiety. In: Berger A, Portenoy R, Weissman DE, editors. Principles and practice of supportive oncology. Philadelphia: Lippincott-Raven; 1998. p. 497–512.

58. Saunders C. Pain and impending death. In: Wall P, Melzack R, editors. Textbook of pain. New York: Churchill Livingston; 1984. p. 472–8.

59. Ingham JM, Layman-Goldstein M, Derby S, et al. Characteristics of the dying process in cancer patients in a hospice and a cancer center. Proc ASCO 1994;13:172.

60. Massie MJ, Holland J, Glass E. Delirium in terminally ill cancer patients. Am J Psychiatry 1983;140(8):1048–50.

61. Tuma R, DeAngelis LM. Altered mental status in patients with cancer. Arch Neurol 2000;57(12):1727–31.

62. Bruera E, Miller L, McCallion J, et al. Cognitive failure in patients with terminal cancer: a prospective study. J Pain Symptom Manage 1992;7(4):192–5.

63. Vortherms R, Ryan P, Ward S. Knowledge of, attitudes toward, and barriers to pharmacologic management of cancer pain in a statewide random sample of nurses. Res Nurs Health 1992;15(6):459–66.

64. Cherny NI, Ho MN, Bookbinder M, et al. Cancer pain: knowledge and attitudes of physicians at a cancer center. In: Dallas (TX): American Society of Clinical Oncology; 1994.

65. Patrick DL. Symptom management in cancer: pain, depression and fatigue. In: National Institutes of Health State-of-the-Science Statement. Bethesda (MD): National Institutes of Health; 2002.

66. Max M, Lynn J, editors. Interactive clinical research textbook. Available at: http://symptomresearch.nih.gov (accessed February 24, 2003).

67. Hileman JW, Lackey NR, Hassanein RS. Identifying the needs of home caregiver of patients with cancer. Oncol Nurs Forum 1992;19(5):771–7.

68. Siegal K, Raveis VH, Houts P, Mor V. Caregiver burden and unmet patient needs. Cancer 1991;68:1131–40.

69. Mor V, Masterson-Allen S, Houts P, Siegal K. The changing needs of patients with cancer at home. A longitudinal view. Cancer 1992;69(3):829–38.

70. Covinsky KE, Goldman L, Cook EF, et al. The impact of serious illness on patients' families. SUPPORT investigators. Study to Understand Prognoses and Preferences for Outcomes and Risks of Treatment. JAMA 1994;272(23): 1839–44.

71. Covinsky KE, Landefeld CS, Teno J, et al. Is economic hardship on the families of the seriously ill associated with patient and surrogate care preferences? SUPPORT investigators. Arch Intern Med 1996;156(15):1737–41.

72. Kristjanson LJ, Ashcroft T. The family's cancer journey: a literature review. Cancer Nurs 1994;17(1):1–17.

73. Manne S. Cancer in the marital context: a review of the literature. Cancer Invest 1998;16(3):188–202.

74. Swensen C, Fuller S. Expression of love, marriage problems, commitment and anticipatory grief in the marriages of cancer patients. J Marriage Fam 1992;54:191–6.

75. Loscalzo MJ, Zobora J. Care of the cancer patient: response of family and staff. In: Bruera E, Portenoy RK, editors. Topics in palliative care. New York: Oxford University Press; 1999. p. 209–45.

76. Katz L, Chochinov H. The spectrum of grief in palliative care. In: Bruera E, Portenoy RK, editors. Topics in palliative care. New York: Oxford University Press; 1998. p. 295–310.

77. Stjernsward J, Pampallona S. Palliative medicine—a global perspective. In: Doyle D, Hanks GWC, MacDonald N, editors. Oxford textbook of palliative medicine. Oxford: Oxford University Press; 1998. p. 1227–45.

78. Whippen D, Canellos G. Burnout syndrome in the practice of oncology: results of random survey of 1,000 oncologists. J Clin Oncol 1991;9(10):1916–20.

79. Mount B. Dealing with our losses. J Clin Oncol 1986;4: 1127–34.

80. Maslach C, Jackson S. Maslach burnout inventory. Palo Alto (CA): Psychologist's Press; 1996.

81. Ramirez A, Graham J, Richards M, et al. Mental health of hospital consultants: the effects of stress and satisfaction at work. Lancet 1996;347:724–8.

82. Penson R, Dignan FL, Canellos GP, et al. Burnout: caring for the caregivers. Oncologist 2000;5:425–34.

83. Abeloff M. Burnout in oncology—physician heal thyself. J Clin Oncol 1991;9(10):1721–2.

84. Subcommittee of the American Academy of Neurology Ethics and Humanities. Palliative care in neurology. Neurology 1996;46:870–2.

85. American Society of Clinical Oncology. Cancer care during the last phase of life. J Clin Oncol 1998;16(5):1986–96.

86. Ferris FD. Palliative care: towards a consensus in standardized principles of practice. First phase working document. Ottawa: Canadian Palliative Care Association; 1995.

87. Berger A, Portenoy R, Weissman S, editors. Principles and practice of palliative care and supportive oncology. 2nd ed. Philadelphia: Lippincott Williams and Wilkins; 2002.

88. Doyle D, Hanks GWC, MacDonald N, editors. Oxford textbook of palliative medicine. 2nd ed. Oxford: Oxford University Press; 1998. p. 1283.

89. Ingham JM, Foley KM. Pain and the barriers to its relief at the end of life: a lesson for improving end of life health care. Hosp J 1998;13(1-2):89–100.

90. MacDonald N. A proposed matrix for organisational changes to improve quality of life in oncology. Eur J Cancer 1995;31A Suppl 6:S18–21.

91. Byock I. Dying well: the prospect for growth at the end of life. New York: Riverhead Books; 1997.

ADDITIONAL READINGS

American Society of Clinical Oncology. Cancer care during the last phase of life. J Clin Oncol 1998;16:1986–96.

ASCO Curriculum. Optimizing cancer care—the importance of symptom management. Alexandria (VA): American Society of Clinical Oncology; 2002.

Berger A, Portenoy R, Weissman S, editors. Principles and practice of palliative care and supportive oncology. 2nd ed. Philadelphia: Lippincott Williams and Wilkins; 2002.

Doyle D, Hanks GWC, MacDonald N, editors. Oxford textbook of palliative medicine. 2nd ed. Oxford: Oxford University Press; 1998.

End of Life Physician Education Resource Center. Medical College of Wisconsin and the Robert Wood Johnson Foundation. Available at: <http://www.eperc.mcw.edu>

Ferrell BR, Coyle N, editors. Textbook of palliative nursing. Oxford: Oxford University Press; 2001.

Field MJ, Cassel CK, editors. Approaching death: improving care at the end of life. Committee on Care at the End of Life. Washington (DC): Institute of Medicine (US); 1997.

Foley KM, Gelband H, editors. Improving palliative care for cancer. Institute of Medicine. National Research Council. Washington (DC): National Academy Press; 2001.

Max M, Lynn J, editors. Interactive clinical research textbook. Available at: <http://www.symptomresearch.nih.gov>

26

Pain Management Techniques

PATRICIA HARRISON, MD

Achieving optimal pain control in patients with germ cell tumors, especially in the occasional patient with resistant or refractory poor-risk metastatic disease, is not usually a problem until the more advanced stages of the disease (see Chapters 14 and 16). The management of acute postoperative pain for those patients undergoing surgery for primary or metastatic disease has been described elsewhere[1-3] and is outside the scope of this chapter. The diagnostic principles and possible therapies for the pain associated with advanced genitourinary cancer have also been covered in a previous review.[4] In the uncommon situations in which germ cell tumors progress despite chemotherapy, pain management techniques should be individualized for each patient and will be determined by the extent of disease and the site of metastasis.

Despite the widespread availability of effective therapy and an increased understanding of the mechanisms of pain, undertreatment of cancer pain remains common.[5] Inadequate assessment of the severity of pain and of associated psychosocial issues, the reluctance of patients to take opioids, and inadequate access to nonpharmacologic techniques for pain control[6] are major obstacles to adequate treatment. Inadequate training of health care providers has also been cited as a contributing factor.[6] In a multicenter study of 1,308 patients with metastatic disease, 67% of patients reported significant pain while 36% of patients had pain severe enough to impair their ability to function.[7] Of these patients, 86 (7%) had advanced genitourinary cancer, making this group the fourth largest group after groups with cancers of the breast, gastrointestinal tract, and lungs.

Several common pain syndromes are more likely to arise in patients with advanced germ cell tumors. These syndromes are caused by direct tumor invasion in the pelvis or as a result of distant metastasis.[8] Pelvic pain may arise from tumor recurrence locally, and abdominal pain may arise with the involvement of para-aortic lymph nodes or hepatic metastasis whereas chest pain may signify mediastinal metastasis or the presence of a mediastinal extragonadal germ cell tumor. When neural structures are invaded, pain will be severe and neuropathic in nature. It is important to understand the etiology of the pain that is described as the success of therapy will depend on accurate assessment and the implementation of appropriate analgesics. This may include pharmacologic or interventional therapy.

Even after a pain management plan has been implemented, patients and their families require ongoing assistance with problems as they arise.[9,10] This ongoing assistance has been found to be more successful in optimizing the regimen than is providing the patient and caregiver with information and education alone.

CLASSIFICATION OF PAIN

Classifications of pain are frequently based on the temporal nature of the pain (acute or chronic) or on the underlying mechanisms (somatic, visceral, or neuropathic). Somatic and visceral pain are also known as nociceptive pain. By using the etiologic classification, the clinician can select an analgesic therapy that is more likely to have efficacy with that specific type of pain.

Somatic Pain

Somatic pain arises from the activation of the pain receptors, or nociceptors, in the peripheral or deep tissues. Transmission of pain impulses is carried via C and A delta fibers to the dorsal horn of the spinal cord. Clinically, the pain is well localized and is often associated with tenderness and swelling. Pain relief is relatively easy to achieve with nonsteroidal anti-inflammatory drugs that act peripherally at the site of injury. In more severe situations, the addition to an opioid analgesic may be helpful.

Bone pain, which may classically be found in metastatic choriocarcinoma or seminoma, is an example of somatic pain. Bone destruction arises from the activity of tumor products on osteoclasts, causing increased resorption and decreased bone density. Periostial stretching, mechanical stress of weakened bone, and the entrapment of small surrounding nerves are thought to be the etiologic factors of the pain.[11] Pain is experienced in the area of the affected bone, most commonly the vertebrae, pelvis, ribs, femur, and skull.[12] It frequently develops gradually, becoming progressively more severe, especially at night or upon weight bearing. The pain is predominantly somatic unless there is invasion of adjacent neural structures, in which case there will be an additional neuropathic component. A sudden increase in pain may signify a pathologic fracture. Hypercalcemia, which is frequently associated with bone metastases, can cause weakness, lethargy, confusion, and constipation, all of which can have an important impact on the patient's long-term quality of life.

Visceral Pain

Visceral pain may occur when tumor growth causes stretching, ischemia, distention, or invasion of pelvic and abdominal viscera. Smooth-muscle spasm, inflammation, or chemical irritation of these structures can also produce this type of pain. Innervation of genitourinary organs arises from sympathetic, parasympathetic, and sensory fibers. Afferent fibers from the pelvic organs travel via the superior and inferior hypogastric plexuses and parasympathetic fibers at the sacral level. In patients with germ cell tumors, obstruction of the ureters by an abdominal mass may cause severe flank pain. Local tumor extension or pelvic metastasis is likely to cause visceral pelvic pain whereas visceral abdominal pain may arise from metastatic disease in abdominal organs or para-aortic nodes. Afferent impulses from abdominal organs are transmitted via the celiac plexus and splanchnic nerves although innervation of these structures is less dense than in the peripheral tissues. The resulting pain is deep and poorly localized pain, frequently described as "squeezing" and cramplike. Referred pain, if present, is experienced in the somatic dermatome that corresponds to the nerve plexus that is involved. Symptoms of nausea and diaphoresis, which are mediated by the sympathetic nervous system, may also accompany this type of pain. Opioid analgesics do provide some relief although patients may experience medication side effects before satisfactory analgesia is achieved. In this case, sympathetic plexus blocks including the superior hypogastric plexus for pelvic pain and the celiac ganglion or splanchnic nerves for abdominal pain frequently alleviate the pain.

Neuropathic Pain

Neuropathic pain occurs as the result of invasion or compression of neural tissue by tumor or, less commonly, as the side effect of the administration of chemotherapeutic agents or radiation therapy. Peripheral neuropathy that arises following the administration of some chemotherapeutic agents (such as the vinca alkaloids, cisplatin, and oxaliplatin) is associated with dysesthesia and burning of the hands and feet and is frequently accompanied by paresthesias. The qualitative nature of neuropathic pain is the sensation of burning, squeezing, or shooting, with electric shock–like feelings in the distribution of the affected nerve. Allodynia, the sensation of pain resulting from a non-noxious stimulus, is common in addition to paresthesia and dysesthesia. Neuropathic pain does not respond well to opioid therapy alone, but the addition of appropriate adjuvant medication (Table 26–1) will provide the most effective relief. Consideration should be given to invasive therapies (such as nerve blocks or infusions) if this type of pain remains refractory.

Table 26–1. ADJUVANT MEDICATIONS FOR NEUROPATHIC PAIN			
Drug	Daily Dose (mg)	Formulation	Considerations
Tricyclic antidepressants			All: sedation, constipation, urinary retention, delirium, weight gain, hypotension*
Amitriptyline (Elavil)	10–150 qhs	10, 25, 50, 75, and 100 mg	
Desipramine (Norpramin)	25–300 qhs	10, 25, 50, 75, 100, and 150 mg	
Nortriptyline (Pamelor)	10–100 qhs	10, 20, 50, and 75 mg; 2 mg/mL	
Imipramine (Tofranil)	10–300 qhs	10, 25, 50, 75, 100, 125, and 150 mg	
Doxepin (Sinequan)	10–150 qhs	10, 25, 50, 75, 100, and 150 mg; 10 mg/mL	
Antidepressants			
Trazodone (Desyrel)	50–600 qhs	50, 100, 150, and 300 mg	No anticholinergic effects; priapism
Anticonvulsants			
Gabapentin (Neurontin)	300 tid to max 4,800	100, 300, 400, 600, and 800 mg; 50 mg/mL	Sedation, dizziness
Carbamazepine (Tegretol)	100–600 bid to max 1,200	100 and 200 mg; 20 mg/mL	Bone marrow toxicity, hepatotoxicity; drowsiness, dizziness, N/V
Phenytoin (Dilantin)	100 tid	100 mg; 50 and 125 mg/mL	GI upset, dizziness, sedation, hepatotoxicity
Topiramate (Topamax)	25 bid to max 200 bid	15, 25, 100, and 200 mg	Renal calculi, weight loss, dizziness, sedation
Oxcarbazepine (Trileptal)	1,200–2,400	150, 300, and 600 mg; 60 mg/mL	Hyponatremia
Local anesthetics			
Mexiletine (Mexitil)	150–600	100, 150, and 200 mg	Dyspepsia, dizziness, insomnia, tremors
Lidocaine (Lidoderm)	q12h/d	5% patch	Dizziness, local irritation
Benzodiazepines			
Clonazepam (Klonopin)	0.5–2 qhs or bid	0.5, 1, and 2 mg	Drowsiness, ataxia, confusion

bid = twice daily; GI = gastrointestinal; max = maximum; N/V = nausea/vomiting; qhs = every night at bedtime; tid = three times daily.
*Less of these effects occur with nortriptyline and desipramine, which are more suitable for elderly patients.

Lumbosacral Plexopathy

A specific type of neuropathic pain occurs in patients with germ cell tumors after radiation therapy to the pelvis or when perineal nerves are infiltrated by tumor. Lumbosacral plexopathy is categorized by initial deafferentation pain radiating down the leg or into the buttocks in the distribution of the involved nerve root. This can be followed by sensory and motor weakness as the larger fibers become involved.[13] Pain from tumor involvement in the epidural space may resemble this pain syndrome but is more likely to be bilateral. Although spinal metastasis is not common in patients with germ cell tumors, it should be considered in young males presenting with neurologic compromise and pain.[14] Coccygeal plexopathy caused by tumors that are low in the pelvis (eg, sacrococcygeal teratoma) may

mimic lumbosacral plexopathy but is more likely to be accompanied by sphincter dysfunction and perineal sensory loss.[15]

Brain Metastases or Intracranial Primary Tumors

A particularly vexing problem is the clinical presentation of the patient with cerebral metastases (frequently from choriocarcinoma) or with a primary intracranial germ cell tumor (see Chapters 17 and 21). The nature and the extent of headache (and the accompanying clinical syndromes) depend particularly on the site and size of the tumor deposit. In this situation, there is often overlap between elements of neuropathic and somatic pain. Frequently, the patient presents with a localized region of headache but will occasionally suffer from global and poorly localized discomfort (especially in the presence of raised intracranial pressure). As outlined in Chapter 17, urgent management with surgery, radiotherapy, and/or chemotherapy is required to control the underlying disease process.

In the interim, however, effective analgesia is essential. It is necessary to avoid over-sedation of the patient, whose conscious state and congnitive function may be essential as parameters of the progress of disease. Nonspecific adjuvants (such as corticosteroids) will reduce intracranial edema, and in the emergency situation, osmotic agents (such as mannitol) may reduce edema and associated pain, as a holding measure prior to surgery. In general, the use of NSAIDs is contemplated because of the risks of exacerbating hemorrhage. The use of opioids is somewhat controversial but occasionally cannot be avoided. In such a situation, it is safest to use agents with relatively short durations of action to allow the effects to diminish relatively quickly if oversedation is a concern.

ASSESSMENT

Evaluation and assessment are important first steps in the management of cancer pain.[16] A pain-related history should be taken as part of a full medical history and should focus on the onset, site, intensity, and quality of the pain and on the relieving and exacerbating factors.

If the onset of pain is sudden, an acute event such as a fracture or local hemorrhage should be suspected whereas a gradual onset might signify increasing tumor growth. Visceral pain is more likely to be episodic in nature, but intermittent pain can also occur during movement of an involved limb. When the source of the problem is bony metastasis, the pain is usually localized to the area or areas overlying the metastasis. Neuropathic pain will be experienced along the distribution of the nerve. For patients with multiple sites of pain, each site should be assessed separately to determine if multiple therapies will be required.[2]

The measurement of pain not only allows quantification of the severity of the pain but also allows documentation of the outcomes of both established and new pain treatments. Furthermore, many regula-

tory bodies now mandate that pain assessment be incorporated with the measurement of vital signs. Visual analog scales, verbal and numerical scales (Figure 26–1), and multidimensional tools such as the Brief Pain Inventory and the McGill Pain Questionnaire can provide added information about the pain, provided that the limitations of their validity are considered.[16] When using the visual analog scale, the patient grades pain from zero (indicating no pain), to ten (which corresponds to the worst possible pain). However, some patients find a scale that uses descriptive terms to be a simpler way of measuring their pain. The other scales attempt to address pain in the context of affective components or functional limitations. Pain intensity assessment should include the current pain score as well as the scores for the least and worst pain over the last 24 hours. Pain scores that are reduced by more than two to three points on the analog scale indicate some therapeutic success.

Physical examination of the patient should include areas of tenderness and swelling or areas of allodynia, indicative of neuropathic pain. A neurologic examination will confirm sensory loss and motor weakness and is essential when cord compression is suspected. Palpation of the abdomen will reveal the presence of tenderness, masses, or bowel obstruction. Diagnostic tests should be used to correlate the pain symptoms with the underlying pathology. Patients who experience severe pain and who find it difficult to lie in one position for lengthy periods will require additional analgesia to enable them to complete the diagnostic tests.

Once the initial assessment has been completed and a treatment plan has been instituted, it is imperative that reassessment is done at regular intervals as complaints of new pain or a change in the initial pain complaints will warrant a change in therapeutic approach.

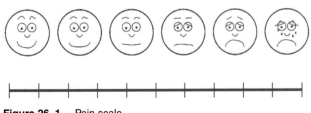

Figure 26–1. Pain scale.

PHARMACOLOGIC MANAGEMENT

The majority of patients with cancer pain will respond to analgesic therapy, provided that it is prescribed according to the type of pain and is titrated to effect. In many instances, analgesic agents with different pharmacologic actions can be added together to achieve optimal control with minimal side effects. This is most important in those patients with neuropathic pain syndromes.

Nonsteroidal Anti-inflammatory Drugs

The action of NSAIDs is predominantly a peripheral one at the site of tissue injury, but NSAIDs also have a central effect. At the cellular level, they inhibit both forms of the cyclooxygenase enzyme (COX-1 and COX-2), the key regulatory enzyme in the production of the inflammatory mediators, prostaglandins, and leukotrines.[17] Therefore, NSAIDs are most effective in patients who have pain associated with tissue inflammation and bone involvement although they have also been demonstrated to have an effect on visceral pain.[18] NSAIDs that selectively inhibit only one form of the enzyme (COX-2) are no more effective as analgesics than are the traditional NSAIDs,[19] but they are thought to have fewer side effects. NSAIDs do not have any action at the opiate receptor level, but when they are combined with an opioid drug, opiate sparing is seen (ie, lesser doses of opiates are required, which consequently have fewer toxic side effects).[20] The predominant use of NSAIDs is in the treatment of mild to moderate pain and as adjuvant medication when pain increases. Tolerance and addiction are not features of these drugs, but a "ceiling effect" occurs whereby progressively higher doses do not produce increased analgesia but do increase the risk of side effects.

The commonly used NSAIDs are listed in Table 26–2. Different formulations, including liquids and suppositories, are available, and many NSAIDs are available without a prescription. Sustained-release preparations will soon be available for the majority of these drugs. Ketorolac (Toradol) is the only available NSAID for parenteral administration; it has found widespread application in the perioperative setting and for short-term use in patients who are unable to take oral medications.

Table 26–2. NONSTEROIDAL ANTI-INFLAMMATORY DRUGS				
Class	Duration (h)	Daily Dose (mg/d)	Formulations (mg)	Considerations
Salicylates				All: displace drugs from plasma protein binding; mostly GI effects; irreversible platelet action; incidence hypersensitivity reactions
Aspirin	4–6	3,000–5,000	Many OTC incl liquid/supp	
Diflunisal (Dolobid)	8–12	500–1,000	250, 500 mg	
Nonacetylated salicylates				
Choline magnesium Trisalicylate (Trilisate)	8–12	1,000–4,500	500, 750, 1,000; 100/mL	All: no platelet action; intermediate side effects
Salsalate (Disalcid)	8–12	1,000–4,500	500, 750, 1,000	
Pyranocarboxylic acid				
Etodolac (Lodine)	4–6	800–1,200	200, 300, 400, 500	Possibly fewer GI effects
Proprionic acids				
Ibuprofen (Motrin, Advil)	4–6	800–2,400	Many OTC; 20, 40/mL 400, 600, 800	All: moderate-risk side effects
Naproxen (Naprosyn)	6–8	500–1,000	250, 375, 500; 25/mL	
Fenoprofen (Nalfon)	4–6	1,200–2,400	200, 300, 600	
Ketoprofen (Orudis)	6–8	100–150	25, 50, 75	
Oxaprozin (Daypro)	12–16	1,200	600	
Oxicams				
Piroxicam (Feldene)	24	20	10, 20	High GI effects
Meloxicam (Mobic)	24	7.5–15	7.5	Fewer GI effects
COX-2 inhibitors				All: predicated low side effects; no platelet action
Celecoxib (Celebrex)	12	200–400	100, 200	
Rofecoxib (Vioxx)	24	25–50	25, 50; 5/mL	
Valdecoxib (Bextra)	24	10	10	

GI = gastrointestinal; incl = including; OTC = over the counter; supp = suppository.

Increased bleeding, gastric irritation, and renal and hepatic dysfunction are well-documented side effects of NSAIDs.[21] For patients who are likely to have renal dysfunction because of the tumor or treatment, doses of these drugs should be reduced and the patients monitored frequently. As NSAIDs are extensively bound to plasma proteins, the intake of other drugs such as warfarin, methotrexate, cyclosporine and the oral diabetic agents will displace them, causing an increase in the unbound serum concentration and thus increased side effects.[22] Many of the NSAIDs produce irreversible inhibition of platelets and a possible prolongation of bleeding time.[23] However, the nonacetylated salicylates (such as sodium salsylate and choline magnesium trisalicylate) and the COX-2 inhibitors have little effect on coagulation and should be considered for use in those patients who have clotting abnormalities or who are thrombocytopenic. As gastric irritation is not an associated prostaglandin effect, the COX-2 inhibitors might not have a profound advantage over the other agents.[24] Most of the side effects of NSAIDs appear to have specificity for individual patients, and it is thus worthwhile to try a drug from a different class of NSAID if these side effects occur.

Although often included in this group, acetaminophen lacks the anti-inflammatory action of the NSAIDs; its major indication over NSAIDs is its antipyretic action. It does not cause platelet, gastric, or renal dysfunction, but it can cause significant hepatic toxicity at doses of greater than 4 g per day.[25] It is formulated alone and in combined preparations with opioids such as hydrocodone, codeine, or oxycodone.

Tramadol is a useful analgesic for mild to moderate pain and for patients who are unable to tolerate opioids because of unacceptable side effects. Although it is a mu opioid receptor agonist, it is classified as a non-opioid medication. There is a "ceiling" effect for analgesia; the starting dose is 50 mg every 6 hours as needed and escalates as tolerated, to avoid nausea. Because of the risk of induced seizures, the maximum dosage should not exceed 400 mg in 24 hours.

Opioids

Opioids bind to specific receptors both within and outside the central nervous system. The majority of available drugs are opioid receptor agonists with effects similar to those of the naturally occurring opioids of the body. The familiarity and ease of use of morphine have enabled it to remain the most widely used drug of this type for the treatment of cancer pain. It is relatively easy to titrate and is available in a variety of formulations for oral use, including a controlled-release pill, a short-acting tablet, and an elixir. It can also be administered rectally, parenterally, or neuraxially (via an epidural or intrathecal infusion). Opioids with mixed agonist-antagonist receptor action (eg, butorphanol, buprenorphine) are not recommended for use in pain management, owing to the risk of opiate withdrawal.

Recommendations for Selection

In 1990, the World Health Organization devised a three-step analgesic "ladder" to guide prescribing physicians in the selection of a "weak" versus a "strong" opioid for mild, moderate, or severe pain.[26] The "weak" opioids (codeine, hydrocodone, and oxycodone) were so named not because of their low efficacy but because their doses were limited by their formulation with acetaminophen. Many of these drugs are now available alone, so that the progression from "weak" to "strong" opioid as pain escalates is less well defined. For pain in the lower range of the linear analog scale, the initial step is to start therapy with a non-opioid medication, with the addition of an appropriate adjuvant drug when indicated. If the pain continues or escalates, a weak opioid should be added to the non-opioid medication. Stronger opioids such as morphine, hydromorphone, or fentanyl are indicated for moderate to severe pain whereas non-opioid and adjuvant medications are continued at all stages. The commonly prescribed opioids and their dose equivalents for both the oral and parenteral routes are shown in Table 26–3. This equianalgesic or relative potency table will assist in the selection of the appropriate dose when a change is being made from one opioid to another or from one administration route to another. However, the values or doses are estimates only and may not take into account such factors as advanced age, hepatic or renal impairment when doses might need to be reduced, or concomitant drug use when doses might need to be increased and titrated to effect.

Table 26–3. EQUIANALGESIC OPIOID DOSES				
Drug	**Dose (mg)**	**Routes**	**Duration (h)**	**Comments**
Morphine	30	Oral	3–6	Solution (2, 4, and 20 mg/mL), tablet (10, 15, and 30 mg); liquid or Kadian granules suitable for G-tube
			8–12	Controlled release (MS Contin, Oramorph, Kadian, Avinza) (15, 30, 60, 100, and 200 mg)
	30	Rectal	3–6	Suppositories (5, 10, 20, and 30 mg)
	10	Parenteral	3–6	Subcutaneous, intramuscular, intravenous
	1 (epidural)	Neuraxial	8–12	Preservative free
	0.1 (intrathecal)	Neuraxial	8–24	Preservative free
Hydromorphone (Dilaudid)	5–7.5	Oral	3–4	Tablet (2, 4, and 8 mg); proposed controlled-release formulation; used in cough syrup
	5–7.5	Rectal	6–8	Suppositories (3 mg)
	1–1.5	Parenteral	2–4	Subcutaneous, intramuscular, intravenous
	0.02–0.04 (epidural)	Neuraxial	—	Off-label use
Methadone (Dolophine)	20	Oral	8–12	Solution (10 mg/mL), tablet (5 and 10 mg); long half-life; action on spinal NMDA receptors; used for opiate detoxification, addiction maintenance
Oxycodone	20	Oral	4–6	Solution (2 and 20 mg/mL), tablet (5 mg) (Roxicodone, OxyIR)
			8–12	Controlled release (OxyContin) (10, 20, 40, and 80 mg); with acetaminophen (Roxicet, Percocet, Tylox); with aspirin (Percodan)
Levorphanol (Levo-Dromoran)	5–7.5	Oral	6–8	Tablet (2 mg), solution (2 mg/mL); proposed controlled-release formulation
Codeine	120	Oral	4–6	Tablets (12, 30, and 60 mg), solution (multiple); high incidence of nausea, constipation as doses increase; often with acetaminophen, aspirin; used in cough suppressants
Hydrocodone	20	Oral	4–6	Not available alone; solution with acetaminophen, tablet (2.5, 5 ,7.5, and 10 mg) with acetaminophen (Lortab, Lorcet, Vicodin, Norco) or with ibuprofen (Vicoprofen); also used in cough suppressants
Fentanyl	Variable*	Transdermal	—	25, 50, 75, 100 µg/h patches; 25 µg/h = 45–135 mg daily oral morphine; usually worn for 3 days

NMDA = *N*-methyl-D-aspartate.
*Published data vary with respect to equianalgesic doses. Individual patient titration to clinical response is necessary.

The aim of opioid therapy is to achieve adequate analgesia while minimizing the occurrence of side effects. In order to achieve this goal, several basic principles can be applied when selecting the optimal regimen (Table 26–4). The most efficacious opioid regimen for a particular patient might involve a trial of several different drugs before the desired response is achieved. Similarly, if increasing side effects develop after therapy with one opioid for a lengthy period, a change to a different drug may reduce the side effects without compromising analgesia. This is known as opioid rotation and is thought to combat the effects of the accumulation of active toxic metabolites and may also exert a possible effect at the receptor level.[27,28] The initial dose of the new opioid

should be reduced by 25 to 50% of the estimated equivalent dose and then titrated as needed.

The preferred route of administration is the oral one due to its convenience and cost-effectiveness. However, the rectal, transdermal, or parenteral (subcutaneous and intravenous) routes should be considered for those patients who experience nausea and vomiting, dysphagia, or bowel motility disorders. Neuraxial or intraspinal techniques are also a means to administer opioid medication at much smaller doses for the same analgesic effect. When opioids are given at regular intervals, large fluctuations in blood levels are avoided, and the occurrence of breakthrough pain and side effects is minimized. Such regular administration can be done conveniently with

Table 26–4. OPIOID THERAPY GUIDELINES

Select the most effective opioid for the pain.

Select the most appropriate route of administration.

Titrate dose to achieve analgesia without unacceptable side effects.

Administer on a regular or round-the-clock basis to maintain a serum level.

Provide adequate rescue or breakthrough doses for incidental pain or pain increase.

Anticipate and treat side effects.

Add appropriate adjuvant medications.

Reassess frequently for effectiveness of therapy and for side effects.

Consider opioid rotation if toxicity persists.

Consider interventional therapy if conservative management fails.

Provide the most cost-effective therapy.

one of the controlled-release oral preparations of morphine, with oxycodone given every 8 to 12 hours, or with the transdermal fentanyl patch. Long-acting preparations of other opioids such as hydromorphone and levorphanol may soon be available.

Following the discovery of an action at both opiate and non-opiate receptors,[29] there has been renewed interest in methadone for the management of cancer pain. Its antagonist action at the N-methyl-D-aspartate (NMDA) receptors appears to delay the development of morphine tolerance and NMDA-induced hyperalgesia, with a potential benefit in neuropathic pain states. One advantage of methadone is its low cost, but it can be difficult to titrate when using the equivalence tables as it has a long and unpredictable half-life. Dosing should begin at 8- to 12-hour intervals, but wide individual variation may require adjustment of the doses at 2- to 3-day intervals, especially at the institution of therapy.

Fentanyl is a highly potent opioid with lipophilic properties that make it suitable for transdermal formulation. Transdermal fentanyl provides a way of bypassing the gastrointestinal tract as well as avoiding invasive therapy techniques in patients who experience protracted vomiting or difficulty in swallowing. The dose of the patch correlates with its size, and the patch has a rate-controlling membrane that allows diffusion of fentanyl below the dermis, where it creates a drug reservoir. Analgesia occurs 6 to 8 hours after application, with a peak effect at 12 to 24 hours; the patch is changed every 48 to 72 hours. This therapy is ideal when sustained blood levels of medication are achieved but is not suitable when rapid dosage adjustment is required. The opi-

oid dose equivalence tables can be used to choose the most appropriate dose by calculating the previous 24-hour opioid requirement.

Parenteral infusions via the intravenous or subcutaneous routes can achieve constant blood levels quickly if pain is severe and when rapid control of pain is required. The most frequently used opioids for this purpose are morphine and hydromorphone although any available parenteral drug could be given. If there is significant pain when at rest, the dose of the baseline medication should be increased whereas a higher dose of the breakthrough medication would be more appropriate when there is increased movement-related or dynamic pain.

A breakthrough dose should be available at all times during opioid therapy, to provide analgesia at times of higher pain (such as during increased physical activity). Breakthrough medications can be administered parenterally, orally, rectally (as a suppository), as a short-acting opioid, or as the oral transmucosal formulation of fentanyl.[30] If the number of daily required breakthrough doses rises or if the patient experiences increased pain at rest, the dose of the baseline opioid should be increased accordingly. If the doses of the baseline opioid are increased, it is recommended that the breakthrough dose also be raised by 5 to 15% of the 24-hour baseline dose.[15]

Several available opioid drugs are not recommended for the treatment of cancer pain. Even though meperidine is an opioid agonist, central nervous system toxicity can occur with repeated doses because of the accumulation of its metabolite, normeperidine[31]; the high oral doses that are required tend to increase this risk. The partial opioid receptor agonist buprenorphine and the agonist-antagonists pentazocine, butorphanol, and nalbuphine should also be avoided due to the risk of precipitating withdrawal in opioid-dependent patients. In addition to these opioid drugs, the intramuscular route should also be avoided due to the unreliable absorption and occasional presence of dependent edema and thrombocytopenia in this population of patients.

Management of Opioid Side Effects

Opioid side effects are generally predictable and can be minimized if they are anticipated and treated early.[32] The substitution of one opioid for another may alleviate idiosyncratic reactions, with the reduction of unwanted side effects. Respiratory depression is extremely rare in patients who are receiving stable doses of opioid therapy or in those who are receiving gradual dose escalations as tolerance to this effect appears to develop rapidly. Only on rare occasions should small incremental doses (0.02–0.05 mg) of the opioid antagonist naloxone be necessary to reverse the respiratory depression without causing a precipitous reversal of analgesia.

Sedation frequently occurs with the initiation of opioid therapy or with dose increases, but tolerance to this side effect usually develops rapidly. Dose titration for both static and dynamic pain levels, as well as consideration of a different opioid, may alleviate this problem. If sedation persists after adequate analgesia has been achieved, a small dose of a psychostimulant (eg, dextroamphetamine or methylphenidate) may reverse this effect and allow further dose escalation. Methylphenidate has been shown to improve cognitive function (including memory and concentration) in patients who are receiving opioids.[33]

Nausea and vomiting have been estimated to occur in 10 to 40% of patients[34] but these side effects usually diminish with time or with the administration of an antiemetic on a regular basis. Metoclopramide is useful as it increases gastric motility, as are antiemetics in suppository form, if there is associated vomiting.

The most troublesome side effect for patients receiving opioid therapy is constipation[35] because tolerance to this side effect does not develop. However, most patients will respond to regular doses of cathartics (eg, bisacodyl, senna, or lactulose) with or without the addition of a stool softener such as ducosate. To avoid compromising analgesia, these should be started at the commencement of opioid therapy.[36]

Adjuvant Medications

Adjuvant medications (or coanalgesics) provide additional analgesia and, when given with opioids, allow the doses to be lowered and reduce the incidence of side effects. While NSAIDs are useful in the treatment of pain associated with inflammation, neuropathic pain tends to respond to medications that affect nerve transmission. The main groups of these drugs that have benefit are shown in Table 26–1, but many others have been tried with varying success. These agents have a variety of actions at the cellular level; as a result, combinations may be beneficial. The tricyclic antidepressants have traditionally been a first line of therapy for neuropathic pain. They have inherent analgesic effects in addition to the improvement of insomnia and underlying depression with increasing doses. Tricyclic antidepressants such as amitriptyline are usually given at night, but if oversedation occurs or a patient experiences unacceptable anticholinergic effects, a secondary amine such as nortriptyline or desipramine can be substituted. Doses should start at 10 to 25 mg and should be increased as tolerated. These doses are usually lower than those required for the antidepressant effect although doses as high as 100 to 150 mg may be required.

Anticonvulsants have been found to be useful for patients with neuropathic pain, especially when there is a lancinating or shocklike component.[37] Gabapentin is as effective as the antidepressants but has a better safety profile with minimal drug interactions and side effects. It is a preferred alternative to carbamazepine and phenytoin for the treatment of neuropathic pain and is used by some practitioners as an alternative to initial therapy using tricyclic antidepressants. Gabapentin is structurally related to the neurotransmitter γ-aminobutyric acid (GABA), but the receptor appears to be different from that of the benzodiazepines, and it may also have an action at the spinal cord level. Gabapentin lacks the hepatotoxicity and bone marrow–depressant effects of carbamezepine and avoids the need for the regular monitoring of hepatic function. Preliminary studies are promising for the newer anticonvulsants oxcarbazepine, which is related to carbamazepine[38] but is without the same side effects, and topiramate, which blocks sodium channels and enhances GABA activity.[39] Recommended doses are shown in Table 26–1.

Mexiletine is structurally similar to lidocaine but is active orally. It inhibits the inward flux of sodium ions along the nerve membrane and reduces the rise of the action potential, similarly to the action of local anesthetics.[40] It appears to have a minimal effect on the cardiac impulse in patients with a normal conduction system. A trial of intravenous lidocaine may predict the response to oral mexiletine in patients with neuropathic pain.[41] Side effects include nausea, dizziness, tremor, and impaired concentration. A local anesthetic patch impregnated with lidocaine can be effective when applied to the skin surface over a small area of neuropathic pain.[37]

Clonazepam is the only benzodiazepine that appears to have a use in therapy for neuropathic pain.[42] It has the additional benefit of providing sedation to those patients with insomnia and anxiolysis. The serotonin-specific reuptake inhibitors have not been shown to have the same analgesic benefits as the tricyclic antidepressants, apart from a mild action by paroxetene, which also has a noradrenergic receptor action.[43]

When neuropathic pain is caused by nerve compression, corticosteroids can reduce the associated edema and provide analgesia.[44] Additional benefits of corticosteroids include their appetite-stimulating effects and mood-elevating properties, but the side effects of hyperglycemia, weight gain, and dysphoria preclude their prolonged use.

INVASIVE THERAPY

Invasive therapies should be considered when pain continues despite adequate doses of appropriate analgesics or when side effects become intolerable. Nerve blocking techniques, neurolytic techniques, parenteral infusions, and implantation technologies improve overall quality of life and become cost-effective when less-invasive therapies fail to produce adequate analgesia.[45]

Regional and Peripheral Nerve Blocks

Nerve blocks may provide diagnostic information about the causes of the pain or may allow time for another anticancer therapy to have effect. Analgesia will be of limited duration although it frequently outlasts the pharmacologic duration of the local anesthetic agent. If a somatic nerve is to be blocked with a local anesthetic agent, it should be done proximally to the locus of pain generation in order to diminish afferent impulses. As it is difficult to spare the sensory and motor fibers, the patient will experience numbness and weakness in the distribution of that nerve.

Sympathetic Ganglion Block

Sympathetic plexus or ganglion blocks are indicated if pain is predominantly visceral.[46] Blocks of the superior hypogastric plexus are intended to relieve pelvic pain due to malignancy or radiation-induced cystitis or enteritis.[47,48] A network of sympathetic nerves lies anterior to the fifth lumbar vertebral body (Figure 26–2). At that level, it is a retroperitoneal bilateral structure that innervates the pelvic viscera via the hypogastric nerves. The block is performed with the patient in the prone position, and needles are inserted 5 to 7 cm from the midline bilaterally at the level of the L4–L5 spinous interspace. The needles are directed under computed tomography (CT) or fluoroscopic guidance until they reach the position of the plexus (see Figure 26–2, B). A diagnostic or prognostic block can be performed with 6 to 8 mL of 0.25% bupivacaine whereas injection of a neurolytic agent such as alcohol or phenol will give a prolonged block. The sacrococcygeal plexus or ganglion impar can also be blocked by a posterior rectal or transsacrococcygeal approach to relieve rectal and perineal pain. Adverse effects, most of which are usually transient, include neuritis, weakness, hypotension, and bladder or bowel dysfunction.

Celiac plexus blocks have been advocated for pain relief in patients with abdominal malignancies. When germ cell tumors metastasize to para-aortic nodes or as the tumor volume increases, patients may experience increasing abdominal pain. The celiac plexus lies anterior to the aorta, at the level of the junction of the twelfth thoracic (T12) and first lum-

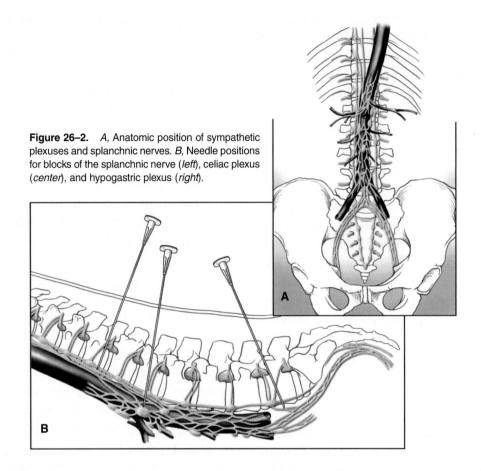

Figure 26–2. *A,* Anatomic position of sympathetic plexuses and splanchnic nerves. *B,* Needle positions for blocks of the splanchnic nerve (*left*), celiac plexus (*center*), and hypogastric plexus (*right*).

bar (L1) vertebral bodies, and is responsible for the transmission of pain impulses from the abdominal viscera (see Figure 26–2). Several approaches to this plexus have been described for neurolysis, depending on the target space where the alcohol or phenol is to be injected.[49] These approaches include posterolateral, transdiscal, and anterior approaches, done with CT or fluoroscopic guidance. Figure 26–3 shows the posterolateral approach to the celiac plexus under CT guidance, with needles placed bilaterally. Verification of needle placement close to the celiac plexus is made with the injection of radiopaque dye. Blockade of the splanchnic nerves with radiofrequency neurolysis has also been described[50] (see Figure 26–2, B). Side effects include hypotension, diarrhea, hematoma, and increased pain due to neuritis.

Neuraxial Therapy

Neuraxial or intraspinal therapy involves the delivery of an analgesic into the epidural or subarachnoid space. In patients with germ cell tumors, this therapy should be considered for patients who have not responded to conservative treatment and who have more than one type of pain. This therapy allows opioid doses (and thus, their adverse effects) to be reduced, with the possibility of adding agents that will be more effective for neuropathic pain. The condition of the patient and the expected prognosis will guide the clinician toward the most appropriate modality. Once a system has been implanted and the therapy instituted, monitoring and titration of medication by trained personnel will still be necessary.[51]

The intrathecal delivery system involves the placement of a subarachnoid catheter, which is then tunneled subcutaneously and attached to a small pump, which, in turn, is placed into a subcutaneous pocket anteriorly (Figure 26–4). The capacity of the pumps is up to 50 mL for the nonprogrammable models and up to 20 mL for the programmable models (Figure 26–5). The pumps can be accessed percutaneously to refill the reservoir, and the infusion rates of the programmable models can be changed with an externally placed programmer. Doses via

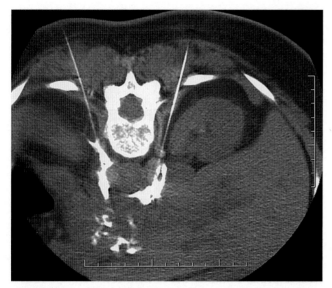

Figure 26–3. Celiac plexus block with computed tomographic guidance. Injection through needle via a left-sided approach shows dye spreading anteriorly away from the celiac plexus. Injection through needle via a right-sided approach shows dye anterior to the aorta, at the site of the celiac plexus.

this route are in the magnitude of 100 times less than the equivalent intravenous dose. Thus, if concentrated solutions and low infusion rates are used, patients will require less frequent visits. However, if changes in the infusion rate are required, the patient will need to visit for the pump to be reprogrammed.

The epidural space has a larger capacity than the intrathecal space and is a space from which the solution is able to diffuse. Therefore, an epidural infusion requires a significantly higher volume to achieve the same analgesia and will necessitate an external pump and drug reservoir. An epidural infusion with a temporary catheter can be used for short periods postoperatively, during painful diagnostic procedures, or while waiting for anticancer therapy to reduce pain. If the decision is made to continue this mode of therapy, a silicone catheter can be implanted (Figure 26–6) and tunneled to a larger percutaneous catheter anteriorly (Figure 26–7) or to a subcutaneous port. Both of these can be connected to an external portable pump and infusion bag or cassette. The proximal catheter tip should be placed as close as possible to the dermatomal distribution of pain and its position verified by the injection of radiopaque contrast dye (Figure 26–8). The combination of medications and the rate of infusion can be changed, and a bolus can be administered more eas-

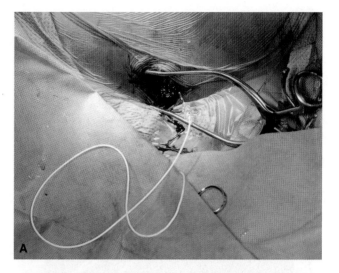

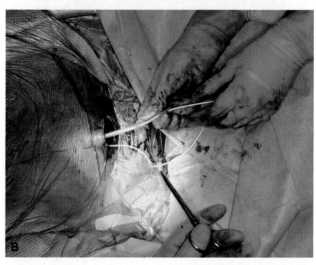

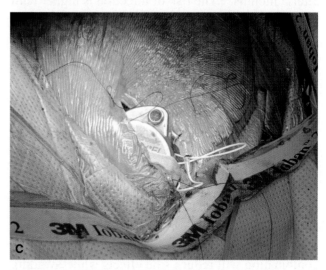

Figure 26–4. Technique of intrathecal pump implantation. *A,* A catheter is threaded into the intrathecal space following verification of cerebrospinal fluid flow through the needle after the dura is punctured. *B,* The catheter is subcutaneously tunneled from the posterior incision to the site of the anteriorly placed subcutaneous pocket. *C,* The catheter is connected to a pump that is placed in the pocket.

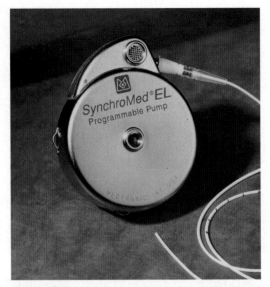

Figure 26–5. A programmable intrathecal pump with an 18 mL reservoir. (Courtesy of Medtronic Inc., Minneapolis, MN)

ily than with the intrathecal infusion. If skilled nursing is available, these changes can be made in the home, avoiding visits to the hospital.

Complications of both infusion therapies include pump failure, catheter leakage or disconnection, inadequate analgesia, urinary retention, and signs of local anesthetic block if a local anesthetic drug is used. A cost analysis of both systems showed that the initial cost was higher with the implanted pump but that the cost of the external system was higher after 3 months.[52] The risk of infection is higher with the epidural infusion, owing to the externalized nature of the therapy.[53] The decision regarding the appropriateness of either therapy is often made according to the prognosis of the patient.

Opioids act on spinal cord opiate receptors and produce analgesia when given via the intraspinal route.[54] The most widely used drug for intraspinal therapy is morphine although hydromorphone, fentanyl, and sufentanil have also reportedly been used. Opioids are the drugs of choice when the pain is predominantly somatic, but when they are combined with a local anesthetic drug, a synergistic effect and improved analgesia for neuropathic pain occur. The combination will reduce side effects while avoiding the development of tachyphylaxis to the local anesthetic, which is seen when it is given alone.

Clonidine can also be administered via the intraspinal route. It is an α_2-adrenergic agonist that

results in an inhibition of the release of substance P and a decrease in the transmission of neuropathic pain at the spinal cord level. Its side effects include sedation, dry mouth, and decreased heart rate.[55]

OTHER THERAPIES

The management of the pain of bone metastasis is usually effective with an NSAID and an opioid. The bisphosphonates, such as pamidronate, inhibit osteoclast activity and were originally used for the management of hypercalcemia. They will reduce pain and the analgesic requirements by 20 to 50% in patients with bone metastasis pain,[56] especially if the pain is predominantly movement related.

Radiation therapy provides effective treatment for bone pain by shrinking an existing tumor and inhibiting further bone destruction.[57] This may prevent a damaged bone from fracturing and thus lessen the need for surgical reduction. In newly diagnosed cases that have not previously been treated with cytotoxics, systemic chemotherapy will usually decrease the pain dramatically over the course of 7 to 10 days. However, for the occasional patient who experiences relapse after initial chemotherapy, salvage treatment of bone metastases with chemotherapy may be less successful, and the principles outlined above become much more important. Of course, in a newly diagnosed patient, pain is a medical emergency, and appropriate analgesia must be provided while awaiting a symptomatic improvement after cytotoxic therapy.

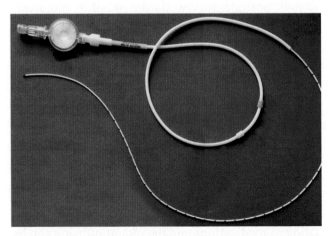

Figure 26–6. The DuPen long-term epidural catheter. (Courtesy of C. R. Bard, Inc., Salt Lake City, UT)

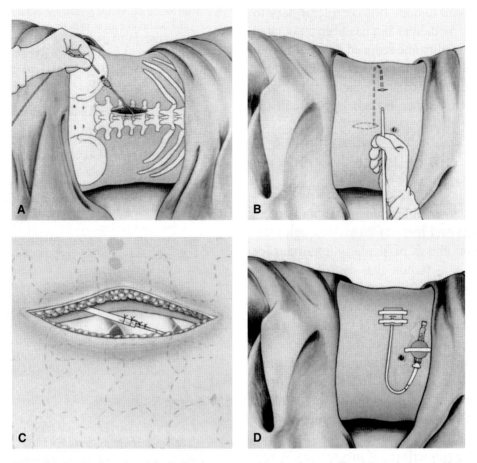

Figure 26–7. Implantation of the DuPen long-term epidural catheter. *A,* The catheter is threaded into the epidural space through a needle after verification, using the loss-of-resistance technique. *B,* A distal catheter is tunneled from the abdomen to meet the epidural catheter. *C,* The two catheters are joined via a metal connector, and the connection is secured with sutures. *D,* The external portion of the system is attached to a filter and secured with tape to the patient's skin.

In some malignancies, such as metastatic prostate cancer, radionucleotides such as strontium 89 have also been used to treat metastatic bone pain[58] although other radionucleotides are under investigation and appear promising. However, this approach is generally not applied to patients with

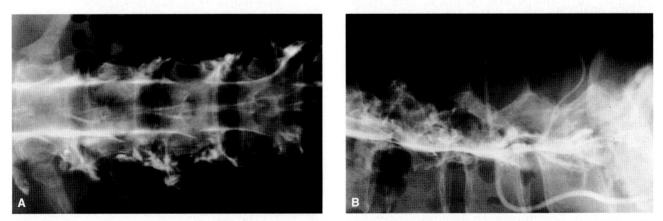

Figure 26–8. Verification of epidural catheter placement with radiopaque contrast dye. *A,* Epidural spread of radiopaque contrast dye in the anteroposterior view. *B,* Epidural spread of dye in the lateral view.

metastatic germ cell tumors. It is complementary to other therapeutic modalities but has been associated with improved mobility and reduced doses of opioid analgesics.[59] The limitations of this therapy include the special requirements for storage of the isotope and the disposal of urine, as well as cost and the potential marrow toxicity.

CONCLUSION

Usually, the relief of pain in patients who have germ cell tumors is not problematic unless the tumor progresses and metastasizes. Although relatively uncommon, this is particularly important for the patient with a tumor that is refractory to chemotherapy or radiotherapy. An improved understanding of the mechanisms and etiology of pain allows a more accurate assessment of the pain syndrome and an optimal choice of therapy. A conservative noninvasive approach with analgesic therapy, frequently an opioid, remains the most effective treatment for the majority of patients. When indicated, non-opioid adjuvant medications can be added to improve the quality of analgesia and to reduce the side effects of medication. A few patients will require a more invasive therapy to control pain, and the physician should be aware of the indications for each technique.

Even in the clinical setting, in which a rapid response to chemotherapy or radiotherapy is anticipated, pain is a medical emergency and requires prompt and appropriate attention. The technologies of pain management have improved in the past decades, and the vast majority of patients can now anticipate swift and skillful control of their symptoms, without excessive side effects.

REFERENCES

1. Heid F, Jage J. The treatment of pain in urology. BJU Int 2002;90:481–8.
2. Jin F, Chung F. Multimodal analgesia for postoperative pain control. J Clin Anesth 2001;13:524–39.
3. Follin SL, Charland SL. Acute pain management: operative or medical procedures and trauma. Ann Pharmacother 1997;31:1068–76.
4. Harrison P. Update on pain management for advanced genitourinary cancer. J Urol 2001;165:1849–58.
5. Cheville AL. Pain management in cancer rehabilitation. Arch Phys Med Rehab 2001;82:S84–7.
6. MacDonald N, Ayoub J, Farley J, et al. A Quebec survey on the issues in cancer pain management. J Symptom Manage 2002;23:39–47.
7. Cleeland CS, Gonin R, Hatfield AK, et al. Pain and its treatment in outpatients with metastatic cancer. N Engl J Med 1994;330:592–6.
8. Banning A, Sjogren P, Henriksen H. Pain causes in 200 patients referred to a multidisciplinary cancer pain clinic. Pain 1991;45:45–8.
9. Schumacher KL, Koresawa S, West C, et al. Putting cancer pain management regimens into practice at home. J Pain Symptom Manage 2002;23:369–82.
10. Lyne ME, Coyne PJ, Watson AC. Pain management issues for cancer survivors. Cancer Pract 2002;10:S27–32.
11. Campa JA, Payne R. The management of intractable bone pain: a clinician's perspective. Semin Nucl Med 1992;22:3–10.
12. Tubiana-Hulin M. Incidence, prevalence and distribution of bone metastases. Bone 1991;12:S9–10.
13. Rigor BM. Pelvic cancer pain. J Surg Oncol 2000;75:280–300.
14. Arnold PM, Morgan CJ, Morantz RA, et al. Metastatic testicular cancer presenting as spinal cord compression: report of two cases. Surg Neurol 2000;54:27–33.
15. Cherney NI, Foley MK. Management of pain associated with prostate cancer. In: Principles and practice of genitourinary oncology. Raghavan D, Scher HI, Leibel SA, Lange PH, editors. Philadelphia (PA): Lippincott-Raven; 1997. p. 613–27.
16. Caraceni A. Evaluation and assessment of cancer pain treatment. Acta Anaesthesiol Scand 2001;45:1067–75.
17. Goodwin JS. Mechanism of action of nonsteroidal antiinflammatory agents. Am J Med 1984;77:57–64.
18. Mercadante S, Casuccio A, Agnello A, et al. Analgesic effects of nonsteroidal anti-inflammatory drugs in cancer pain due to somatic or visceral mechanisms. J Pain Symptom Manage 1999;17:351–6.
19. Cannon GW, Caldwell JR, Holt P, et al. Rofecoxib, a specific inhibitor of cyclooxygenase 2, with clinical efficacy comparable with that of diclofenac sodium. Arthritis Rheum 2000;43:978–86.
20. Weingart WA, Sorkness CA, Earhart RH. Analgesia with oral narcotics and added ibuprofen in cancer patients. Clin Pharm 1985;4:53–8.
21. Eisenberg E, Berkey CS, Carr DB, et al. Efficacy and safety of nonsteroidal antiinflammatory drugs for cancer pain: a meta-analysis. J Clin Oncol 1994;12:2756–65.
22. Jacox A, Carr DB, Payne R, et al. Management of cancer pain. Clinical practice guideline no. 9. Rockville (MD): Agency for Health Care Policy and Research, US Department of Health and Human Services, Public Health Service; 1994.
23. Stuart MJ, Murphy S, Oski FA, et al. Platelet function in recipients of platelets from donors ingesting aspirin. N Engl J Med 1972;287:1105–9.
24. Silverstein FE, Faich G, Goldstein JL, et al. Gastrointestinal toxicity with celecoxib vs nonsteroidal anti-inflammatory drugs for osteoarthritis and rheumatoid arthritis. The CLASS study: a randomized controlled trial. JAMA 2000;284:1247–55.
25. Whitcomb DC, Block GD. Association of acetaminophen hepatotoxicity with fasting and ethanol use. JAMA 1994; 272:1845–50.
26. World Health Organization. Cancer pain relief and palliative

care. Report of a WHO expert committee. WHO Tech Rep Ser 1990;804:1–75.

27. De Stoutz ND, Bruera E, Suarez-Almazor M. Opioid rotation for toxicity reduction in terminal cancer patients. J Pain Symptom Manage 1995;5:378–84.

28. Mercadante S. Opioid rotation for cancer pain: rationale and clinical aspects. Cancer 1999;86:1856–66.

29. Davis AM, Inturrisi CE. D-methadone blocks morphine tolerance and N-methyl-D-aspartate-induced hyperalgesia. J Pharmacol Exp Ther 1999;289:1048–53.

30. Payne R, Coluzzi P, Hart L, et al. Long-term safety of oral transmucosal fentanyl citrate for breakthrough cancer pain. J Pain Symptom Manage 2001;22:575–83.

31. Eisendrath SJ, Goldman B, Douglas J, et al. Meperidine-induced delirium. Am J Psychiatry 1987;144:1062–5.

32. Portenoy RK. Managing cancer pain poorly responsive to systemic opioid therapy. Oncology 1999;13(S):25–9.

33. Bruera E, Miller MJ, Macmillan K, et al. Neuropsychological effects of methylphenidate in patients receiving a continuous infusion of narcotics for cancer pain. Pain 1992;48:63–6.

34. Campora E, Merlini L, Pace M, et al. The incidence of narcotic induced emesis. J Pain Symptom Manage 1991;6:428–30.

35. Bruera E, Suarez-Almazor M, Velasco A, et al. The assessment of constipation in terminal cancer patients admitted to a palliative care unit: a retrospective review. J Pain Symptom Manage 1994;9:515–9.

36. Thorpe DM. Management of opioid-induced constipation. Curr Pain Headache Rep 2001;5:237–40.

37. Carter GT, Galer BS. Advances in the management of neuropathic pain. Phys Med Rehabil Clin N Am 2001;12:447–59.

38. Carrazena E, Beydoun A, Koblentz S, et al. An open-label, prospective trial of oxcarbazepine in the treatment of painful diabetic neuropathy. J Pain 2002;3:S38.

39. Jenson MG, Royal MA, Ward S, et al. Topiramate for the treatment of neuropathic and chronic pain syndromes: an open label trial. Am J Pain Manage 2002;12:16–23.

40. Sloan P, Basta M, Storey P, et al. Mexilitine as an adjuvant analgesic for the management of neuropathic cancer pain. Anesth Analg 1999;89:760–1.

41. Galer BS, Harle J, Rowbotham MC. Response to intravenous lidocaine infusion predicts response to oral mexilitine: a prospective study. J Pain Symptom Manage 1996;12:161–7.

42. Khouzam HR, Highet VS. A review of clonazepam use in neurology. Neurologist 1997;3:120–7.

43. Gray AM, Pache DM, Sewell RD. Do alpha2-adrenoreceptors play an integral role in the antinociceptive mechanism of action of antidepressant compounds? Eur J Pharmacol 1999;6:161–8.

44. Byrne TN. Spinal cord compression from epidural metastases. N Engl J Med 1992;327:614–9.

45. Krames ES. Interventional pain management. Appropriate when less invasive therapies fail to provide adequate analgesia. Med Clin North Am 1999;83:787–808.

46. de Leon-Casasola OA. Neurolytic blocks of the sympathetic axis for the treatment of visceral pain in cancer. Curr Rev Pain 1999;3:173–7.

47. Plancarte R, Amesua C, Patt RB, et al. Superior hypogastric plexus block for pelvic cancer pain. Anesthesiology 1990;73:236–9.

48. Patt RB, Reddy SK, Black RG. Neural blockade for abdominopelvic pain of oncologic origin. Int Anesthesiol Clin 1998;36:87–104.

49. Eisenberg E, Carr DB, Chalmers TC. Neurolytic celiac plexus block for treatment of cancer pain: a meta-analysis. Anesth Analg 1995;80:290–5.

50. Kopacs DJ, Thompson GE. Celiac and hypogastric plexus, intercostal, interpleural, and peripheral neural blockade of the thorax and abdomen. In: Cousins MJ, Bridenbaugh PO, editors. Neural blockade: clinical anesthesia and management of pain. 3rd ed. Philadelphia (PA): Lippincott-Raven; 1998. p. 451–85.

51. DuPen SL. Epidural techniques for cancer pain management: when, why, and how? Curr Rev Pain 1999;3:183–9.

52. Bedder MD, Burchiel K, Larson A. Cost analysis of two implantable narcotic delivery systems. J Pain Symptom Manage 1991;6:368–73.

53. DuPen SL, Petersen DG, Williams A, et al. Infection during chronic epidural catheterization: diagnosis and treatment. Anesthesiology 1990;73:905–9.

54. Carr BC, Cousins MJ. Spinal route of analgesia: opioids and future options. In: Cousins MJ, Bridenbaugh PO, editors. Neural blockade: clinical anesthesia and management of pain. 3rd ed. Philadelphia: Lippincott-Raven; 1998. p. 915–83.

55. Eisenach JC, DuPen SL, Dubois M, et al. Epidural clonidine analgesia for intractable cancer pain. The Epidural Clonidine Study Group. Pain 1995;61:391–9.

56. Fulfaro F, Casuccio A, Ticozzi C, et al. The role of bisphosphonates in the treatment of painful metastatic bone disease: a review of phase III trials. Pain 1998;78:157–69.

57. Arcangeli G, Giovinazzo G, Saracino B, et al. Radiation therapy in the management of symptomatic bone metastases: the effect of total dose and histology on pain relief and response duration. Int J Radiat Oncol Biol Phys 1998;42:1119–26.

58. Kalkner KM, Westlin JE, Strang P. 89 Strontium in the management of painful skeletal metastases. Anticancer Res 2000;20:1109–14.

59. Serafini AN. Therapy of metastatic bone pain. J Nucl Med 2001;42:895–906.

27

Acute Toxicity of Chemotherapy

LISA G. HORVATH, MBBS, FRACP

MICHAEL J. BOYER, MBBS, PHD, FRACP

The development of effective chemotherapy regimens for metastatic germ cell tumors has resulted in dramatically improved survival for patients over the past 25 years. While cisplatin remains the mainstay of treatment and has a well-described toxicity profile, there are several other agents that are used in combination chemotherapy, each of which has distinct side effects. These include vinblastine, bleomycin, ifosfamide, and etoposide. More recently, paclitaxel and gemcitabine have also been used in the treatment of testicular cancer.

In parallel with advances in treatment, there has been an increasing awareness of the adverse effects of chemotherapy, along with the development of strategies to minimize toxicity. The introduction of serotonin receptor antagonists revolutionized the treatment of chemotherapy-induced nausea and vomiting.[1,2] In the past decade, granulocyte colony-stimulating factor (G-CSF)[3,4] and (more recently) recombinant erythropoietin[5-7] have been used to ameliorate bone marrow suppression secondary to chemotherapy. In addition, amifostine (Ethyol) has been used to reduce the nephrotoxicity of cisplatin treatment.[8,9]

Despite these advances, most men undergoing chemotherapy for testicular cancer experience at least some toxicity. This chapter will review the acute adverse effects of chemotherapy for germ cell tumors.

GASTROINTESTINAL TOXICITY

The major acute gastrointestinal side effects of chemotherapy for germ cell tumors are nausea and vomiting; diarrhea, paralytic ileus or constipation, and mucositis occur less commonly. Cisplatin and vinblastine as used in the cisplatin/vinblastine/bleomycin (PVB) regimen are responsible for the majority of this toxicity,[10,11] with a lesser contribution from ifosfamide, methotrexate, and actinomycin D in men receiving salvage therapy or treatment for poor-prognosis disease.[12] The vinca alkaloids and paclitaxel, in particular, can cause ileus presumably related to effects on the autonomic nervous system. The degree of gastrointestinal toxicity in many patients has been reduced by the use of more serotonin antagonist antiemetics such as ondansetron, granisetron, or tropisetron.[1,2] In addition, the replacement of vinblastine by etoposide[13] and changes in the dosing schedule of cisplatin from 100mg/m^2 on day 1 to 20mg/m^2 on days 1 to 5 have been shown to decrease the rate of World Health Organization (WHO) grades 2 to 4 nausea and vomiting from 74% to 57%.[14]

The replacement of vinblastine by etoposide in first-line treatment has also resulted in a substantial decrease in the rate of ileus such that abdominal cramps, which occurred in 20% of patients treated with PVB, now occur in only 5% of men receiving bleomycin, etoposide, and cisplatin.[13] A less common gastrointestinal side effect is explosive diarrhea, which occurs in 10 to 20% of patients[15] and which can easily be treated with conventional antidiarrheal agents such as loperamide.

NEPHROTOXICITY

Nephrotoxicity was noted initially in early-phase studies of cisplatin-based chemotherapy; a decreased glomerular filtration rate and elevated serum creatinine occurred in up to 36% of patients.[16] Modern cisplatin administration schedules incorporating forced saline diuresis[13,17] have decreased the rate of significant renal impairment to fewer than 5% of patients.[14,17,18] Less commonly, damage to the proximal convoluted tubules can result in a magnesium-wasting nephropathy, which can cause hypomagnesemia severe enough to precipitate cerebral seizures.[19,20] This can be prevented using intravenous and oral magnesium replacement.

When renal biopsy specimens from patients with cisplatin-induced renal damage have been examined, several histologic patterns have been observed. These include acute focal necrosis of the distal convoluted tubules and collecting ducts, dilatation of the convoluted tubules, and the formation of casts[16,21] (Table 27–1).

Although cisplatin is responsible for the majority of the nephrotoxicity observed during the treatment of germ cell tumors, a number of other drugs may contribute to the problem. In particular, methotrexate is also excreted by the kidneys and can cause an interstitial nephritis when used as a single agent. In combination with cisplatin, such as in the cisplatin/vincristine/methotrexate/bleomycin and actinomycin D/cyclophosphamide/etoposide (POMB/ACE) regimen used for poor-prognosis tumors,[22] these nephrotoxic effects may become synergistic (see Chapter 14). Additional nephrotoxins may also be introduced in the form of aminoglycoside antibiotics used in the management of febrile neutropenia and may exacerbate renal impairment due to cytotoxic agents.

Downstream from the kidneys, ifosfamide is well known to cause hemorrhagic cystitis.[23] Once established, hemorrhagic cystitis is difficult to treat; thus, prevention is important. Aggressive hydration, continuous infusion schedules, and the use of mesna (a sulfhydryl compound that binds the degradation products of ifosfamide within the bladder) have reduced the incidence of this complication from 18 to 40% of patients to 5 to 10% of patients.[9,23]

NEUROMUSCULAR TOXICITY

Acute neurotoxicity after cisplatin-based combination chemotherapy may take many forms, including those of peripheral neuropathy (in particular, sensory), autonomic dysfunction (orthostatic hypotension, ileus, and esophageal dysfunction), and auditory impairment.[24,25] While cisplatin can produce each of these effects, other cytotoxics such as the vinca alkaloids and paclitaxel may increase the occurrence of neuropathies.[11,17,26,27] Metabolic disorders such as hypomagnesemia may also contribute to the incidence of acute neurologic side effects.

Peripheral neuropathy manifesting as distal symmetrical paresthesia occurs in up to 80% of patients receiving first-line cisplatin-based chemotherapy. For the majority, these symptoms resolve after completion of cytotoxic treatment, with the reported incidence of persistent paresthesia ranging from 7 to 51%.[28–35] On the other hand, 50 to 76% of patients have asymptomatic peripheral nerve damage that can be detected only by neurophysiologic testing.[29,33]

Drugs other than cisplatin may influence the rate of neurotoxicity. Patients treated with regimens containing etoposide instead of vinblastine have a lower incidence of acute peripheral neuropathy.[13] With regard to newer agents, paclitaxel is known to cause WHO grade 2 to 4 peripheral neuropathy in 29% of patients when used as a single agent after prior chemotherapy.[36,37] When paclitaxel is used in combination with cisplatin and ifosfamide to treat relapsed germ cell tumor, the incidence of WHO grades 3 to 4 paresthesia has been documented as only 7 to 20% although only small numbers of patients treated in phase II trials have been reported.[38,39]

Table 27–1. ACUTE NEPHROTOXICITY SECONDARY TO CISPLATIN CHEMOTHERAPY			
Site	Histology	Physiology	Clinical Effect
Proximal convoluted tubules	Acute tubular necrosis	Impaired magnesium absorption	Hypomagnesemia
Distal convoluted tubules and collecting ducts	Focal tubular necrosis; dilatation of tubules; casts	Tubulo-glomerular feedback compromises glomerular perfusion and filtration	Decreased glomerular filtration rate

Autonomic neuropathy is a less common but well-recognized side effect of cisplatin-based combinations for patients with germ cell tumors.[24,40] Orthostatic hypotension may occur in the phase that occurs shortly after the completion of treatment but usually resolves spontaneously.[24] This appears to be mediated through the parasympathetic system as most patients have intact sympathetic function.[40] In addition, acute autonomic dysfunction can manifest as paralytic ileus.

Acute ototoxicity (Figure 27–1) is most commonly associated with cisplatin treatment,[41,42] with potential contributions from the vinca alkaloids and aminoglycoside antibiotics. The pathologic basis of cisplatin-induced auditory damage is believed to be the death of hair cells in the organ of Corti. Clinically, this manifests most commonly as persistent tinnitus in 11 to 33% of patients.[29,31,43] High-frequency hearing loss (ie, above the frequency of normal speech) occurs in up to 30% of cases.[9] Practically speaking, this means that these patients have difficulty hearing against a noisy background although the audiometric changes of bilateral sensorineural hearing loss have been detected in 28 to 75% of patients in large series.[29,30,44,45] A weak association between the dose of cisplatin and the severity of hearing loss has been demonstrated in men receiving cisplatin-based chemotherapy for germ cell tumors, but such a relationship has been documented in patients receiving cisplatin for other cancers.[41] In addition, the schedule of cisplatin administration may be an important determinant in the degree of auditory toxicity.[14,41] Single-day

administration schedules are certainly associated with higher peak plasma levels, and this may result in greater ototoxicity than that resulting from a 5-day schedule.

Although not life threatening, the myalgia associated with some chemotherapeutic agents can be debilitating. The combination of cisplatin, vinblastine, and bleomycin can cause severe myalgias in up to 14% of patients, due mainly to the latter two agents.[13] Similarly, paclitaxel is well known to be associated with muscular discomfort in the first 2 to 4 days after treatment.[46] A myopathy has also been described in patients receiving high doses of paclitaxel in conjunction with cisplatin.[47]

BONE MARROW SUPPRESSION

Acute tri-lineage bone marrow suppression occurs after chemotherapy for germ cell tumors; the predominant pattern reflects the selection and doses of agents. Although cisplatin causes a mild progressive anemia with only modest neutropenia and thrombocytopenia, carboplatin, etoposide, vinblastine, and paclitaxel all cause more significant neutropenia and thrombocytopenia. Cisplatin-induced hemolysis has also been described.[48] The most commonly used first-line regimens that incorporate cisplatin (> 100 mg/m^2 per cycle) and a vinca alkaloid or etoposide cause WHO grade 3 or 4 neutropenia in 50 to 60% of patients and grade 3 to 4 thrombocytopenia in up to 15% of patients.[13,14,49–51] Second-line regimens such as vinblastine, ifosfamide, and cisplatin (VIP) or, more recently, paclitaxel, ifosfamide, and cisplatin (TIP) cause higher rates of neutropenia and neutropenic sepsis (up to 70%) as well as significant anemia and thrombocytopenia that may necessitate transfusion (see Table 27–1).[50,52] In contrast, gemcitabine, one of the newer drugs for cisplatin-refractory germ cell tumors, is relatively well tolerated, with only 25% of patients developing thrombocytopenia and 12% of patients developing granulocytopenia.[53,54] Predictably, the combination of paclitaxel and gemcitabine also results in moderate to severe neutropenia and thrombocytopenia.[55]

Although grade 3 to 4 neutropenia occurs in up to 60% of patients, febrile neutropenia is an uncommon complication whose reported rates range from

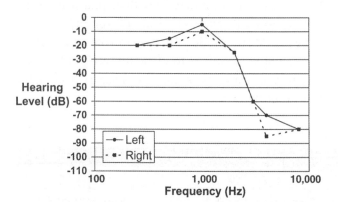

Figure 27–1. Audiogram of a patient who had received two cycles of cisplatin (100 mg/m^2 per cycle) shows bilateral high-frequency hearing loss.

1 to 5%.[13,14,51,56] The use of growth factors such as G-CSF may have further reduced the incidence of febrile neutropenia in men receiving treatment for germ cell tumors. However, there are no randomized studies of growth factor use with the standard cisplatin/etoposide/bleomycin (PEB) regimen.

Hemopoietic growth factors have also been demonstrated to be of benefit in the setting of high-dose chemotherapy for patients with poor-prognosis or relapsed germ cell tumors.[3,4] Bajorin and colleagues[3] showed that granulocyte-macrophage colony-stimulating factor (GM-CSF) reduced the incidence of infection during the first cycle of ifosfamide-based chemotherapy but had no benefit in subsequent cycles. Moreover, GM-CSF was discontinued in 14% of cycles due to toxicity specifically related to the growth factor.[3] A more recent phase III trial using G-CSF in patients receiving six cycles of either etoposide and cisplatin, plus or minus bleomycin (BEP/EP), or bleomycin/vincristine/cisplatin and etoposide/ifosfamide/cisplatin/bleomycin (BOP/VIP-B) demonstrated a significantly decreased rate of neutropenic fever and a decreased rate of toxic deaths in the G-CSF arm (9 in the non-G-CSF arm vs 3 in the G-CSF arm).[4] In addition, the use of G-CSF was associated with improved delivery of the planned treatment schedule. However, there is no direct evidence to support the routine use of hemopoietic growth factors during the administration of standard regimens of cisplatin, vinblastine, or etoposide and bleomycin (PVB/PEB/BEP) although G-CSF is used commonly.

A number of groups have treated cisplatin-induced anemia successfully with recombinant erythropoietin (EPO).[5–7] Randomized trials have shown that EPO can improve serum hemoglobin and consequently reduce blood transfusion requirements as well as improve quality of life for patients who are already suffering the fatigue of cytotoxic treatment.[7] In addition, the increasing awareness of the risks of blood transfusion (even in developed countries with a well-screened blood supply) makes EPO treatment an attractive option. However, for the majority of patients treated with first-line treatment (BEP/PEB/PVB), anemia is not a significant problem. By contrast, EPO may be useful for patients receiving salvage therapy or a more intensive treatment for poor-prognosis disease.[57]

PULMONARY TOXICITY

The most common acute pulmonary toxicity is pneumonitis secondary to the use of bleomycin, an important component of germ cell tumor treatment.[58,59] This usually manifests as dyspnea with a variety of radiologic findings, including increased interstitial markings, patchy reticulonodular infiltrates, consolidation, or nodules.[60] This syndrome may be exacerbated by cigarette smoking or prior pulmonary irradiation and may progress to pulmonary fibrosis in a small proportion of patients.[60,61] Although deaths from bleomycin pulmonary toxicity have become rare, they can still occur. Monitoring of the diffusing capacity of the lung for carbon monoxide (DLCO) and measurement of lung volumes are used widely in an attempt to predict the development of bleomycin pulmonary toxicity and to modify treatment to prevent the progression of this complication. A drop of more than 20% in the DLCO compared to baseline values is commonly used as an indication for the suspension of bleomycin. However, this value is somewhat arbitrary, and controversy remains as to whether other tests or even clinical signs are more appropriate indicators.[59,62]

VASCULAR TOXICITY

While there is good evidence for the association between chemotherapy for germ cell tumors and chronic small-vessel toxicity manifesting as Raynaud's phenomenon,[29,31,32,35] the relationship between such chemotherapy and acute vascular events is less clear. Both acute cardiac and cerebral ischemic events have been reported after the administration of vinblastine alone,[63] vinblastine and bleomycin,[64] vinblastine and cisplatin,[65] and PVB.[29,30,43,66–68] Implicating these chemotherapeutic agents in a direct causal relationship to these events is difficult, given the comorbidities that may be involved such as tobacco smoking, mediastinal irradiation, and family history. Furthermore, most reports of vascular toxicity are from relatively small series. In large modern trials of chemotherapy (usually with PEB) for testicular cancer, acute vascular toxicity has not been reported.[14,18,51]

Venous thromboembolic disease may also occur in men who are undergoing chemotherapy for germ cell tumors. Possible causes for this include the presence of tumor in the retroperitoneum, with associated compromise of flow in the great veins, and the well-described association between chemotherapy and venous thrombosis.[69] In addition to the above problems, paclitaxel as a single agent is known to cause cardiac arrhythmias such as bradycardia.[70,71]

ALLERGIC REACTIONS AND OTHER TOXICITIES

Acute allergic reactions to a number of cytotoxic agents used in the treatment of germ cell tumors have been documented; these agents include bleomycin,[60] paclitaxel,[72–74] and (rarely) carboplatin or cisplatin.[57,76] These can manifest as minor reactions such as flushing and rashes or as more severe symptoms such as urticaria, periorbital edema, bronchospasm, and hypotension. In the majority of cases, the hypersensitivity syndromes can be treated with corticosteroids and antihistamines, and the patient can be rechallenged after pretreatment with these medications.[74,76] Hypersensitivity reactions are so common during treatment with paclitaxel (up to 30% of patients) that patients are routinely treated prophylactically with corticosteroids, cimetidine, and antihistamines.[46]

One of the most common acute side effects of germ cell tumor treatment is alopecia. The principal agents that cause alopecia are etoposide, ifosfamide, and paclitaxel; only WHO grade I hair loss is associated with cisplatin, vinblastine, and bleomycin, as single agents. With combination chemotherapy, used predominantly for treating this disease, the majority of patients will suffer significant alopecia.[13,15,50]

By contrast, acute endocrine side effects occur in only a handful of patients. The syndrome of inappropriate antidiuretic hormone secretion can occur as a consequence of vinca alkaloid and/or cisplatin administration.[77,78] The electrolyte imbalances spontaneously revert to normal on cessation of the relevant cytotoxic agent.

PREDICTION OF TOXICITY

The predicted toxicity of combination chemotherapeutic regimens depends on the toxicity profiles of each of the drugs, the dosage of the drugs, and the duration of treatment. A number of investigative

groups have shown that increasing the dose of vinblastine in the setting of the PVB regimen increases toxicity without any associated improvement in survival.[79–81] Similarly, prolonged treatment schedules of vinblastine (maintenance regimens) did not demonstrate a survival benefit. Increasing the dose of cisplatin also has the effect of increasing its side effects.[17,82] The toxicities of the most commonly used chemotherapeutic regimens are summarized in Table 27–2, which emphasizes studies that used modern agents (such as serotonin antagonists, mesna, and G-CSF) to treat side effects.

STRATEGIES FOR REDUCING THE TOXICITY OF THERAPY

While improvements in chemotherapeutic treatment have increased the chance of long-term cure in patients with germ cell tumors, attempts have also been made to decrease the toxicity of therapy. A number of strategies have been used, including reduction in the intensity of treatment and the use of new agents to protect normal tissues from damage.

Reduction of the Intensity of Treatment

To improve the toxicity profile, several investigative groups have attempted to modify the chemotherapy regimens used in the treatment of germ cell tumors. These modifications have included a reduction in the number of cycles of chemotherapy administered to patients with good-prognosis disease (from four to three cycles),[83] the substitution of etoposide for vinblastine,[13] and the omission of bleomycin.[56,84]

Although the omission of bleomycin results in reduced toxicity, it also results in a lower likelihood of complete response and an increased risk of death from cancer.[18,84,85] While it is appropriate to continue to attempt to devise less toxic regimens, this must not be at the price of treatment efficacy and usually should not be done outside the context of carefully structured clinical trials.

Agents for the Protection of Normal Tissue

Several agents, such as mesna, G-CSF, EPO, and (more recently) amifostine, have been developed

Table 27–2. TOXICITY PROFILES OF CHEMOTHERAPY REGIMENS USED TO TREAT GERM CELL TUMOR						
Toxicity*	PVB[†] (%)	BEP[‡] (%)	PEB[§] (%)	PE[∥] (%)	VIP[#] (%)	TIP[**] (%)
Gastrointestinal	94	74–90	57	> 50	90	3[††]
Nephrotoxicity	< 5	0–2	1–5	6	23	7
Neuromuscular						
Peripheral neuropathy	11	4–8	10	NR	17	7–10
Auditory impairment	NR	6	2	NR	10	10
Myalgias	19	0	NR	NR	NR	10–35
Pulmonary	15	30	12	0	0	NR
Bone marrow (grades 3 or 4)						
Anemia	NR	7	1	2	> 50	70
Myelosuppression	59	65	59	25	84–89	53–75
Thrombocytopenia	5	8–14	2	18	28–51	45

BEP = beomycin/etoposide/cisplatin; NR = not reported; PE = cisplatin/etoposide; PEB = cisplatin/etoposide/bleomycin; PVB = cisplatin/vinblastine/bleomycin; TIP = paclitaxel/ifosfamide/cisplatin; VIP = vinblastine/ifosfamide/cisplatin.
*World Health Organization grades 2 to 4.
[†]See references 13 and 17.
[‡]See references 14 and 56.
[§]See references 13, 14, and 18.
[∥]See references 18 and 56.
[#]See references 50, 52, and 88.
[**]See references 38 and 39.
[††]Grades 3 or 4.

specifically to protect normal tissues from the toxic effects of chemotherapy. The use of G-CSF, mesna, and recombinant EPO was discussed earlier in this chapter. Amifostine, a thiol, is thought to protect cells from damage by scavenging oxygen-derived free radicals and by donating hydrogen to repair damaged target molecules.[9] A large randomized trial demonstrated that amifostine could selectively protect against cumulative nephrotoxicity associated with cisplatin-based combination chemotherapy for ovarian cancer.[8] In addition, there was a trend toward a decrease in peripheral neuropathy in the group treated with amifostine and, to a lesser extent, a decrease in ototoxicity. While there is evidence from phase I and II trials that supports the finding of protection against nephrotoxicity,[86,87] additional data on benefit with regard to neurotoxicity are inconclusive.[9] Only one small randomized trial has been undertaken to assess the effect of amifostine in patients undergoing chemotherapy for germ cell tumors.[39] In that trial, 40 patients who were receiving paclitaxel/ifosfamide/cisplatin followed by peripheral stem cell transplantation with carboplatin and etoposide were randomized to receiving amifostine or no treatment. No differences in toxicity were detected between the two groups. However, given the small benefit demonstrated in the other trials described, this study may have been underpowered

to detect a difference.[39] Although there is no specific evidence of an effect of amifostine in the treatment of germ cell tumors, the current recommendation from the American Society of Clinical Oncology is that amifostine may be considered for the prevention of nephrotoxicity in any patient who receives cisplatin-based chemotherapy.[9]

CONCLUSION

While significant progress has been made in the last three decades in the treatment of patients with germ cell tumors and while most patients can now reasonably expect to be cured, chemotherapy regimens for this disease continue to have significant side effects. However, progress has been made in ameliorating the toxicity profiles, and significantly fewer patients now experience such morbidities as renal failure, hemorrhagic cystitis, and bleomycin-induced pneumonitis. Newer chemotherapeutic agents such as paclitaxel and gemicitabine have distinct patterns of side effects and must be assessed carefully to establish how their toxicity interacts with the conventional cytotoxic agents that are used in patients with this disease. As new approaches for reducing side effects are evaluated, the efficacy of current management must be maintained and not sacrificed in pursuit of a more attractive toxicity profile.

REFERENCES

1. Einhorn L, Nagy C, Werner K, Finn A. Ondansetron: a new anti-emetic for patients receiving cisplatin chemotherapy. J Clin Oncol 1990;8:731–5.

2. Marty M, Pouillart P, Scholl S, et al. Comparison of the 5-hydroxytryptamine₃ (serotinin) antagonist ondansetron (GR 38032F) with high-dose metoclopramide in the control of cisplatin-induced emesis. N Engl J Med 1990;322:816–21.

3. Bajorin D, Nichols C, Schmoll H, et al. Recombinant human granulocyte-macrophage colony-stimulating factor as an adjunct to conventional-dose ifosfamide-based chemotherapy for patients with advanced or relapsed germ cell tumors: a randomized trial. J Clin Oncol 1995;13:79–86.

4. Fossa S, Kaye SB, Mead G, et al. Filgrastim during combination chemotherapy of patients with poor-prognosis metastatic germ cell malignancy. European Organization for Research and Treatment of Cancer, Genito-Urinary Group and the Medical Research Council Testicular Cancer Working Party, Cambridge, United Kingdom. J Clin Oncol 1998;16:716–24.

5. Cascinu S, Fedeli A, Del Ferro E, et al. Recombinant human erythropoietin treatment in cisplatin-associated anemia: a randomized, double-blind trial with placebo. J Clin Oncol 1994;12:1058–62.

6. Miller C, Platanias L, Mills S, et al. Phase I-II trial of erythropoietin in the treatment of cisplatin-associated anemia. J Natl Cancer Inst 1992;15:98–103.

7. Itri L. The use of epoetin alfa in chemotherapy patients: a consistent profile of efficacy and safety. Semin Oncol 2002;29:81–7.

8. Kemp G, Rose P, Lurain J, et al. Amifostine pretreatment for protection against cyclophosphamide-induced and cisplatin-induced toxicities: results of a randomized control trial in patients with advanced ovarian cancer. J Clin Oncol 1996;14:2101–12.

9. Hensley M, Schuchter L, Lindley C, et al. American Society of Clinical Oncology clinical practice guidelines for the use of chemotherapy and radiotherapy protectants. J Clin Oncol 1999;17:3333–55.

10. Einhorn L. Testicular cancer as a model for a curable neoplasm: the Richard and Hinda Rosenthal Foundation Award Lecture. Cancer Res 1981;41:3274–80.

11. Peckham M, Barret A, McElwain T, et al. Non-seminoma germ cell tumors (malignant teratoma) of the testis: results of treatment and an analysis of prognostic factors. Br J Urol 1981;53:162–72.

12. Levine E, Raghavan D. Treatment of refractory testis cancer: salvage or savage chemotherapy. Eur J Cancer 1991;27:932–6.

13. Williams SD, Birch R, Einhorn LH, et al. Treatment of disseminated germ-cell tumors with cisplatin, bleomycin and either vinblastine or etoposide. N Engl J Med 1987;316:1435–40.

14. Toner G, Stockler M, Boyer M, et al. Comparison of two standard chemotherapy regimens for good-prognosis germ-cell tumors: a randomised trial. Lancet 2001;357:739–45.

15. Vogelzang N. Toxicities of chemotherapy for metastatic testicular cancer. In: Horwich A, editor. Testicular cancer: investigation and management. London: Chapman & Hall; 1996. p. 381–401.

16. Prestayko AW, D'Aoust CJ, Issell BF, Crooke ST. Cisplatin (cis-diamminedichloroplatinum II). Cancer Treat Rev 1979;6:17–39.

17. Levi J, Thomson D, Sandeman T, et al. A prospective study of cisplatin-based combination chemotherapy in advanced germ cell malignancy: role of maintenance and long-term follow-up. J Clin Oncol 1988;6:1154–60.

18. de Wit R, Stoter G, Kaye S, et al. Importance of bleomycin in combination chemotherapy for good-prognosis testicular nonseminoma: a randomized study of the European Organization for Research and Treatment of Cancer Genitourinary Tract Cancer Cooperative Group. J Clin Oncol 1997;15:1717–9.

19. Dirks J, Alfrey A. Normal and abnormal magnesium metabolism. In: Schrier R, editor. Renal and electrolyte disorders. Boston and Toronto: Little, Brown and Company; 1986. p. 348.

20. Schilsky R, Barlock A, Ozols R. Persistent hypomagnesemia following cisplatin chemotherapy for testicular cancer. Cancer Treat Rev 1982;66:1767–9.

21. Gonzales-Vitale J, Hayes D, Cvitkovic E, Steinberg S. The renal pathology in clinical trials of cis-platinum (II) diamminedichloride. Cancer 1977;39:1362–71.

22. Newlands ES, Bagshawe KD, Begent RH, et al. Current optimum management of anaplastic germ cell tumors of the testis and other sites. Br J Urol 1986;58:307–14.

23. Zalupski M, Baker L. Ifosfamide. J Natl Cancer Inst 1988;80:556–66.

24. Vogelzang N. Vascular and other complications of chemotherapy for testicular cancer. World J Urol 1984;2:32–7.

25. Cowan J, Kies M, Roth J, Joyce R. Nerve conduction studies in patients treated with cis-diamminedichloroplatinum(II): a preliminary report. Cancer Treat Rep 1980;64:1119–22.

26. Kaplan R, Wiernik P. Neurotoxicity of antineoplastic drugs. Semin Oncol 1982;9:103–30.

27. Thompson S, Davis L, Kornfeld M, et al. Cisplatin neuropathy: clinical, electrophysiologic, morphologic and toxicologic studies. Cancer 1984;54:1269–75.

28. Moul J, Robertson J, George S, et al. Complications of therapy for testicular cancer. J Urol 1989;142:1491–6.

29. Boyer M, Raghavan D, Harris P, et al. Lack of late toxicity in patients treated with cisplatin-containing combination chemotherapy for metastatic testicular cancer. J Clin Oncol 1990;8:21–6.

30. Bissett D, Kunkeler L, Zwanenburg L, et al. Long-term sequelae of treatment for testicular germ cell tumors. Br J Cancer 1990;62:655–9.

31. Aass N, Kaasa S, Lund E, et al. Long-term somatic side-effects and morbidity in testicular cancer patients. Br J Cancer 1990;61:151–5.

32. Roth B, Greist A, Kubilis P, et al. Cisplatin-based combination chemotherapy for disseminated germ cell tumors: long-term follow-up. J Clin Oncol 1988;6:1239–47.

33. Hansen S, Helweg-Larsen S, Trojaborg W. Long-term neurotoxicity in patients treated with cisplatin, vinblastine, and bleomycin for metastatic germ cell cancer. J Clin Oncol 1989;7:1457–61.

34. Fossa S, Kreuser E, Roth G, Raghavan D. Long-term side effects after treatment of testicular cancer. Prog Clin Biol Res 1990;357:321–30.

35. Gietema J, Sleijfer D, Willemse P, et al. Long-term follow-up of cardiovascular risk factors in patients given chemotherapy for disseminated nonseminomatous testicular cancer. Ann Intern Med 1992;116:709–15.

36. Bokemeyer C, Beyer J, Metzner B, et al. Phase II study of paclitaxel in patients with relapsed or cisplatin-refractory testicular cancer. Ann Oncol 1996;7:31–4.

37. Motzer R, Bajorin D, Schwartz L, et al. Phase II trial of paclitaxel shows antitumor activity in patients with previously treated germ cell tumors. J Clin Oncol 1994;12:2277–83.

38. Motzer R, Sheinfeld J, Mazumdar M, et al. Paclitaxel, ifosfamide, and cisplatin second-line therapy for patients with relapsed testicular germ cell cancer. J Clin Oncol 2000;18:2413–8.

39. Rick O, Beyer J, Schwella N, et al. Assessment of amifostine as protection from chemotherapy-induced toxicities after conventional-dose and high-dose chemotherapy in patients with germ cell tumor. Ann Oncol 2001;12:1151–5.

40. Hansen S. Autonomic neuropathy after treatment with cisplatin, vinblastine, and bleomycin for germ cell cancer. BMJ 1990;300:511–2.

41. Vermorken J, Kapteijn T, Hart A, Pinedo H. Ototoxicity of cis-diamminedichloroplatinum (II): influence of dose, schedule and mode of administration. Eur J Cancer Clin Oncol 1983;19:53–8.

42. Fleming S, Peters G, Weaver A, et al. Ototoxicity associated with cis-platinum in three chemotherapy multi-drug regimens. Cancer 1983;51:610–3.

43. Stoter G, Koopman A, Vendrik C, et al. Ten-year survival and late sequelae in testicular cancer patients treated with cisplatin, vinblastine, and bleomycin. J Clin Oncol 1989;7:1099–104.

44. Osanto S, Bukman A, Van Hoek F, et al. Long-term effects of chemotherapy in patients with testicular cancer. J Clin Oncol 1992;10:574–9.

45. Stuart N, Woodroffe C, Grundy R, Cullen M. Long-term toxicity of chemotherapy for testicular cancer—the cost of cure. Br J Cancer 1990;61:479–84.

46. Rowinsky E, Donehower R. Antimicrotubule agents. In: DeVita V, Hellman S, Rosenberg S, editors. Cancer: principles and practice of oncology. Philadelphia and New York: Lippincott Raven; 1997. p. 472–9.

47. Chaudhry V, Rowinsky E, Sartorius S, et al. Peripheral neuropathy from Taxol and cisplatin combination chemotherapy: clinical and electrophysiological studies. Ann Neurol 1994;35:304–11.

48. Getaz E, Beckley S, Fitzpatrick J, Dozier A. Cisplatin-induced hemolysis. N Engl J Med 1980;302:334–5.

49. Dearnaley D, Horwich A, A'Hern R, et al. Combination chemotherapy with bleomycin, etoposide and cisplatin (BEP) for metastatic testicular teratoma: long-term follow-up. Eur J Cancer 1991;27:684–91.

50. de Wit R, Stoter G, Sleijfer D, et al. Four cycles of BEP vs four cycles of VIP in patients with intermediate-prognosis metastatic testicular non-seminoma: a randomized study of the EORTC Genitourinary Tract Cancer Cooperative Group. European Organization for Research and Treatment of Cancer. Br J Cancer 1998;78:828–32.

51. Horwich A, Sleijfer D, Fossa S, et al. Randomized trial of bleomycin, etoposide, and cisplatin compared with bleomycin, etoposide, and carboplatin in good-prognosis metastatic nonseminomatous germ cell cancer: a Multiinstitutional Medical Research Council/European Organization for Research and Treatment of Cancer Trial. J Clin Oncol 1997;15:1844–52.

52. McCaffrey J, Mazumdar M, Bajorin D, et al. Ifosfamide- and cisplatin-containing chemotherapy as first-line salvage therapy in germ cell tumors: response and survival. J Clin Oncol 1997;15:2559–63.

53. Bokemeyer C, Gerl A, Schoffski P, et al. Gemcitabine in patients with relapsed or cisplatin-refractory testicular cancer. J Clin Oncol 1999;17:512–6.

54. Bokemeyer C, Kollmannsberger C, Harstrick A, et al. Treatment of patients with cisplatin-refractory testicular germ-cell cancer. Int J Cancer 1999;83:848–51.

55. Hinton S, Catalano P, Einhorn L, et al. Phase II study of paclitaxel plus gemcitabine in refractory germ cell tumors (E9897): a trial of the Eastern Cooperative Oncology Group. J Clin Oncol 2002;20:1859–63.

56. Bosl G, Geller N, Bajorin D, et al. A randomized trial of etoposide + cisplatin versus vinblastine + bleomycin + cisplatin + cyclophosphamide + dactinomycin in patients with good-prognosis germ cell tumors. J Clin Oncol 1988;6:1231–8.

57. Albers P, Heicappell R, Schwaibold H, Wolff J. Erythropoetin in urologic oncology. Eur Urol 2001;39:1–8.

58. Ginsberg S, Comis R. The pulmonary toxicity of antineoplastic agents. Semin Oncol 1982;9:34–51.

59. Comis R. Detecting bleomycin pulmonary toxicity: a continued conundrum. J Clin Oncol 1990;8:765–7.

60. Cheson B. Miscellaneous chemotherapeutic agents. In: DeVita V, Hellman S, Rosenberg S, editors. Cancer: principles and practice of oncology. Philadelphia and New York: Lippincott Raven; 1997. p. 494–5.

61. Boyer M, Roth B. Side effects of treatment. In: Raghavan D, Scher H, Leibel S, Lange P, editors. Principles and practice of genitourinary oncology. Philadelphia: Lippincott-Raven Publishers; 1997. p. 741–50.

62. McKeage M, Evans B, Atkinson C, et al. Carbon monoxide diffusing capacity is a poor predictor of clinically significant bleomycin lung. New Zealand Clinical Oncology Group. J Clin Oncol 1990;8:779–83.

63. Lejonc J, Vernant J, Macquin J, Castaigne A. Myocardial infarction following vinblastine treatment. Lancet 1980;2:692.

64. Vogelzang N, Frenning D, Kennedy B. Coronary artery disease after treatment with bleomycin and vinblastine. Cancer Treat Rep 1980;64:1159–60.

65. Subar M, Muggia F. Apparent myocardial ischemia associated with vinblastine administration. Cancer Treat Rep 1986;70:690–1.

66. Edwards G, Lane M, Smith F. Long-term treatment with cis-dichlorodiammineplatinum(II)-vinblastine-bleomycin: possible association with severe coronary artery disease. Cancer Treat Rep 1979;63:551–2.

67. Bodensteiner D. Fatal coronary artery fibrosis after treatment with bleomycin, vinblastine, and cis-platinum. South Med J 1981;74:898–9.

68. Doll D, List A, Greco F, et al. Acute vascular ischemic events after cisplatin-based combination chemotherapy for germ-cell tumors of the testis. Ann Intern Med 1986;105:48–51.

69. Levine M, Gent M, Hirsh J, et al. The thrombogenic effect of anticancer drug therapy in women with stage II breast cancer. N Engl J Med 1988;318:404–7.

70. Rowinsky E, McGuire W, Guarnieri T, et al. Cardiac disturbances during the administration of Taxol. J Clin Oncol 1991;9:1704–12.

71. Arbuck SG, Strauss H, Rowinsky E, et al. A reassessment of the cardiac toxicity associated with Taxol. Natl Cancer Inst Monogr 1993;15:117–30.

72. Rowinsky E, Donehower R. Drug therapy: paclitaxel (Taxol). N Engl J Med 1996;332:1004–14.

73. Rowinsky E, Cazenave L, Donehower R. Taxol: a novel investigational antineoplastic agent. J Natl Cancer Inst 1990; 82:1247–59.

74. Rowinsky E, Eisenhauer E, Chaudhry V, et al. Clinical toxicities encountered with Taxol. Semin Oncol 1993;20 Suppl 3:1–15.

75. Cheng E, Cvitkovic E, Wittes R, Golbey R. Germ cell tumors (II): VAB II in metastatic testicular cancer. Cancer 1978; 42:2162–8.

76. Wiesenfeld M, Reinders E, Corder M, et al. Successful re-treatment with cis-dichlorodiammineplatinum(II) after apparent allergic reactions. Cancer Treat Rep 1979;63: 219–21.

77. Antony A, Robinson W, Roy C, et al. Inappropriate antidiuretic hormone secretion after high dose vinblastine. J Urol 1980;123:783–4.

78. Ginsberg O, Comis R, Miller M. The development of hyponatremia following combination chemotherapy for metastatic germ cell tumors. Med Pediatr Oncol 1982;10:7–14.

79. Krikorian J, Daniels J, Brown B, Hu M. Chemotherapy for metastatic testicular cancer with cis-dichlorodiammineplatinum (II), vinblastine, and bleomycin. Cancer Treat Rep 1978;62:1455–63.

80. Einhorn L, Williams SD. Chemotherapy of disseminated testicular cancer. A random prospective study. Cancer 1980; 46:1339–44.

81. Stoter G, Sleyfer D, ten Bokkel Huinink W, et al. High-dose versus low-dose vinblastine in cisplatin-vinblastine-bleomycin combination chemotherapy of non-seminomatous testicular cancer: a randomised study of the EORTC Genitourinary Tract Cancer Cooperative Group. J Clin Oncol 1986;4:1199–206.

82. Einhorn L, Williams S, Troner M, et al. The role of maintenance therapy in disseminated testicular cancer. N Engl J Med 1981;305:727–31.

83. Einhorn L, Williams S, Loehrer P, et al. Evaluation of optimal duration of chemotherapy in favorable-prognosis disseminated germ cell tumors: a Southeastern Cancer Study Group protocol. J Clin Oncol 1989;7:387–91.

84. Levi J, Raghavan D, Harvey V, et al. The importance of bleomycin in combination chemotherapy for good-prognosis germ cell carcinoma. Australasian Germ Cell Trial Group. J Clin Oncol 1993;11:1300–5.

85. Loehrer PJ Sr, Johnson D, Elson P, et al. Importance of bleomycin in favorable-prognosis disseminated germ cell tumors: an Eastern Cooperative Oncology Group trial. J Clin Oncol 1995;13:470–6.

86. Bennett C, Golub R, Calhoun E, et al. Cost-utility assessment of amifostine as first-line therapy for ovarian cancer. Int J Gynecol Cancer 1998;8:64–72.

87. Glover D, Glick J, Weiler C, et al. Phase I trials of WR-2721 and cis-platinum. Int J Radiat Oncol Biol Phys 1984;10: 1781–4.

88. Harstrick A, Schmoll H, Wilke H, et al. Cisplatin, etoposide, and ifosfamide salvage therapy for refractory or relapsing germ cell carcinoma. J Clin Oncol 1992;9:1549–55.

28

Late Toxicity of Chemotherapy

CHRISTOPHER J. SWEENEY, MBBS
DEREK RAGHAVAN, MD, PHD

After more than 25 years of experience with curative cisplatin-based chemotherapy, it has become clear that the important advances that have increased the cure rate for patients with advanced germ cell malignancy from around 20% to greater than 85% have also led to some unexpected costs. As a result, attention in the past decade has been directed to defining more clearly the long-term toxicities of this therapy. This has been the subject of many long-term follow-up studies, including detailed sequential studies of small cohorts of patients as well as overviews of population-based treatment groups and broad assessments of long-term survivors from several centers of excellence.

However, the data must be interpreted with a number of caveats in mind. One of the most troubling and contentious issues is the prevalence and frequency of second malignancies in this population of patients. The data drawn from these studies include data from patients treated with extensive irradiation (mediastinal and/or abdominal) or alkylating agents. These therapies are not necessarily relevant to patients receiving therapy today as the current radiation fields are smaller and as alkyating agents are less frequently employed; however, experience with the late effects of some of the newer agents that are currently in use is less defined.

Another issue is the distinguishing of treatment-induced malignancies from malignancies that are associated specifically with a history of germ cell tumors, such as contralateral testis cancer or a range of myelodysplastic conditions that may culminate in leukemia. Therefore, when determining the incidence of iatrogenic malignancies in a treatment group, a valid judgment can only be made when that group is compared with a group of patients with the same characteristics who did not receive therapy. For example, patients with stage II disease treated with chemotherapy or radiotherapy should be compared with patients with stage II disease treated with surgery alone. This will allow the distinction between common factors that pertain to all groups (such as genetic risks or prenatal exposures) and treatment-related effects. The same is also true for the definition of the incidence and causes of other late events that are unrelated to cancer.

It is also important to recognize that the young patients who had germ cell tumors that were treated in 1970 to 1980 with combination chemotherapy are only just now entering the peak age group for the incidence of cardiovascular and malignant disease, and ongoing scrutiny will be essential to define (for the first time) the true incidence and prevalence of intercurrent and iatrogenic disorders in this population as it ages.

After considering these provisos, the available data provide a framework to facilitate the counseling of patients who are about to be started on chemotherapy, as well as long-term survivors. This is especially important in some of the decisions that have arisen with the advent of adjuvant chemotherapy for patients with high-risk clinical stage I germ cell tumors and for patients with small-volume metastatic disease identified at retroperitoneal lymph node dissection.

PULMONARY TOXICITY

In the initial period of the use of bleomycin for advanced germ cell tumors and other malignancies, it rapidly became clear that patients treated with high cumulative doses, especially doses > 300 to 350 U, were at increased risk of developing progressive respiratory symptoms that sometimes culminated in death from pulmonary failure. At Indiana University, 1 of 50 patients died from from this toxicity in the original cisplatin/vinblastine/bleomycin (PVB) study.[1] The first Australasian Germ Cell Trial recorded bleomycin-related pulmonary toxicity in 46% of cases and in 4% of pneumonitis-related deaths from PVB use.[2] This led to a randomized trial of cisplatin/vinblastine versus cisplatin/vinblastine/bleomycin in which pulmonary toxicity was recorded in 34% of patients receiving bleomycin and culminated in death in 4% of the patients treated with this agent.[3] Of importance, there was a higher cancer-related death rate when bleomycin was omitted.

In a large recent European Organization for the Reasearch and Treatment of Cancer trial comparing four cycles of bleomycin/etoposide/cisplatin (BEP) (360 units of bleomycin) with four cycles of etoposide/cisplatin (EP), there were two deaths attributed to bleomycin (1% incidence) and a 3% incidence of chronic dyspnea in the BEP arm. This chronic dyspnea was not observed in the EP arm. In this study, a median 20% decrease in the diffusion capacity of the lung for carbon monoxide (DLCO) was noted for the whole BEP group when compared with baseline, versus a 2% decrease in the EP group.[4] Similar results were recorded for the combination of cisplatin, etoposide, and bleomycin in trials conducted by the Eastern Cooperative Oncology Group assessing the elimination of bleomycin.[5] As discussed in Chapter 13, etoposide replaced vinblastine in the standard treatment regimens, dramatically ameliorating acute nonpulmonary toxicity. The rate of pulmonary toxicity that occurs with the administration of 270 U of bleomycin (three cycles of BEP) has been clearly delineated by several prospective studies and is minimal in the "good-risk" patient population. Pulmonary fibrosis, the long-term complication of bleomycin exposure, occurs in about 5% of patients and is fatal in 1 to 2% of patients.[3–5] Risk factors for these abnormalities are age greater than 70 years, prior chest radiotherapy, impaired renal function, high inspired oxygen concentration, higher cumulative doses (especially > 360 U), and a history of cigarette smoking.[4] For these reasons, at Indiana University and the University of Southern California, the eleventh and twelfth doses of bleomycin are often withheld, especially if a patient is to receive four cycles of BEP with planned elective post-chemotherapy surgery. It is very rare to have toxicity in the absence of these risk factors. However, if a patient has risk factors for bleomycin toxicity and has good-risk disease, four cycles of EP can usually be substituted for three cycles of BEP. If a patient has advanced disease and requires four cycles of therapy but is unable to receive bleomycin, then etoposide, ifosfamide, and cisplatin (VIP) can be used.[6]

In addition to tailoring therapy to avoid bleomycin when contraindicated, close monitoring of therapy is essential. Although widely used, corticosteroids are frequently ineffective in preventing bleomycin-induced pneumonitis, and the withholding of therapy at the first sign of toxicity is thus of paramount importance.[6] The earliest findings of pulmonary toxicity from bleomycin include an inspiratory lag (chest excursion decreased on one side when compared with the other) or inspiratory crepitations. If these are found, the bleomycin should be discontinued. Symptoms and signs are bibasilar crepitations, a nonproductive cough, and/or an altered pattern of dyspnea on exertion. Pulmonary function tests may reveal a decrease in DLCO (Table 28–1), and very advanced disease is associated with hypoxia and hypercapnia. Chest radiography may reveal pleural nodules or ground-glass and linear opacities, predominantly at the posterior lung bases (Figure 28–1). If therapy is stopped as soon as the problem is recognized, the radiographic findings usually disappear. When pneumonitis is established and the patient is deteriorating, a prolonged course of corticosteroids at a high dose, with gradual tapering, may abort the process; at that point, further administration of bleomycin is completely contraindicated.

NEPHROTOXICITY

It is well known that cisplatin can cause acute renal impairment (see detailed discussion in Chapter 27). In the acute setting, this is characterized by proximal tubule defects and is clinically evident as magnesium wasting, often with associated hypokalemia.[8] Acute

Table 28–1. PULMONARY FUNCTION TEST DEMONSTRATING CHARACTERISTICS OF DIMINISHED DIFFUSION CAPACITY OF LUNG FOR CARBON MONOXIDE AND A RESTRICTIVE DEFECT			
	Without Bronchodilator M		
Spirometry	**Predicted**	**Pre**	**% Pre**
FVC (L)	5.20	2.84	55
FEV.5 (L)	3.35	2.04	61
FEV1 (L)	4.31	2.53	59
FEV1/FVC (%)	83	89	108
FEF 25–75% (L/S)	4.53	3.12	69
FEFmax (L/S)	9.58	7.27	76
PIFR (L/S)		4.61	
FEF50/FIF50 (%)		169	
	Pre-drug* Averages		
Diffusion	**Predicted**	**Pre**	**% Pre**
Dsb mL/min/mm Hg	39.04	11.75	30
Dsb (adj) mL/min/mm Hg	39.04	13.63	35
D/VA	5.91	3.21	54
D/VA(adj)	5.91	3.73	63
VA(sb) (L)		3.66	
	Hb = 10.5		

adj = adjusted for hemoglobin; Dsb = diffusion in a single breath corrected for hemoglobin; FEF = forced expiratory flow; FEV1 = forced expiratory volume in 1 second; FVC = forced vital capacity; Hb = hemoglobin; L/S = liters er second; PIFR = peak inspiratory flow rate; Pre = before; Va(sb) = alveolar volume per single breath; D/VA = diffusion per single breath.

decreases in glomerular filtration rate (GFR) and effective plasma filtration are also well characterized. There have been varied reports regarding the long-term effects of cisplatin. Some investigators have reported that the glomerular defects persist and do not improve over the months to years that follow the chemotherapy.[8–10] Others have reported improvements over years.[11] In one study, 34 patients with germ cell cancer were observed for a median of 65 months. None of the patients experienced relapse

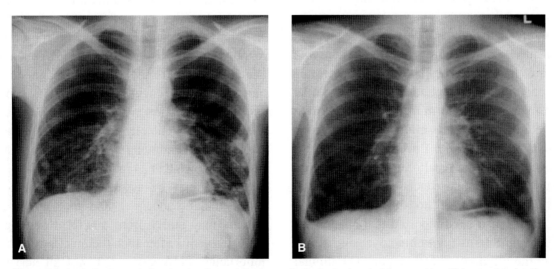

Figure 28–1. *A,* Posteroanterior chest radiograph from a patient who had underlying renal insufficiency, showing the peripheral distribution of ground-glass opacities after administration of 270 units of bleomycin. *B,* A radiograph made 6 months later reveals persistence of the lung nodules (teratoma or necrosis) but resolution of the opacities.

during follow-up. During treatment, the GFR decreased by 18% ($p < .05$). In follow-up, kidney function recovered in 10 patients and partly improved in 8 patients.[11] In contrast, other studies reported that GFR changes were found to progress during the first year after the initiation of chemotherapy; specifically, a significant increase in serum creatinine was observed to occur at 6 months after the initiation of treatment.[12] This discrepancy may have been due to the short follow-up in this study.

One group of investigators reported on the prospective evaluation of 85 patients with germ cell tumors more than 10 years after retroperitoneal lymph node dissection alone, radiotherapy alone, or chemotherapy with or without surgery or radiation.[13] Nuclear medicine assessments of renal function (ie, GFR) were done at baseline and at follow-up (after 10 years). After a minimum of 10 years of follow-up, a group of patients who had had surgery alone ($n = 14$) had no change in GFR, patients in the radiotherapy group ($n = 18$) had an overall 8% reduction, and patients in the chemotherapy group ($n = 53$) had a an overall 14% reduction in renal function. Two of the patients who had undergone surgery only, 5 of the patients who had been treated with radiation only, and 18 of the patients who received chemotherapy had renal impairment (GFR at or less than 70% of the lower normal limit). In our study of patients treated with a regimen that included 1-day cisplatin (100 mg/m²), 43% of patients had impaired creatinine clearance more than 5 years after treatment[14] although it is emphasized that the 1-day regimen appears to be more nephrotoxic than the standard 5-day approach.

Renal microscopic features after treatment with cisplatin are characterized by hydropic degeneration of the renal tubular epithelium, thickened tubular basement membranes, and mild interstitial fibrosis (Figure 28–2). Electron microscopy revealed phagolysosomes filled with flocculent material.[8] It should be noted that the renal injury in the majority of patients with testicular cancer remains subclinical, with a persistent 20 to 30% reduction in GFR.[14,15] It has also been reported that coadministration of nephrotoxins (eg, aminoglycosides) may exacerbate the glomerular dysfunction. The tubular defects, on the other hand, have been shown to improve with time.[16]

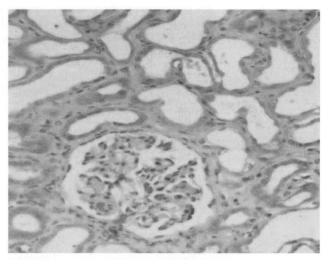

Figure 28–2. Renal biopsy specimen at 5 months after four courses of cisplatin therapy, showing flattening of tubule cells, luminal dilatation, and widening of intertubular space resulting from interstitial fibrosis (hematoxylin and eosin; ×200 original magnification). (Courtesy of Moo Nahm Yum, MD, Department of Pathology, Indiana University.)

Associated with the presence of long-term renal dysfunction is the risk of hypomagnesemia and hyperuricemia, both of which may be found in up to 35% and 30% of patients, respectively.[14] The presence of hypomagnesemia may be of particular importance in a patient with established cardiac disease.

VASCULAR TOXICITY

It has been known since the 1970s that patients being treated with bleomycin, vinca alkaloids, and cisplatin, alone or in combination, occasionally may suffer a broad range of vascular complications, including pulmonary emboli, myocardial infarction, venous thrombosis, and Raynaud's phenomenon. The initial reports identified these phenomena as sporadic occurrences[17,18] although subsequent reports of larger series suggested a possible pattern of events.[14,19,20] The physiologic mechanisms underlying these phenomena are not known although it has been shown that an increase in the level of serum cholesterol may be associated with chemotherapy for testicular cancer[21,22] and that up to 20% of patients may suffer from newly presenting hypercholesterolemia after such therapy (Figure 28–3). Of importance, however, is that not all surveys have confirmed these data.[23] Nonetheless, patients cured of advanced testicular cancer by chemotherapy

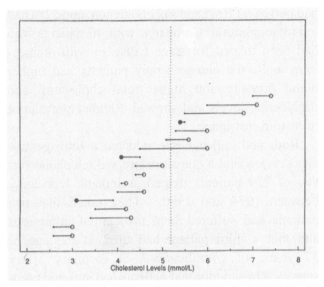

Figure 28–3. Pattern of emerging hypercholesterolemia with cisplatin/vinblastine/bleomycin (PVB) chemotherapy. (Reproduced with permission from Raghavan D, Fitzharris BM, George PM, et al. Fasting plasma lipid measurements following cisplatin chemotherapy in patients with germ cell tumors. J Clin Oncol 1992;10:1609–14.)

should be monitored, and hypercholesterolemia should be treated as clinically indicated.

Raynaud's phenomenon is one of the more dramatic and visible after-effects of chemotherapy for germ cell tumors, and the nature of the vascular change is easily identified (Figure 28–4). The main culprit is bleomycin although the incidence is higher when vinblastine and bleomycin are combined. In a retrospective review of 60 patients, Raynaud's phenomenon occurred in 22 (37%) of patients treated with vinblastine and bleomycin with or without cisplatin for germ cell testicular cancer.[17] In our series,

we identified 10% of patients presenting with persistent Raynaud's phenomenon in a long-term follow-up series.[14] In the Vogelzang series,[17] patients with and without Raynaud's phenomenon did not differ with respect to median age; tumor histology; total doses of vinblastine, bleomycin, and cisplatin; or frequency of vinblastine-induced neuropathy and bleomycin-induced cutaneous toxicity. Digital ischemia occurred in 21% of patients treated with only vinblastine and bleomycin and in 41% of those treated with PVB. Cigarette smoking was more common in patients with Raynaud's phenomenon. The median time to onset was 10 months. A follow-up study by Hansen and colleagues confirmed this high frequency but also reported a high prevalence of asymptomatic Raynaud's phenomenon.[18] Thirty-two patients with germ cell cancer were observed for a median of 78 months (range, 49 to 106 months). The arterial vasoconstrictor response to cold in the finger was measured by cuff- and strain-gauge techniques at 30°C, 15°C, and 10°C. Arterial closure was provoked in 9 patients. The remaining 18 patients (56%) had no finger symptoms but had an exaggerated response to cold in comparison with controls, and Raynaud's phenomenon was provoked in 2 patients. Another long-term follow-up study has reported that 49% of 146 patients treated with PVB have persistent symptoms after a median time of 8.5 years and a minimum of 6 years since completing chemotherapy.[19] It should be noted, however, that the functional status of patients after chemotherapy with PVB is maintained, and 95% of the patients return to their

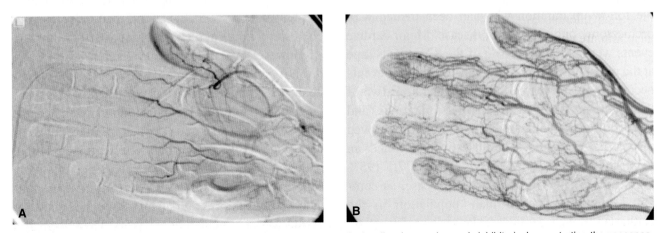

Figure 28–4. Angiograms made before (*A*) and after (*B*) administration of tolazoline (an α-adrenergic inhibitor), demonstrating the vasospastic changes seen with Raynaud's phenomenon induced by bleomycin. (Courtesy of Matthew Johnson, MD, Department of Radiology, Indiana University.)

pretherapy status. Unfortunately, substituting etoposide for vinblastine has not eliminated the problem.[23] Nifedipine, a calcium channel blocker, has been reported to have some efficacy in limiting this problem.[24] Avoidance of precipitants (such as cold exposure) is the mainstay for preventing this toxicity. In general, it appears that Raynaud's phenomenon in this context is seen more frequently in colder climates, with higher incidence figures having been reported in studies from Minnesota and Scandinavia.

A more contentious question is whether coronary artery or cerebrovascular events occur at an increased rate in patients treated with platinum-based chemotherapy for testicular cancer. One case series described four patients who had acute vascular ischemic events after treatment with cisplatin-based combination chemotherapy; two had myocardial infarctions, and two others had cerebrovascular accidents.[25] All patients were less than 30 years of age and had no significant risk factors for atherosclerotic cardiovascular disease. Others investigators have reported similar findings.[26,27]

One interesting finding is that up to 20 years after administration of cisplatin-containing chemotherapy, circulating platinum is still detectable in the plasma of patients cured of testicular cancer by this treatment.[28] The same group of investigators identified 87 patients who were treated with cisplatin-containing chemotherapy before 1987 who had been in remission for at least 10 years and who were less than 50 years of age at the time of analysis.[29] Their cardiovascular risk profile was compared with that of 40 patients of comparable age and with comparable follow-up duration who had been treated with orchiectomy only for stage I disease. Major cardiac events were found in 5 (6%) of the 87 patients (age at the time of the event was 30 to 42 years; the events occurred 9 to 16 years after chemotherapy). Two of these patients suffered myocardial infarctions, and three presented with angina pectoris with proven myocardial ischemia. The investigators found an increased observed-to-expected ratio of 7.1 (95% CI, 1.9–18.3) for coronary artery disease, as compared with the general male population in the Netherlands. The cardiovascular risk profile of 62 chemotherapy patients was as follows: 79% had hypercholesterolemia, 39% had hypertension, 25%

had persistent Raynaud's phenomenon, and 22% had microalbuminuria. Compared with 40 patients who had been treated for stage I disease with orchiectomy only, the chemotherapy patients had higher blood pressure and higher total cholesterol and triglyceride levels and showed a higher prevalence of insulin resistance.

Roth and colleagues conducted a retrospective chart review and a questionnaire and telephone survey of 229 patients treated at Indiana University between 1974 and 1980.[19] They noted that two patients had suffered fatal myocardial infarctions and that a third patient had died, at the age of 37 years, of complications of coronary artery surgery. Three additional patients had suffered coronary artery disease (total cases, 3%) although the investigators noted that all were smokers and that three had undergone mediastinal irradiation. Of the 147 surviving patients, nearly 50% reported variants of Raynaud's phenomenon.

In a study of 53 patients previously treated with cisplatin-containing chemotherapy (predominantly the PVB regimen) at Royal Prince Alfred Hospital in Sydney, Australia, we identified only one case of myocardial ischemia (in a 63-year-old smoker) but did detect 8 cases of Raynaud's phenomenon, 4 cases of mild hypertension, and 4 patients in whom ST elevation occurred during exercise electrocardiographic testing (but in whom stress thallium tests were normal).[14] Four of the patients who experienced Raynaud's phenomenon had been smokers or were current smokers. Of interest, 9 patients were noted to have hypercholesterolemia at presentation, but 20 patients had raised serum cholesterol levels at the time of long-term follow-up.

However, one systematic evaluation of this issue did not confirm an increased incidence.[30] The incidence of vascular events was evaluated in a Testicular Cancer Intergroup study that randomized patients to observation versus two cycles of PVB if found to have nodal disease at primary retroperitoneal lymph node dissection.[28] If there was recurrence on observation, four cycles of PVB were given. Questionnaires were sent to 459 patients when the follow-up period was at a median of 5.1 years. There were 270 replies, equally distributed among patients who were randomized to adjuvant chemotherapy, observation with no relapse, and observation with relapse. Although persistent sensory neuropathies were more frequent in patients who were treated with chemotherapy, there was no apparent increased incidence of vascular events (two myocardial infarctions in the treatment observation group, one myocardial infarction in the adjuvant therapy group, and no reported cerebrovascular accidents. There are limitations to this study because (1) it is a retrospective self-reporting questionnaire study; (2) there is a potential case selection bias, and outcomes are not known for the 189 patients who did not respond; and (3) follow-up was relatively short.

Another relevant issue is that patients with advanced germ cell tumors have been noted to suffer from pulmonary emboli. Although the majority of cases appear to be classic emboli of vascular origin that are perhaps due to toxicity of chemotherapy per se, it has been documented that this may, in fact, be due to vascular invasion by tumor cells.[31]

NEUROTOXICITY

Cisplatin has been well documented to cause neurotoxicity and ototoxicity. The peripheral neuropathy is predominantly sensory, manifested mostly by paresthesia and dysesthesia. These symptoms have been reported to persist beyond 6 years in about 30 to 40% of patients.[14,19] The long-term toxicity has been confirmed by other investigators.[11] Nerve conduction studies have shown that the changes in conduction along peripheral and central pathways after tibial nerve stimulation are compatible with a toxic effect on the sensory root ganglia causing an axonal degeneration of central and peripheral nerve fibers. An increasing cumulative dose of cisplatin and simultaneous development of Raynaud's phenomenon increases the risk of neurotoxicity.[15] The presence of abnormal nerve conduction studies in 50% of cases studied in the Royal Prince Alfred Hospital series[14] suggests that higher single doses of cisplatin (eg, 100 mg/m^2) may be more neurotoxic than are the more standard repeated daily low doses.

The clinical trial that resulted in BEP replacing PVB showed that the former is clearly a better option in the context of neurotoxicity. Specifically, the major toxicity of PVB is neuromuscular toxicity

due to vinblastine, and the etoposide-containing regimen caused substantially fewer paresthesias ($p = .02$), abdominal cramps ($p = .0008$), and myalgias ($p = .00002$). These toxicities can impair manual dexterity for life and occupational activities, as well as cause significant discomfort from abdominal cramps, ileus, and myalgias. Thus, the difference in the rates of neuromuscular toxicity was both statistically and clinically significant.[23]

The ototoxicity associated with cisplatin is high-frequency hearing loss and is related to the cumulative dose and rate of infusion.[32,33] It occurs in 20 to 40% of patients.[15] Older age, serum creatinine level > 1.5 mg/dL, cumulative doses of cisplatin, and preexisting hearing impairment are predictive for ototoxicity (Figure 28–5). Although there may be some improvement over months to years, recovery to normal hearing is rare if a clinical or symptomatic hearing deficit is noted by a patient. When higher single doses of cisplatin are used, up to 60% of patients may exhibit occult audiometric changes.[14]

SECONDARY MALIGNANCIES

Several international studies have used information from tumor registries in an attempt to determine whether there is an increased incidence of secondary malignancies in patients with testicular cancer and,

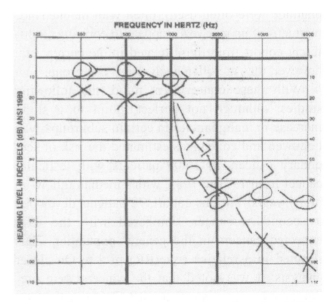

Figure 28–5. Audiometry assessment of a patient after cisplatin-based chemotherapy, demonstrating bilateral hearing impairment, most notably at higher frequencies. O = right ear; X = left ear.

specifically, whether radiotherapy and/or chemotherapy increases the incidence. Several tumor types have been identified in this context, including second primary testicular cancer (probably unrelated to treatment), soft-tissue sarcomas or neuroendocrine carcinomas (especially associated with prior radiotherapy or chemotherapy and sometimes arising from unresected immature teratoma), malignant melanoma (perhaps associated with the syndrome of multiple atypical nevi), and acute myelomonocytic leukemia (associated with etoposide).

However, the situation is complex. As outlined by Nichols and Loehrer,[34] two issues have to be considered when attempting to assess the prevalence and causes of second malignancies in patients treated for germ cell tumors. First, when the incidence in a treatment group is being determined, a valid judgment can be made only when that group is compared with a group of patients who have the same characteristics but who did not receive that treatment (eg, as previously noted, patients treated for stage II disease with chemotherapy or radiotherapy should be compared only with those treated for stage II disease with surgery alone). This is an important issue as it is likely that common factors such as genetic risks or prenatal exposures pertain to all treatment groups. Second, patients treated with dose-intense chemotherapy regimens from the early years (in which alkylating agents such as cyclophosphamide were often used), often with maintenance regimens of up to 2 years, appear to constitute a different cohort from those treated in the current era; however, they are often analyzed as one group.

With these concerns in mind, the following studies, although not perfect, point to a slight increase in malignancies in certain subgroups. Van Leeuwen and colleagues estimated the risk of secondary cancers in 1,909 patients with testicular cancer from 1971 to 1985, with a median follow-up of 7.7 years.[35] In this cohort, 78 patients developed a secondary cancer, compared with the 47.6 expected cancers in the general population. This resulted in a relative risk (RR) of 1.6. On closer analysis, it was noted that the cancers were predominantly gastrointestinal (RR, 2.6) (particularly stomach cancer [RR, 3.7], contralateral testicular cancer [RR, 35.7], and leukemia [RR, 5.1]).

Patients who received radiation therapy had a RR of 6.9 for developing stomach cancer whereas those who received chemotherapy had no increased risk of solid malignancies (RR, 0.83).

Moreover, patients who underwent surgery as sole treatment had an increased risk of contralateral testicular cancer, and those who had chemotherapy had no increased risk when compared with the general population. The latter finding was postulated to be due to the elimination of carcinoma in situ. In those who received chemotherapy, the observed-to-expected ratio (O/E) of leukemia was 1:0.05, with an RR of 20 and a 95% confidence interval (CI) of 0.51–111, and was not statistically significant. This cohort did not receive etoposide. However, the risk of leukemia was significantly increased in the radiation therapy group (O/E = 3:0.58; RR, 5.2; 95% CI, 1.1–15.1).

A similar study by Travis and colleagues evaluated 28,843 patients with a history of testicular cancer between 1935 to 1993 from 16 different tumor registries in North America and Europe.[36] There were 1,406 cancers (excluding contralateral testicular cancer) and an RR of 1.43. In this cohort, 64 leukemias were identified, with a fourfold risk overall and an 11- to 15-fold increase when associated with chemotherapy. Acute nonlymphoblastic and lymphoblastic leukemias were both identified and also found to be associated with radiation therapy. The risk of solid tumors was noted to be increased, especially after 20 years, in a 3,330-patient cohort, with an RR of 1.54. Excess cancers of the bladder, stomach, and pancreas were mainly associated with radiotherapy. Other cancers with an increased incidence were colon cancer, rectal cancer, melanoma, prostate cancer, kidney cancer, thyroid cancer, and sarcomas. Further to this, Jacobsen and colleagues found that of 6,187 men with testicular cancer, 10 patients developed sarcoma, 8 of these 10 having received radiation therapy and 2 having had unknown therapy.[37] The relative risk was approximately threefold.

HEMATOLOGIC TOXICITY

Leukemia and myelodysplasia are the other major long-term toxicities associated with the BEP regimen. These phenomena usually occur within 5 years of chemotherapy, were not reported with the PVB regimen, and also appear to be dose related. Nichols and colleagues reported that 2 (0.37%) of 538 patients receiving a cumulative etoposide dose ≤ 2,000 mg/m^2 developed an acute leukemia.[38] Pedersen-Bjergaard and colleagues reported no incidence of leukemia in 130 patients with a cumulative etoposide dose ≤ 2,000 mg/m^2.[39] In contrast, when the cumulative dose of this DNA topoisomerase inhibitor was > 2,000 mg/m^2, 4 of 82 patients developed an acute leukemia and 1 patient developed myelodysplasia. Of note, we have previously reported a case of acute leukemia in a patient who received only four cycles of cisplatin/etoposide/bleomycin (PEB) chemotherapy with a cumulative etoposide dose of < 1,500 mg/m^2.[40] The classic leukemia associated with etoposide is an acute monocytic leukemia (Figure 28–7), which is sometimes characterized by an 11q23 translocation (Figure 28–8) and, less often, 21q22.

Unfortunately, this complication has been recorded in long-term survivors of pediatric germ cell tumors (GCTs).[41] In one series, 6 of 442 patients receiving chemotherapy with cisplatin, ifosfamide, etoposide, vinblastine, and bleomycin developed acute myelogenous leukemia.[41] This represented about 1% of patients treated with chemotherapy alone and 4% of patients treated with combined chemotherapy and radiation therapy. In each case,

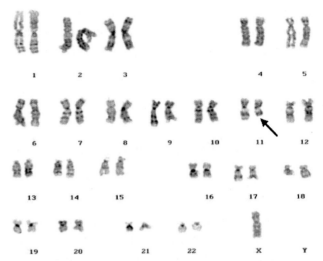

Figure 28–7. Karyotype demonstrating the characteristic deletion of 11(q23) seen with etoposide-induced acute monocytic leukemia. (Courtesy of Gail Vance, MD, Cytogenetic Laboratories, Department of Medical and Molecular Genetics, Indiana University.)

the patient had been treated for nontesticular germ cell cancer (ovarian, coccygeal, pineal, or mediastinal). Despite the small case numbers, these investigators carried out intensive biologic studies and concluded that most of these leukemias were more likely to be therapy related than GCT related, based on the pattern of chromosomal abnormalities.

It should, however, be noted that the occurrence of hematologic malignant disease in patients with primary mediastinal nonseminomatous GCTs (NSGCTs) appears to be part of a broader syndrome that is not necessarily related to treatment.[42]

EFFECTS ON FERTILITY

The issue of fertility in the patient with testicular cancer is a complex topic. Patients with testicular cancer often have testicular dysfunction and infertility prior to the diagnosis of the tumor and before the commencement of any therapy. Some (but not all) patients have persistent dysfunction after the completion of treatment. The variables to be considered when discussing this issue are baseline (pretreatment) semen characteristics, exposure to chemotherapy, the type and amount of chemotherapy, and the availability of experienced surgeons to perform a nerve-sparing retroperitoneal lymph node dissection (when feasible), to preserve ejaculation. It must also be realized that oligospermia does not translate into

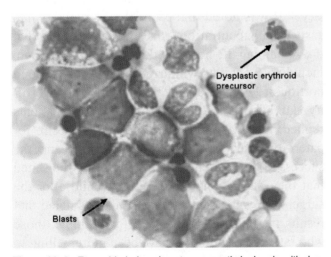

Figure 28–6. Etoposide-induced acute monocytic leukemia with dysplastic features. (Courtesy of Carol A. Bradford, BS, MT(ASCP)SH, Department of Medicine, Division of Hematology and Oncology, Indiana University.) (Original magnification ×50.)

absolute infertility. In one study, 8 of the 30 patients who received chemotherapy were able to father children, and 3 of the 13 patients with oligospermia caused conception; there was no difference in sperm motility, count, or concentration between those who fathered a child and those who did not.[43]

Baseline Characteristics

Semen obtained prior to chemotherapy from a cohort of 30 patients with disseminated testicular cancer who had not undergone a retroperitoneal lymph node dissection (RPLND) revealed oligospermia (sperm count < 20 million/mL) in 77% of patients and azoospermia in 17% of patients, and only 6.6% of patients met the criteria for sperm banking.[44] In another series, impaired spermatogenesis in patients with clinical stage I disease was found in 11 of 22 patients, with 2 patients having azoospermia and 5 having oligospermia.[45] This has been attributed to the malignancy itself, the presence of carcinoma in situ, the presence of only one testicle, and the increased incidence of cryptorchidism in this population.[46] Objective evidence supporting this stance was provided by Berthelesen and Skakkabaek,[47] who performed biopsies on the contralateral testicle of 200 patients with testicular cancer before chemotherapy or radiotherapy. No sperm production was found in 8% of patients, and spermatogenic impairment was evident in 16%. These defects were thought to be irreversible because they were associated with tubules that contained only Sertoli's cells, spermatogenic arrest, and hyalinized obliterated tubules. Of the remaining patients studied, 60% had a decreased number of late spermatids, which was considered to be a reversible defect. Also noted was a 9% incidence of cryptorchidism, a 1% incidence of cancer, and a 5% incidence of carcinoma in situ. It is unknown whether the aberrations of spermatogenesis and the development of testicular cancer are related by a common genetic and/or environmental factor.

In addition to impaired spermatogenesis, patients with testicular cancer often have testicular failure as evidenced by a low testosterone level or by a normal testosterone level with a compensatory increase in gonadotropins (luteinizing hormone [LH] or follicle-stimulating hormone [FSH])[46,48] Berthelsen and colleagues noted that 10 of 75 patients with a normal beta–human chorionic gonadotropin (β-hCG) level had an LH level higher than the 97.5 percentile and/or a testosterone level lower than the 2.5 percentile.[47] Moreover, 54 of 74 patients had an FSH level higher than the 97.5 percentile. It should also be noted that an elevated β-hCG level can decrease the FSH level and can be associated with impaired spermatogenesis. Leitner and colleagues observed an elevated LH level in 19 of 22 patients who had been treated with chemotherapy and in 5 of 6 patients treated with orchiectomy alone.[48] These investigators also noted that peak LH and FSH responses to gonadotropin-releasing hormone (Gn-RH) infusion were significantly greater ($p = .051$ and $p = .003$, respectively) in the patients who had received chemotherapy than in those who had not received cytotoxic therapy.

Recovery of Fertility

Hansen and colleagues evaluated the baseline and follow-up semen samples of a cohort of patients with clinical stage I disease.[49] About 60% of patients in this series had oligospermia or azoospermia after orchiectomy, and about 30% retained low sperm counts after at least 1 year of follow-up.

Foster and colleagues evaluated retrospectively the fertility via semen analysis and ability to father children among 51 patients who underwent nerve-sparing RPLND at Indiana University.[50] It was noted that 39 of the 51 patients had a sperm concentration > 10 million/mL and that the remaining 12 had less than this concentration, including 5 patients with azoospermia. The second portion of Foster and colleagues' study was a fertility survey. In the survey, 69% of 289 patients replied; they were grouped according to desire for paternity, previous attempts at paternity, and the success of those attempts. Of 66 patients who stated that they had attempted to father a child after the surgery, 50 were successful. The authors noted that results may have been skewed; for example, those who fathered a child may have been more willing to reply. Nevertheless, it was demonstrated that although most of these patients are fertile, the incidence of fertility is less than the general population.

Moreover, the impairment in patients who have undergone nerve-sparing RPLND (without chemotherapy) is not always due to an inability to ejaculate as the patients in this series had 98% normal ejaculation after surgery.

Semen Analysis after Chemotherapy

Azoospermia has been shown to be almost uniform during chemotherapy. Drasga and colleagues found that 2 months after starting the PVB regimen, 96% of 23 patients developed azoospermia.[44] With a follow-up of 6 to 18 months after the same regimen, Hansen and colleagues found that the median sperm count of 21 patients was 1 million/mL, with 9 patients having azoospermia and 7 patients having counts of < 1 million/mL.[49] Lange and colleagues also found that each of 10 patients evaluated within 18 months of administration of four cycles of PVB had an elevated FSH level and/or azoospermia.[51]

Recovery

Although the effect of chemotherapy is profound during treatment, recovery does occur in a significant proportion of patients. Recovery appears to be related to a number of factors, as discussed below.

Time

The recovery of the gonads from chemotherapy has been shown to occur about 2 years after chemotherapy. Leitner and colleagues observed that the mean LH level was significantly higher ($p = .01$) in 8 patients evaluated within 18 months than in 14 patients evaluated 18 months after treatment.[48] Nijman and colleagues noted that in 25 patients with stage II/III disease, the sperm concentrations per milliliter prior to chemotherapy were 0 in 1 patient, 1 to 20 million in 17 patients, and > 20 million in 7 patients, with a mean of 14 million.[52] At 1 year after four cycles of PVB (with some patients receiving 1 year of maintenance vinblastine), the concentrations per milliliter were 12, 9, and 4 million, respectively, with a mean concentration of 9 million/mL. These numbers improved at 2 years, with 7 patients being found to produce no sperm, 5 patients having 1 to 20 million/mL, and 13 patients with a concentration

> 20 million/mL; the mean concentration for the group at 2 years was 38 million/mL. It was observed that the semen analyses of patients 2 years after chemotherapy did not significantly differ from the semen analysis of 17 patients treated with orchiectomy alone (detailed above).

Lampe and colleagues had longer-term follow-up data and found that the number of patients who recover to oligospermia or to normospermic status continues to increase until about 5 years.[53] Other reports have supported these findings.[44,49,51] Of note, Hansen and colleagues reported that 18 months after a course of six cycles of PVB, the median sperm count of 21 patients increased to 20 million/mL from 1 million/mL and the median FSH level decreased from 30 IU/L to 19 IU/L.[50] These values were not significantly different from those of the 17 patients on surveillance. It was also noted that 5 years after therapy, 54% of the patients who received chemotherapy had not achieved their pretreatment sperm counts, and 55% of patients on surveillance had sperm counts below the reference range.

Baseline Semen Analysis

Lampe and colleagues studied the semen of 178 patients before and after various chemotherapeutic regimens for testicular cancer, including BEP, PVB, EP, and carboplatin plus EP.[53] Of the group, 170 patients had sperm counts conducted more than 1 year after chemotherapy. It was reported that of 89 patients who were normospermic (ie, with sperm counts > 10 million/mL) before chemotherapy, 64% remained normospermic after chemotherapy, 16% developed oligospermia (sperm counts of 1 million/mL to 10 million/mL), and 20% developed azoospermia (sperm count < 1 million/mL). Of the 41 patients with oligospermia, 24% became normospermic, 41% continued to have oligospermia, and 34% developed azoospermia. Of the 40 patients with azoospermia, 15% became normospermic, 30% progressed to oligospermia, and 55% remained with azoospermia.

Age

In the study by Lampe and colleagues, the RR of patients older than 30 years recovering to oligospermia was 0.4, compared with patients younger than 30 years.[53] This finding is supported by Leitner and colleagues, who found that the mean FSH level of the 8 patients in their study who were less than 25 years of age was significantly lower ($p = .01$) and that the LH level tended toward significance ($p = .065$), compared with the 14 patients who were more than 25 years of age.[48]

Number of Chemotherapy Cycles

Lampe and colleagues also noted that if a patient received more than four cycles of chemotherapy, the chance of recovery to a sperm count of at least 1 million/mL (oligospermia) was markedly decreased (9 [35%] of 26 patients in comparison with patients who had received four or fewer cycles (107 [70%] of 152 patients).[53]

Type of Chemotherapy

Lampe and colleagues also noted that the 59 patients who were treated with carboplatin were 3.9 times more likely to recover to oligospermia than those treated with cisplatin-based therapy.[53]

Dose

Data that demonstrate that there is a dose-dependent impairment of gonadal function in patients treated with BEP have also been published. Petersen and colleagues[43] reported that 19% of 27 patients who received four cycles of standard therapy with a median follow-up of 79 months had azoospermia, compared to 47% of 17 patients who received double-dose cisplatin (40 mg/m^2 for 5 days) and etoposide (200 mg/m^2 for 5 days) in three or more cycles. The sperm density was also significantly greater in the standard-therapy arm, with a median of 5.83 million/mL, compared with 0.005 million/mL in the high-dose group. The median FSH level was significantly higher in the high-dose group ($p = .018$), and whereas the baseline level was elevated in 22 (73%) of 30 patients in the standard-therapy arm, it was elevated in 20 (95%) of 21 patients in the high-dose arm. Although there was no significant difference in the median LH levels, the basal level was elevated in 8 (27%) of 30 patients of the standard group and in 9 (43%) of 21 patients of the high-dose group.

GONADAL TOXICITY

In addition to impairment of spermatogenesis, injury to Leydig's cell function is a potential toxic effect of chemotherapy. Elevations of FSH levels were observed in 24 of a cohort of 32 patients who received platinum-based chemotherapy.[54] Of these 24 patients, 15 had elevated LH levels. Two patients, each with a remaining testicle, had low testosterone levels. This underscores the problem of compensated (and sometimes uncompensated) Leydig's cell function. Testosterone replacement can be implemented if clinically indicated.

NEUROCOGNITIVE IMPAIRMENT

Cisplatin is derived from a heavy metal with known neurotoxicity and may also be associated with neurocognitive impairment (as has been observed with mercury and manganese).[55] This topic has been poorly investigated in regard to testicular cancer. One small study compared patients with testicular cancer who were treated with chemotherapy ($n = 13$) to patients who were not treated with chemotherapy ($n = 9$) and to controls who had no history of cancer ($n = 17$). In this study, the group of patients who had been treated with chemotherapy performed at a lower level, according to measures of the visual-motor scanning component of attention. However, more work needs to be done in this area before firm conclusions can be made.[56]

SUMMARY

The treatment of testicular cancer has some notable long-term toxicities; however, the curative potential in the face of metastatic disease far outweighs this problem. This issue requires very careful consideration and is an argument against adjuvant chemotherapy for patients with clinical stage I disease, for whom a risk-benefit analysis must govern decisions. What is absolutely clear is that patients who first received curative chemotherapy for advanced testicular cancer in the 1970s are just entering their maximum-risk period for cardiovascular and oncologic problems as they approach their fifth and sixth decades of life. Accordingly, it is crucially important that such patients be monitored closely during therapy for toxicities and that they continue to be followed closely by clinicians who are aware of the scope and spectrum of potential late toxicities and who are able to identify them, treat them, and report them to the medical community at large.

REFERENCES

1. Einhorn LH. Testicular cancer as a model for a curable neoplasm: the Richard and Hinda Rosenthal Foundation Award Lecture. Cancer Res 1981;41:3274–80.

2. Levi JA, Thomson D, Sandeman T, et al. A prospective study of cisplatin-based combination chemotherapy in advanced germ cell malignancy: role of maintenance and long-term follow-up. J Clin Oncol 1988;6:1154–60.

3. Levi JA, Raghavan D, Harvey V, et al. The importance of bleomycin in combination chemotherapy for good prognosis germ cell carcinoma. J Clin Oncol 1993;11:1300–5.

4. de Wit R, Stoter G, Kaye SB, et al. Importance of bleomycin in combination chemotherapy for good-prognosis testicular nonseminoma: a randomized study of the European Organization for Research and Treatment of Cancer Genitourinary Tract Cancer Cooperative Group. J Clin Oncol 1997;15:1837–43.

5. Loehrer PJ Sr, Johnson D, Elson P, et al. Importance of bleomycin in favorable-prognosis disseminated germ cell tumors: an Eastern Cooperative Oncology Group trial. J Clin Oncol 1995;13:470–6.

6. Nichols CR, Catalano PJ, Crawford ED, et al. Randomized comparison of cisplatin and etoposide and either bleomycin or ifosfamide in treatment of advanced disseminated germ cell tumors: an Eastern Cooperative Oncology Group, Southwest Oncology Group, and Cancer and Leukemia Group B study. J Clin Oncol 1998;16:1287–93.

7. Jensen JL, Goel R, Venner PM. The effect of corticosteroid administration on bleomycin lung toxicity. Cancer 1990; 65:1291–7.

8. Dentino M, Luft FC, Yum MN, et al. Long term effect of cis-diamminedichloride platinum (CDDP) on renal function and structure in man. Cancer 1978;41:1274–81.

9. Fjeldborg P, Sorensen J, Helkjaer PE. The long-term effect of cisplatin on renal function. Cancer 1986;58:2214–7.

10. Meijer S, Sleijfer DT, Mulder NH, et al. Some effects of combination chemotherapy with cis-platinum on renal function in patients with nonseminomatous testicular carcinoma. Cancer 1983;51:2035–40.

11. Hansen SW, Groth S, Daugaard G, et al. Long-term effects on renal function and blood pressure of treatment with cisplatin, vinblastine, and bleomycin in patients with germ cell cancer. J Clin Oncol 1988;6:1728–31.

12. Groth S, Nielsen H, Sorensen JB, et al. Acute and long-term nephrotoxicity of cis-platinum in man. Cancer Chemother Pharmacol 1986;17:191–6.

13. Fossa SD, Aass N, Winderen M, et al. Long-term renal function after treatment for malignant germ-cell tumours. Ann Oncol 2002;13:222–8.

14. Boyer MJ, Raghavan D, Harris PJ, et al. Lack of late toxicity in patients treated with cisplatin-containing combination chemotherapy for metastatic testicular cancer. J Clin Oncol 1990;8:21–6.

15. Hartmann JT, Kollmannsberger C, Kanz L, Bokemeyer C. Platinum organ toxicity and possible prevention in patients with testicular cancer. Int J Cancer 1999;83:866–9.

16. Jongejan HT, Provost AP, Molenaar JC. Potentiated nephrotoxicity of cisplatin when combined with amikacin comparing young and adult rats. Pediatr Nephrol 1989;3:290–5.

17. Adoue D, Arlett P. Bleomycin and Raynaud's phenomenon. Ann Intern Med 1984;100:770.

18. Vogelzang NJ, Bosl GJ, Johnson K, Kennedy BJ. Raynaud's phenomenon: a common toxicity after combination chemotherapy for testicular cancer. Ann Intern Med 1981; 95:288–92.

19. Hansen SW, Olsen N. Raynaud's phenomenon in patients treated with cisplatin, vinblastine, and bleomycin for germ cell cancer: measurement of vasoconstrictor response to cold. J Clin Oncol 1989;7:940–2.

20. Roth BJ, Greist A, Kubilis PS, et al. Cisplatin-based combination chemotherapy for disseminated germ cell tumors: long-term follow-up. J Clin Oncol 1988;6:1239–47.

21. Raghavan D, Cox K, Childs A, et al. Hypercholesterolemia after chemotherapy for testis cancer. J Clin Oncol 1992; 10:1386–9.

22. Gietema JA, Sleijfer DT, Willemse PHB, et al. Long-term follow-up of cardiovascular risk factors in patients given chemotherapy for disseminated nonseminomatous testicular cancer. Ann Intern Med 1992;116:709–15.

23. Ellis PA, Fitzharris BM, George PM, et al. Fasting plasma lipid measurements following cisplatin chemotherapy in patients with germ cell tumors. J Clin Oncol 1992;10: 1609–14.

24. Williams SD, Birch R, Einhorn LH, et al. Treatment of disseminated germ-cell tumors with cisplatin, bleomycin, and either vinblastine or etoposide. N Engl J Med 1987; 316:1435–40.

25. Hantel A, Rowinsky EK, Donehower RC. Nifedipine and oncologic Raynaud phenomenon. Ann Intern Med 1988; 108:767.

26. Doll DC, List AF, Greco FA, et al. Acute vascular ischemic events after cisplatin-based combination chemotherapy for germ-cell tumors of the testis. Ann Intern Med 1986; 105:48–51.

27. Cantwell BM, Mannix KA, Roberts JT, et al. Thromboembolic events during combination chemotherapy for germ cell-malignancy. Lancet 1988;2:1086–7.

28. Vogelzang NJ, Frenning DH, Kennedy BJ. Coronary artery disease after treatment with bleomycin and vinblastine. Cancer Treat Rep 1980;64:1159–60.

29. Gietema JA, Meinardi MT, Messerschmidt J, et al. Circulating plasma platinum more than 10 years after cisplatin treatment for testicular cancer. Lancet 2000;355:1075–6.

30. Meinardi MT, Gietema JA, van der Graaf WT, et al. Cardiovascular morbidity in long-term survivors of metastatic testicular cancer. J Clin Oncol 2000;18:1725–32.

30. Nichols CR, Roth BJ, Williams SD, et al. No evidence of acute cardiovascular complications of chemotherapy for testicular cancer: an analysis of the Testicular Cancer Intergroup Study. J Clin Oncol 1992;10:760–5.

31. Stockler M, Raghavan D. Neoplastic venous involvement and pulmonary embolism in patients with germ cell tumours. Cancer 1991;68:2633–6.

32. Bokemeyer C, Berger CC, Kuczyk MA, Schmoll HJ. Evaluation of long-term toxicity after chemotherapy for testicular cancer. J Clin Oncol 1996;14:2923–32.

33. Reddel RR, Kefford RF, Grant, JM, et al. Ototoxicity in patients receiving cisplatin: importance of dose and method of drug administration. Cancer Treat Rep 1982;66:19–23.

34. Nichols CR, Loehrer PJ Sr. The story of second cancers in patients cured of testicular cancer: tarnishing success or burnishing irrelevance? J Natl Cancer Inst 1997;89:1394–5.

35. van Leeuwen FE, Stiggelbout AM, van den Belt-Dusebout AW, et al. Second cancer risk following testicular cancer: a follow-up study of 1,909 patients. J Clin Oncol 1993;11:415–24.

36. Travis LB, Curtis RE, Storm H, et al. Risk of second malignant neoplasms among long-term survivors of testicular cancer. J Natl Cancer Inst 1997;89:1429–39.

37. Jacobsen GK, Mellemgaard A, Engelholm SA, Moller H. Increased incidence of sarcoma in patients treated for testicular seminoma. Eur J Cancer 1993;5:664–8.

38. Nichols CR, Breeden ES, Loehrer PJ, et al. Secondary leukemia associated with a conventional dose of etoposide: review of serial germ cell tumor protocols. J Natl Cancer Inst 1993;85:36–40.

39. Pedersen-Bjergaard J, Philip P, Larsen SO, et al. Therapy-related myelodysplasia and acute myeloid leukemia. Cytogenetic characteristics of 115 consecutive cases and risk in seven cohorts of patients treated intensively for malignant diseases in the Copenhagen series. Leukemia 1993;7:1975–86.

40. Segelov E, Raghavan D, Kronenberg H. Acute leukemia following chemotherapy including etoposide for testicular carcinoma. Aust N Z J Med 1993;23:718–9.

41. Schneider DT, Hilgenfeld E, Schwabe D, et al. Acute myelogenous leukemia after treatment for malignant germ cell tumors in children. J Clin Oncol 1999;17:3226–33.

42. Nichols CR, Roth BJ, Heerma N, et al. Hematologic neoplasia associated with primary mediastinal germ-cell tumors. N Engl J Med 1990;322:1425–9.

43. Petersen PM, Hansen SW, Giwercman A, et al. Dose-dependent impairment of testicular function in patients treated with cisplatin-based chemotherapy for germ cell cancer. Ann Oncol 1994;5:355–8.

44. Drasga RE, Einhorn LH, Williams SD, et al. Fertility after chemotherapy for testicular cancer. J Clin Oncol 1983;1:179–83.

45. Carroll PR, Morse MJ, Whitmore WF Jr, et al. Fertility status of patients with clinical stage I testis tumors on a surveillance protocol. J Urol 1987;138:70–2.

46. Meistrich ML, Vassilopoulou-Sellin R, Lipshultz LI. Gonadal dysfunction. In: Devita VT, Hellman S, Rosenberg SA, editors. Cancer principles and practice of oncology 5th ed. Philadelphia: Lippincott-Raven; 1997. p. 2758–73.

47. Berthelsen JG, Skakkebaek NE. Gonadal function in men with testis cancer. Fertil Steril 1983;39:68–75.

48. Leitner SP, Bosl GJ, Bajorunas D. Gonadal dysfunction in patients treated for metastatic germ-cell tumors. J Clin Oncol 1986;4:1500–5.

49. Hansen PV, Trykker H, Helkjoer PE, Andersen J. Testicular function in patients with testicular cancer treated with orchiectomy alone or orchiectomy plus cisplatin-based chemotherapy. J Natl Cancer Inst 1989;81:1246–50.

50. Foster RS, McNulty A, Rubin LR, et al. The fertility of patients with clinical stage I testis cancer managed by nerve sparing retroperitoneal lymph node dissection. J Urol 1994;152:1139–43.

51. Lange PH, Narayan P, Vogelzang NJ, et al. Return of fertility after treatment for nonseminomatous testicular cancer: changing concepts. J Urol 1983;129:1131–5.

52. Nijman JM, Jager S, Boer PW, et al, The treatment of ejaculation disorders after retroperitoneal lymph node dissection. Cancer 1982;50:2967–71.

53. Lampe H, Horwich A, Norman A, et al. Fertility after chemotherapy for testicular germ cell cancers. J Clin Oncol 1997;15:239–45.

54. Strumberg D, Brugge S, Korn MW, et al. Evaluation of long-term toxicity in patients after cisplatin-based chemotherapy for non-seminomatous testicular cancer. Ann Oncol 2002;13:229–36.

55. Troy L, McFarland K, Littman-Power S, et al. Cisplatin-based therapy: a neurological and neuropsychological review. Psychooncology 2000;9:29–39.

56. Troy LA, Littman-Power S, McFarland K, et al. Impact of cisplatin-based therapy on attentional processes in testicular cancer patients [abstract]. Proc Am Soc Clin Oncol 1996;15:507.

Index

Page numbers followed by f indicate figure. Pages numbers followed by t indicate table.